Indexers on Indexing

Books written or compiled by L. M. Harrod

Lending Library Methods (London, England: Grafton, 1933)
The Libraries of Greater London (London, England: Bell, 1951)
Library Work with Children (London, England: Deutsch, 1969)
Librarians' Glossary and Reference Book, 4th rev. ed. (London, England: Deutsch, 1977; Boulder, Colorado: Westfield, 1977)

Indexers on Indexing

A Selection of Articles Published in *The Indexer*

Edited by

Leonard Montague Harrod

for the Society of Indexers

R. R. BOWKER COMPANY
New York & London, 1978

The Society of Indexers is grateful
for the cooperation of those
authors whose articles are being
republished in this volume.

Published by R. R. Bowker Company
1180 Avenue of the Americas, New York, N.Y. 10036
Copyright © 1978 by Society of Indexers of the United Kingdom
International Standard Book Number 0-8352-1099-5
Library of Congress Catalog Card Number 78-56880
Printed and Bound in the United States of America

Contents

Preface

This selection of articles is being published to mark the formation of the Society of Indexers in England twenty-one years ago as the first society of its kind. One of its early, and probably most effective, continuing actions was to begin the publication of *The Indexer*, which was, and still is, the only publication in English dealing solely with indexing.

The main objective of *The Indexer* through the years has not been to provide basic instruction. (This is available in *Indexing Your Book: A Practical Guide for Authors* by Sina Spiker [University of Wisconsin Press]; in several books by R. L. Collison; in *Training in Indexing*, edited by G. Norman Knight [London: MIT Press]; and in *Book Indexing* by Mrs. M. D. Anderson, which replaced *Making an Index* by the late G. V. Carey in the Cambridge [University Press] Authors' and Printers' Guides series.) Instead, *The Indexer* has dealt with some of the debatable problems that challenge even experienced back-of-the-book indexers. Indexing is not a science but an art and poses many problems to indexers, especially those who deal with long and complicated texts. The solutions to some of these problems, as presented from time to time in *The Indexer*, have been included in this selection.

An examination of past issues of *The Indexer* indicates a shift in the activities of indexers from the original, and still predominant, indexing of books to the application of basic indexing principles, combined with the use of mechanical and technical developments, for the prompt production of indexes to periodical literature. This volume reflects this shift. It contains articles on simple indexing, which often uses the British Standards Institution's *The Preparation of Indexes to Books, Periodicals and Other Publications, BS 3700: 1976* as a guide and is the basis for the various forms of indexing. It also includes articles on the construction of subject headings and thesauri for specialized practices, such as the production of indexes to abstracts, bibliographies, and literature sources. Such indexes, in order to be produced quickly using various mechanical and electronic methods, require scientifically designed subject headings and often thesauri.

Beginning as a slim periodical (116 pages in the first volume and increasing—as far as finances in the period of inflation would permit—to 216 pages in Volume 10), *The Indexer* now has subscribers in fifty-two countries and serves, as well, as the official journal of the British, American, and Australian societies of indexers. At the time of writing, consideration is being given to its becoming the official journal of the newly formed Indexing and Abstracting Society of Canada.

Bearing in mind that *The Indexer* also is used extensively in library schools, I asked the heads of a number of British and American library schools to suggest articles that might be included in this book. I am happy to state that six British schools and eleven American schools have been good enough to send me suggestions, which have served as a very helpful guide in choosing articles. Unfortunately, not all suggested articles could be included. At times it was necessary to choose between two or more articles on the same subject.

I trust that the final result, which combines the library schools' suggestions with my own personal selection, is a balanced and representative collection of the more important articles and will be of use to indexers of all kinds. Readers who have access to a ten-volume set of *The Indexer* (all issues of which are still kept in print) will be able to find other articles on the same or similar aspects of indexing as are included in this volume.

L. M. HARROD
Former Editor of *The Indexer*

Harpenden, England
March 1978

I. The History of Indexing

The Beginnings of Indexing and Abstracting:

Some Notes towards a History of Indexing and Abstracting in Antiquity and the Middle Ages

Francis J. Witty

Some eight years ago when the writer was asked to prepare a course in indexing and abstracting for his graduate library school, he felt that the first lecture ought to be devoted, at least in part, to the history of the subject. However, a search of the standard texts revealed either nothing at all in this area or an almost complete lacuna prior to the sixteenth century. Wheatley, for example, in his pioneering text, *How to make an index,* misunderstood the term *index* in Roman antiquity and unfortunately tells us:

> Cicero used the word 'index' to express the table of contents of a book, and asked his friend Atticus to send him two library clerks to repair his books. He added that he wished them to bring with them some parchment to make indexes upon.[1]

The pertinent letter to Atticus (IV.4a), in the writer's translation, reads as follows:

> ... and bid them bring a bit of parchment from which title-tags [*indices*] are made. You Greeks, I believe, call them SILLYBOI.[2]

Although scholars might argue about the exact meaning of the diminutive *membranulam,* there is no doubt that *index* and SILLYBOS meant the little parchment title tag which hung down from the papyrus roll to identify a work on a library shelf.

Accordingly the writer began to gather as much as possible on the subject from works on the history of the book and from collections of facsimiles of papyri and of mediaeval manuscripts. The following notes, of course, are far from exhausting the subject; but they might provide a point of departure for a comprehensive history.

Our investigation into the history of indexing and abstracting must go back to the time when man first began to do something to make information in written records more easily accessible, either by arranging the salient features in a known order, or by condensing long documents into convenient abstracts or epitomes.

The most ancient of either of these devices known to the writer is used on some of the clay envelops enclosing Mesopotamian cuneiform documents of the early second millennium B.C. The idea of the envelop, of course, was to preserve the document from tampering; but to avoid having to break the solid cover, the document would either be written in full on the outside with the necessary signature seals, or it would be abstracted on the envelop, accompanied likewise by the seals.[3]

Indexing itself finds its primitive origins in the arrangement of chapter heads or summaries at the beginning of historical or other non-fiction works. The Bible—in the absence of concordances and indexes—was in the

Reprinted from *The Indexer* 8, no. 4 (October 1973): 193–198.

early centuries of this era outfitted with such summaries (*tituli, capitula, capita,* KEPHALAIA). It should be noted that the chapter/verse arrangements of our modern Bibles were still a long way off in the future. These summaries (*tituli*) are mentioned a number of times by Cassiodorus in his *Institutiones*[4], which he furnished with such headings at the beginning of each book to aid in finding information contained therein. While this seems somewhat far from indexing, as we know it, it did permit easier searching of data and enable Cassiodorus to cross-reference his text. Among other works from the early centuries of this era, which were furnished with summaries either by their authors or later editor/copyists, were the *Attic nights* of Gellius, Pliny's *Natural history*, the *Antiquities* of Josephus, and Bede's *Ecclesiastical history*. Undoubtedly a search into similar works would reveal a host of other titles so equipped.

An essential element in any index is the arrangement of the entries according to a known order. This may follow the usual order of the Roman alphabet, but the arrangement might follow some system of classification; or, for some kinds of works, it might be chronological or numerical. Since, however, alphabetic order is the most generally known arrangement in the West, we should take a quick glance at its use in ancient times. For this aspect of our inquiry we are indeed fortunate to have the relatively recent work of L. W. Daly, *Contributions to a history of alphabetization in antiquity and the middle ages* (Collection Latomus 90; Brussels 1967). This excellent work is to be recommended strongly to anyone interested in the history of indexing; the writer found most of his own previous researches confirmed in it and a myriad of additional data.

Why the letters of the alphabet are arranged as they are is a problem which has never been solved, although ingenious explanations have been presented.[5] The order of *aleph, beth, ghimel* goes back probably to the second millennium B.C., since this order

was already obviously established when the Greeks adopted and adapted the Semitic writing system in the early eighth century B.C. (or earlier?). In Hebrew the letters of the alphabet were sometimes used for numerals, as is evidenced by their use in some books of the Bible, e.g. Psalms 9, 24, 33, 36, 110, 111, 144 and the Lamentations of Jeremiah, where the letters of the alphabet precede individual lamentations. The Greeks inherited the order of the letters along with the alphabet itself and used it for one of their numeral systems.

Under the Ptolemies the Hellenistic Greeks of Egypt seem to have begun using alphabetic order for complicated lists of names such as one would find in a library catalogue or the tax collector's office.[6] From a close study of the fragments of Callimachus's catalogue of the Alexandrian Library and the literary references to it, it would appear that he used alphabetic order for the arrangement of authors under broad subjects. And papyrus fragments from the 'rubbish heaps' of Egypt show that alphabetic order was sometimes used in the centuries just preceding this era for lists of taxpayers from various villages and districts, which themselves also appear sometimes in alphabetic order. But the virtues of this arrangement seem not to have been universally received among the Greeks, to judge by the many lists among extant papyri which seem to have no recognizable order at all.

When we speak of alphabetic order in antiquity, we do not mean the detailed, 'letter-for-letter-to-the-end-of-the-word' arrangement so dear to the heart of the librarian. This precision was not deemed necessary either in antiquity or the middle ages, and, according to Daly, it has not completely won out even in modern times.[7] Actually, the order might be considered relatively close if it were kept through the first three letters of a word; but often only the first letter is considered in these documents. Nevertheless, these represent a start towards progress. Later on in this era there can be found, particularly among Greek writers, an interest in alphabetic verses of an acrostic nature for presenting certain aspects of Christian thought in a mnemonic form. These so-called *Erbauliche Alphabete* are cited extensively in Karl Krumbacher's history of Byzantine literature.[8]

Religious literature was not unique in its employment of the alphabet for mnemonic purposes. The second-century author, Sextus Pythagoreus, arranged his so-called *Pythagorean sentences* in alphabetic order—a group of 123 maxims reflecting the thoughts of the Pythagorean school. And the first and second centuries of this era also saw many lexicographical compilations in alphabetic order— glossaries of terms in various fields.[9]

Also closely associated with efforts to bring out pertinent information rapidly from documents is the employment of symbols in textual criticism and hermeneutics. Aristophanes of Byzantium and Aristarchus, Hellenistic scholars at Alexandria, are probably the most outstanding for the invention of critical symbols, but a man like Cassiodorus, though of the sixth century of this era, is not to be ignored; for he worked out an elaborate system of symbols to be used in biblical commentaries, so that the student could readily find the kind of information he needed on a particular passage.[10] However, although we have in Græco-Roman times the use of alphabetic order and the employment of the *capitulatio* or placing of summaries at the beginning of certain non-fiction works, we do not—as far as the writer has been able to ascertain—have anything like an alphabetic index to a work before the Middle Ages. But now let us take a look at abstracting in classical times.

The Alexandrian scholars at the *Museion* realized the problem of the large book not only for the library, but for the reader. Callimachus may have had large, uninspired epics in mind when he wrote that a 'big book is equivalent to a big nuisance',[11] but this could well be applied practically in his days to any large work which would occupy a number of papyrus rolls; after all, his own work, the *Pínakes*, occupied 120 rolls.[12] Therefore, from Alexandrian times many works, particularly histories and other non-fiction, were epitomized, i.e. abstracted; and often our only sources are the epitomes. But the Alexandrian critics also decided that editions of the plays of the great dramatists would be more useful if preceded by abstracts of the plots. These were called HYPOTHESEIS in Greek, and appear at the beginning of each play (sometimes in verse) along with a list of the characters. The following is the abstract (hypothesis) found at the beginning of the *Agamemnon* of Aeschylus, in the writer's translation:

> Agamemnon upon departing for Troy had promised Clytemnestra that, if he sacked Troy, he would signal by beacon on the same day. Consequently Clytemnestra set a hired watch to look out for the beacon. Now when he saw it, he reported; she then sent for the assembly of the elders—of whom the chorus is composed—to make an inquiry concerning the beacon. When they hear, some sing a song of triumph. Shortly afterwards Talthybios (herald) makes an appearance and describes in detail the events of the voyage. Then Agamemnon comes on a chariot followed by another chariot in which are the booty and Cassandra. While he then goes forth to enter the house with Clytemnestra, Cassandra, before entering the palace, prophesises about her own and Agamemnon's death and the matricide of Orestes; then rushing in like one ready to die she casts down her insignia. This part of the play is admirable because it arouses fear and proper pity. Characteristically Aeschylus has Agamemnon slain off-stage; says nothing about the death of Cassandra until he displays her corpse. He has Aegisthus and Clytemnestra each rely on personal arguments for the murder: hers is the slaying of Iphigenia; his, the misfortunes of his father at the hands of Atreus. The play was staged during the archonship of Philocles in the second year of the eightieth Olympiad (459/8 B.C.). Aeschylus won first prize with the *Agamemnon, Libation bearers, Eumenides,* and his satyr play, the *Proteus*. Xenocles Aphidnaios led the chorus.[13]

It will be immediately noted that the abstract, concise as it is, contains a bit of literary criticism towards the end and includes historical data based on Aristotle's *Didascaliae*. Later on in Roman times the comedies of the playwrights Plautus and

Terence were graced with such abstracts, except that these summaries were all composed in verse.[14] The use of the abstract, however, was not confined to belles-lettres in ancient times, as is evidenced by the custom of abstracting documents of sale, forfeitures, and contracts at Tebtunis in the third century B.C.[15]

Later in the Middle Ages one can find in manuscripts of scholarly works, like histories, marginal summaries of a page's contents, a custom that has been carried over into modern times.[16] Marginal summaries can be noted in some of the ninth and tenth-century manuscripts of Justinian's code also.[17]

Another device which can be associated with the origins of indexing is the work carried out on the text of the Scriptures by Eusebius of Caesarea in dividing the Gospels into sections, numbering them, and arranging related material in the ten *Canones evangeliorum*.[18] While again this is not indexing as such, it does provide for relatively quick consultation of data hidden in long, connected textual matter.

But it is really with the general adoption of the codex form of the book that the idea of an alphabetic index becomes practical. The papyrus roll obviously did not—nor does the microfilm roll—lend itself to ready reference.

The earliest approach to an alphabetic subject index that the writer has been able to find appears in an anonymous work of the fifth century of this era, the *Apothegmata*, a list of the sayings of various Greek fathers on certain theological topics. Although originally composed in another order, it was arranged into alphabetic order in the sixth century.[19] Of course, in this age of manuscripts we must remember that exact citations are a rarity. Some authors divided their works into chapters and numbered sections, which is very helpful for citations; e.g. Cassiodorus in his *Institutiones* can cross-reference his work by referring not only to the chapter number, but also to the *titulus* of the chapter.[20] However, the 'book con-

sciousness' of Cassiodorus is almost a unique phenomenon for antiquity.

Two centuries later we encounter what amounts to an alphabetic subject index to the great fathers of the church and the Bible in the *Sacra parallela* by John of Damascus.[21] In his introduction he calls attention to his summaries or table of contents which appear at the beginning of the text:

> Furthermore, the easier to find what is sought, a list of headings PINAX TON KEPHALAION or summaries (TITLOI) in alphabetic order has been compiled; and each subject that is sought will be found under its initial letter. (Col. 1041.)

Then there follows in rough alphabetic order the theological statements arranged by keyword, with passages from the Bible and the Greek fathers illustrating them. Some examples of the subjects from the table of contents read as follows:

Letter A (Col. 1045)
The eternal Divinity PERI *Aïdou* THEOTETOS, etc.
The inevitability of God PERI TOU *Apheukton* EINAI THEON.
The incomprehensibility of God PERI TOU *Akatalepton* EINAI TON THEON.

Letter B (Col. 1050)
The kingdom of heaven PERI *Basileias* OURANON.
The counsel of God PERI *Boulês* THEOU
The help of God PERI *Boêtheias* THEOU.

Aside from this eighth-century work, however, the writer has been unable to find any other indexes of such a nature before the fourteenth century. L. W. Daly corroborates this for the Vatican Archives: 'Evidence indicates that alphabetic indexing was not introduced into papal record-keeping as represented in the Vatican Archives until the fourteenth century'.[22]

Before leaping over to the fourteenth century, however, mention should be made of the famous, early sixth-century codex of the *Materia medica* of Dioscorides Pedanius. Although the author seems not to have been very systematic in the composition of his treatise, those responsible for the now famous Vienna manuscript[23] decided to arrange the work in alphabetic order. Since the treatise deals with various herbs and other medical materials, each having a numbered paragraph of its own, the alphabetic re-arrangement, like a dictionary, requires no index. The Vienna codex does have a *capitulatio* or listing of the *materiæ* in the front and, of course, this naturally falls into alphabetic order. However, it might be added that this outstanding codex, often called *Codex Julia Anicia,* is more famous for its rich illumination than for its introduction of the alphabetic approach to medicinal herbs.

With the rise of the universities in the late twelfth and following centuries and the renewed interest in theology, philosophy, and law, and particularly the passion that seemed to prevail for scholastic disputation, one is not surprised to see the beginnings of alphabetic indexing, as we know it. Disputation (debate) would require ready reference to the authorities (Aristotle, Thomas Aquinas, Peter Lombard, *et al.*).

The indexes that the writer has been able to examine from the fourteenth century are extremely simple in their make-up, but not particularly easy to read. For this was the period when Gothic script was prevalent throughout Western Europe, and when this hand is done with any speed, it sometimes becomes almost illegible for the unpractised reader. The texts of these manuscripts are usually done with some care, but the indexes seem to show all the characteristics of haste and impatience. Perhaps the texts of the manuscripts examined were copied by professional scribes, while the indexes were compiled and written by the owners.

The texts which the writer has found of fourteenth-century manuscripts in facsimile so far have all been either philosophical-theological or of the *Materia medica* of Dioscorides. In the article (*supra*) on 'Early Indexing Techniques' two such works were examined in some detail: a commentary on the first book of the *Sentences of Peter Lombard* by Egidio Colonna and two Vatican manuscripts of Dioscorides. Since the Colonna work is written in the usual scholastic way, it consists of a number of *theses*

(statements to be proved) with explanations of terms and syllogistic arguments. These are all numbered as *distinctiones* and *quaestiones;* thus the index which lists these propositions by catchword makes citation fairly simple, e.g. ' d :. 24. q. 3 ' means *distinctio* no. 24, *quæstio* no. 3. There seems to be no effort made to bring out more than one catchword from each proposition; e.g. the statement *Actio et passio sunt una res et duo predicamenta* gets an entry under *actio* but not under *passio*, etc. While such superficial indexing is easily criticised now, it must be admitted that it represents a great step forward from the mere listing of *theses* at the beginning of a work, as will usually be found in manuscripts of this century as well as in incunabula of the next. The Dioscorides manuscripts are just as simply treated in their indexes, for the numbered *materiæ* are easily cited in an index. But nothing beyond the principal item is mentioned in the index. The example of ' ink ' (MELAN) is used in the article (*supra*); ink is described in section 825 of the work, and so the index entry is merely ' OKE. MELAN ' or ' 825. Ink '.

Although the alphabetic listing of chapter headings and *theses* represents some progress in information retrieval, it would seem, even from a survey of books printed in the next century, that our own concept of indexing is some distance in the future. For the writer surveyed as many incunabula as possible either at first hand or through facsimiles or catalogue descriptions, but he was forced to conclude that indexing was still not a very common practice, even after the mechanical multiplication of texts through printing had made the notion of an index much more feasible and practical. The writer's article cited above presents an analysis of the *Nuremburg chronicle* (1493) of Hartmann Schedel printed by Koberger.[24] Briefly it was found that most of the index entries (the index is in the front) were taken verbatim from the text and sometimes not entered under what would seem the proper keyword; e.g. the statement about the invention of printing in Germany is entered under *Ars imprimendi libros* with no entry at all under any form of *imprimere, impressio, Germania,* or *liber.* It should be added that Koberger included his usual numbering of leaves, but the index citations give only the leaf number with no designations of recto or verso. Alphabetization, as can be expected, is rough— not ordinarily past the first syllable.

The sixteenth and later centuries are beyond our scope, but it might be mentioned that the writer found tremendous improvements in book indexes of the sixteenth century. But with the appearance of the first scholarly and scientific periodical literature in the seventeenth century, indexing in that area leaves a lot to be desired. A brief example can be seen in the index to the *Acta eruditorum* (Leipzig): in the volume for the year 1682 the *Index auctorum ac rerum* (author and subject index) divides the subjects into six general categories and under each group is an alphabetic listing of authors with the titles of their articles. But how often in the twentieth-century periodical indexes have we not found similar or even poorer treatment?

References

(1) (London 1902) p. 6.

(2) M. Tulli Ciceronis *Epistulæ,* ed. W. S. Watt, v. 2, pt. 1 (Oxford Classical Texts; Oxford 1965) p. 126.

(3) G. Contenau, *Everyday life in Babylon and Assyria* (New York 1966) p. 177.

(4) Cassiodori Senatoris *Institutiones.* Edited from the Manuscripts by R. A. B. Mynors (Oxford, repr. 1961) p. 18 (1.2.13), p. 27 (1.6.5).

(5) D. Diringer, *The alphabet, a key to the history of mankind* (3rd ed., London 1968) v. 1, pp. 169-70.

(6) *Tax lists and transportation receipts from Theadelphia,* edited by W. L. Westermann and C. W. Keyes (Columbia Papyri : Greek series, no. 2; New York 1932), 'Papyrus Columbia 1 recto, 1 a-b', pp. 3-36, and 'Papyrus Columbia 1 recto 2', pp. 37-78.

(7) *Op. cit.,* p. 92 : in his epilogue he remarks: 'Finally there is a curious irony in the fact that in the middle of the twentieth century there

appeared at Alexandria, the birthplace as it were of alphabetization, a book which reverts to the simple first-letter alphabetic order of the third century B.C. This is the *Catalogue of the patriarchal library of Alexandria'.* He then quotes part of this list showing the following order : 'Ioannes, Ierotheos, Isidoros, Ignatios, Ieronymos'.

(8) *Geschichte der byzantinischen Literatur* (2nd ed., Munich 1897) pp. 717-720.

(9) E.g. LEXEIS RHETORIKAI 'rhetorical terms' in no. 1804 of the *Oxyrhynchus papyri.*

(10) The pertinent passages have been cited and discussed in the writer's *Writing and the book in Cassiodorus* (Ann Arbor, Mich. 1967) pp 46-49.

(11) *Callimachus,* ed. R. Pfeiffer (Oxford 1949-53) v. 1, frag. 465.

(12) F. J. Witty, 'The Pínakes of Callimachus', *Library quarterly* 28 (1958) pp. 132-36.

(13) Aeschylus. *Septem quæ supersunt tragoediæ* recensuit Gilbertus Murray (Oxford Classical Texts; 2nd ed., Oxford 1957) p. 205.

(14) *Oxford classical dictionary,* edited by N. G. L. Hammond and H. H. Scullard (2nd ed., Oxford 1970) : 'Hypothesis" pp. 535-36 and 'Epitome' p. 402.

(15) *The Tebtunis papyri,* edited by B. P. Grenfell and A. S. Hunt (London 1902-38) v. 3, pt. 1, nos. 814-15.

(16) The use of marginal summaries as the basis for the index entries is seen in G. Budé, *De asse et partibus eius* (Paris 1541), an index studied by the writer in his 'Early indexing techniques : A Study of Several Book Indexes of the Fourteenth, Fifteenth and Early Sixteenth Centuries', *Library quarterly* 35 (1965) pp. 141-148; cf. pp. 147-8.

(17) E. Chatelain, *Paléographie des classiques latins* (Paris 1884-1900) plates 184, 186.

(18) D. S. Wallace-Hadrill, *Eusebius of Cæsarea* (London 1960) p. 70.

(19) L. W. Daly, *Op. cit.,* p. 64; other pagan *apothegmata* are mentioned on p. 62.

(20) *Op. cit.,* p. 47 (1.15.10).

(21) *Patrologia graeca* (Migne) 95. 1039-1588, 96. 9-442; also L. W. Daly, *Op. cit.,* pp. 63-4.

(22) 'Early Alphabetic Indices in the Vatican Archives', *Traditio* 24 (1963) p. 486.

(23) *Ms Vindobonensis suppl. graec.* 28.

(24) Hain 14508.

Book Indexing in Great Britain:

A Brief History

G. Norman Knight

The origin of indexes

Indexes must have had their origin in the tables of contents which were fairly frequently to be found in mediaeval manuscripts. Their alphabetical arrangement came into use—very slowly—after the European invention of printing in the middle of the 15th century.

The name 'index' itself, which had been used in this sense by Cicero, had a long struggle to oust such competitive synonyms as not only 'table' but also 'calendar', 'catalogue', 'inventory', 'register', 'summary' and 'syllabus'. Shakespeare in his *Troilus and Cressida* (Act I, Sc. 3), 1609, writes:

And in such *indexes*, although small pricks
To their *subsequent volumes,* there is seen
The baby figure of the giant mass
Of things to come at large.

[The italics are mine.] H. B. Wheatley[1] remarks regarding this passage that Shakespeare has established for all time the correct literary plural form. We must therefore leave the Latin 'indices' to the mathematicians.

Some early indexes

Four years ago I was able to inspect some ancient indexes in the British Museum, through the courtesy of the Superintendent of the Reading Room (incidentally the present Chairman of the Society of Indexers).

Reprinted by kind permission of the author and of *The Journal of Library History* in the April 1968 issue of which journal it appears.

The earliest indexed book I could discover was *Provinciale seu constitutiones Angliae* by K. Lyndewoode (1525). The index, which is entitled 'Tabula', is, like the text, in Latin and no page references are provided. The entries are in alphabetical order but the whole thing is more in the nature of a table of contents.

Very interesting examples I found in the two editions of *Urbinatis Anglicae historiae* by Polydore Vergil (1546 and 1555), both beautifully bound and produced. The index to the latter one, which is dedicated to the reader ('Index hic tibi lector Angliae'), occupies no fewer than 31 pages and is in Latin, like the text, with an occasional Greek word. The entries are given in strictly alphabetical order, except that the archbishops of Canterbury (under the heading 'Cantuarii') are arranged chronologically. What is more remarkable, after each page reference there is shown the actual *line number* on the page on which the item appears. The index user is not, alas, similarly pampered nowadays.[2]

Similar consideration for the user is shown in John Speed's *The history of Great Britaine* (1611), where the 'Index or Alphabetical Table' refers inquirers not only to the text page numbers but also to the section numbers in each chapter. The order again is strictly alphabetical, but I noticed that the Monastery and the Battle of St. Albans both occur under Alban, whereas we should place them today under Saint. Another odd practice in this index is that the names of persons when used as keywords are not inverted.

Thus we have in the Bs:

Roger Baldock, Bishop of Norwich
Walter Baldock, Prior of Laund

None the less, both this and Polydore Vergil's are remarkably useful indexes.

The index to *The naturall historie* of C. Plinius Secundus, translated by Philemon Holland (1601), was the earliest that I came across in the English language. This has a heading: 'Haire shedding, how to be retained and recovered' followed by no fewer than 40 page references in solid unbroken rows. The next entry is 'Haire of mans head medicinable' and there are sixteen other main headings starting with 'Haire', the alphabetical arrangement going sadly astray.

The pillorying of Prynne

An early index of both historical and legal interest that I was able to inspect in the British Museum is that to *Histrio-mastix: the players scourge* by William Prynne (1633). Had the author, described as 'an utter-Barrister of Lincolnes-Inn', confined himself to writing the text, which is practically unreadable,[3] he would not have landed himself in the pillory and been deprived of both his ears. But he was so proud of his invective against stage plays that he compiled a full and florid index of 40 pages, four of which he devoted to his idol, Bishop Hooper, whose sermons and letters are there quoted at length. It was entries like the following one (which I have actually abbreviated) that were Prynne's undoing:

'Women-Actors notorious whores ... and dare then any Christian women be so more than whorishly impudent as to act, to speak publikely on a stage perchance in man's apparell and cut haire here proved sinful and abominablle in the presence of sundry men and women? ... O let such presidents of imprudency, of impiety be never heard of or suffered among Christians, 385'.

This was scarcely a tactful utterance at a time when Charles I's Queen, Henrietta Maria, was preparing with her court ladies to act in a pastoral, and when Prynne was prosecuted in the Star Chamber Attorney-

General Noy took care to quote the above and other similarly breathless outbursts from the index. He was sentenced to the savage penalties I have mentioned, together with a fine of £5,000 (the equivalent of at least £50,000 in today's currency). Justly, some might think, not because of the index's contents but for its prolixity.

It is interesting to note that this must have been about the first occasion on which an indexer used preliminary notes (so often and usefully employed in modern substantial indexes) to explain the meaning of abbreviations, symbols or other devices occurring in the index. Thus, Prynne supplies a note: 'p. signifying the page, f. the folioes from pag. 513 to 545 (which exceeded the Printer's computations), m. the marginall notes ...'.

18th century indexes

Hitherto indexes to books had been compiled mainly by their authors. The 18th century saw the advent of the professional indexer. He was usually of inferior status—a Grub Street hack—although well-read and occasionally a university graduate. We get some idea of his condition in life from a passage in Dean Swift's pamphlet *A further account of the most deplorable conditions of Mr Edmund Curll, bookseller, since his being poisoned on the 28th March* (1716):

'At the laundress's at the Hole in the Wall in Cursitor's Alley up three pair of stairs ... you may speak to the gentleman, if his flux be over, who lies in the flock bed, my index maker.'

Again, in Oliver Goldsmith's *Citizen of the world* (1762) a certain pretentious character is contemptuously dismissed as one who 'writes indexes to perfection'. Although he may have ceased to dwell up three pair of stairs at the Hole in the Wall, it may be worth remarking that up to quite recent years the indexer always tended to be the Cinderella of the British publishing world.

In 1737 appeared that great index, *Cruden's concordance*. Although Alexander Cruden was not the first (by nearly two centuries) to publish a concordance of the Bible and although he himself was so eccentric that he had to be confined at times in a madhouse, his work after 230 years is still in daily use.

Samuel Johnson's famous *Dictionary of the English language* was published in 1755. Robert L. Collison[4] points out that Cruden indexed only the Bible—Johnson indexed the English language itself. To assist him he employed six 'scribes', or professional indexers. It was Dr. Johnson who asked his friend Samuel Richardson, usually regarded as the first true English novelist, to add an *Index rerum* to *Clarissa*, and Richardson complied in its third edition (1751). Four years later he published as a separate work what is described in the preface as a 'General Index both of Maxims and Reflexions' for *Pamela, Clarissa* and *Sir Charles Grandison*. This is not the place to discuss whether or not novels should be provided with indexes.[5]

During this century analytical indexing of subjects had grown to a peak that is rarely approached today and the habit arose of making a study of the index serve as a substitute for reading the entire text. Thomas Fuller (1608-61) had previously written about 'indical learning' and now Alexander Pope was to deride the practice in his *Dunciad* (1728):

How index-learning turns no student pale,
Yet holds the eel of science by the tail.

The indexes to British Government publications have almost invariably borne a very high reputation, largely due no doubt to paying a satisfactory rate of remuneration. We learn that in 1778 a total of £12,000 was voted for indexes to the (pre-Hansard) Journals of the House of Commons. The items of this amount, as quoted by Wheatley, were:

'To Mr. Edward Moore £6,400 as a final compensation for thirteen years labour; Rev. Mr. Forster £3000 for nine years labour; Rev. Dr. Roger Flaxman £3000 for nine years labour; and £500 to Mr. Cunningham.'

Other government indexes that have proved their usefulness down to the present day include those to: the excellent series of *Calendars of state papers*; Parliamentary papers (although several important 'Blue

Books' have unaccountably made their appearance unindexed!); 'Hansard' and the *London Gazette*.

Indexing in the 19th century

By 1800, indexes had greatly improved both in quantity and quality. The 7th edition of the *Encyclopaedia Britannica*, Edinburgh (1827-42), included as its 22nd volume a separate index to the whole. Its great rival, *Chambers's encyclopaedia*, followed suit in 1874, as have other similar publications since. Some publishers of the cheaper cyclopedias continue to shuffle out of their responsibility for providing an index under the pretext that the articles are already arranged in alphabetical order of their titles. But the fact is that an index is more vital in an encyclopaedia than in almost any other work of reference. Thus, for instance, while the *Britannica* has a long article on GREAT BRITAIN in the text, its index entry on that country comprises nearly five columns containing references to a mass of information *in related articles* throughout the 23 volumes. As Collison points out:[6] 'For the great majority of its users the encyclopaedia is a poor tool without its index'.

In the preface to his *Lives of the chief justices of England* (1849-57) the 1st Baron Campbell, who was himself at different times Lord Chief Justice and Lord Chancellor, made his famous declaration:

'So essential did I consider an index to be to every book, that I proposed to bring a Bill into Parliament to deprive an author who publishes a book without an Index of the privilege of copyright; and moreover to subject him for his offence to a pecuniary penalty.'[7]

Alas, no such legislation was ever enacted. Also Lord Campbell confesses that he himself had previously sinned.

In 1877 Dr. Wheatley and some fellow enthusiasts founded the Index Society (not to be confused with the present Society of Indexers) with the laudable aim of providing indexes for important works that had been published without any. It performed some valuable work and published a variety of indexes (1879-91), notably the fine index to Sir George Trevelyan's *Life and letters of Lord Macaulay* (1876) compiled by Perceval Clarke in 1881. Unfortunately it failed for lack of support; Wheatley considered that its aim had possibly been too general. Had it been confined to history and biography, it might have been more successful.

Other excellent examples published during that century include *The analytical index to the works of Jeremy Bentham* (1843), compiled by J. H. Burton, George Birkbeck Hill's index to his own edition of *Boswell's Life of Johnson* (1887)—the *Life* (1791) had originally been indexed in characteristic fashion by the biographer himself—and the index to Wheatley's edition of the *Diary of Samuel Pepys* (1893-9).

The 20th century

In the present century authors, publishers, the reading public and literary critics alike became more index-conscious, and the last-named have come to point out frequently in their reviews the absence or deficiencies of an index.

The three outstanding events in the British indexing world took place in the second half of the century. They were the foundation of the Society of Indexers in 1957, the institution in 1961 by the Library Association of the Wheatley Medal for an outstanding index of the year and the publication of the British Standard Institution's *Recommendations for the preparation of indexes* (B.S. 3700: 1964). The second and third were largely the result of the first.

The Society of Indexers, which started with about 100 members, has now trebled that number and some 35 reside in the United States. It has the following aims: to improve the standard of indexing; to provide a liaison with authors, editors and publishers for the supply of qualified indexers and to advise about remuneration; to publish or communicate books and papers on indexing; to raise the status of indexers.

As regards the penultimate aim, while the Society has not so far got down to publishing an index for any important work originally issued without one, as did the old Index Society, it has from almost the start published every half-year its own journal, *The Indexer,* consisting of an average of 48 pages and containing a number of weighty articles, which are duly abstracted in *Library science abstracts.*

Among other useful activities, the Society promoted a Course of Training in Indexing in 1958, and since 1961 this in an expanded form has become an annual event.

The annual award of the Wheatley Medal for a book index of outstanding merit published in the United Kingdom during the preceding year was instituted by the Library Association in 1961. The qualifications and the adjudication are both strict and for three years none of the nominated books has been judged worthy of the award. Of the four indexers who have so far received the award no fewer than three have been the authors of the books concerned. In this connexion it has been suggested (possibly unfairly) that the author-indexer possesses a pull over his professional rival in that it is thought he can claim almost unlimited space for his index from his publisher. The first medal went to Mr. Michael Maclagan, Senior Tutor of Trinity College, Oxford, in respect of his index to his own work, *Clemency Canning* (1962). Undoubtedly by instituting the award the Library Association has succeeded in stimulating the production of good indexes.

The British Standard for the *Preparation of indexes* (1964) was the result of a suggestion made by the Society of Indexers. It followed (both in time and to some extent in essential recommendations) the American Standards Association's Z39.4 — *Indexes* (1959). The sub-committee that prepared the British Standard included four members of the Society of Indexers. The standard has certainly proved its usefulness in influencing indexers but already stands in need of slight revision, so that the sub-committee is about to renew its labours.

Among the many notably excellent book indexes that have appeared during the present century, mention may be made of the following: E. T. Cook and Alexander Wedderburn's edition of the *Works of John Ruskin* (index volume No. 39, 1912); Dr. L. F. Powell's revision of Birkbeck Hill's edition of Boswell's *Life of Johnson* (1934-50)—the index is an improvement in many respects; the Centenary edition of *The complete works of William Hazlitt*, indexed by Mr. James Thornton (Vol. 21, 1934); Anthony Spalding's *The reader's handbook*

to Proust: an index guide (1952), containing a rare example of an index to characters in fiction; Dr. Esmond de Beer's index to Evelyn's *Diary* (1955); and the facsimile edition of Richard Hakluyt's *Principall navigations* (1965), which gained for its indexer, Mrs. Alison Quinn, a Wheatley Medal.

Considerable as has been the progress achieved during recent years, there are still, alas, far too many books published without the needed indexes or with only indifferent ones.

---

[1] Henry Benjamin Wheatley, D.C.L., F.S.A. (1838-1917), a noted bibliographer and sometimes described as 'the father of modern indexing'. His *How to make an index* (1902) is still one of the most valuable treatises on this subject.

[2] The most that he can hope for today is such a device as that used in the *Encyclopaedia Britannica* index, where a small a, b, c or d after each page reference denotes in which of the four sections of the large page of the text the item is to be found.

[3] Thomas Carlyle refers to *Histrio-mastix* as a book 'still extant, but never more to be read by mortal'.

[4] *Indexes and indexing* (2nd ed., London, Benn, 1959).

[5] Students of such classics as *Don Quixote* by Miguel de Cervantes Saavedra (1605) would undoubtedly welcome the assistance of an index. The late Evelyn Waugh possessed a fully indexed translation of Count Tolstoy's *Resurrection* (1889), published in New York, while the present writer knows of a librarian who has compiled a comprehensive index to John Galsworthy's complete *Forsyte saga* (1922).

[6] *Encyclopaedias: their history throughout the ages,* New York, London, Hafner, 1964.

[7] A distinguished American lawyer, the Hon. Horace Binney, held the same views.

II. The Practice of Book Indexing

IIa. Principles and Techniques

The Purpose of Indexing

L. R. McColvin

In a paper presented at the Conference of the London and Home Counties Branch of the Library Association in June,[1] Mr Philip Unwin wrote: 'Some reviewers, especially those in one of our most respected weeklies, delight to pounce with governessy righteousness upon any publisher guilty of producing a book without an index. Of course every substantial specialist work must have one but I contend that there are many "general" books to which an index is superfluous. A good list of contents gives an intelligent reader all he needs and an index is not provided for nothing.'

Listening to him I thought of the books I had encountered that I had had to read through, suffering agonies of boredom, just to find that after all there was, as I had expected, nothing therein of any significance relating to the matter with which I was concerned – just because they had no index. And, to be quite frank, I remembered that when my own report on public library services[2] was, in 1942, being prepared for the press, I weakly agreed with someone who shall be nameless who said: '*You don't want an index, Mac. If you have one all they'll do will be to look up what you've said about "them" and no one will read it all right through.*' And being humanly frail I confess to feeling flattered when told that one librarian whom I could not honestly call a 'librarian friend' had handed it over to one of his staff with the words '*I suppose I'll have to read it but for heaven's sake make an index to it. Fancy charging five bob for the damned thing – and no index*'.

However, I was pondering Philip Unwin's remarks, agreeing with him that some books definitely need indexes and others do not, when the Editor wrote to me asking for an article on the purposes of indexes. 'Yes', I thought, 'if we had a clear idea of the purposes for which an index is provided we should know better when one is necessary – and, also, what kind of index it should be.'

Having assured the Editor that I knew nothing about indexing and having been assured by him that as it was the user's point of view he sought and that consequently my ignorance was a positive asset, I began by studying all the books on indexing I could find to see what others, better informed, regarded as the purposes of an index.

I naturally turned first to my friend Collison's[3] book. There I found an admirable phrase: '*The one purpose in making an index to any book is to make all the information in that volume fully available to any reader without delay*'. I thought to myself 'what else is there to be said?' until I realized that it wasn't the 'one purpose' – but I anticipate. Nowhere else could I find, after studying some ten volumes on indexing, any reason why one should index excepting a reference to Seneca who wrote of providing indexes to certain books so that the recipient of

Reprinted from *The Indexer* 1, no. 2 (September 1958): 31–35.

the volumes 'might be spared the trouble of examining them entire' – which is, of course, a very important purpose.

To my mind the salient point about every index is that it is a guide to the contents of a book (or whatever it may be that is indexed) which is arranged differently from the contents themselves. Usually an index is alphabetical, with maybe some classified sub-arrangement under the alphabetical headings. The book itself is arranged according to the author's treatment. Now the author's treatment may be the only one possible, or at least sufficiently satisfactory as to make demand for any other treatment unlikely. I cannot say impossible. The novel, the poem and the play are examples of books of which most readers are prepared to accept the author's treatment, i.e. they begin at the beginning and read through to the end. Few people want to look back for an episode or a passage in a novel they had read and if they did they would have some recollection of the book's sequence to guide them; one would not expect someone who had not read the book to seek therein any isolated item as he would not know what he might find. Nevertheless even for novels and poems the time may come when indexes – and even that most detailed of all indexes, the concordance – will be required, i.e. when the author's works have become a subject for quotation, study and research.

Apart, however, from works of 'pure' literature most books contain facts or ideas that could be of value in isolation from the context as a whole, both to people who had read the book and those who had not. If the book's own pattern, maybe as disclosed by the list of contents, makes it simple to find every such isolated item again an index may be unnecessary. Usually, however, the specific item cannot be found with certainty unless an index is provided. Clearly the first purpose of an index is to enable he who does not want or does not need to read a book as a whole to find the particular passage in it, the particular item of information that he does need.

One can go further and say that the index must enable the user to find *all* that there is in the volume dealing with a particular theme, etc.

But that is not its sole purpose.

As I have mentioned above, the book is arranged according to the author's treatment and just as the books on the shelves of a library can only be arranged according to one classification system, so can the items of which that book is made up. The librarian knows well that the classification system adopted can at best be that which serves most users, that for other users it does not necessarily bring related material together. On the contrary, it disperses it. He knows that for some people classification does not *disclose* desiderata, it *loses* them. So he does his best to overcome the limitation of one place classification by means of cross references, added entries, analytics, indexes and all the other paraphernalia of the modern cataloguer. It is the same as regards most individual books. The author chooses to arrange his work in a particular way because he believes that thereby he will help and please most readers. If he is not unaware that thereby he will hinder and displease others, he adds an index. No index could render it possible for anyone to use a book as a whole to serve some purpose for which a different arrangement was needed but at least it could enable the student for which that different arrangement was suitable to find, from time to time, the relevant data as given in the book in question. Let us, for example, think of a book on French cathedrals which could be arranged in numerous different ways. Each cathedral could be described in the sequence of the author's tour of visiting, or according to provinces or departments or even alphabetically by place. It could be arranged according to historical or architectural factors though no arrangement by date or style could be very rigid, because probably in every cathedral one would find work of different dates and in different styles. My point is that however it is arranged some users will not be satisfied unless it is well indexed – unless indeed the index caters for all possible lines of approach (name, period, style, etc.). Even this will not be completely sufficient. The index must also be a guide to detail of all kinds. Some users may be concerned with architectural features, e.g. fonts, reredos, organ lofts, others with architects, others with materials and processes, others with historical and biographical associations.

When an index of this kind *is* provided, however, not only does it serve varying approaches, it also discloses relationships which, perhaps not previously manifest, may lead to further and different lines of research or explain the previously inexplicable.

If we revert to our previous example: the index to the book on French cathedrals will tell the man interested in Chartres where to look and it will also tell the man who seeks information about stained glass, or carved screens or organ lofts the various places in which to look.

Usually, to be frank, that is all. Since, for example, all churches have fonts and most have stained glass, the good index will in effect more or less provide two entries for the same thing – one under place and one under the thing itself. It is not always so, however. Some places will have some things but not other places and vice versa. Thus, if the book is sufficiently thorough and the index sufficiently specific the index could disclose that a particular kind of font, of a particular stone, or design, was found in certain places, perhaps certain regions and not elsewhere, or in certain periods, and so on. To change my metaphors, a good index could be a guide to 'ecology' – and show that in a certain soil particular plants grow and particular annuals flourish. Probably these relationships would be of little significance to the author or the user concerned with *his* pattern of presentation but could be of great significance to the 'outsider' whose approach is from another angle.

Thirdly, of course, an index can indicate what one will *not* find in a book – which can be a great saver of time. For example, if the index to a description of the Tyrol has no reference to Fieberbrunn I am saved detailed study of the book *if that is all I want from it* at the time. In other words indexing saves time, not only positively (in that it guides the user at once to the required information) but also negatively.

I think these are the main purposes, i.e. (*i*) *to facilitate reference to the specific item;* (*ii*) *to compensate as far as possible for the fact that a book can only be written in one sequence, according to one plan; (iii) to disclose relationships, and (iv) to disclose omissions.* But there are others. Of them I can think of (v) *to provide a living for indexers*, if indeed any of them are able to keep alive on what they earn as indexers, and (vi), quite seriously, *to limit wear and tear on the items indexed.* So far as books are concerned this seldom arises but with newspapers and maybe other periodicals it can be important. Files of newspapers, printed on very inferior paper, would soon disintegrate were there not indexes to limit the handling to which they would be subjected.

Whether in fact indexes can fulfil these purposes depends entirely upon their thoroughness and the method of presentation adopted.

To ensure the finding of specific information an index must be complete, it must give entries or reference under all the headings likely to be used, and any necessary sub-division under a heading must be given. When I say complete I do not mean that it should be cluttered up as indexes often are with useless references which can only cause annoyance, i.e. entries which in fact do not lead to information about the specific item. For example, it is quite absurd to refer an enquirer on Mittersill to page 47, when all that is there is a statement that 'Those wishing to travel to the Tyrol [from X] must go via Lofer or via Zell am See, Mittersill, etc.'. There is need for discretion, nevertheless. In certain instances even a casual relationship might have significance. For example, the biography of B might tell that in Paris in 1869 he met C, D, E, F, G and H. If it is at all significant that B and, say, F ever met or met there, then an entry under F would be useful. The test for inclusion or exclusion is whether the entry leads to the discovery of any information which might be of interest to anyone who would look under that entry in an index.

It is axiomatic that in a good index whenever one reference is to the pages where the major or systematic treatment will be found, that reference should be given prominence. To return to my travel book, probably there will be a page or more where the author, as it were, stops and describes a place and though he may make many references in passing, it is the former that most users seek.

I believe that whenever a heading can be sub-divided it should be so treated, not only to save time but to show the relationship discussed earlier. The indexer should not be deterred if this involves a great deal of repetition. Similarly, unless it is both complete and detailed the index cannot tell what is not in the book.

Incidentally an index can be of value when selecting books to borrow from a library or buy from a bookshop. The selector who is chiefly interested in certain matters can readily see whether, and how extensively, the book covers them. To others the index may offer a brief summary of the kinds of material covered and the extent of coverage.

Is it going too far to say that where a good index is not thoroughly justified, no index is necessary. I do not think it is. Any kind of selection of entries, any deliberate omission, implies that some of the things are more likely to be sought than are others. It is highly debatable whether this is so. I do not suggest that some entries may not attract more users, these being references to matters of most general interest, but such matters will be few and, excepting these, choice will be extremely hazardous.

So it becomes a question of to index (well) or not to index. Despite the foregoing it must in many cases be a matter of personal choice. For many books it is obvious that there must be a good index; conversely, others manifestly can be without one. What of those in between? I think the real deciding factors are these. Firstly, is the book capable of being indexed. Some – few perhaps – are not. Such are books which are essentially argument rather than fact presentation, books which at any particular place are often not about one thing but several, books where the threads interwind but cannot be disentangled sufficiently for an indexer to relate them to specific pages. For such books indexes probably would be quite useless and misleading.

Secondly, is the book sufficiently serious and systematic? The index to a popular superficial travel book or volume of reminiscences might well say so little about so many things that no index user would find worth-while reward. By all means let Mr Unwin and his fellow publishers save money on such books.

Maybe, however, more money would be saved if such books were not published at all – unless, of course, they are so profitable that they can help pay for indexes for other books which deserve them.

---

[1] *Libraries and the book world*, Hastings, 6th–8th June, 1958.

[2] *The public library system of Great Britain: a report on its present condition with proposals for post-war reorganization.* ix, 218p. The Library Association, 1942.

[3] *Indexes and Indexing.* 155p. Benn, 1953.

Introduction to Book Indexing

M. D. Law*

Introduction

For the betterment of men's condition, the world today, as a thousand years ago, has two basic needs: wealth and knowledge. Even the most compassionate and generous, the most highly skilled administrator, cannot share out what does not exist, and the most brilliant intellects cannot apply powers of reasoning and imaginative deduction to information they do not possess.

It is not for us to consider how to increase wealth. But it is for us to consider how to increase information—or rather to make it increasingly available. We all acknowledge the need for information and for spreading it about: books, films, radio, television, strip cartoons, teaching machines, learned transactions, blue books, white papers, reports of commissions, even opinion polls, all proliferate—'Communication', used no doubt in a variety of meanings, is indeed, one of the great vogue words.

Rôle of the Indexer

In the task of spreading, communicating information and perhaps, who knows, of even increasing it, the rôle of the indexer is, I often think, insufficiently recognized. The work is certainly all too often inadequately remunerated. I cannot encourage you to believe you will directly add to any substantial increase of personal wealth. But you may indeed be lending an indirect hand, your little personal push, to the better grasp of events and ideas and thus to the improvement of human understanding.

---

* The introductory lecture to the 1970 Course in Book Indexing.

An Index: its essential purpose

You will forgive me, I hope, if in now turning to consider the essential purpose of an index, I begin at the beginning and discuss, in too elementary a fashion, concepts and techniques with which you, or some of you, are already familiar. But it may be useful, I hope it will be, to think again about such matters.

In the first place, the purpose of an index is to re-organize the information in the book (or other printed material) to turn it inside out, as it were. The information has to be broken down, and re-assembled into its component parts. These components have then to be collated and arranged in a form at once planned and consistent and therefore easily consulted.

An index is not a table of contents and must never be confused with one. A table of contents is a summary of the author's plan of his book, how he has chosen to present his theme in the most interesting and thoughtful way. An index is the indexer's plan of the information given by the author, how the indexer is re-presenting the author's material in the most convenient way.

Qualifications for an Indexer

There are several attributes the possession of which will make life easier for the intending professional indexer. High among them is an orderly mind, the kind of mind which tends automatically to sort and classify. If you put your things back where they belong, and where they belong is the logical place, this is the attitude. Next, one needs wide general knowledge and a passion for accuracy. You need not be a polymath or a computer. But you ought to cultivate that kind of background knowledge which rings

Reprinted from *The Indexer* 7, no. 2 (Autumn 1970): 46–48.

a bell when you encounter a phrase, event, person only barely familiar and not really comprehended; warning you that although you may not know, there is something there that ought to be checked. Thereupon, without enough context, the Sublime Porte, the Eastern Question, Batavia, should, unless you happen to know, at least remind you that the first had to do with Turkey, the second did not begin with Zionism, and make you query which Batavia–the island of the former Dutch empire or the short-lived republic of the Low Countries. People, too, can be pitfalls, especially politicians who become ennobled halfway through their careers; persons known by different names in widely separated fields of endeavour; and of course, the elegant alias.

It is good, also, to be a rapid reader; and unless you are expert with a typewriter and indeed even if you are, to have neat and legible handwriting.

Procedure for Beginners
May I suggest how absolute beginners should begin?

First, have a good look at the publication before you accept the commission, and do not accept as your first undertaking a work which may prove too vexatious, e.g. a series of philosophical essays, a work on economic or political theory, or a scientific work, unless you have a high degree of specialized knowledge. Nothing is more difficult to deal with than abstract concepts and ideas or technical jargon, especially if this happens to include a large number of ordinary words used in a highly technical sense.

Secondly, find out from the publisher the proposed length of index, number of pages, size of type, number of columns per page, and thus the number of headings and references.

Then set to work
Start by reading or thoroughly scanning the whole book, noting the scope of the subject matter and its treatment, e.g. whether chronological or by topics or themes.

Secondly, relate the number of references available to you to the number of pages in

the work, thus discovering how many references per page you can take out *on average*.

Supposing it is a shortish work, say 222 pages of text. The index is to occupy 5 pp., each of 2 columns. The size of type used will permit a maximum of 47 headings per column. This would be a maximum of 470 headings in the finished index, each heading with no more references, i.e. page numbers, than would fill the line of type, say 4 or 5 references per heading. You cannot however allow for this; you have to allow one blank line of space between each letter of the alphabet; you have to reckon that a proportion of headings will carry more than four or five references and thus occupy two or more lines; and you may need to subdivide some headings into classifications. I suggest you allow two-thirds or possibly three-quarters as many headings as the maximum, i.e. instead of 470, say 300 plus.

Now for the references (or page numbers). These may average, say, five or six per heading, allowing for headings that have only one reference and those which have six to twenty. Say you allow 150 references (or page numbers) per column. This means 1,500 references for 222 pages of text or about six per page.

Third, start reading carefully, underlining the items, persons, places, events, ideas and topics you propose to index.

As you go, write out in ink (or type) a card or slip for each item, the heading in the top left-hand corner, followed by a description which will identify the heading. In the middle put the modification, i.e. the word or phrase which points to the particular aspect of the heading, and in the bottom right-hand corner (but give yourself space) insert the page number.

Two important points must be borne in mind. Do not use two headings which are synonymous, with some references under one and some under the other; the synonym if included as a heading should be cross-referred to the chosen heading. Of course, make sure that the headings *are* synonymous and not merely similar. Also it will often be necessary to make two or more cards with different headings (but the same reference) for one item, e.g. in a book about the drama, a discussion on Shakespeare's views on tragedy as exemplified in *Hamlet* could well qualify for index entries under the headings ' Shakespeare ', ' tragedy ', and ' *Hamlet* '. In a work on agriculture an important reference to wheat should be indexed also under the headings ' cereal ' and ' grasses '.

When you have finished and have your 1,500 or more probably 2,000 cards or slips they must be sorted into alphabetical order. They must then be edited. This means arranging all the references for one heading together in some planned order, page order, order of importance (when the subordinate references should be prefaced by modifications in alphabetical order) or classified.

Equipment

Start with the minimum—you will find as you go on that you develop your own habits of work and need equipment accordingly. A supply of cards or slips, soft pencils, a good india rubber, paper clips, rubber bands, and a small shoe box will serve you more than adequately. I do heartily recommend you, however, to provide yourself with a few reference books, e.g. *Whitaker's Almanack,* a good dictionary, a printer's guide to proof-reading and type sizes, and, if possible, a reliable encyclopaedia or at the least easy access to one.

Some Do's and Don'ts

Do take plenty of time for the initial planning—mistakes made here will never be retrieved.

Do be accurate. Never guess or rely on being virtually certain—check up.

Do check up all queries before you put the cards into alphabetical order. If you have been misled by an alias or pseudonym or an elevation to the peerage or one of several places with the same name, the query may be lost because it is in the wrong alphabetical place.

Do train your memory.

Don't, I will repeat, enter different references to the same person, place, thing, event or topic under different headings.

Don't make references to similar things or topics under one heading. This is back to the Table of Contents fallacy.

Don't over-index the first fifty pages.

Don't, for your convenience in editing, skimp descriptions and modifications. This will help you too to prune the index at the very last to the required length.

How to Recognise a Good Index

Geoffrey Hamilton

Discusses criteria for evaluating printed subject indexes, based on those used as guidelines by the Wheatley Medal selection committee. Some common faults in indexes are mentioned. The intention of the article is to suggest a method of assessing indexes which can be applied by anyone who needs to do this, as well as to indicate what the characteristics are of an outstanding index.

It has been initially gratifying to note that in recent years the number of indexes entered for the Wheatley Medal seems to provide evidence that the compilation of high-quality indexes in Britain is a thriving activity. However, it has subsequently been disappointing to find after only a brief preliminary examination that several of these indexes are not outstanding in any way. This article has been written in an attempt to show how a good index can be recognised. The criteria discussed are those which serve as guidelines for the Wheatley Medal award. The comments are the author's personal views, and the article is in no way an official statement on behalf of the Wheatley Medal selection committee. It is hoped that its publication may encourage nominations for the Wheatley Medal, but it is intended to serve also as a guide to anyone who has occasion to assess the quality of a printed subject index.

The Wheatley Medal is awarded for an outstanding index. This is perhaps not sufficiently appreciated, and there may be some who regard it as the reward for a perfect index. It is unlikely that a perfect index, in the sense of one that is universally recognised as being incapable of improvement, has been or will be compiled. Outstanding indexes certainly exist, good indexes are numerous, but there are unfortunately many indexes which are of indifferent quality or downright inadequate. How can an index be placed correctly, after a brief examination, within this spectrum? Several criteria will be put forward and discussed, of which some are objective in nature, while others—a majority—involve some degree of subjective assessment. Some are concerned with features which inevitably occur in all indexes (such as length of the index and the arrangement of entries in it). Others relate to features which are not necessarily present in every index (such as an introductory note). Thus, not all of these criteria will apply in every case, and the odd fault under any of them will not invariably disqualify from the highest grading. Shortcomings under several headings are a clear indication that an index is not in the top class.

The order in which the various criteria are considered can be varied according to circumstances and personal preference. An early indication of a good index can be found without even examining a single index entry, by considering the length of the index in pages as a proportion of the number of pages in the work indexed. If this proportion is less than five per cent it is unlikely that the index can be sufficiently detailed. However, due regard should be paid to the format of the index. If it is set in two or more columns to a page, the proportion may fall below five per cent without necessarily indicating insufficiently detailed indexing. Another point to watch for is whether the work indexed includes a significant number of pages of illustrative or tabulated matter, which would thus call for a comparatively small number of index entries. Regardless of the size of the work being indexed, it is reasonable to assume that any index which amounts to about fifty pages or more deserves further scrutiny.

In turning attention to the index itself, probably the first item to claim attention will be the introductory note, if there is one. Points which should always be noted include a statement of what the location references refer to, if this is not page numbers; the meaning of any abbreviations which occur in the index; the significance of variations in type-faces within entries, such as the use of bold numerals for major references or of italic numerals for illustrations. Any deliberate limitations of coverage should be explained, such as the exclusion of references to illustrations and appendices, or the omission of entries for topics which are mentioned only in passing in the text. It is advisable to carry out some spot checks to make sure that the indexer has consistently done what the introductory note proclaims. So far as statements of limitations are concerned, if these are reasonable in relation to the work being in-

Reprinted from *The Indexer* 10, no. 2 (October 1976): 49–53.

25

dexed then the indexer should be credited for the decision and for drawing attention to it. Conversely, if, after further examination of the index limitations are found which have not been noted, this may be counted a serious fault. As well as considering the content of an introductory note, attention should be paid to its style. A good introductory note will be clear and well expressed, without an unnecessary word.

In forming a judgment on the quality of an index several characteristics must be taken into account. The first of these relates to the coverage of significant items in the text. An obvious difficulty arises in determining the criteria for deciding which items in a given text are significant, and the assessor must be on his guard against an inclination to apply standards which are too closely based on subjective criteria. What were the author's objectives in writing the book? For what level of readership is it intended? How has the author organised his text? What kinds of information are conveyed by the work, and to whom will the information be of use? These are the kinds of question the assessor should continually be asking, and to obtain answers to them it will often be necessary to peruse introductory sections and examine contents lists, as well as selecting sample passages in the work for particular scrutiny and checking against the index. If you have special knowledge of an aspect of the subject-matter of the work, the appropriate section may be selected for this scrutiny. Bear in mind, however, that the object of the exercise is to see how good the indexer's judgment of significant items is, and not to find out how well the author treats the subject. In other words, it is possible to have a good index to an indifferent work. The Conditions of Award for the Wheatley Medal stipulate that 'the index must include all headings that common sense would expect, and scholarship need to find in an index'. It is important to take a broad view of the needs of scholarship, and particularly to be aware of the possible value of certain information contained in a work within one field of learning to scholars working in another field. For instance, some otherwise very good indexes to scholarly editions of the correspondence of great men give little or no assistance to scholars whose interest lies in ascertaining, through the recorded views of notable personalities, what attitudes were taken in relation to contemporary problems and issues, which might range from copyright through the conduct of the Crimean War to cremation. Thus, although indexers, and judges of indexes, must take account of the readership the author set out to address, they must also consider the possible wider uses of the resulting work.

In indexing the items which have been selected as worth an entry, has the indexer used appropriate and well-chosen terms in a consistent manner? The appropriateness of the chosen terms should be assessed with reference to the nature of the work and to its intended readership. For instance, in the case of a work dealing with natural history, will the intended readership more likely to approach it through popular or scientific names of species? In a historical work, are contemporary or current forms of names more useful? Have the indexer's decisions been consistently applied? If inconsistencies do occur it may be because the author has been inconsistent, but in such cases the indexer should make sure that a user can rely on the index to be free from such discrepancies. Consistent use of terms in the 'language' of an index is a greater virtue than rigid adherence to the author's usage. Apart from the question of inconsistencies, is the indexer's choice of terms generally based on those used by the author, or has he preferred terms which perhaps more closely relate to current general use? Some indexes are particularly likely to be used as access points by readers who expect the work to contain information they need, while others are likely to be used more often as a convenient way of finding again parts of a text which has already been read. Many indexes need to be capable of satisfying both kinds of users, and hence in choosing index terms the indexer should have regard both for the author's terminology and for that in common use. To test this the assessor may put himself in the position successively of a reader already familiar with the work and of one who seeks via the index information about topics which may be reasonably assumed to be treated in the work.

Conflicts between variant terminologies can be resolved by careful provision of cross-references. Scrutiny of any index should include an examination of the network of cross-references which may serve to connect related topics and to lead the user from an unused term to its synonym, or from an inverted form of a multi-word term to the form in which it is entered. It is best to spend a little time looking particularly at such references as appear, trying to deduce the basis on which they have been supplied, and then by checking examples of references suggested by certain headings to see if they have in fact been provided. How easy would it be for a reader with little prior knowledge of the relationship between various aspects of a subject, all of which are dealt with in the work, to find all the relevant headings in the index? While it is more common to come across an index which has an insufficient provision of cross-references, it is also possible to find the occasional example of an index which has an unnecessarily generous provision of references. If the cross-reference structure gets in the way of the user, for instance by diverting him along unprofitable byways where he will find very little relevant information, this is as much a fault as failing to provide cross-references which would be helpful. Another common failing in this area is the provision of 'see' references instead of duplicate entries where there are only a very small number of locations to be recorded, for which it is not necessary to provide sub-headings to differentiate between them.

The extent to which subheadings are used to prevent the occurrence of large numbers of un-differentiated location references should be separately considered. If there are numerous examples of strings with more than about six undifferentiated references the index is almost certainly not going to achieve an outstanding grading. This may not, of course, be the indexer's fault, since if there have to be limitations in space allocated for an index it is natural to achieve this as much as possible by cutting out sub-headings rather than by leaving entries out altogether. From the user's point of view, however, it is definitely a disadvantage not to be able to select from the index the one or two out of perhaps a dozen location references which are relevant to his needs. This scrutiny should also embrace headings which have been exten-sively subdivided. Do the subheadings clearly define the aspect of the main topic which is dealt with at a particular location? According to what principle are they arranged? It is sometimes found that the organisation of subheadings under a heavily subdivided heading is by a pseudo-classification, or in an order which corresponds to the order of the first occurrence of each aspect in the text of the indexed work. The assessment of the index for a work about a single subject or the biography of an individual person will be much influenced by the treatment of that subject or person in the index. In theory, a book about a single subject need have no, or only a very few, entries under the heading for that subject, the various aspects dealt with being scattered under headings appropriate to each

aspect. The index to a biography is far more likely to have a lengthy entry, sometimes ex-tending over several pages, for the biographee. How easy is it for users of the index to find a particular reference in such a long entry? In cases where the arrangement of subheadings follows the order of treatment of the text it may be concluded that the resulting sequence has more use as an aide-mémoire to the author than for many of the book's users.

How well does the index serve its text? This question has been an underlying one during the examination of various characteristics which have been discussed above. Can all significant items of information in the text be located by any reasonably intelligent person through use of the index? Are there any signs of bias in the index, such as uneven treatment of different subjects? Are there inconsistencies of any kind? Deliberate variations in the treatment of subjects which have been explained in an introductory note may be acceptable, provided they are reasonable. It is also appropriate to consider under this head cases in which two or more indexes, or separate sequences of entries are provided. Does this serve the text more effectively, and is it more convenient for users, than a single sequence? It may be generally helpful to have separate indexes of persons, places and subjects for a large-scale work, but in some instances it is doubtful whether the user should be required to select the appropriate index before he can even begin to look for the headings that are relevant to his enquiry.

In the process of carrying out checks of the kind suggested in the preceding paragraphs it may already have become clear that the location references are always accurate. If there is any doubt on this point some further spot checks should be made, working from the index to the text in every case. Inaccuracies in location references are a particularly serious fault, and an inaccurate page number not only renders the entry to which it is attached completely useless but casts doubt over the reliability of the entire index. The occasional very slight error, such as the citation of page 59 for an entry indexing an item of information which actually turns up in the first few lines of page 60, may be overlooked. Such instances are probably due to a reallocation of type by the printer after the return of the page proofs from which the indexer took the location references. But if, as sometimes happens, there is a large number of entries all with location references one or two page numbers removed from the correct location the index cannot be given an outstanding rating, even though the error may in no way be the indexer's fault. Another point to check while examining the accuracy of location references is whether they are consistently given with each related entry. It is surprising how often it is found that comparison of location references attached to two related entries reveals that a common core of shared location references is accompanied by further references attached to one of the headings only. This casts doubt on the indexer's consistency and thoroughness.

It will also have become apparent by this time how the entries in the index are arranged. It has been pointed out that alphabetical order is not the only arrangement that may be followed. Whatever principles are followed, is the arrangement accurate? And are the principles consistently followed? A misplaced entry is little more use than no entry at all, but an occasional lapse involving a single entry is likely to be less serious than an incorrectly filed sequence of entries. Once more, slight faults are not necessarily attributable to the indexer's carelessness. The printer may have chosen to bring forward a short entry to fill a space at the end of a column so as to avoid splitting a longer entry.

In each of the assessments made so far, attention has been focused on the content, structure or organisation of the index. It is now time to consider critically its presentation on the printed page. Many otherwise good indexes fall at this hurdle, and yet again this may not be the indexer's fault, if he has not been permitted to instruct the printer in the layout which should be adopted. The effective and consistent use of different typefaces, spacing, indentation and punctuation can make a notable contribution to the ease of use and intelligibility of an index. What use has been made of them in the index under scrutiny? Where it has been necessary to carry over entries under a particular heading to another page or column, has the heading (and subheading if one is involved) been repeated at the head of the continuation sequence? This seems such an obvious thing to do, yet it is often not done.

The presence of unusual or original features in an index should always be taken into account. Some indexes serve also as vehicles for conveying additional information, not given in the text, about some of the subjects indexed. An index which has been compiled later than the work indexed, e.g. for a reprint edition, may correct errors in the original work. Special problems may have called for the development of special solutions, for instance, in the index to the proceedings of a committee of enquiry which has to cope with questions, answers, written and oral evidence, and the ensuing report and recommendations. Unusual procedures may have been used in its preparation, for instance involving the use of mechanical aids. In all such cases it is not simply the fact that an unusual or original feature is present that is to be noted. Their suitability and the success they achieve in relation to the text that is indexed should be assessed.

The criteria which have been discussed above in the context of indexes to books apply also to the indexes to serial publications. For the latter there are also certain other points to consider during an assessment. In the case of indexes to single volumes of a serial, one of the important considerations is continuity throughout successive indexes. Can they be used satisfactorily to support a search for references to a particular topic over a period of time? There are bound to be instances of a change in terminology. How have these been dealt with? Can the user get from the old term to the new one when searching forwards in time, and from the new term to the old one when searching backwards in time? In many serials certain sections contain numerous brief news items, of which there may be twenty or more on a page. Does the index make it easy to find the particular item to which the index entry refers, for instance by using the cross-heading captions as subheadings in the index? An introductory note, explaining the treatment of special features, is particularly likely to be needed in a serial index. Among special features one which should often be present is a list of issue pagings and dates for the benefit of those who may not have individual issues bound. The other type of serial index to be considered here is the cumulative index, which will almost certainly be issued as a separate volume. Here the problems of maintaining continuity may be more easily observed. Again, the treatment accorded to topics which have been affected by changing terminology should be noted. There are likely to be some headings which cover very large numbers of references. Have they been effectively subdivided? For all serial indexes, as for book indexes, their suitability for use by any reader to locate within the text any item which may reasonably be expected to be sought is ultimately the basis for recognising a good index.

Appended to this article is a list of the 15 special criteria which are employed as guidelines by the Wheatley Medal selection committee. If there is difficulty in deciding whether an index is really outstanding, or if it is desired to determine which of several indexes should rank highest, it is possible to use this list to award marks on a four-point scale. Allot three marks for each criterion which achieves a rating of 'good' in the index under consideration, two marks for those which have an 'average' rating, one for those rated 'poor', and no marks for any criterion which does not apply. There is potentially a highest score of forty-five, which is unlikely to be achieved, but any index which gets a score above thirty on this scale will probably be outstanding in at least some respects. However, it is perfectly possible for an index which achieves a score lower than thirty to be successful when judged by a sixteenth criterion, not on the list, which recognises that a proven record of successful use to retrieve information from the text is a sufficient measure of a good index.

Appendix

Criteria used as guidelines by the Wheatley Medal Selection Committee

1. If there is an introductory note, it should be clear and well expressed.

2. The index must be accurate. The location numbers given in the index must tally with the text.

3. Significant items in the text must appear in the index.

4. Where related entries in the index are each given location references, these must be consistent.

5. An index must have enough subheadings to avoid strings of undifferentiated location references.

6. An index must be arranged in correct alphabetical or other order.

7. Items and concepts in the text must be represented in the index by appropriate, well-chosen terms.

8. The terms must be chosen consistently.

9. There must be enough cross-references to connect related items in the index.

10. There must be cross-references to relate out-of-date or idiosyncratic terms in the text to those in current use.

11. The layout must be clear and help the user.

12. An index must be comprehensive (though certain limitations on comprehensiveness may be allowable if clearly explained) and neither scanty nor unnecessarily full.

13. The index should serve the text and not be a vehicle for expressing the indexer's own views and interests.

14. If the index departs from conventions the departures should be explained in the introductory note.

15. Abbreviations, etc., should also be explained.

The Inadequacies of Book Indexes:

A Symposium

From time to time we find the expression of members' views on a particular topic both interesting and stimulating. I sent the following theme to a number of members recently and asked for their views. I have pleasure in printing their contributions.

HON. EDITOR.

A member has recently had occasion to refer to a large number of books for information on a specific subject and has been appalled at the inadequacies of their indexes. On reading many of the books concerned he has frequently found that the information he was seeking was in them but not indexed. Often personal names only were indexed. Where it was obvious, all well and good —but disappointing; in other cases it was impossible, from examining the indexes and reading the text, to determine what criterion there had been for deciding what to index and what to ignore. There were no entries for either the subject matter concerned or for the place concerned with it—and the place was important.

None of the indexes contained an introductory and explanatory paragraph, and as the indexes appeared adequate, it was assumed that they were comprehensive.

It is very frustrating for the person who has to read much of a book in order to find information which he suspects is in it but which he cannot trace through the index.

Librarians, especially those dealing with readers' enquiries, are constantly having to use indexes to trace information, and their work is rendered much less effective, and the readers' opinion of the book stock much less favourable, than it should be.

from K. G. B. Bakewell

Some years ago *The indexer* included a report of a survey by a number of library school students of indexes to periodicals, which commented very unfavourably on such indexes in the field of management.[1] This situation is not—alas—confined to periodicals but is also true of books on management, and it is with this area that I wish to deal. I became very conscious of this between 1961 and 1964 when I was librarian of the British Institute of Management and my opinion has been reinforced during recent years when I have had occasion to consult a large number of management books in connection with a particular project. There are *some* very good indexes but many are completely inadequate and make retrieval of specific information very difficult.

What concerns me more, however, is the complete absence of indexes from many books including some of the more important standard material. The noted British writer E. F. L. Brech justifies the absence of an index from his *Management: its nature and significance* (Pitman 4th ed. 1967) by arguing in his preface that the book is an essay rather than a textbook. So what? The 'essay' extends over 238 pages and contains useful information on a large number of management topics. Mr. Brech's excessive modesty should not have been allowed to prevent librarians, managers and students from being able to trace this information. Brech's *Managing for revival* (Management Publications, 1972. 292p.) also lacks an index, as do at least three contributions by the late expert on work study, Russell M. Currie: *The measurement of work* (British Institute of Management, 1965. 416p.), *Simplified PMTS*

Reprinted from *The Indexer* 9, no. 1 (April 1974): 1-9.

(British Institute of Management, 1963. 202p). and *Financial incentives based on work measurement* (Management Publications, 2nd ed. 1971. 175p.). Another major book on work study without an index is the International Labour Office's *Introduction to work study* (2nd ed. 1969. 436p.).

A feature of management literature is the large number of 'readings', which collect several previously published writings (and sometimes some original material). Very rarely are such works provided with an index, except perhaps an author index, although the papers included in them are presumably regarded as outstanding contributions to their subject. One example is *Managing people at work*, compiled by Dale S. Beach (New York: Macmillan; London: Collier-Macmillan, 1971), which contains 515 pages of readings on organisation, employment and development of personnel, motivation, financial rewards, health and safety, collective bargaining, ethics and social responsibility but has no index. There are many similar examples, and the number of pages in works I have examined ranges from approximately 400 to more than 800.

Similarly, conference proceedings and collections of case studies are often provided only with indexes of authors and/or companies. It has not occurred to the editor or publisher of such works that a subject index could perform a very useful service for the student of, say, job evaluation by enabling him to locate different views on or experiences of the subject which have been scattered throughout the publication. Proceedings of the Third International Congress on Project Planning, published as *The practical application of project planning by network of techniques* by Almquist and Wiksell (Stockholm) and the Halsted Press of John Wiley (New York), contains 110 papers in more than 1,600 pages spread over 3 volumes. It has an author index but no subject index.

Publishers really should appreciate that if material on a subject is worth publishing it is also worth indexing properly so that it can be retrieved when required. Librarians and readers should see that publishers are made aware of this fact by being quick to complain when they are inconvenienced by the absence of an adequate index.

---

[1] *The indexer,* 7 (2) Autumn, 1970, pp. 70-79.

from Kathleen Binns

It is some time now since I used indexes in order to find information for reference library users and I leave this aspect of the inadequate index to others. Recently my main use of indexes has been for assistance with indexes I was compiling to other books, and often that assistance has been of negative value; at least in some cases I was shown what to do.

In books for the general reader, and those which are not intended to be the last word on the subject and are of no scholarly depth it is easy to see from one's own experience how the inadequate index can come into being.

There is the seemingly inevitable haste in which the indexer is required to work and this is bound to affect his judgment. There is the restriction on space and this calls for a judicious assessment of every entry. Sometimes the restriction is so severe that it is possible to take only one theme for the index and to provide names only or subjects only; it can be so bad that one has to be selective even of these and that is worse than having no index at all, since no one selection is going to meet all demands. On occasion I have refused to do indexes with this last instruction.

These two factors in indexing at least have some cause behind them, however unreasonable it may seem, but occasionally one receives an instruction that can only leave one disclaiming responsibility for the final result, since neither judgment nor skill play any part in it. There is the list of 'keywords' provided by the author and the 'indexer', so-called, is expected to pick up the references in the text—not so much an indexer, more of a mind-reader. In my own experience of a book by a very well-known author, published by a highly reputable firm, I had to index the word 'daffodils' in a guide book to London; the author was merely describing a photogenic sight in spring, but no matter how silly, this author's word was law to his publisher however strongly I protested against this and other non-entries. Not all are as bad as this and one editor allowed me to construct my own index when such entries were pointed out.

One of the worst kinds of indexing to come my way is that of re-paging the entries of an index to a reprint of a book which has actually been re-set. This is in many ways worse than mind-reading, and a most effective way of showing how inadequate the index was in the first place. Nevertheless one has to go ahead with the work, regardless of the fact that it might have proved cheaper to compile a new index. If one has the original edition the pain can be over quite quickly but is more usual to be given the old index and the new proof and to have to sort it out from there. Recently I took on holiday to Greece a guide book (borrowed I'm glad to say) with '1973 Edition' prominently printed on the jacket – so it may have been, but the index was an old one and I soon learned to look several pages ahead of the numbers given in the index!

Sometimes the old index is used to a new edition of a book and the 'indexer' has to try somehow to fit the two together. I have had the misfortune to do only one index of this kind and was nearly driven frantic by it. There would be a couple of chapters intact, another two fused into one, whole sections deleted, some sentences fitted into other paragraphs, there was new material. The original had been profusely illustrated and from the excisions it was clear that some of the illustrations would not be reproduced in the new edition. They had been indexed in the original and I had not been given a list for the new one. My question how to deal with this problem brought the response that I could forget about the illustrations because they hadn't been finalised yet! There was more which I will leave to the reader's imagination—it begs an entirely different question about publishing!

from Miss V. M. Carruthers

In the preface to his *'Lives of the chief justices of England* (1849-57)' the 1st Baron Campbell wrote: 'So essential did I consider an index to be to every book, that I proposed to bring a Bill into Parliament to deprive an author who publishes a book without an index of the privilege of copyright and moreover to subject him for his offence to a pecuniary penalty'. However it sometimes seems to me, as a librarian, that no index to a book is preferable to an inconsistent, misleading one. Preliminary notes to an index are vital and so is the indexer's familiarity with the British Standards Institution's *Recommendations for the preparation of indexes.*

Literary critics nowadays frequently point out the deficiencies of an index when reviewing a book and this has led to some improvement.

I think the subject indexed should be as specific as possible and that every book should be treated separately on its merits. Nothing is more daunting than a large number of page references after an entry. Inconsistency must be avoided at all costs.

An example of an inadequate index: '*Royal Society of Arts journal* 1952-1962. 77p. 1964'. This must have been compiled without forethought or planning. The indexer must determine the relative importance of a subject. An item not indexed is an item lost.

from Bruce Harling

A list of faults which would make an index less than adequate might include: alphabetical confusion, errors in page references, misprints and too few entries. Such faults as these—and there are many more—concern the index in an individual book; but if we extend our vision to include the indexes in a collection of books, then two weaknesses, neither of which is necessarily the fault of the individual indexer, become apparent: lack of consistency in the choice of (a) subject headings, and (b) cross-references. (Although there are undoubtedly many problems in the indexing of proper nouns, such as names of people and places, I am here concerned with topical, or subject, entries.)

This lack of consistency contributes to a third problem, which is that the user can never be certain whether the information he seeks has not been indexed or is not in the book.

"As yet no method has been discovered for indexing material that is not included in a book but which one might reasonably assume might have been there" (*The indexer*, 8 (1), April, 1972, p.16). Before writing that sentence I had quoted Samuel Butler's remark about Erewhonian scholarship and good breeding not allowing the expression of a definite opinion on any subject; I should have extended the quotation to include the qualification that it referred particularly to having an opinion which might be shown to be mistaken.

In the next issue of *The indexer*, Pastor Luther Poellot explained an interesting practice that he had employed to deal with this problem. Another technique might simply be to give the entry followed by the page number '0', with an explanatory note about this usage at the beginning of the index.

However, I might claim that I was more concerned with a method for assessing what might reasonably have been included rather than with the technique of expressing it.

If we take the whole problem of headings, cross-references and excluded matter, the situation could be compared with that in which librarians were placed before the production of standardized classification schemes such as the Universal Decimal Classification and the Colon Classification. The existence of such schemes has led to a more consistent approach to classification although individual classifiers must remain creative in relating the scheme to their own stock and requirements. Might not the same sort of approach, *mutatis mutandis*, be similarly beneficial if applied to book indexing?

"Although an alphabetical index should not be classified, yet it is necessary to gather together the synonyms, and place all the references under the best of these headings, with cross-references from the others" (Wheatley: *How to make an index*, 1902, p. 70).

Would it not be valuable if the individual indexer did not have to do all this work himself with the inevitably idiosyncratic results involving the searcher in more effort? I would suggest that the time might have arrived for indexers to come together—perhaps through the medium of a sub-committee or working party of the Society of Indexers—to produce their own "classification" schemes.

These I would expect to be on the lines of the information retrieval system thesauri (such as the English Electric *Thesaurofacet*) that have been appearing over the last twenty years or so. Constructed with book indexing in mind, a series on different subjects would offer both the indexer and user guidance on preferred terms and cross-references together with an indication of topics which the subject embraces but the particular book does not.

The need for the individual indexer to make decisions concerning the particular work in hand is not denied; but I am suggesting that much intellectual effort is being duplicated unnecessarily in an anarchic situation which contributes to the discrepancies and inconsistencies which are apparent when the information store is seen, not as an individual book, but as a collection.

An index which takes no account of other indexes in books on the same topic which might be consulted during the same search might be regarded as less than adequate. An attempt to harmonize the approach to indexing books in a similar field could help to avoid the need continually to re-formulate the search strategy every time a different book is consulted. This, in turn, could lead to greater efficiency in the retrieval of the information and this, surely, is one of the main aims of indexing.

---

from Dr. J. E. Holmstrom

The hindrance to improvements in indexing practice aimed at making the end product more useful to the searcher—especially if he is a reference librarian who may at any moment have to search any kind of subject matter whatever—is not so much technical as economic. Obviously the greater amount of effort expended by the indexer in using his skill to combine specificity of detail with comprehensiveness of coverage (both for names and for subject entries) the smaller will be the risk of the user being left unaware of something in the text or footnotes that might be of value to him.

If the indexer could be given a free hand and did not have to rush, this would be an enjoyable exercise, but all too often the finalised page proofs of the book in question may have been delayed and the printer's copy for the index is impatiently awaited as the last thing outstanding before it can go into production. Moreover, the publisher may at heart be only half convinced of the value and necessity for an index. It is he who has to pay not only the indexer but also for the additional paper and printing, which in turn will affect the price and selling prospects for the book. And indeed there is no gainsaying the fundamental fact that governs the economics of indexing, which can be stated as follows:

Limiting the index entries to only one or two for each chapter in the book would be pointless as that much information is given anyway in the list of contents. On the other hand, trying to index the purport of every sentence throughout the text would be futile, and indexing also the names cited in footnotes may or may not be desirable, according to the nature and purpose of the work. Somewhere between these two extremes a line must be drawn, and where to draw it must ultimately be decided on a basis of personal judgement informed by background knowledge. Furthermore, however well versed in the subject matter of any given book its indexer may happen to be, he cannot foresee what items may at some future time chance to be of interest to some individual reader. Perhaps nine-tenths of his index entries may never be looked at again by any human eye. In this sense, indexing is analogous to insurance, and the only rational statement one can make about its economics is that if, over a long period of years, the value that has been gained from its existence as a whole exceeds the value of the work originally invested in it, the premium paid in advance will not have been excessive. Unfortunately from the publisher's point of view it is he who has to pay the premium as a lump sum once and for all, the amount of which is all too evident, whereas the benefits (if any) will accrue to an unpredictable number of people possibly including some who are not yet born.

Whereas life assurance premiums are able to be scaled in accordance with precise actuarial calculations (made possible by the fact that everyone will eventually die, so the only thing that has to be averaged from past experience is how soon) a closer analogy here is the insurance of boilers and other industrial plant which is based on the ascertainment that the things to be insured satisfy established technical standards and on the fund of experience gained by the inspectors who certify this. It may not be too fanciful to suggest that a study of the principles on which these inspectors work might indirectly yield ideas for improving the observance of proper qualitative standards in indexing and the checking of indexes, especially if it were linked with a scientifically controlled investigation aiming to correlate different styles and details of indexing with the opinions formed by index users.

The outcome from such a survey could be valuable as an objective indication of the rates of payment that qualified indexers may reasonably expect, also as a basis for the education of publishers and book buyers as regards what is worth paying for. Clearly the most suitable body to sponsor it would be the Society of Indexers, but it would need a good deal of work by experts whose time is valuable. The question arises whether there is any source from which a grant of funds for the purpose might possibly be obtained.

Meanwhile, can anything be done to improve book indexing, as at present conducted, without taking up more space? The following ideas are suggested at random as a few starting points for thought:

(1) The frequent practice of following a name or a subject keyword by a long string of undifferentiated page numbers is more often irritating than useful, for the searcher in a hurry cannot bother to turn up each page number in succession if he has no means of knowing beforehand which of them are more likely than others to coincide with what he wants and he suspects that even if some of the references are apposite they are as likely as not to be too trivial. Rather than this, it is better to give ranges of page numbers like 139-45 (meaning that the name or topic in question recurs on each of the intervening pages with not more than one exception) or 237-53 *passim* (meaning that it is more or less continuously relevant even though it may not necessarily be printed on all the intervening pages).

(2) This device—to be explained, of course, in an "Important Note" at the beginning of the index—is one of several ways that commonsense advantage can be taken of the faculty acquired by every experienced reader, of noticing a particular word if he knows it occurs in a stated range of text, without actually having to read all of it.

(3) In some books each chapter is subdivided into sections with headings of their own, or the text of each chapter is preceded by a summary of the matters treated in it giving the page numbers at which each topic starts. This is a practice to be encouraged for, among other advantages, the alphabetically arranged index entries can then be shortened without losing specificity if the reader is recommended to cross-refer from them to the chapter or section headings which will enable him to judge how exactly they correspond with what he wants to find.

(4) In subject indexing, the only possible criterion for deciding what needs to be indexed and what can be omitted would seem to be the

indexer's understanding of the background to the subject matter, fortified wherever possible by consultation with the author or some other specialist. In other words, efficient indexing depends on ability to make value judgements; it is therefore an art not a science. In name indexing the criterion is even more difficult to establish; there may be cases where either every name without exception must be indexed or none at all. But the name entries can be made more useful if, in appropriate cases, they are followed by the word "cited" to mean that sufficient detail is given of a publication by the named author for it to be findable in a library or by "quoted" if some of his own words are reproduced verbatim. ("Quoted" will normally imply also "cited".)

---

from Mrs. H. B. King

From personal constant daily use of books with children and with teachers, I endorse the view that indexes are often inadequate. I speak from experience of books of information written specifically for school libraries, but also of text books, and adult general books which are necessary in a large school of very mixed ability, ranging in age from eleven to nineteen.

I began my enquiry by asking the teachers their opinion of book indexes that they were using. Older teachers retorted that even 'A' level candidates had no knowledge of the alphabet, could not use a dictionary easily, and had to be led by the hand and shown the use of the index. Here I felt that school librarians and tutors in teacher training colleges were to blame for failing to give adequate frequent instruction and guidance.

Given the fact that a book had an index and that children were prepared to use it—how then did they fare? I quote from a clever VIth former studying 'A' level history. "Indexes?" says she, "I don't trust them. I use them, but more and more I study the table of contents and am forced to read great chunks to find just what I want". I took her up on this, and studied the index of a social history text book universally used. I found an entry under *FULL Employment* but nothing at all under *Employment*—an entry under *Department of Education* but nothing under *Education*.

Several years ago I wrote that not all books intended for school libraries were indexed, but that the provision had now increased, although often the quality was poor and frequently no explanation of the index was given to the children—that is whether pictures were indexed, and the meaning of italics and bold type when these were used.

In the last three issues of the *School librarian* some two hundred and fifty-five non-fiction books were reviewed. As far as I can ascertain, only twenty six made any mention of an index whether good, bad or indifferent. Here are a few comments "The index does not seem complete". "The index lists all composers mentioned in the text and some other items haphazardly chosen. The reader will not find it adequate". "The index is derisory". "Reference is difficult in the absence of an index!". "Missing—an INDEX". "Highly selective index is of limited use". On the credit side are clear complimentary references, praising clear cross-references and using such terms as 'substantial index', 'comprehensive index' and 'first class'.

From my own experience, I do not find the indexes to school library books so appalling, although some could be improved. I am always grateful in my busy single-handed day to find an index at all! The lack of confidence in indexes negates surely much of the scholarship which has gone into even the simplest of books. An introductory explanation should head every index. Adequate cross-referencing and simplicity as well as comprehensiveness should be taken for granted—but cannot be—at present!

---

from Oliver Stallybrass

My first reaction to the Editor's request for this contribution was: Why have I not, all my adult indexer's life, maintained a card index on inadequate book indexes? My second: generalities are useless—but if in search of specific examples I spend my spare moments during the next twelve days burrowing in putative IBIs, how can I be sure they are not the handiwork of fellow members of the Society of Indexers? (With the corollary: which of *my* unsigned IBIs is about to be publicly pilloried?) My third: there flashed upon the inward eye the weirdest and most incompetent index I have ever needed to consult—consult, moreover with a constancy found perhaps only in reviewers and translators. In this case I was the checking-editing-polishing- and - getting - the-technical-and-historical-terms-right half of a two-man translation team engaged by an American university press for a work kinkily entitled *L'Amérique et les Amériques;* and since, surprise, surprise, it is written in French, the likelihood of my treading on any reader's toes is negligible.

With a French book one is, of course, lucky to find anything more substantial than a *table des matières. L'Amérique et les Amériques* offers the dubious advantage of providing not one index but three: of *personnes, lieux* and *sujets.* Such a scheme results in some curious classifications. 'Diable (Le)' has one entry as a person and one (without his article) as a subject. 'Rhett Butler héros d'*Autant en emporte le vent* de Margaret Mitchell' ranks as a person, while those rather more substantial people the English, French etc. figure as subjects. 'Places' include such oddities as '*Bible Belt*', 'Chrétienté' (with a subheading 'occidentale'), 'Extrême-Occident (chrétien)' 'Megalopolis', 'Nord soviétique', '*Old West*', other variations on the points of the compass, 'Pampa (La)', 'Paralléle (Le 40e) américain', 'Quadrilatére industriel Atlantique-Grands Lacs', 'Thulé' and '*Sea Bord*' (*sic*)—with a cross-reference from '*Tide Water*' to '*Sea Borel*' (*sic*); after which one is mildly surprised to find 'Raleigh Tavern (Williamsbury)' (*sic*), '*Tumuli*', 'Utopie', '*Wall Street*' and '*Western*' among the subjects.

The 'index de sujets' is in reality a concordance —a concordance limited, however, to words with initial capitals, words in italic or quotation marks, and words with certain easily identified characteristics: for example, nouns denoting products or ending in -isme. The idea of indexing concepts rather than words is wholly alien to the indexer. Thus '*Red Coats*' are indexed when they are so designated, otherwise not. Similarly, when the statement that (in our translation) 'the vocabulary used to denote racial nuances is astonishingly inventive' is followed by 24 examples drawn from Mexico and Peru, there is no entry under 'racisme' (to give the suitable term actually found in the index); instead there is an entry under each example, from *mestizo* and *mulato* all the way through to *salto atrás* and *tente en el aire.*

Such catalogues go a long way towards accounting for the indexes' delusively impressive extent: 41 triple-column pages. Another factor is that they cover not only the 342 pages of text (including illustrations), but all the bits and pieces as well (except for one or two which *follow* the indexes). Pages 350-79, for example, consist of fifteen double-page, four-column spreads of 'Tableaux Chronologiques'. Every time that 'États-Unis', 'Canada', 'Mexique' or 'Antilles' appears at the head of a column it receives an index entry. Rather surprisingly, the column-heading 'Le monde et l'Amérique' is not indexed; but, as far as I can see, every single item under it is from 'Australopithéciens', 'Pithécanthropiens' 'Néanderthaliens' and 'Homines Sapientes' down to 'Spoutnik I' and 'Lunik 2'. Similarly, several hundred authors' names from the 'Orientation bibliographique' are solemnly repeated in the name index. But the prize for fatuousness must go to the indexing (for all three indexes) of the list, facing the title-page, of the twelve volumes in the series to which this one belongs; thus volume 1, *L'Homme avant l'écriture,* is indexed under 'écriture' as well as under its author, while the author of *L'Amérique et les Amériques* itself has a string of index entries which includes references both to this list (2) and to the title-page (3). After that, one only wonders why the indexer stopped short of indexing the index.

If headings are chosen on a purely verbal as opposed to a conceptual basis, so too are the rare subheadings. Thus 'Méxique' has 98 undifferentiated entries, followed by five for '-humide' and a few others for other phrases which the author happens to have used. Perhaps the most useless wodge of all is the half-column and more under 'États-Unis', which gives no fewer than 198 unadorned page numbers, from 5 (for chapter-headings in the 'Sommaire') to 396 (actually it's 400, but what of that?), on which page there is a caption for a facing plate that includes the words '. . . à Salt Lake City, États-Unis'.

As the last parenthesis may have suggested, the indexes are no more accurate in matters of detail than their conceptual framework is intelligently constructed. To start with, no fewer than 100 headings—26, 25 and 49 in the three indexes respectively—are either wrongly alphabetized or correctly alphabetized under a wrong spelling—so that, for example, 'Amstrong [*sic*] (Duff)' is half a column away from 'Amstrong' (unspecified but Louis), which itself follows instead of preceding 'Armytage (Francis)'. Of the misfiled index cards a number have resulted in duplicate or near-duplicate headings; thus there are, correctly alphabetized in the index of places, entries under 'Potosi (ville, Bolivie)', 'Prairie (États-Unis)' and 'Prairie (États de la), Canada', while on the next page, between 'Punta del Este' and 'Pyrénées', there occur further entries on 'Potosi (Bolivie)' and 'Prairie (Ouest des États-Unis)'. Similar duplications arise from inaccurate versions of names; thus the author of *Prejudices* has two entries as 'Mencken (Henry)' and one as 'Mencken (M.L.)'. Of the bogus names, some—such as 'Amstrong' and 'Chesman (Caryl), criminel'—are the invention of the indexer; but for the most part—as with Mencken, Lord Seldkirk (*sic*), Book (*sic*) T. Washington, Thornstein (*sic*) Veblen, Roger William (*sic*) and Postdam (*sic*)—he or she has merely been all too faithful to the text. Peers and other possessors of complex or outlandish names are treated with predictable eccentricity: 'Rhett Butler', already mentioned, rubs shoulders with 'Cochrane (Lord)' (i.e. Thomas Cochrane, later Earl of Dundonald), 'Beecher Stowe (Harriett)' (*sic*), 'Brigham Young', 'Dred Scott' and many more.

I could go on all night. But what is the *English* index like? It doesn't, and won't, exist. With our translation I submitted 30 foolscap pages documenting our repeated and repeatedly ignored assertion that, despite an illustrious author's name on the title-page, the book, like its index, was a disgrace that should never have been published in the first instance. Sadly the prospective American publisher agreed that he had made a ghastly and costly mistake, and kissed the abortion goodbye. Perhaps, at least, it has provided readers of *The indexer* with a little relief, as well as a supreme demonstration of how *not* to make an index.

---

from John L. Thornton

I have generally found indexes to medical and scientific books inadequate, mainly because indexers tend to carry out what they believe to be a routine job, urged on by publishers who have given them insufficient time to perform the task properly. Every index should be tailored to fit the specific book, catering specifically for the person who has already read the book, and wishes to check certain information, but also for the potential reader who is searching for any book containing the information he requires at

that time. Librarians frequently consult in vain the indexes to books which they know must contain the answers to queries that have been posed. The problem is sometimes solved by consulting the list of contents, or running through the chapter headings. This should not be necessary. These should all appear in the index, but I have found successive chapters of thirty pages devoted to subjects which are not featured in the index.

There is a similar reluctance on the part of some indexers of scientific literature to index plates, diagrams, tables and other supplements to the text. They often contain useful information that is not readily available by reference to the text, and are sometimes located pages away from the text to which they refer. Some years ago I indexed a book on forensic medicine which contained very extensive lists of poisons, with information relating to them. These had not been included in the index to the previous edition, but I made entries for every single item mentioned—and appreciated why some indexers ignore these time-consuming, but extremely important, tabulated facts!

Many scientific books contain bibliographies, or lists of references either at the ends of chapters, or at the back of the book. References to authors quoted in the text, as footnotes, or in separate lists of references should all be indexed, even if these are arranged alphabetically by names of authors at the end of the volume. This will ensure that joint-authors, editors, translators, etc. can all be traced by reference to the index. This is important in tracing scientific literature—and not only to those who want to see if their work has been quoted by other authors!

Appendices should be indexed as fully as the body of the text, not just from the heading, since they may contain vital information. Lists of staff of institutions, drugs, etc. might well be found relegated to the end of a book, but they should be traceable individually by means of the index.

Prefaces and introductions are often overlooked, and they probably seldom contain anything of significance that does not also appear in the text. However, an introduction can be lengthy, informative, and possibly contain useful historical material that is worthy of being indexed.

These features should certainly be perused for possible entries. In 1949 a colleague in America wrote words to this effect: "You say the nicest possible things about my work in your Introduction, but there is no reference to this page in your index!" I have since read introductions with a view to indexing them, but have seldom found this necessary.

I appreciate the provision of introductory notes to indexes, and usually include them in my own books, but I must confess that I never deliberately look at the beginning of an index to see if there is an explanatory paragraph. I know that it would usually be in vain! However, in lengthy, complicated indexes with unusual features I consider that they are essential, and such books constantly used for reference purposes demand these time-saving devices. Without them it can be like consulting a very complicated map with no scale, and no key to the symbols provided!

The Uses of Indexes

John L. Thornton

The uses to which indexes are put are many and varied, depending upon the type of literature indexed and the person for whom the contents of the book are intended. Just as a map reference is the key to a position on an atlas, so the index should permit one to pin-point required information in a book, although this is generally limited to a page reference. How does one determine what should be included in an index? Firstly one must decide for whom the book is intended, and who, having read it, might later refer to it as a potential source of information. Is the title likely to attract a wider audience than suspected by the author, possibly to unfamiliar fields, and if so, should the indexer cater for these readers by including additional non-technical terms, or further cross-references?

Every index should be tailor-made to fit the book, taking into account its purpose and potential readership. Too many indexers launch forth into the fray on receipt of a few page-proofs, without adequate consideration and subsequent planning. Not that I advocate reading the entire text before starting to index. This is quite impossible with medical and scientific books, for example, but one should read the preliminaries, peruse the contents, study the lay-out, and base one's index on the results of careful consideration. It *is* possible to change course mid-way through an index, or to make additions or alterations when editing, but it is far more satisfactory to spend time planning the campaign before starting the battle.

Ideally, indexes should cover the *complete* contents of books; chapters and sub-headings, plates, tables, diagrams, footnotes, references, bibliographies, and even prefaces and introductions if these contain useful information that is not available elsewhere in the book. Many books in the fields of science and medicine are inadequately in-dexed, and regrettably one must record that this also applies to the majority of books on librarianship. Some books are over-indexed, containing unnecessary entries that are not only useless, but clutter up the index. Perhaps these are compiled by indexers paid by the number of entries! Certain indexes appear to concentrate on the ephemeral, for example, including the titles of journals given in references, but failing to index the titles of chapters devoted to specific subjects. These are frequently omitted, the indexer erroneously assuming that because these are listed in the table of contents they need not be included in the index. The provision of inclusive pages is invaluable. This indicates lengthy treatment, and although major entries can be indicated by the use of bold or italic type, it is very useful to note that a specific number of pages is devoted to a particular topic.

An introductory note to an index can be very useful, particularly if it elucidates unusual arrangement, or innovations, yet how many readers urgently in search of information turn to the beginning of an index to see how it is arranged? Working in a library one can consult dozens of indexes within a short period looking for sources of information. Familiarity with the reference tools enables this to be done quickly and efficiently, but it is easy for the novice to overlook useful material.

The above notes suggest the main features of the ideal index, and this depends upon the nature of the book and its potential users. An elementary textbook requires a simple index, and as one progresses through more advanced textbooks, monographs, handbooks, reference works, and encyclopaedias rather more complex indexes are needed. Symposia, congress proceedings, colloquia and similar publications require adequate indexes, but seldom have them. Journals have indexes of varying standards, and it is usual for these

Reprinted from *The Indexer* 8, no. 1 (April 1972): 17–19.

to have entries based almost entirely upon the names of the authors and the titles of the articles. Titles *can* be self-explanatory, and this should be insisted upon by editors, but they sometimes bear no relationship whatsoever to the text of the article. Indexers must devise their own subject headings, using the text, and particularly the summary. Fortunately there are excellent abstracting and indexing bibliographical tools in medicine and science, and periodicals are not generally used by readers in search of routine information.

This classification of the literature into various types enables one to attempt an investigation into the indexes we *do* find in these types, as distinct from what we *should* find. It is obvious that more comprehensive indexing is needed, and that the index should not be looked upon merely as a few pages of alphabetically arranged names and subjects mainly provided to placate reviewers. The index is the key to the contents of the book, and the continued use of any book as a reference source of information is dependent upon the adequacy of its index.

A random selection of six books devoted to scientific subjects was taken, and the indexes were examined:

(a) A book on intermediate physics with a chapter on isotropic dielectrics covering twenty pages has no entry under either heading in the index. There is a chapter devoted to vibrations of strings, rods and columns of gas, but there is no entry under 'Strings', although there are two page references under 'Stretched string, frequency of vibration', and a single page reference under 'Vibrations of strings'. There are chapters on electrostatics (18pp.) with no entry in the index, and on calorimetry (29pp.), with a page number followed by 'et seq'. These are a few examples from a very unsatisfactory index.

(b) A book on biology for medical students with a nineteen-page index in three columns. An extensive chapter on plant physiology (83pp.) is not mentioned in the index under either term, although there are entries under 'Plant histology', and 'Plant movement', but the references are not to this chapter. Inclusive pages are not provided, but where an extensive section is included, the words 'et seq' are given. To provide the final figures would require less space, e.g. 87-98, instead of 87 et seq. Apart from these criticisms, this index is fairly comprehensive and adequate, but I was momentarily stunned by the entries:

White Ants
— of egg

(c) An elementary book on botany has a ten-page index containing entries under the Family but not the Order of the flora described. Only the initial pages are given except for the subjects of chapters, for which inclusive pagination is provided. The term 'Thallus' has eight sub-headings, but is incomplete, there being no entries for *Penicillium* and *Mucor*, for example. The entry 'Control of fungi' is an example of several entries of doubtful value.

(d) A monograph on the renal circulation has a five-page index headed by a note stating that illustrations are noted by the use of bold type. The entries 'Circulation of kidney', and 'Kidney, circulation of' are followed by 'see Renal circulation', under which heading there are a few entries. All these headings are of doubtful value since the entire book is on this subject. The entry 'Kidneys, human (see also Human kidneys)' is followed by page references which are duplicated under the latter, in addition to numerous sub-headings not under the former heading. The references to authors in the text and in the bibliography are not indexed. Some of these are extensively quoted, and should appear in the index, which is quite inadequate in a research tool.

(e) A concise textbook on biochemistry has a note preceding the index stating that references to formulae are given in bold type, and the index itself is comprehensive and ideal for a work of this nature.

(f) The chemistry of terpenoids and steroids suggests a complex index containing terms incomprehensible to anyone except a chemist. There is a chapter on plant steroids (19pp.), but no entry under this, or under 'Steroids, plant'. Nor are the chapters on the Triterpenoids, the Sesquiterpenoids, and the Monoterpenoids represented in the index.

A similar sample of clinical books was taken, with the following results:

(g) A textbook of medical microbiology, containing a good index in which inclusive pagination is given to entries, but the contents of the Appendices are not individually indexed.

(h) A book on the clinical aspects of autonomic pharmacology has two indexes, one general (1½pp.) and the other a 'Compound index' (1⅔pp.). This separation is unnecessary, and the index is very selective, many paragraph headings not being included, and inclusive pagination is not consistently given.

(i) An introductory book on fractures has an index in which the main references are printed in bold type, but under 'Fractures' all aspects of fractures are given as sub-headings, and are duplicated under bones, types, etc. This is unnecessary.

(j) In a general textbook of medicine, two pages of 'Useful data' are included after the index, and are neither paginated nor indexed, although they are included in the table of contents. Only the first page numbers are given, even where an entire chapter is devoted to a subject, and since numerous topics are mentioned several times, it is impossible readily to locate the major references.

(k) A monograph on tumours has a forty-one-page index in single columns to a text of over a thousand pages. Inclusive pages are provided to headings, but the heading 'Cancer (see *Carcinoma, etc.*)' has six sub-headings. There are numerous sub-headings and sub-sub-headings, but this is unavoidable, and the material is clearly set out. It is a good index.

(l) The indexes to the individual volumes of an encyclopaedia of medical practice have so many sub-sub-sub-headings, covering in some instances several pages, single-column, that it is hopeless to attempt to use them. The separate index to the set is a great improvement, and gives inclusive pages, but it contains some very peculiar entries, e.g.:

Muscles, cervical rib, causing wasting of
Ophthalmia neonatorum, reservoirs of infection
Pregnancy, diet in, goitre, prevention of

These examples indicate that few indexes to medical and scientific books are adequate, and one suspects that many of them were compiled by the authors, their wives or secretaries, with no flair for the task. An index is an integral part of a book and should be designed to fit the text. An advanced research work should have an index that will enable readers to locate required information without delay. The elementary textbook should be indexed with the same objective. Even if one expects readers to peruse the entire text, it is often necessary to refer back to sections. Schoolchildren should be taught how to use indexes properly, and teachers should appreciate their potential value. But firstly we must have sound, comprehensive indexes which will guide readers precisely to the information they require, indicate its extent, and truly serve as essential appendages to the text matter. A shoddy index is a particular abomination in the fields of research concerned with science and medicine, where time is especially precious, and the speedy location of accurate information can be vital.

The Society of Indexers as a Servant of the World of Letters*

G. V. Carey

At the close of a business meeting on a Saturday morning what most of you want, I'm quite sure, must be to get away as soon as possible, and not to be talked to by anybody—least of all by a last-minute substitute for someone really worth while. So I promise to be brief.

Since you did me the great honour of election to the presidency I've seldom attended Council meetings, in the belief that society presidents are expected to emerge only rarely from their proper place: which is the Shelf. But it happens that I did attend the last Council meeting, and I'm very glad I did; for the Council had decided that this, the seventh year of our Society's existence, was the right time for a reappraisal (though not an agonising one, it's to be hoped) of our progress and of our policy in general. I was thus able to be present at their first deliberation on this subject. Our talk, based on a thoughtful paper submitted by a wise and experienced member of our staff,** was purely exploratory; no decisions were taken; any conclusions reached hereafter will naturally be laid before you in due course. Meanwhile it would be premature and quite out of place for me now to attempt any detailed report of our discussion, but I think that I may be

permitted just one, very general, reflection prompted by it.

The occurrence in the aforesaid paper of a warning against 'grandiose' notions was criticised by another wise and experienced member of the Council; and in so far as it was liable to misinterpretation in the particular context in which it appeared, it was perhaps open to criticism. Nevertheless 'grandiose' struck me at once as a very apt cautionary word that we, as a Society, should do well to keep at least at the back of our minds; for aren't we perhaps just occasionally tempted to forget that our part on the literary stage, essential though it be, is not and never can be a star part? (I'm referring of course to literary indexing only. The various forms of scientific indexing remain, I'm ashamed to say, in spite of the admirable expositions that we're privileged to hear or read from time to time, a profound mystery to me, and I'm inclined to regard all concerned with them as stars of the first order.)

Believe me, I'm not myself immune from this temptation—to think of our calling just a little more highly that we ought to think. The longing to *create* is common to nearly all of us, and some of you, I dare say, may have experienced something of the feeling that often comes to me on the completion of an index—the flush of pride, soon tempered by the thought: 'IF ONLY I could write a book, paint a picture, compose a song, de-

---

* Written by the then President from notes of his address given at the A.G.M., 1964.

** The then Secretary, E. Alan Baker.

Reprinted from *The Indexer* 5, no. 2 (Autumn 1966): 78–80.

sign a building, that will live after me. But no: my Creator has seen fit to let *me* create nothing better than an index. And, even so, nobody will ever know that it was I who created it—will never even have heard of me. Oh well, perhaps in the course of time quite a lot of people may use the thing; it's even *just* possible that one or two may be moved to say: " Funny—this index seems to get me quite quickly on to exactly what I want "`.'

Isn't that verdict, even though it may never actually reach our ears, in itself the one thing that really matters? So then, if in the theatre of literature we can be thoroughly efficient and helpful door-keepers, dressers, property-men, backstage hands, let's not be too concerned about our names not appearing in lights.

The aims of our Society, as set out in our Constitution, are five in number. The first is: ' To improve the standard of indexing'; and—rightly, in my opinion—fifth and last comes: ' To raise the status of indexers'. Let us firmly resolve to *keep first things first*. We are already doing much to improve the standard of indexing; the Society is already more than justifying the faith and foresight of its founder, Norman Knight. Of that I'm certain. We can be equally certain that, in so far as we succeed in attaining Aim No. 1, assuredly Aim No. 5 will be added unto us.

On a lighter note I start the last lap. If you can bear with me a few minutes longer, I'd like to mention a couple of items of ' indexers' shop'.

The first arises out of a bloomer *announced*, and duly *denounced*, just as the Council meeting I've referred to was breaking up: in a recently published book there was reported to be an entry ' Morrison, W.S. ' that referred in fact to Herbert (later Lord) Morrison. Though I didn't say so at the time, as we were all in a hurry to be off, I know a better—or, rather, a worse—instance of that kind; for, after all, the two Morrisons *were* contemporaries and in the same line of business, but my example hasn't even that excuse.

I bought each volume of Churchill's *The Second World War* as issued, and as soon as

Vol. I was in my hands I turned at once to the index. Incidentally, the fact that this was immediately preceded by no less than two and a half pages of Errata seemed to presage that some of the backstage hands on that great work hadn't been up to their job. In the index itself almost the first entry that happened to catch my eye was:

Boothby, Guy, 93*n.*, 242

My first reaction was: ' Now, what on earth can Churchill possibly have had to say, in relation to the Second World War, about Guy Boothby, an ephemeral writer of thrillers popular in the 1890s? ' Then almost simultaneously came the deduction: ' Elementary, my dear Watson; obviously the references must be to Robert Boothby.' After which I looked up both contexts, and found that that of course *was* the answer. I further deduced, incidentally, that the compiler of that index must have been nearly as ancient as myself—again, ' Elementary, my dear Watson '; Guy Boothby died in 1905 and within a year or two was almost forgotten; at any rate nobody born later than about 1895 would *instinctively* associate with the surname Boothby the christian name Guy.

The elderly indexer anyway earns no marks on that question.

My second and last point relates to a subject often discussed or written about; indeed we had an entertaining paper on it after a General Meeting only a year or two ago: ' Humour in indexing ' (*The Indexer*, Vol. 3, pages 60-63). But whereas this is normally dealt with from two angles only—index entries that are themselves humorous (*a*) unintentionally, (*b*) intentionally—I'd like you to consider another facet of the subject that I've never yet seen or heard referred to: How far can or should a humorous *context* be indexed simply on the ground of its humour?* I apologise for an overdose, from now on, of the first person singular, but it's only from personal experience that I can illustrate exactly what I mean.

---

* This subject was dealt with by Mrs. E. M. Hatt in her talk on ' Humour in Indexing ' on May 19, 1962 (*The Indexer*, Vol. III, pages 60-63).—*Editor.*

More than ten years ago (1953, to be precise) I was indexing Noël Coward's *Future Indefinite,* one of those light autobiographical works that are easiest of all to deal with, needing few entries other than names of persons and places. But in a description of the author's stay in a Moscow hotel occurred the following passage:

> I turned on the bath tap marked 'Hot' and was astonished to see a tadpole come out of it and vanish down the plughole. Later on . . . I spoke to the manager about it. I explained, as politely as I could, that although he might consider what I was saying to be alien propaganda, in England when we turned on a hot tap, as a general rule, hot water came out of it, whereas if on the other hand we wished for a hot tadpole, we turned on a tap marked 'Hot Tadpole' and, owing to the efficiency of our Capitalist State, a hot tadpole usually appeared. The manager received this gentle reprimand with the utmost courtesy.

Now, that made me laugh aloud (whereas, to tell the truth, I'd found some of the book rather tedious), and I said to myself, 'I'm sure there must be lots of other people whose sense of humour isn't very different from mine; and, what's more, that some of them at some time or other might want—as I certainly should—to remind themselves of, or point out to others, that passage. Very well, then: into the index must go that tadpole.

But that's not quite the end of the story. Years later, in fact not much more than a year ago, at some party or other a lady, launching out spontaneously on the subject of books, asked me whether I'd ever happened to read a book of Noël Coward's called *Future Indefinite,* and—believe it or not—almost before I had time to reply went on: 'If so, I wonder whether you remember his absurd description of a tadpole incident—I particularly enjoyed it'. I could have embraced her there and then (she was in fact more than ordinarily attractive). Instead I exclaimed, 'I'm eternally grateful to you for that bit of evidence that my life has not been wholly wasted. If ever you should pick up the book again and want to find that tadpole, you'll be able to, in the index, under "Tadpole, encounter with a"'. I know, because I put him there myself'.

Which brings me to my final point: namely the conviction that there are occasions when humour, *as such*, should be indexed. I hope you'll agree with me.

Indexing Children's Books

Brenda Miller

The question to be decided before writing this article was whether to deal with the subject in a general or a specific way, and whether to try to encompass children's books in general, or only those published in Australia. My solution has been to try to do a little of both. I have strong views on indexes in general, some of which have been aired here. Since, however, I live and work in Australia, my remarks on specific book indexes refer mainly to children's books published in Australia during the last two or three years. In my selection of these books I relied mainly on those reviewed in *Reading Time,* a journal published by the Children's Book Council of New South Wales, along with others which came to my notice. I collected as many of the recently-published books as could be easily borrowed or bought, and worked from them. The books published in England, whose indexes have been examined in some detail, are a random selection of recent publications borrowed from the shelves of the school library on the last day of term; I tried only to have a representative of several well-known series by well-known publishers. The absence of American books reflects only their absence from the library shelves. It should also be pointed out that when writing of children I am thinking of those between the ages of say nine and fourteen.

It has long been my opinion that many people think that expert knowledge of a subject is not necessary when writing a book for children. The evidence for this belief lies in the number of series in which books on widely differing subjects are written by the same author. Surely the writer of a children's book needs a detailed knowledge of his subject in order that he may know when and how to simplify his subject matter without resultant confusion and inaccuracy. Far too many children's books are merely watered-down versions of adult books, written by people whose knowledge of the subject is completely superficial. The same is equally true for indexes. It is vital that the index for a children's book be accurate, comprehensive and easy to follow. In order to achieve this the indexer needs some knowledge of the subject matter, and of the basic rules of indexing, and should keep in mind ' the user over his shoulder '.[1] Children are often slower readers than adults; some are very slow by the average literate adult's standard, but at school they are expected, more and more, to use reference books, and to find their own information. For some children, even finding a specific entry in an alphabetical index is a labour, and they are easily frustrated if the index is at all difficult. Indexes would be easier for children to use if a space was left between each letter of the

Reprinted from *The Indexer* 8, no. 3 (April 1973): 140–144.

alphabet, and if the print were always of a reasonable size, not significantly smaller than that used in the text, as is sometimes the case.

I remember in particular a twelve-year-old boy who had been told to look up Henry Lawson, and then told by me that he must look this up in *The Australian encyclopaedia* under L. He stood in front of the complete set, and it was after some time with much prompting from me, that he picked out the volume entitled Hospitals to Marsh. He is not a naturally timid boy, and I am quite sure was not rendered incapable by fright. Although I knew that many children had difficulty with alphabetizing, this was the first time it was brought home to me how the omission of some letters from the spine of encyclopaedias could impede the user.

This is not, of course, the indexer's responsibility, but it does indicate the difficulty of his task. I have watched children laboriously reading through the index to an encyclopaedia to find the entry they want, and then be baffled by a multiplicity of volume and page references. *The Oxford junior encyclopaedia*, presumably to avoid confusion, gives the volume reference in roman figures, and the page reference in arabic numerals, but the volumes themselves are numbered on the spine in arabic numerals. This causes that very confusion the indexer hoped to avoid.

While on the subject of encyclopaedias and their indexes, perhaps a mention should be made of *Newnes pictorial knowledge*. The index to this was incomplete, with many entries missing. A member of the Society was commissioned to do the additional indexing necessary for a new edition some years ago, and when he pointed out the deficiences of the index to the publishers, was told that his job was purely to provide the references for new material. My method of finding material not listed in this index was to skim rapidly over pages in what I thought were the relevant sections. This is something beyond the capabilities of the children for whom the encyclopaedia is intended.

Many children's books are published without an index. The most recently published volume in the Australian Way Series, *Athletics the Australian way*, edited by Ron Clarke (Lansdowne, 1971), received a glowing review in *Reading time*, and will certainly be very popular with the eleven to fourteen age group. It is a well-produced book, and contains many photographs of well-known athletes in action, but there is no index, and the table of contents only identifies the event dealt with in a specific chapter, and the author of the chapter. Two other recently published Australian books contain neither index nor table of contents. *Australia's insects*, with text by John Child and John Currey (Lansdowne, circa 1971) is a lavishly produced book with some beautiful colour photographs of various insects, and a certain amount of text about each. The second section of the book is more technical, with many diagrams explaining such things as the parts of an insect, and appears to my inexpert eye to be well and clearly written. A nine-year-old would enjoy the pictures, while a twelve-year-old would appreciate it more fully. In the Young Nature Library Series the volume entitled *Possums* by Bruce Edwards (Lansdowne, 1972) is a less expensive but still attractive production of the same sort. As well as lacking an index, in neither book, so far as I can discern, is there any logical order to the contents, and the second has no pagination. How the publishers rationalize their actions is hard to imagine. Another book, *Australian stamp collecting*, by Ian F. Finlay (Lansdowne, 1971), aimed probably at the twelve plus age group, endeavours to overcome the lack of an index in an unusual way. The table of contents is fairly extensive, and after the first chapter, which deals with the history of stamps in general, the topics in each chapter are dealt with alphabetically, and listed thus in the table of contents, a compromise which might be satisfactory if the reader were sure under which chapter heading he should look. Lest I should be thought to be unduly severe on Australian publishers, perhaps I should say that English publishers also do the same thing. Three recent books published without table of contents or index are: *The story of the alphabet* by John Biggs (O.U.P., 1968), *Ships and seafarers of the South Pacific*, and *Ships and seafarers of the Orient*, both by Victor Hatcher (Collins, circa 1970). All three are aimed at the ten to twelve age group.

In many other recently-published children's books, the indexes are inaccurate or inadequate, or both. In volume 3 of the Seeing History Series, called *Colonies to Commonwealth* by K. M. Adams (Lansdowne, 1971), the entry in the index for 'Aborigines' cites pp. 109-112, but there is no reference to aborigines on p. 109, which deals mainly with kanakas; the section on aborigines starts on p. 110. As kanakas are different from aborigines (the former terms being used to describe the natives of the South Sea Islands, brought here, willingly or unwillingly, to work in the sugar plantations of Queensland), and yet can be easily confused with them in a child's mind, this must be regarded as a serious error. In the same volume there is a chapter entitled Education, but there is no heading 'Education' in the index. Various schools are mentioned by name in this chapter, and there are illustrations of several of them, with brief descriptions of their foundation and early days, but only two of these schools appear in the index. Neither is there a heading 'Schools', although 'National Schools' and 'Independent Schools' appear under N and I respectively. In volume 1 of the series, *The first Australians*, Dirck Hartog (a name well-known to generations of Australian school children) is listed in the index under his christian name. This dismal catalogue of errors could be continued indefinitely. A further puzzling aspect is that the index to volume 1 has a hundred and seventy-seven entries, that to volume 2 two hundred and fifty-five, and that to volume 3 one hundred and forty, although the text here is the longest.

By contrast, the index to *The story of China* by Lo Hui-Min (Angus and Robertson, 1970) is accurate and reasonably comprehensive. The indexer has, rightly in my opinion, omitted references to Voltaire and Leibnitz made by the author to illustrate his arguments. The main criticism that can be made is that the illustrations are not indexed. Thus both the pictures of Kublai Khan and Mao Tse-Tung are likely to be overlooked by the child researcher, as it is necessary to turn over the page from the reference given in the index to see them.

More examples of poor indexing can be given from *Wildlife of Australia* by Vincent Serventy (Nelson [Aust.], 1971). Here again the illustrations are not indexed, a very serious defect in a book in which the illustrations play such a major part. The index entry for 'Frogs' refers the reader to pp. 56-58, but between pages 52 and 53 are large colour photographs of the burrowing frog and the green and golden tree-frog, neither of which appears in the index. It should also be pointed out that pages 52, 53 and 56 have no page numbers. In this same section there are headings in the text devoted to different species of frogs, some of which appear in the index, and some do not. The selection seems to be completely arbitrary.

Another question arises: should an index have explanatory notes or not? The problem here is that many readers, both children and adults, will not read these notes, especially if they run to more than a few lines, but for those who will, a few rules, simply stated, will give assistance. The use of bold type should be explained, and also the use of italics.

In *Tortoises, terrapins and turtles* by John Goode (Angus and Robertson, 1971), italics are used in the index to identify the scientific names of individual species, but there is no explanation of this. The illustrations are not indexed, but as they seem to be always on the same or adjacent page to the reference in the text, this is not such a serious omission as in some other cases.

The index to *Australian animal behaviour* by Harry Frauca, one of the Periwinkle Series (Lansdowne, 1971), tells us that 'Numbers in italics indicate illustrations', but my eye finds it difficult to discern which figures are in italics. A similar although more expensive series is published by A. H. and A. W. Reed: in *Australian crustaceans in colour* by Anthony Healy and John C. Yaldwyn (1970), and *Australian insects in colour* by Anthony Healy and Courtenay N. Smithers (1971), the indexes are prefaced by the brief note that 'Bold figures indicate colour plates or black and white figures'. In addition to this, each such entry is labelled either 'pl.' or 'fig.', and all illustrations are numbered. In *Australian spiders in colour* by Ramon Mascord (1970), however, this admirable practice has not been followed, and the index is much more difficult to understand. Here again italics are used to indicate the names of individual species, but no explanatory note is given. A publisher's representative with whom I discussed this matter claimed that it could be too complicated to do this, as italics are used for so many proper names, such as ships, aeroplanes, newspapers, titles, etc., but since in most children's books only one class is involved, surely it could be done. It is depressing to have to add that the index to *Australian insects in colour* is the only one of the last four books mentioned in which errors and omissions were not easy to find. My favourite is the entry in *Australian crustaceans in colour* which reads, 'Elegant coral shrimp', surely a case of a misplaced adjective. The last two series considered are probably not written specifically for children, but are widely used by them.

Comments on a few English books now follow. *Ships and shipping* by Michael Palmer (Batsford, 1971), has a short note at the top of the index saying that 'numerals in bold type refer to the page-numbers of the illustrations', and this bold type is very easy to identify. The index does not list the names of ships separately, but lists them together, in italics, under the main entry 'Ships'. This is probably a good idea, although to have listed them separately as well would not have required any further pages, as the fourth and last page of the index is only one quarter used. A similar book is *Travel by sea* by R. J. Hoare (A. and C. Black, 2nd ed. reprinted 1970). Here the names of ships are listed in italics, with no explanatory note, while illustrations are not indexed. The entry for 'trireme' is in italics, but those for 'bireme' and 'quinquireme' are in ordinary type. Such inconsistencies make the use of an index more difficult. The index to *Russian revolution* by Ronald Hingley (Bodley Head, 1970), gives no explanation of italics, nor are the illustrations indexed. It is in the New Adults Series, but even so, thirteen page references under the heading 'Moscow', with no sub-headings, seem a little excessive. Selective indexing could eliminate many of them.

From my observation indexes to children's books, whether published in Australia or elsewhere, contain few sub-headings, and this, I am sure, is a good thing. When helping children to find information in encyclopaedias, it is obvious that they are usually confused when faced with a number of sub-headings. Some may be necessary, to avoid a large number of unidentified references, but great care should be taken that page references are not given unnecessarily. Sometimes the reader turns to a page to find that a single word or phrase of little relevance is his only reward. As stated earlier, selective indexing can help to overcome this problem, and a few well-chosen sub-headings will give additional assistance. 'See' and 'See also' references should also be used sparingly, especially as in most children's books it is a comparatively easy matter to duplicate the reference under a second heading. This does make me wonder, as a librarian, about the value of these references in my catalogue, much as the prospect of cataloguing everything under all possible headings daunts me.

Children's books need indexes, but they need good indexes. For short simple books, a fairly detailed table of contents is sometimes sufficient, but a simple index can replace this, as in *Prehistoric animals*, in the First Library Series (Macdonald, 1970), where thirty-one pages of text, interspersed with illustrations, have a two-page index. Every species mentioned in the text is illustrated on the same page, so that the lack of indexing of the illustrations cannot be felt to be a fault.

It appears from a cursory glance at some illustrated adults' books, mainly of a biographical and historical nature, that it is not necessarily the custom to index illustrations, but for children's books this should be the general rule. Almost without exception the books I have catalogued for the school library over the last two years have been illustrated, and the illustrations are usually an integral part of the text. The index should also differentiate clearly between verbal and pictorial references, except perhaps in the case of a very simple book such as *Prehistoric animals*, which is discussed in the previous paragraph.

Children need to be taught how to use indexes, and this is the responsibility of the teacher and librarian, but having so learnt, they have a right to expect that the indexes they consult should be accurate, comprehensive, and simple, also that there should be an index to consult. My research has led me to the inescapable conclusion that much is lacking in these respects. I have written both to Lansdowne Press and to Angus and Robertson asking for information on the subject. Angus and Robertson replied promptly, saying that the question of the inclusion of an index was decided jointly by the author and the editor, and that the index might be compiled by any of the three possibilities I had suggested, the author, a member of the publisher's staff, or an outside indexer. Their reply does not, however, make it clear that there is any firm policy on this matter. Lansdowne Press has not replied to my letter after six weeks. Angus and Robertson also mentioned a book recently published by them with an index, a junior edition of *What bird is that?* by Neville Cayley, but I was unable to borrow a copy. I think it is true to say that these two firms publish a large number of the non-fiction books written specifically for children, and excluding those in a more strictly educational category, in this country. My sample of English publications is small, but I think representative, and reveals that although the position is probably better there, the situation is far from perfect, especially when publishers of high reputation can produce books without either index or table of contents. I do not know whether any member of the Society specializes in indexing children's books, but there is certainly 'Room for improvement in Australia '.[2]

References

(1) 'What is a good index" by F. H. C. Tatham (*The Indexer*, volume 8, no. 1, April 1972).

(2) Title of article by Mr. H. Godfrey Green (*The Indexer*, volume 8, no. 1, April 1972).

Indexes to Children's Books Are Essential

Mrs. H. B. King

When I was at school, long before the Second World War, school text books were standardized and dreary. If they were illustrated then the pictures were for the most part in black and white, dull and smudgy. There was a great dearth of information books for children of all ages and abilities.

No one today can be unaware of the great revolution that has taken place in children's book publishing. There is now an embarrassment of choice for the children's librarian. The radio and television give publicity to new books, to exhibitions, and to writers, and more and more book reviews appear in newspapers and periodicals of all kinds.

In spite of the claims of visual aids, language laboratories and television, books are still the 'bare bones' of learning. The text book in the class room is bright, illustrated and attractive. The shelves of the school libraries in many schools are blossoming— from picture book A B Cs to Skira art books—depending on the ages of the children and the size of the school. Public libraries appoint children's library advisers, provide quiet rooms for homework and reference material for further study. I have seen primary school children absorbed in making their own small books with the help of their own little classroom library, consisting mainly of Ladybird books and Black's *Children's encyclopaedia*.

As many adults will be aware, the new C.S.E. examinations entail a lot of individual research by children of lesser academic ability. A large folder of work has to be produced at the end of the school year on a particular topic—a year's work of finding, searching, writing and drawing. I have made a short list of some of the subjects studied this year. 'The world's wool', 'Tobacco and the dangers of smoking', 'Crime and punishment through the ages', 'Transport', 'Local Government', 'Fruits of the world',

'Lace'—to mention just a few. All these subjects demand books to answer the questions, to produce the material—books from the very simplest to the most advanced.

So now I make my plea. However simple the book, however inexpensive the production, please, *it must have an index*. Children are taught the use of books today—they are shown title-pages, lists of contents, pictures, lists for further reading and so forth; then when the teacher says 'Turn to the end of the book for the index' it is most daunting to find no index there.

Children are busy, impatient and young. They approach a book, however simple, for a specific fact or piece of information, and expect to have speedy access to the relevant pages. An index for them is the key. I have here on my desk a small selection of books intended for children about news and newspapers: They range from the very simplest 'Look' book in large print to 'The pageant of progress' advanced series. Freedom of the Press was the subject sought. Four of seven books possessed an index and listed the subject. The other three contained some relevant material, but each lacked an index, and it was difficult for children to sift out the facts that they needed.

More and more book reviews appear for children. In the *School Librarian*, the official journal of the School Library Association, the presence or absence of an index is frequently noted. I quote two typical examples from reviews from the current issue. " This is one of the most exciting books that has been published for many years, and I hope that in future editions the only real fault, the *absence of an index*, will be corrected." And, a review of a new series ends, " It would be useful, however, if each book had an index! " Mention of the inclusion or absence of an index is made also in the non-fiction reviews

Reprinted from *The Indexer* 5, no. 3 (Spring 1967): 130–131.

in Mrs. Anne Wood's *Books for Your Children.*

Margery Fisher, in her magazine of children's book reviews, *Growing Point,* makes particular mention of indices—to quote but **one**—" **My only criticism is that the index is too selective if the book is to be used for reference** ". From *The Junior Bookshelf*: " **If a book of this nature is to be used as an information book, then it will rely greatly on the quality of its index** ". From the current *Children's Book News*: " **I greatly missed an index** " and again " **There is a useful bibliography and a full index . . . the book is a model of what a biography for young people should be** ". The Autumn Children's Book number of the *Times Literary Supplement* has this to say in a review of one book: " **The index is a very sketchy affair** ". The Consumers' Association magazine *Which* in their analysis of children's encyclopaedias makes a point of mentioning the presence and quality of each index. Their summary is brief: " **A good index is essential for children over eleven** ". Any non-fiction book is a book of reference to a child. If I am faced with two books of otherwise equal merit on a particular subject, only one of which has an index, then that is the one that I choose for the school library.

INDEXES FOR CHILDREN'S BOOKS

' Every book that is to be used for reference, even by young juniors, needs an index. It takes very little time for an average nine-year-old to find his way with one. A variety of 'hide and seek' with the children racing to discover the reference is practically all that is needed. There is a special art in compiling an index to meet the needs of young children, and expert advice at this stage in the production of a book is too rarely sought.'— From *Books and the teacher* by Antony Kamm and Boswell Taylor (University of London Press).

Dealing with the problems of choosing books for use in class, these authors say: ' Beware of any book intended for reference, even at a junior level, which has no index. It will be virtually useless in the classroom or library. And a glance at an index will often give a much better idea of the scope of a book than an examination of the contents page. A very good way of making a quick assessment of the value of a book, or of comparing two similar books, is to use the index to find a reference to an aspect of the subject which particularly interests you.'

Index Specifications

Charles L. Bernier

Specifications, already found useful for audio amplifiers, automobiles, and the like, should also be helpful for indexes. Index specifications can include, amongst many others: existence of an index, kind of index, size, indexing density, error percentage, percentage of omissions, breadth and adequacy of modification, incorrect references, and non-subject entries. Specifications should help users to evaluate indexes for acquisition and use. Once specifications are found to be useful, then standards can be developed. Indexers should find specification to be useful as goals and as recognition of quality work. The index-publisher should find the same and also be able to justify extra expenditure for indexes of high quality. He can also take pride in publishing indexes of quality as advertised by specifications.

Specifications have been found useful for audio amplifiers, automobiles, books, bridges, buildings, cameras, equipment, highways, and the like. Specifications for indexes should likewise be helpful to index-users, indexers, and index-publishers. It seems likely that standards can be developed after specifications have been published and found to be useful. It is unnecessary that all specifications become and remain standardized. For example, in the early days of radio, the number of tubes in sets was invariably specified; today, the number of transistors and tubes is virtually meaningless.

The simplest possible specification for indexes is whether or not the work has an index. This specification could helpfully appear on advertising, bibliographies, catalogue cards, citations, references, and reviews. As a convenience, a microform insert on a catalogue card or a microfiche could carry, for example, the table of contents in full. The same could be in a book catalogue as microprint. In ultra microform, the entire index to a work could appear on its catalogue microfiche.

The kinds of indexes are the next most simple specification, e.g., author index, concordance, molecular-formula index, patent-number index, subject index, table of contents, or taxonomic index.

Quantitative specifications are also possible. The size of indexes, expressed as the number of pages, seems useful, but not so useful as is the number of entries—in order to remove dependence upon type size from the number. An even more significant specification is the number of entries per page of material indexed (indexing density). Indexers and publishers could specify these numbers. Bibliographers could estimate them. Another specification is indexing density as related to the subject area of the work indexed.

A more complicated and more useful specification is of scattering among index headings. Scattering of similar entries is the bane of all indexes. The amount of scattering is an inverse measure of one quality. Scattering among synonyms is common and measurable. Synonyms for a random sample of subject headings can be found in dictionaries and indexes, and these synonymous index headings can be searched for entries in the index. Measured scattering can be expressed as a percentage of the total number of entries in the index or as a percentage of entries under the headings sampled—thus obtaining percentages of scattering for the entire index or for an average index heading. Scattering places a worthless burden upon the user by making him seek synonyms and then look for entries under all of them. If he misses a synonym, he may miss relevant entries and then have to accept responsibility for missing information. Index users certainly have enough responsibilities without having to accept this one. Elimination of this kind of scattering can easily be made the responsibility of the indexer and index-publisher.

Reprinted from *The Indexer* 9, no. 1 (April 1974): 9–12.

There may also be scattering among generic and specific subject headings. This comes about when, at times, the indexer uses the more-generic term; at other times—the more specific term. Searchers look up both generic and specific headings, as an added load, if they wish to avoid loss of pertinent material. For high-quality indexes, generic indexing is normally done only when the author generalises. Indexing to the maximum specificity is customary otherwise. Consistent "posting-up" (indexing under both specific and general headings) is usually found to be impracticable because of difficulty in achieving consistency and because of the bulky index produced. Also, separation or generalisation that is an artifact of title construction or of shortening statements, from valid generalisation by authors, is often difficult and probably never done completely. Separation of trivial examples or samples from valid specificity is difficult and also never done completely. Thus, index-users are required to look under both general and specific headings. Measurement of the amount of this kind of scattering is difficult and probably must always be made by subject experts or by indexperts (indexers who are subject experts). Such scattering can also be expressed as percentages.

Scattering also occurs among headings related by other than synonymy and as the genus-species relationship. Relationships that bring about scattering are: antonymy, cause-effect, product-use, part-whole, and mathematical. For examples, entries of interest to a person searching under "Electrical resistance" may also be found under "Electrical conductivity". Entries related to "Tuberculosis" may also be found under "Mycobacterium tuberculosis". Those interested in "Nutrition" may find related data under "Bread". A searcher under "Lenses" may discover useful entries under: "Cameras", "Microscopes", and "Telescopes". For those interested in long division, related entries might appear under "Dividend" and "Quotient". Determination of the amount of this kind of scattering requires the services of an expert or of the indexpert. This kind of scattering can also be expressed as a percentage of the number of entries in the index. "See also" cross-references take care of this kind of scattering. So, when an appropriate "See also" cross-reference is found, scattering can be discounted.

Another kind of scattering occurs among modifying phrases (modifications, subheadings) under a given heading. For indexes in which only one modification is made under a given heading for a given document, this kind of scattering is inescapable. It can also be measured and requires the services of experts or indexers.

Of all kinds of scattering, that among synonyms is the most serious and seems likely to be the most usefully expressed as a specified percentage. Once scattering of various kinds has been specified, standards for scattering may become obvious. Such standards seem likely to depend upon: kind of index (e.g., a concordance may be found to have most scattering), subject field, indexing rules, and publisher dicta. Elimination or reduction of scattering economically burdens the index-publisher but economically relieves the user. The economic balance between these two is calculable. It depends upon number of users, time to compensate for scattering, cost of publication, salary plus overhead for users, etc.

One way to reduce load of scattering upon the user is, as has already been indicated, to use syndetic apparatus. Cross-references are the most common kind of apparatus. Other syndetic apparatus include: introduction to the index (especially useful for standard nomenclatures and terminologies), notes at certain headings in the index, and heading-term inversion, e.g., "Indexes, author", "Indexes, formula", and "Indexes, subject". The syndetic apparatus of an index can be specified. The simplest specification is whether or not any syndetic apparatus exists. Next simplest is a list of kinds of syndetics used. For example, "See", "See also", "See under", "Introduction", "Notes", and "Heading inversions" can be listed as truthful. Quantitative measures are also specifiable. The number of cross-references can be specified by type. Calculation from a random sample of index pages is a method of determining the specification. More refined is the number of cross-references per page of index and/or of text. Standards may become obvious after specifications are viewed for a number of indexes. Content of the introduction to the index can be listed in a specification. The number and percentages of notes defining headings can be used. The number and percentages of inversions of headings can be obtained.

Cross-references external to the index and in the form of a list or as a "thesaurus" place several burdens on the index user. First, he must remember that there is an external source of guidance. Then he must search the list or thesaurus for guidance. This is an extra step. Finally, he turns to the index with the discovered guidance in mind or noted (if it is complicated or detailed). For most, if not all, systems with external guidance, there is no guarantee that terms found in the external list or thesaurus will, indeed, be found in the index. Thus, every term in the list or thesaurus is potentially dangling (blind, frustrated). Dangling guidance is not only frustrating and irritating to the sophisticated user, but also it wastes his time. The external source of cross-references may have to be consulted several times during a search. Repeated consultation wastes time and is irritating. Thus, cross-references and notes interfiled in the index gives the most convenient product. A specification can be that the syndetic apparatus is interfiled or is external to the index.

Another measure of index quality is absence of error. Incorrect references from index to text can be counted and calculated as percentage of number of index entries. An incorrect reference obviously makes the entry worthless; less obviously, it makes the entry worse than worthless— it may place time consumption as a burden on the index-user as he attempts to find the correct reference. Entries in a subject index that do not lead to subjects is another error that wastes the time of users. This error, one usually of word-indexing instead of subject-indexing, can be measured by those acquainted with the subject field, and calculated and expressed as a percentage of the number of subject headings in the index.

A very serious error is that of omission of valid entries. This may be costly to measure, but can be done by re-indexing or by checking the indexing. Sometimes documents are re-indexed inadvertently and omissions can be determined as a benefit of this error. A random sample of documents re-indexed can yield data on the number of unnecessary entries and other errors as well as on the number of omissions. From these data, percentages of omissions can be calculated, based upon the number of entries in the index. Another error may result from misinterpretation or misunderstanding. For example, "Automatics" might be indexed under "Guns" rather than under "Lathes". Two other types of error, much more subtle and difficult to measure, are modifications that are too broad or too narrow. One that is too broad, forces the user to look up the entry only to discover that there is nothing of interest for him in the reference. A modification that is too narrow may cause the searcher to disregard the entry and thus miss relevant information. These errors can be measured by checking the indexing, by re-indexing, by predicting what will be found if a sample of entries is looked up, and by comparing prediction with findings. The omission of modifications, as in some book indexes, may place an unreasonable load on the index-user. An index entry should enable the user to

say, "Yes, I want to look up the entry", or "No I do not want to look up the entry". The entry should not make him say, "Maybe I want to look up the entry". Lack of modifying phrases or those perceived to be too broad cause the searcher to say, "Maybe" and to look up the entries— only to find that many references are irrelevant to his interests. The percentage of entries without modifications can be measured from a random sample of index pages and calculated as a percentage based on the number of entries in the index. In some indexes 100% of the entries have no modification.

There are doubtless many more specifications that can be derived for indexes, such as point size of type, set solid or leaded, quality of typography, type face, presence or absence of running headings, line length, width of gutter margin, quality of paper, and legibility. Which of these specifications will actually be found useful can be determined by trial. While guesses could be made for values and usefulness of the specifications described here, guessing seems to be a waste of time. Measurement, calculation, and reporting of specifications will serve the purpose of establishing those most useful. Feedback (stimulated and spontaneous) from users of specifications should suffice. Specifications should help users in deciding to acquire the index and in how to use it, as well as in upgrading indexes in general. Once specifications are found to be useful, then standards for them can be developed. Such development may take years or decades. There seems to be no useful purpose served in depriving users of accurate specifications while standards are being developed.

Users should find specifications for indexes to be useful for the same reasons that they now find specifications for automobiles, books, bridges, buildings, phonograph pickups, and weather to be useful. Indexers should find specifications useful as goals to surpass and as recognition of quality work. The index-publisher can benefit for the same reasons. He can also justify extra expenditure for high-quality indexes on the basis of valid specifications and can take pride in publishing indexes of top quality as advertised by specifications. In the early days of automobiles, no purchaser or driver knew horsepower, acceleration, miles per gallon, expected mileage for tyres, or much else that is now taken for granted. Today, specifications are very useful in choosing among automobiles and in their use and maintenance. Indexes have been produced longer than have automobiles. It is time that valid specifications were published and used for indexes.

Indexing Hints for Beginners—With Special Emphasis on Time-Saving

Jessica M. Kerr

When I started my self-taught career in indexing, I had no equipment apart from my own experience working in libraries and Mr. G. V. Carey's admirable little book published by the Cambridge University Press. Consequently I had to make all my mistakes and gain my experience the hard way, and even now, after several years, I still fall into grievous errors and learn by them.

So it may be helpful to others like myself, to read about some of the traps which can be so frustrating and the way to avoid them. Every indexer is by no means a typist (even a hit-and-miss typist like myself) and there are publishers who will accept neat cards, or hand-written slips. But here in the United States (where I am living now) typing is expected. My own experience has been that typing from index cards is just another opportunity for mistakes and, in fact, I believe that most slips and errors occur when the entries on the card are transferred to the typewriter. Most of what follows applies to a typed index, but some of the suggestions are appropriate to any kind of index.

1. From the very first card, make every entry as clear, neat and accurate as if it were to be used by the printer; if a card is untidy in any way, tear it up and make another.

2. Before placing a card in the correct position in the box you are using, *check it again* with the text. This may seem over-careful and time-consuming, but actually it will save many a minute in the final stages when mistakes, oversights and errors have a way of piling up!

3. Galley-sheets are difficult to cope with in revision (at the beginning it is all only too easy!) and with a big index it saves much fruitless handling and confusion if the sheets are clipped firmly together in groups of ten and identified by a label marked clearly ' 1-9 ', ' 10-19 ' and so on. Then they should be laid out in sequence on the table. Galley-sheets have an uncanny way of getting tangled up and out-of-order; and, as the work goes on and the indexer begins to feel a little pressed, this becomes more and more frustrating. In an index of, for example, 1,000 entries, one mislaid card may mean an extra hour's work. In any case, be sure to underline clearly every subject used even though it may appear more than once on the same page. There is another method which

Reprinted from *The Indexer* 5, no. 3 (Spring 1967): 131–132.

—if space permits—is a great time-saver. Lay the whole batch of galley-sheets on the table. Check page 1 for entries. Then mark it in the top right-hand corner (preferably in red pencil) ' 1 '. With a drawing-pin (or thumb-tack) pin it lightly to the wall and so on right through the proofs, with as many pages as possible on the top row, and then start a second row, and so on. The rows *may* slightly over-lap as it is easy to lift the lower half of a sheet. Should a problem of any kind arise it is amazingly easy to check back to the proof, added to which the sheets remain in proper sequence and tidy.

4. Keep an extra box or tray for ' Pending ' cards—entries requiring special research or presenting a temporary problem. Mark such cards just as clearly as the others but keep separate until ' cleared ' for the index. Never allow stray cards to lie around where you are working.

5. Never let a card go into the box without its page numbers. This is a common and costly error which will be decidedly unpopular when your index arrives at the publisher's office. Being particularly prone to this mistake (especially when distracted for a minute in order to look up a reference) I have had a rubber stamp made which says in large red ink print ' Page-numbers ' and I hope that this particular trap will cease to torment me.

6. Be sure to keep the cards in correct order after typing. It is tempting and easy to cast them aside in a pile and then have to hunt wildly for one of them at some later stage. It is just as easy to put them back in correct alphabetical order.

7. Stack required reference books within easy reach.

8. Many publishers state definitely at the outset how many ' units ' to a line of index can be allowed—usually 34 or 32. The counting of these ' units ' (punctuation, spaces, brackets, etc.) *must be accurate* and it takes up a considerable amount of time no matter how it is done. But it is certainly much easier when done on the card with a line clearly drawn to mark the limit of each line of entries. It is difficult, tedious and time-wasting to do this while typing.

9. Keep both galley-sheets and cards until the index is finally cleared with the publisher.

The moral of all this really is: *do as much of the work on the cards as possible.* Not only will this lighten the typing work but it will also provide a substitute index which can be used in an emergency. Do not write little notes, abbreviations, or symbols to yourself—60 cards or so later you will have forgotten why you put them there!

All this will seem rather obvious and elementary to expert indexers of long experience, but they represent my own problems and mistakes in the early stages, and will, I hope, be helpful to those who are also teaching themselves.

Some Snags in Indexing

G. Norman Knight

Substance of talk given at the Society's A.G.M., 1958

Every indexer encounters his own difficulties and problems, and the points I am going to mention are for the most part those which I have come up against in my own practice. Many of them are not dealt with in the recognised text-books and some of my solutions may appear highly controversial.

My first snag is the vexed question of the indexing of hyphenated words. It is generally accepted, I think, that these should appear under the initial letter of the first of the hyphenated words. But where in relation to other entries of that same word? Some indexers, I am aware, put all hyphenated words immediately after the last entry of the unhyphenated word. Thus:

> Slaughter of animals
>
> Slaughter-houses

But the rule I have adopted—I cannot now remember where I first saw it suggested—is to treat all cases where the first of the hyphenated words has an independent standing of its own as if they were separate words. This would result in reversing the order of the two " slaughter " entries above. On the other hand, where the first word can only be used in conjunction with another word, then both words should be treated as if they were one word and should be given in the appropriate order. Examples of words which in our language and in the hyphenated sense are incapable of being used independently are as follows:

Ante- Anti- Auto- Hyper- Inter- Non- Post- Pre- Pro- Pseudo-

We should accordingly expect to see (though in what work I cannot imagine!) the following order:

> *Non compos mentis*
>
> Nonage
>
> Non-aged persons
>
> Nonagenarians
>
> Non-barking dogs
>
> Nonchalance

What of hyphenated proper-names? Sir Henry Campbell-Bannerman, the Liberal Prime Minister before Asquith, was plain Mr. Campbell when he entered the House of Commons. Bannerman was his mother's maiden name and he adopted it in hyphenated form on the death of a rich uncle. In this case, if both forms of the name occur in the text of the book, I suggest that a cross-reference from Campbell is needed, or (perhaps preferably) the one entry could read:

> Campbell, Henry (later Sir Henry Campbell-Bannerman)

Again, Lord Swinton first gained fame as Sir Philip Lloyd-Graeme. Later, following the example of another earlier M.P., Mr. Ashmead-Bartlett, who married the Victorian heiress, Baroness Burdett-Coutts, he took his wife's name as his own

Reprinted from *The Indexer* 1, no. 4 (September 1958): 104–109.

and became known as Sir Philip Cunliffe-Lister. Here, two cross-references, from Lloyd-Graeme and from Cunliffe-Lister, may be required.

It may not be generally known that Sir Winston Churchill is correctly Sir Winston Spencer-Churchill and up to the end of 1951 the always punctilious *Court Circular* invariably referred to him as such. But only a pig-headed pedant would think of indexing him under S, unless he happened to be referred to in the text as Spencer-Churchill, in which case I suggest that there should also be a cross-reference from Churchill, or vice-versa.

Far more difficult are the cases of people with no hyphens but whose fore-names have become inextricably woven with their true surnames. I suppose it would be agreed that strictly Bonar Law should be indexed under Law, Andrew Bonar, and Lloyd George (before he became Earl Lloyd-George of Dwyfor) under George, David Lloyd.

A year or two ago I observed that Robert Blake, the author of the standard biography of Bonar Law, had in his index (which he had compiled himself) listed his hero under B. Having to write to him for permission to quote a passage in one of my own works, I called attention to this. He justified his practice by saying that his readers would think of the statesman as Bonar Law and would instinctively look for him under B. I replied that in that case there should at least have been a cross-reference from Law. I notice that my encyclopaedia (correctly, as I hold) inserts him in the L volume, as does the *Dictionary of National Biography* (with a cross-reference from Bonar).

The case of Lloyd George is rather more complicated. When he entered the House of Commons it was as plain David George, but later the whole world was to know him as Lloyd George, and when towards the end of his life he was ennobled, he took the title of Earl Lloyd-George of Dwyfor. Again, his second son, Gwilym, caused his name to be hyphenated in *Hansard* before he also entered " another place " as Lord Tenby. On the other hand Lady Megan, as revealed by *Who's Who*, has eschewed the family preference for the hyphen. It is somewhat odd to find that *Dod's Parliamentary Companion* omits the hyphen in the case of the present Earl as well as that of his sister.

Whichever plan we adopt with these names, I don't suppose we shall go far wrong so long as we recognise the inevitable necessity of a cross-reference from the name we reject for the main entry.

Speaking of peers, it is customary to follow the fashion of Burke and Debrett rather than that set by the *D.N.B.** and to index them under their titles. There are, however, exceptions to this rule. No one would think of either Sir Robert Walpole or Horace Walpole as the Earl of Orford, in spite of their both having assumed that title before the end of their lives. Again, Lord Passfield is far better known as Sidney Webb. In all three cases I suggest that the titles need be given in the index only if expressly referred to in the text and then with appropriate cross-references.

---

* The *D.N.B.* does give cross-references from titles to surnames, but while Debrett supplies cross-references from surnames, Burke does not.

As with peers, so with cardinals, archbishops and bishops, who should normally be indexed under the names of their sees. But here we must be careful. With peers it is easy to differentiate by stating, e.g.: Salisbury, 3rd Marquess of. But Salisbury, 78th Bishop of, (unless followed by the dates of his holding the office in brackets) would convey very little. Consequently in indexing a book where, shall we say, several Archbishops of Canterbury are mentioned I find it best to distinguish them as follows:

Canterbury, Archbishops of, *see* Davidson, Randall; Fisher, Geoffrey; Temple, Frederick, *and* Temple, William.

As regards cross-references, I always try to save the time and patience of the users of my indexes by not employing them where there are but few page entries and no sub-headings. Thus, to take an instance from Collison's *Indexes and Indexing*:

Flowers, Scilly Isles, 87-9
Scilly Isles, flowers in, 87-9

This applies equally where there may be more than two indexable references. Thus:

Dead Sea Scrolls, electronic indexing of, 53,119
Electronic indexing of Dead Sea Scrolls, 53,119
Indexing, electronic, Dead Sea Scrolls, 53,119

In these cases it is just as easy to supply the page numbers each time as to write cross-references.

Talking about the Scilly Isles reminds me that I always invert the Isle of Wight to Wight, Isle of, and the Isle of Man to Man, Isle of. (In parenthesis, perhaps Members may recall one explanation of the naming of the Virgin Islands in the West Indies; it was supposed that they must have been so called because they were so far away from the Isle of Man!)

While we are dealing with place names, I would venture to suggest that the method of alphabetical classification adopted in the Post Office Guides is an unsafe one for indexers to follow and that places consisting of two words ought to be kept separate from those of one word. Thus:

Not	New Brighton	But	New Brighton
	Newcastle		New Zealand
	Newfoundland		Newcastle
	New Zealand		Newfoundland

Every indexer knows the rules about indexing Mac and St. Mc and M' are to be treated as if they were Mac, which indeed they really are. The British Museum Catalogues go so far as to spell them so in each case, actually expanding, for instance, McPhail and M'Phail to MacPhail, but I should scarcely recommend this practice to indexers; it seems to me to be taking liberties with the owners' actual names and might also be confusing to inquirers. Again, St as if it were spelt out, S-a-i-n-t. Thus:

Sails
St James's Square
St Moritz
St Paul's Cathedral
Saints and Sinners

Please note the position of St. Moritz. "St" here really stands for "Sankt" but I think that only the pig-headed pedant already referred to would accordingly place St. Moritz at the end of the above list, since the ordinary user of the index would naturally look for it in its present place.

On the other hand, where the saint himself is referred to, he should appear under his name ; thus:

> James, St
> John the Baptist, St
> Paul, St

Next we come to the somewhat vexing problem of foreign names. The usually accepted rule is that for actual foreigners mere prepositions come after the names, but definite articles or articles combined with prepositions (e.g., Du, Des) are placed before. Thus:

> Bismark, Prince Otto von
> Costa, da
> Des Moines
> Du Plessis
> La Fontaine, Jean de

This is how they would be indexed in the countries concerned. But now we meet with the further difficulty that the Italians themselves put the prepositions Di and Da before the names in their indexes. Thus they use Di Monti, Da Capezio, etc. Accordingly in an index I recently compiled for Rosenthal's *Two Centuries of Opera at Covent Garden* I arranged all such Italian singers (e.g., the tenor Enzo di Martino) or characters (e.g., Di Luna in *Il Trovatore*) under D. Mrs. Hatt has kindly called my attention to a curious oddity to be seen in the index to Hutton's *Highways and Byways in Somerset* :

> Robbia, work at Nynehead, Della

With English or Anglicized or Americanized names it is usual to put the preposition first. Thus:

> De la Mare, Walter
> De Morgan, William
> De Quincey, Thomas
> Van Dyck, Sir Anthony

The question arises as to whether Anglo-Norman names during the first two centuries after the Conquest should count as English for this purpose, for I notice that practically all the history works and encyclopaedias classify Simon de Montfort as Montfort, Simon de, although it is true that the *Shorter Cambridge Mediaeval History* indexes him under Simon (with no cross-reference from either Montfort or De Montfort).

In compiling the index I have just alluded to, I came across a reference to Baron de Rothschild (the English one) as having been a member of the Covent Garden Syndicate. But, judging that anyone wanting to look him up would look under R, I boldly indexed him as Rothschild, Baron de. I think that we must treat all these rules with a grain of common sense. For instance, the French co-discoverer of radium was actually Mme de *la* Curie, but is always thought of as Mme Curie and I am emboldened in indexing her under C by the British Museum catalogue entry, which runs:

    Curie, Marie de la

Also I cannot see any indexer in his senses putting the French seaport of Le Havre under L.

While on the subject of French names may I mention that, given a newspaper called *L'Industrie,* I would of course index it under I, but would keep it as it stands rather than as *Industrie, L',* which looks and is awkward. But I have found that this occasionally offends the printer's sense of symmetrical fitness and he changes it back. If he does, then is the time to keep a firm hand when correcting the proofs and to insert a note in the margin " See copy ".

Equal firmness with the printers is sometimes necessitated by my way of treating abbreviations. As may have been noticed in some of the preceding examples, I do not insert a full point where the last letter of the abbreviated form is the same as that of the full word. Thus, " Rev.", " Prof.", " foll.", but also " Dr ", " Fr ", " Mme ", " St " (for both " Saint " and " Street "), etc.

There is one curious Dutch name which has puzzled indexers. This is " im Thurn ". But in the case of Sir Everard im Thurn, who was a distinguished Governor of British Guiana, I would have no hesitation in indexing him under I.

In the Covent Garden book I have mentioned there was an allusion to a M. Bouvet, a French singer. Having ascertained from the author that M. here stood for Monsieur and that he was unable to trace either Christian names or initials, I proceeded to index him as follows:

    Bouvet, Mons. (*tenor*), 572

I consider that " Mons." is always preferable to " M." in an index, as avoiding fear of confusion with the initial M. (for Marcel or Maurice).

In indexing the same work I largely used dates to avoid long strings of page numbers, putting the years in italics (to avoid confusion with page numbers). To quote an extract—the full entry is far longer:

    Barbirolli, Sir John (conductor), 468, 471 ; *1932-7*...478, 483 ; as guest-
        conductor at C.G., *1951-2*...611-2, 614-5—*1952-3*...621.

Here the snag was that Sir John was a guest-conductor for three seasons in all. If I had put an ordinary semi-colon after 614-5, it might have been assumed that the remaining dates referred to a resumption of his ordinary career. This particular problem I solved by employing dashes instead of semi-colons.

The following snag has been suggested by Mr. René Hague, and I have experienced similar instances. It concerns the identity of proper names. In a volume, for example, on the Reformation the author may refer to the same person in different places as " John Frederick ", " Frederick of Saxony ", " the Saxon Elector " and " the Elector John ", and (since there is also another Elector John) the indexer has to keep all his wits and be uncommonly careful if he is to compile an index that will be of any use.

For another somewhat similar snag I am indebted to Mr. Hewitt. This does not relate to proper names but to the difficult decision as to which term or phrase to use when the nomenclature of some particular field is in process of change.

For instance, mental illness and persons of unsound mind are replacing lunacy and lunatics, while affiliation proceedings are taking the place of bastardy proceedings. Often the author does not help because of his own constant chopping and changing, and the index-user may well be infuriated by not finding the term to which he is accustomed. The only solution I can suggest in such cases is a copious use of cross-references for such synonyms.

Again, the indiscriminate use of such expressions as Infant/Child/Young Person/Minor makes the choice of a suitable catch-word a difficult one, since a Minor is not necessarily a Young Person, while an Infant may (according to the context) mean either a babe-in-arms or else a person suffering incapacity (i.e., under 21 years of age).

My final snag concerns the indexing of a really serious work, such as a Constitutional History. In such a case it may be important for the student to cast his eye over every reference to a given personage. Now suppose this personage to be Lord Palmerston and that he is referred to on page 54, lines 3, 8, and 12 and also on the last line, where the reference runs on to the first few lines of page 55. In such a case: Palmerston, Lord, 54-5, would be scarcely adequate since the student might confine his attention to the last reference. Better would be: Palmerston, Lord, 54, 54-5, that is, if the secondary theme is in all cases the same and does not warrant separate sub-headings. But best of all, I would submit, as accounting for all the references, is: Palmerston, Lord, 54(3), 54-5. It should be noted that some indexers prefer (bis) or (ter), as the case may be, to the bracketed numerals.

Do Members consider that such a method provides unnecessary spoon-feeding for the index-user, who should be expected to read the whole of any page to which his attention is directed ? I do not agree. Provided that the practice is confined to references of importance, I believe that anything that may be helpful to the student is worth while. Of course, carrying it out postulates the indexer's being allowed plenty of time for his task. How rarely is this the case !

Making an Index to a Specified Length

M. D. Anderson

An indexer faced for the first time with the task of making an index to a specified length may wonder how best to set about it. It is hoped that the following gleanings from experience may be helpful.

First get exact information about the length. The publisher may have said: we can allow you twelve pages. Ask how many columns to a page (almost always two), how many lines from top to bottom of the page, how many characters across the column. Suppose the answer is two columns, 50 lines, 35 characters. It is now possible to tell whether the space allows of a long or a short index. The calculations are best done in lines rather than in pages, because of the great variation between books in the ratio of number of lines per page of text to number of lines per page of index. Suppose that the 12-page index with 50 lines per page (600 lines) is for a book with 300 pages, and 40 lines per page (12,000 lines); the index will amount to 5 per cent of the book. This is an average length for indexes to non-specialist but serious books. Let us take it that the imaginary book is of this type.

The indexer can now begin work, knowing that there is room for adequate but not intensive coverage of the book. The 600 lines of index, in two columns, would mean 1,200 entries if no entry was longer than the width of the column. In practice, a considerable number of entries are sure to be longer than this, and a few lines have also to be spared for the heading of the index, and for spaces between letters of the alphabet, so that 800 to 900 entries is the most that should be aimed at. Do not take alarm from the conclusion that 900 entries for 300 pages allows only three entries per page. This is true enough, but remember that an entry may be followed by several page numbers, so that 900 entries may include 2,000 or 3,000 references, or more.

When entries have been made for about one-quarter of the book, it is as well to do a rough check of the number of index cards used, and the percentage of cards with more than one line of writing, so that coverage may be adjusted if necessary. For large numbers of cards, measurement may replace counting; the thickness of, say, 200 cards closely pressed together may be found to be, say, 1.4 inches, and this figure is quite accurate enough for approximate calculations.

When all the entries have been made, and revised, the indexer must set the typewriter to allow for 35 characters in the line, and proceed to the typing, which will show how nearly the desired length has been attained. Knowing the number of lines per page of typescript, and consequently how many pages should be occupied by an index of the required length, the indexer is apt to go through a variety of stages of hopefulness, doubt, and despair, before the typescript is completed. But it is consoling to keep in mind that pruning an index is not necessarily a disaster, and may even improve it. It will be found that assessing the length correctly becomes easier with practice.

Suppose that coverage has not been very successfully calculated, and that the typescript extends to 18½ pages, when only 17 are wanted. Some more arithmetic will show that, say, 50 lines must be deleted, three from each page on the average. If the sub-headings have originally been 'set-out', each on a separate line, the necessary space may perhaps be saved by arranging them in continuous or 'run-on' form, separated by semi-colons. Another method of shortening is to remove a whole class of entries, if one can be found suitable for sacrifice. But sometimes there is nothing for it but a patient reconsideration of the entries, compressing a long one here, deleting a short one there, combining another two together, gaining a line by omission of an unimportant word, and marking each line removed on a score-card, until the 50 lines have been accumulated.

Reprinted from *The Indexer* 7, no. 3 (Spring 1971): 121–122.

The reaction of one reader to the last paragraph was: 'I jib at the idea of having to delete entries . . . deletions result in a less comprehensive index, for the deleted ones may be the very ones the reader is needing'. This attitude is very natural, and the indexer doing the deletion may feel the same. But it is really an objection to any limit on length. No index can include every possible reference without becoming a concordance; the process of indexing is one of selecting the entries that readers are most likely to need out of a mass of possible ones. If the index has to be shorter than the indexer would naturally make it, selection has merely to be more stringent. Slightly over-indexing, and then making deletions, is merely a double process of selection. In my experience, it tends to give a better result than attaining the desired length by what feels like under-indexing from the start—that is, omitting entries of marginal importance. If these are included, then after working through the book the indexer is better able to judge which of them ought to be included, and which may safely be discarded.

And furthermore, shortening is not all deletion. Some, or even much, of the space saved in revising an index to a given length can be obtained by alterations that make it more concise and compact, and thereby improve it. In fact, making an index to a specified length is an interesting challenge to the indexer's skill. But both indexers and publishers should recognise that it requires extra time.

Chapter Headings

M. D. Anderson

The following words recently caught my eye: ' . . . chapter headings, which are seldom or never indexed . . . ' The statement as it stands is certainly too sweeping, and it may be nearer the truth to say 'not always indexed', or 'sometimes not indexed', but whether to include chapter headings or not is a matter worth consideration when planning an index.

Any decision must depend on both type of index and nature of chapter headings. It is obviously not necessary to index chapter headings where the chapters themselves mark no very definite divisions of the subject matter, as may happen in discursive memoirs or travel books. It may even be that the chapters are headed only by numbers. For such a book, a simple index of names of persons and places is all that is required.

Again, it would be misleading to index a chapter heading with page references covering the whole chapter when the heading has been used in a rather vague way, and actually refers to part only of the following pages. For example, in Green's *Short History of the English People,* the chapter called The Great Charter has seven sections, of which one only deals with Magna Carta; the references to the Charter in the preceding and succeeding parts of the chapter are few and only incidental. The index directs the reader to this section in the entry 'Charter, the Great' (although with three single page numbers rather than with a comprehensive 128-32). Another chapter, called Puritan England, opens with a section on the Puritans, pages 460-74; six of these pages are referred to under 'Puritans' in the index, along with three later pages in the chapter. From both of these chapters the indexer has justifiably selected the pages specifically devoted to the subject of the heading, instead of giving what would have been rather meaningless references to the whole chapters.

In the same book, however, the chapter called The Reformation, covering the reigns of the Tudors from 1540 onwards, receives no entry under 'Reformation' in the index, where two page numbers refer the reader to an account of Luther in an earlier chapter. Here the indexer should surely have considered the chapter heading, and inserted 'in England', with appropriate page numbers from the chapter, in his entry for 'Reformation', or alternatively should have given a cross-reference to 'Protestants', in which entry adequate references to the Reformation chapter are provided.

A type of chapter heading that cannot easily be indexed is the obliquely descriptive epithet, resembling the title of a novel, such as several of the chapter headings in A. J. P. Taylor's *English History 1914-1945*—The Years of Gold, Unexpected Crisis, Half-Time, Appeasement, Finest Hour, etc.

Chapter headings in G. M. Trevelyan's *English Social History* have been curiously treated by the indexer. Chapters I and II, headed Chaucer's England I and Chaucer's England II, are indexed as 'Chaucer's England, Chapters I and II', with no page numbers. The headings of the next three chapters (England in the Age of Caxton, Tudor England, and England during the Anti-Clerical Revolution) are not indexed. Chapters VI and VII (Shakespeare's England I and II, pages 139-72 and 173-205) are indexed as 'Shakespeare's England, 60, 97-8, 134, 235, and Chapter VII', Chapter VI be-

Reprinted from *The Indexer* 6, no. 3 (Spring 1969): 116–118.

ing ignored. The remaining chapter headings are not indexed, although they include Defoe's England, Dr. Johnson's England I, II and III, and Cobbett's England I and II. For consistency's sake, either these chapters should have had index entries to correspond with those for Chaucer's England and Shakespeare's England, or the two latter entries should have been omitted, which would undoubtedly have been the wiser course. Readers seeking matter relating to Chaucer, Shakespeare, Defoe, Johnson, and Cobbett will be satisfied with the index entries provided for these writers themselves, and are unlikely to want references to chapters about the periods in which they lived. Such chapter headings may be classed as too general in their scope to be indexed, and are often found.

But there remain books in which the headings of the chapters are clear indications of the whole of their contents, and are indexable in form and meaning; here we can rightly expect to find chapter headings included in the index. Take for example Anthony Sampson's *Anatomy of Britain*, in which the thirty-nine chapter headings are of the type Parliament, Press, Civil Service, Bankers, Trade Unions, and so on. All but two appear in the index, in the form ' Parliament, 51-65 ', usually with added page numbers from other parts of the book. The last chapter heading is a repetition of the name of the book, and is understandably omitted, and we must suppose that Chapter 7, with the heading Opposition, escaped indexing by accident.

Such an omission of a chapter heading is not uncommon, and—perhaps in consequence—the contents of the chapter may not be referred to in the corresponding index entry. An example of this may be taken from C. R. L. Fletcher's *The Making of Modern Europe, Vol. II*. Chapter VI is headed France 1000-1180, and covers pages 238-98. In the index entry for France, there is no page number from this chapter. The entry for Spain, on the other hand, leads off with: ' (see also Chapter VII) ', and gives some page references to the chapter as well.

The insertion of chapter headings in indexes brings various problems. If a chapter is not long, and contains practically all that is said on the subject in the book, an entry might simply run:

France, 21, 52, 67-83, 110,

where 67-83 is easily seen to refer to the main account. It can be emphasized by heavy type, or by placing first, if such a convention has been established. But suppose that the book is a large history of Europe, with chapter 5 headed France, and many references to France scattered through other chapters. Then it will not suffice to produce an entry like the above in expanded form:

France, 150-200
    army of, 45-7, 203
    literature of, 209-14
    relations of, with England, 29-30; with
      Spain, 314
    etc.,

in which the page numbers for the sub-headings are all from chapters other than chapter 5. The topics of the sub-headings are almost certainly mentioned also in chapter 5, so that the sub-headings are incomplete as they stand, and page numbers from within chapter 5 must be added to them. The entry form for France will then become something like this:

France, 150-200
    army of, 45-7, 163, 172, 203
    literature of, 183, 209-14
    relations of, with England, 29-30, 150-2,
      197; with Spain, 195-6, 314
    etc.

But in chapter 5 there are other comparable topics *not* found elsewhere in the book, and it becomes necessary to add more sub-headings:

France
    navy of, 166, 167
    relations of, with Italy, 189; with the
      Papacy, 194
    etc.

As this process continues, and the contents of chapter 5 are dissected into their component topics, and divided into sub-headings, the entry ' France, 150-200 ' covering the whole chapter, comes to seem super-fluous. Some indexers delete it, or never put it in, and this may be defended on the grounds that the chapter heading is in the table of contents at the beginning of the book. However, I think that the overall entry still has value for the index user, in that it prevents the trees of the sub-headings from hiding the forest of the chapter.

Furthermore, a large index of this kind is liable to contain many duplicate sub-head-ings under different entries, such for example as military references, collected both under 'France, army of', and also in the entry 'armies, of France . . . of Spain . . . etc.' In order to keep the index to a permissible length, it may be necessary to cancel the longer duplicate sub-headings, by means of cross-references to the other entries under which they may be found. It usually seems best to do the cancelling in the major entries, hoping thus to simplify the reader's search. Thus under France, in the imaginary index we are dealing with, a final sub-heading might be added:

see also under armies, literature, navies

and these sub-headings would then be cancelled from the France entry. The further this process is carried, the less will chapter 5 be represented in the sub-headings, and the more advisable it will be to keep 'France, 150-200' at the beginning of the index entry.

I hope that these preliminary reflections may encourage other indexers to give their views on the problem of indexing chapter headings.

IIb. Case Histories

The Modern Index to Richard Hakluyt's *Principall Navigations**

Alison M. Quinn

I started indexing the *Principall Navigations* in September 1961. I was approached to do this partly, I think, because I was available in the sense of not being gainfully employed, partly because I had already indexed two publications for the Hakluyt Society, publications that covered a considerable part of the third section of *PN*, the enterprises of Sir Humfrey Gilbert and Sir Walter Raleigh. A third qualification was that I had permanently in residence a member of the Hakluyt Society who could supervise the work in progress. There was, I think, some advantage in having editor and indexer under one roof especially for the indexer who soon found that it was quicker to ask a question than look up a book. In the course of time when many, if not most, of the pages of *PN* seemed to have been photographed on to my mind by some tele-lithographic process I could give the editor a reference not only as to page but where on the page without having to look at a card. I don't regret the fading of this parlour trick. It is enough to feel that your head is a ragbag, without the certainty of remaining an automated ragbag. What has not faded is the pleasure and satisfaction the reading of the entire 1589 edition gave me from the table of contents to the index. Parts I and II I had read before only in selection. I had been introduced to *PN* as literature when I was at school and had to remind myself more than once that what I was supposed to be

doing was indexing and not literary appreciation or even making a glossary. Yet re-reading a passage that I found vividly descriptive or graceful or effective provided relaxation from the inevitable tedium with which indexers are all familiar.

Copy arrived first of all in the negative impression, single sheets, white letter on black, rather ghostly. Most of the first reading was done from these sheets. I soon became accustomed to this but it is not as clear as the positive, black on white. When the positives arrived they were in gatherings and in this form much easier to handle for checking and much easier to assemble if they became misplaced. To upset a pile of black sheets was a minor disaster. By the following summer, that is 1962, an index was ready but not as full as the one that was printed. What remained to be indexed was the introduction but this was not ready in page. One reason for delay was that Cambridge was in the middle of re-organizing, moving house. This gave me more time to extend the index and pursue identifications. Copy was sent to Cambridge in April 1963 in order that decisions could be taken on presentation. With so large a page a decision had to be made about number of columns and samples printed of selected entries. The copy was then returned to me for adjustment and finally sent back, as far as I can recall, about the beginning of June. An amusing coincidence was that the number of typescript pages was exactly the number of pages in *PN*.

The following month I set off with the editor for a year in the United States, study-

* A talk given to the Society on 16th March by the winner of the Wheatley Medal for an outstanding index published in 1965.

Reprinted from *The Indexer* 5, no. 3 (Spring 1967): 106–112.

ing at three libraries, the John Carter Brown, the Huntingdon and the Folger, and it was at the last mentioned that the galley proofs caught up with me in the spring of 1964. I was very happily situated there, together with the Library of Congress across the road, for any further checking. The proofs went with me to the John Carter Brown for the summer where, again, I had every facility for checking voyages of discovery. The galleys were returned to Cambridge about the beginning of September shortly before we, ourselves, returned to Liverpool. Two sets of page proofs followed fairly rapidly and just after Christmas 1964 I had finished my part in the index to *PN* (1589).

I will deal now with the general policy outlined for the start of this project. It was decided that this should not be only a name and place index but should also incorporate a wide range of subjects. The index to the MacLehose edition of the 1598-1600 *Principall Navigations* is almost wholly name and place, with subjects, apart from Ships, barely touched on. Even so it occupies almost an entire volume and is complicated by having volume as well as page references. It is an index for which I have the greatest admiration. I used it extensively and seldom found a mistake. The 1589 edition being paginated straight through greatly simplified the indexing of subjects, indeed the indexing of everything. Such complications as there are in the pagination I will refer to later.

As this was to be a modern index it was decided that all place names should be given their present form where they could be identified and that the modern name should be the main entry. Names of persons were to be treated in this way also and persons who were mentioned by office or in any other indirect way should be identified and indexed under their proper names, again where this could be done accurately. A preliminary working list of subjects was agreed on with the understanding that I could introduce any further subjects that might arise from indexing. An initial list of subjects was not difficult to arrange. Hakluyt's motives in compiling *PN* and his special interests were well known. Anything connected with

voyages of discovery and anything connected with plans for settlement in new discoveries would be a suitable category. Such subjects as Ships and allied topics, Commodities, embracing both Fauna and Flora, Maps, Navigation, Money, Measures, Weights, Merchants suggested themselves. Colonization and colonists implied native peoples, Indians, Eskimos, Negroes and the questionnaires with which all discoverers descended on societies, then as now. They were to take note of customs, ceremonies, religion, weapons and tools, houses, clothing and diet. They were to attempt to collect words of the language and bring back some of the natives to learn English and teach their language. Some I tried out of curiosity. In what was very much a man's world I wondered what sort of information there was about women and was interested to find that Hakluyt himself had indexed women. How much was there about games, about music, about diseases? I was asked to index rain. Out of the search for references to rain it became clear that the English were interested mainly in its absence. Hakluyt's index entry for Egypt is ' Aegypt hath raine very seldome'. Apart from these general directives I had a gloriously free hand, enough rope to rig the ' Golden Hind '. There was not even a limitation as to size. As the second volume was to contain only Part III the index could swell itself importantly into Part IV. And swell it did. This index was another voyage of discovery. I had very little idea of what I might find or what the final index would look like.

I come now to the technical points which had to be settled before indexing could begin. The pagination presented certain problems which were resolved by Mr. Skelton. The narratives are paged straight through from 1 to 825. The index which follows is not paginated and was silently numbered 826 to 834 as far as the reader is involved. The indexer got busy with a pencil immediately. The introduction was numbered in roman as introductions so frequently are. The introduction to *PN* is sixty pages and touches what I consider to be the upper limit for the use of roman numbering. An introduction of over two hundred pages numbered in roman which I have recently indexed reduced me to counting on my fingers. Such references take up a disproportionate amount of space in the actual index. Italic arabic is a more efficient and effective method, I think. To return to *PN*. Italic arabic was used for the Preliminaries which, again, were without page numbering. So far we have roman, arabic and italic arabic. There are still two sections to be dealt with, the Drake narrative and the alternative version of the Bowes report. This account of Drake's circumnavigation, inserted after *PN* had been printed, is not paged. For this the device of using capital letters was used with the number of the page immediately preceding, working out as 643A to 643L, in italic. Sir Jerome Bowes' account of his experiences as ambassador to Ivan IV ran from pages 491 to 505. The amended version, diplomatically revised, runs from pages 491 to 501 and these numbers are in italic to distinguish them from the first state, obviously necessary when both versions are to be indexed. Need I tell indexers what a constant anxiety these numbers were. Most people have experienced neurotic anxiety feelings about gas and water taps when leaving home on holiday. In the same way I was in a constant state of neurosis about whether I had remembered to underline or had underlined the proper number. How I wished that Sir Jerome Bowes had been illiterate, or perhaps more discreet. In all there are five kinds of numbering, roman, arabic, italic arabic, Drake, Bowes—six if you include invisible numbering—seven if you include wrong page numbers, silently corrected.

Punctuation came under scrutiny next. There was some discussion on how to present the two place names, ancient and modern, resolving itself into putting the text name into round brackets after the modern name which was the main entry, with, of course, a cross-reference from the text name. This rule applied also to personal names but was used only where there was a marked difference as, for example, in the English rendering of Russian names. Where there was an identification by office the name is followed by the description and there is a cross-reference from some key word such as consul or ambassador. Commas and semi-colons only were used and the material could be paragraphed or divided by subheadings.

Subjects were to be grouped with cross-references from the particular to the group. The reverse arrangement was never canvassed for this index. The size of some of these groups was estimated to be potentially too large as it turned out. A long list of items to be looked up separately on different pages would be too cumbersome as well as adding to the wear and tear on pages. A list can suggest relationships. It did add considerably, as more than one reviewer has pointed out, to the number of cross-references but as I was not limited in space I indulged to the full. I did consider giving a list of Subjects at the beginning of the index but rejected this as being out of tune with Hakluyt whose own index is discursive and gives up its information only to the browser. In this modern index, to the browser the subject headings are readily apparent. This arrangement of grouping subjects has been described by an American reviewer as 'instant research', including I think much of the analysis under place names and leading characters. I think this is an apt description and partly what I found, as I progressed through *PN*, I was for various reasons led into doing.

It was not practicable to read through the entire *PN* before starting to index, so that many decisions were taken as the index grew in bulk and sample analyses were made. There was the size of the page. One page of this facsimile is the equivalent of two and a half pages of the MacLehose edition, many of them with scarcely a break for paragraphing. Black letter is not easy to scan quickly nor is it possible in a facsimile to employ any technical device to assist in finding a reference, such as dividing a page into three sections or numbering the lines in tens. Some other assistance in finding a reference, I felt, would be desirable and this could only be descriptive in that it might help to show on which part of the page the reference would be found. In pages that contain so much reading matter changes of topic are frequent. This is why so many references, apparently trivial, have a label. Much more labelling of references is necessary too when making an analytical index, for working purposes, especially when the indexer is not also the editor, the compiler or the author. Such labels do not necessarily appear in the final index but many were retained in the index to *PN* for this reason. It also seemed to me to be helpful to readers to give in the index some definitive information especially about persons. If there is a run of John Browns time is saved if they can be described by occupation or pinned down in time by giving dates of birth or death. Subject items were put into a context as an aid to selection for those using the index for specific information. This is ' instant research ' in that the information may be to hand in the index without reference to the text. Why not? Miss Paulin in her address to the 1966 Annual General Meeting of the Library Association underlined the need for such time-saving help to researchers faced with ever proliferating books and papers. If this analytical work has been done, either by indexer or editor, there is everything to be said for passing it on. This is particularly desirable for a work known to be or published with the intention that it should become a standard reference book. After nearly four hundred years *PN* qualifies.

I found as details began to accumulate and sample presentations were tried out that a formula, especially for places, emerged. This might well illustrate something of Hakluyt's method when editing the texts for publication. There is on record what he selected, what he stressed. In his re-editing of some of the narratives for the 1598-1600 edition there are indications of what he may well have eliminated for the 1589 edition. Some of the information might have been considered too common-place for the sixteenth century. The repetitive narrative worked up from a ship's log called for his blue pencil yet it is from these that a glimpse is given of how people occupied their time

on long sea voyages or during long sojourns in a foreign harbour. By cutting much from Hugh Smith's journal describing the voyage of Pet and Jackman in search of the Northeast passage I think he toned down or almost destroyed its dramatic effect. I admit that I indexed this description of the struggles of two tiny ships to get out of the ice east of Vaygach during a cold January with the snow falling. It made its mark. A little earlier I had been indexing the description of Ivan IV's annual review of the ordnance at the time when the Russians exploded that powerful bomb somewhere in the region of Novaya Zemlya. It may have appeared a menace to everyone else but to me it was just the annual review of the ordnance taking place at the traditional time of the year. The formula worked out for places was descriptive details first, one or two paragraphs, followed by historical details, again paragraphed according to the nature and amount of material. Miscellaneous references were kept to the end and the final reference was to the Hakluyt index where this applied. Persons, as one would expect, were more idiosyncratic. Here, such personal information as was given was put first, followed by references to documents such as letters and then historical information. The order of paragraphs was never intentionally alphabetical but governed by some logical order inherent in the material—time, geography, documentation, etc. The Volga, for example, is indexed from its source to its delta in the Caspian Sea. Native peoples are indexed, at a guess, in the order of the questionnaire, the order which appears again in the Cook *Journals*. Lists were, of course, alphabetical but an exception was made for the ships' complement. Here the order is rank, supplying an extra piece of information. An exception was also made for those entries beginning with " Saint " in sundry languages. These were kept together as a section indicated by extra space, as a *cordon sanitaire,* at the beginning and end. Some subjects are mixed alphabetical and associative, such as houses and navigation. The assortment of structures under houses is brought together because they are called mostly some kind or other of a house such as trading house or sugar house and I thought it would be useful when looking for a reference to know that the word ' house ' was the clue. Navigation proved the most intractable of the subjects for everyone concerned. How could this seemingly endless supply of assorted observations be put into some order that could be of use or meaning. The model I used seems to me to be that of the BBC weather bulletin, region by region, gale warnings and all, keeping Atlantic and American regions together, Arctic and northeast regions together.

The physical apparatus I used for making the index was 5″ x 3″ cards and, eventually, shoe boxes to hold them as they soon outgrew the two filing drawers I have. Cards for persons and places were kept in one alphabetical section, subjects in another, as this cut down the labour of finding cards. These cards contained eventually the name, labelled page references, and at the bottom the source for an identification. Many of these entries ran to several cards, each numbered in sequence. Cards with the cross-references were put in when the need arose. In all about 10,000 cards were used. When the last page was indexed the labour of typing had to be faced, as there was no alternative. Ten thousand cards holding information some of which was not intended for the index could not be sent to a publisher. Some help was essential and a typist was employed to do the persons and places. Subjects I typed myself together with those persons whose entries were long enough and complicated enough to rank as subjects, such as Hakluyt himself, Ivan IV, Queen Elizabeth. For the guidance of the typist a green card was inserted into her group of cards wherever a subject intruded, with instructions to start a new page. Three copies were made with triple spacing to allow for corrections and additions. It was clear that a point had been reached before every entry was ready when the overall impression of the shape and nature of the index that would reveal itself in typescript was desirable. It would be easier to check for consistency and cross-references. It was not

typed to fit any specific column width as this had not been decided and the internal punctuation was left as simple as possible to make corrections easier. It took the typist from A to C to become accustomed to my writing and the shape of the entries so that quite a number of these early pages had to be re-typed. I worked ahead of the typist once I realised what her difficulties were, editing the cards into exactly what was to be typed. I had lived with these cards for so long I could no longer appreciate how bizarre some of them must have appeared.

As can be seen from the list of acknowledgments in the preface to *PN* much expert information was incorporated into the index. This list mentions the most assiduous and hard worked members of the research panel with the exception of the editor. For him there was no escape from my importunity. He could and did turn the tables on me and we decided that our mutual votes of thanks should be as silent and implicit as the invisible page numbering. Behind these names there is a cohort of friends in many places whose brains I picked if they happened to come my way with the possible answer to an unsolved query. What better person to ask about owners of copies of *PN* than Mr. Lawrence Wroth who had known so many personally. If I mention here Mr. Peter Petcoff who read the galleys and Mrs. Clara LeGear, both of the Library of Congress, it is because the acknowledgment had already been printed before they gave their invaluable help. Much information was picked up from books both here and in the States, much from Hakluyt Society editors past and present and from the editor's collection of books on voyages of discovery available at my elbow. Some gave advice on presentation and checked the final form. I suspected that I was becoming known as that Hakluyt bore.

This research work is to be found largely distributed between the place names and the subject entries, some in the foreign words used, some in the list of books. Most of the identifications of people were readily found in standard reference books. There are the notes in Money, Weights and Measures, the identifications in Fauna and Flora and also of Commodities. There are the different types of cloth, of furs, of drugs, the attempts to find how many ships of the same name were, in fact, the same ship. Gradually the list of unknowns grew smaller but right up to the last proof reading I hoped to be able to find something on the obstinate few. One that eluded me for a long time was the word 'tisik' used apparently to mean a Persian merchant. I was taken in the Library of Congress to a Persian expert. He replied to my query without a pause, 'Tisik—a Turkic word meaning head man, obsolete now, but widely used in the Caspian Sea area in the sixteenth century.' Not all dropped into my lap quite so neatly.

It is obvious, however, that an index is not the most satisfactory medium through which to present the fruits of investigation. It is much too arbitrary, while footnotes to an index does not commend itself as an innovation. That would introduce a nightmare quality. The use of question marks or other ways of indicating something less than certainty can be merely irritating. The desire for a footnote was expressed more than once in order to explain why one conclusion was preferred to another. In short a great deal of interesting material was being collected about the sixteenth century and more specifically about Hakluyt himself or was pointing to the usefulness of fragmented studies of Hakluyt's collections and methods. This has led in turn to a proposal for a series of studies of Hakluyt to be incorporated in a Hakluyt Handbook for which there is now a provisional plan. Suggested topics are Hakluyt as a translator, an editor, a geographer, a historian; his use of language, his nautical terms, his maps; his use of materials available to him on the various parts of the world covered by his narratives.

In PN there is a considerable body of narrative in Latin as well as some translations from Portuguese or Spanish. For most of the Latin Hakluyt provides a translation. The exceptions are the extract from Pliny on monsters and the Mandeville Travels. These two items I left until the end for indexing. A translation for the Pliny was easily found but there is no direct transla-

tion for Hakluyt's version of Mandeville. My Latin had lain for too long in disuse to be of much help in disposing of Mandeville quickly. I collected one or two editions of Mandeville, several Latin dictionaries and the medieval word list. Thus embedded I tracked down in one edition or another the passages that were misplaced. Here I found a good index invaluable. I was advised not to attempt identifications for Mandeville— as if I were competent to do any such thing—a piece of advice I was only too pleased to take. One other category of foreign language deserves mention, the vocabularies collected in the field and brought back to England, Eskimo, Lapp, Algonkian, Javanese and African dialects. When extra time was available I thought that it would be interesting to test how good or bad, in the light of current scholarship, had been these attempts to transcribe words from what were, to English ears, completely unfamiliar languages. The linguistic experts mentioned in the preface responded most willingly to my requests for such an assessment and went to a great deal of trouble to send me the results in a form that could be incorporated in the index. Where words could be recognised the modern form is given. The interest of this section would be much more apparent if the results of the comparison were given more fully than the index permitted.

A fitting conclusion to this account would be some notice of Hakluyt's own index. Indexes are normally the ending. It is in alphabetical order but follows its own rules. Persons are indexed by their Christian names, Steven Borough appearing in 'S' and Walter Raleigh in 'W'. Sir Humfrey Gilbert appears in 'H' as Humfrey Gilbert, kt, but Sir George Peckham is found under 'S' for Sir. You won't find Ivan IV under 'I' but under 'M' for Muscovite emperor. Places follow a more conventional order. Subjects, when they are not embedded in an analysis belonging to a person or place seem to be chosen for their quality of surprise. You have marvels of nature and the odd ways of foreigners; fishes that fly, dogs that catch fish, springs of tar, lions, leaves, reeds of a huge bigness; fire forced of two sticks, kissing used in Moscow, as in all the Greek churches, lawyers not suffered nor maintained in Russia, nails of the hands suffered to grow very long. There are two entries for the Scots; the first, ' gifts sent to Queen Mary from the emperor of Russia; the same gifts spoiled by the barbarous Scots '; the second one, ' Scots theft, and spoil of English goods '. Two unfavourable mentions is notoriety. It would seem that he did not like the Scots. His choice seems to be governed by disapproval where other nations are concerned with complaints of treachery and double dealing towards the English. No doubt he thought it necessary to warn intending discoverers and planters of the pitfalls in their way. All the subject categories I used can be found in Hakluyt's index, if only by one example. It is obvious that Hakluyt had, in common with all indexers, to hurry. Evidence of this haste is easy to find; such material as he had assembled for some time is extended in analysis. There are long entries for the Crusades, for Mandeville, for the early history of the Muscovy Company. But the later English voyages to America

have been rushed and noticed only here and there. There is an entry for Virginia but John White does not appear. This may be because he was not considered important enough as there is a longish entry for Cavendish who did not return from his circumnavigation until 1588. But as the purpose that prompted Hakluyt to publish *PN* was the promotion of voyages to America the weighting in the index is misleading.

As I have said Hakluyt did not like the Scots. This is what he selects for women in his index: ' women of Arabia, their apparell and ornaments; women paint their faces in Muscovy; breasts of women very long; women deadly and very hurtful in their looks; the undecent manner of riding used by the women of Muscovy; women bought and sold, and let out to hire in Persia; the manners of the young women amongst the savages of America '.

What would Hakluyt have said of an index to his *PN* made by a woman and a Scot? Barbarous and undecent.

How I Indexed Dickens's Letters

James Thornton

—Or at least the first volume! There are eleven more to follow—coming up in a celebratory sort of way to 1970, the centenary of Dickens's death. The plan is that the final volume should contain a complete index, including a common-noun subject index and a full index of Dickens himself. Meanwhile the index of each volume is confined to persons, publications and places.

None better than an indexer to know the shortcomings of his own index. To write about it now after one volume is to whistle in the dark. Still, I must welcome this chance of formulating principles *post facto,* thus to further my education through succeeding volumes and maybe to help others to know at least some of the vicissitudes of the long literary index.

The first lesson is that there can be no waiting for a comfortable beginning with a nice clean set of page proofs. With complex and scholarly editions of major authors, the indexer may have to begin with the typescript, as I did, or at latest with the first slip proofs. It is now over fifteen years since my friend Humphry House sought me out with the exciting news that Rupert Hart-Davis the publisher had invited him to edit a definitive edition of the Letters. He asked me to join his editorial committee as indexer. For editing purposes he clearly saw that he would need a card-index far ahead of publication. So I began with the typed copies of the letters, many of them un-

The substance of a talk given at the Society's A.G.M. on 29th May, 1965.

dated or with putative dates since found to be erroneous. What I should have done was to give each letter a number and raced through them, carding the names and numbers mechanically. A computer would have done it better. Instead, I plodded on slowly, reading for interest, letting myself be taken along by-ways, doing a bit of delving here and there. I had not got very far when Humphry House died in 1955. What would have been a great and personal contribution to Dickens scholarship for all time was ' untimely stopp'd '. That the edition survived at all was owing, first, to the fact that Humphry House had meticulously laid down the principles of the edition and had educated his editorial committee in carrying them out; secondly, Rupert Hart-Davis, himself a skilled editor, who was a member of the editorial committee, remained steadfast to his original vision of the Complete Letters; and thirdly, the Pilgrim Trust, which was supporting the edition, did not lose heart. So the indexer was not let off; and Volume One, edited by Madeline House and Graham Storey, was published by the Clarendon Press in February of this year.

I dwell upon this background history because I want to emphasize the advantage to the indexer of being associated with his editor or author from the very beginning. I cannot regret this even though much of the early indexing work was wasted effort. I smile at myself now when I look back at the simple-minded enthusiasm with which I sat down to a pile of Dickens's correspondence. But it

Reprinted from *The Indexer* 4, no. 4 (Autumn 1965): 119–122.

77

suited me, whose method is always more empirical than doctrinaire. I always put off any decision about what an index is going to look like until the last possible moment. Thus to splash about for a long time in the shallows without getting any-where would enable me, I hoped, to swim better in the deep end.

The deep end was to be the final mon-ster volume with everything in it. But, as it became clear that volumes would be published at intervals of a year or even two years, I felt that each volume should have at least a proper name index. The hope at that time was for enough space at the end of each volume for names and page numbers—not so much an **index** as a check-list, what I came afterwards to call ' a contemptible collection of digits '. Clearly it had to be more than that. I began to think that an analytical index would be possible in the space available. The extent of the analysis seemed to me to be not only a question of space. The cen-tral problem was that the indexer cannot derive the relative value of any item in the text from the text alone. All of it may be trivial, all of it may be important. No one knows for what uses the Letters will be consulted in future years, nor what breadth of interests they will serve. What may be important for one purpose may be insignificant for another. The indexer must not therefore be selective nor impose a scale of values either of his own or de-rived from Dickens. All is equal—the publication of Pickwick and the six-o'clock bus from Brompton.

What was wanted was a break-down of the material under broad heads. The index sins again and again against the rule that there should not be more than four or five undifferentiated references. To have introduced a great deal more descriptive matter simply out of regard for this rule would often have given a signifi-cance which was not borne out by the

text nor justified by anticipation of the interests of future readers. It would also frequently have meant that readers would find little more in the text than they already knew from the index. To make reference to the text unnecessary is often for me an ideal of indexing, but to have followed this ideal with Dickens would have made the index unbearably long and confusing, with sub-classification carried to the fourth or fifth degree.

A biographer of Dickens once told me that he would expect an index to show the number of times Dickens dined with Forster. This my index will show. It does not, however, say whether they dined at home, at a pub or a club, or the house of a mutual friend (although with a little ingenuity a reader can find that pages 331 and 506 indicate that Ainsworth was also present at dinner). Better, it seemed a straight run of dinners with Forster than to break the sequence (and the chrono-logy) by giving each occasion a separate significance and a keyword of its own. The food was not necessarily better at the Athenaeum than at the Freemasons' Arms, or if it were, Dickens did not men-tion it.

Even in a straight run of numbers, it was possible, where advisable, to identify a reference by putting a descriptive word, often a quoted word, in brackets after the page number. This is quite a good trick and gives the indexer a little leeway out-side the strict classification, and without breaking the page sequence. This last may be important where the consultant is likely to want to look up all the references in order but may also wish to pick out one in particular. The following extract is an example of this device where it has been rather heavily used :—

DICKENS, Mrs. Charles : *Courtship and mar-riage* : comments on her feelings and senti-ments (*see also below* cross) 61 (' coldness '), 79 (' anxiety '), 87 (' forebodings '), 97 (' unjust '), 99 (his 'pleasure' in not being with her), 104 ('amiable and excellent'), *ib.* (CD to love her 'once more'), 109 (his letters 'stiff'), *ib.* ('objection' to CD's riding), 110 ('distrustful').

Then follow the reference to 'cross'. The two related blocks of references come together because the helpful alphabet makes 'cross' follow 'comments'. Dickens called his future wife cross, or in his baby language 'coss', seven times, and these seven references have been taken out of the 'comments' sequence and promoted to a sub-group of their own.

The longer articles are arranged in paragraphs, each with its own italicized heading, and the alphabetization of the headings decides the order of the paragraphs. The recurrent heading '*CD, relations with*' comes nearly always early on in any articles in which it occurs, and as an author's writings are generally better listed at the end of other material about him, I chose the heading 'Works' rather than 'Publications' (an indexer I often think is fortunate in that birth begins with a 'b', career with a 'c', and death with a 'd').

Within the paragraphs the sub-headings are also arranged alphabetically. Where further classification was called for I used the bracket device mentioned above, but occasionally had to insert the em-rule to indicate the repetition of the sub-head. For the most part, however, I managed to avoid sub-sub-indexing by taking it out and putting it elsewhere with a cross-reference. But this sometimes has its disadvantages as I shall show.

The two goals—completeness and compression—posed two major questions: the extent to which subsidiary subjects should be brought under one subject head, and the extent of the cross-referencing. For instance, I followed my masters, Dr. L. F.

Powell, editor and indexer of Boswell, and Dr. E. S. de Beer, editor and indexer of Evelyn, and assembled topographical information under the one place-name. There is to my mind a great advantage, for instance, in having all the localities and buildings in London listed together. Those places in London which have a good deal of descriptive matter to themselves are cross-referenced out to separate articles, but space allowed few cross-references inwards to the main article. This may sometimes infuriate the consultant. Thus, if he wants a reference to the Freemasons' Arms, he has to learn to find it under 'LONDON: *Hotels, inns*'. Having grasped the principle he may find it tiresome when he looks up 'LONDON: *Theatres*' to find he is referred to separate articles for Covent Garden and Drury Lane in the main alphabetical sequence. The reason for this is obvious, but it is nevertheless a drawback. Up to a point cross-references are a great saver of space, but the point has to be carefully watched.

From these few observations it will be seen, I think, that the intended virtue of the index to the Letters does not lie so much in a multiplex analysis as in its synthesis—or to be less philosophic in its compression. This aim meant that when the entries on the cards on any one subject were brought together, all the cards had to be laid out and the entries looked up afresh. It was then possible to see how a sub-heading could be devised to bring together this half-dozen or so of entries, or how by modifying the sub-heading or introducing a sub-sub-heading a link could be established with a further batch of cards. So the entries were slimmed down to their essentials, grouped and re-grouped and grouped again. For me the fascination of indexing lies in this vast game of patience.

Indexing the Life of Sir Winston Churchill*

G. Norman Knight

At our Annual General Meeting this time last year we were privileged to listen to an exceedingly interesting talk on 'How I Indexed Dickens's Letters' by Mr. James Thornton (*The Indexer*, Vol. IV, pages 119-122). But our now newly elected President was careful to state in his first sentence: 'Or at least the first volume!'

Exactly the same modification applies to this talk. It is only the first volume, dealing with Winston Churchill's earliest 25 years until the turn of the century that I have so far indexed. This volume is due to be published by Messrs. Heinemann in October and will be previously serialized in *The Sunday Telegraph* in September.

A Cumulative Index?

It will be followed by at least nine other volumes, four more of straight biography, with at least five companion volumes of documents and records. It is planned to publish them at the rate of one main volume together with its companion or companions each year. As regards the companion volumes, I have inspected the proofs of the first and can only say that, so far from being dry (as might be expected from a volume of archives), from the fact that it deals more fully with certain incidents and aspects and even scandals related in the biography, it is to anyone interested in those incidents and aspects even more exciting than its parallel volume. Each volume will carry its own index of course, but I rather gather that it has not yet been decided whether there shall be a final volume

containing a cumulative index for the whole series. My view (for what it is worth) is that in the case of a valuable work of this nature, which is bound to be used as a work of reference for many, many years to come, such a cumulative index is indispensable.

The author has lavished and is lavishing such immense pains on his presentation of his father's *Life* that I feel certain that, when publication is complete in five years' time, the whole work will take its permanent place in literature as the standard and definitive biography of Sir Winston Churchill. This could be so, indeed, if only by reason of the vast amount of material to which the author has exclusive access.

Author's Co-operation

Before I come to describe the index itself I ought perhaps to mention that never can there have been an instance of more complete co-operation between the indexer and the author or his representatives, of whom I hope to say a word or two a little later. Mr. Randolph Churchill indeed took the greatest interest in the index and on three occasions invited me to stay at his home in East Bergholt, Suffolk, in order to discuss my methods and progress. These visits were most enjoyable. The house, in its beautifully kept grounds of 23 acres, is mainly eighteenth century but its fine central staircase dates from the reign of Charles II. Now East Bergholt was the birthplace of John Constable and where he did much of his painting—some even from the very house which is now Randolph Churchill's home, so that from almost any window one is confronted

* The substance of a talk given after the A.G.M. on May 19, 1966.

Reprinted from *The Indexer* 5, no. 2 (Autumn 1966): 58–63.

with an authentic Constable landscape. In this connection I would especially mention the famous 'Haywain at Flatford Mill'.

Here, amid an assemblage of stirring Churchilliana, the author has a regular team of research workers and secretaries helping to produce the biography, with the result that William Hardcastle, the B.B.C. announcer, speaking rather out of turn, referred to the place somewhat unkindly in a radio talk as 'the Churchill factory'.

The Galley Proofs

I found that compiling the index was on the whole fairly straightforward. None the less, certain problems presented themselves. In the first place, because of the time factor it was necessary to start my work from the galley proofs of the text. I must say a word about these particular galleys. All my hearers will be familiar with the drab, elongated, straggling strips of paper, tiresome to handle and temper-fraying to use, that normally pass for galley-pulls. Imagine my delighted surprise at the actual form that the Churchill galleys took. The proofs consist of cunningly fastened loose-leaf pages, each only slightly longer than a page in the book, the pages are printed on good paper and have wide side, top and bottom margins and are bound together to give the impression of a paper-back, complete with the title inscribed in gilt lettering on the cover. All that was needed to complete the illusion would have been a tastefully decorated jacket!

They certainly proved a joy to· read through and work from. When I tackled the author about the unusual elaborateness of the galley proofs, he explained that his father had always insisted on *his* proofs being submitted to him in just that form. It may sound as somewhat of an anticlimax if I add that when the galley proofs of my index arrived they consisted of the ordinary elongated straggling strips! Possibly, to round off my description of those wonderful text galley-proofs, I ought to mention that at the head of each page is the following formidable caution:

I have previously indexed books completely from their galley proofs and there is an account of two of my experiences in this connexion in *The Indexer* (Vol. III, pp. 90-2). As my hearers will appreciate, the process is rarely wholly satisfactory, while the whole job inevitably takes much longer when even merely started in this way.

In the present instance, after my typed headings and subheadings on the 5 x 3 cards I inserted the galley page numbers in pencil, and when the paged proofs eventually reached me, the actual page numbers were substituted in ink by a young lady assistant from a local public library, Miss Linda Warden, whose services had become necessary, again because of the time factor. This lady was later to prove extremely useful also in checking the accuracy of the page reference numbers in the index galley proofs.

Indexing Problems

But now a complication arose. A number of text additions and deletions having become necessary, fresh sets of galleys were issued with the resulting changes in galley page numbers. Similarly the paged proofs were not the final versions, since the foundry plate pulls contained several alterations, owing to important matter having been received at the last moment—one lady who had been indexed under her married name actually reverted to her maiden name between one page proof stage and the foundry pulls, I am bound to confess that ensuring that all these changes were duly reflected in the index became somewhat of a headache; some indeed were too late to be inserted on the cards and could only be made on the index proofs.

One problem that presented itself concerned the alphabetical arrangement of the Churchill family. It may not be universally known that Sir Winston himself had a hyphened surname and the ever rightfully punctilious *Court Circular* right up to the end of 1951 invariably referred to him as Winston Spencer-Churchill. But it is related how much he resented coming at the end of the school roll-call (or 'Bill', as it was named at Harrow) and in a letter he wrote to his father as early as 1888 he explained: 'I never write myself Spencer Churchill but always Winston S. Churchill'. In any case, since scarcely anyone would dream of looking for his name or those of his parents, Lord and Lady Randolph, under 'S', they were indexed under 'C'. For the meticulous-minded, however, cross referencing is provided in the entry under 'Spencer-Churchill'.

Another problem I had to face was how to treat the entry for the central character of the book, the subject of the biography. The other two chief characters, Winston's parents, Lord and Lady Randolph Churchill, I dealt with at some length and normally, except that I devoted a separate section (under the same main heading) to Lord Randolph's political career. But with Winston himself I was mindful of the words of wisdom and warning uttered by our President emeritus, Mr. G. V. Carey, when he addressed our Society in 1961 (*The Indexer*, Vol. II, pages 120-3). Taking an imaginary example of a *Life and Letters of the Rt. Hon. Tarquinius Proudman,* he showed how utterly unnecessary were most of the subheadings which would normally clutter up the several pages of index devoted to a synopsis of his entire career; the vast majority could be far more conveniently placed, and were more likely to be looked for, under appropriate separate entries.

Perhaps the outstanding example of the lengths to which an indexer can go in overloading the entry for the subject of his book is furnished by the American indexes to the well-known Boswell series. Under BOS-WELL, JAMES, we are treated in *Boswell on the Grand Tour* to 3½ pages of index; in *Boswell's London Journal,* to 4½ pages; and in *Boswell in Holland* to no fewer than

5½ pages (or eleven columns)! In the carefully compiled index to *Boswell in search of a wife* it is not pretty to find as many as 38 references to Boswell's catching, escaping from, or being treated for, the pox. I suggest that these had better been relegated to an entry under the letter 'V'. With all this haystack piled up around the index-user's needles, he almost needs (as Mr. Carey pointed out in connexion with his 'Tarquinius Proudman') an auxiliary index to find the object of his search.

In the case of CHURCHILL, WINSTON LEONARD SPENCER, I felt that it would be wrong to omit the heading altogether. What I have done, therefore, is to limit the full-blown subheadings to CHARACTERISTICS, FINANCES, HEALTH, HOBBIES and POLITICAL INTERESTS. Under EDUCATION I simply cross-referenced to his schools and the various subjects he was taught, while under MILITARY CAREER similarly to the regiments, places and campaigns in which he served. Or so I had planned. But my galley-proofs were edited by other hands and when the page-proofs arrived I found that the subjects, such as English, French, Latin, Mathematics, etc., had been deleted as separate entries and transferred to the EDUCATION subheading of CHURCHILL, WINSTON LEONARD SPENCER.

For those of his WORKS that are quoted or referred to in the text the reader is cross-referenced to the entries under their titles. Even with this limitation the complete entry for Winston Churchill occupies over two pages.

Fullness of Entries

As regards my entries generally, these will be found to be somewhat fuller than is common in today's practice. That is to say, I was not content with providing a mere list of proper names and subjects, but in nearly every case supplied either a brief description of the item forming the heading or else briefly what happened to him, her, or it, in the text. I will give a sample entry a little later, to show my meaning. In making these fuller entries I have reverted to some extent to the custom of former days. In Alexander Pope's time, to study the index was regarded as a short cut to knowledge of a book's contents, as he shows and derides in his *Dunciad*:

How index-learning turns no student pale
Yet holds the eel of science by the tail

Not that I would claim that anyone could pass an examination on the early life of Sir Winston Churchill after reading my index. Nor would I approve the florid style of indexing adopted by William Prynne in his *Histriomastix: the players scourge (1632)*. Let me quote one entry, yes one single heading (which I have actually abbreviated!):

Women-Actors notorious whores . . . and dare then any Christian women be so more whorishly impudent as to act, to speake publikely on a stage perchance in man's apparell and cut haire here proved sinful and abominable in the presence of sundry men and women? . . . O let such presidents of imprudence, of impiety be never heard of or suffered among Christians, 385.

This and similar breathless outbursts in the index were duly quoted by the Attorney General when Prynne was prosecuted in the Star Chamber and was sentenced to stand in the pillory and be deprived of both ears. Justly, some may think—not for the index's contents, but for its prolixity.

In the Preface to *Winston S. Churchill, 1874-1965*, it is stated that 'the necessary details of rank and identification' will be found 'in the index'. Fulfilling this requirement necessitated supplying dates in most cases and other details not available in the text, and involved a good deal of research in encyclopedias and other works of reference and of telephoning public libraries, embassies, etc., etc. Let me give just one instance. When he was at his preparatory school, Winston twice wrote to his mother expressing a desire to see Buffalo Bill. I felt that the mere heading: 'Buffalo Bill, 90 *bis*' rather lacked point. Accordingly my entry runs:

Buffalo Bill (W. F. Cody, 1845-1917), WSC wants to see (1887), 90 *bis*

A somewhat unusual feature of this biography is that, at the author's suggestion, short biographies of the major characters who make their appearance are provided at the front of each volume. Their names in the index are printed in small capitals and the entries are correspondingly shortened, details being confined to those mentioned in the text proper. This is to be the standard practice throughout the five main volumes.

I am aware that it is unusual in an index to give a character's dates after his name, although it was successfully done in a previous work of Randolph Churchill's, his *Lord Derby, 'King of Lancashire'* (1959), which was indexed by Mr. Michael Wace, a member of the Society's Council. I notice, moreover, that Mr. Michael Maclagan, whose own index to his *Clemency Canning* (1962) won the first award of the Wheatley Medal for an outstanding index, supplied the dates of death for most of his characters. I think that in historical works particularly, the practice is a useful one, although of course it involves more work for the indexer. In the present instance, however, I have most gratefully to acknowledge having received considerable help in obtaining these dates from two gentlemen who are acting as research advisers to the author and to whom I referred earlier as his representatives. These are Mr. Michael Wolff, the well-known editor of *Crossbow*, and Mr. Andrew Kerr, both of whom I am glad to welcome to this meeting.

Length of Index—Ratio to Text

But there was one rather unfortunate result of these fuller entries. They caused a serious miscalculation on my part as to the length of the index. My index cards (which, after being carefully edited, went to the printer in that form) totalled 1,656 and, judging from previous experiences, I estimated that these should produce about 40 pages, or at the most, 48 pages. Imagine my dismay when it was discovered that in fact they made 66 pages of index. What had happened was that in my previous indexes the majority of entries had consisted of single-line headings, whereas in the Churchill index it is the exception to find an entry consisting of fewer than two lines. Now every indexer knows how disheartening it is to have to make substantial cuts in his or her index, and in this case it became necessary to cut four pages or eight whole columns. One of the first casualties had to be the very extensive list of acknowledgements. I am grateful for very substantial help in making these cuts from Mr. Wolff and Mr. Kerr, who also gave valuable assistance in correcting the proofs. It is my contention that proofs cannot be corrected too many times or by too many people, provided, of course, that the corrections are submitted to the original writer, who must remain the final authority. I am mindful of a late chief editor of Penguin Books, with whom I was acquainted. He was not only a fine indexer, but also had such a reputation as a proof-reader that it was said that scarcely a printed page (whether published or not) could be put in front of him in which he could not detect at least one error!

I must admit that in the matter of correcting my index galley proofs my mentors and I did not invariably see entirely eye to eye. I have already mentioned the instance of Winston's education. There was also the controversy over the spelling of abbreviations. I always use a full stop after every abbreviation except where the last letter corresponds to that of the unabbreviated form, as in Dr, for instance. I did not mind so much seeing the stops disappear altogether in H.M.S., V.C., and A.D., and the letters being joined up into HMS, VC and AD, but did protest over the loss of the stop after 'no.' for number (as in No. 46, Grosvenor Square), because of the danger of its being mistaken in its naked form for the adjectival form of 'no'. 'House-rules (in this case, the East Bergholt house-rules) however, have to prevail and in this matter the indexer had to yield.

But to return to the length of the index. I do not consider that 62 pages of index—it is printed in 9 pt. type—to 550 pages of text is an excessive ratio. I am fortified by the fact that the modern tendency is towards long, comprehensive indexes to important works. For example, A. J. P. Taylor's *English History, 1914-45*, published last year by the Oxford University Press, contains 78 pages of index to 601 pages of text, while Michael Maclagan's biography that I mentioned just now has 35 to 370. The British Standard for the *Preparation of Indexes* (B.S. 3700: 1964) has an even greater ratio, $10\frac{1}{2}$ to 21, but then that is only a pamphlet, and the index is printed in single column. Here are two other outstanding examples: John Askling's index to *Statistics of deadly quarrels* by the late Dr. Lewis F. Richardson (Stevens & Sons, 1960) ran to 49 pages of index to 300 pages of text excluding bibliography, while Mrs. Alison Quinn's index to the new C.U.P. edition of Hakluyt's *Navigations*, which ran away with the recently awarded Wheatley Medal for last year, extends to 140 (three-columned) pages, making 420 columns, compared with 889 pages of text.

Devices used

It will be found, I think, that in the Churchill index, I have pulled out nearly every stop available to the indexer, including the open diapason of using bold type for page references for items to which more than a few lines are devoted in the text. Similarly I put page references in italics to denote illustrations or maps. I also use *bis* and (more occasionally) *ter* after a page reference to indicate that the subject is referred to quite separately twice or thrice respectively on the same page. I know that this practice is derided by some indexers as providing unnecessary spoon-feeding to the index user, who, it is contended, should always read through the whole of each page to which his attention is called in the index. But I do not agree. Having been caught myself, I know how easy it is, in the absence of a specific direction, to find one reference at the top (shall we say) of a given page and then, since this is not the object sought, hurry on to the next page indicated, finally giving up the quest in disgust, when all the time it was to be found lower down on the original page looked at.

All these devices are explained in preliminary notes at the top of the index, as recommended in the British Standard. But I have also made occasional use of another device which is somewhat frowned upon by the British Standard, chiefly because of its employment in the wrong sense. I allude to the word *passim*. '196-200 *passim*' should mean that the subject of the heading is referred to, not continuously (which would require plain '196-200'), but in scattered passages throughout those five pages. Used correctly in this way, the word can be responsible for a considerable saving in page reference numbers and is in this way useful.

My subheadings are run-on and are mainly in chronological order, even when this involves inverting the page number order. One innovation I did make. When there was a mass of subheadings, I divided them up into paragraphs. This gives them a more inviting appearance, for nothing (to my mind), is more distressingly tiresome in an index than unbroken blocks of subheadings, unless it be solid rows and rows of unbroken page reference numbers.

I have tried in this talk to give an idea of the methods I used in compiling this index, as also of some trials and tribulations while I was engaged in the exercise. I forgot to mention that at one period the indexer was carted off to hospital for an operation, so that for three weeks the 'Norman Knight factory' had to close down.

When I was asked to undertake the index to the *Life* of this great statesman, I considered it an exceptional honour and also somewhat of a challenge.

Whether I have been able to produce a really worthwhile index, useful to reader and reference hunter alike, and worthy of the book to which it is appended or whether it will prove merely an 'also-ran', time alone will show.

.   .   .   .

The lively discussion that developed after the talk mainly concerned the question of a cumulative index and whether this should include the companion volumes, or should these have a separate one.

IIc. Indexer-Author-Publisher Relations

Relations between Authors and Indexers

M. D. Anderson

[*When the* Library Association Record *announced in its June* 1976 *issue that Mrs M. D. Anderson had been awarded the Wheatley Medal for* 1975, *it stated* "Some part of the credit for the particular index, says Mrs Anderson, should go to Judith Butcher, the author, for her advice and collaboration." *The Hon. Editor asked Mrs Anderson if she would be good enough to enlarge on this for the benefit of readers of* The Indexer. *She was kind enough to comply with this request.*]

Strange as it may seem, there are often no relations between the author and the indexer of a book. The publisher may commission the index, and deal with any questions about it, and the author may not concern himself with the matter at all. To an indexer who is also an author, this is hard to understand, particularly since many publishers require the author to pay for the index.

There is, of course, a contact of minds. The indexer of a book of any considerable length acquires a kind of acquaintance with the author, whose ways of thought and writing, prejudices and peculiarities, talents and achievements, become gradually apparent. The indexer may then be able to divine to some extent how the author might wish the index to develop, but this can hardly take the place of real collaboration.

Some authors take the trouble to read and amend the index typescript, often to good effect. But though author participation in the indexing process would seem in every way desirable, in practice it is not always welcome. I have had experience of a few authors whose additions and alterations to the typescript were sometimes ill-judged and unnecessary, who tended to ignore the conventions of the index, especially with regard to order of sub-headings, and who occasionally flouted the basic rules of indexing. A good sub-editor may submit an author-mutilated index to the indexer for repair, but usually any rescue work has to be done on the index proof—supposing the indexer is given the chance of reading it. The intervention of such an author may appear little short of disastrous, and the indexer can only be thankful for anonymity.

I might add that authors of this kind are not alone in committing acts of sabotage against indexes. Inexperienced and enthusiastic sub-editors can also do much damage by inconsistent meddling with punctuation, capitals, indentation, and other important details. Even spelling may not be spared; one sub-editor altered my 'rat-borne disease' to 'rat-born disease'.

An indirect relation between author and indexer arises when the author makes an index that the publisher considers inadequate or bad —or starts to make an index and gives up in despair—and the indexer is called in to save the situation, often in minimum time. It would sometimes be easier, if not quicker, to start the index again from the beginning, but this would be unduly discouraging to the author, and it is interesting to exercise ingenuity in using as much of his work as possible, without allowing his errors to affect the revised index.

Genuine collaboration between author and indexer does occur. I have several times worked with authors who had themselves commissioned their indexes. Preliminary discussions about the scope and arrangement of the index were followed by one or more meetings or exchanges of letters in the course of the work, to settle any difficulties, and the typed indexes were read by the authors, and on occasion sent back for alterations. The indexes were undoubtedly improved by the authors' help, and the indexer would wish for such participation more often. The chief obstacle is the usual tight schedule for indexing, and the expectation of many publishers that time lost earlier can be recovered at this stage. Little opportunity may remain for consultation.

Reprinted from *The Indexer* 10, no. 3 (April 1977): 137–138.

The Author, the Publisher and the Indexer*

Oliver Stallybrass

For weeks my waking and sleeping hours have been tormented by a vision of judgment: of a publisher getting up at the end of my talk and saying: 'But in 1953 you defaulted on an index'—or an indexer: 'But in 1965 you paid me a fee that worked out at four shillings and ninepence an hour'—or an author: 'But in 1968 you threw a tantrum when I dared to criticize your beastly index'. All these accusations would, I am sorry to say, be more or less true. Though perhaps the sorrow is not quite one hundred per cent genuine: *qui s'accuse, s'excuse*, or, as Swift put it, 'a man should never be ashamed to own he is in the wrong, which is but saying, in other words, that he is wiser today than he was yesterday.' Out of my new-found wisdom, then, I venture, as an occasional indexer and a one-time publisher, to address you.

A Questionnaire and its Victims

At an early stage in the preparation of this talk I realized that it would be presumptuous for me to start telling publishers what they ought to be doing in respect of indexes without at least testing my strong suspicion that they were not already doing precisely that.

Twenty-five publishers were therefore selected as the victims of a small piece of research. The main criteria for their selection were in most cases two: the presence on the board or the editorial staff of somebody whom I hoped I could con into answering a questionnaire [. . . . .] that ran to forty-three questions; and second, since I had to be my own postman, an address in Bloomsbury or Soho or Saint James's rather than in Newton Abbot or Cambridge or even the Euston Road. This is certainly not a sound sampling method, and in any case twenty-five—in the final count twenty-four—is far too small a sample to have any statistical validity. (If I use an expression like 'most firms' I do so as shorthand for 'most of the firms completing the questionnaire'.) The answers to the questionnaire are, however, likely at least to be indicative of tendencies; and the twenty-four firms, ranging in age and size from Longman or the Oxford University Press to Maurice Temple Smith, do in fact seem to represent some sort of a cross-section of the more serious-minded London publishers. They are, in alphabetical order, Allen & Unwin, Edward Arnold, Barrie & Jenkins, A. & C. Black, The Bodley Head, Butterworth (the managing editors of whose Legal, Medical, and Scientific and Technical Books divisions completed separate forms), Chatto & Windus,

* A paper read at a meeting of the Society on 9 March, 1971, when a number of publishers were present and took part in the ensuing discussion.

Reprinted from *The Indexer* 7, no. 4 (Autumn 1971): 156–171.

87

Collins, Constable, André Deutsch, Duckworth, Faber, Victor Gollancz, Hamish Hamilton, Michael Joseph, Allen Lane The Penguin Press, Longman, Macmillan Press (academic publications company of Macmillan & Co.), Methuen, O.U.P., Penguin Books, Secker & Warburg, Temple Smith, Thames & Hudson. Not one firm refused to help me; and, although one or two respondents had some occasional mild fun at my expense, only one was incapacitated, it seems, by my barrage of questions. To all who fought their way through I am enormously grateful.

I propose to attempt two things: to summarize the state of play as revealed by the thousand or so answers received, and then to outline what I would regard as an ideal case history. From both halves of this programme I shall depart frequently for polemical, hortatory and other purposes; and before even embarking on the first half I need to issue two caveats. First, several firms restricted the applicability of their answers to, for example, ' general books only '. Second, I invited respondents to regard the pronoun ' you ' as singular rather than plural whenever this made a particular question easier to answer. A device for pinpointing the exercise of this option was not always utilized; and in any case elaborate differentiation seems in many instances uncalled for. It is thus possible that when I refer, say, to ' fifteen firms ' I really mean ' eight firms, one department, four individual editors and two more whose practice in this respect may or may not be that of their colleagues '. Whenever I have mentioned a firm by name, however—and nearly half my respondents preferred to remain corporately as well as individually anonymous—I have tried to make any necessary distinctions.

The State of Play

Only five of the twenty-four firms—two of them, moreover, related by marriage—have a standard set of instructions about indexes. (In addition, two mention Carey as a constant source of counsel.) Of these five sets of instructions, one is aimed solely

at editors, while three, and perhaps all four, of the others form part of authors' guides to house style. Neither of the extracts that I have seen strikes me as beyond criticism, and at one point they contradict each other: one states that printers will, the other that they will not, accept cards to print from.

Although a quarter of the firms have one person who commissions and supervises all indexes, *policy* over indexes is virtually everywhere uncoordinated: each editor, that is, makes most of his own decisions. The first and most critical of these, of course, is the decision whether a given book is to have an index at all; and the answers hereabouts were rather encouraging. Question 9 read:

> Certain categories of books clearly need no index : fiction (adult and juvenile), poetry, drama, illustrated books with little or no text, self-indexing books such as dictionaries. Are there any other categories of book for which you would *never* provide an index? If so, what?

None of the few tentative suggestions—the simple textbooks, highly topical quickies, ' perhaps short collections of lectures or case studies ' (O.U.P.)—sent a real shiver down my spine; and Macmillan Press earned a bonus by challenging my ill-considered assertion that a novel needs no index. (How could I have forgotten R. A. Spalding's magnificent index volume to Proust?). Full marks too to the three editors at Butterworth—one of whom said I could name their firm, so I am stretching a point of confidence to record that they alone gave an unqualified ' All ' in answer to question 10 which asked: ' Excluding these categories, for roughly what proportion of your books do you provide an index? ' Of the other firms, I am happy to say that no fewer than twenty gave answers ranging from ' roughly, all ' or ' virtually all ' to ' majority '—and only three ' a small minority '.

Criteria of Need

Question 11 asked what criteria were applied in the decision whether a book should have an index. At first I had intended making this, like so many others, a multiple-choice question; later I decided to leave it open-ended, with the result that only fifteen publishers attempted an answer. These answers were in one respect highly gratifying; not one publisher mentioned financial criteria—if a book from any of these firms needs an index, it will apparently get one.[1] What constitutes need? Here are two sets of answers which, between them, cover most of the points made. Bodley Head:

1 Will the reader be inconvenienced by the lack of an index?

2 Does the author want the book to have an index?

3 Are reviewers likely to complain if an index is not provided?

And Maurice Temple Smith:

1 Extent to which book will be used for reference as opposed to single reading.

2 Size and complexity: we wouldn't necessarily index a short book where it was easy for the reader to find any major subject from the list of contents.

No less than eight respondents used the word 'reader' and seven 'reference' (or 'refer'). But hardly one made it clear beyond doubt that he remembered the legitimate reference needs of somebody who might well be described as a *non*-reader—the hard-pressed writer or research worker or civil servant or professional man who doesn't want to have to read a word more than he can help in the hundreds or thousands of books that he is ransacking for his particular purposes. And it is not only the textbook or academic tome that is in question. Almost any book, however lightweight, is liable to contain odd nuggets of more or less unique information. The most obvious example is the biographical snippet; but there is also the piece of local history or folklore or sociology which a mere index of names will fail to reveal. Hence Stallybrass's First Law: A good index is important even when the book isn't.

[1] The expense involved relates to paper, printing and editorial time—not generally, as will appear, to an indexer's fee.

Indexes or Ads?

Stallybrass's Second Law is plagiarized from a forgotten source, and reads: Ideally the index should be by the author—even when the book isn't. The key word here is of course 'ideally'. It is evidently the ideal of that overwhelming majority of publishers who (questions 12 and 13) place the onus of providing an index fairly, squarely and indeed contractually upon the author. And now I am going, it may seem, to contradict my own second law by proclaiming the view—which as an editor I have more than once put into practice by fiddling the accounts or doing the index myself—that to set the indexer's fee against the author's royalties is quite wrong.[2] The ability to write a book and the ability to compile a good index are two quite different skills, and although the ideal author is also his own ideal indexer there is no more justification for *demanding* such versatility than there would be for expecting an author to design his own jacket—or pay the artist. If Constable, to whom all credit, can afford to pay for indexes, so, surely, can other publishers.[3] If they really cannot, then I suggest that they make equivalent cuts in their advertising budgets: trade journals apart, and with rare exceptions, publishers' advertisements are notoriously aimed at the author and his agent rather than the prospective buyer—and if the equation was pointed out to them both author and agent would be quick to see the point.

The Cost—Accountancy Iceberg: A Polemic

Questions 16 and 17 touched on a subject of deadly importance: cost-accountancy systems. Seventeen out of twenty-four firms normally or invariably considered it neces-

[2] Still worse is the practice of one firm which *never* employs an outside indexer—if one particular editor-indexer feels out of his depth with a book unindexed by its author, unindexed it stays.

[3] Constable are not quite unique in paying for all commissioned indexes. One managing editor at Butterworth not only does this, but as a logical corollary pays the author a fee if he chooses, and is competent, to do his own index.

sary—of the minority, Gollancz thought it
'absurd'—to estimate the cost of a commissioned index before an indexer has had
a chance of seeing the book. Four respondents qualified this answer by adding 'at
least approximately' or some such phrase;
but four others gave an unqualified, and
eight a qualified, 'yes' to the question 'Do
you then consider it imperative to keep
strictly within the estimated figure?' (One
of these said, quizzically or perhaps sternly,
'One always tries to keep within estimate
figures.')

Here, it seems to me, there peeps out the
tip of an iceberg that could well sink many
of the best books being written or about to
be written. I will come to that in a moment.
My immediate point is that in most cases it
is quite impossible for an indexer—or anybody else—to estimate with any accuracy the
cost of his labours on a book which he hasn't
even seen. Even if he is supplied with an
accurate word-count and a fair general description of the book, the variables and im-
ponderables are far more numerous and
serious than even an experienced editor
might guess. Or, for that matter, an inexperienced indexer: the first book I attempted
to index (the one I reneged on in 1953) was,
I knew in advance, well over a thousand
pages long and consisted entirely of fif-
teenth- to eighteenth-century diplomatic
documents in Latin, French, Italian, German
and, as a rare treat, English; what I was *not*
told was that almost every page was thick
with references to innominate monarchs, am-
bassadors and functionaries of every kind
and nationality, all of whom had to be
identified by name.

Another major variable, which only the
actual compilation of the index will reveal
in full, is the author's attention or inatten-
tion to detail, coupled with the question of
whether the copy-editing has been done
well, badly or not at all. If almost every
name has been spelled in at least two different ways, the indexer may have to spend
longer in establishing the correct versions
than in actually making the index.

It was with these factors in mind that I
included a series of questions (38-40) about
the stage at which those publishers who ask
the indexer for an estimate do so. Of the
thirteen firms who commonly ask for an
estimate (including three who only do so
with new indexers, or in exceptional cases),
five normally ask for an estimate based on
(a) their description of the book, and eight
for one based on (b) an actual sight of
proofs. The question, what percentage of
error would be regarded as reasonable in
cases (a) and (b) respectively, drew only a
few answers. For Bodley Head, Deutsch and
Gollancz, the problem hasn't arisen—which
probably means both that they employ a
small number of regular indexers and that
their copy-editing is consistently good.
Rather more sharply, Michael Joseph said:
'We hope our indexers don't make mistakes.' Three firms regarded ten per cent as
reasonable where the indexer had seen proofs.
For cases where he had not done so, only
two firms hazarded a figure: one gave ten
per cent, the other 100! The 100 per cent
firm was also prepared to concede twenty
per cent even when the indexer had seen
proofs. These admirable and, as I have tried
to suggest, far from excessive figures are, I
like to believe, partly inspired by an invoice
of mine for £27 which, following a rough
estimate of £20 to £25, led—or so the rumour
reached me—to the convening of an extraordinary general meeting of shareholders!

If the rigid application of cost-accountancy
methods to book-publishing did nothing
worse than lead to occasional acrimony over
indexers' fees, or to inadequate indexes, or
even the absence of indexes where they are
clearly needed, it would be bad enough. I
would like to take this opportunity of saying
that it is wholly pernicious and, even by the
half-baked standards of those who institute
such practices, ultimately self-defeating. In
a recent letter to myself the distinguished
American publisher Helen Wolff spoke of

the accountants and their destructive habit of
looking at cost and profit sheets for each *single*
book instead of considering the overall operation—
and further their way of applying rigid ratios to

each year's operation—as if we were producing shirts. I asked Claude Gallimard whether they kept such separate cost sheets, and he threw up his arms in horror—he knows that certain books *have* to be published, regardless of present sales, and is content as long as the entire *department* does not lose money. I . . . cling firmly to the conviction that there are lean and fat years in publishing, and one has to feed the other—it comes out in the end if the people involved have knowledge and dedication and are given sufficient leeway to experiment.

Experiment: how many of the best—which in the long run so often means also best-selling—creative writers would ever have got started under present-day conditions? In October 1905 a first novel called *Where angels fear to tread*, by an obscure young man called E. M. Forster, was published by William Blackwood and Sons in an edition of 1,050 copies at a price of six shillings. I doubt if even a second impression of 526 copies in January 1906 resulted in a profit margin that would have satisfied the on-rushing fools who effectively control so many of our latter-day conglomerates. Need I say more?

Flexibility

Back to my last. In all twenty-four firms the decision whether a book should have an index has normally been made—several respondents emended 'normally' to 'always'—before the typescript is sent to a printer for casting-off; in the great majority of cases the extent also has been determined, at least roughly, by this stage, and the designer and/or printer instructed accordingly. The degree of subsequent flexibility over extent and design proved, not surprisingly, to have some correlation with the degree of flexibility over cost. An ambiguity in question 20—about the degree of latitude over extent given to the indexer—precludes any attempt to summarize the answers. Here are some of the more interesting ones:

Before compiling the index, the indexer will discuss with the editor here . . . how many pages should be necessary, and why. (Gollancz.)

If the index would [otherwise] be impaired . . . I would instruct indexer to exceed an even working. (Macmillan Press.)

We give him a fairly free hand. We have a rough idea from our brief how long the index is likely to be. Any variation can normally be accommodated in the pages allowed by varying type-size, leading, etc. (Bodley Head.)

I attempt to estimate to the nearest signature working. (Butterworth, medical books only.)

Instruct the indexer to fill a convenient number of pages. (Constable.)

Budgetary problems are always acute nowadays, so indexer will be told the number of pages available to him—their number having been determined at design stage. (Deutsch.)

When allowable extent known we then give indexer clear instruction of number of entries required.

Try to fit into available space but if too difficult and costs not too tight we occasionally allow an extra four or eight pages.

We realize that a fairly free hand is important on certain books, e.g. legal texts where efficient indexes are absolutely vital.

We tell him how many pages are available, and give an estimate of what this means in terms of entries or lines of type.

Briefing

On the briefing of indexers in matters other than extent it is also hard to generalize. Fewer firms seem to offer guidance on (a) unvarying preferences (such as Allen & Unwin's 'initial caps for all entries') than on (b) matters specific to the particular book (such as the same firm's 'chronological or alphabetical order for sub-entries'). In most cases the amount and kind of briefing given doubtless depend on the degree of confidence which the individual editor has in the individual indexer. Here is another selection of answers:

I convey any author's views and any recommended by the copy-editor. (Macmillan Press.)

(a) Seldom, and only very generally. (b) A good indexer should know this himself, but it is sometimes useful to get an author/editor to give a short list of important subject-headings that must appear in the index. (O.U.P.)

(a) We use experienced indexers who do not usually need instructions about method. (b) This is left largely to the indexer, who, however, often discusses directly with the author.

Normally we discuss the book in general terms: any specific points are raised at this stage or as indexing progresses if any problems arise.

The mention of the author, in three of these answers, anticipated my next question. A majority of firms normally—and wisely—make a point of seeking out the author's views on the nature and scope of the index, and about half send him a copy of the typescript for approval irrespective of whether he has specifically requested this. About half, in addition, normally send the author index proofs in all circumstances; some do so only if he is himself the indexer, or alternatively if he has not previously seen the typescript. The majority of publishers normally send proofs likewise to indexers, irrespective of whether they have asked to see them. Understandably, the qualification 'if time allows' kept cropping up hereabouts; harder to understand are the two firms who *never* send indexers proofs of their work. The most frequent answer to the question 'How many copies of the [typescript] index do you normally request?' was 'two'—the two firms who said 'six' probably thought I was referring to index *proofs*.

Warning, Scheduling, Timing

The next group of questions (28-30) concerned the amount of warning given to a potential indexer and the time he was expected to need. Only one firm took the opportunity of pointing out the relationship between these two time factors—and none, rather surprisingly, distinguished between the indexer who has, and the indexer who hasn't, a regular full-time job. The majority of publishers seem to start approaching indexers as soon as they have worked out either an approximate or a precise schedule (about fifty-fifty as between the two). Three adopt a counsel of perfection ('at the earliest possible moment'), one of defiant imperfection ('*last* possible moment'), while of the five who wait until page-proofs arrive—this being, of course, the last possible moment—the one who adds 'Alas! We are trying to do better' is probably speaking for the rest. The periods quoted as the average allowed for making an index ranged from minus twenty-four hours to four weeks. The question, 'Do you, in working out preliminary schedules, allow longer for longer books?' now strikes me as being on a par with 'Do you breathe?', but one firm said 'No', so perhaps it has hidden depths. I applaud the firm that likes to allow at least three weeks, with the rider that 'a long and complex index may take very much longer than this', and the firm that gave a range of one week to six months, with a suggested two to three weeks for 40,000 words. All these figures, I should add, apply specifically to indexes where all the work is done on page-proofs (or page-on-galley). Only one firm makes a fairly regular practice of asking indexers to work from a set of marked-up galleys; the others would use this, or some still more radical expedient, only, if ever, in exceptional cases, or (Michael Joseph) if the book is being done in litho.

The great majority of publishers always, or usually, or whenever possible, wait until the indexer has completed his index before starting to print off the text; and most of them, on those occasions when they are not going to wait, specifically request indexers to inform them immediately of any inconsistencies of spelling ('etc.' was accidentally omitted from the question) that they may discover. One firm that does not take this precaution adds: 'But perhaps we should.' There is no 'perhaps' about it; nor is it true, as Barrie & Jenkins suggested, that if indexers 'don't do so automatically . . . they can't be doing their job properly'. The key word in the question is *immediately*: the indexer may not unreasonably assume that the publisher will wait for the index as constituting a final check on the text, and that he will prefer a consolidated list of errors and discrepancies to a bombardment of telephone calls.

The Delicate Question

Turning at last to the delicate question of payment (questions 33-37), I asked first: 'Do you have a standard *method* of payment for indexes?' One firm gave the enchanting answer, 'Yes—by cheque through our accounts department'. Of the nine firms using a standard method of the kind I had in mind, Methuen usually agrees an outright fee in advance, based on such factors as 'length and complexity of the book, specialist knowledge of the indexer, proven ability of the indexer'. Constable does much the same, while of the rest, two firms always base payment on the length of the book, three on the extent of the index, and two on the time taken. The only actual rates quoted however, all refer to this last method, and range from sixty-three pence to £1 per hour. Two other firms quoted, as normal, sums ranging, in one case from £15 to £20, in the other from £12 to £25. The second of these in particular, being a firm with a substantial academic list, must be lucky not to get some insufficiently substantial indexes. Most firms are normally guided, in the matter of payment, by the indexer—Macmillan Press restricting this to 'proven indexers'. Penguin Books, however, are guided by the Society of Indexers' suggested fees; as a Society we can but applaud this answer.

Any Complaints?

My last two questions asked respondents whether they were satisfied with the state of affairs described above ('What state of affairs?' asked one, in real or assumed indignation), and invited them to voice any particular dissatisfactions. No less than fifteen professed themselves satisfied or even (Maurice Temple Smith) 'delighted'. (The respondent at Macmillan Press added, 'And I believe my indexers are also'—a pleasant thought, which speaking for myself I am happy to confirm, though my guess is that the overall satisfaction rate of indexers, authors and even readers is lower than that of publishers.) Two publishers were 'reasonably satisfied' ('Is one ever satisfied?' asked one), two 'not altogether' and three 'downright dissatisfied'.

Of the causes of dissatisfaction, one that recurred was the lack of standardization over payment. Two publishers lamented the deficiencies of certain author-made indexes,

three of certain outside indexers. Of the latter group, one (Butterworth Medical Books) castigated 'the vast number of self-styled indexers who . . . put the minimum of effort and thought into the task' and felt that 'there should be provision for rejecting bad work without payment as with other literary efforts'. More mildly, Barrie & Jenkins noted 'a tendency among most indexers to over-index'. The most pertinent and trenchant criticism of indexers, however—though the need for it may in this case reflect surprisingly low rates of pay—came from the O.U.P.:

> In general, the apparent shortage of really efficient, intelligent indexers able to put themselves in the potential reader's place. Too many seem to work to a rigid formula, not always producing the most helpful, common-sensical results.

An Ideal Case History

'A rigid formula'—that is the last thing that I wish to advocate, or to appear to be advocating, when I now attempt my promised 'ideal case history'. The very phrase 'case history' is intended to suggest that in a different set of circumstances a quite different procedure might have been appropriate. And if from time to time I lapse into dogmatism I hope you will put this down to youthful arrogance rather than the rigidity of incipient *rigor mortis*.

It is good, perhaps, for an audience of publishers and indexers to be reminded that books begin—sometimes—with authors. Picture, then, our author—whom I will refrain from naming Bloggins or Scroggins—scratching his head or stroking his beard (any resemblance between case-historical characters and living persons is, of course, entirely coincidental) as he tries to think of a subject for his next book. Eureka: municipal elections in Ruritania, the next round of which he, as an expert on all things Ruritanian, is about to cover for the *Custodian*. He phones his agent—by all means let us complicate the issue with an agent—and presently a synopsis is conjured into being, together with a letter from the agent full of words like 'uniquely qualified' and 'magisterial' and 'definitive' and 'no monograph on the subject since 1573'. We are now in 1973, and in the last year or so the world has become increasingly aware of the information explosion and the enhanced need for, among other things, good indexes. Responsibility for their provision is assumed by a growing number of publishers; and it is one of these who is given first option on *Municipal elections in Ruritania.*

I am not enough of a poet to evoke the varieties of mystical experience by which publishers decide whether to commission, or publish, a book. So I will present you with the *fait accompli,* the *livre* being as yet *in-accompli,* of a contract drawn up by the agent and signed by the author and publisher. Whether this contract does or does not spell out the publisher's agreement to provide the index, the publisher has already had this feature in mind; he has even made a guess at its likely extent and cost—though he has *not* committed himself to any rigid costings, nor indeed allowed the likely economics of this book *in isolation* to dominate his thinking.

At some convenient moment between signature and delivery the publisher—or editor, as from now on I shall call this member of the band—asks the author if he wishes to index the book himself, and, if not, whether there is anybody else he would particularly like to do the job. The letter, which may be a standard one or a variation on it, will commonly include some indication of what is involved—an inexperienced author may well underestimate the difficulties and probable tedium. The editor will add that a final decision need not be reached until, say, two months before page-proofs are due, but that earlier notification, especially of a negative decision, would be helpful. Logic notwithstanding, I doubt if it is wise, as a rule, to offer an author more than token payment— perhaps a few more free copies—for doing the index himself. If there is a strong financial inducement—whether this takes the form of scoring a plus or of avoiding a minus—there is a real danger of an author

undertaking an index even if he has no talent whatsoever in that direction. Conversely, the ideal author who is his own ideal indexer will not readily be deflected from the latter role.

Had our present author been such a one, you would have been ten minutes earlier out of school. Much of what follows would, *mutatis mutandis,* still have applied; but much would have gone by the board. The main mutand would be the amount and kind of briefing given to an author who might be an inexperienced indexer, as against a professional, experienced or inexperienced.

Our Ruritanian authority, at all events, is lazy where indexes are concerned. But he is punctilious, and he answers the editor's letter by return. It would be pleasant to record that he suggested the name of Oliver Stallybrass, who had indexed an earlier work of his so admirably. But alas for this *dé-nouement*: the work in question was the *Diplomatic archive of Ruritania, 1453 to 1763*—the index to which, you may remember, had a chequered history. So it is up to the editor to find an indexer.

Indexers and Self-styled Indexers

How the editor does that is his business. But a word or two on indexers and self-styled indexers may not come amiss. Ideally, a publisher has a small panel of excellent and regular indexers who between them account for most of his books. And to any publisher who finds himself employing a first-rate indexer I can only say, as Frederick J. Praeger said recently[4] of first-rate translators: Grapple him to your soul with hoops of steel, meet his every demand, pay him outrageously . . . But every first-rate indexer needs a first commission, and every publisher needs from time to time to renovate his panel. How does he do this?

Basically there are two, mutually complementary, ways, the systematic and the *ad hoc.* The systematic involves the building-up and maintenance of a register of indexers—

---

[4] In the *Publishers' Weekly*; I quote from memory.

known and unknown, and the known-to-be-bad as well as the known-to-be-good. Edge-notched cards or coloured slips can be used to signal specialisms, knowledge of languages or other information. A card with a black clip top left, for example, might mean ' never again '; such a card would only be examined if the indexer in question wrote to solicit fresh work. Names can be added—when ascertainable; more of this anon—as editors encounter conspicuously good or bad indexes in published books. But the bulk of the names are likely to be culled from the Employment Wanted column of the *Bookseller* and from those letters pleading for work of one kind or another with which most publishers are deluged.

How to assess these indexers, self-styled indexers and would-be indexers? The easiest are those who enclose, or offer to send, samples of their work in the form of carbon copies. I emphasize the format because there are dangers in judging an indexer by published work which he claims as his own. At the worst, the claim may be totally unfounded; although I have never heard of such a case, it might well be tried on by, say, an enterprising undergraduate anxious to eke out his grant, thwarted by the no-experience-no-commission-no-commission-no experience barrier, and ready to profit from the anonymity so widely enforced on indexers. More probably, the index or indexes claimed may have needed a lot of editorial attention; and, although a really good index is almost certain to be the work of one man, a passable-looking one may well have been patched up by a hard-pressed editor from a thoroughly shoddy piece of work. Here is one tip to publishers: beware of the man who submits an indicography as long as your index finger in which (a) almost every item has a different publisher, or (b) this presumed fact is obscured by the omission of publishers' names, or (c) authors are not cited, or cited by their surnames alone—not only is this last practice slovenly in itself, but it may be designed to reduce the risk of your examining the books in a library.

As for the avowedly untried indexer, the most usual course is to try some young or elderly hopeful with a shortish, lightweight book that will make comparatively few demands, and to keep one's fingers crossed. But I see no reason why a would-be indexer should not be required to submit to some sort of test of competence. Literary editors sometimes ask aspiring reviewers to write spoof reviews (naturally, of actual books; and, naturally, unpaid); why not turn aspiring indexers loose on spare proof copies of a short and straightforward book for which, nevertheless, an indexer of proven ability has been lined up, so that a ready-made yardstick will be available?

I have been talking, I realize, as if publishers' editors had nothing to do but browse in the London Library and read *The Indexer* and shuffle the cards in their own indexes of indexers. I know all too well that life is not like that. And most publishers, however well organized, will need, once in a while, to supplement their system with the *ad hoc* employment of a new indexer. Probably the book will be a specialized one for which no known specialist indexer is available. Here are three resources: the grapevine; the well-tended grapevine known as the Society of Indexers' Register of Indexers; and the indexers (once again, if ascertainable—with or without the help of a friendly fellow-publisher) of recent books in the same subject area.

That was a long digression, occasioned by our publisher's need to find an indexer for *Municipal elections in Ruritania.* Having mentally earmarked one or two people, he does nothing else until delivery of the typescript. (I once edited a book that arrived just twenty-five years after its deadline, and there is no point in keeping an indexer keyed up all that time.) From this point—and possibly earlier—he has plenty to think about; I will mention only those thoughts and actions that concern the index. It may be, of course, particularly in a big firm, that such thoughts and actions are delegated, in part or in whole, to somebody else; and there is much to be said for matters relating to indexes being largely concentrated in the hands of one person—almost anyone who happens to have a flair and a feeling for those final pages of a book. But for simplicity's sake we will assume that the editor in question is also the index-wallah.

A Pas-de-Deux

It is now March 1974. The editor reads the book, satisfies himself that there is no need for extensive further work by the author such as might cause undue delay, and gets it scheduled for publication in March 1975—when Ruritania's next batch of biennial elections will help sales along. While reading it he has been giving part of his skilfully divided attention to the requirements of the index. He has also done a rough word-count; and he has got as far as thinking in terms of, roughly, 280 pages of text, 12 pages of prelims, 8 of bibliography, 20 of index: total 320 pages. He now writes to his first-choice indexer, giving him this information, adding that page-proofs (or page-on-galley) are likely to arrive in October or November, and perhaps enclosing a copy of the draft blurb. Is the indexer interested in principle? If so, can he commit himself now, or only on receipt of a more precise schedule? Would three weeks be sufficient? Does twenty pages of index sound about right? Would he like a preliminary view of a duplicate typescript?

Nothing, so far, directly about money. But the whole approach might have been quite different with a different editor or indexer. I am assuming an editor and an indexer who have worked together before and trust each other, so that each has a fair idea of what these probable twenty pages of index are likely to mean in cash terms. Where this is the case, the precise method of assessing the fee is not particularly important. And indeed I find it quite impossible to pontificate over questions of payment. Having said that, I will now pontificate. All in all, payment by the hour is probably the least inequit-

able; a slow or idle worker will soon put himself out of business. But personally I detest the complicated timekeeping which, if one has a conscience, payment by the hour entails. Even if one is celibate, which I am not, the gas man cometh, the cleaner cleaneth, and the phone it ringeth all the day. One needs a pair of chess-clocks; and even then, as in chess, one may forget to depress the appropriate lever. As for estimating, I have already tried to explain why it may be harder to estimate the cost of an index than of the Sydney Opera House.

Our indexer, also, replies by return of post. Yes, he would like to do this book, and yes, twenty pages sounds the sort of thing, and yes, three weeks should be feasible, though four would be nice. Only thing is, other commitments, irons in the fire, how soon must he give a definite answer? To which the editor—but I don't need to itemize the steps in this elegant *pas-de-deux*; the essential point is that each remembers to convey to the other at once any fresh clarification of what lies ahead, up to and including the stage of ' proofs will be forty-eight hours later than scheduled ' and ' I shall/ shall not be able to return them within twenty-four hours instead of seventy-two '. Much of this sort of thing will probably be done over the telephone; but at some stage it is desirable, in order to avoid misunderstandings, for letters to be exchanged over the main issues. A formal contract is hardly necessary, but it is well for both parties to be quite clear whether, for example, the indexer is, or is not, assigning his copyright. (Unless he explicitly is, he isn't.)[5]

---

[5] While writing this paper, I was engaged in friendly correspondence with the hardback publisher of *The collected essays, journalism and letters of George Orwell*, the four volumes of which had just appeared in paperback—complete with my indexes, only the page references having been changed. I have since received the additional fee I had suggested as appropriate—' as an *ex-gratia* payment since I do not under any circumstances accept, nor could any publisher accept, your contentions concerning the copyright of the index'.

Double-Dutch Papers Please Copy

At the publisher's end things are proceeding apace. The typescript has been edited in consultation with the author, with cuts here and additions there; and a copy or copies, definitive as to extent, has or have been through the hands of the designer, the production manager, the printer and the copy-editor, inspiring a succession of ever more complicated sums, and accumulating pencil marks in a variety of colours. I am being deliberately vague about these processes, partly because they are double-Dutch to most indexers, partly because the sequence of events and the demarcation lines between departments vary so much from firm to firm. Whoever does what when, the important points in the present context are three. First, since an even working—i.e., a book whose pages number a multiple of thirty-two—is desirable, it is also desirable that a specific number of pages should be provisionally assigned to the index at an early stage, so that the rest of the book can be designed to fill an appropriate number of pages. Second, although the type area and type face for the index ought clearly to match the rest of the book, it is surely unnecessary for the type *size* in the index to be determined at this stage. I have seen well-designed books whose indexes were in the same type size as the text, and others where the index was three, four or perhaps even five points smaller; and a skilful designer should be able to design a book—as appears to be done at Bodley Head—where either possibility will be at least acceptable. One can fit almost exactly twice the amount of type into the same type area using Baskerville 7 on 8 as one can using Baskerville 11 on 12; and to double the flexibility over the extent of a vital, but not entirely pre-calculable, part of the book is surely worth a possible slight loss in elegance. There are, of course, other devices for accommodating an index that comes out longer (or shorter) than expected: the substitution of run-on for indented subheadings (or *vice versa*), or the allocation of four, eight or even sixteen extra pages. But this latter resource, in particular, should probably be kept as a second line of defence, since not only will it add relatively more to costs but it may even hold up publication if extra paper of the same kind is not immediately available. Even an index occupying the same number of pages will, of course, cost a little extra if it is set in, say, 7-point when the estimate has been for 9-point. And this leads me to my third point: the budget—and I am far from regarding a budget as superfluous—must include some sort of contingency allowance, and it must be recognized that an increase in the cost of an index is one of the more legitimate contingencies.

We seem to have lost track of the author. Here is a letter, or part of a letter, such as an editor might send him about the time that *Municipal elections in Ruritania* is going to press:

> You may remember my asking you if you wished to do your own index, and your answering fairly emphatically that you didn't. So you'll be glad to know that I've arranged for X to do the job. He's an able and experienced indexer, but there may be points he'd like to consult you about; would you object to my giving him your address and phone number, so that he can contact you direct if the need should arise? You will, of course, be keeping me informed of any variants around page-proof stage, and these too I could pass on.
>
> More positively, are there any headings which you feel the index ought to include, and which X might miss? I myself have a number of ideas on how this index should be organized, e.g. on how best to bring out each of the various facets (time, place, party, issue) in a paragraph on the Christian Communists' attitude to housing in the 1951 Micropolis election; and these I could amalgamate with any views of your own, and let X have the lot.
>
> Perhaps you could be thinking about this and drop me a line or give me a ring some time. If I haven't heard from you by the time proofs arrive, I shall assume you're content to rely on X. But even so I *would* like you, unless the whole subject bores you stiff, just to run your eye over a copy of the index, in typescript rather than in proof—though if you'd like to see proofs as well, that should be possible.

To which the author replies that he has full confidence in the expertise of his editor and indexer, unless the latter asks for guidance, in which case he will try to supply it. He would certainly like to see the typescript, and could even face another round of proofs.

The Last Stage

The stage is now set for the last act of this singularly undramatic drama. It has been decided that the book can safely go straight into page-proofs, which has the incidental advantage of allowing the indexer four weeks instead of three, and a little more slack all along the line. With four weeks, there is no need for the indexer to be sent batches of proofs as they are pulled—still less can there be any question of his doing some preliminary work on non-existent galleys. So one fine late October day, as predicted, he receives a neat parcel of page-proofs. Possibly, if the schedule is really leisurely, they may even be a corrected set. But if it is a choice between indexing corrected proofs in two to three weeks and uncorrected ones in four, most indexers, unless a notoriously bad printer is involved, will opt unhesitatingly for the second alternative. If the printer employs a good reader, the literals at least will already have been picked up, and can quickly be transferred to the indexer's set of proofs; and any other alterations which might affect the indexer can be phoned through as they come to light.

With the proofs is a letter from the editor. General instructions there are none— the indexer knows by now that this firm likes, for example, no commas between heading and first page reference, and the other whims that would need to be spelled out to a new boy. There are merely a few suggestions—no more—about those facets and the like; a reminder of the date for completion; the author's address and telephone number; and—most important—a summary of the state of play as regards copy-fitting requirements. Since the text has come out two pages longer than anticipated, there are now only eighteen pages available for the index. Double column, fifty-two lines averaging thirty-five characters/spaces, is the target to aim for, but up to twenty per cent

over-matter can be accommodated without undue embarrassment.

The indexer sets to work—which means, or should mean, that he first reads the book through from beginning to end, making no more than a few notes as he goes. All too often there isn't time, and all too often this is all too apparent. Take a book on Beethoven. One would not normally, when indexing a musical book, use keys as headings; and no indexer who didn't know Beethoven's work fairly well would think of devoting one of his precious cards to 'C minor'. Indexing the book without a preliminary reading— and/or an intelligent briefing from author or editor—he might well reach the 5th Symphony, well over half way through the book, before the author makes it explicit that C minor was for Beethoven a key with a peculiar significance. By now the indexer is past the Trio Op. 1, No. 3, the Pathétique Sonata, the Violin Sonata Op. 30, No. 2, the 3rd Piano Concerto, and the 32 Variations. Does he backtrack? If he takes his craft seriously he does, cursing the publisher who has only allowed him a week for the job. If he doesn't he doesn't—to the reader's loss.

Portrait of an Indexer Indexing

The present indexer, speeding through *Municipal elections in Ruritania,* becomes aware that again and again certain subjects—housing, unemployment, education— occur sometimes as background information, sometimes as election issues. Many readers will be seeking one kind of context rather than the other. To distinguish each reference by a subheading or sub-subheading would be space-consuming and cumbersome. Inspiration: why not distinguish references to election issues by the use of, say, an asterisk, with an explanatory note at the head of the index? Unorthodox, possibly unprecedented. Better consult the editor. Telephone call; editor says: Fine, only why not italic type? Looks neater, saves space.

Having assembled his material in the form of several hundred cards, the indexer sets about typing them out. I regard a modicum of typing dexterity as an essential part of the indexer's craft, and I hold no brief whatsoever for those indexers who regard it as beneath their dignity. It is *not* a mere mechanical operation: while typing, the indexer is also editing, designing, copyfitting. In this case—a very common one, by the way—he has as target a fifty-two-line column. Half of fifty-two is twenty-six, and with double-spaced quarto, the use of an appropriate space at the head results automatically in a page of twenty-six lines. The indexer sets his margins to produce an *average* line of thirty-five characters/spaces. By allowing for the drop head on the first page, and a line between each initial letter of the alphabet, he can produce a typescript of x pages which will make, as near as dammit, x over 4 pages of print.

In this instance the indexer suspects from long experience that even with the twenty per cent margin of error he will be running over the limit. He considers using run-on subheadings, but with these particular subheadings—most frequently the names of towns, and seldom if ever a random collection of phrases—this would be a pity. He decides to have a go with indented subheadings. (If he forgets to indent a line, he uses the approved sign to correct this; if he overtypes in a proper name or page reference, he repeats the name or the entire number, parenthetically, in the margin.) The result is eighty-eight pages of typescript—two or three too many for comfort, even in the smaller type size (7-point instead of 8) implied by that figure of twenty per cent. Damnation! Shall he mark up for run-on subheadings after all? Or can some category of entries be eliminated without undue detriment? Authors cited in footnotes? A gift to reviewers, of course: 'Mr. Bloggins, who leans heavily on the work of Scroggins . . .' —sorry, there was no avoiding it after all. But who else? Phone call to the author: would it matter too much? The author dislikes reviewers, and says so. To hell with them. Conscience almost clear, the indexer goes through his typescript—all three

copies—deleting every name followed only by ' (cited) ' and one or more page references. In the case of double-barrelled names he remembers to delete the ' see ' references from the other barrel.

The indexer sends in two copies as requested, keeping the third—for checking against proofs, demonstrating his *savoir-faire* to potential future employers, and as a basis for the index to the book's next edition. In a covering letter he draws attention to such literals and other errors as he has noticed, and explains that the index *is* within the twenty per cent limit—eighteen per cent, near enough—when the deletions are taken into account. He is right: set in 7-point, the index fits neatly into eighteen pages.

Ruritanian Papers Please Review

There is little more to say. The author is lost in admiration of the index, writes to the indexer to say so, and adds a final sentence to the Preface, expressing his gratitude. In addition, need I add, the indexer's name appears at the head of his work. Proofs, which the indexer checks with scrupulous care, give rise to no fresh problems. The editor duly sends the indexer a complimentary copy of the book. No reviewer comments on the indebtedness of Bloggins to Scroggins; but several comment on the excellence of the index, and a hundred or so additional librarians, correctly inferring that when care has been taken over the index, it has been taken over much else besides, buy this (for their purposes) marginal book. Another good index, another piece of sensible collaboration between all concerned, have justified themselves.

DISCUSSION

Mr. Norman Knight stated that in his experience typed index entries on cards with extra references in writing had never been refused, although on one occasion they had been grudgingly accepted. On the matter of authors compiling their own indexes, he knew of no case where an author had been paid a fee for doing this. Commenting, Mr. Stallybrass said that one firm pays a fee to the author, but he does not encourage this because authors often are not good indexers; they should not be encouraged to compile indexes to their own books. He also reiterated that the typing of the index should be considered part of its compilation.

Miss Coole considered that indexers should not be expected to type their entries, for many of the older indexers were not able to type. She agreed with the Society's recommendation to submit entries on cards as most publishers will accept them. Mr. Stallybrass stated that indexers should at the very least supervise the typing of their entries but that the publisher should pay the cost.

Mr. Tatham said that up to three years ago an indexer always saw the proofs of his index but that this does not happen now. Commenting, Mr. Stallybrass said that this reflected the general haywire state of the publishing and printing industries. Another member of the audience said that this was a question of time. Mr. Stallybrass considered it was essential that the indexer should see the proofs if there were many corrections; otherwise his work might be undone.

Mrs. Wallis asked if a small delay in publishing mattered, to which Mr. Stallybrass replied that with topical books or academic texts it did; moreover, if proofs were returned late the publisher might lose his place in the printer's queue, and the small delay become a major one.

Another member of the audience stated that it was common for printers not to keep up to time; they try to keep to the agreed time schedule but often cannot do so and will 'phone the publisher and tell of any hold-up.

A publisher's representative expressed strong views on the bad indexes compiled by authors.

The Editor and the Indexer

Liz Stalcup

Three things are essential to the production of a good index—a good book, a good editor and a good indexer.

The *Random House dictionary* defines an index as a *more or less* detailed alphabetical listing of names, places and topics along with the numbers of the pages on which they are discussed. Like the old New England land deeds that describe acreage as more or less some figure, this definition leaves several values to be determined:

An index is a list of names—all names? or only certain names? An index is a list of places—again all or which? As to topics—in what detail and how arranged?

Unless there is logic in the way those questions are answered, you will have, in my estimation, only a list and not an index. I would like to include in that definition a modification of a phrase that occurs in another statement of the meaning of the word index—'something used or serving to point out; a sign, token or indication: *a true index of his character*'. Let us say 'a true index of the character of the book.'

Unless an index *does* reveal the character of a book, it remains a list. Not that a list does not have value, but it is not the effective tool an index should be.

So, who determines the logic of an index? Is it the editor, who often actually knows more about the book than does the author? Is it the author?—but most editors will agree that, with rare exceptions, there is no greater abomination than an author-developed index. Is it the indexer, the person who simply does the physical work of compilation? Is the reader involved? After all, he *is* going to use the index.

All these individuals are editorially involved, and the index we are discussing is an editorial, not a file clerk, function. Unfortunately, however, all too frequently the final determinant of the size, and hence the logic, of an index is a non-editorial factor: how many pages are left for the index? If too few for the character of the book, too bad; just scrunch what should occupy 5,000 lines (and *did* in the previous expensive edition of one reprint) into 1,500 lines (as was done in one instance I personally experienced—and the difference between the two editions was not in text content but in the number of illustrations). If too many pages are left, then devise what I call a 'tarantula in left boot' index. That name comes from what, sadly, has become a family joke as I groan that I have another of those padded indexes wherein under the heading 'Boots', to use up lines, I shall have to insert two subheads. The first will read 'Left boot, no tarantula in' and the second will read 'Right boot, tarantula in'. Those subheads will add lines, will they add utility?

Reprinted from *The Indexer* 7, no. 3 (Spring 1971): 114–117.

But no experienced editor will box himself into that nasty corner, unless, and this is an almost inconceivable notion, there is never an editorial/production consultation on the ultimate size of the book under considera- tion. Generally, such consultation is part of the cost and pricing procedure, and the knowledgeable editor will include in his estimating a reasonable projection of the length of the index. As long as a manuscript is available, it is possible to do a rough, reasonably accurate cast off of an index. Select, say, twenty representative manuscript pages. Count names, places and topics that you, the editor, consider important. Multiply the average number of entries by the total pages of manuscript. Behold! a working number of entries for determining the num- ber of pages needed for an index representa- tive of the book.

If by accident, the art director or the pro- duction department later influences the actual number of pages available, the editor is in a good position to help determine the logic of the index. He can suggest that the emphasis be upon names rather than sub- jects if the renown of the names, or the potential reader's familiarity with them, will imply the subjects, or that the emphasis be upon the subjects because they will carry the names.

The reader—the user of the index—must be considered in any compilation. Certain projected readerships and sales are obvious— the 'juvenile' will not normally be con- fused with an adult 'trade book', nor that 'trade book' with a 'graduate student text'. But does the author or the editor feel that that juvenile text is geared to a specific read- ing level? May the indexer introduce words not used in the text? That adult 'trade book'—if it has been written or edited using familiar or short forms of names, should the complete, formal names be sup- plied by the indexer? Is that college text to be used primarily as part of a series of in- terrelated texts, and therefore, hopefully at least, should it have an index reflecting the relatedness of the series? Will it be used by a highly specialized faculty, or is it to be supplemental reading? If index length is not a problem, the professional indexer will index for the broadest use; if length is a problem, should not the editor's, rather than the indexer's, judgment of the index logic hold?

There is a theory that footnotes have no place in a well-written book—if the material is important enough to be included, etc. But footnotes do exist. Some books are even written in hybrid fashion so that, in theory at least, reading the footnotes makes you a scholar and ignoring them an improving- your-own-mind reader or a member of the Book-of-the-Month Club or something else less than a scholar. To index footnotes or not to index? Surely the decision should reflect the editor's and the author's thinking as well as the indexer's.

I think one reason why an author-de- veloped index is so frequently a horror is that the author is so close to his book and his subject that he cannot see the forest for the proverbial trees. He can see the logic in, as well as for, his work; he fails to see the various logics the reader brings to any index. These logics are determined partly by the reader's familiarity with the subject: not everyone seeking information already knows the correct jargon of the discipline for a given concept. The reader is not necessarily the author's peer. Also, an author is likely to organize his index as he organized his book, which can—in fact, should—be quite an individual approach. But the index-user does not know that organization. He brings to an index his working knowledge, which may be limited, of other indexes.

A good index, therefore, must meet such conventional concepts while retaining the individuality of the book. If the author has, for example, pet terminology that may not be the always-accepted usage, it should appear in the index; but so, at least, should a cross-reference guide to his particular usage appear under the more conventional, even trite, expressions.

If an editor has no strong feelings about alphabetization, fine—leave it to the indexer. I know what an editor would get from me, but does the editor? Will alphabetization be letter-by-letter (dictionary) style? Will it be word-by-word regardless of the type of entry? Just this one choice can give quite a range for looking up any given item. Letter-by-letter will, for example, give you:

Browne, Illinois
Browning, Alfred
Brown, Xavier.

Word-by-word will give:

Brown, Xavier
Browne, Illinois
Browning, Alfred.

Quite a reversal, and if the index is lengthy enough, could place each entry on different pages in each instance.

Without a house style being given to me, has any editor any way of anticipating that perhaps I belong to the school of indexers that use neither of the above approaches alone, but either, depending on choice, in combination with an entry sequence that puts people ahead of places and places ahead of things? In that case, our friend Brown, Xavier might be first or third, but Browne, Illinois would have to be third.

So, unless an editor has no particular feeling on the subject and is content to have the indexes of the books on his list alphabetized without uniformity, it behoves him to develop a house style. I personally have strong preferences, but, like any professional indexer, I will follow the editor's house style even if I disagree with it.

Numbers are important in an index. How are they to be handled? Full hundreds, as 111-117? or only the decades repeated, as 122-28? or (perhaps for space reasons) to use only the digits—122-8? The last is not my own cup of tea, but if consistent use in any given index saves even ten lines to the column in an index that is being compressed, I certainly prefer that form to dropping items—and that is what I would provide unless directed otherwise.

How are subentries to be handled? Is there to be a cut off point of number of page references after which subentries are a must? Are they to be alphabetically arranged, each beginning a new line under each preceding larger head? Are they to be 'run-in', paragraph style, in the same alphabetical arrangement, with a semicolon between items? Or to be 'run-in' paragraph form *but* arranged in sequential page order—that is, by the first page entry after each item and regardless of the item alphabetization?

These and other matters of style (the use of ff. or *passim*; illustration references . . . italic with or without *illus.* before the page number; *see also*'s at the end of a series of réferences or after the main words—to name only a few) must be determined by someone until there is one single definitive usage. That will probably come some day, partly because of computerization. It is not generally feasible to program idiosyncratic usages.

Should an index be submitted always, or never, on cards? May it be handwritten (Heaven forbid, except in dire emergency!)? Should it be typed on sheets (with or without a carbon) to word- and line-count length?

Such matters of style and format are, to my mind, important. To be intelligible, content needs form.

So now the editor has in his possession an index on cards or otherwise that meets his (or the indexer's) stylistic standard. Is it a good one?

Unless the editor is thoroughly familiar with the physical and mechanical accuracy of the indexer, page references should be spot-checked if possible, and if length of index and time available permit, every page reference, name spelling, and word usage should be checked in the index of a first-time indexer. The editor's favourite indexers could be spot-checked. They too can goof, sometimes for so simple a reason as the arrangement of pages and the location of folios. The previous job a particular indexer handled had the folios on the bottom of the pages; in this book they were on the top—both jobs, of course, three pages atop each other on a galley sheet. Want to bet on the possibility of visual error? Personally, I prefer working with side-by-side pages, but such proofing seems rare.

Names could be checked for initials and trick spellings.

If the editor had edited the manuscript, then it is possible he would scan the entries to determine that pertinent topics and important names have been picked up. This is particularly important if inadequate space has meant the exercise of judgment in omissions.

The index should be tested by selecting several pages of text at random and then looking for the topics covered in the index. If names or topics are omitted that should appear, the indexer should be asked why over the phone quickly. A good indexer will be able to justify the omissions by the logic of his indexing. If it is decided that the editor's opinion should prevail and the omission is not justifiable, a quick scan or reworking by the indexer, who must naturally have become thoroughly familiar with the book, will at the least pick up most of the related references.

But all such checking must be done quickly, while the material is fresh in the minds of everyone concerned, not at some indefinite time in the future.

It is a paradox only in a limited sense, but those no-good-indexer authors are frequently very good index critics. If the index meets the requirements of their logic, at least one of the two hurdles of use—the author's and the reader's—will have been overcome.

As an indexer, I am only too well aware that the index and the indexer are that last-gasp chance to get back on schedule. The author lost a month, the editor a week, the printer another—that leaves one week for preparing an index that should take three. Miracles have been performed—but not with dependable regularity.

Why not supply an indexer with unpaged galleys at the time the author gets his? No book can be indexed without being read, and early galleys permit the indexer at the least to become familiar with content and organization.

The truism is that no index is better than the book (it can, of course, be worse). The corollary should be: No index is better than the editor's standards of indexing. Editors determine *who* does the indexing and *how*.

The Indexer as Proof Corrector

M. D. Anderson

The page proofs sent to an indexer are usually uncorrected. In reading them through, the indexer may notice misprints, and also mistakes in spelling, grammar, and arithmetic, and inadequacies and inconsistencies in punctuation. He may occasionally see reason to question a matter of fact.

It should not be supposed that it is necessarily someone else's business to put these matters right. Each person who reads a set of proofs attentively is likely to find a few errors missed by other readers. An indexer has to be a particularly attentive reader, and will probably observe not only the more obvious mistakes, but also discrepancies that are not very noticeable to others. For example, in scientific papers with lists of references at the end, the names of authors are sometimes not spelt in the same way in the text of the paper as in the list of references. A statement, date, or name may appear on one page in a form inconsistent with a reference on another page. A reference may be made to something supposed to be found on another page, but actually omitted. The indexer becomes aware of these doubtful points in the course of deciding what index entries to make.

Hence the indexer can often do a service to the author and publisher by noting corrections and suggestions for the attention of the " official " proof corrector. I have even known this proof-correcting function of the indexer to be advanced as one of the reasons for having an index at all.

Reprinted from *The Indexer* 3, no. 4 (Autumn 1963): 163.

IId. The Ownership of Indexes

The Problem of Copyright:
An Indexer's Triumph

G. Norman Knight

Not many indexers seem to be aware that the copyright in their indexes belongs to them, unless and until they have expressly assigned it. In certain circumstances it may prove a property of some value.

Under the Copyright Acts of 1911 and 1956—there are doubtless similar enactments in the United States—a literary copyright is defined as 'the sole right to produce or reproduce an original literary work'. There must be some originality in the work—originality either in expression or arrangement—for it to enjoy the benefits of copyright. The expression 'literary' does not involve any qualification of style—a directory or railway guide, or even a list of football fixtures, can be the subject of copyright—but covers any work expressed in print or writing, so long as it is substantial enough to involve some literary skill and labour of composition. Normally the author is the first owner of the copyright, the author being the person who actually 'writes or compiles' the work.

A book or periodical index satisfies all the above conditions. Possession of the copyright in it is often of only academic interest, since clearly the original publisher has paid for the right to produce the index. But the practice is spreading of a British publisher's selling the right of reproducing some particular work in some territory overseas (probably the United States or some Commonwealth country) to a quite separate publishing house in that territory.* In this case, of course, the indexer is under no contract with the new publisher and if the latter decides to use the original index he should expect to pay a small copyright fee.

Just such an instance occurred recently in my own experience. Half-way through indexing an important biography for a prominent publisher I learnt (quite by chance) that the American rights had been sold to a New York publisher, who intended to use my index. I thereupon stated on my bill: 'Please note that this sum does *not* cover assignment of my copyright in the index', and received a written reply: 'Your statement is noted'. Later I was rung up by the publisher's editor to ask what exactly I had meant. I explained patiently, as at the end

---

* It sometimes occurs also in this country, e.g. in the production of a separate paperback edition by a fresh publisher, in which case my contention is equally applicable.

Reprinted from *The Indexer* 7, no. 1 (Spring 1970): 17–18.

of last paragraph, and said I intended to charge the American publisher for copyright fee. I was implored not to do that, so proposed assigning my copyright to the London publisher.

' How much? '

I replied that I should be satisfied with a token fee of £10 to ' establish the principle '. When I was told that such a proposal was unheard of and was quite out of the question, I suggested starting a friendly test action in the courts. This won the day. The publisher gracefully gave way and I was paid what I had asked, in addition to my indexing fee. (It was a slight disappointment not to have the chance of suing, for I feel certain I should have won and the action might have provided excellent publicity for the Society of Indexers.)

My one fear is lest the extra ten pounds may be foisted upon the unfortunate author, who was already liable to pay the normal indexing charge. But, as an author is rarely consulted about the transfer of publishing rights abroad, it seems to me that he should not be liable for any cost arising therefrom.

The expression ' *small* copyright fee ' has been used above. Any indexer who decides to follow my example and ' have a go ' is warned not to set his (or her) sights too high. It is suggested that he should tell the publisher of his views on assigning the copyright when he starts his original negotiations and should ask for a modest sum not exceeding ten per cent of his total indexing fee. (In my quoted case the percentage was somewhat smaller.) Any attempt at greed may defeat its own ends.

One thing remains to be said. The use of the original index in books published abroad rarely applies to translated books. This is because the whole of the alphabetical order will have to be upset, since (to take one example) the French for ' horse-power ' would come under C for ' cheval vapeur ', and so the foreign publisher would quite likely choose to start afresh with a new index. A French publisher would probably decide to have no index at all. That, at any rate, is my impression of the majority of French books.

Copyright in Indexes

At the last meeting of the Council the question of an author's right to the ownership of copyright in an index he compiled was discussed and it was decided that the President of the Society should write a letter to *The Times* on this subject, following an article on copyright in general, by Ronald Irving, which had recently been published.

This letter was duly printed on 27th January and is reprinted by permission of the editor and the author:

Sir, The highly informative article on copyright by Mr. Ronald Irving, *Business News*, January 15, covers the ground of this complex subject very clearly indeed, and all concerned with books and other media are indebted to you for it.

But may I be permitted to point out that there appears to be one important omission—the copyright of indexes—which is currently engaging the attention of the council of the Society of Indexers, of whom I have the honour to be president.

The index, whose signal role in a book I need not stress, is, I am afraid, too often regarded by publishers as the cinderella of production; it is ironically pertinent in this connexion that your book reviewer, Mr. Michael Holroyd, in his notice, *The Times*, January 20, of a 'publishing book', feels constrained to comment specially that 'the index of this book . . . is appalling'.

There is not a scholar or academician, or graduate, undergraduate, student, researcher, or even dilettante in any subject anywhere today who is not indebted to indexes for facilitating his work, study or interest.

For reasons which are obscure, especially as in many cases the index is not compiled by the book's author but by a professional indexer, the claim is sometimes made, and acted upon in fact, that there is no copyright in an index. But the courts have decided that even so simple a thing as a football fixture list is deemed to be copyright.

How much more so, then, the index compiled with special skills and knowledge. Indeed, some publishers have been found ready to acknowledge that a printed index qualifies automatically for copyright just as other literary compositions.

In probably eight instances out of 10 the indexer's possession of this right is a matter of purely academic interest, since the publisher who has commissioned an index clearly pays for the right to reproduce it. But, although Mr. Irving did not, unfortunately, pursue this theme, I fancy that he will agree with my contention that any agreement between publisher and indexer, whether it be a written contract (as by the interchange of letters) or a verbal contract (e.g.

over the telephone), applies to that particular publishing house alone.

Should the original publisher sell the right to reproduce the whole book to some independent publisher overseas or to a separate paperback publisher in this country who intends (as he probably will) to use the existing index, then I contend that, unless the index copyright has been assigned, the situation is changed; now the compiler is free either to arrange an assignment or else demand a copyright fee from the new publisher.

Yours obediently,
NORMAN KNIGHT,
President,
The Society of Indexers,
Scio House, Portsmouth Road,
Roehampton, London, SW15 3TD.
January 23.

* * *

Subsequently, the editor received the following:

In view of the recent stir over the question of copyright in indexes, the following extract from a letter received lately by a member of the Society from an editor employed by a prominent publishing house may prove of interest:

. . . I was, however, very perturbed to notice on your invoice your statement that the fee did not include copyright in the index. I have now looked back at the files for the other index you did for us and see that this question arose there too and that you settled the copyright for that one on us for an additional fee of ten guineas. I hope you will agree to accept a fee of 15 guineas for this one.

This offer was accepted by the joint indexers concerned and the following Agreement was signed both by the indexers and on behalf of the publishing house:

THIS AGREEMENT made the second day of February 1972 between Mr.   of
                    and Mrs.
of   on the one hand, being the compilers of the index to   by
                    (hereinafter called the Indexers)
and   of   on the other hand, being the publisher of the said work, hereinafter called the Publisher.

WITNESSETH that in consideration of an assignment fee of the sum of fifteen guineas the Indexers hereby assign the copyright of the said index to the Publisher.

(signatures)

Reprinted from *The Indexer* 8, no. 1 (April 1972): 74–75.

It is not thought to be necessary, in a simple matter like this, for the signatures to be witnessed.

The above legally worded Agreement may perhaps prove useful as a model for those members of the Society who are disposed to sell the copyright in their indexes.

It should be made clear that in the above instance the fee of 15 guineas offered in the letter from the publisher's editor represents a copyright assignment fee. The whole of the indexers' charge for their index amounted to 50 guineas.

Readers may remember that this matter, with payment by a publisher in respect of a paperback edition of a book indexed for a hardback edition, was referred to in Mr. Stallybrass's article (*The Indexer*, Vol. 7, no. 4, p. 165).

There has also been some interesting correspondence on this matter in the pages of *The Bookseller* of 15 January and 5 and 26 February; this correspondence is continuing at the time of going to press.

COUNSEL'S OPINION

Following the publication in *The Bookseller* on 4th December, 1971, of an article by Mr. Oliver Stallybrass on the subject of indexes, and the publication in *The Times* of articles on Copyright by Mr. Ronald Irving, there has been dispute in the correspondence columns of these periodicals as to whether or not copyright subsists in an index. Mr. Roger Cleeve considers it 'mischievous nonsense' to assert that such a right exists, and I shall therefore consider first why it might not. Concluding that it does exist, I shall then consider who is entitled to it.

Existence of Copyright

A written work may be deprived of copyright protection

(1) because the copyright period has expired; or

(2) due to some inherent characteristic of the work; or

(3) because the labour of the producer of the work is not such as to attract copyright.

On these points,

(1) is not relevant in the present case.

(2) excludes works which are seditious, scandalous, blasphemous or immoral (Byron suffered under this head—he lost both Cain and Don Juan), and also arrangements of words which do not convey to the mind of the instructed reader any intelligible proposition. Thus aggregations of pure gibberish are not protected, and it has been held that there is no copyright in a cardboard pattern sleeve bearing printed scales and instructions, nor in the ingeniously printed face of a barometer, 'because both are really instruments to be used in conjunction with something else, and though there may be words or sentences on them, by themselves they convey nothing to the reader'.

It might be argued that an index also is 'an instrument to be used in conjunction with something else', and that it has no meaning when divorced from the corresponding text; this, however, involves a misunderstanding of the cases. The printed words on a barometer face convey no information whatsoever, unless the face is attached to the barometer and the needle is pointing; thus copyright could only have subsisted, if at all, in the barometer as a whole, and this would have depended upon registration at Stationers' Hall, which, needless to say, had no facilities for the registration of barometers.

By contrast, the words of an index lose none of their meaning through being separated from the text—the reader is still informed that, for example, Erasmus is referred to on p. 135—he is merely unable to pursue the matter further. An index is rather to be compared to a railway timetable, which is similarly 'to be used in conjunction with something else', but is not deprived of copyright because the reader happens to be in a foreign country, and so unable to catch any of the trains, nor, indeed, because the trains cease to run altogether. I am in doubt as to whether copyright can subsist in an index to a text which did not exist, but it is a problem which is unlikely to arise.

(3)   Almost the only labours in connection with a text which do not give rise to independent copyright are correction and transcription. There will be copyright in a translation, in editorial comment, and in a particular form of re-arrangement. There can be no doubt that the preparation of an index involves the exercise of selective and grammatic skills of the utmost nicety, and that the index cannot be refused protection on the ground that the indexer is a mere copyist.

I therefore conclude that an index is the subject of copyright, independent from that in the appurtenant text.

Ownership of Copyright

Statutory provisions as to the initial ownership of copyright are contained in Section 4 of the Copyright Act, 1956, and are perfectly clear in the present case. Where the indexer is a freelance contractor, and not an employee of the publisher, then the copyright vests in the indexer, whether or not he was commissioned to do the work, and remains his until he disposes of it.

Assignment of Copyright

Section 36(3) of the Act provides that ' no assignment of copyright (whether total or partial) shall have effect unless it is in writing signed by or on behalf of the assignor '. From the description in The Bookseller article of the 'elegant pas-de-deux' between indexer and publisher, it does not appear that there is, in general, any such written assignment of copyright, and it therefore remains, in law, vested in the indexer. It may be, however, that it is the intention and understanding of both parties that for the agreed fee the publisher shall obtain full rights in the index, to deal with as he wishes. If that is the case, there has been a good equitable assignment of the copyright, and the absence of legal formalities is relatively unimportant—the

publisher can call for a legal assignment to be executed in his favour by the indexer.

I should mention that since 1957 it has been possible to assign, both in law and equity, the copyright in a work which has not, at the time of the assignment, been written; the assignment takes effect as soon as the copyright comes into existence.

Existing Contracts

I am not told that any dispute has so far arisen as to ownership of copyright in an index. The only reported case that I know of which concerns an index is H. Blacklock & Co. Ltd. v. C. Arthur Pearson Ltd. [1915] 2 Ch. 376, where the index to Bradshaw had been copied. It was not argued that copyright did not subsist in indexes, and since this one had been compiled by the publisher, no question of ownership arose. I am therefore unable to give more than a general analysis of what the position might be.

When the contract between two parties is silent on the point over which a dispute arises, it is necessary to determine what was the intention of the parties at the time when they made the contract, and the Court will imply such terms as are necessary to give business efficacy to the contract. At the least, the publisher must obtain, if he pays anything, an irrevocable licence to use the index in the particular edition for which it was prepared. At most, he may, as I have said, become the owner, in equity, of the entire copyright.

An indexer who denies that he intended to assign his copyright, or the whole of it, is asserting that he expected to be able to demand further payment, should his index be used, for example, in a second edition or in translation. It is not easy to justify such an assertion unless it has been customary for indexers in general to receive payment for such further use of their copyright material, or unless it has been customary as between the particular indexer and publisher.

Mr. Cleeve is wrong to suppose that if copyright is allowed to an indexer then the entire publishing staff will be entitled to it also—the copy-editor, blurb-writer, etc., are employees of the publisher, so that copyright in their literary efforts vests in him, while the labours of typist and proof-reader are not such as to attract copyright.

Future Contracts

For the avoidance of disputes, it is desirable that there should be certainty as to what rights in the index the publisher is to enjoy. It should not be supposed that such clarification will necessarily result in increased rewards for the indexer, for while he is certainly at liberty to restrict the rights enjoyed by the publisher—he could licence the printing of one copy only if he wanted to—it is to be expected that the publisher will correspondingly restrict the remuneration. Furthermore, separate ownership of copyright is somewhat inconvenient, and the publisher will prefer to buy it outright. If, for example, the copyright in the index is not vested in the publisher, then he should, under the word INDEX, display the notice provided for in Art. one hundred and eleven of the Universal Copyright Convention—the symbol © accompanied by the indexer's name and the year of first publication.

The question of ownership of copyright should be raised when the indexer and publisher are negotiating their contract. If the indexer agrees to part with the copyright, then he should make a written assignment. If it is decided that the publisher should enjoy limited rights only, then this may be implemented either by a partial assignment of copyright, or by a licence to print, publish and sell, subject to the limitations agreed upon.

III. Index Typography

The Typography of Indexes

S. I. Wicklen

There are many aspects to the study of indexes. The Society has enumerated a few in its aims and objects. I would like to discuss one aspect which so far has received little attention – namely the typography of indexes.

An experienced indexer might well ask what has typography to do with indexing? But when we understand that typography simply expressed means the arrangement of type and printed matter on a book-page then the subject becomes relevant. I should like to attempt an answer to this question of how typography is worthy of the attention of the indexer.

In his essay on the *First Principles of Typography*, Mr Stanley Morison has this to say: '*Typography may be defined as the craft of rightly disposing printing material in accordance with specific purpose; of so arranging the letters, distributing the space and controlling the type as to aid to the maximum the reader's comprehension of the text*'. These principles are as applicable to an index, even more than the text of a book. If we substitute the word index in place of text in the quotation, then we as indexers have our starting point; for it is of greater importance to aid the reader 'to the maximum in comprehension of the *index*' even more so than in the text of a book.

It is, I think, agreed that the virtues of a good index should be: clarity in presentation; be easily understood in the way it conveys its message to the reader; and lastly – concise in the telling of its information, handy and of easy reference. An index that is vague and difficult to read (and I mean in the manner of its presentation) is a bad index. Yet how many indexes which have been carefully compiled by a skilled indexer are found when printed to be inadequate? The reason for their apparent failure is sometimes difficult to define. I suggest that many owe their inadequacy to poor typographical presentation. The index, as one indexer remarked recently, 'is regarded by the publisher as an afterthought and the printer as a nuisance'.

The average printer lavishes his skill and attention on the title-page of a book, which allows him to show type-arrangement in an attractive and pleasing design. Although the title-page, as William Morris pointed out, has little historical tradition behind it – the modern form being a degenerate style of self-advertisement introduced in the nineteenth century. An index, on the other hand, has a long established tradition behind it, dating back to the printer-scholars of early years of printing. It is perhaps evidence of the present standard of values that the index is now regarded as being among the oddments of the book. The very term will suggest to indexers how low in esteem the printer now considers the index. It is not surprising that the index being among the also-rans gets shabby treatment at the hands of printers. It follows logically that the

Reprinted from *The Indexer* 1, no. 2 (September 1958): 36–41.

best indexes are those to be found in the books of the University presses who, with a background of scholarship, have given some thought to the typography of indexes.

In the constitution of the Society of Indexers provision is made for the setting up of committees in special fields of knowledge and research. I should like to outline some of the points that a special committee in typography would have to consider in relation to the typography of indexes.

It will be in the preparatory stage of book-making that matters of typography will have to be considered. This is part of the increasing detail known as preparation of copy – for it is now accepted that copy should be prepared before presentation to the printer, thus saving the wasteful cost and time in adjusting the copy of a book when it has reached the setting stage.

It is not my aim here to give an account of what is involved in the preparation of copy for the printer, but merely to state that it is at this stage that typography should be settled – preferably by a typographer prior to handing out to the printer and thence to the operators engaged in mechanical composition. Again it is not my purpose to examine the merits of line composition (i.e. linotype and intertype) as against the monotype – although this topic is worthy of exploration – but not here.

I would again like to emphasize that the typographical details of a book should be decided before setting; for when the make-up stage after correcting is reached then it is too late for alterations in style and type to be made. Such alterations *are* made but at considerable addition to the cost of book-production.

In the make-up of a book the Index will be the last item among up to seventeen parts of a book. For those unacquainted with the technical terms in printing these parts are as follows:

Commencing with a *Half-title* then *Title-page*.
History of Book (containing the date of publication, and dates of reprints and revised editions) with imprint.
Dedication (if any).
Acknowledgements.
Contents.
List of Illustrations.
List of Abbreviations.
Preface to the book.
Introduction.
Corrigenda or *errata* (if any).
Text of Book.
Appendix.
Author's Notes.
Glossary.
Bibliography
and finally *Index*.

So it will be seen that from a printer's point of view the index is relatively unimportant.

It must be the aim of the Society to change this view and make the printer more index-conscious. William Aldis in his *The Printed Book* sums it up nicely when he writes that *'with the exception of Dictionaries and Cyclopaedias almost every book that aims at being useful requires an index to make its store of knowledge accessible'*.

ON THE SETTING OF INDEXES

'The labour and patience, the judgement and penetration which are required to make a good index, is only known to those who have gone through this most painful, but least praised part of a publication.' Sympathetic members of the Society will recognize that William Oldys, the eighteenth-century bibliographer who made this comment, knew all about indexing, and we share his lament. But please remember that the printer, too, has his problems in setting indexes.

The printer after all is only following what he considers to be the author's or publisher's scale of values. If those that compile indexes give the matter the thought and attention that it merits, then the printer will give the index the typographical treatment that it justly deserves. This is where our Society can give a lead by setting an example in index-typography and by providing an authoritative voice. One of the problems that the Society will have to contend with will be the highly conservative and traditional outlook of the printing industry, which will look askance at any proposed change in the format of the traditional book. There is, however, the opportunity for the Society of Indexers to work with typographers and by so doing getting their ideas across.

Of indexes there are many in shape and form. All are subject to considerable typographical ingenuity by the printer, sometimes with intelligence and discrimination. It is clear, however, that an index in whatever form that it may be must conform to certain principles.

In his book *Introduction to Typography*, Oliver Simon gives advice on the setting of indexes, and as the one-time director and typographer at the Curwen Press his words incorporate much that is worth while in the manner of setting good typography in the trade today. This book, which has been reprinted in the Penguin series, can be recommended to anyone desiring an authoritative introduction to book-typography.

Oliver Simon suggests that *'an index of two or more columns is to be preferred, set in type two points smaller than the text of the book. Begin each letter of the alphabet with even small capitals if an initial letter is not specified. Print page numbers immediately after the last word, with a comma before the figures. Divide columns by white space and not a rule.'*

These comments are worthy of study. Firstly, let us consider the recommendation for setting an index in two columns. One reason is that the eye has less distance to travel along the line when it is set in a narrow measure. The advantage of this is partly physical and partly psychological. The eye tires in the physical sense if it has a long distance to travel. In the text of a book this physical tiredness is compensated to some extent by the easy understanding of the printed words or sentences, for it has been proved that we really read groups of words and not individual words. The mind therefore by its comprehension counteracts the physical tiredness of the eye; this, together with the accustomed motion across the printed page from left to right, allows for easy reading. In an index the reverse happens, the eye is faced with a mass of individual words – and rebels. Our aim as indexers must be to split up these masses of words and give the printed page some resemblance of order by means of type-arrangement, in other words plan the index-page for easy reading. This can be achieved in some measure by splitting the page into columns. Another point is that in an index we are dealing with short lines of type-matter; when type-set in the full width of the page measure, such lines would appear unsightly giving a result confusing to the reader.

A second point arising from the suggested rules for setting an index is the use of white space instead of a printed rule to divide the index columns. Many printers continue to use rules – not because of any thoughtful and useful purpose, but because they have always done so. Modern trends in typography have shown that white space – or what is known sometimes as paper colour – is a useful aid to illuminate and define the printed area. A division or channel of white space dividing columns of closely arranged type – as an index must be – serves as a guide to the reader's eye. It is more effective than the printer's rule, which is a printer's device (or distraction) which is of greater value to him in his work than of assistance to the reader.

These basic principles have now to be applied to the various forms of indexes – of which there are many.

The general rules suggested above are suitable for a General Index at the end of a book and also a Subject Index which serves much the same purpose in some books. We also have an Index of First Lines which, as the title suggests, is an index of the first lines of poetry or a hymnal. Such an index has to have a different treatment from the typographic aspect from that of a general index. This index has to be set the full width of the printed area (i.e. text-page width) in the form of lines. It is the exception to the rule of dividing an index into columns. The lines will range on the left-hand side of the page finishing as they will, with white space or leaders (dots) leading to the page number set at the extreme right-hand edge of the type-measure. Books on typography suggest that white space should be left in the middle between the end of the line of poetry and its corresponding page number. I do not myself agree with this principle, for if the line ends rather short, as it may often do, there is a tendency for the eye to halt and lose its way to the page reference – this is obviously bad. If leaders are used, which as the name says lead the attention of the reader, this fault is avoided, the eye being led as desired by the author. It is good practice, however, to divide alphabetical groups in an Index of First Lines by white space as this aids understanding.

A Glossarial Index may be set in many ways. Such an index may contain more information than other forms of index. One character or term may contain quite a lengthy explanation including a number of references which will call for the setting of a number of lines. The item should stand out in some way from its explanatory matter. This may be achieved as follows: Setting to the full width of the type-measure in capitals ranging on the left-hand side, or alternatively in small capitals of the type-face in use, with a combination of capital and lowercase letters in the explanatory matter following – which should have an indention (a printer's term for indentation), the item thus standing out.

As a general rule the index starts on a right-hand (recto) page, this principle will apply to whatever form the index may take. It should be set as stated earlier in a type-face two points smaller than the text. Names of books and titles of periodicals should be set in italic.

Alphabetical groups can be divided by various devices. The setting of a large initial letter let-in to the first item of an alphabetical group, or a display initial centred in a line to itself appended to the group it refers. Again, the first words of each alphabetical group may be set in small capitals and each group divided by white space.

Other indexes are: Index to Proper Names, Index to Subjects, etc., and for these the general principles and treatment remain the same. A two-columned index may be separated by a channel of white space as stated previously. This is preferred to a rule – there is, however, an exception to this principle when it is considered preferable to use a rule. This is when the main headings in an index are followed by numerous sub-headings. To save repetition and space, dashes are used ranging on the left-hand side of the type-measure – sometimes these dashes are omitted and the two-columns appear ragged; to avoid this, and give some assistance to the reader, a rule may be inserted between the columns.

A book without an index has been described as like a country without a map. I would go further and say that the disposal and arrangement of types are the signposts to guide the traveller in this land of knowledge. If the signposts are vague and not easily seen (as they frequently are not) then the reader loses his way.

Ease of reference is an elementary matter frequently overlooked by printers of indexes. Whether it be a straight-forward historical narrative or a complicated work on science with numerous cross-references, an improvement can be made by judicious selection of typesizes and typefaces with an assortment and range of type styles, i.e. by setting in roman, italic, bold, etc.

Legibility at all times must be the key-note. The type size must not be so reduced that the entries are difficult to read. Often sub-headings are so closely set-up under the main headings that they are confusing to the reader. It might be suggested by the planning of some indexes that the author, publisher and printer were together in some dark mysterious plot to defeat the reader's understanding. Only the other day I came across an example of this plotting – a book on early Welsh poetry printed by the authority of the University of Wales Press Board (who, one would have thought, knew better). This book containing some three hundred pages with many scholarly references was ill-served by an index of one and three-quarter pages!

It is customary to set the index in a size of type smaller than that of the text matter. This is a reasonable rule to follow – but it should be set in a fair size. One would gather from the way that some printers set indexes that they are ashamed of its inclusion with the text of a book – and try to hide it. If distinction is made in the typographical size, let it be a reasonable one consistent with legibility and the usefulness of an index. The index deserves at least as good a treatment as the dust-jacket – which is thrown away. The index on the other hand remains an indispensable part of the book. The dropping in size of say a book set in 12 pt. text matter to an index set in 6 pt. or 8 pt. is excessive. A better proposition would be to reduce the size for setting the index by two points. This would avoid the misapprehension of the printer who, on instructions of the publisher, reduces the index by two sizes – a book set in 12 pt. type size may, in this way, get an 8 pt. index due to the printer not having an 11 pt. typeface. As the printer will hasten to point out *he* has followed instructions.

A word of caution here. Some consideration must be given to the selection of type faces, especially in relation to the x-heights of type designs. This refers to the actual part of the type that appears in print, the term derived from the lowercase x of the type face in use. A type face such as Times New Roman may have a large x-height, this will have the effect of appearing very large and prominent if used in an index. Types that have a large x-height require leading, that is the insertion by the printer of material to give the appearance of white space between lines. This matter of x-height, also seemingly only a detail, becomes important when a printer for some reason uses a different type face for the index than that used in the text of a book. Such is the position that if a book is set in Bembo, a very popular book face with a small x-height on its body size – that size being 12 pt., and the index for the particular book was set in Times New Roman 10 pt. The result when printed would be that the index would be equal in apparent size on the printed page – due to the large x-height of the type face used in the index.

It will be seen then that typography does have its contribution to make in the arrangement and disposal of printing material, thus aiding the indexer and the reader. Each book should be treated individually as a problem in design. Whether the book is a 'popular' work or a learned treatise its particular index should have individual treatment. The plan should conform to the character of the book – and the printer should have enough pride in his product to aim at good typography in his index as well as his text.

The Typography of Indexes

Robin Kinross

As against the typography of the body of a book, the more complex content of the index, and the heavier demands made on it by the reader, help to give the typography of the index special qualities. Through consideration of examples, certain arguments are advanced: that the typography of indexes cannot be considered separately from their content; that the typographic conventions of indexes that have been evolved are often sound and well adapted to the needs of the reader; that the particular problems of index typography can stimulate fresh typographic treatment, particularly when there is mutual understanding between indexer and typographer.

In contrast to the continuous text matter of the body of a book, the index has certain special features that make it a subject of interest to the typographer. The material of indexes is non-continuous and takes the form of a list. One reads both vertically and (within entries) horizontally. The language of indexes is compressed, and abbreviations are much employed. These things give the text matter of indexes their characteristic complexity. And one may see this complexity of content as placing demands, to which the editorial and typographic form of the index must correspond.

Another kind of demand is made by the reader of the book. The nature of this demand will be indicated when one says that most indexes are not read but used—flipped through and scanned. The time spent by the reader in thus using the index becomes a factor for consideration—as it is not in the usual reading process. Again, the typographic and editorial form of the index must

be adequate to these demands, in doing what can be done to assist—or, at least, not to impede—the reader.

In addition to meeting the requirements and constraints of the production process (which will be touched on at the end of this article), the index may therefore be seen as having to satisfy two sets of demands: those made by its content and those made by its readers. But this distinction is hard to maintain in consideration of any specific example. Thus, one may ask 'is this system of alphabetization appropriate?', or 'should the subheadings have been broken off rather than run on?'. But these questions can only be answered by a reader (or by the reader imagined by those making the index), and will therefore be decided in readers' terms, rather than in the illusory terms of 'what the content demands'.

Here one should mention another set of demands on an index—those made by the publisher. The limits on the space allowed to the index, and on the time and money allowed to the indexer, will have their effect on the final product. Such constraints need not be disadvantageous to the quality of the product. But whatever the outcome of these external pressures, in that they are unrelated to the essential issues of the typography of indexes, they need not be considered further here. One can simply notice that the publisher's typical demands on the index serve to add further complications to the process of making this most complex part of the book.

These special demands may lead to the suggestion that typographic form may make some difference to the ease with which a reader is able to use an index. The complexity of the material, and the reader's demands of speed and

Reprinted from *The Indexer* 10, no. 4 (October 1977): 179–185.

121

ease of discovery, suggest that appearance and configuration of material might be factors of significant importance to the process of use— as they do not seem to be in the case of simple continuous text matter. The question of what typography could do for an index will not however be addressed directly here. Rather, what will be considered are these necessary prior questions: is it possible to consider the typography of an index separately from its contents that is, what the indexer generates)? what happens if these two things, typographic form and the content, are considered separately? if— as will be suggested—the form and content of an index are inseparable, then what part could a typographer play in the making of an index?

MALMAISON.   *See* Napoleon.

MALMESBURY, Lord, xiii. 317.

MALONE, Edmond, Chatterton (*q.v.*); *Life of Reynolds*, xvi. 182; also ref. to, iii. 184; xi. 220, [358].

MALTA, English occupation of, i. 99; xiv. 163, 189, 190, .194, 196, 198; importance denied, i. 101; Knights Hospitallers (*q.v.*); Napoleon (*q.v.*); also ref. to, iii. 173, 175.

MALTHUS, Thomas Robert:
   American tribes, on the, i. 298.
   ' amorous complexion,' i. 242.
   answer to, vii. 221.
   argument summarized, i. 205.
   authors studied by, i. 189.
   character of (*The Sp. of the Age*), xi. 103–14.
   Cobbett's apostrophe to, vii. 351.
   ' cockney,' a, i. 288.
   Condorcet (*q.v.*).
   corn, on the monopoly of, i. 363.
   cultivation, on (quoted), i. 213.
   doctrines examined, vii. 332–7.
   Edinburgh Review, encouraged by, xi. 129.
   equality of man, argument against (quoted), i. 208.
   errors, two capital, i. 219.

Figure 1.   From the 'General index', compiled by James Thornton, to *The complete works of William Hazlitt*, Dent, 1934.

Figure 1 indicates the impossibility of treating as separate the content and the typographic form of an index. The details of typography— the system of punctuation and of capitalization, the use of italics, for example—are coincidental with, and follow from, the generation of the matter of the index. That subheadings in important entries are broken off rather than run on, for example, can only be described as a decision of editorial-design policy.

This index was produced before the specialized 'typographic designer' had begun to play much part in book production. And such a typographer might now question the decision to justify the lines (that is, where possible, to set lines of equal length), or the use of full points at the end of entries. But such reservations do not affect our judgement of this index as exemplary in its typography. And this high quality seems to stem largely from the standard of the editorial and indexing work. This is just one example of a body of model indexes that are well-designed in the widest sense—products of a particular (British) tradition of serious publishing.

Another example may help to show the soundness of conventional index typography. Looking at the index to Hart's *Rules* (Figure 2) one sees nothing remarkable. But consider this in relation to the contents pages list in the same book (Figure 3). The contents pages function as a preliminary index, giving the user an outline of the matter of the book. The typography of these pages, whereby page references are pushed to the right of the page, certainly discourages the reader from connecting heading and page number. Though, one might argue that this arrangement gives the page numbers an emphasis that they do not enjoy in the index. Both this emphasis and an easier horizontal connection could however be obtained by setting page numbers to the left of headings. But this would destroy the symmetry of the page. And this aim of symmetry and balance is, one suspects, the main consideration behind the convention adopted. When nowadays type is not set by hand in rectangular 'chases' (frames) the argument that this arrangement arises naturally in production no longer applies.

The different typographic treatment of the essentially similar material of index and contents page suggests that indexes have been comparatively free from the purely formal considerations of symmetry and balance—the 'dis-

138 INDEX

References generally, 48 ff.
  abbreviations in, 49, 56
  in bibliographical matter, 17
  in scientific works, 49
  least number of figures, 17
  to Acts of Parliament, 50–1
  to footnotes, 18
  to Government and official papers, 52
  to law reports, 51–2
  to library numbers, 17
  to manuscripts, 50, 52
  to page and footnote, 56
  to pagination, 17, 18
  to plays, 50
  to printed works, 48–52
  to symbols in line-blocks and plates, 12
  to the Bible, 6–7, 50
  to unpublished sources, 52
Roman numerals, 17, 18
  type, *see* Italic and roman type
Russian language, works in the, 110 ff.
  abbreviations, 112
  bibliographical lists, 112–13, 114
  capital and lower case, 113–15
  Cyrillic alphabet, 111–12
  dash, 115–16, 119, 120, 121
  division of words, 116–17
  en rule not used, 115 n.
  hyphens, 117
  letter-spacing, 112, 113, 117, 118–19
  marks of omission, 120
  New Orthography (1918), 110
  numerals, dates, etc., 118
  plays, stage directions, etc., 118–19
  punctuation, 115–16, 118, 119–21
  quotation marks, 112–13, 116, 117, 120–1
  reference figures, 118
  Slavonic languages, 110–12
  spacing, 121
  transliteration, 111, 113, 121

S., St., etc., 4

INDEX 139

ſ and ß, use of, 102
Scientific work generally, 52 ff.
  abbreviations for units, 53
  abbreviations in metric system, 5–6
  chemical names, 55
  degrees of temperature, 4
  displayed formulae, 54, 55
  italic for theorems, 23
  italic or roman for symbols, 53
  numbers above 9999 to be spaced, 55
  omit rule from square-root sign, 54
  preparation of copy, 52–3
  punctuation of formulae and equations, 55
  reduction of handwork, 53–5
  references to footnotes, 18
  symbols easily confused, 52–3
  text references to symbols in plates, 12
  titles of papers, how to print, 49
Scripture references, 6–7, 50
Semicolon, 38–9
Shakespeare's plays, references to, 50
Signs for reference indices, 18
  special, 57
Singular forms with plural numbers, 67
Slang terms, quotation marks for, 42
Slavonic languages, *see under* Russian language
Small capitals, accented in French, 85
  when to use, 12
Spacing generally, 56
  in abbreviated titles of books, 56
  in abbreviations of honours, etc., 56
  in French, 92, 95–6
  in Greek and Latin, 107
  in Italian, 108–9.
  letter-spacing in Russian, 112, 113, 117, 118–19, 121
  of German words for emphasis, 101
  of Greek words for emphasis, 107
  of last line of paragraph, 56
  of poetry, 56
  of references, 56
Spanish language, works in the, 122–4
  accent, 122–3

Figure 2. From *Hart's rules for compositors and readers*, Oxford University Press, Thirty-seventh edition, 1967.

play' values usually unrelated to use or to meaning. This may, it is suggested, be connected with the peculiar characteristics of indexes noted at the start of this article—their unusual clarity of function. This is something that is harder to attribute to a contents page list or, say, a list of illustrations. Such parts of a book simply do not have to meet the kind of demands made on an index. And one might go on to wonder whether indexers (and editors), having been left to get on with their work without much interference from book designers, have not thus been at an advantage, in being able quietly and unselfconsciously to develop conventions firmly based on the reader's needs.

It is suggested then that it has been characteristic of index typography (more so than the typography of other parts of a book) to employ conventions that best suit the reader—rather than, say, the designer or the printer. The effect that certain typographic practices, outside the indexer's sphere of influence, can have on an index is shown in Figure 4. In this index to a cookery book the majority of entries relate to only one page reference—recipes being the only items indexed. This fact perhaps encouraged the decision to set an em space between heading and page reference, rather than the conventional comma and word space. However, the printer's decision to justify has meant that—while this em space is consistently maintained—the spaces elsewhere will not be of fixed dimensions. To squeeze 'Gammon 18; Baked gammon 183' into a line, the compositor had to set '18;Baked' x CONTENTS

Punctuation marks and references to footnotes 47
Points in title-pages, headlines, etc. 47
Quotations 47
References to Printed and Manuscript Sources 48
Printed works 48
MS. and unpublished sources 52
Government and official papers 52
Scientific Work 52
Spacing 56
Special Signs and Symbols 57
Thorn, Eth, Wyn, Yogh 57
Vowel-Ligatures (Æ and Œ) 58

SPELLINGS

Alternative and Difficult Spellings 59
Doubling Consonants with Suffixes 63
Fifteenth- to Seventeenth-Century Works 65
Formation of Plurals in English 65
Words ending in -e and -y 65
Words ending in -o 66
Compounds 66
Formation of Plurals in Words of Foreign Origin 67
Hyphened and Non-Hyphened Words 70
Words ending in -able 75
Words ending in -ible 78
Words ending in -ize, -ise, and -yse 78
Words ending in -ment 79

DECIMAL CURRENCY 80

RULES FOR SETTING FOREIGN LANGUAGES

French 81
Abbreviations 82
Accented capitals 84
Awkward divisions: abbreviated words and large numbers expressed in figures 85
Capital and lower case 85
Division of words 89
Grave and acute accents 90
Hyphens 91
Italic and roman type 91
Metal-rules 92
Numerals 92
Punctuation 93
Quotation marks 93
Reference figures 95
Spacing 95

CONTENTS xi

German 96
Abbreviations 97
Accented letters 98
Apostrophe 98
Division of words 98
Double letters 99
Hyphens 99
Initial capitals 100
Letter-spacing for emphasis 101
Numerals 101
Punctuation 101
Quotation marks 102
Use of ſ and ß 102
Greek 102
Aspirates and accents 103
Cardinal numbers 105
Division of Greek and Latin words 105
Punctuation 107
Spacing 107
Italian 107
Division of words 107
Spacing 108
Oriental Languages in Roman Type 109
Russian 110
Abbreviations 112
Bibliographical lists 112
Capital and lower case 113
Dash 115
Division of words 116
Hyphens 117
Italic and letter-spacing 117
Numerals, dates, reference figures, fractions 118
Plays 118
Punctuation 119
Quotation marks 120
Spacing 121
Transliteration 121
Spanish 122
Accent 122
Division of words 123
Orthography 123
Punctuation 124
Quotation marks 124

BIBLIOGRAPHY 125

INDEX 126

Figure 3. From *Hart's rules for compositors and readers*, Oxford University Press, Thirty-seventh edition, 1967.

without intervening space. And thus the dislocation occurs, whereby one groups page reference ('18') and entry ('Baked gammon') wrongly. This unfortunate incident illustrates the fundamental objection to justification of lines: the variation of word space entailed introduces an arbitrary element into the system of words and space that constitutes text matter.[1] In normal continuous text matter this may not be of great concern. But in the more complex configurations of an index, where horizontal space carries more precise meanings, justification begins to become a significant factor and, one would suggest, an unhelpful one. The conventional narrowness of width of the lines of an index contributes to the problems attendant on justification. The mistake of Figure 4 could have been avoided by setting equal spaces between words and by carrying whole items over onto new lines. But in any case, whether justified or not, the more conventional, watertight system of punctuation and normal word space would prevent such misreading.

Objections, similar to those made against the example of Figure 4, could be applied to the index shown in Figure 5, where lines are justified and an unconventional system of space and punctuation is employed. But, though the risk of confusion is there, in practice the composition avoids the dislocations of Figure 4. This index is an interesting example of the kind of typographic innovations that are possible

Fritter batter 55
Ham fritters   160
Normandy apple fritters   110
Split pea fritters 99
Fudge, chocolate 226

Gammon 18; Baked gammon   183
   Stuffed gammon rolls 129
Garbure 158
Garlic soup 120
Gazpacho 165
Gingerbread men 224
Gingerbread, Orkney oatmeal 224

Figure 4.   From Jocasta Innes, *The pauper's cookbook*, Penguin Books, 1971.

---

photopolymer 222
pica – about 12-point: as 12-point, used as a
   unit of typographical measurement – 34
Pickering, William 90 100
pitch-line – line across bed of press to show
   how far printing-surface can extend without
   fouling grippers – 235-6
planographic – see *surface processes*
Plantin, Christophe 84: *Plantin* (type)
   84-5 401-7, x-height of 73, & paper 74, &
   Times 106, proportions of 110, & verse
   124, examples 132 136-7 154
plastic stereos 220
plate – illustration printed separately from
   text – 321-3, numbering of 143 282, &
   list of illustrations 194, & colophon 203,
   & paper 300 304 310 365, & imposition
   318, folding 323, & estimating 367, &
   proofs 374-5, & tenacity 375: *plate-glazing*
   – method of smoothing paper surface –
   298-9 302: see also *albumen plate, duplicate
   plate*
platen-press – press which brings paper and
   printing-surface together as plane surfaces
   – 233 236
plays 109 124 128 255
pochoir – stencil process – 252
poetry – see *verse*

Figure 5.   From Hugh Williamson, *Methods of book design*, Oxford University Press, Second edition, 1965.

in indexes—given the particular needs of a particular index. That such innovations were carried out in this case, and that this index seems to be good and useful, may follow from the fact that author, indexer and typographer were one man. The inclusion here of definitions of terms (between en dashes) is an example of an author's involvement with the index. Some of the practices adopted seem uncomfortable. For example, the use of a colon to mark a conclusion, where one is used rather to connect items on either side of this mark. But, taken as a whole, this index is a good instance of the unity of typography and indexing, and it is a good argument for indexing done with full awareness of typographic possibilities.

That indexes are a peculiar and distinct part of a book is again suggested by the next example (Figure 6). The width of indentation of the vertically aligned sub-headings is determined by the natural length of words in the main heading. In this feature, therefore, the content of the heading and subheading (before the point of indentation) determines its visual or typographic form. This is, however, something that has often been the aim of selfconsciously radical typographers, but it is achieved here (unselfconsciously, one supposes) in a book that is elsewhere traditional in appearance. This system does of course use more space than the traditional narrow column setting; on the other hand, the reader may find a readier access through it. However one judges this, the point that may be made here is that this typographic innovation derives (one supposes) from the author-indexer considering the nature of her material—and not from any considerations of the designers or producers of the book; for elsewhere in the book the typographic configurations are imposed on, rather than derived from, the content.

One should make clear however that the 'content' here referred to is the apparent or surface content of the words, as against the deeper content of the meaning of the material—its hierarchies and system of internal relationship. The visual patterns which the surface content produces depend merely on how much space the words occupy, and, in that words have no intrinsic relationship with the things that they denote, the visual patterns of words are arbitrary. In order to carry the deeper content of the material, a non-arbitrary visual system (of indentation, word-space, line space, punctuation, capitalization and so on) must be devised—one that provides a suitable coding system for the

The English Book Trade | *Index*

Quarterly-book, 257–8, 442
in binding, 342

Rags, 190–1, 337
bleaching, 327
gatherers, 193, 196
importation, 326–7, 333, 336
scarcity, 325, 333–4
taxation, 327, 335
Railway bookstalls, 415, 432
Reformation, 30, 32, 49
Refugees, paper-makers, 194–5
type-founders, 177
Remainders, definition of, 434
destroyed, 326
exported, 421
prices, 433–4
sold at dinners, 405
Remigius, 192
Renaissance, 49
Rents, 165–9
Reprints, American, 421, 424–7
French, 420–3
German, 421
Prices, 414–16
Re-sale price maintenance, 432–44
Reviews, 409, 430
Rolling machine, 347–8
Roman Empire, book production in, 17–18
Rotary press, 280
Routledge, introduced esparto, 336
Roworth's press, 271
Royalties, 410, 416
on reprints, 428
paid in copies, 219
Rubber, use in offset printing, 320–1

St. Monday, 383
St. Paul's Churchyard, 81–2, 85–6, 165–6, 253
Sale dinners, 405
Sanitation of factories, 363–4
Savage's wood engravings, 313
Schäffer, 327–8
Scholar-printers, 32, 149
Schools, effect on demand, 36–40, 53–4, 446–7
Search of printing-houses, 125, 136, 144

Seasons, The, copyright, 119–20, 420
Secondary occupations, 95–7
Senefelder, invention of lithography, 306
Seres, patents, 101, 103
Series, publishers', 432
Service books, early editions, 24–5
patent for, 101, 106–7
prices, 240
Sewing, 345
machine, 350
Shares in books, 110, 225–6, 429–30
Sheepskin, 213, 342, 354
cost, 212, 243
fines for using, 207
See also Parchment
Size, of books, 95, 418
of the edition, 92–5, 300, 331, 404, 412, 414, 416
of the firm, 86–8, 356–9
of binderies, 348
of the industry, 80–86, 449
Skiver, patent for, 213
Soap, ingredient of ink, 323
Social conditions, 150–3, 367–72
Socialism among printers, 381–2
Society for the Encouragement of Learning, 223–4
Solaces, 146, 158–9
Sörensen's composing machine, 283
Specialisation, by apprentices, 367
in manuscript production, 24
of demand, 448
of production and distribution, 59–79
due to shortage of type, 175
effect on costs, 407
encouraged by patents, 109
Spilman, 192–4
Stalls, 82, 254, 415, 432
Stanhope, press, 271–2, 287
stereotype process, 301
Star Chamber decrees regarding bookselling, 255–6
importation of books, 261
licensing, 31, 33
number of apprentices, 133–4
number of presses, 86–7, 171
number of printers, 83
provincial printing, 81
type-founding, 62
unemployment, 154

494

Figure 6. From Marjorie Plant, *The English book trade*, Allen and Unwin, Second edition, 1965.

material, rather than an attempt at literal representation of it. But this non-arbitrary system of visual coding is, couched in theoretical language, no more than the aim of any serious index.

Examples such as those of Figure 5 and (perhaps) Figure 6 would seem to confirm the suggestion that the peculiar demands of content of an index encourage clear (and fresh) thinking about typographic form. For, as well as exhibiting a body of sound typographic convention, indexes also show a capacity to innovate and experiment in response to the needs of the occasion. Figure 7 is included here as a warning against the acceptance of such a suggestion without qualification. It is taken from an index with which almost everything is wrong, in its construction and in its typography. One may mention the lack of system and indentation, punctuation, capitalization, and the separation of headings and page references that necessitates the use of 'leaders'. Such an example summarizes all the possible sins of making indexes. But, though a counter example, it does serve to support a thesis of this article—that the content of an index and its typographic form are related intimately and organically. Typographic disorder inevitably follows from disorder in construction; and, equally, typography by itself (if it could be 'by itself') cannot be effective with bad copy.

These examples may suggest the diversity and the particularity of each index. As every indexer knows, there are limits to the application of rules and conventions—there will always be awkward decisions to be made. For this reason

Figure 7.   From Low Warren, *Journalism from A to
Z*, Herbert Joseph, Third edition, 1935.

one may be suspicious of the prospects of empirical research supplying useful advice on
making indexes. The attempt to apply such
research seems to rest on the fallacy that one
can draw general conclusions from particular
(and often rather strange) instances. And, given
the typical complexity of an index, it seems unlikely that much can be learnt from the necessarily
simplified indexes that supply the test pieces for
experiments.

Also, empirical research isolates factors for
evaluation, hoping to report on the effectiveness
of certain conventions. This isolation of features
denies the essential unity of form and content
in an index. One cannot discuss, or test, the
effectiveness of, say, letter-by-letter alphabetization or bold type without considering the
function of such conventions in a particular
case. And this consideration will bring in all
the issues that relate to the decision about
alphabetization or bold type.

This brief investigation of the typography of
indexes has suggested that the content of an
index and its typographic form are organically
related. The stress laid on this may have implied that a typographer can contribute nothing
to index making. Such a suggestion would be
misleading. For although much of the typo-

graphic form will be generated by the indexer
and editor, decisions that they take in this work
of generation could, and should, be significantly
affected by advice from someone with specialist
typographic knowledge. Coding conventions
such as the use of bold or italic or small capitals,
or the use of special signs, depend on the facilities
offered by the system of composition used. A
thorough understanding of typographic possibilities may, as the case of Figure 5 indicated,
help to meet the special demands of a particular
index.

This function for the typographer of supplying
advice concerning composition becomes especially important with the demise of hot-metal
composition. Such systems (Monotype, Linotype and Intertype) have been the traditional
means for setting books; Monotype, as the
most complex composition system, has been
able to provide rich possibilities for typographic
coding. The use of much less sophisticated
systems in book production introduces different
sets of typographic conventions. Indexes to be
set on a machine that cannot supply italic, say,
need to be designed to allow for this—designed,
that is, from the point when the indexer starts
work. And with the growing practice of printing
books set on the typist's (or author's, or indexer's)
own typewriter, this need to incorporate design
considerations at an early stage becomes even
more acute.

One might suggest then that indexers would
benefit from an education in typography. Equally,
it will be clear that typographers must understand the procedures of indexing—for even the
more purely typographic decisions, such as the
determination of line length or space between
lines, will proceed from an appreciation of the
nature of the copy. The work of indexing and
of typography forms a unity that is ideally
taken on by one person. It would not be realistic,
however, to see the indexer-typographer as more
than the rare exception. But one may say that
the indexer and the typographer should certainly
get to know each other better.

All the figures are reproduced by kind permission
of the respective publishers.

Reference
1.   Hartley, J. and Burnhill, P. Experiments with
unjustified text. *Visible language*, **5** (3) Summer
1971, 265-278.

Card Indexes or Printed Pages:

Physical Substrates in Index Evaluation*

E. J. Coates

General ideas on indexing have been greatly influenced by performance testing, which began in the 1960s. It is suggested that the exclusive use in these tests of the single-record-per-index-card form could limit the generality of the ideas to be derived from the tests. Panoramic display forms of index (of which the printed page is the commonest example) offer users enhanced mobility in relation to the file, which in turn facilitates recognition of elements of structure in the displayed sequence. Structured data may be preferentially accessible to enquiry or comprehension.

Typographical resources supply structure to printed indexes, in particular by forming visual blocks of conceptually homogeneous material— to the extent that the mechanics of filing order and the grammar of the indexing language allows or facilitates this. Examples from BNB (PRECIS) and BTI are given for illustration, the problems of the classified printed index are mentioned briefly, and suggestions are made on the lines of research on printed indexes which might usefully be pursued.

Substrates in index performance tests

The Cranfield Projects of the 1960s mark the beginning of systematic evaluation of indexing systems.[1,2,3] More than a decade later the Aberystwyth study on Printed Subject Indexes seems poised to undertake a closer examination than has hitherto been attempted on the manner and extent to which typography and the display of a swathe of index records on a printed page influences index performance.

*Based on a talk given at the Study Institute on Printed Subject Indexes, Aberystwyth, July 1975.

The time-lag between the two events gives food for thought. In the interval, tests involving printed indexes have been carried out,[4,5,6,7] but there seems to have been no concentration upon typographical factors as such, apart from the ergonomic study of Spencer, et al.[8,9] Nor has there been attention to the possible interaction between indexing language properties and the possibilities of page display. Moreover, in this same interval it is Cranfield, rather than the later projects, which has shaped what has become the accepted wisdom. It may be wondered whether this wisdom may have been slanted by the total absence from the Cranfield view of things of typography and of the panoramic display of index records on pages. Without any question, the exclusion was justified; equally without question, both the design of the Cranfield tests and their results were to some extent influenced by the use, as physical substrates, of index cards, each bearing a single index record, filed in drawers. For example Cranfield 1 compared the performance of four indexing languages, two of which were based on the alphabet alone, and two of which used a classified output supported by alphabetical indexes. There was thus a fundamental difference in the capabilities offered by the two kinds of indexing language. The classified languages were designed to utilise the effect of graduated collocation of related subjects. The other two languages were designed expressly on the basis of ignoring this effect. The test did not in fact evaluate the capability of the classified collocation of related subject items as a possible aid or hindrance to retrieval. As far as the test was concerned the classified files of the two classified index languages might well have been arranged in random subject order, as long as the randomly ordered subject locations were correctly given in the supporting alphabetical subject indexes. It is hard not to relate this

Reprinted from *The Indexer* 10, no. 2 (October 1976): 60–68.

apparent anomaly to the single-record-on-card substrate, to the unstated assumption that physical related subject collocation that is not immediately accessible to sight (the card index file situation) is of so marginal a significance that it was not worth designing an experiment to test it. An instance of the effect of the single-item-on-card substrate on test results occurs in connection with the problem of defining a cut-off point in the tests, at which searchers should end a search. In fact in Cranfield 1 this cut-off point was largely at the uncontrolled discretion of the searcher. The question of effort and endurance in searching is one of the most elusive aspects of indexing, as anyone who has had to train others in reference searching skills knows, and it was not necessarily a design fault that search cut-off point was left uncontrolled. Nevertheless search cut-off decisions contributed to the results on performance of the systems tested, and the actual level of cut-off in a given instance would ultimately be affected by the particular effort of grasping the sides of a manageable batch of cards in the drawer, separating each card in turn from the batch, turning each over, the turning over of a given card often taking longer than the time in which it takes to forget precisely what was on the preceding card. This necessary series of actions gives rise to a characteristic cut-off level in searching. With a substrate of a different kind, involving only eye or head movements in passing from one index record to the next, a very different cut-off level would possibly have been recorded. In view of the existence of such substrate dependent effects, tests involving a different substrate form might be expected to generate some modifications to the Cranfield inheritance of basic notions about indexing.

Visual mobility and structure recognition in "panoramic output"

Though not totally alien to card index files (there are, after all, printed catalogue card files, printed index cards for publishers' forthcoming new books) typography has a relatively minor role in any system in which each index record is seen in isolation by the user. A project on evaluation of Printed Subject Indexes must be concerned with the page-in-codex substrate.

The essential new factor in the page form of index is that the user has, compared with the user of a card file, an *enhanced mobility*, viz., eye mobility as opposed to the relatively cumbersome manipulation-dependent mobility of the card index user. Present understanding of the effect

upon retrieval performance of this ability to shift attention, with little effort up and down the file from the point of entry, is minimal. Does it improve or degrade precision? Does it encourage the user to refine, reformulate or adjust the stated search target? And if so is the encouragement acted upon? Is its effect only diffusely stimulative? Is the panoramic view which it offers of a wide band-width of knowledge in some significant way representative of our experience of knowledge as a continuum rather than as discrete units of this and that? Considerations such as these might seem to have almost exclusive application to classified indexes alone, but we must bear in mind that a certain amount of incidental collocation of related topics does occur in the purely alphabetical index too.

It is reasonable to think of the printed page as the *output* of the total information storage system representing the work of preparing and producing a printed index. The mechanisation lobby in the information field will normally stress the separateness of the output from the rest of the system. This emphasis is part of the process of drawing attention to the fact that a single mechanised information system may be switched at will to produce several different outputs. Research on printed indexes would be unwise to accept the demarcation line between a system and its output as an entirely clear one. Or to put the same point in differently slanted terms, it should be looking for possible interactions between indexing language and structure factors on the one hand and printed page output on the other. In this connection the purview of the research should not exclude a close look at the system/output demarcation line in computerised information-retrieval systems, for which typographical questions may be remote. The concept of multiple, variable, or adjustable outputs may be validly extrapolated from the general properties of digital data processing, and yet not be readily realised in practice. Too often even small changes in output program modules are found to involve unwanted repercussions in other parts of the total mechanised indexing system. PRECIS is perhaps a rather instructive example of the problems in this area. Formally in PRECIS the division between indexing system as such and the output design is very clear. Indeed, the contrast between the forms of the input and the output is quite striking. The possibility of flexible output is one of the promotional features of PRECIS, yet, though the system has been in operation for five years, it has not yet output a single-sequence file of subject entries and cross-references. The time scale here is perhaps some measure of the effort that may be involved in implementing the inherent potential for flexible output which mechanised systems undoubtedly have.

When we look at a manual indexing system designed primarily with the conventional substrate—the single record-bearing index card—in mind, we observe that what lies between indexing system and indexing output is not so much a sharp demarcation line, but a middle grey band where practices contributing to the index structure are in force. These practices markedly affect output, but they are often not specifically prescribed in the rules of the indexing language. Filing and alphabetisation rules belong to this category of procedures. They are often omitted from the rules for using index languages, and when they are included it is not unheard of for the system to lay down prescriptions which prove disastrous. Two examples which come to mind are the former practice of the Library of Congress in the filing of subheadings in its subject catalogue, and the filing of punctuation symbols in the Universal Decimal Classification. The result in both cases is complicated without compensating benefit to the user. It is interesting to note that it is only the mechanisation prospect which has brought the question of file order and alphabetisation into prominence, generating in the process the somewhat dubious concept of 'filing order for mechanised files', which suggests that the file order is for the convenience of the machine rather than a vital factor in presenting information to the user. For indexes in the printed page format, file order may make or mar the possibility of the material organising itself into block structures.

Block structures assume some importance when the index user is thought of as an active entity capable of moving through the file. The extent to which the user is regarded as having an active or a passive role in the process of extracting information from store is very much a function of available hardware. When economic and methodological difficulties weigh heavily upon the planners of indexing systems, and when computers are at the same time available, planners tend to cheer themselves with the reflection that the user is an intelligent and enterprising being, for whom it is good that he should be obliged to shoulder those parts of the information processing task that simple quasi-clerical procedures leave

undone. Many ongoing information systems are founded upon this convenient point of view, despite the fact that there are often awkward problems in justifying on social economic grounds repeated effort by individual users carrying out searches at different times in order to establish something which could perhaps have been indicated once and for all at input.

On the other hand, when only the conventional card-file substrate is available, it becomes highly convenient for information specialists to see the index user as a passive detector. As conditioned by this substrate, the system supplies the user with the called-up output set within a frame or surround designed to rivet attention upon a single index record. Thus a premium is set upon a user's *immobility* in relation to the file. Each record displayed precludes anything approaching a near-instantaneous sight of any other record. It is true that file guides may be inserted with the object of encouraging the user to move into another part of the file, but they are a very limited asset. Anyone who has tried to guide a short file knows of the inconvenient tendency of guide tabs to mask each other. Anyone who has tried to guide a very long file knows that there are never enough lateral tab positions and that, accordingly, logic has to be compromised, thus misleading users. It is very doubtful whether guiding significantly mitigates the immobilising effect of the single record-per-card substrate.

Immobility in relation to the file inhibits user recognition of any elements of structure that the sequence may display, and this effect is in no way offset because of the facility which cross-referencing offers for 'hopping' mobility between distantly separated points in the file. Is structure important in the display of information? Some support for an affirmative answer can be discerned in the manner in which knowledge itself has developed. For instance, in natural science crystallographers and solid-state physicists have built up over a few decades a vast and detailed corpus of knowledge of ordered states of matter. By comparison, much less is known about disordered states such as liquids and glasses, and much of what is known about them is in relation to intermediate or semi-ordered states, such as those which may occur in melts adjacent to a solidifying interface. The disparity in the amount and detail of knowledge in these two areas may, of course, be temporary only, but this hardly affects the picture of human enquiry grappling first with what is ordered, later with what is not ordered. Is the disparity just a historical accident, does it merely result from the coincidence of particular instrumentation and mathematical tools, all leading to the preferential detection of ordered states, or have we here a basic epistemological factor—viz., that what is ordered is somehow preferentially accessible to human enquiry and comprehension? Do we take more kindly to, do we more easily take cognizance of, structured as against unstructured data. If so, the existence of elements of structure in the output data of indexing systems may be of some importance.

cable adapter, for information communication cable 1–22310
cable adapter 1–22310
CAMAC scheme 1–17747
Captor, for natural-language keyboarding 1–22317
channel to control unit interface 1–24508
channel-to-channel adapter for I/O interface switching 1–12788
components for computer communications, review 1–15314
computer connections, principles 1–20194
computer interface, hardware arrangements 1–15315
computer interface, turnkey message switching, cyclic and queueing executives 1–15317
computer terminals evaluation, for information retrieval systems 1–19667
concentrator for remote operation, systems 1–17760
conf. Neuilly-sur-Seine, France, (1970) 1–14584
controller for output devices, cct., patent 1–22326
curved-line drawings, incremental encoding, data comparison 1–14196
data transmission conference, Lausanne (1970) 1–22319
detector circuit, for function sensing in data-carrying pulse signals, patent 1–15165
digital information buffer function, queueing operation and memory 1–15303
digitisers, functions and home assembly 1–20191
display terminal for conversational communication 1–12818
e.c.g. transmission from patient to cardiologist via telephone system 1–23593
elastic loop interface for data insertion and extraction 1–12781
electro-pneumatic convertor, for computer operation of hydraulic integrated adder 1–21030
electrolytic cells for remote timing 1–24505
Firmware programmable read-only memory packages 1–15307
gathering, design 1–24517
Hewlett-Packard 3360A design considerations 1–12771
human factors in telecommunications, symposium, London, (1970) 1–23531
hybrid computer interface, patent 1–22404
I/O control, patent 1–15323
input devices, analogue, for process computers 1–24519
input-output devices organisation for control computers 1–17716
input/output module, for processor interface 1–22312
instrument connections to computers 1–22315
integrated computer network, development 1–12787
inter unit coupling of computer systems 1–20202
interface, CAMAC with small computer, characteristics 1–17729
interface, clip-on design for process control 1–17733
interface, for CDC 3000 computer 1–24521

Figure 1

Block structure

An alphabetical index in its raw (or free-text) state is perhaps analogous to disordered matter. Fig. 1 shows an example of such material culled from free-language modifiers used to amplify controlled index headings. By itself the sequence of modifiers appears rather uninviting and unlikely to generate much optimism in a searcher. However, if we submit such raw material to a certain amount of interventionist processing, it will exhibit 'condensed' or 'solid' areas of a relatively tightly connected nature. These areas form visual blocks, each associated with a high degree of conceptual homogeneity. This block structure is a very simple phenomenon arising out of the clumping together of identical lead-in terms or phrases. It arises only in panoramic files where the records are individually short—as in indexes. It does not appear in files of longer records, such as abstracts. In contrast to the free-text example, Figs. 2 and 3 exemplify indexes

Pilotage. Shipping. Great Britain
— *Inquiry reports* 387.1'66
Pilots' navigation instruments. Civil aeroplanes 629.135'1
Pineal eye. Vertebrates 596'.01'823
Pinter, Harold. Drama in English
Homecoming — *Critical studies* 822'.9'14
Pipe fittings. Engineering components
— *Standards* 621.8'672
Pipe organ building industries. Durham
Harrison and Harrison Limited, *to 1973*
338.7'68'1816624281
Pipe organ playing. Great Britain
Organisations: Royal College of Organists — *Yearbooks*
786.5'06'242
Pipe organs built by Renn, Samuel. Musical instruments
786.6'22'4
Pipelines
See also
Countryside adjacent to proposed Amlwch-Stanlow pipeline
Pipelines
Concrete water pipelines 621.8'672
Construction — *Standards* 621.8'672
Pipes
See also
Hoses
Tubes
Pipes
Carton steel compression couplings & stainless steel compression couplings — *Standards* 621.8'672
Concrete water pipes 621.8'672
Pitch-impregnated fibre drain pipes — *Standards*
621.8'672
Propylene-ethylene copolymer pressure pipes — *Standards* 621.8'672
Pipework *See* Piping systems
Piping systems
See also
Pipe fittings
Pipelines
Pipes
Piping Systems
Thermoplastics piping systems — *Standards* 621.8'672
Pips. Fruit
See also
Cultivation from pips, seeds & stones
Pirates
to 1973 — Juvenile literature 910'.453
Pisces
See also
Blue whiting
Cichlidae
Eels
Salmon

Figure 2

il.
PILES : Legs : Platforms : Off shore drilling : Petroleum. See PETROLEUM : Drilling, Off shore : Platforms : Legs : Piles
PILOTS' CABINS : Aircraft. See AIRCRAFT : Cabins, Pilots'
PIPELINES : Off shore terminals : Tankers : Ships. See TANKERS : Ships : Terminals, Off shore : Pipelines
PIPELINES; Steel : Petroleum. See PETROLEUM : Pipelines; Steel
PIPELINES : Town gas. See GAS, Town : Pipelines
PIPES
Related Headings:
DUCTS
PIPES; Copper : Water installations : Buildings. See BUILDINGS : Water installations : Pipes; Copper
PIPES, Curved : Turbulent shear airflow. See AIRFLOW, Shear,, Turbulent : Pipes, Curved
PIPES : Detonation : Waves : Velocity fluctuations : Measurement : Interferometry, Microwave
Study of unstable detonations using a microwave interferometer. D.H. Edwards, G. Hooper & J.M. Morgan. *J. Phys. D: Appl. Phys.*, 7 (21 Jan 74) p.242-7. *il.refs.*
PIPES : Flow : *n*-Hexane. See *n*-HEXANE : Flow : Pipes
PIPES : Flow : Measurement : Tracers
Indicator dilution measurement of mean transit time and flow in a straight tube. D.A. Lane & J.A. Sirs. *J. Phys. E: Sci. Instrum.*, 7 (Jan 74) p.51-5. *il.refs.*
PIPES : Molecular flow : Cold neutrons. See NEUTRONS, Cold : Molecular flow : Pipes
PIPES (Sewers) Concrete,, Damaged : Diamond sawing
Damaged sewerage pipe removed by diamond sawing. *Ind. Diam. Rev.* (Mar 74) p.102-3. *il.*
PIPES; Steel : Cooling systems : Sodium cooled fast nuclear reactors. See NUCLEAR REACTORS, Fast,, Sodium cooled : Cooling systems : Pipes; Steel
PIPES, Thin walled : Flow : Vibrations
On the stability of thin pipes with an internal flow. D.S. Weaver & B. Myklatun. *J. Sound Vib.*, 31 (22 Dec 73) p.399-410. *refs.*
PISTONS (Hydraulic machinery) Heads : Seals
Heavy duty gland and piston head seals. *Hydraul. Pneum. Pwr.*, 19 (Dec 73) p.481-2. *il.*
PITCH, Bituminous : Spectroscopy, Infra-red
Infra-red identification of asphaltic and coal-tar pitches. A.B. Moustafa. *J. Oil Colour Chem. Assoc.*, 57 (Jan 74) p.44-5. *refs.*
PITCH, Bituminous—P.V.C. . See P.V.C. —PITCH, Bituminous
PITCH, Bituminous—Polyvinylidene chloride : Spectroscopy, Infra-red
Modification of pitches by poly(vinylidene chloride) and poly(vinyl chloride). Y. Yamashita & K. Ouchi. *Fuel*, 53 (Jan 74) p.3-7. *refs.*
PITCH, Bituminous—Polyvinylidene chloride : X-ray diffraction
Modification of pitches by poly(vinylidene chloride) and poly(vinyl chloride). Y. Yamashita & K. Ouchi. *Fuel*, 53 (Jan 74) p.3-7. *refs.*
PITCH : Coal tar. See COAL TAR : Pitch
PITCHBLENDE : Flotation : Collectors : Cupferron—Fuel oil
Flotation of pitchblende with a chelating agent and fuel oil. A.M. Marabini & G. Rinelli. *Trans. Instn. Min. Metall.*, 82 (Dec 73) p.C225-8. *il.refs.*
PITOT TUBES : Response
Response of Pitot probes in turbulent streams. H.A. Becker & A.P.G. Brown. *J. Fluid Mech.*, 62 (8 Jan 74) p.85-114. *refs.*

Figure 3

which show block structure, the *British National Bibliography* using the PRECIS system and *British Technology Index*. Evident here is the simple reinforcing effect of repetition of vertically aligned terms not too far separated by other text matter. It is almost certainly the block formed by the repetition of the leading terms which constitutes the first impression on the initial sight of a column or page. Conversely a continuously varying lead term sequence without the stable intermissions caused by such repeats may well be off-putting to a user consulting files of over a certain threshold length or degree of complexity. Possibly we have here the valid perception behind the sometimes misconceived advocacy of limited vocabularies. A heavily blocked alphabetical index structure will indeed yield fewer lead terms and phrases than will a free-language index file of the same material.

Putting typography to work

Typographical resources have to accomplish certain essential discriminations in addition to the discrimination of blocks. Functionally different types of record which appear in the same file may have to be distinguished. Individual records of the same type must be distinguished from each other. It may be necessary to use typography to identify particular parts of records. If special measures are put into force to emphasise block structure, it must not be at the cost of omitting these other features. The typographical resources at disposal for this multiple task are: (1) type-face variations, (2) upper/lower-case variations, (3) left-indentation variations, (4) vertical space variations, and (5) type-size variations.

Neither the PRECIS nor the *BTI* samples individually or together demonstrate all the possible typographical means of drawing attention to block structure. The repeating lead-in terms may be typographically emphasised, or they may be left with the normal typographical features of the rest of the file with reliance placed upon the weight of repetition itself to supply emphasis. Alternatively and perhaps paradoxically, the necessary emphasis may be achieved by deleting all repeats after the first example, thus exposing a set-off left indentation of a series of subheadings. The last possibility is more often than not the rule in book indexes. Fig. 4 is an example.

Considering the PRECIS and *BTI* specimens in more detail, it is apparent that PRECIS relies upon the bold type which it uses for all of its lead-in terms to form visual blocks where the file-ordering rules and structure of the PRECIS language allow them to be formed. *BTI*, on the other hand, relies upon upper case whether in plain Roman or Bold to emphasise possible blocks. Neither of the two specimens uses left indentation (a blocking device in continuous text) for the purpose. On the issue of whether blocks are to be emphasised by the weight of vertically adjacent repeating words, or by the device of deleting the repeats, both samples try to make the best of both worlds in somewhat similar ways. PRECIS drops repeats of identical 'Lead-Qualifier' lines, and also drops repeats of the left-hand side of its 'see also' cross-references. *BTI* uses the dropping-off of repeats to form blocks of its entry-type records and of its 'related heading' cross-references. On the other hand, *BTI* retains repeats to form blocks of its inversion-type cross-references. The *BTI* use of both repeat-dropping and repeat-retaining techniques thus contributes not only to block formation but also to discriminating between various types of record. Other record-type

Train control, automatic, 18 41 *et seq.*	Trickle charging, 7 99
lighting, 18 48	Triode(s), 20 2
-stopping device, 18 33	detector type, voltmeter, 13 20
Transducers, 13 84; 20 77	electron gun, 20 20
ferroelectric, 3 90	gasfilled, 20 34
Transfer (divertor) switches, 4 17	voltmeters, 20 10
Transformation, 1 137	Trip coil, earth leakage, 11 53
Transformer(s), Sec. 4; 30 22, 24, 27; 32 11	guards, 23 41
analysers, 6 44	wires, 23 48
comparing, Arnold, 13 93	Trip-pole oil-immersed isolator, 7 56
connections, 3-ph., 4 20	Tripping and operating circuits, D.C., 7 93
current and voltage, 7 72	Trolley buses, 18 55
drying out, 11 55 *et seq.*	locomotives, mining, 24 28
equations for, 22 11	Trough-belt conveyor, 21 27
factory distribution, 11 6	Trunking, '' power-line '', 30 78
fittings, 4 10 *et seq.*	Tube(s):
substations, 6 47	anode, 20 65
impedance and resistance, 4 33	insulating materials, 3 73
instruments, 13 14, 41, 95	television camera, 20 20
losses, 4 30 *et seq.*	X-ray, 20 65
magnetic field effects, 1 52	Tungsten, 1 37; 3 13; 20 24, 73
oil, 3 53; 6 30 *et seq.*	arc lamp, 12 22
oil, site purification, 11 63	as contact material, 7 11
operated meters, 13 45	copper, 7 14
power station, 2 68	lamps, 12 10, 22, 31, 33
protective systems, 7 99	silver, 1 19; 7 14
ratio, Dannatt, 13 95	steel, as magnet, 3 13; 13 46
short-circuit calculations, 6 42	Turbine(s):
single, protection with relay, 7 85	-electric propellers, 19 4
small, 4 30	gas, 2 50; 19 14
small, 4 30	impulse, 2 57
starting polyphase motors, 8 39	reaction, 2 58
steels, 4 2, 4	ship's propulsion, 19 4
surge protection, 4 42	steam, 2 17
testing, 11 59; 4 42	water, 2 57
welding, 4 26; 18 4	Turbo-alternators, 2 64
Transients, 1 33, 121, 135	-generators, steam, 30 6
and oscillographs, 13 30	Turbulator, 7 28
	Turbulence, 1 40

Figure 4

differentiation techniques used by *BTI* are bold type for headings of entry-type records, and special left indentation for the right-hand side of 'related-headings' references and locality references. PRECIS relies entirely upon the last-mentioned method for discriminating 'see also' cross-references from entries. For the purpose of discriminating individual records from their immediate neighbours both systems use special left indentation. As for distinguishing parts of records by typographical means, PRECIS uses bold and left indentation to pinpoint the right-hand side of cross-references, while *BTI* correspondingly uses either upper case alone or upper case plus indentation for identifying the right-hand side of cross-references. Concepts in headings are distinguished typographically only by PRECIS, which uses italics for common subdivision terms and in one or two special cases such as 'study fields'. *BTI* uses italics to distinguish the source journal field in its entry-type records. As to the use of typographical means to indicate syntactic subject relationships, only *BTI* uses punctuation and space character combinations for this purpose. Neither sample makes use of type size variations. PRECIS makes rather lavish use of vertical space, while *BTI* is set more nearly solid.

Block structure, filing order and indexing language

Both the mechanics of filing order and certain basic features of the indexing language itself have a bearing upon the appearance of block structure and upon its inhibition. Alphabetisation is too often regarded as a minor matter which can be safely considered in isolation from other factors. As is well known, the basic alternatives here are the methods described as 'word-by-word' and 'letter-by-letter'. More precisely, we have to decide whether the space between words is to be given an earlier ordinal value placing it before the alphanumerics, or whether it is to be ignored altogether in filing. Within the 'word-by-word' method there is the additional issue of what to do about the ordinal value of punctuation. The free language, PRECIS and *BTI* systems use 'word-by-word' filing, but the book-index specimen (Fig. 4) uses 'letter-by-letter'. 'Word-by-word' filing systems tend to encourage the formation of blocks, and it is no coincidence that this is the generally favoured alphabetisation system for bibliographical indexes. It should be noticed, however, that in a few cases where established conventional names are highly variable in their use of single- or multi-word

forms to represent the same concept in different settings, the 'letter-by-letter' method produces a *conceptually* homogeneous block, though not a visually homogeneous one. One well-known example of this variability occurs in the fusing or splitting of the names of organic radicals when they form the leading part in the names of chemical compounds. A similar situation occurs in personal name indexes where the same individual may choose to fuse or separate the prefix in a prefixed surname. If it is desirable to file both forms together, filing must be 'letter-by-letter'. It is quite feasible even within a computer sorted system to retain 'letter-by-letter'-sorted areas within a generally 'word-by-word'-sorted file. Another question in filing order which has implications for block formation is the sorting of identical lead-in terms on records of different types. At a casual glance both PRECIS and *BTI* appear to follow the same policy here, but the practices diverge where there is an entry without a 'display line' (PRECIS parlance) or without a 'subheading' (*BTI* parlance). PRECIS has the sequence

> Cross reference
> Entry (without display line)
> Entry (with display line)

while *BTI* has

> Entry (without subheading)
> Cross reference
> Entry (with subheading)

The PRECIS alternative gives the better visual block, but there is much, perhaps, to be said for not immediately redirecting a user at the head of his first access point, when that access point itself may perhaps contain relevant entries.

The second major factor inducing block formation is one which has dogged discussion on indexing languages from time immemorial and is still far from resolved. It is broadly whether phrases needed as headings should be given as they stand or as split forms consisting of headings followed by one or more subheadings. Phrases as lead terms are related to block structures in the following way. A user's normal expectation—assuming that he is without preknowledge of a particular index—is that he will try to match a single word, which may or may not form part of a complex phrase. Single words then tend to have more impact as block formers than phrases, though phrases repeated still form useful blocks. More serious weakening occurs when blocks of mixed phrases are formed with only the first word of the phrase being common, e.g.,

CHEMICAL BALANCES
CHEMICAL ENGINEERING
CHEMICAL KINETICS
CHEMICAL MACHINING

In principle, then, it appears that single-word headings-plus-subheading forms are more conducive to block formation than are phrases. However, there are limitations on the possibility of always using heading-subheading forms as substitutes for phrases. Some established phrases have acquired a meaning over and above what might seem to be implied in the conjunction of the constituent single-word concepts. Or the splitting may suggest a meaning other than the correct one. Thus a capacitance detector is not a device for detecting capacitance as an end-purpose, but it might appear to be so if the phrase were split as CAPACITANCE: Detectors, especially if CAPACITANCE: Measurement, representing measurement of capacitance as such, is a neighbouring heading. Most attempts to codify subject indication procedure rely in this instance upon a supposed distinction between established and unestablished phrases. It is not surprising to find Charles Ammi Cutter—a father-figure in this field—advocating such a distinction in the relatively static mental environment of 1876. It is surprising to find it still apparently employed as at least a partial operating principle in PRECIS in 1976. As an example of the problems produced, Fig. 2 gives Pipe fittings as a phrase, but Pipe couplings, i.e., variety of Pipe fittings, are embedded in the subheadings of Pipes. It is also noticeable that a stronger block structure would have formed if Pipe organ playing and Pipe organ building had been rendered as

Pipe organs : Building
Pipe organs : Playing

Both PRECIS and *BTI* place limits on the use of phrase headings, and, of the two, the *BTI* limits are considerably more drastic. Accordingly the *BTI*, especially in its annual cumulations, presents a more definite impression of a series of compact blocks (true, with some less striking mortar in between them) than the PRECIS indexes do to the *British National Bibliography*. This is not to say that the typographical layout of PRECIS does not score in other ways. The question of the rendering of phrase headings is an example of a long chain of cause and effect, beginning in the rules for the syntax of the indexing language and reaching down to the typography of output, and the effect that the appearance of this output may be expected to have upon users.

Classified printed indexes

The typographical questions raised by the classified printed index merit brief consideration. Whereas in the case of the alphabetical index it is possible through appropriate measures at the levels of the index language grammar, of the filing order, and of the typography, to produce a series of blocks of material emergent from an alphabetical medley, the classified indexing system itself directly prescribes, not blocks strung in series, as in the alphabetical domain, but a pattern of nesting boxes. This is a much more complex proposition typographically than anything that an alphabetical file might require. Twenty-five years ago, the *BNB* introduced verbal 'features' translating the meaning of classification notation attached to entries. This added enormously to the intelligibility of a classified file, but there were three residual problems on the typographical plane that were never completely resolved. They were, first, that there were never enough type-sizes and non-clashing type-faces available to differentiate all the stages of the hierarchical boxes. Secondly, even with the type differentiation available, pyramids of 'features' tended to overwhelm the descriptive information in the entries. Thirdly, a typographical solution might have been expected as an answer to the obtrusiveness on the page of long classification symbols, but has not been found. Since the *BNB* now no longer relies upon classification for the essential business of information retrieval, these problems are less immediately urgent; but, in the context of the testing of printed indexes, the whole question of classified indexes, which never gained a hearing given the single-card-per-record substrate, merits consideration.

Matters for research

There are some fairly obvious matters which could profitably engage typographically-oriented index evaluators. Thought might be given to designing a test to study the effectiveness of user mobility over panoramic output in 'expanding' a query and how this compares with the procedure of 'expanding' by consulting a thesaurus and re-interrogating the system. Both the single-term index to the classified file and the chain-index technique for alphabetical and classified files demand a certain mobility by the user. It would be of value to try to discover experimentally how realistic this demand is, given the printed page index form. Closely related to this is the question of 'distributed relatives' in all systems of term manipulation using less than full permutation. How well does the visual mobility afforded by panoramic substrates offset the loss of recall to which in a card file 'distributed relatives' might be expected to give rise? Not very distantly related to the 'distributed relatives' problem is the question of non-significant terms embedded in composite pre-coordinated index headings. These non-significant terms are sometimes essential to clarify a relationship between significant terms in a composite heading. Unfortunately, being non-significant, they set up noise for a searcher looking for significant terms. In what form can they be given which least obstructs the searcher? Finally there are two very simple matters on which designers and producers of printed indexes would find hard data useful. What is the effect of packing density in the column and page? And what, in this day of new cheap technology not yet quite up to standard quality in graphic output, is the effect of bold type with less than the usual contrast?

Acknowledgement is hereby made to INSPEC, The British Library (Bibliographic Services Division), The Library Association, and Syndication International Ltd. for permission to reproduce index excerpts.

References

1. Cleverdon, C. W., & Mills, J. Testing of index language devices. *Aslib Proc.*, **15** (4) April 1963, 106-130.
2. Cleverdon, C. W. Cranfield tests on index language devices. *Aslib Proc.*, **19** (6) June 1967, 173-184.
3. Cleverdon, C. W., Mills, J., and Keen, E. M. *Factors determining the performance of indexing systems.* Cranfield-Aslib Research Project. 1966.
4. Aitchison, T. M., and others. *Laboratory evaluation of printed indexes.* Inspec Reports R 70/5 and R 73/17. Instn. Elect. Engrs. 1970.
5. Hall, A. M. *User preference in printed indexes.* Inspec Reports R72/7. Instn. Elect. Engrs. 1972.
6. Hall, A. M. *Case Studies in the use of printed subject indexes.* Inspec Reports R 72/8. Instn. Elect. Engrs. 1972.
7. Lancaster, F. W. Evaluation of published indexes and abstracts journals. *Bull. of the Med. Libr. Assoc.* **59** July 1971, 475.
8. Spencer, H., and others. Spatial and typographical coding in printed bibliographical materials. *J. Doc.*, **31** (2) June 1975, 59-70.
9. Spencer, H., and others. Typographic coding in lists and bibliographies. *Appl. Ergonomics*, **5** (3) Sept. 1974, 136-41.

IV. Indexing Periodical and Multi-Volume Publications

IVa. Some Principles and Techniques

Case History of the Compilation of a Large Cumulative Index

Jacqueline D. Sisson

Admittedly with great trepidation and some reservations, I accepted a request to submit an article for *The Indexer* because I felt that by relating the trials and tribulations of a foolhardy novice, I might help others to avoid similar pitfalls. My recent experiences, even though limited to a cumulative index, have resulted in a renewed awareness and greater appreciation of the complexity of the indexing process.

My first piece of advice to beginners is to read all issues of *The Indexer*. To my great regret I only discovered this journal a little over a year ago while preparing a lecture on indexing for a librarians' workshop on our campus. Instead of reading the articles directly pertaining to the lecture topic, I read all of the current and back issues and found numerous suggestions which would have been invaluable in the planning stage of my two-volume 1,461-page *Index to A. Venturi's Storia dell'arte Italiana*. One statement, for which I cannot cite page or issue, amused me greatly. If my memory is correct the author said 'Any fool can write, but it takes a genius to index.' In my case it would be fitting to add '. . . however it also takes a fool to index the impossible.'!

Attempting the impossible depicts perfectly the project I am about to describe. In all honesty it must be said that the Index would never have been attempted if I had known from the start that it would take six years of intensive work to complete it. Articles appearing in *The Indexer* would have warned me that the figures computed during pre-indexing time studies should be doubled or even tripled in order to arrive at a valid time estimation. The latter would have resulted in an exact computation. I had estimated that the project would take two years working from forty to sixty hours per week after

my normal forty-hour work week at the library. It took exactly six years.

Published between 1901 and 1940, Adolfo Venturi's 24,845 page *Storia dell'arte Italiana* is still an important source of documentation on Italian Early Christian through sixteenth century painters, sculptors and architects. Like Bernard Berenson, Venturi was the advisor of a large number of individuals whose private collections, through donations or purchases, are now housed in museums. Since many of the attributions for these works of art were made by Venturi, museum curators frequently consult Venturi's monumental work when preparing collection catalogues. However, due to the lack of a cumulative index, locating specific information in the eleven-volume-in-twenty-five-parts *Storia* has been a frustrating, time-consuming task. Each Venturi part contains a location index, an index of artists' names and, as is true of most publications on the Continent, an extremely comprehensive table of contents intended to serve as a subject index. The second volume of my Index includes a reprint of these important tables of contents. I was pleased that my publisher agreed with my suggestion that they be included even though this is unusual in an index.

Basically my location index is simply a corrected, expanded and reorganized cumulative index derived from Venturi's individual indexes. The reorganization consists of establishing categories for each listing. Column one of Figure 1 illustrates the Venturi index and on column two the Sisson cumulative index arranged by categories.

The artist index, while based on the location index, is totally new. Unlike Venturi's simple listing of artists' names and page references,

Reprinted from *The Indexer* 10, no. 4 (Autumn 1977): 164–175, 194.

my index includes listings of bibliographies, *catalogues raisonnés* and, arranged by medium or categories, listings of works by their titles or descriptions. Figure 2 compares the Venturi artist index on column one with the Sisson index on column two. It is difficult to understand why authors of multi-volume works often do not maintain cumulative indexes as each volume is published. This would result in continuity in methodology and terminology thus avoiding variants in place and personal names—essential in any work of the size of Venturi's which is dependent on a large and fluctuating staff.

My Index now provides convenient access to both a wealth of information and an enormous corpus of illustrations which are impossible or difficult to locate in other publications.

All of the above leads to the first question to be faced by the compiler of a cumulative index. Is an index needed? Up to the present four reviewers have stated that my Indexes are important contributions to research. In the September 1976 issue of the *Art Bulletin*, Creighton Gilbert claims in a lengthy, highly critical review, that the index should not have been published since, in his estimation, the Venturi *Storia* is in part obsolete. The *Storia*, originally published in a small edition of about 200 copies, has been reprinted, at great cost, by Kraus-Thompson Reprints. The $2,000.00 reprint is selling quite well. It does not seem logical that at this time of severe budgetary restrictions, libraries throughout the world would invest such a large sum for an obsolete publication. I am not going to use this article as a vehicle for rebuttals since there are other avenues for this but some of Gilbert's statements are pertinent to this article and it might be interesting to readers to compare the critic's point of view against those of a compiler.

Prior to making any serious commitments to the index, I took advantage of a national conference of the College Art Association to seek the opinion of a large number of scholars. In every case my proposal was greeted with enthusiasm, and to my great surprise, later in the week, I heard a scholar whom I had not consulted, mention in the course of his paper that he had heard that a much needed index to Venturi was forthcoming! While all those consulted approved of the general subject categories I was planning to employ, they suggested that, contrary to my plans, the cumulative index should be in English, that all the locations should be brought up to date, and finally, that the index should include an iconographic index. The

first two suggestions are discussed further in this article. Gilbert, in his review, states that an iconographic index would have been far more useful than the location and artist index. I was, and am, in full agreement that it is needed but not to the exclusion of the location and artist index. When my consultants at the CAA meeting suggested the inclusion of an iconographic index I couldn't help thinking that it would not be feasible unless I could be guaranteed that I would be a second Methuselah. Furthermore, while my language background and good knowledge of art history qualified me for the compilation of the cumulative indexes, I felt that an iconographic index should be compiled not only by an art historian but by one who is also a specialist in Italian art. In his review Gilbert implies that I didn't have the language and art history background to compile the indexes and, if I may paraphrase and read a little between the lines, that art historians if they could stoop so low as to perform such a menial task, should have published the indexes. Yet further in the article he states that I, or someone else, should publish an iconographic index. As stated in many articles in *The Indexer*, the criteria for establishing qualifications in the field of indexing go further than subject knowledge. Too high a percentage of authors' indexes are either poor in quality or too complex for the average user. I do not feel that a scholar would have employed as logical a user-orientated system as the one I developed for the *Storia*. It is especially in this area that I feel the greatest satisfaction in my Index. As an art librarian I have had occasion to assist thousands of library users in their research and I was determined to organize a gigantic amount of information into a user-orientated format. Except to state incorrectly that my indexes are simply duplicates of those in Venturi, Gilbert did not mention this point in his review.

Jean Adhemar, the highly respected art historian and editor of the *Gazette des beaux arts*, was thoughtful enough to write a warm letter congratulating me on the index and specifically on the simplicity of its arrangement. This letter alone made the six years of hard labour worthwhile: I had succeeded in one of my primary objectives. The other objective of course was accuracy. I am certain that my fiches were correct since I double-checked every entry prior to the filing of the fiche *and* in the course of the filing we had constantly to refer back to the text for clarifications of the variants. In every case the volume and page listings were correct. I am afraid that my proof reading of the typescript was not perfect. Also errors may have occurred during the final revision of the filing when the constant discovery of variants required a large number of corrections between the two files, but here again every effort was made to eliminate mistakes.

Gilbert states that the indexes are only 90% correct. If this is true my margin of errors is far too great. I had hoped for none but knew that this was impossible. If I had been asked what percentage would be acceptable I would have said less than one percent of the over 100,000 entries. I still find it difficult to believe that my index contains 10,000 or more errors. Gilbert did not state what statistical measurements were employed in establishing a 10% figure. I do know that none of the students and faculty members using my index in the library have brought errors to my attention even though I have asked them always to let me know in order to publish errata in the Art Libraries Society *Newsletter* both in Great Britain and in North America. Since many of the users of my indexes are not aware that I compiled them, and they don't hesitate to ask for assistance when running into errors in the *Art Index to periodicals* and the *Répertoire d'art et d'archéologie*, I am taking it as a sign that the 10% figure is incorrect.

Pre-planning

Unless the work is commissioned by a publisher and sold for an extraordinarily high sum, the compiler of an index such as the one being discussed must accept the fact that the work is a contribution to scholarship and not a profit-making enterprise. This is equally true of publications by most scholars. Since this article is appearing in a journal for career indexers, I feel it is essential that I discuss frankly the financial setbacks encountered by the compiler, not the publisher, of a work of any size.

I had no intention of making a profit of any great size but I did expect to cover all my expenses plus perhaps a modest compensation for my time. My publisher is not to be faulted for the personal financial fiasco of my Index. I was asked to establish the list price and was provided with the normal 10% royalties. Knowing the limitations of library and museum book budgets, I determined that $85.00 for the two volumes

was the maximum we could charge if we expected reasonable sales. Only one reviewer stated that the cost was too high but he cannot be criticized for that statement since only those involved in indexing can fully realize its complexity. In the distant future, once all copies of the indexes to Venturi have been sold, the royalties will not fully cover the wages of my typists, let alone all the other expenses and my time. In addition to the typists there were costs such as the rental of two electric typewriters, the 100,000 plus index cards, the thousands of guide cards, photocopying costs, purchase of dictionaries and finally, last but not least, the indexer's time computed at one third of my salary as a senior librarian. The total disbursements by the compiler in time and cash mounted to $59,300.00. The additional $5,000.00 most gratefully received from The National Endowment for the Humanities for the filers' wages bring the total conservative cost of the compilation of the *Index to A. Venturi's Storia* to $64,300.00 or 38,734 British pounds! The publisher's expenses are of course not included in the above sum. It is therefore obvious that, if totally subsidized by a publisher, the list price of an index of any size would be beyond the reach of libraries. I have been gently criticized on several occasions for having emphasized the time expenditures in the preface of the Index, and for having stated that if lined up end to end there are over one hundred and thirty feet of cards. Admittedly I wanted to bring to the attention of possible critics that the project was difficult. But most importantly, I wanted to make the general public aware of the complexity of indexing. Because my indexes resulted in my receiving a promotion to Associate Professor on our campus, quite a few of my colleagues have been looking around for similar projects not realizing what they will have to face. Until I worked on this index I often took indexes for granted, and I have in the past been guilty of questioning the high prices of various indexes in the book reviews I write for several journals. In this age of civil liberty crusades, I have become the defender of career indexers, the unsung heroes and heroines of scholarship.

The system established for the project prior to the beginning of its compilation proved to need few changes. The major alterations were:

1. Translating the entries into English, as suggested by scholars, was going to be confusing to the user. My original plans, changed on the advice of scholars, had always been that except for the

category headings, an index to an Italian work should remain in that language.

2. It would not be economically feasible to continue hiring students, Italian literature majors, to translate and transcribe the Venturi location indexes on to 3 x 5 cards. More importantly, the work of several hands would be detectable and result in inconsistencies.

Even with comprehensive written directions there were visible nuances in the interpretations of the three students assisting me. I was also able to detect similar nuances in the various volumes of Venturi's monumental work. Each of his numerous assistants had his or her own method and some volumes reflected the fluctuations in the capabilities of his changing staff. Indexing is after all subjective in its processes of creation even though highly objective in its written plans and procedures.

An amusing incident is worth relating at this point. In the early phases of the project while double checking the work of the students, I was rudely shaken out of my midnight lethargy by an entry reading 'Florence-San Lorenzo-Sacristy-Verrocchio-Washstand, VI 707'. Since my helper was a literature major, not an art historian, he had naturally translated lavabo to its everyday equivalent, not realizing that when referring to ecclesiastical use the word was left in its original Italian. Although the image of a washstand in the midst of the San Lorenzo Sacristy was amusing it was also the cause of a series of nightmares in which I was drummed out of the College Art Association in a manner befitting the most stupendous of Hollywood productions. On the following day, since my contracts with the student assistants had nearly expired, I paid them in full and dismissed them. During the night I realized that the time consumed revising the work of others was equal to the time it would take for me to do the work myself and that the index would take far longer than I had anticipated. Therefore I could not afford to spend a large portion of my salary on student wages. Even at this point, even though the time required for the project was beginning to dawn on me, I was still totally ignorant of exactly how long the project would take. What I did realize was that it was a perfect opportunity to go back to my original plan of using English terms for the categories but in all instances keeping the index in its original language, making cross-references from English to Italian whenever absolutely necessary. I destroyed several months' work, and being an eternal optimist, with great excitement, began all over again.

As can be seen in a small scale on Figures 1 and 2, every effort was made to reduce an enormous amount of information into a reasonably uncomplicated format. Establishing categories was at times difficult. This was expecially true of the *catalogues raisonnés* whose entries were frequently not mentioned in the text. Some errors may have been made in those cases but through extensive research in other publications every effort was made to locate the required verifications. Nearly half way through his gigantic work, Venturi ceased listing the catalogue entries in his location indexes and since I felt that consistency was essential, it was necessary for me to pick them up. This proved to be the source of enormous difficulties and the cause, I am sure, of a large percentage of the questionable entries since these catalogues included a large number of variants in place names, and frequently omitted the names of the cities where located, sometimes only listing building names. In other cases the titles of specific works were variations of the titles mentioned in the text. A considerable amount of research was required to consolidate these variants and in most cases I found that I could merge textual references with the catalogue entries. When it was impossible to verify that the works were one and the same they were left as separate entries. It is in this area that my reviewer, Creighton Gilbert, was most critical. Whereas other reviewers read the introduction and thus were aware of the difficulties I encountered, Gilbert expresses no sympathy or understanding, nor does he mention that I pointed out areas requiring some vigilance on the part of the user. Gilbert states that my *Index* is misleading and could well result in serious errors in scholarship by having added non-existent works of art to the repertoire of Italian artists. It is surprising to learn that even though Gilbert stated in his review that hardly anyone seems to use my *Index* at Queens College in New York, he later implies that my mistakes in judgement are going to cause permanent damage to Italian art scholarship. Even though such ambiguities are amusing, I am not taking his charges lightly. In retrospect I deeply wish that rather than adding the entries, I had simply gone through all of the earlier listings for the *catalogues raisonnés* and removed them from my files. If I had done this the chances of errors would have greatly decreased and the total time required for the completion of the indexes would have been reduced by several months. On the other hand, important works of art would not have appeared in the indexes but presumably users of Venturi's *Storia* would have consulted the catalogues whether I listed the items individually or not. It is also true that scholars do not always check primary sources and errors are consequently compounded from one publication to another, corrections only being made when a fastidious scholar traces references to the primary sources. I had never realized that the indexer's responsibilities could be such a heavy burden. Similar problems were encountered in the frequent variations between the textual references to the titles of works of art and those appearing under the illustrations. Whenever possible I determined whether they were in fact one and the same and employed the most descriptive title or the one most often used in other publications. Cross-references were always made.

All of these problems compounded as the work progressed and my estimate for the completion of the index went through a series of new computations. I had signed a contract with Kraus-Thompson Reprints in Liechtenstein shortly before I discovered the omission of the catalogue entries in the last third of Venturi's work. No publisher could have been more patient and understanding. My miscalculations of the time required kept multiplying as the problems grew.

Categories

The assignment of categories was not as simple as anticipated and works of art frequently fell into several categories. Whenever this occurred, I made extra cards for the same work of art. For example a piece of sculpture on a façade appears under architectural ornament, architecture, and sculpture. If not ornamental but rather a statue, the categories were architecture and sculpture. The so-called minor arts were the source of similar aggravations. Medieval objects such as coins, mirror backs, crosier heads, *châsses*, reliquaries, etc., are often listed, according to the Library of Congress cataloguing system, as minor arts yet they are also to a certain extent sculpture. Such items were always listed twice, once under minor arts and again under sculpture. By employing categories the user can go directly to the medium fitting the item desired without having to plough through literally hundreds of listings. For example under Rome there are seventy-four

pages of listings in my location index. Without categories a user would have to run through all the pages in order to make a list of Venturi's references to sculptures located in Rome. By employing categories, only fifteen pages need to be checked. The same is true of the artist index. However, in that index the location is listed only in the case of architecture or when several works of art have the same title or descriptions.

The categories employed throughout the two indexes are: Architectural Drawing, Architectural Ornament, Architecture, Drawing, Graphics, Minor Art, Painting, Sculpture. The codes I used on my index cards were AD, AO, A, D, G, MA, P, and S. My admiration for Venturi's monumental work grew throughout the six years of close association with his publication, and if I seem to emphasize overmuch the inconsistencies in his work, it has been only in order to explain that my task was not simply one of copying existent indexes and merging them into a cumulative one. My path, like Venturi's, was beset with problems. Venturi has stated that he had personally seen every work discussed in his publication. How he was able to publish such a vast history, plus numerous articles appearing in scholarly journals, and undertake consultant work, is beyond comprehension.

Location index

Seventy years and two world wars have gone by since the first Venturi volume was published and there is no doubt that many of the location listings are now incorrect. Works have been destroyed or lost, or have changed hands. Establishing the present locations would have been a formidable, if not impossible, task. As mentioned earlier, my consultants invariably suggested that I at least make the obvious changes. For example, American millionaires collected with great fervour from the 1920s through the 1940s, and due to recent bequests by these collectors, many of the former private European collections are now in major museums of the United States. These works of art are still listed in Venturi's *Storia* under the names of the original owners or even under the names of the American collectors. The same is true in Europe where inheritance taxes have forced the dispersal of many private collections, resulting in their purchase by national museums. Recent laws forbid the export of great works of art without the approval of governing bodies, but this was not the case during the time span of Venturi's publication. I decided, perhaps incorrectly, that in the interest of consistency no changes should be made and this fact is explicitly stated in my introduction. After all I was not rewriting the *Storia*.

Using the Venturi Location Indexes (Figure 1, column one), I made separate 3 x 5 cards for each entry. Although extremely expensive for a project of this size, using hard cards was well worth the expense because of the ease of handling during photocopying for the artist file and the filing. Knowing that the index would take some time to compile, two years I thought, and because the cards would have to be handled frequently, I avoided smudging by using indelible pens. Since the index was in a foreign language and would be bound to cause difficulties

---

SPALATO

Duomo: Porta intagliata, **105-113,** 102-104; Campanile, rilievi, 350; Arcone, **349,** 350; Annunziazione, 350; Natività, **351,** 350.
Palazzo di Diocleziano: Sfinge, **796,** 796.

SPELLO

Santa Maria Maggiore, 807.

SPOLETO

San Salvatore: Facciata, 806, 899, 904; Fregi, 903.

Duomo, 806, 899; Pavimento, 904.
Sant'Ansano, 806; Ornati, 901.
San Gregorio, 806; Rilievo, 901, 904.
San Ponziano, **808,** 806.
Municipio: Porta, **893,** 900, 901.
San Pietro: Rilievi della facciata, **895, 897,** 900, 902, 903.
Proprieta privata: Sarcofago, **900,** 904-907.

STILO (CALABRIA)

Chiesa, 502, 503.

SPOLETO

<u>Architectural Ornament</u>
MUNICIPIO
   Maestro Melioranzo: Porta, III 900,
   901, fig. 795
S. ANSANO
   Ornamenti della porta laterale,
   III 901
S. GREGORIO
   Porta laterale (rilievo), III
   901, 904
S. PIETRO
   Rilievi della facciata, III 900,
   902, 903, fig. 796, 797
S. SALVATORE
   Fregi, III 903
<u>Architecture</u>
DUOMO
   Sec. XII: III 806, 899
   Barocci, Ambrogio e Pippo Fiorentino:
   Portico, VIII^1 702, fig. 530
   Fiorentino, Pippo e Ambrogio Barocci:
   Portico, VIII^1 702, fig. 530
   Pippo d'Antonio da Firenze e Ambrogio
   d'Antonio da Milano: Portico, XI^1
   942, fig. 860
S. ANSANO
   Sec. XII: III 806
S. GREGORIO
   Sec. XII: III 806
S. SALVATORE
   Sec. XII: Facciata, III 806, 899, 904
<u>Mosaics</u>
DUOMO
   Musaico, II 416
   Pavimento, III 904

A. Venturi. *Storia* . . .   J. Sisson, *Index* . . .
vol. 3, p. XXIV   vol. 1, p. 605

Figure 1

for the typist, it would have been preferable if the entries had been typed instead of handwritten. If the project had been less gigantic I would have employed that method but the index was compiled after my working hours at the library and during vacations. Having to sit at a typewriter would have been too fatiguing. It is fortunate that I did at least use indelible ink since during a working vacation I became irritated at having to stay indoors and took my work, on a calm day, to the boat landing-stage of my parents' summer cottage. A sudden wind blew cards off the bridge table I had set up and dozens of cards landed in the lake. A laundry line full of cards was an amusing sight for some but not for me. Needless to say that was the end of attempting to enjoy fresh air while indexing.

The layout of the cards remained the same throughout the project. First line: city and building. Second line: artist if known, otherwise century. Third line: title or description of the work. Fourth line: volume, page and illustration numbers. I double-checked for copying errors immediately upon completing each card. An extra card for the artist index was not made. I had rejected making a carbon copy due to the smudging problems invariably resulting from the use of carbons and had also decided to avoid adding to the chances of errors surrounding the writing of a second card. Instead, at a later date, I made photocopies of the location cards and used them for the artist index. Due to library training, an authority file of artists' names was maintained throughout the project. For this file I used pink slips and these entries were always filed immediately, as were the cross-references for variants of personal names. The latter were done on blue slips. This file was checked prior to writing each location card. Once all of the location listings for a particular volume were completed, the cards were arranged numerically by the first page listed, and the total book was scanned page by page comparing the text against the cards. When the page listings for a specific location were not consecutive the other pages were also checked at this point. Frequent omissions were found and location cards made. The page by page check did result in some duplication since cards were made for items which later appeared on other cards having multiple but not consecutive page listings. Having to merge or delete these cards at a later date added to the total time required, but it was well worth the time since important

omissions were discovered. Some might wonder why I bothered using the Venturi index as a guide. The reason was that the location of a work of art did not always appear in the textual discussion. While Venturi presumably knew which work of art he was referring to, I would not have always been able to determine the location from the text.

In order to be certain that all the illustrations were accounted for in the Venturi indexes, I typed a list of numbers and photocopied enough copies to have one for each volume. As each entry was verified the proper illustration number was circled. Omissions were found in every volume, and the illustration numbers were added to the already existent textual references or, if there were none, new entries were made.

Errors in Venturi's page listings were not frequent but they did occur. At first, as I came to the problems, I attempted to find the proper pages but soon realized that since I was making cards for seemingly omitted items, it would be a waste of time to search. The problem cards were set aside in a special box until later findings allowed their correct completion. In nearly all cases this proved to be a satisfactory system.

Variants in the titles of works and in personal names began appearing frequently as work progressed. For the variants in personal names I chose the most commonly employed name and made cross-references for all the others, always making entries for the authority file as well. The variants in the names of cities and buildings were also handled as I came across them, but I did not maintain a location authority file. Instead I made blue slip cross-references which were filed in the location file once a complete volume was checked. I probably should have compiled an authority file for the cities and buildings but it would have been far too large to keep within reach while working. As the project grew, the variants became an enormous problem. Some artists, locations and works were mentioned in different volumes with up to four or five different names and no clues to earlier names. It is in this area that I fault Venturi and his staff for not having maintained authority files of their own. Publishers of multivolume works would be advised to insist that their authors or compilers establish consistent methods through authority files of terminology, place and personal names.

The category headings were placed on the upper right corner of each card as the entries were compared against the text. The categories I chose may have been too simplistic, but I felt that it would be confusing to the user if I employed too many. The following list provides an idea of some of the problems encountered in determining categories and my solutions:

Architectural Drawing: These materials are of interest in two ways. The drawing is in itself a work of art but some users' approach would be the building represented and not the sketch *per se*. For example: Antonio Sangallo's sketch for the fortifications of Perugia is housed in the Uffizi in Florence. I made extra cards for listings of this type, thus there are references to the above work under Perugia-Fortificazione and also under Firenze-Uffizi, Gabinetto di Stampe e Disegni. Entries were also made under both cities using the category Architecture. These drawings are of immense importance to architectural historians since they are often the only remaining evidence of monuments destroyed in wars, by fire and, regrettably, sheer neglect and indifference.

Architectural Ornament: Cards were made for the location of the ornament if it is still part of a building but in the case of fragments, ornaments are listed under their original location with the notation 'gia' (formerly). In many cases architectural ornament entries were repeated under both sculpture and architecture.

Architecture: This category was straightforward except for the frequent changes of the names of the buildings which soon grew to nightmarish proportions. These problems are discussed in the section pertaining to filing.

Drawing: Except for cases such as those discussed above, these entries were usually listed under the location of the drawing or sketch. In cases of drawings for the minor arts or sculpture, cards were also made for those categories. Cartoons for tapestries are one example.

Graphics: Listed under both the location of the work and its subject if it was architectural.

Minor Arts: Listed by the location of the work of art. If at present in a museum but formerly in a church or private residence, the listing will also appear, if known from textual evidence, under its former location with the notation 'gia' and its present location in parentheses. By present I mean present at the time Venturi wrote the text.

Painting: The only problems encountered in this category were changes in the names of the building where housed and variants in the titles of the paintings. Cross-references were made in each case.

Sculpture: If the sculpture is presently in a museum or private collection but was originally part of a building, the listing will also appear under its former location with the notation 'gia' and its present location in parentheses. Extra cards were also often made for the categories Architectural Ornament, Architecture, and Minor Arts. Sketches for sculptures appear under both Drawing and Sculpture.

Filing location cards

The filing system for the location cards was made as simple as possible. Unlike other indexes of large histories of art I did not use sub-categories such as private collections, public buildings, secular buildings, churches, etc. I personally find such indexes difficult to use. Instead the location index is in strict alphabetical order by the name of the city, then by category and under each category by the names of the buildings or the collections. Since art historians often need to know what works of art are in specific areas of churches, sub-divisions were often made under the names of the churches. Creighton Gilbert found some errors in my listings of private collections. For example under London I have listings for Coll. Duveen and again under Casa Duveen. He is correct in his objection. I cannot remember at this point exact examples I encountered but they were numerous, always having to do with decisions when I could find no resources providing the answers. In the above examples I believe that I could not verify whether Venturi was referring in the first case to the private collection of a gallery owner and in the second case to a painting for sale in Duveen's gallery. Since gallery owners more frequently than not also have private collections, I felt that the entries should remain as listed by Venturi. Gilbert feels that they were both meant to be Duveen's gallery. The listings should probably have both been under Duveen with sub-divisions under Casa and under Collection. The two entries would then not have been separated in the alphabetical listing. But I had wanted to file all private collections together and had adopted Venturi's system of using Coll. as the first word. My British readers might be interested in knowing that the Venturi listings for Great Britain were awful to resolve. Many of the paintings were in private collections on country estates. Venturi sometimes listed the locations as simply London (near); at other times the same residence was listed under the name of the nearby village or town and in still other cases no city or town was specified. The term 'near London' was employed by Venturi for estates located as far as thirty miles from London. Hampton Court was listed as Hampton Court in some volumes and in others as London (near). Due to the vastness of the location files for any large city it was often not possible to detect these inconsistencies since they could be several volumes apart, but often sheer intuition took over. If the paintings were well known I was able to determine their locations from other sources in our library. Needless to say I also used atlases and multi-volume publications on the buildings of England in order to try to trace the estates. I did not go as far as to use our large histories of counties since I would have had to check all of them and more often than not they are not indexed. In the case of Scotland, Venturi listed no towns, just the names of the collections or museums.

The vagueness of some of the location listings was not limited to England. For example: Maiano. Chiesa di S. Martino was also listed in another volume under Firenze (dintorni). S. Martino a Maiano! Perhaps I should have given up the project when the filing problems began mounting and I became aware that I would be repeating and perhaps compounding some of Venturi's ambiguities, but it is still my belief that even though I did not catch all of the variants, an enormous amount of detective work resulted in providing good access to Venturi's text and greatly improving his own indexes. I have been told that in some major museums the curators have requested private copies of the index for their offices. I cannot believe that they would go to that expense unless the *Index* and Venturi's *Storia* do in fact assist them in their research.

As the filing problems mounted I came to the realization that I had reached a point when assistance was essential. I applied for a coveted National Endowment for the Humanities grant, and much to my surprise and pleasure was awarded $9,000.00, four thousand of which went to my institution to cover the inevitable expenses of a bureaucracy. The remainder was used to employ two filers, one working on the location file full time in the library for ten months, the other working on the artist file in her home twelve hours a week for five months. They both developed uncanny sixth senses for possible problem areas and I soon found myself running a steady flow of deliveries of corrections to be made in their files. If I had read *The Indexer* prior to the compilation of my *Index* I would have been warned not to carry cards in the process of correction. Instead the author of one article suggested that notes be made in a ledger in order to avoid the possible loss of cards. I hope that I didn't lose any, but with hindsight I realize that the suggestion is an excellent one. I did keep a ledger beside me at all times in order to jot down ideas as they came to me. These notes were invaluable when writing the introductions to my indexes.

As implied earlier, a word-by-word approach was used except in the case of churches having San, Santa or Santi as the first word. All of these were filed as though spelled S. Articles and numbers were ignored in the arrangement of titles and the first key words employed. My location filer and I used every available edition of guide books, atlases and literally hundreds of art books in attempting to resolve some of the problems. By comparing city maps of early guide books with those of subsequent editions we were able to determine that some of the listings were simply variants. For example in some cities, listings such as Pinacoteca Civica, Galleria Civica, Palazzo Communale and Galleria Nazionale were all one and the same but in other cities they were not. A similar problem was centred around the following listings which turned out to be one and the same: Biblioteca Marciana, Biblioteca Sansoviniana, Palazzo Reale, Libreria Sansoviniana. Gilbert faults me for not having caught all of the discrepancies and suggests that an art historian would have been able to catch all of them. I do not believe this since there were often thousands of cards for one large city and Venturi's own staff consisted of art historians and students. Furthermore none of my consultants brought up the fact that there were inconsistencies in Venturi's *Storia*. Let it suffice to say that we discovered literally hundreds of variants, and that cross-references were made in each instance and the changes also made in the artist file.

Artist file

It is important to remember that one of the greatest values of Venturi's work is that he frequently included discussions of the work of lesser known artists. His publication in some cases is the only source of information available to most users of small to medium sized art libraries, that is libraries ranging from 20,000 to 60,000 volumes.

The artist index was compiled by simply photocopying six location cards at a time. Cutting them was time consuming and a dreadful task but relatives volunteered to do this for me.

These paper slips were much more difficult to handle than the card stock employed for the location cards, but it still was a time saver to use this method since the initial corrections made while checking the cards against the text only had to be made on one card. The total cost of photocopying was $370.00, a significantly lower figure than the time cost of making two cards for each entry.

Corradini, detto Fra' Carnevale, 478-482.
Bartolommeo di Giovanni di Miniato, 714, 715, 745-746, 748, 751, 758, 761, 764, 773.
Bartolommeo da Lendinara, 434, 473.
Bartolommeo di Pagolo del Fattorino, poi Fra' Bartolommeo da S. Marco, 693, 696, 706.
Bartolommeo di Tommaso, 529-530.
Bartolommeo Vivarini, 316-318, 524, 533.
Bastiani, v. Lazzaro Bastiani.
Bastiano Mainardi, 713, 714, 715, 721, 724, 729, 748, 751, 759, 760, 761, 764, 768, 770, 771-773.
Bellini, v. Gentile, Giovanni, Jacopo.
Bembo, ·v. Benedetto e Bonifacio Bembo.
Benedetto Bembo, 288-289, 291.
Benedetto Bonfigli, 356, 510, 538-544.
Benedetto Ghirlandaio, 586, 713, 746, 768, 770, 774.
Benozzo di Lese, detto Benozzo Gozzoli, 58, 70-72, 77, 252, 402-430, 530, 532, 533, 538, 540, 547, 678, 681-682, 683, 716, 717, 718, 721, 722.
Benvenuto di Giovanni di Meo del Guasta, 505-510.
Berengario Picaluli, 152.
Bernardino Betti, detto il Pinturicchio, 773 in nota.
Bertoldo, 735, 776.
Bicci, v. Lorenzo e Neri di Bicci.
Bicci di Lorenzo, 22, 24-25, 28, 431, 434.
Boccati, v. Giovanni Boccati.
Bon [Scultori della famiglia], 291.
Bonaiuto di Giovanni, 22.
Bonaventura di Parigi, 137.
Bonifacio Bembo, 288-291.
Boninsegna da Clocego, 228.
Bonfigli, v. Benedetto Bonfigli.
Bono ferrarese, 268, 320.
Botticelli, v. Sandro Filipepi.
Botticini, v. Francesco di Giovanni e Raffaello Botticini.
Brea (Famiglia nizzarda de' pittori), 148.
Brunellesco, v. Filippo Brunellesco.
Buffalmacco, 204 in nota.
Buonarroti, v. Michelangelo.

BICCI DI LORENZO   (continued)
Painting   (continued)
Battista, Iacopo e Agostino (sportelli), VII^1 24n; Sportelli d'altare (Brunswick, Museo ducale), VII^1 24n; Sposalizio di Santa Caterina (trittico), VII^1 24n; Sposalizio di Santa Caterina e i Santo Uberto, Giovanni Battista e Antonio Abbate, VII^1 24n
Sculpture
Lunetta sulla porta (terracotta, Firenze, Santa Maria Nuova), VI 232

BICCI   see also   LORENZO DI BICCI

BIDUINO
III 946-949, 953, 955, 958n
Sculpture
Architrave (Lucca, San Salvatore), III 946-949, fig. 840-841; Bassorilievo (San Cassiano, Chiesa), III 958n; Sarcofago (Pisa, Camposanto), III 955

--(?)
Sculpture
Porta (Lucca, San Giovanni), III 953, fig. 844

BIFFI, ANDREA
X3 508-516, 518
BIB X3 511
Sculpture
Busto di Carlo Borromeo (bronzo), X3 511; La disputa di Gesù nel tempio, X3 511, 516, fig. 422; La fuga in Egitto, X3 511, 516, fig. 421; Istorie della Santa Vergine Maria (rilievi), X3 511, 516, fig. 392, 420-423; La Purificazione, X3 511, 516, fig. 420; Il transito di Maria e l'Assunzione, X3 511, 516, fig. 423

--e aiuti
Sculpture
La Virtù cardinale (per il sepolcro di S. Carlo Borromeo), X3 518

A. Venturi. Storia...   J. Sisson, Index ...
vol. 7, pt. 1, p. XLVI   vol. 2, p. 76

Figure 2

In the course of filing the artist cards, a large number of variants in the names of locations became apparent to the filer even though the first line carrying the location was ignored in the actual filing. The entries were alphabetically arranged by the name of the artist. Da, de, dei, di, della, etc. were ignored in the alphabetizing. For example, Andrea del Castagno was filed before Andrea da Formigine. Cumulative listings of pages for each volume as well as page listings of bibliographies and the *catalogues raisonnés* preceded the descriptive categorized entries. The listings were then arranged by category and within each category the following order was employed: sole work, in collaboration with others, attributed to, in manner of, and finally, school of.

These nuances in attributions are extremely important and most users of materials on the history of art are conscious of them. In the categories of Drawing, Painting and Sculpture, the locations were used only when several works had the same title or if the title or description was too general. It soon became evident that there was no way for us to notice all the variants in personal names without checking the whole authority file against the universally recognized forty-two volume *Allgemeines Lexikon der bildenden Künstler* by U. Thieme and F. Becker. This unforeseen task, undertaken once the artist filing was completed, took over 160 solid hours of work on my part. In order to avoid interruptions I spent a great number of hours in the library after closing time but since our Fine Arts Library is open to the public until ten in the evening, I was forced to work a good part of the time in the open. Our students were overjoyed to see me in the library during the evening hours and I soon found myself swamped with reference questions. Finally in desperation I made a large sign stating 'I am a figment of your imagination. Please do not disturb this ghostly presence'! Some of our graduate students who are working on their doctorates reminded me of that sign quite recently after they had read Gilbert's suggestion that I had not consulted reference tools. One student wished someone had taken a photograph of me and my sign surrounded by Thieme-Becker in order to send it to Gilbert! Thanks to Thieme-Becker I discovered hundreds of variants which we had not previously detected, but a large number of artists' names appeared only in Venturi even though I used all types of combinations of spelling and arrangement to locate them. The Venturi artist index, Figure 2, column 1, was often alphabetically arranged by the artists' first names. In the case of Andrea del Castagno and many others our index was too, but in the case of those underlined in Figure 2 it was not.

Once the corrections were transposed from the authority file to the artist file, we of course had to make hundreds of changes and cross-references in the location file. All of this caused further delays resulting in more letters of apology to my long-suffering publisher. Meanwhile I was receiving letters and phone calls from colleagues asking when the index would be available.

One amusing incident occurred in the course of the final check of the files just prior to the beginning of the typing. My location filer asked me orally how to file AIX. I replied with the correct French pronunciation 'under Aix (pronounced X) of course'. She looked at me strangely but I didn't catch on. Lo and behold, when proof reading the last page of the typescript I found Aix under X. Being Franco-American I cannot understand why the name Aix seemed so strange to my more than capable assistant who had been working with thousands of foreign listings. I only recount this episode to reinforce the fact that nothing should be left to chance when it comes to the compilation of any work, and that specificity on the part of the project director is essential. We had to make an addendum on the final page and also squeeze Aix on its proper page with a note stating 'see addendum'. Both of my filers were remarkable, intelligent and devoted assistants and were given full recognition, as was the final typist, in my acknowledgements and prefaces. Their work left its toll on them, they dislike Italian art and hope that they never see another Madonna and Child for the rest of their lives!

Typing

I had always planned on typing the typescript myself but I had to face the fact that it would be impossible even though my grant funds were depleted. Once again I miscalculated the time required and decided I could afford to rent two electric typewriters and hire two full-time typists. My library administrators were kind enough to permit their typing in my library so that I could continue working but always be available for questions arising in the process of typing. I thought that with each typist working on one of the indexes it would take about two months at forty hours a week. My first calculation was that I had thought that it would be a simple task to locate typists familiar with foreign languages since many of our dissertations are written in foreign languages. Wrong. I called person after person and all I had to say was the word Index and they suddenly had prior commitments. Finally I turned to an employment agency and two persons reported to work. One was scared and slow but extremely accurate; however she was available for only a few weeks and the agency had told her not to tell me. The other was very young, leading a complex and tragic life and was absent half the time. After one prolonged absence I finally learned that she was in prison. I finally located an excellent, reliable typist who also had a fine sense of humour and loyalty. I hesitate once again to confess my stupidity but it took her eight months of forty-hour work-weeks. The total cost of the typing alone came up to $4,300.00.

My indentations for the typescript are not as noticeable as I would have liked but the indexes were going to be done by offset and the number of pages was going to be sizeable. I employed two columns per page. It is possible that it would have been preferable if I had not for a work of that size. Figures 1 and 2, columns 2 show only half a page.

I was not able to hire a professional proof-reader due to financial reasons, and each night I attempted to keep up with that day's typing since the omission of one or two entries would require the retyping of all subsequent pages. This is one very good reason for avoiding having to

furnish a perfect copy for offset processing. The completion of the typescript should have been a day of celebration but somehow none of us felt like celebrating. We just wanted to forget all about it.

My advice to novice indexers or compilers of indexes similar to mine is to believe every word printed in *The Indexer*. Don't question the judgement of professionals and when they say double or triple the estimated time, believe them. Also be certain that you have an adequate supply of index and guide cards and most importantly of boxes for filing the cards. I had to beg, borrow and nearly steal the large number of boxes required for my over 130 feet of cards. In addition I was caught by a paper shortage resulting from the energy crisis during the oil embargo and depleted the stock of index and guide cards in every shop in our large city.

I cannot presume to call myself an indexer since most of my efforts were to compile a cumulative index. But I do have a keener knowledge of the complexity of that profession and feel that it is time that indexers be given full credit for their important contributions by having their names appear either in the acknowledgements or on the title page of the publication they are associated with.

I hope that this account of my miscalculations will be of assistance to other would-be compilers of gigantic projects and that it has been a source, not of ridicule, but rather of amusement, for those of you who would have had the intelligence not to undertake it.

The Indexing of Multi-Author, Multi-Volume and Periodical Publications

J. Edwin Holmstrom

1. Introduction

The indexing of volumes made up of contributions by different authors raises questions which do not arise in indexing a treatise, textbook or narrative by a single author. Such a book is a coherent whole. Its chapters, sections and paragraphs are balanced so as to create in the reader's mind the pattern of knowledge or ideas and the distribution of emphasis the author intends. The language and style are uniform. The same special terms are used with the same meanings and implications throughout. All this makes it possible for the indexer to distinguish the wood from the trees and decide which kinds of trees call for more notice than others by scanning right through the book before he starts considering the details.

None of this is true of a volume, still less of a series of volumes, made up of contributions from a multiplicity of authors treating varied topics in a variety of styles. Even if the compiler of a combined index to a series of volumes could read the whole beforehand he would not be able to retain in his memory a detailed enough picture of their total contents to be of practical help. The problem is still more difficult in the case of a weekly or monthly periodical publication whose successive issues, containing many miscellaneous small items as well as longer articles, are later to be bound into volumes—especially if the volume index is required to be ready for sending to the printer within a few days of the last issue, in which case the indexer when dealing with the earlier issues has no means of knowing what may be sprung upon him in the later ones such as might, had he known it, have made him develop a different pattern of keywords and adopt a different distribution of emphasis at the start.

The object of this paper is to set down and invite discussion on certain recommended principles and procedural techniques which are the outcome from experience in such work during the past six years. The principles are listed in the next following section, in which they are numbered for easy reference from the examples described in the remaining four sections. These relate, respectively, to the indexing of a weekly technical journal, the preparation both of separate volume indexes and of a five-year cumulative index to the proceedings as well as other publications of an engineering institution, the indexing of a bi-monthly journal along with its quarterly bibliographical supplements, and the compilation more recently undertaken of a single name index and a single subject index covering the first fifty annual volumes of the proceedings of a learned body whose interests extend over a very wide range.

Reprinted from *The Indexer* 8, no. 1 (April 1972): 31–43.

The four different jobs are described in the order they were started. The writer is grateful to all four of his clients, as named below, for their permission to do so and to reproduce extracts from this work by way of illustration.

2. *Recommended principles*

R.1. It is assumed that the purpose of indexes is to make it possible to find out readily whether a volume or set of volumes contains references to any particular topic or person in which the index user may be interested, and if so where. The minimum requirement for this purpose is a subject index and a name index, either separate or combined, but in some fields there may be need for others such as an index of places, of organisations, of chemical compounds, etc. The relative importance of name and subject entries may vary according to the nature and purpose of the publication, the eminence of the named persons, and other factors. In the case of a combined index to many volumes containing contributions by many authors it should be remembered that the index user may not have all the volumes conveniently within reach and it is desirable, therefore, that the names of these authors should be distinguished (typographically or otherwise) from other names and be followed by the titles of their respective contributions. The entries in the subject index should not, however, be limited to what is implicit in these titles, for indexes can be made more effective as aids to stimulating the spread and applications of knowledge if they also pinpoint references that may be of value although occurring only incidentally to the main theme of any given text.

R.2. How far the coverage of the indexing ought to be extended into details such as these must be governed ultimately by its sponsors' judgment in their balancing of desirability against financial means. At present there is a lack of firm data able to be adduced for determining this balance and an evident need for research (a) as to the relation between fulness of indexing and its utility to index users, and (b) on the comparative economics of different methods. In anticipation of such research, individual indexers can and should keep records of the ratio between number of index entries and number of pages they consider to be more or less adequately indexed.

R.3. Disregarding the question whether a systematic classification of subject heads to correspond with a hierarchical pattern of the concepts they denote (such as the Universal Decimal Classification provides) may or may not be better in card indexes or for computerised indexing, it is assumed here that alphabetical sequences of names and of subject keywords are to be preferred where indexes are printed in page form for use by independent readers. On this assumption most of the following principles apply to all alphabetical indexing, though for multi-author and multi-volume publications their importance is greater.

R.4. Provided that all names without exception are to be indexed, name indexing can be done by almost anyone who is capable of obeying a set of rules. If not all names are to be indexed it may be difficult to formulate any objective criteria to govern the inclusion of some and the omission of others: to what extent, for instance, should the names of authors quoted verbatim or cited bibliographically in the text or in footnotes be indexed? In the absence of such criteria, selectivity in name indexing requires that the indexer should be in a position to judge what kinds of references are more likely than others to be of value either now or in the future, which in turn implies that he must be well versed in the subject matter himself or have ready access to advisers who are.

R.5. In subject indexing the ability to make value judgments is essential in order to distinguish between what ought to be indexed and what it would be uneconomic to index as well as time-wasting to the user of the index. It is important to notice that this ability to interpret the word ' ought ' is something that can inhere only in a human mind which understands the subject field and knows the needs and mentality of people concerned with that field. A computer cannot make value judgments; it can indeed be programmed to pick out items that have been coded to indicate that they have a particular relevance but it cannot be programmed to decide that item A is 'better', 'more suitable' or 'more useful' than item B.

R.6. Specificity of reference is an advantage which has to be balanced against the economic need for brevity. Every subject index entry should begin with a keyword carefully chosen to catch the searcher's eye by telling him the most distinctive point of interest or novelty in what is referred to. Thus under the main heading 'Computer applications' it is better to enter 'Ship design programmes library', and under 'Shipbuilding' to enter 'Computerised design: programmes library', than to put these words the other way round. In either case it would be unintelligent to begin with the word 'Library'. (Another detail, illustrated in the second of these entries, is the utility of a colon as a means of introducing a sort of sub-sub-heading which makes for clarity.) A string of undifferentiated page numbers after a single index entry irritates the reader and may, if it often occurs, even defeat the purpose of providing him with an index by making him feel rightly or wrongly that it would be quicker for him to scan through the pages of the text itself. If, therefore, the same name or the same topic is mentioned more than two or three times it should be made into a collective heading with separate specifically worded sub-headings under it. If, however, the matter does not seem important enough to warrant this a range of page numbers may be cited, followed by the word 'passim'.

R.7. As terminology is far from being fully standardised and as almost every word has both synonyms and homonyms (which, to make matters worse, are seldom exact) it is particularly important in the alphabetical indexing of subjects, on the scale being considered here, that headings or entry words should be protected against the risk of a searcher not finding what he wants because the indexer has hidden it in another part of the alphabet than expected. It must not happen, for instance, that he looks in vain under 'Heart diseases' because the indexer has chosen to call these 'Cardiac diseases' and has omitted to insert cross-references at the places in the alphabet where the same concept might reasonably be looked for. What would be still worse would be for the indexer to use sometimes the one term and sometimes the other. This risk can be avoided, either by taking all the subject heads and entry words from an existing 'thesaurus' which distinguishes the preferred from the non-preferred terms and gives the necessary cross-references, or by the indexer progressively building up such a thesaurus of each subject field and embodying the cross-references in the index as he goes along. In the examples that follow the latter alternative has been adopted.

R.8. Apart from this, a perennial moot point in alphabetical indexing is whether, or according to what criteria, the keywords with which the subject entries begin should be grouped under collective main heads or should each be inserted independently according to where their initial letters come in the alphabet. Should, for instance, 'Feudal law' be made a sub-head under 'Law' or should it be inserted, independently of that, directly among other entries beginning with F? In the examples that follow the second alternative is adopted as a rule, but an exception is made where the same entry keyword is shared by several different references, or where the entry keyword does not make sense or might be ambiguous without the context supplied by a 'higher collective' main heading. Where, however, a searcher of the index might reasonably be in doubt where to look either on this account or because a synonym exists, a cross-reference is given in one of the following ways:

Airports and airfields
    Pavements —)   (meaning 'see Pavements as a separate heading')

Earth pressure
    Measuring cells —) Load cells/ (meaning 'see these as a sub-heading under Load
                                cells')
    (Seismology) —) Earthquakes   (meaning 'see instead the preferred synonym Earth-
                                quakes')

A further advantage of this device is that the same cross-reference for Pavements, for instance, can be given under other main heads where appropriate, such as under Roads. In typing the draft for an index the arrowhead is imitated by two hyphens followed after back-spacing by a bracket closure, thus —).

R.9. For the reason already suggested at R.1, and because nothing exasperates an index user more than being caused to waste time following up what appears at first sight a useful clue only to discover that it leads to something different from what he expected or too trivial to be of use, it is important that the index entries themselves should indicate the authorship, date and length of each reference. In the examples below this is achieved by the device of following each entry in the Subject Index by a 'Harvard reference'—i.e. the author's name and the year of publication—before giving the page number or range of page numbers where the subject in question is treated. If the Harvard reference is preceded by the word 'In' this means that the subject is treated only incidentally to the main theme of the paper or article whose full title and full range of page numbers will be found after the stated author and year in the Name Index. Thereby the subject entries can often, without loss of specificity, be made shorter than they would otherwise have to be and the space saved can be used for increasing the number of entries (see R.2).

R.10. The military precept that 'time spent on reconnaissance is seldom wasted' applies also to indexing (and to many other activities). In practical terms this means that before doing anything else the indexer should take a preliminary look at all the ground he has to cover—or as much of it as is accessible to him within the limitations referred to in the Introduction here—distinguishing its more obvious features from those that seem to demand more thorough consideration. A good method is to scan rapidly through the text, underlining the names and making a mark against these in the left margin, side-lining on the right the passages that suggest a need for subject index. These marks should be made in pencil so that the names and sub-entries finally chosen can be distinguished by marking with a ball pen.

R.11. Copying and recopying thousands of names, technical terms and page numbers without error is difficult to achieve unless all are checked. Because of this, and also for overall economy, it is advantageous to devise methods whereby the successive phases of indexing work can be shared between an indexer who has the necessary professional knowledge and capacity for judgment (see R.5) and an assistant able to concentrate wholly upon accurate copy-typing, co-operation between them being systematised in such a way that each automatically checks the other's work, as is exemplified below.

3. *Indexing of 'The Engineer'*

This weekly journal founded in 1856, the oldest of all British journals in its field and one of the oldest in the world, maintained until 1968 an unbroken tradition of covering all branches of the profession and related industries from an always updated standpoint. Two volumes a year were produced, each made up of 26 weekly issues and each provided with a Names Index containing about

3,000 entries, a Subject Index containing a still larger number and a title index to about 250 book reviews. Allowing for the large format of the pages and also for the space occupied by the numerous illustrations, the total number of index entries in the volume indexes of recent years probably corresponded to an average of between five and six per thousand words of text, including the longer articles (usually several taking up about half the space in each issue) as well as very many shorter notes on engineering equipment and products, contracts awarded, etc. Apart from this a large, but selectively compiled, author and subject index to the permanently or historically interesting contents of the journal during the first 104 years of its life had appeared in 1964 (the work of Mr. C. E. Prockter who is the editor of *Kempe's engineers year book* published by the same company).

Until 1965 the volume indexes were produced in the publisher's own library by staff who drafted the entries for the current issues week by week and typed them on 'Copystrips' which were interlocked with one another in alphabetical order to build up copy for the printer. For three years from then onward the work was performed under contract by the present writer (himself a Chartered Engineer) in the manner now to be described; but in 1968 the editorial policy of the journal was radically changed in accordance with the description now appearing under its title as 'The weekly for engineering management', and indexing was discontinued altogether.

In the intervening three years the style of indexing remained nearly the same as before apart from some rationalisation of the subject index heads to improve their mutual exclusiveness, but at the publishers' request a different procedure was developed and it may be of interest to mention here the experience gained from it. The object of this new procedure was primarily to make it possible for the spare capacity of punched card machinery, already installed for the purpose of printing the addresses of subscribers to the journal on

wrappers, to be utilised both for sorting the index entries into alphabetical order and for intercalating them with earlier ones in the event of a decision to produce another index cumulated over a period of years. On balance, however, the experiment was not a complete success and if the indexing had been continued a changeover to the use of gummed labels as described and illustrated in the next section would have been recommended. One reason for this was that the card sorter was too apt to be in use for other purposes when wanted for the indexing work. A more technical reason, which may be worth mentioning here, was that typewriting an index entry lengthwise below the top edge of each card— so that after the cards had been sorted into the right order and shingled over one another as shown at (c) in Fig. 1 they could temporarily be stuck together with adhesive tape and the succession of entries photocopied in list form for the printer to set in type—necessarily involved the cards becoming bent round the platen of the typewriter and this bending was apt to jam and mutilate them when they were afterwards fed into the sorting machine. Looking back, it seems doubtful anyway whether the punching of cards for the purpose of having them sorted once (or possibly twice) in their lives by machine takes any less time than sorting gummed labels by hand.

Using punched cards, it was found helpful, if not essential, to have a system of code abbreviations both of names and of subject headings, these being so devised that cards punched in accordance with the abbreviations would be sorted by machine into the same alphabetical order as the full names (whether personal or corporate) or main subject headings should occupy. Abbreviations to five letters, needing ten of the 80 punchable columns on the cards, were found sufficient to ensure this but it would have been better to add a sixth letter so that any index entries subordinated to a particular name or main subject head could be arranged in the right order by machine instead of having to rely on visual inspection and hand sorting for the final step. So far as it went, the coding system evolved may be understood from the following examples:

assEI	Associated Electrical Industries Ltd.
eurNE	European Nuclear Energy Agency
hamAH	Hamilton, A. H.
pilBL	Pilkington Brothers Ltd.

AGRm	Agricultural machinery
DISh	District heating
EARme	Earth moving equipment
VEHse	Vehicle safety enginering

As will be seen, the principle is that the first three letters are those with which the first word in the name or subject head begins and the following two are the initial letters of the next two words. Exceptions are made, however, in parts of the alphabet where there are many names or subject heads beginning with the same two or three letters. Thus the code abbreviation for British is distorted to brj so as to ensure that cards punched with this will come after those for Bristol, and Institute is denoted by inr to ensure that cards so punched will come before those punched ins for Institution. Likewise for the subject index:

AUTac	Automatic control, automation
AUTad	Automatic data processing
AUTb	Automobiles
AUTct	Automobiles: car types
AUTrt	Automobiles: racing types and engines

RAIw	Railways
RAIwe	Railways, electrification
RAIwr	Railway, rolling stock
RAIws	Railway signalling and train control
RAIwt	Railway terminals

If punched card machinery is to be used not only for sorting into alphabetical order but also for first separating the Name, Subject and Book review references into three

sequences these can be denoted by 1, 2, 3 written in front of the code abbreviations and one additional column must be punched.

(Using the gummed label system, code abbreviations are required only for main subject headings under which sub-headings will be arranged and they need not necessarily consist of five letters each.)

The procedure developed for sharing the work between an indexer and a copy typist so that each is likely to detect any error made by the other (R.10) is illustrated in Fig. 1 as follows:

(1) The indexer reads the text, decides what to index and drafts the index entries in page number order as at (a); but to save having to write out all the necessary words in full he underlines most of them where they are printed in the text or titles and denotes these by ringed numbers as at (b). (It is convenient to begin the ringed numbers from one over again for each fresh article, or for each fresh page of text if the items are crowded.)

(2) His assistant types each index entry, preceded by its code abbreviation, below the top edge of a card as at (c).

(3) She or another person punches the code abbreviation letters in the appropriate columns of the cards.

(4) The indexer checks the typing and punching of each card, then deletes the code abbreviation in red ink as a sign that he has done so and to prevent its being printed. Any error due, for instance, to the ringed numbers in (b) having been confused is at once apparent from the fact that the words in the order they are typed do not make sense (R.11).

(5) All these operations can be completed during the week following each issue of the journal. If it is desired that the cards up to date should be available as a means of referring to the contents of recent issues before the current volume is completed, each weekly

batch of cards can at once be sorted into alphabetical order and intercalated with the
previous ones by machine. Otherwise the
sorting and intercalating can be deferred until the volume index is due to be printed.
Thereupon the cards are shingled over one
another as at (c) and are temporarily held
together by adhesive tape (of the kind that
can be stripped off without damaging the
cards) while a photocopy is made of the
typing on them, for sending to the printer.
An extract from a volume Subject Index is
reproduced at Fig. 1 (d). Afterwards the
cards can, if desired, be re-separated and kept
for later intercalation among those referring
to other volumes in order to produce a cumulative index over a run of years. At this point
it may be of interest to mention in passing an
untried suggestion on which comment is
invited, for producing without the use of
punched cards a kind of cumulative index
which, while perhaps not quite so convenient
to search as a conventional one, would be
very much cheaper. This might be of advantage because what too often happens is that
the people who would be prepared to pay for
cumulative indexes are too few to justify the
cost of publishing them, although to those
few they would be extremely valuable.

The proposal is, therefore, that cuttings
from successive volume indexes each covering
the same range of the alphabet, such as for
instance from vols. 27 to 36 covering the
range Ear to Ellipse as shown in Fig. 2,
should be pasted side by side on a large sheet
and photographed. This would enable sets
of photocopies from A to Z to be produced
manually and stapled together, as and when
required, in very small batches or even one
by one. Furthermore, as soon as the index
to vol. 37 became available the corresponding cuttings from this could be pasted on the
right of those from vol. 36, while at the same
time removing the cuttings from vol. 27 on
the left if it were preferred to file the older
ones separately. Thus the publisher would
then be in a position to supply indexes covering the ten most recent volumes at any
moment.

4. Indexing the publications of the Institution of Civil Engineers.

The *Proceedings* of this professional institution, founded in 1818, appear as a monthly
journal with about 170 pages. A typical
issue may contain about twenty titles : several
papers describing either completed engineering projects for oral discussions or research
presented for oral discussion at meetings or
for written discussion; several summaries of
such discussions on earlier papers; summaries
of 'informal discussions' that have taken
place on questions propounded orally by their
introducers at meetings for that purpose;
some short technical items and a few obituaries.

Every four numbers of the *Proceedings*
constitute a volume for which an Author Index, a Subject Index and what is now called
a Place and Project Names Index are provided. The Institution also publishes a quarterly journal *Géotechnique* on behalf of the
International Society for Soil Mechanics and
Foundation Engineering, which contains articles, occasionally a lecture, correspondence
and book reviews on those subjects, each four
numbers constituting an annual volume with
similar three indexes.

Since 1968 the indexes to each volume of
the *Proceedings* and of *Géotechnique* have
been prepared by the methods about to be
described. At the same time a single five-year
index has been compiled and published, in
which name, subject and place references to
the contents of both journals over the years
1965 to 1969 inclusive are cumulated as well
as references to various supplements and
shorter reports and to the proceedings of over
forty conferences and symposia held at various times during these years, each forming a
separate volume with several hundred pages.

The methods developed for compiling these
indexes may be understood from Fig. 3 which
represents (a) the beginning of a paper in
the *Proceedings* marked with ringed numbers
against the words to be indexed, (b) a 'drafting slip' containing these numbers, (c) the
upper half of a sheet of gummed labels with

perforations for tearing them apart (known in the trade as Ivy Series TWL 31) on to which the nine index entries have been copied in accordance with the drafting slip, and (d) the appearance of the Subject Index as printed from copy prepared by separating the labels and rearranging them in alphabetical order of the subject abbreviations typed in their top left corners. These abbreviations are on the same principle as described above for punched cards (though they need not, of course, be limited to five letters), the meanings of those in the present sample being:

damBR	Dams, barrages and reservoirs.
testE	Testing and experimental techniques
soiM	Soil mechanics
desSA	Design and stress analysis
straM	Strain measurement

The letters and figures on the drafting slip have the following meanings and where they are double-underlined this indicates that the words they represent are to be typewritten in capitals for printing in bold type:

(H) is the slightly abbreviated 'Harvard reference' which serves to identify the paper by citing its first mentioned author's name (followed by &c if there are joint authors) and the year of publication (which is not necessarily the same year as a meeting on it was held), in order to shorten the index entries (see R.9 above).

(V) stands for the *Géotechnique* or *Proceedings* volume number as the case may be. In the case of a paper contained in the separately published report of a conference, for example the conference on World Airports published in 1970, the Geo. and P symbols are deleted and replaced by a symbol like ICE (1970 wa). The range of page numbers occupied by each paper as a whole, within that volume, is written under (p). The symbol (T) tells the typist that the full title of the item under reference is to be copied out. If the latter is something other than a full-scale paper for discussion or an article its nature is indicated by adding after (T) the

appropriate description (A), (B), (Cr), (Id), etc.

The entries in the Subject Index relate to topics whose potential interest to a reader is not confined to a particular locality, whereas those in the Place and Project Names index are such as a reader would naturally expect to find there (e.g. Severn Bridge, Kariba Dam, Victoria Line in London, etc.). Many of the papers, or parts of them, are referred to in both these indexes. If a topic so indexed is only incidental to the main theme of a paper the (H) and (V) are preceded by the word 'In' and the pagination following the (V) is limited to the topic in question. This enables a user of the index to judge its importance relatively to the paper in which it occurs (as well as to find out the context) by referring, via the author's name, to the title and full pagination (see R.2 above).

The labels intended for the Author Index are distinguishable by the names on them being typed in capital letters, those for the Subject Index by the presence of code abbreviations for subject headings and those for the Place and Project Names Index by the absence of any abbreviations. Checking the typed labels is facilitated by the fact that they remain in page number order until they are separated. After separation, their sorting into alphabetical order is easily and quickly done by hand on to a large sheet of paper divided into 24 rectangles (or using 24 empty yoghourt cartons) marked with the letters of the alphabet (PQ and XYZ being combined).

When the first five-year index on these lines (covering the years 1964-1969 inclusive) was being prepared the gummed labels themselves were produced in duplicate by carbon copying on to a second sheet of them, one lot being separated, sorted and stuck on to backing sheets in alphabetical order to serve as printer's copy for the current volume index while keeping the other lot for cumulation over the five years. At the same time, and as is still being done, two carbon copies on ordinary paper were made, one for filing at the Institution in case the originals should be lost in some disaster and the other kept by the indexer for reference when he has to link the indexing of a subsequent discussion with that of the original paper to which it relates. For various practical reasons, however, the carbon-copied labels did not prove altogether satisfactory, so the avoidance of repetitive typing and checking is now being achieved by a better method, as follows.

Only a single copy is typed on gummed labels. As soon as a volume is complete, the labels for the last issue included in it are checked, separated and intercalated among those for the previous issues in alphabetical order. They are then tacked temporarily on to back sheets in that order, not moistening the gum over the whole of the back of each label but only over a spot in the middle. The backing sheets bearing the labels are photocopied. As the typing denoted by (V) in Fig. 3 (b) is not wanted in the volume index this is crossed out on the photocopies; also the subject heading abbreviations are deleted and the full subject headings are typed in the appropriate positions on the photocopies, enabling the latter to be used as printer's copy for the volume indexes.

As so little of each label adheres to its backing sheet they can easily be pulled off for later re-use to build up the cumulated five-year index. Meanwhile, however, as their number runs into many thousands it is obviously undesirable to run the risk of any being lost or misplaced. To avoid this the labels after being used for the volume index are permanently stuck on to sheets which are themselves filed in alphabetical order, leaving ample gaps between the labels first collected so that later ones can be inserted in the right alphabetical positions between them. Quarto-sized sheets are convenient as tens of these with their top edges shingled over one another and labelled with successive ranges of the alphabet, stapled together, can be kept in foolscap-sized folders or boxes. This arrangement, as sketched in Fig. 4, makes individual labels much quicker to find than separately filed cards or slips as many can be seen at a glance, although no guide cards or tabs are needed. If the total number of index entries to be anticipated is roughly known, existing indexes or dictionaries can be helpful for estimating how many sheets will be needed to spread out corresponding ranges of the alphabet, but the tendency is always to underestimate. Therefore, until the compilation of the index is well advanced the labels should be placed only in the right hand half of the sheets, leaving the other half free for interpolations when there is no more room between those on the right.

Four golden rules may be stated: do not be afraid of what may initially appear to be a waste of paper; keep the gaps as large as possible for as long as possible; do not place two labels in immediate contiguity until respect for the alphabet compels it; if and when this does happen and a third has to be inserted between the two, cut the sheet across and start a fresh sheet between the severed parts.

The successive steps in compiling the index entries for each issue of a journal or conference report on this system can be recapitulated as follows:

(a) The indexer first scans each paper or other item (R.10), then considers the essential parts of it in greater detail, deciding what to index and marking the appropriate words with ringed numbers.

(b) He then prepares a drafting slip for each item which he inserts in the journal at the page where that item begins. If some of the ringed numbers are on pages other than the first he also inserts small slips of paper where these are, to guide the typist. Before passing the publication to her he makes sure that no item has been overlooked, and facilitates later checking, by writing the number of labels to be typed in the bottom right corner of the drafting slip and also against the title in the list of contents of the journal, where the total can be added up, which is useful also for statistical purposes (R.2).

(c) The labels are typed as listed on each drafting slip. The typist checks that their number is correct, then separates the block of labels that refer to each item from those that refer to other items and inserts this with the drafting slip at the page where the item begins.

(d) Receiving it back, the indexer checks the typing of the labels by comparing the words on them with (a) any discrepancy (other than simple spelling errors) due to a mistake by himself or by the typist being immediately apparent as it will have resulted in the sequence of the words denoted by the ringed numbers not making sense (see R.11).

(e) The indexer, or someone supervised by him, separates the labels, sorts them into alphabetical sequences of Name, Subject and Place references and sticks them on to backing sheets to constitute printer's copy first for the volume index and later for the cumulative five-year index as described above.

5. Indexing of ' Science Policy News '

The Science Policy Foundation, founded in 1966 as the Science of Science Foundation, is not concerned with the technical content of the various sciences but with studies of the planning, financing and social repercussions of research and development nationally and internationally. It holds meetings, organises conferences and sponsors various projects in support of these interests, and jointly with the Organisation for Economic Co-operation and Development it began in 1969 the publication of a bi-monthly journal *Science Policy News* (now *Science Policy*). Each issue of this contains one or more signed articles, addresses delivered by eminent persons or reports on conferences, followed by a great many shorter notes received from countries and international organizations all over the world, as well as occasional book reviews, filling 16 pages in all. Three times a year the bulletin includes as a supplement a List of Current National Publications which gives briefly annotated bibliographical references to well over one hundred reports and miscellanea, submitted by national correspondents who are appointed for this purpose in all the OECD member countries.

The indexing of the bulletin and its supplements may be of interest because their characteristics are at the opposite pole to those of the publication to be described in Section 6 here. On the one hand, understanding the text calls for no specialised knowledge of any kind so R.5 presents no problem and the annual volume comprising six issues of the bulletin with three supplements totals less than 150 pages; hence not much time will be wasted if very occasionally an index entry is not specific enough to prevent the reader setting off on a false scent. On the other hand, apart from the opening pages of each issue nearly all the rest consists of multitudinous disconnected summaries or citations of information whose potential value relatively to one another it is impossible to assess; hence every such item must be indexed or none at all, and as most of them are very short it would be meaningless to express the density of indexing as so many entries per thousand words of text.

To meet these conditions a Name Index and a Subject Index are provided shortly after the completion of each annual volume. In each of them the references are to page numbers in the case of the text but not hitherto in the case of the Supplements, the reason for this being that the numbering of the pages in the latter starts from one in each issue instead of continuing through the volume and that the pages therein are very crowded. Therefore the index references to the Supplements are given in the form exemplified by Maddock, I., S(5)2 : L8, meaning that a publication by him is mentioned in Supplement no. 5, page 2 thereof, in the left hand column about 8/10ths of the way down. The indexes to vol. 2 (1970-1) of SPN are printed as a four-page folder, whereof the portions reproduced in Fig. 5 here show the end of the Name Index and the beginning of both parts of the Subject Index.

The Name Index contains all individual names. Those of the personal authors of publications cited in the Supplements are included but not corporate names of organization as the latter can easily be discovered via

(*Continued after illustrations section*)

Rules for automatic sprinkler installations revised

The Fire Offices Committee has just published a new set of rules for the installation of automatic sprinkler systems in Great Britain and Ireland. The new rules, based upon a series of full-scale fire tests, represent a scientific approach to the problem of automatic extinction of fires to meet the wide variety of conditions existing today, particularly the heights to which goods are stored and to the growing use of new hazardous materials such as foam plastics. In drafting the rules, full regard has been paid to the need to keep the capital cost of installations as low as possible without sacrificing efficiency, and some saving in costs should result in many cases.

For sprinkler systems fire risks are arranged in three classes in the new rules—extra light, ordinary and extra-high hazard—depending on the hazard and fire load involved in any particular building. The new rules applied from 1 January, and, while systems installed under the previous rules will be accepted until July 1969, all sprinkler systems installed thereafter will have to conform to the new requirements.

The new rules are also the basis for the model rules adopted by the Comité Européen des Assurances, comprising insurers of all countries of Western Europe including the United Kingdom. The Fire Offices' Committee played an important role in the preparation of these model rules, which it is hoped will be ultimately followed in Europe and elsewhere.

Copies of the rules are available from the Fire Offices Committee, Aldermary House, Queen Street, London, E.C.4, price 10s 6d.

I.R.D. MAKES A 15 000 A HOMOPOLAR GENERATOR

A large homopolar generator of 600 kW is being built by I.R.D. (International Research and Development), for the Rutherford Laboratory, Chilton, England. The contract is for a generator rated at 15 000 A, 40 V, d.c., designed to have a very low ripple in the output voltage and to energize a septum magnet in the final stage of the ejection of a proton beam from the Nimrod proton synchrotron. The magnet current will be

Schematic diagram of 15 000 A, 40 V homopolar generator

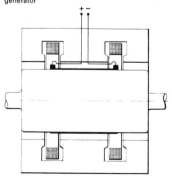

pulsed to a peak of 21 000 A, with a trapezoidal waveform.

To satisfy these conditions the generator will be a homopolar machine: in this respect it will resemble the superconducting motor being developed by I.R.D. but it will differ from it by being air/water-cooled instead of cryogenic.

The accompanying diagram (not to scale) outlines the proposed machine which will have the following (approximate) dimensions: length 12 ft (3·6 m), stator diameter 5 ft (1·5 m), rotor diameter 3 ft 3 in (1 m). The steel stator will be solid, bored out to carry the rotor and the stator coils, wound from aluminium foil. The rotor will also be solid, surrounded by a conducting sleeve fitted with sliprings. Brushgear, bearing on these sliprings in the air-gap will conduct the output current to the external terminals as indicated.

Generators of this kind can be made with current outputs up to 500 000 A and voltages up to 100 V, suitable for electric furnaces, electroplating, electrochemical machining, large-scale battery charging and chemical processing, such as the production of chlorine.

For further information write to International Research & Development Company Ltd, Fossway, Newcastle upon Tyne, NE6 2YD. Or use the post-paid card opposite p. 26, circling **157.**

Shipyard celebrates 125th anniversary

Last month A.G. 'Weser' with shipyards at Bremen and Bremerhaven, and a member company of the Krupp concern, celebrated its 125th anniversary. Originating from an iron foundry and engineering works, the shipyard became famous with the construction of such vessels as the Bremen. Today it is one of the most modern yards for the building of large tankers; No 5 slipway (illustration) can build oil tankers with capacities of up to 500 000 ton.

The enterprise was founded in 1843 by the engineer Carsten Waltjen and his friend Heinrich Leonard, and soon after both came to England to study the construction of iron ships for which there were no facilities in Bremen at the time. Waltjens built his first iron steamer in 1846, the Roland. Its hazardous launch caused Leonard to withdraw from the partnership. In 1872 the firm was converted into a joint-stock company with the name A.G. 'Weser'. In 1926 it was merged into the Deschimag group, but resumed its old name after 1945. The company employs about 7 500 people, and builds ships of all sizes from seagoing tugs to large tankers, as well as being a well-known marine engineering firm.

PETROL PUMP ACCEPTS BANKNOTES

Following upon the introduction a few years ago of coin-operated petrol pumps, a pump which accepts DM10 banknotes as well as coins has been produced by A.E.G.-Telefunken. Money can be inserted in any order desired. As the valve of the filling nozzle is pressed and petrol begins to flow, the counter startes to operate and an electronic circuit ensures that the total discharge corresponds correctly to the amount paid. If the tank fills up more quickly than was thought, or for any other reason filling has to be stopped sooner than intended, the filling hose is replaced on the pump column and unused coins are returned; however, no provision is made for giving change.

For further information please write to A.E.G.-Telefunken, 6 Frankfurt (Main) 70, A.E.G. Hochhaus, German Federal Republic. Or use the post-paid card facing p. 26, circling **158.**

2 FIRE – Automatic sprinkler installations: rules revised. Fire Offices Committee, 12

1   Fire Offices Committee. Automatic sprinkler installations: rules revised, 12

1   Weser AG (GFR). Shipyards 125th anniversary, 12 i

2 EL'Le Homopolar generator, 15 000A, 40V, d.c. International Research & Devt. Co. Ltd. for Rutherford Laboratory, Chilton, 12 i

1   Rutherford Laboratory, Chilton. Homopolar generator, 15 000A, 40V, d.c. by International Research & Development Co. Ltd., 12 i

1 intRD – Homopolar generator, 15 000A, 40V, d.c., for Rutherford Laboratory, Chilton, 12 i

2   PETROL PUMPS accepting banknotes. AEG–Telefunken (GFR), (12)

1   AEG–Telefunken (GFR). Petrol pumps accepting banknotes, (12)

2 SPAr – Man-on-the-moon project: dependence on lunar model; 13

FIG. 1(c)

Relays
 Armature Arms. Failure, T. R. F. Williams and D. T. Stevens, (TC) 826-7 i
 Compact, low-cost. Londex Ltd., (NP) 600 i
 Controlled reed type, plug-in modules. McMurdo Instrument Co. Ltd., (NP) 711 i
 Miniature, for safety circuits in railway signalling, (Paper) 838 i
 Overload, with single-phase protection and ambient temperature compensation. Telemecanique Electrique (GB) Ltd., 870 i
 Solid-state, for telegraph equipment. Plessey Automation Group, (NP) 24 i
Remote Control. Completely centralized remote control for boilers and generators, valves, dampers, motors, &c, at West Thurrock Power Station, 539-40 i
Research
 Application of results. R. G. Stansfield, (Paper) 340, (Letter) 453
 Collaboration between Government research departments, industry and the universities. Leading article in *State Service*, Institution of Professional Civil Servants, 90
 Joint working party between Universities and industry, 194
 Organization and benefits. (Papers at British Association symposium), 339-41
 Science, Technology and Society. Presidential address to the British Association for the Advancement of Science. Lord Jackson of Burnley, (Leader) 277, 279-80
 Sophistication Factor in Science Expenditure. Report by Department of Education and Science, (Leader) 849-50

Research and Development. Proportion of gross national product. Department of Economic Affairs, progress report, 201
Road Breaker and Rock Drill. Dual-purpose, petrol-engined. Holman Brothers Ltd., (NP) 162
Roads, Construction and Maintenance
 (An) *Experiment Comparing the Performance of Roadstone in Surface Dressing.* RRL Report No. 46, D. S. Wilson, 863
 Heated roadway made from pulverized fuel ash. Electro-Agricultural Centre, (41)
 Performances of surfaces evaluable in bridge deck panels testing frame, full scale. Road Research Laboratory, (Colour photo &c), 40 i
 Submarine Tunnels: see separately
Roads Development, Economics and Policy
 Discussion at joint meeting of British Road Federation and Institute of Highway Engineers, (Leader) 578
 Investment programme of Greater London Council, (Leader) 754
 Parking. R. A. Parker and N. V. E. Seymer, (Paper) 801
 Traffic Control: see separately

FIG. 1(d)

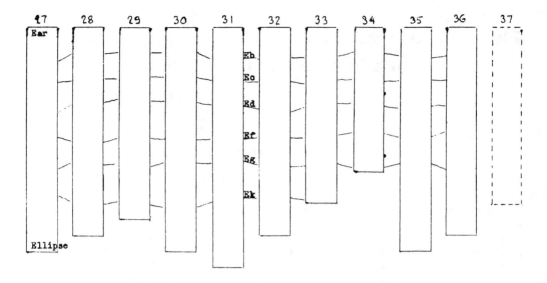

FIG. 2

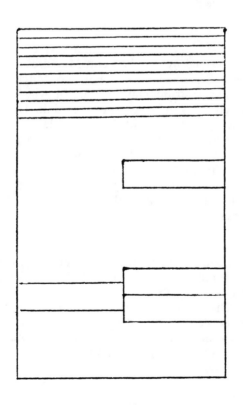

FIG. 4

7403 (T.1) Observed and predicted deformations in a large embankment dam during construction

A. D. M. PENMAN, MSc, FICE*

J. B. BURLAND, MSc(Eng), PhD, MICE*

J. A. CHARLES, MSc(Eng), ACGI, MICE*

Detailed measurements are being made of the movements of a large number of points on the main cross section of Scammonden Dam and these movements are compared with those calculated from an analysis based on a finite element technique. The agreement is encouraging and the analysis offers a method of estimating the expected movements in an embankment type dam. Design against complete collapse using a suitable safety factor gives little indication of expected movements, which can damage a core, outlet works, etc., and at present there is a need for a design method which will allow internal deformations to be estimated. Although the analysis given in this Paper uses many simplifying assumptions which may be improved in future work, it gives a method which can be used now and which is compared here with the observed behaviour of a fairly large dam.

Introduction

Scammonden Dam, the highest dam in Great Britain, is of earth/rockfill construction and has been described by Mitchell and Maguire[1] and Winder.[2] Its initial behaviour has been described by Penman and Mitchell.[3] It has been fitted with comprehensive instrumentation, part of which consists of horizontal plate gauges which are similar to those used in Gepatch Dam (Lauffer and Schober).[4] They consist of rigid PVC pipes laid to an outward fall of about 1:40 during construction and fitted with steel plates at about every 15 m length, as indicated by Figs 1 and 2. Sensing units passed through the pipes detect the steel plates and enable their horizontal and vertical positions to be measured relative to terminal plates at the end of each gauge in small instrument houses on the downstream slope of the dam. Details of the horizontal plate gauge are given in Appendix 1.

Observations

2. To obtain the total movements of the plates, the movements of the instrument houses were measured in relation to a reference pillar (shown by Fig. 3) founded in bedrock far enough downstream of the dam to be unaffected by its stress zone. The pillar was protected from ground movements by a cylinder of concrete manhole rings to a depth of 5 m. The level of each terminal plate was referred to this pillar by use of a Wild N3 precision level. This was a fairly difficult task over the rough terrain with large level differences

---

Ordinary meeting 5.30 p.m. Tuesday 9 November, 1971 jointly with British Section ICOLD and British Geotechnical Society.

Written discussion closes 30 November, 1971, for publication after February 1972.

* Building Research Station, Garston, Watford.

Fig. 3(a)   1

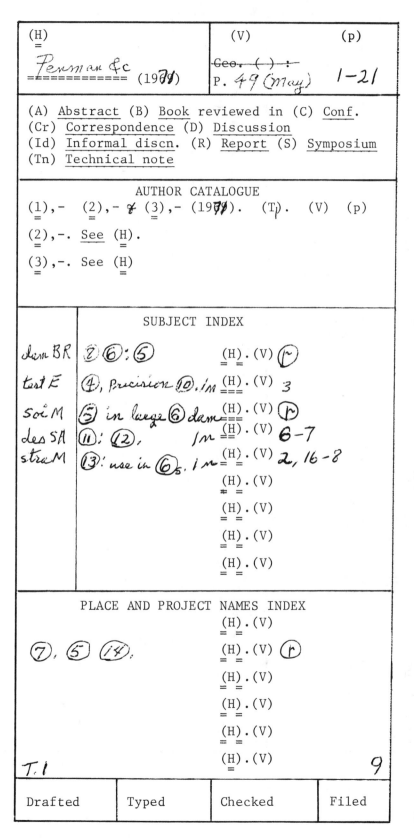

| Drafted | Typed | Checked | Filed |

Fig. 3(b)

PENMAN, A.D.M., BURLAND, J.B., and CHARLES, J.A. (1971). Observed and predicted deformations in a large embankment dam during construction. P.49 (May) 1-21	BURLAND, J.B. See PENMAN &c (1971)
CHARLES, J.A. See PENMAN &c (1971)	damBR Earth/rockfill embankment: deformations. PENMAN &c (1971). P.49 (May) 1-21
testE Mekometer, precision electro-optic distance measuring apparatus. In PENMAN &c (1971). P.49 (May) 3	soiM Deformations in large embankment dams. PENMAN &c (1971). P.49 (May) 1-21
desSA Finite element analysis: deformations of earth dams. In PENMAN &c (1971). P.49 (May) 6-7	straM Horizontal plate gauges: use in embankments. In PENMAN &c (1971). 2, 16-8
Scammonden Dam. Deformations during construction. In PENMAN &c (1971). P.49 (May) 1-21	

Fig. 3(c)

Fig. 3(d)

Subject Index

FIG. 5   iii

23	POLfs	infDL	Switz	27
24	—	invnP	UK	(24), 27
25	—	res	"	Contract research offered by (25), 27
26	MEDh	reptA	"	Dept. of (26), 27
27	MEDh	infDL	"	(27) booklist, 27
28	TECH	soclR	USA	(28), 27
29	ENVep	—	USSR	(29), 27
30	SPAC	econ	"	(30), book on economic uses of space vehicles, 28
31	—	invnP	EC	(31) conventions, 28
32	AGR	—	FAO	Output in 1970, 29
33	—	pers	WHO	Assistant D-G, 29
34	ENVep	—	"	Waste disposal: (34) issuing 'IRCWD News', 29

FIG. 6(a)

POLfs/infDL Switz: 27	/invnP UK:Patent Office, 27
/res UK: Contract research offered by Technion (Israel), 27	MEDh/reptA UK: Dept. of Health & Social Security, 27
MEDh/infDL UK: Ciba Foundation booklist, 27	TECH/soclR USA: Harvard program to end, 27

FIG. 6(b)

FIG. 7

62-3	
0	
1	S
2	
3	N
4	
5	
6	
7	
8	N
9	N

ⓡ   **AB CD EF GH IJ KL MN OP QR ST UV WX YZ**   FRAZER (1917) 8. ⓡ

57	.1	FRAZER, J.G. (1917). Jacob + the mandrakes. 8 , 57=79
	mand	Mandrake (mandragora) ≠
	mand.1	⎧ Pregnancy-promoting power affirmed ⎫
		⎪ in 'Genesis' ; associated legends ⎪
		⎨ (15 modern ancient + about 65 ⎬ -79
		⎩ modern citations, passim). ⎭
	mythL	Mandrake's pregnancy-promoting power → ≠
	chri	Genesis : esp.. " " " → Myths + legends
	folkl	" " " → ≠
	jewH.8	Dudaim (mandrake) plant. ln -9
58	grkA.9	Aphrodite , ~~goddess~~ goddess of love. ln
	.9	Harris, Rendel. Cited on Aphrodite +
		mandrake legend, in
59	.1	Maundrell, Henry (17c.). Quoted on
		visit to Nablus (ancient Shechem), in
	.4	Tristram, H.B. Quoted in , 73-4
62	.3	Dioscorides. Greek medical writer, quoted in
63	mand.1	Habitat + forgeries, selling in modern times. ln -4
	.8	Brown(e), Sir Thomas. 18c. physician. Cited in
	.9	Grimm, J. " "
67	.2	Joan of Arc. ln
	.2	Jeanne d'Arc, Jeanne Darc → Joan of Arc ≠
68	.8	Gerard, John. 17c. herbalist. ln
	a.7	⎡ Anaesthesia. Mandrake (mandragora) used in ancient ⎤
		⎣ + medieval times. ⎦ ln -9
	med.	Anaesthesia → ≠
	mand.7	Anaesthetic use. ln -9
69	warf. 3	Soporific stratagems. ln
73	castl. 4	Machaerus, near Dead Sea. ln
78	relig. 4	Personification of nature. "

Fig. 8

mand Mandrake (mandragora)	mythL Mandrake's pregnancy-promoting power --)	folkL Mandrake's pregnancy-promoting power --)	grkA.9 Aphrodite, goddess of love. In FRAZER (1917) 8, 58	.1 Maundrell, Henry (17c.). Quoted on visit to Nablus (ancient Shechem), in FRAZER (1917) 8, 59
FRAZER, J.G. (1917). Jacob and the mandrakes 8, 57-79	mand.1 Pregnancy-promoting power affirmed in Genesis: associated legends. (15 ancient and about 65 modern citations, passim). In FRAZER (1917) 8, 57-79	chri Genesis: Mandrake's pregnancy-promoting power --)	jewH.8 Dudain (mandrake) plant. In FRAZER (1917) 8, 57-9	.9 Harris, Rendel. Cited on Aphrodite and mandrake legend, in FRAZER (1917) 8, 58

Fig. 9

the country symbols in the Subject Index. Authors of articles or other texts occupying more than one full page have their surnames in italics followed by the titles, for ease in cross-reference to them (R.9).

The structure of the Subject Index is dictated by the main purpose of the bulletin as a whole, which might be described as that of combining broad generalised expositions of science policy with the diffusion of numerous short items which have been assembled from many countries because people concerned with parallel problems in other countries may be able to profit from them. That being so, and seeing that most of them are presented under headings which relate them to their countries of origin, it is desirable that the indexing should cut across this arrangement and juxtapose the items in such a way as will facilitate international comparisons. To achieve this, each element of information is characterised by a ' Relevance ' term to which an ' Aspect ' term is related as may be understood from the following examples :

RELEVANCE		Aspect
Agriculture	:	Productivity
Energy and fuels	:	Economics
Mathematics	:	Universities and other higher education
Pharmacy	:	Manufacturing
Transport	:	Bibliography

The Relevance terms are designations of about forty sciences and technologies with their applications. As some are of wider scope than others (e.g. Physics is wider than Electronics) the rule, where they overlap, is to choose whichever is the most specific term that will cover the subject matter being indexed. Experience has shown that the interest of any item of information occurring in the text or Supplements can be sharply enough specified (R.9) with a minimal need for further annotation, by choosing the most appropriate Aspect term from a list of about thirty.

As can be seen in Fig. 5 the Subject Index is divided into two sections containing respectively I. References to aspects of all subject fields (which are grouped directly under Aspect terms) and II. References to aspects of specified subject fields (which are grouped first under Relevance terms and within those under Aspect terms). In both sections the actual references are arranged in the alphabetical order of symbols denoting the countries or international organizations from which they emanate, those whose interest is international apart from any organization being put first.

In preparation for name indexing the indexer simply underlines the names wherever they occur in the text or Supplements (numbering them consecutively in the margin so as to be able to check later that none are left out), and his typist copies them on to labels ready to be checked, sorted into alphabetical order and stuck on to backing sheets as copy for the printer. For the subject indexing he reads through the text and Supplements, marking with ringed numbers (in a different colour of ink) and underlining the words that the typist is to copy, then drafts the entries as at (a) in Fig. 6 for them to be typewritten on labels as at (b). When the labels have been checked and the abbreviations of Relevance and Aspect terms on them crossed out, these likewise are stuck on to backing sheets in the appropriate order, the Relevance and Aspect terms are typewritten between them in full where needed and the copy for the printer is thereby completed. (As what has to be typed on each label takes up very little space and can when necessary be continued on to an additional label it is convenient to use self-stickers. These are easily typed upon, and separable by using scissors, while still adhering to their original backing sheets of glossy paper. It is easy to peel them off the separated strips and transfer them to the printer's copy sheets after they have been sorted.)

5. Indexing the 'Proceedings of the British Academy'

The British Academy was established by Royal Charter in 1903 for ' the promotion of the study of the moral and political sciences, including history, philosophy, law, politics and economics, archaeology and philology '. In these widely varied fields and their many subdivisions it has the same standing, its Fellows are of corresponding eminence and its functions are comparable with those of the Royal Society in the physical and biological sciences.

The *Proceedings* of the Academy were at first published biennially but since 1926 they have appeared in annual volumes up to 400 pages, each containing some ten to twenty papers or lectures as well as lengthy obituary notices which provide material for history of scholarships, but there are no reports of oral discussions. The texts are not meant to be popular reading matter but are learned dissertations, or presentations of the outcome from research into detailed aspects of questions affecting the various sections of the Academy's interests. Often they serve also as frameworks for numerous bibliographical citations.

A classified catalogue of the Academy's publications up to 1968, with an index of the authors' and lecturers' names as well as the names of persons appreciated in the obituaries, appeared in that year but otherwise the *Proceedings* have not hitherto been indexed. In 1970 a pilot project was carried out to see whether it would be practicable to index them in detail by an adaptation of the methods described, for a very different field, in Section 4 here. Accordingly a sample of eighteen papers or lectures on various subjects and four obituaries was chosen from three volumes of widely separated dates so as to be representative, for which a name index with 192 entries and a subject index with 174 en-

tries were compiled. After these had been discussed by the appropriate committee and some minor changes agreed upon in principle a contract was entered into for preparing, on the same lines and in about the same proportions, a single Name Index and a single Subject Index to the contents of the first fifty volumes, dating from 1903 to 1964. This work is now in hand and will be completed, it is hoped, in 1973. A statistical analysis made when four early volumes had been indexed in alternation with five of more recent date showed that indexing practically every name in the text and footnotes resulted in an average of 0.87 name entries per page of nearly 500 words. The corresponding average density of subject entries judged by the indexer to be appropriate (see R.4) worked out at 0.61. These densities fluctuate very widely from paper to paper but they seemed to have no correlation with differences in the subjects written about. If they are maintained for all fifty volumes the two indexes together will be about as thick as one of the annual volumes. (Probably, however, each index will be separately bound so as to make cross-references between them easier.)

The most conspicuous difference from the indexing described in Section 4 is the much greater importance of names here—no doubt natural enough seeing that all humanistic studies relate ultimately to people whereas engineering is concerned with physical phenomena. In the Name Index several categories are distinguished as follows:

(a) Authors of contributions to the *Proceedings*: surname to be in bold type followed by initials, year, title of the paper or lecture, volume number, full pagination (to which cross-reference is made from all the other index entries: see R.9).

(b) Persons of whom biographical appreciation is given: names in full followed by years of birth and death.

(c) Persons quoted verbatim, cited bibliographically or mentioned incidentally in the text or footnotes: surname followed by initials (or hyphen in lieu) if modern; name followed by a period indication or other clue if died before 19c. and if not well known; form of name by which known to contemporaries if died before 16c.

The Subject Index when printed will look like Fig. 4(d) though of course with ' humanistic' instead of engineering headings. In principle the entry keywords are the words commonly used by writers on any given subject to designate the concepts that concern them, but care is taken to provide cross-references to these from any non-adopted synonyms or quasi-synonyms they may have under which a searcher of the index might look, especially if the synonym is one whose use is deprecated—e.g. (Mahommedanism) —) Islamic studies. When any given keyword has occurred in different contexts more than three times it is adopted as a collective main heading and entered in a Thesaurus of such headings, of which at present there are about 140. (For the advantage see R.8.)

Apart from the scale of the operation the indexing procedure being followed is so similar to that already described at the end of Section 4 that it will suffice here to mention the differences affecting the two steps (a) and (b), the remaining steps (c), (d) and (e) being unaffected:

(a) As the indexer is not well versed in all the subject matter (nobody but a genius could be!) and therefore cannot make the necessary value judgments unaided (R.5), yet the indexing has to be done by one person for the sake of consistency, continual use is made of background reference books and of personal advice from subject specialists.

(b) As the Academy has only a few copies left of the early volumes the indexer does not mark them even in pencil; instead of the ' ringed numbers' device and the drafting slips a narrow slip as shown in Fig. 7 is inserted between each two facing pages such as 62-3 (this one has 64-5 on the back) and is marked N or S as the case may be in the positions where name or subject entries appear, on first perusal, to be necessary. That being done, and any necessary background research accomplished, the text is read again and the index entries are drafted in the form exemplified in Fig. 8. The object of beginning each index entry in the column headed by its initial letter is that this makes it much easier to rediscover that entry in the draft when the same name or topic is mentioned again later in the text, in order to add the later page numbers after the vertical line on the right. Paper with quarter-inch squares is used as the accurate alignment makes for clarity; also, being in school arithmetic books, it is a cheap form of stationery. Fig. 9 shows a few of the gummed labels typewritten by copying from Fig. 8.

IVb. Periodicals

Standards for Indexes to Learned and Scientific Periodicals

These standards approved by the Council of the Society of Indexers are put forward in an attempt to improve indexes to periodical publications. Addressed mainly to editors and publishers, they outline the minimum requirements for adequate indexes, which are of vital importance to librarians and research workers.

1. The value of any journal is enhanced by an adequate index, and no learned or scientific periodical should be published without this essential feature.

2. Every volume of a journal should be provided with an adequate index. While it may not be possible for each number or part of a journal to contain this feature, these issues should have tables of contents displayed in prominent positions either on the cover (front or back) or in the pages preceding the actual text. An alphabetical list of authors in each issue is most useful.

3. The index to a journal should be issued in or with the final part of the periodical, failing which it should be published as soon as possible after the publication of the final issue. Preferably it should be printed separately, or in a manner permitting ready extraction for binding purposes. It should not be stitched or stapled in such a way that the folds of paper forming an issue must be mutilated in order to extract the index.

4. A dictionary index combining author, subject and title entries may be preferable to separate author and subject indexes, but where separate indexes are provided their functions should be clearly defined at the beginning of each index and at the top of each page.

5. The names of all co-authors should be printed in the index, cross-references only being provided if space is limited.

6. Special features should be indexed under such headings as Book Reviews, Editorials, Obituaries, *etc.*, but the items should also appear under author, title and subject headings. Corrections of printers' or authors' errors, additional material in the form of letters, *etc.*, should be noted by page numbers under the appropriate entries.

7. Abbreviations used in the index should be listed at the head of the entries, and any special form of arrangement should be noted, as well as indications of the purpose of any special type (bold or italics) used for page numbers.

Reprinted from *The Indexer* 2, no. 2 (Autumn 1960): 63–64.

8. Articles in journals should be indexed under authors, titles, significant words in titles, and under the subjects dealt with in the text. Some articles may require many entries for subjects, synonyms, and for authorities quoted. There is no reason why entries in bibliographies should be omitted in indexes to journals when they are considered useful in indexes to books.

9. Cumulative indexes are invaluable to librarians, bibliographers and research workers. Certain journals publish an index to the first part of a volume, and cumulate it through the parts until it appears in the final issue as the index to the complete volume. Five-yearly, decennial, or indexes covering longer periods are of vital importance in libraries, and these are usually sold separately. It is appreciated that a cumulative index to a weekly journal might be large and costly, but most libraries would subscribe to all indexes to periodicals in their files.

10. It is useless to provide indexes set in type too small for reading under normal circumstances. 8 point is preferable, but 6 point should be the smallest employed. Adequate spacing and intelligent layout are also necessary to facilitate quick reference to an index.

11. A table of contents, with or without an alphabetical list of authors' names, does not take the place of an index.

12. Indexes should be compiled by competent indexers having some knowledge of the subject being indexed. A journal badly indexed is liable to acquire the reputation of a bad journal.

The 'Jewish Chronicle' Index, 1841–

John M. Shaftesley*

First let me say a few words about the 'Jewish Chronicle' itself. It is a weekly newspaper with a national—indeed, an international—circulation, devoted primarily to news and features of Jewish interest.

Established in 1841, it is the oldest surviving Jewish newspaper in the world, with the biggest circulation of Jewish weekly newspapers anywhere. Two Jewish newspapers on the Continent ran it close as centenarians, but they unfortunately may be classed as casualties of the pre-war Nazi era.

In a sense, the 'Jewish Chronicle' was also a sufferer from the Nazis, as it sustained heavy material losses in the blitz on London in the early part of the last war. By good fortune, arrangements had been made to print the paper in the country not far from London if war should break out—a precaution taken by a good number of papers at that time. Owing to the exigencies of the evacuation, however, only the absolute necessaries in the way of reference material were taken to the country office—various well-known books of reference and directories, etc., and a large index volume of alphabetical references to the contents of the paper covering the previous few years only. It was enough, in the circumstances, with which to get by.

A complete run of the volumes of the 'Jewish Chronicle' from 1841 was deposited in the underground basement of the paper's premises in London, but when the City was blitzed in December 1940, the building and all its contents, including the records, were destroyed. From the point of view of reference, therefore, a vast historical period became virtually blank.

For several years after the war we persistently sought for other volumes in order to build up the run again, and gradually acquired those for various periods until the set was almost complete. There are still some blanks, but fortunately there are one or two other libraries, public and private, which have a fair number of volumes from which one may bridge the gaps. Even the British Museum, however, did not have a copy of Volume I, and I was therefore very fortunate in 1952, during a visit to Canada and the U.S.A., to be offered this rarity as a gift by the Canadian Jewish Congress, who possessed it, after I had addressed a luncheon party they gave in my honour in Montreal.

Some few years ago, it was decided, as a safeguard against any future catastrophes to this laboriously built-up new run, to have the 'Jewish Chronicle' micro-filmed from its first issue onwards. The 'Jewish Chronicle' is a widely known source of Jewish historical material and in constant demand for research, but the researcher is obviously hampered by the lack of an index. As former Editor and, before that, Assistant Editor of the paper for many years, I felt particularly fitted for such a task as compiling one, and so the arrangement was come to with the Company on which I am now engaged. The task, on which I began a little over three years ago, is that of writing a cumulative index of the 'Jewish Chronicle' from 1841 up to the 1940s.

---

* Talk given to the Society of Indexers, Thursday, November 28, 1963.

Reprinted from *The Indexer* 4, no. 1 (Spring 1964): 3–13.

In preparation, among other things I studied, by kind permission of their various Editors and librarians, the systems followed in the libraries of nearly all the daily newspapers in Fleet Street, the larger Sunday newspapers, some of the serious weeklies, newsagencies such as Reuter's-P.A., and Jews' College Library and the Wiener Library. I already had some knowledge of provincial newspaper libraries, as I had received my original training in the provinces. Their systems varied considerably.

It was finally agreed in my office, where I had consultations with the Chairman and Managing Director, Mr. Kessler, that this index should be alphabetical, on cards (the usual 5″ x 3″), and cumulative, not annual. From my experience, I believed this to be best for the circumstances of newspaper production, where speed in research is a prime consideration. I do not think that in such an index the various 'decimal' systems are so suitable, especially as the spectrum of researcher ranges from office boy to Fellow of All Souls. Subsequent publication of the index is to be microfilming also, but this of course does not rule out printing for wider circulation at any time, and therefore a plain alphabetical system seemed best.

I have said 'plain alphabetical system', but perhaps it is not quite so simple as that. Bearing in mind the needs of internal newspaper office inquiry, as well as the yearning for learning often evinced by members of a curious public, I divided the index into broad categories, six in all, but each with its own subdivisions, each shown by coloured guide cards.

The six categories are: GENERAL; HOME; ABROAD; PROVINCES; SPECIAL; PERSONALIA.

These titles largely speak for themselves, except that HOME in this context means London, the place of publication, or, in the early stages even more, the East End, where the bulk of the Jewish community lived in those days and had done so since the Resettlement under Cromwell. SPECIAL covers a wide field, including, among other sections, leaders, letters to the editor, special articles, sermons, poems, and so on—even a gossip column. The 'gossip' column is not, as is so often thought, an invention of the popular press of today; the 'Jewish Chronicle' had a regular column of that description, ponderous in style perhaps, as early as 1855. This ran for ten years and was only dropped when, as was laconically recorded one week, the copy just failed to turn up. But later, 'gossip' returned for different periods, in the form of regular discursive 'letters to the editor', written by the same pseudonymous author each week.

Now for a few words on the mechanics of the matter. It did not all spring up ready made—I made adjustments as I went along, in accordance with experience and with an eye to labour-saving. I now have all my 'working' cards within arm's reach as I sit at my desk. In front of me I have nine shallow shelves the complete width of my table, each shelf carrying seven 15-inch-long cardboard trays, in which the cards repose. The trays have several advantages over the usual index boxes; they are lighter for handling, they are longer than the normal and so contain more cards at once, they are shallower and thus allow for easier extraction and replacing of the cards, and more can be contained in the height within reach than the deeper index cabinets.

Without standing up, therefore, I can reach to about sixty boxes, each capable of containing approximately 1,100 cards. At present, my 'revolving' complement is about 40,000 cards, with a capacity for expansion to about 70,000 on the existing shelves. As cards are completed they are transferred in order to stock boxes, for further transference in due course to the office index cabinets.

Gradually I have introduced refinements to save the routine work. For example, the cards are now preprinted in batches with the various sectional headings; there are printed columns at the right-hand side headed 'Date / page / col.' As far as possible, I use rubber stamps for regular entries, such as the year, in bold figures stamped at the top of and, where necessary, across the columns. My 'date / page / col.' rubber stamps contain the months and not the years, and fit in like a cash-column. I have counted 'columns' on the page by letter: 'a', 'b', 'c', etc., in order to avoid conflict with the page numbers. For cross-references, I have revolving rubber stamps which will give me either plain section headings or such headings with 'see' in front of them; for example, all the six main categories mentioned above, and additionally, such references as 'see PARLT', 'see SERMONS', etc.

Everything, however, depends on the written entries on the cards (I could, I suppose, type them, but that would not be any quicker, with the mechanical movements involved, and the machine would simply add a bulky piece of equipment to my desk without compensating advantages). The subject title or name at the top left-hand side of each card is in block letters—caps.—but the rest is in handwriting. I have introduced a system with my cross-references which provides instant recognition: whenever a word or name in any entry is underlined (which would be italics in printing), that means automatically that there is an entry under that name or subject elsewhere, in the appropriate—it might be the same or a different—category. The main entry I make on any card I call my 'key' entry, from which cross-references may branch.

This is where I introduce my next labour-saving device—my wife. When : have written the key entry and marked the cross-references, I clip the cards relating to the cross-references to the top card and place them in a rack on my wife's desk beside my own. She in due course, with a rubber date stamp set at the same date as my own, fills in the reference on each and then stacks the cards and restores them to their places in the trays from which I am working, for re-use as they turn up again.

There are certain difficulties in working from these old newspapers which do not apply to current newspapers. Normally, in a newspaper office, cuttings are taken from the editions and from other newspapers and the necessary key words marked for entering up according to the particular method adopted in that office. I am quite unable to make cuttings or marks, as the volumes I am working from are sacrosanct; some are irreplaceable. So I read and work 'off the cuff'. I have to make a quick assessment and write the entries direct on to the cards, without preliminaries. Years of practice at sub-editing and headline-writing are a wonderful preparation for this!

The entries on the cards are in the form of 'abstract' or 'digest' wherever possible. It has been my experience that this is well suited to the needs of the newspaper office, although it is, I suppose, not particularly necessary to do it that way. But where perhaps hundreds of entries under one title are found, it is of great help and a time-saver to, say, a leader-writer or a sub-editor if he can run down them and see the particular connections he is seeking and skip over those inappropriate to his thesis.

It is impossible in the time at my disposal to mention more than a few of the problems found in this particular work—including, I may say, having to be on the look-out for changed meanings in the language even during the last century. For example, one must not assume that any criticism is implied in such a report as 'The sermon of the Rev. —— at the Sabbath service last week was truly pathetic'; the word 'pathetic' did not bear the scornful meaning we nowadays give it, but meant simply some subject which drew pitying regard from his congregation. Nor does the report that a reverend gentleman addressed a public meeting in 'forcible language' mean in 1871 quite what we might think it does today.

There were many differences in journalistic practice 100 years ago from that of today. Display types were hardly thought of; solid columns of type contained the news, with barely a cross-heading of relief. One meeting might take up four solid columns of report, while, especially in foreign news, a dozen different—quite different, all needing separate entries—reports might appear in half a column, run on, two or three lines to each.

'Copy' was naturally handwritten, with all its hazards of misconstruction (remember that the typewriter as a practicable machine was not invented until 1873). I remember that for 1857 I had to enter the name of a New York Deputy District Attorney as 'JOACHIM, sen.,' as it appeared in the paper. There was no occasion to query this, as the especially American habit of calling people 'sen.' and 'jun.' was not uncommon. But in 1859, and later, this turned out to be a gentleman with a name of Scandinavian spelling, Lt.-Col. P. J. Joachimsen, ap-

pointed Judge Advocate of the National Guard, and I had to amend my cards accordingly. This is one small instance, by the way, of the advantage of a good memory—I cannot too strongly support somebody's dictum that one virtue a good indexer must have is a good memory!

Then one must remember that geography is not a static subject, nor history, nor, for that matter, most other branches of learning! On the subject of geography, is it better to enter, say, 'TRIESTE' under 'Italy', as we know it today, or under 'Austria', as it was recorded in the last century? In many of these cases, where the place is so well known, I compromise by entering it under its modern locale and by placing a cross-reference card under the other country, reading (in the case above) 'Austria, TRIESTE . . . see under Italy'. But then, what does one do about, say, 'ALSACE-LORRAINE', which suffered sudden changes in 1870 and again in 1918? The safest way seems to be to enter the events according to historical chronology, but to put under France 'see also Germany' and under Germany 'see also France'.

Nor was spelling, especially of names of places, always consistent nor in accordance with modern orthography. For example, the impulse on seeing the Russian name 'Charkov' is to pronounce it as 'ch' in 'church', unless one happens to know that it is pronounced with a Russian guttural 'kh' and would appear better under 'K' in an English index than under 'C'.

One particularly frustrating habit in those old newspapers is that of reporting names without initials. This is very frequent, even with the most common names. The name 'Cohen', for example, is very common among Jews (quantitatively, not genealogically!), yet time after time reports are printed referring to 'Mr. Cohen' in different connections which could not possibly refer to the same person. Wherever possible, therefore, on each Cohen's card (assuming he is newsworthy and therefore index-worthy) I fix some distinguishing mark, which may be his occupation, his address, or the organisation or society with which he is connected. If the Cohen is a foreigner, then he is distinguished also by his country and (where it is known) town; if he is a dweller in the provinces, his town appears also at the top. From these considerations, I have built up a 'code' system at the top of the index cards which you might almost liken to the punch-hole entries on computer cards! I give here a hypothetical instance of an 'ISAAC COHEN', of France. This Isaac Cohen is a doctor, from the town of Lyons, where he first appears in the news in 1860. His first card therefore reads:

number is not strictly necessary, but it is an additional, and bolder, way of identifying the place of the card in the index besides the natural sequence of the dates. The word *doctor* is underlined because there is a series of cards headed 'Doctors'. Normally one might not think a separate section for doctors or other occupations is necessary, but in the particular circumstances of a Jewish index dealing with past centuries it is of importance. One has to bear in mind the persecutions inflicted on the Jews, one of whose manifestations was that of preventing Jews from taking up many of the trades and professions (in somewhat later history the phrase 'numerus clausus' bore a sinister meaning to Jews in the high schools and universities). Thus for Jews to become doctors, etc., was something of a feat in many countries, and the fact takes its place in history and sociology. In this connection also, the

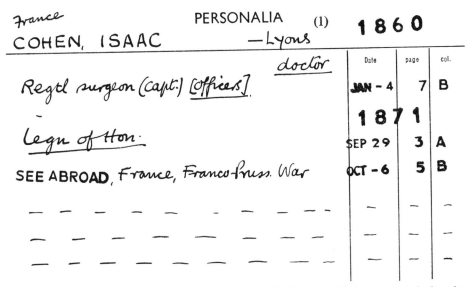

The 'code' at the top tells us that he is of France, in the town of Lyons, and that he is a doctor. The figure (1) in a circle is not added until the card is filled and a number (2) is under way. The

word 'officers' will be seen underlined in Isaac Cohen's first entry. There was a constant canard (not unheard-of even today) that Jews did not become soldiers. In fact, there were actually hundreds of thousands of Jews in European armies in those days, but in many of those armies they were prevented from attaining commissioned rank. Thus early records of Jewish officers are of some significance. In our example, 'Legn. of Hon.' is also underlined, because there is elsewhere a section for that distinction, and Isaac Cohen's name is entered in it under this date as a cross-reference.

The next hypothetical reference says simply 'SEE ABROAD, France, Franc-Pruss War'. This is, in its turn, a cross-reference from a key entry on the card under France 'Franco-Prussian War', in which Isaac Cohen appears among a number of people named as having secured distinctions or been wounded, etc.

Various further entries as time goes by fill up Isaac Cohen's card (you will see we have gone into 1871), and then, as we begin card (2), we find that he has been appointed to the Mount Sinai Hospital, New York (underlined for the usual reason), and been awarded in addition the Fileman Prize. His consequent emigration to the U.S.A. in 1872 causes some alteration in the 'code' at the top, and we see at a glance that he is now in the U.S.A., in New York. It is not really necessary to repeat the word 'Doctor' in the right-hand corner.

Now settled in New York, his third card, (3), needs only the notation U.S.A. and N.Y. (which will appear on all his future cards, unless he moves again), with the reference-back in this one instance '(ex France)'. (See illustration on next page.)

It will be seen that such a system helps to settle the place and identity wherever possible of the subject of the cards, especially when there are many of them of the same name. I give here an imaginary series of 'ISAAC COHENS' based on these principles:

All
London,   COHEN, ISAAC   *dentist*
requiring   COHEN, ISAAC   *Gt. Synag.*
no corner
title: COHEN, ISAAC   Middlesex St.

Following the name is given a distinguishing description, in alphabetical order—including occupation, or organisation to which attached, or address.

In alpha-   Africa, N.
betical   COHEN, ISAAC —Algeria
order ac-   *Spanish Vice-Consul*
cording to   France
place of   COHEN, ISAAC —Paris
residence:
                Hungary
                COHEN, ISAAC —Budapest

                New Zealand
                COHEN, ISAAC —Auckland
                                   mayor
                Southampton
                COHEN, ISAAC

France / U.S.a.   PERSONALIA   (2)   **1872**
COHEN, ISAAC   —Lyons / N.Y.

Appointed Mt. Sinai Hosp, N.Y.—Fileman Prize award	Date	page	col.
	MAR 14	15	C

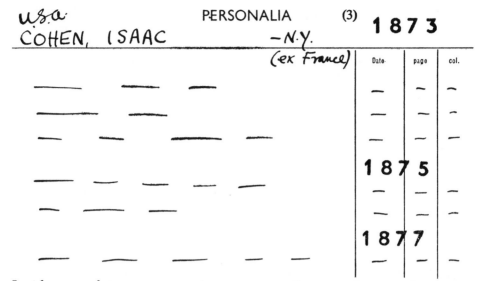

usa.
COHEN, ISAAC   —N.Y.   PERSONALIA   (3)   **1 8 7 3**
                      (ex France)

Date·	page	col.

1 8 7 5

1 8 7 7

Jewish nomenclature may present certain difficulties to the non-Jewish indexer. I might summarise it by saying there are three main styles: Biblical; of the Middle Ages; and modern. My own style of listing, therefore, takes on the following aspect:

JACOB
    (Bibl.)
        —which, of course, is plain enough.
JACOB OF NIMES
JACOB OF ZANZIBAR
        —imaginary names, but of the Mid. Ages 'territorial' style, where the first name is still the criterion.
JACOB BEN DAVID, Rabbi
    (11th cent.)
        —another Mid. Ages style, but the compound is now religious, with the first names still of most importance.
JACOB, ALBERT
JACOB, NATHAN
        —now we have reached the modern period, where surnames are normal practice and, in listing, take precedence over first names.

It should be added, in explanation of the list above, that Jews long used their religious names and it is only in comparatively late times that they adopted regular sur-

names ('surnames', as we know, are a comparatively late invention in any case). Very often they had surnames of a ridiculous or 'smearing' character imposed on them by the anti-Jewish officials of despotic governments.

I revert to the entry above, 'Rabbi Jacob Ben David'. The word 'Ben' carries particular difficulty for the non-Jew unversed in Hebrew, for here it is not a diminutive of Benjamin, but is the Hebrew word meaning 'son (of)'. Every Jew is given a Hebrew name for religious purposes. Usually his first Hebrew name is the same as, or the equivalent of, his ordinary forename, but to that is always attached the first name of his father. The rabbi above is therefore Jacob the son of David. I, being 'John', am Jochanan in Hebrew, and therefore, if called up to read a portion of the Law in the synagogue, would be addressed as 'Jochanan ben David' (my father's name); his Hebrew name was 'David ben Shelomo' (=Solomon, *his* father's name).

But in more modern times, there has also grown up a custom, especially in the State of Israel, to adopt permanent surnames beginning with ' Ben ', whether joined or disjoined. The most famous example today is probably David Ben Gurion, the former Prime Minister of that country. He would be indexed, not under ' G ' for Gurion, but ' B ' for ' Ben Gurion ', David.

The closest parallel I can think of is the Norman French style, *Fitzmaurice*, where Fitz is equivalent to the French ' fils ', ' son '. (A member of the audience called out also ' Mac, Scottish ', with which I agreed, and added, 'Also "Ap" in Welsh ').

A slight complication is provided by the variation ' Ibn ', the Arabic equivalent of the Hebrew ' Ben '. Many famous Jewish scholars of the centuries of Moslem ascendancy in Southern Europe were known as ' Ibn ' this or ' Ibn ' that. The best plan is to index them under ' I ', but the Jewish papers of the last century had their own peculiar custom of spelling such names as ' Aben '. I normally index such names under 'Ibn '.

Sometimes there seems to be confusion over names in the news, which differ in different reports. One lovely example I have found concerns an unfortunate little boy who was run over and killed. In the first report of the accident, in 1871, he was named *Jacob Michaels*. A letter in the following week's issue, complaining of some aspect of the report, names the boy as *Michael Jacobs* (without, however, stating that the earlier name was wrong). The following week, the paper, reporting the inquest, refuses to be caught on the wrong foot, and this is what appears:

' THE FATAL ACCIDENT IN SPITALFIELDS.—An inquest on the body of the poor little boy killed by being run over by a van in Bell Lane was held on Thursday, 23rd ult., when a verdict of "Accidental Death " was returned.'

On a serious level, the only solution in such cases is to index the two names, with an appropriate cross-reference in each.

Owing to the peculiar journalistic standards of the day, it is necessary, at least in the earlier years, to keep an eye on the advertisement columns as well. Much of what we consider as ' news ' today was not considered so—in newspapers—a hundred years ago. ' Personalities ', as they were called, for example, but never specifically interpreted, were ruled out—unless you wished to publish them as paid-for advertisements. There were even ' letters to the editor ' published under this rule, with the legend in small capitals at the top, ' Advertisement '. Often in the small advertisements news appeared of significant resolutions passed by the various organisations paying for the announcement; important appointments of the clergy or other officials sometimes appeared only in this form. It is necessary, too, to keep an eye on the death announcements, as obituary notices were treated in the most haphazard manner, the news of the death of quite distinguished persons sometimes being omitted altogether. And we know from experience that there are constant calls from the public for the dates of obituary notices, whether for the purpose of ferreting out wills or chasing up family trees!

It was from a death notice of a lady that I found the only notification of a change of name which, although perhaps not of the greatest importance, at least has a tiny place in the history of Jewish journalism. The lady was the wife of a ' Herschell Phillips ', and I should not have noticed it further if it had not added the name (Filipowski) in parentheses. It happens that Herschell Filipowski had occurred in my index many times several years before in connection with his pioneering efforts in Jewish journalism in England. This simple death notice therefore called for an added notation in the index.

Hebrew words naturally occur frequently in a Jewish newspaper, and for ease I have generally indexed them under a transliteration into Latin characters (with a simple cross-reference card under the Hebrew). But, as in all other branches of learning, it is hard to get two scholars to agree on the exact form of transliteration, and the International Phonetic Alphabet is scarcely of general application, so I have adopted generally the forms used in the ' Jewish Chronicle' today. Many Hebrew references, words and phrases, however, do not lend themselves to transliteration as a guide, and so I have added a small Hebrew section to those subdivisions where they occur.

Indeed, in one subsection under GENERAL, that of ' Pen-names ', I have had to include a small run of pseudonyms which, in the coy manner of the day, consist only of the conventional reference marks that are usually employed to denote footnotes: stars, daggers, paragraph marks, etc., in the order in which they are normally used. The Editor was not averse to giving a pseudonymous correspondent such a ' signature ' to his letter, and one such ' award ', of *three* daggers, was the subject in subsequent correspondence of some acrimonious comment by the correspondent himself, who had not liked it. At the risk of overloading—and I would rather have too much than too little—I find it necessary to index these pseudonyms, especially as I know that some of them turned out to be quite important in the Jewish literary and communal fields later on.

Our Secretary, Mr. Baker, in his circular letter inviting members to this meeting,

described my task as ' gigantic '. I admit that it is, and you may therefore wonder whether I have not thought of the possibility of employing some computer method on it. The answer is that I have, often. But before I deal directly with that, I want to interpolate that as early as 1872 a Jewish scholar, S. M. Drach, had an idea, which he expressed in a letter to the editor, of using ' numbers ' instead of letters, especially by non-Jewish scholars, for ' transliterations ' of Hebrew words in their English or other writings. It almost has the ' computer ' ring about it! It is simply, to avoid error or argument, to substitute figures for the Hebrew letters, the figures being in proper sequence according to the place of the letter in the Hebrew alphabet, which is shorter than the Latin alphabet. Although Hebrew is written from right to left, this would not affect the non-Jewish scholar's use of figures, because he could write the appropriate figures from left to right in any case. Furthermore, this would have the advantage of avoiding confusion over names, Drach pointed out, which, though spelt the same in English, are different in various places of the original Hebrew Bible. One example he gave was ' Noah ', which occurs in Genesis v and Numbers xxvii. In the former it is spelt ' *nun, het* ', but in the latter ' *nun, ayin, hai* '. Translating these Hebrew letters into figures according to their place in the alphabet, you get accordingly:

NOAH נ ח 8, 14
NOAH נ ע ה 5, 16, 14

I discussed the matter of the whole index thoroughly with a big computer company, and we had several conferences at my place and theirs. After much study, they gave me their answers, which were, very briefly, ' Yes, it can be done '; ' You would have to do the programming, nevertheless' (which would be on a less flexible scale than my free-hand efforts now); 'It would cost you over £40,000.'

I compute that I have used up rather more time than that allotted to me, so I shall sit down!

Dealing with some of the points which arose at question time, Mr. Shaftesley said:

The 5 x 3 cards are used, rather than larger ones, because of ease of handling (I can have many more in front of me) and in order not to have odd sizes of cabinet for their keeping. Many of the cards have only a few entries on, but one can get a surprising number even of abstracts on to this size.

The whole index could of course be one general one, in alphabetical order, instead of being divided up into six sections. But I find it better for consulting if it is divided into recognisable sections; there are often possible confusions, for example, between proper names and geographical names. 'Germany, KONIGSBERG' may be either the name of a man or the name of the town, but there is no doubt at all if one is headed by the sectional indication PERSONALIA and the other by ABROAD. In any event, this index is so constructed that, if it is thought better ultimately to make one long general index of it, 'one and indivisible', this can be done without any other trouble than by redistributing the whole of the cards in their proper alphabetical order in one continuous sequence.

'Doctor' as an indication of occupation refers only to medical men, not Ph.D., etc. The reason is the sociological one explained above.

The changes in features in the 'Jewish Chronicle' can be followed easily by the index. The earliest date under such entries as 'Children's Page', 'Gossip', etc., will tell the inquirer immediately when such a feature began. Furthermore, I have devoted a special section to the 'Jewish Chronicle' itself, under the subdivision 'Newspapers' (in GENERAL), which records the changes in the paper, important dates in its record, policy declarations (as in leading articles or editorial footnotes), and references to it from other sources. The historian who wishes to write a history of the paper from its own pages has now at hand a good part of the framework ready made. This of course goes for many other subjects as well.

I have such a section as 'Newspapers', under which the 'Jewish Chronicle' appears, rather than putting the 'Jewish Chronicle' simply under 'J' in GENERAL, because I believe that self-evident groupings together are a help and not a hindrance. Anyone looking for, say, the 'Norfolk Chronicle' (assuming it appears in the index) would know very well that it was a newspaper.

There will in due course be a 'guide' to the index, attached to the beginning, so that the system of sections and subsections will be explained.

I estimate index-worthiness more or less on the basis of news-worthiness. In other words, I substitute for the old legal test of the reasonable person, 'the man on the Clapham omnibus', 'the man in the Piccadilly Tube', reading his newspaper and saying to his wife when he gets home, 'Did you read about the *murder* in *Tottenham Court Road?*'

I could not possibly index every name in the Births, Marriages, and Deaths columns from the beginning. It would take me a hundred years! All I can do in that respect is to keep an eye on the columns, especially in the early years while the index is being built up, for names which I know became well known or distinguished later. As it is, I am up to the 1870s now, and I reckon I have made at least a quarter of a million entries already.

The 'London Gazette' Index

Grace Holmes*

The London Gazette is a government publication in which various official or individual acts are set out in print and thus acquire legal status. The phrase 'gazetted', used of honours and military appointments, can also be employed for any other announcement made.

The *Gazette* appears twice weekly throughout the year, on Tuesday and Friday, including public holidays. A quarterly Index is compiled, and two years ago the contract for this work was put out to tender. I understand that, immediately before this step was taken, the Index was compiled by full-time staff at H.M.S.O. However, when I visited H.M.S.O. after obtaining the contract, there were intriguing references to an elderly lady who had earlier carried out the task for many years, apparently working single-handed and in solitude in a small office. I now feel a bond with this unknown person.

The contractor's price for the Index has to include all expenses, notably paper and postage. A further requirement is that one should be accessible both personally and by phone when needed, and hence must live within reasonable distance of London. The final important condition of the contract is the strict timetable laid down for both indexer and printers. The average number of entries per quarter is 35,000, and these must be stuck up and delivered within 21 working days from the end of the quarter. It follows that one must work intensively in January, April, July and September, and arrange one's personal affairs accordingly. At the Stationery Office everyone who discussed the work with me was very affable, but no one admitted to any knowledge of the methods so far used in compiling the Index. An old copy and two specimen texts were provided, and the rest was up to me. The composing-room overseer at St. Stephen's Parliamentary Press was very helpful over layout, and made it seem less complex than had at first appeared.

The first step after undertaking this work was to find suitable and inexpensive material for the typing and sticking up. A large newsagent-stationer's firm with many branches sell rolls of gummed perforated address labels at 21/6 each, and these can be fed into the typewriter and used until exhausted. Subsequently the long strips are cut up, sorted, and pasted on to newspaper strips which are numbered consecutively. I hoped to get a discount from the stationers on my enormous purchases of label rolls, but was unsuccessful. My local branch now keeps a permanent stock, and the shop assistant once asked if I was running an agency.

To avoid confusion, which could easily arise, each of the seven sections of the Index has its own alphabetical symbol which always appears on every slip. Occasionally we have sorted into the wrong box, which could be disastrous if not noticed quickly. However, the distinguish-

* The substance of a paper read at a Discussion Meeting on February 27, 1964.

Reprinted from *The Indexer* 4, no. 1 (Spring 1964): 13–16.

ing symbols enable these mistakes to be corrected. After sticking up, the symbols are crossed off in red ink, together with any other superfluous indications which need not be printed. While crossing off one can make a final check for errors.

As the assignment is so large, my next step was to break the work down into skilled and unskilled sections. The typing of the simpler entries (lists of names) was offered to a disabled ex-serviceman who has been very reliable and accurate, and being house-bound is delighted to find a remunerative occupation. His work is checked by me, and then cut up by my husband, who can be relied upon not to snip off a vital page number. This has happened once or twice, and necessitated a search through the whole quarter's issues. We try to avoid it. Discarded boxes from the gummed rolls are stapled together in rows, lettered and placed in shallow cardboard dress boxes. The cut slips are sorted into these. If possible, the cut and sorted slips ought not to be left in a warm room, as they tend to curl up and are then difficult to handle.

I now come to the various sections of the *Gazette*. The first is State Intelligence. This includes, and largely consists of, Ministerial announcements. If these are made by virtue of a specific Act of Parliament, they are entered under that Act, with reference from the Ministry, otherwise under the Ministry concerned.

Example:

Agriculture, Fisheries and Food, Ministry of:
  Diseases:
    Returns of outbreaks:
    Diseases of Animals Act, 1950
    see heading

Institutions such as Church Commissioners, Bank of England, Electricity and Gas Boards and Land Registry form main headings under which announcements are listed. The use of classifying symbols saves time and ensures accuracy.

Example:

Church Commissioners:
  Church Patronage Act:
  Symbols s (State Intelligence)
      CC/CPA
        followed by the name of the
        parish concerned.

Many of these institutional entries have corresponding personal name entries, especially where appointments are involved.

Example:

Gas Boards:
  North-West:
    Part-time Members   3456
  Jones, E., part-time Member,
    North-West Gas Board 3456

Announcements under the Factories Acts are also frequent and in the case of Factory Doctor appointments require personal entry as well as place entry under the heading of the Act. Other announcements concern the Privy Council, appointments to the Queen's Household, diplomatic appointments and the various orders of chivalry.

In the last case, the names of the persons appointed are listed in Section II of the Index, namely Honours, Decorations and Medals. All typing, cutting and sorting of State Intelligence slips is done by me, so that I can observe the vital classifying symbols.

Section II, Honours, Decorations and Medals, is typed by my war pensioner. Lists of persons to whom the Imperial Service Medal has been awarded are frequently published. There are also military honours and Baronetcies and Knighthoods. The latter appear in State Intelligence, but the names of the recipients are listed in the Honours section.

Example:

s   Knights   4567, 5678
        (See also Honours, Decorations
            and Medals)
H   Smith, J. H.   4567

No details of the honour are given, but if a titled person is given an additional award, he is listed by title.

Example:

Brentford, Earl of   5678

You will notice that it is the practice to index under the title, and not under the family name: indeed, no reference is made from this name. In this I am following precedent, as set out in the terms of the contract to the effect that my Index must be consistent with earlier ones.

Twice a year the publication of the Honours List swells the number of entries considerably. If two persons have the same name and initials they must be distinguished by their town or government department. Periodically a long list of appointments to the Order of St. John appears in State Intelligence and the names are indexed under Honours.

Section III, Naval, Military and Air Force Appointments, is the largest. It too is typed for me, but checking, cutting, sorting and sticking are a considerable task. Identical names are distinguished by service numbers. Quixotically, Admiralty appointments appear in State Intelligence, and, having no service numbers, can only be distinguished by the letters R.N. Appointments of Aides de Camp to the Queen are listed in State Intelligence with other Royal Household appointments. As with Honours, names only are listed in this section, without details of announcements.

Section IV, Advertisements, is complex in the same way as State Intelligence, but differs from it in that the announcements are made by Local Authorities, non-Government institutions such as the Royal College of Surgeons, and by individuals. Announcements under Water, Clean Air, Road Traffic and Town and Country Planning Acts form the bulk of this section. They are listed by the name of the authority. A considerable number of changes of name appear regularly, and both the abandoned and the assumed name must be indexed. Another large item is the registration of places for the solemnisation of marriage, and cancellation of registry.

Example.

Marriage:
    Cancellation of Places for the Solem-
        nisation of:
            Acton, Gospel Hall,
                High Street   1234

For this, the classifying symbols are a/mc while an entry in the registration section is a/mr. The Industrial and Provident Societies Act and the Friendly Societies Act also head cancelling and dissolution notices. Page references only are needed for these, and the society concerned is listed alphabetically in the main body of the Advertisements index.

Example:

Friendly Societies Acts:
    Cancelling of registry   5678
    Dissolution notices   5679
    (Symbol: a/FS/c
                  a/FS/d)
a   Todmorden Sick Benefit Society,
        cancelling notice   5678

Notices under the Companies Act form Section V. There are few complications here, but the successive notices concerning the same company, appearing at infrequent intervals, have to be collected together after sorting.

Trustee Act notices are also straightforward and are put out for typing. Here again, identical names must be distinguished by adding the town of residence.

Example:

Jones, Mary Eliz. (Cardiff)
—   —   —   (Swansea)

Bankruptcy notices form the final section of the Index. Here, as with companies, references occur at intervals and have to be assembled. Aliases and alternative names must be entered, and also the names of any firm with which the bankrupt has been associated.

Example:

Brown, Henry (also known as John Smith) trading under the style of Handy Stores

The copy is posted to St. Stephen's Press in batches as ready, and galley proofs come back in instalments for checking. The final stage is the counting of entries for the submission of the quarterly account. When all this has been completed, a month's *Gazettes* of the current quarter have accumulated and the whole process begins again.

———

The discussion following this talk was mainly concerned with the following points:

1. *Abbreviations.* These are sparingly used in the Index, according to established precedent. Some members thought that lists of quarterly returns, a recurring feature, might well have the names of months shortened in the recognised manner. Others pointed out that while this particular point might be valid, it was inadvisable to use many abbreviations in an Index which might be widely used abroad.

2. Various suggestions for tax claims based on expenses were made, bearing in mind that the **Contractor (Indexer)** must meet all costs from the price agreed with H.M.S.O. The initial problem here is to establish precedents with the Inland Revenue over expenses incurred while working at home.

3. It was generally agreed that once the system of headings and entries, already established in the past, had been mastered, the major task and satisfaction of this work was found in organising the enormous volume of entries so that all participants were kept employed without bottlenecks, and the work delivered in accordance with the time table.

Some Notes on the Indexing of a Library Science Periodical:

The Index to *Libri*, Vols. 1–25

Leif Kajberg

This paper gives a summarized description of the main points to be considered in connection with the compiling of a cumulated index to *Libri: International Library Review* vols 1-25. Also touched on are the general problems facing the indexer concerned with the indexing of periodical publications including the assignment of priorities to special parts of the textual material to be indexed, the maintenance of consistency, and the difficulties stemming from the poor state of terminology in library and information science.

Cumulative or collective indexes to periodical publications in library and information science are not an unknown phenomenon. They range from the decennial index to the scholarly journal *Zentralblatt für Bibliothekswesen, 1957-1966,*[1] to the recent *LISA Cumulative Index 1969-1973.*[2] Other recent products are the Collective Index to the *Journal of the American Society of Information Science*, Volumes 1-25, and the other ASIS publication, Cumulative Index to the *Annual Review of Information Science and Technology* Volumes 1-10 which supersedes the Cumulative Index to Volumes 1-7 published by ASIS in 1972. Besides, mention may be made of the collective index to *Nachrichten für Dokumentation*, covering the period 1950-1969, published by the German Society for Documentation.

The subject indexes included in this index are UDC-classified sequences. Finally, a notice in *Information Science Abstracts* vol. 11, 1976, No. 2 informs us that a cumulated index to vols. 1-10 (1966 through 1975) is to be prepared for publication.

The literature concerned with serial indexes and multi-volume or multi-author indexes is rather modest. However, a few contributions that deserve consultation do exist, For example, mention may be made of articles by J. Edwin Holmstrom on the indexing of multi-author, multi-volume and periodical publications.[3]

Thus, the indexer being confronted with the task of compiling or constructing an index of this category may find some help and guidance in the written sources as far as the procedural steps, the technical approaches and innovations are concerned, but it seems to me as if less treatment has been given to the more fundamental problems which arise in compiling this type of index, as a result of their specific nature.

Before concentrating on this set of problems a few words on the profile of *Libri*. As stated on the cover *Libri, International Library Review* is a quarterly journal 'bringing original papers on all aspects of librarianship, including the history of books and publishing.' Within these limits the spectrum of topics covered has been very wide. An index to it implies that it is possible

Reprinted from *The Indexer* 10, no. 4 (October 1977): 191–194.

191

to locate articles ranging from the study of manuscript fragments to the nature of information science, to mention two extremes. Many outstanding contributions are of a scholarly nature, especially those dealing with themes such as book history, bindings and manuscripts. Included in the corpus of articles are many high-level contributions by well-known theoreticians and professionals in the field. The articles concerned with research libraries, mainly university libraries, have preponderated over the years, but it is my personal observation that a shift in coverage and orientation has occurred during recent years leading to a broadened coverage of the area of librarianship, and quite in harmony with *Libri*'s orientation and scope there has been a considerable number of papers reporting on national developments in the library field all over the world, thus parallelling other international library periodicals such as *International Library Review* and *Unesco Bulletin for Libraries*. Another salient feature that emphasizes *Libri*'s international orientation is the section entitled 'IFLA Communications' which appeared regularly for many years as a separate section devoted to the reporting of meetings, conferences and other activities of IFLA sections and committees. On the other hand, an analysis of the recent volumes reveals that the number of papers falling within the sphere of book arts and historical bibliography has decreased, or even disappeared.

Design of the index apparatus

During the initial phase of preparation several issues were to be considered, including the structuring and dimensions of the index and its components, its scope, including the degree of selectivity and the physical size of the index, and the modes of indexing. A number of possible index structures based on combinations of such basic index components as author index, index of names, subject index, and a classified sequence were outlined, and after some consideration it was agreed that two separate sections covering authors' and subjects' names respectively would be sufficient to meet the minimum requirements for a journal of this nature.

When determining the design and composition of the index apparatus several points must be clarified, above all the obvious factors affecting the framing and elaborateness of the index, such as the space allocated—limited by the funds made available—and the time allowed for the compilation and production. In the case of *Libri*, a physical framework equivalent to 60-80 pages —being similar to a normal issue—was taken as a guideline before the project was implemented.

Among the alternatives rejected was the classified section that groups articles under broad subject headings or categorizes them according to some classification scheme (e.g. UDC or the Classification Research Group scheme). Comparing the systematized sequence with the alphabetical subject index is a debate often encountered in articles or discussions on indexing problems. The classified section displays the range of subjects and reflects the distribution of the material included, but although the systematic approach has its qualities —including the browsing feature—and may be of value to some users it cannot compare for ease of use with the alphabetical subject index.

Subsequently, a choice of indexing mode had to be made. In theory, several index systems might be chosen, ranging from the more 'dirty'* machine-aided approaches (e.g. KWIC) to sophisticated systems like, for instance, PRECIS. However, selecting the latter would undoubtedly cause problems, since a specially trained indexer would be required. The decision was made to adopt a more traditional system in the back-of-the-book-index mode.

As indicated, the rather limited amount of space allowed necessitated a highly selective coverage implying that certain categories of material had to be rejected out of hand (e.g. book reviews). Besides, a vast number of items was sifted out during the indexing process including corporate names, names of individuals mentioned incidentally in the text or in footnotes, geographical locations, bibliographical references, and titles of books considered peripheral.

Efforts were made to isolate the subject matter regarded as relevant, and the concept indexing approach thus attempted involved scanning or reading all contributions and features within the categories of material to be indexed. As expected, difficulties in determining which items were to be considered for inclusion were often encountered, and a clear impression of the delicate problem of maintaining the consistency of indexing within a wide range of heterogeneous contributions emerged.

Choice and form of entries

When analysing in detail the overall body of textual material contained in the set of volumes

---

*In this connection, 'dirty', which is of American origin, coupled with the word 'quick', denotes a rough machine-produced index based on the extraction of words from titles. The generation of the index requires no intellectual effort, and no refinement, such as control of synonyms, is aimed at.

to be indexed a number of special problems relating to weighing and assigning of priorities turn up. Do, for instance, the more recent contributions deserve a more thorough treatment implying an expanded coverage in the index? In other words should the factors of obsolescence and topicality be allowed to underlie the indexer's judgements? And is the indexer capable of performing an evaluation like this which involves a determination of the weight to be ascribed to various parts of the textual material? Although some items, for instance those concerned with themes in the fields of historical bibliography, are still valuable, it is clear that the factor of obsolescence does occur. It should be borne in mind that 25 years represent a wide span, even within the fields of library and information science, and the ravages of time may affect some articles. As an example mention may be made of *Libri* vol. 3 (1952) which is solely devoted to the proceedings of the First International Congress on Medical Librarianship including a wide range of contributions which doubtless would be of minor interest to professionals active in medical libraries to-day. In addition, it will be possible to locate other items of a technological nature, dealing with operations and processes that can be considered less relevant in 1976. On the other hand, it must be admitted that a number of contributions will be of some importance and relevance from a library historical point of view. Or perhaps an observation of this nature is hypothetical, trifling and irrelevant?

Another difficulty is that of maintaining consistency, due to factors such as scope and structuring of individual articles, the subject matter itself, its heterogeneity and shifts in emphasis, and variations of style among contributors.

When embarking on a periodical indexing project (subject indexing approach) it is advisable to rely on a thesaurus or an 'authority list' so as to ensure some control in the selection of entry words and subject headings, for the sake of consistency and uniformity. However, here the indexer is faced with another basic problem arising from the weaknesses of library and information science terminology—ambiguity, lack of standardization, consolidation, and systematic development. This phenomenon, being one of our profession's 'shoemaker's children' syndromes, is true of any language, so far as I know. In Danish, for instance, the terminology of librarianship, let alone information science, is rudimentary and very poor.

Nevertheless, a plethora of terminology lists, glossaries, vocabularies, dictionaries, and index languages exists, partly as monographs and partly as sections of books and serial publications —but which are the appropriate ones, to help the indexer to distinguish the preferred from the non-preferred terms? A universal library and information science thesaurus possessing some recognition and authority has, so far as I know, not been constructed yet. One of the recent attempts in this area is the multilingual vocabulary entitled *Terminology of Documentation* issued by Unesco,[4] a work which is not blameless in all respects. This was clearly illustrated by Mr Anthony Thompson in a presentation dealing with the translation of specialized terminology at the conference of documentalists in West Germany, October 1976. It appears that some of the terms included are questionable or even erroneous.

An alternative solution would be to try to build a 'thesaurus' of one's own during the indexing process. But I consider that the indexer will be faced with the same basic problems due to the lack of a codified terminology/vocabulary.

Among the sources I preferred to consult when compiling the *Libri* index were *A Classification of Library & Information Science* by Daniel & Mills[5] and the index terms to be found in the *LISA* subject indexes.

Also related to the field of terminology is the problem of determining English language counterparts of items which occur in German or French contexts—*Libri* is a multi-lingual journal accepting articles in all three languages. Precision is required during the process of translation so as to prevent erroneous index entries.

If the list of problems is to be continued, mention may be made of a classical one, that of making sure that the concepts and index terms selected constitute appropriate and relevant representations of the subject matter embodied in the set of volumes indexed. Do they actually meet the user's needs, and do they conform to his search approaches? Having adopted a precoordinate indexing mode, as is the case with back-of-the-book indexes or 'micro-indexing', the indexer cannot deny that he is left with a feeling of uncertainty, a feeling of operating in a vacuum. Perhaps the concepts displayed by the indexer appear to be too broad or too rigid to provide an adequate surrogate that expresses the various facets in an acceptable way. In addition, the adherence to a subject heading for reasons of uniformity may result in formulations that are too narrow, thus leading to inadequate subject characterization. In other words, information may be lost during the process of reformulation and translation into controlled vocabulary terms.

It is hoped that the desultory observations and reflections embodied in this account will serve to highlight the theoretical problems relating to the indexing of multi-volume and periodical publications.

References

1. *Generalregister zum Zentralblatt für Bibliothekswesen 71.-80. Jahrgang 1957-1966.* Bearbeitet von Gottfried Rost. Leipzig: VEB Bibliographisches Institut, 1968, 120p.

2. *Library and Information Science Abstracts Cumulative Index 1969-1973.* Oxford/New York: Learned Information, 1975, 309p.

3. Holmstrom, J. Edwin. Innovations in the indexing of contributions to series of volumes. *J.Doc.* **31** (2) June 1975, 71-92.
    Holmstrom, J. Edwin. The indexing of multi-author, multi-volume and periodical publications. *The Indexer.* **8** (1) April 1972, 31-43.

4. *Terminology of documentation. A selection of 1,200 basic terms published in English, French, German, Russian and Spanish.* Compiled by Gernot Wersig and Ulrich Neveling. Paris: Unesco Press, 1976, 274p.

5. *A classification of library & information science.* By Ruth Daniel and J. Mills, with the assistance of R. Selwood and Pirkko Elliott for the Classification Research Group. London: The Library Association, 1975, 127p. (Library Association Research Publication, 15).

IVc. Encyclopaedias

Indexing *Chambers's Encyclopaedia**

Dorothy Law

The editions of *Chambers's Encyclopaedia* appearing betwen 1858 and 1948 had no index. But the new Chambers's for which I was responsible comprises a limited number of long main articles, many shorter articles dealing with the principal points of the main articles and a very large number of brief descriptive entries. Such a scheme seemed essential because one department of knowledge, investigation and thought constantly overlaps and impinges on another.

The special problems of such an index lead off with the simple matter of size. This particular *Encyclopaedia* has an index of about 200,000 references, some 400 pages, each page set in 4 columns of 7 point type. This is a lot of index. The second distinctive factor is the subject matter to be indexed. It is comprehensive. It embraces some 15,000,000 words covering as far as is feasible, recorded human history over 5,000 years, with the events and discoveries, the ideas and hopes of the human race. No neat little specialisms for the indexer here. nor even a *magnum opus*, one scholar's life work. The third distinctive point is the time factor. The time at the editor's disposal, including the time taken by the printer and the dealing with galley and page proofs, was well under a year.

From these points flow a number of consequences. The index had to be made not by a single expert but by a staff of indexers of whom none (except the scientists and mathematicians) can be specialists. The organisation and physical labour required to isolate, classify and distribute entries on specific intellectual disciplines (which after all appear on the page proofs in alphabetical order) is beyond contemplation, and secondly disciplines overlap and, therefore, the articles may well cover more than one sphere of interest. We therefore had to choose a staff of generalized intellectual capacity who could be taught the techniques necessary for this particular labour. For the most part our indexers were seconded from the editorial work they had been carrying out on the text.

An important consequence of having to use a team of indexers was that consistency of approach and of attitude of mind (if I may so describe it) to the weight and significance of items of information indexed had to be secured: and, of course, uniformity in the actual techniques of the operation.

Agreeing that the object of making a classified subject index is to turn the information in the *Encyclopaedia* inside out and to indicate the whereabouts of a vast range of information in a different and more specific form, this form, in addition to the obvious entries, titles of articles and the like, will embrace (1) different terms from those shown for the titles of articles; (2) specific items of information lumped together in the text under a general heading; (3) alternative terms, names or spellings.

The index has by no means been restricted to the listing only of persons, places and things. Subjects, topics and ideas as well as names, receive their full share of attention.

* A lecture given at a meeting of the Society.

Reprinted from *The Indexer* 7, no. 1 (Spring 1970): 13–16.

It was also the policy to include as many entries as possible on those rather more obscure persons, who, buried in the folds of time and having no outstanding claim to fame, are perhaps not likely to be met with in other works of reference.

On the problem of what references to take out, the main criterion was whether the reference conveyed material information about the subject of the actual index heading: allusions incidental to some other subject had to be passed over. A useful rule-of-thumb we suggested was that, to be worthy of an index entry two hard facts must be given in the text, i.e., the reference indexed must contain two specific and concrete factual statements about the topic specified in the index heading. There being few rules, however, without their exception, it proved useful on occasion to relax this to one 'hard fact'. Small references to matters or people not dealt with elsewhere in the *Encyclopaedia* are sometimes as valid for inclusion in the index as longish references to subjects also treated elsewhere. Bear in mind, we said, that as indexers cannot index from the text something that is not there, so the editors will not be able to collate into any sensible shape (a) cards that are not there; (b) cards which are in error; (c) cards which are in any way misleading or ambiguous. It is therefore better to write too much in the way of explanation on any card taken out than too little. It is better, generally speaking, to over-index than to under-index. Excess can be dealt with at a later stage; deficiency cannot.

Our indexers were reminded that they should also bear in mind allied subjects to the one under consideration. It is not always enough merely to index what is in front of one. Thus, an important reference to *wheat* in the article, say, on *Agriculture* should be indexed not only under *wheat* but probably under *cereal* and *grasses* (whether these words actually occur or not), as well as possibly under any names mentioned of leading wheat-growing countries, to be classified by the editors later under sub-section Agri-

culture of such country index headings. Similarly a discussion, for instance, in the article *Drama* on Shakespeare's views on tragedy as exemplified in *Hamlet,* could well qualify for index entries under Shakespeare, Tragedy and Hamlet (but N.B.—NOT under Drama).

To pick out of the text the names of persons, places or things about which at least two hard facts are given is relatively easy. Nor is it especially difficult to think of additional but *not* of course synonymous headings under which the reference should also be made. It is more difficult to recognize a discussion or description of an idea, concept or general topic which the contributor may not have labelled with a definitive name. Such references have nevertheless to be identified and taken out. The choice of the heading under which such references are entered requires thought.

Two separate groups of entries dealing with the same subject, e.g., liberty and freedom, would never do. All such entries had to be brought together under the heading with a cross-reference from the other.

Such chosen names and their alternatives (as cross-references) were specially noted and made available for inspection by all indexers. When an article existed under one of the possible names, that name was preferred as the selected index heading and was if necessary cross-referred to from the others. This did not exclude, of course, that references to the subject might also be made under still other headings: e.g., under *Totalitarianism*. Special difficulty arose in the indexing of ideas in distinguishing between two related but not identical concepts, e.g., *Absolutism* and *Divine Right*.

We had to impress upon our indexing staff that a full, accurate and precise description was vital, as without correct identification of the person, place or thing later editing and proper collation would be impossible. There are several meanings of the one word 'strike' for example: each separate reference to 'strike' had to be gathered together and sorted at the final stage into its proper category—the strike entries boiled down to four, plus two under 'striking'. Again, in the index to the 1950 edition, there are four separate entries on 'cat': the island, the animal, the type of ship and as a military term. It is obvious that references in the text to the domestic animal accidentally indexed under the island in the Bahamas will be misleading to say the least.

Similarly, with 'modifications' it was important to be accurate, pinpointing the nub of the matter under discussion, dating treaties, battles, political events, inventions, scientific discoveries and the like; or otherwise indicating place and period of time. Thus there might be more than one reference in the work to Gladstone's attitude to 'the Turkish question'. With index cards properly filled in editors would be able to collate them under the appropriate modification and the reader who wished to know exactly what his attitude was would be able to find the reference immediately. Never sacrifice, we begged, clarity to brevity and avoid abbreviations, e.g., not, please, 'pol. in Pol.', but 'policy in Poland'.

The indexing of persons posed problems. The prime object was to identify the person named. It was really necessary to distinguish accurately between, say, the various Charles II's (The Fat, of France, of England, of Epirus, of Naples, of Navarre, of Parma, of Spain, of Wurttemburg, of Brunswick, and, of course, the Holy Roman Emperor). Difficulties arose when an entry had to be taken from an article which gave insufficient data for easy recognition. This problem, which was incessant, necessitated our employing a number of research workers as adjuncts to the index team. All doubtful identifications were set aside and handed over to our researchers for pinpointing. This difficulty did not relate only to potentates. There is a dismaying tendency in scientific articles to describe the important work of Jones and Davies who are said to be the first persons to have isolated some vital something or other. Such eminent characters cannot be just pushed into the index under 'Jones'.

Let us hope that the great man turns out to bear as a first name a really distinctive appellation.

Then there are the medieval polymaths who are known to the scientists under the name which may be Mohammed something or other and to the literary specialists under another, which may be Abdul something or other.

We may all recognize Buonarotti to be Michael Angelo or the earl of Beaconsfield to be Disraeli, but you really have to have your wits about you to equate Ab Aquapendente with Hieronymus Fabricis or Abu Raihan Mohammed with Al Biruni. There were also the people unknown to such ignorance as mine, with single names such as Toun, which turned out to be the name of a Japanese metal worker. How important it was to those who ultimately edited the index that the descriptions and dates should be full and accurate will be readily grasped if one looks at the index entries on Frederick which occupy well over a column and a half and start off with Frederick the Penniless and run through Frederick the Fair, Frederick the Wise, Barbarossa, of course, and Frederick the Great, moving on to the Frederick Augustuses, the Frederick Charleses, the Frederick Christians, the Frederick Henrys, to end up with Frederick William IV.

The accumulation of index entries for some countries was very large and for the main countries the index entries were classified. In practice I found it necessary to delegate the classification and editing of the entries on countries to one member of the index team to ensure a reasonable degree of consistency. I need not trouble you with any cries from the heart caused by those regions, countries and nations which have changed their boundaries, changed their names, changed their sovereignties, during the course of history. You will be able to imagine these for yourselves.

With books, pictures and music, the question arose whether to take out the names of works of art and if so, which. Generally speaking, works taken out had to be important, historically or artistically.

The rule-of-thumb of at least two facts was strictly applied; and from biographies of writers, painters, etc., works were taken out very sparingly. But famous works by minor performers were favoured, e.g., *Uncle Tom's cabin*.

Indeed, we made a real effort to index the names of well-known works the authors of which most of us are hard put to specify. Who of us could now remember off-hand the name of the writer of ' Rule Britannia '? James Thomson is better remembered for ' The Seasons '. Or for that matter who wrote *The Star Spangled Banner*? This became the national anthem of the United States by Act of Congress in 1931, 117 years after it was written by Francis Scott Key.

I have made no reference to the indexing of the scientific articles. One of the leaders of the team who undertook this specialised work is a member of our Society and I could not possibly venture to offer a word on this topic except to express, once again, my thanks for her expert labours and those of her colleagues, including Mr. Skelton.

The *Encyclopaedia*, indeed, was marvellously well served by its indexers. On the first round Mr. Laurance Fitch was in general charge and the late Mr. Hubert Fitchew's team checked most of the galley proofs. And on the second round, Mr. Merton Atkins was in general charge, with Mr. Sandison added to the scientists.

The Index of the *Encyclopaedia Judaica*

Raphael Posner

Editorial Decision

The making of the index for the *Encyclopaedia Judaica* (*EJ*) was governed by various decisions taken by the Editorial Board in conjunction with the publishers. Both bodies felt that a work of the scope of the *EJ* required a comprehensive index; so much information is buried within entries that without such an index the encyclopaedia loses a great deal of its value. It should be noted that the text of the encyclopaedia comprises thirteen and a half million words in 24,000 entries. It was further felt that an index would obviate the need for 'see' references within the text of the encyclopaedia; taking into consideration the fact that concepts and people are known by different names and that, at times, the same name is spelt in several different ways, plus the fact that a great deal of Hebrew is used in the encyclopaedia, these references would clutter up the text unbearably.

In order to stress to the reader the importance of the index it was decided that it should appear in Vol. 1 together with the introduction. No limit was set on the size of the index.

It was further decided that the whole *EJ* would appear at once, including Volume 1, and that, considering the large financial investment involved, the encyclopaedia would

not, under any circumstances, be able to wait for the completion of the index. In other words, the task was to finish the printing of the index simultaneously with the completion of the printing of the encyclopaedia text. The *EJ* was published in January 1972, but the actual printing started in August 1970, and the work on the index began in November 1969. The encyclopaedia was printed by the offset method and a computer-aided typesetting programme was used. Entries were set at random as they were ready and when all the entries for any volume were complete they were transferred on to one tape. The computer tape activated a Photon electronic film setter and the film produced was made up into printing plates.

Scope

There were long discussions in the Editorial Board of the encyclopaedia with regard to what type of index should be incorporated in the *EJ*; there was even a suggestion that the index should include articles of the *Jewish Encyclopaedia* which appeared at the beginning of the century and which has no index. This idea was, however, discarded as being beyond the scope of our index, which, it was decided, would be fully comprehensive. This meant that: (1) all entries would be listed; (2) all persons mentioned in the *EJ*—including those in charts and picture

Reprinted from *The Indexer* 8, no. 2 (October 1972): 101–111.

captions—would be indexed; (3) all places would be indexed; (4) all concepts would be indexed and (5) all books of major importance would be indexed. It was decided that the index would not include lists of professions or callings, i.e. there would not be an index entry ' doctors ' followed by a list of all the doctors mentioned in the encyclopaedia. The very nature of the encyclopaedia would make such a listing impracticable; a listing of, say, rabbis or Hebrew authors would run into tens of thousands and would hardly be of any real use to anybody. However, for certain subjects of special educational importance, lists were included.

In order to make the *EJ* as useful a work as possible we decided that all the information on a specific subject found throughout the encyclopaedia should be gathered as subentries under that subject in the index. We realised that this would inevitably lead to some duplication of information but we felt that the advantages greatly outweigh the disadvantage of occasionally seeing the same information twice.

Indexing from Manuscript

Normally indexing is done from page-numbered galley proofs or from the printed, numbered pages themselves. We realised that such a system would be unworkable for us; although it would have been possible to have indexed the early volumes by the conventional method, the time available to us for the last eight or nine volumes—from their being paginated until the completion of their binding—would be far less than the minimum required to index them adequately. Furthermore, even were we to enlarge the staff very greatly (more about this later) and manage to do the actual indexing, we would never have enough time to order and edit the index adequately. It must be borne in mind that in a work of this scope the objective indexing problems are enormous. The number of people mentioned in the encyclopaedia with the same name is very large and while in most cases identification is relatively easy, in a significant minority of cases a great deal of research (which means time) is required to arrive at an adequate identification. In a very few cases it is impossible.

Another difficulty is the person who was known by many names and is referred to, in different entries, by different names. This is a problem which, to my knowledge, no index has succeeded in solving completely; the amount of work required to achieve at least a reasonable level of correctness is very great. In addition to all this we realised that a great deal of work would be needed to put the index in order and to arrange the subentries into sub-divisions in those entries where there was a great number of subentries. Because of all the above-mentioned considerations we decided to index the entries in manuscript form after the manuscript had received the final authorization from the Editor-in-Chief's office and was ready for press. This, of course, created the problem of corrections and additions that were made to the entries after that stage and indeed right up till the final printing. Taking everything into consideration, however, we felt that this method would still give us the best chance of success and arrangements were made that any change or addition to a manuscript after it had left the index department was required to be sent to our department before going for setting; it was examined to see if the changes or additions required any change to the indexing and, if they did, the necessary adjustment would be made in the index cards. All in all, we succeeded in making the whole *EJ* staff very ' index-conscious '; both the management and the senior editorial staff were co-operative, and all levels of staff quickly learned that it was totally forbidden to alter an article once it had passed the indexing stage without informing the index department of the change.

The computer programme used for printing the encyclopaedia called for each article to have a distinctive number. This number was made up of the first four letters of the name of the article (or all the letters if there were less than four) followed by a six digit number which was not random but built according to an internal logic. A number which did not fit the logic was rejected by the computer. For the index we utilised this number plus specific index numbers which were added to it. The purpose was to use computer code numbers in the index instead of volume and page numbers. This would enable us to build our complete index, edit it and prepare it for press without knowing in which volume or on what page our information appeared. At a very final stage the computer would convert all the codes into real volume and page numbers. For the overwhelming majority of the index this system worked perfectly.

The Work System

The actual working arrangement was as follows: The indexer received the manuscript of an entry and made out a 'title card' which consisted of the name of the entry as it appeared at the head of the article, followed by a brief description in parenthesis and the code number of the entry. Ordinary 3½in. by 4¾in. index cards were used. A typical title entry card looked thus:

*Tunis, Tunisia (tn, ctry, Africa)   TUNI 058562

The name was underlined in red and preceded by an asterisk for easy identification as a 'title entry'; this convention was later used as an instruction for typesetting. All writing on the card was in block capitals to ensure legibility; the red underlining indicated capitalization. The indexer then read the article and marked all the passages that he felt needed indexing. This included all places and people mentioned in the article as well as subjects and concepts. The article, thus marked up in pencil, was examined by the chief editor of the index, who made additions or otherwise corrected it. The manuscript then returned to the indexer, who made out index cards for all the points marked and, at the same time, marked up the article in ink at those points. Thus, the article referred to above reads at one point: 'This tradition also relates that

the *kohanim* (i.e. priests) escaping from Jerusalem in the year 70c.e. carried one of the Temple's doors to the island (Djerba) and it is believed to be walled in the synagogue called Ghriba . . . ' An index card for the *kohanim* was made as follows:

Priests
- Carried Temple door to Djerba, 70c.c.   TUNI 058562-5

one for the Temple:

Temple, Second*
- Door carried to Djerba, 70c.c   TUNI 058562-5

and one for Ghriba:

Ghriba (Syn., Tun)
-Temple door incorporated in   TUNI 058562-6

In the manuscript the indexer inserted the code [I|5] before the word *kohanim* and [I|6] before the word Ghriba. These marks were included in the text of the entry as it was type-set for the computer (punched on to the tapes) by the keyboard operators. The [I] was the instruction to the computer that this was the index code and it appeared on all galleys of the encyclopaedia articles produced (in the margin opposite the line of text where it occurred) until justified copy. For the article in question 178 index marks were made on the manuscript; some index marks carried more than one card as above for *kohanim* and Temple.

The article was then sent for type-setting and, for the time being, the cards for it were stored together. Later on the cards were put in alphabetical order; we delayed that stage as long as possible to facilitate easy retrieval should any change be made to the entry.

For this stage we had decided that every card should include a description of the subject in order to help in the editing at a later stage although we already realised that in the final stages a great number of descriptions would be omitted. Indexers were also encouraged to write on the card, in pencil, any additional information they felt might be of help in editing. A very definite decision was taken that no card should contain more than one item of information. As the work progressed we began to develop abbreviations

Pages from the Index of the *Encyclopaedia Judaica*

for the terms most commonly used. For the duration of the work on the index an average of seven or eight people was employed. Of these some were indexers and others were editors. The latter also worked as indexers until the later stages when they took up the actual editing of the cards and even then occasionally had to help out with the indexing. One of the great problems was the uneven flow of material into the department; at times huge quantities of material would descend and great pressure would be applied for us to process it quickly so as not to cause difficulties in the production stages following ours. Usually indexing is not a part of the production flow but rather outside it and parallel to it; it is therefore free of this problem. Since we were indexing from manuscript we were, in fact, the last stage of the editorial process and thus the natural address for the complaints of the production people. At other times the index department would be without material for days on end. At the beginning the slack periods were utilized for reviewing what had been done and for preliminary discussions of policy for the editing stages. Later on, the quiet days, which became fewer, were used to catch up on filing and alphabetization.

Illustrations

The illustrations for the *EJ* were prepared by a separate department. Occasionally illustrations were specifically ordered by authors or editors but a very large proportion was initiated by the researchers of the illustration department who ultimately had to receive the authorization of the editor-in-chief with regard to suitability and correctness of captions, etc. The term 'illustration' here includes photographs, maps, diagrams, musical notations and family trees. The administrative and co-ordinative problems involved in indexing these before printing were insurmountable and so they were indexed only when the actual numbered page proofs were ready. The system followed was the same as above except that actual volume and page numbers appeared on the cards instead of computer code numbers.

Filing

When some 25,000 cards had accumulated we started filing them. The cards were filed according to the words appearing on the first line and alphabetization was by letter up to the first punctuation mark; the system followed in putting the encyclopaedia entries in order.

What resulted was a situation in which all the cards on a specific subject were grouped together. In the case of title-cards, they always came first, followed by the cards with all the other references to the subject which would become sub-entries; in the case of main entries, such as the Ghriba card above, a decision would have to be taken later whether to arrange them as a main entry followed by sub-entries, in which case the most substantive reference would be taken for the main entry or, if the number of cards or the nature of the information did not justify that, to arrange the cards as one main entry followed by several page references. Actually the Ghrîba card shown above was the only one on the subject. For title entries, only one page number could follow, with some exceptions for 'capsule' articles; all other information had to take the form of sub-entries. We felt that this was the best way to indicate to the reader where the actual entry was and thus to differentiate between the entry and secondary material: the system used in the index of *Encyclopaedia Britannica* and the *New Catholic Cyclopedia*, by which even a title entry is followed by more than one number does, to our mind, create a certain confusion even if the number listed first indicates the actual article.

At this stage the editing consisted of putting the cards in the proper order and starting some order for the sub-entries. We developed a system of crossing out unwanted words in green felt-tip pen so that the text would still be legible. The 'Priests' card shown above was filed behind the title-card, 'Priests and Priesthood' for that was the actual name of the entry, and the word

'Priests' on the first line was crossed out. Thus, this card was now a sub-entry to the title entry.

The cards were stored in open boxes which held about a thousand cards each. Boxes were never filled and the labels showing the scope of each box were constantly being changed as new material flowed in. The editors took responsibility for the boxes in series of five or six; we felt it advisable to spread the editors over the index as widely as possible. Every few days the new cards which had accumulated were alphabetized and put at the back of the box where they belonged; a wooden block was kept in each box to keep the cards upright and separate the integrated cards from the new ones. Periodically the editors reviewed their boxes and integrated the new cards. The plan of the index entries was constantly changing, due to the insertion of the new cards, and as yet no serious effort was made to put the sub-entries in order. At this stage the editorial work consisted mainly of checking problematic cards. The cards from the indexing of the illustrations were kept separate as long as possible so as not to complicate the editing.

Details of Index Policy

As the number of index cards increased, editing became more intensive. Index entries began to be created; final abbreviations and conventions were decided and general policy took form. We decided that persons listed in the index would not have a description attached unless there were others of an identical or very similar name. In those cases dates were given to differentiate; where the dates were not sufficient, the occupation or profession was given and where that was not sufficient, the country. There were few cases where all three were not sufficient and in those the reader will have to examine all the entries concerned. For names of people which are not easily so identifiable, a description was given, as was the case with certain groups of people such as kings or *amoraim* (rabbis of the Talmud). All other index entries were described except when

absolutely obvious. People preceded places and places preceded things. In the case of persons with identical names the order followed was chronological.

A further decision was that for large encyclopaedia entries (we took 3,000 words as the criterion although there are many in the 10-20,000 range and not a few in excess of 50,000) we would include a list of contents of the article in the index entry for the convenience of the reader who is interested in some specific aspect of the subject.

When the number of sub-entries justified it, we arranged them into **sub-divisions** according to their content. The sub-divisions follow a logical order not necessarily alphabetic but the sub-entries were always arranged alphabetically

'See' and 'See also' cards

All alternative names of a subject were indicated by *see* cards:

Menaker, Abraham, *see* MOREWSKI, ABRAHAM

as were alternative spellings. Such cards were also used when the subject was treated in another article: Engineers, *see* INVENTORS AND ENGINEERS. Cognate subjects or entries likely to be of interest to the reader were indicated by *see also* references at the end of the index entry thus:

CAMPS (Concentration and Extermination) has more than 120 sub-entries which are followed by: *see also* FORCED LABOR;GHETTO;HOLOCAUST

The criteria by which another encyclopaedia article was listed as a sub-entry or as a *see also* reference were (1) subject matter, i.e. whether the information was directly relevant to the entry, and (2) the size of the article referred to; the Holocaust article is full of information about concentration camps but that information is spread throughout an article of more than 70 pages.

Special Problems

Some of the index entries were so large as to pose special indexing problems. The ISRAEL (STATE OF) index entry contains in excess of 1,100 sub-entries and, obviously, any reader other than the most expert is going to have difficulty finding his way through it. We therefore decided that in such cases—there were a few—the index entry would begin with a guide to itself indicating how it had been sub-divided. Further, important sections of it also appear as independent index entries in their correct alphabetical position. Thus, WATER AND IRRIGATION IN ISRAEL appears in the index of both the ISRAEL encyclopaedia entry and the ISRAEL index entry.

Many of the above problems are based on the question 'What is an index for?' and the solutions found will be based on the answer to that question. Is an index merely an aid to finding the information you are looking for or should it perform an independent function as well? We wanted the index to the *EJ* to be, in some degree, a useful study guide for major subjects, particularly since no other Jewish encyclopaedia has an index. One of our aims when we made index entries such as BIBLE and ZIONISM was to give the reader a comprehensive study programme to the subjects as far as the information in the *EJ* was concerned and not just an aid to help the reader who knows what he wants to find in it.

Typography and lay-out were considered after the work on the index had been under way for about nine months. Several trial pages were made up and we decided that: (1) title entries would be in upper case; (2) main entries would be in upper and lower; (3) sub-divisions would be in upper and lower; (4) sub-entries would be in lower except for proper names; and (5) sub-divisions and sub-entries would be indented, and that indentation marks would be used.

Thus the title or main entry is always flush left and if there are only sub-entries these are indented one space and the indentation is indicated by an indentation hyphen. If, however, the sub-entries are sub-divided, the sub-division title receives one indentation and its sub-entries two. In a very few cases we resorted to special typography to avoid creating four levels of indentation. Here, considerations of space were important; we felt that four columns to

a page was the best number and it was obviously desirable to minimize as far as possible the number of over-run lines. With this in mind we also tried to keep the text of the sub-entries as brief as possible.

The Computer Stages

We had realised that if the *EJ* was to be published in January 1972 we would have to start setting the index in August 1971. At that time not all the encyclopaedia articles had been through the index department. The *EJ* was prepared in less than five years and during the last six months of that period the pressure was, to say the least, extreme. An encyclopaedia is a dynamic organism until the very last page is printed; omissions are constantly being noticed and article-structure changed. Although a master-list of entries had finally been completed in April 1969, it was by no means complete and was open to change right up till the last stage of the encyclopaedia. We had devised a system for the index by which we would send it for typesetting and update each successive round of galleys with the index cards that would accumulate in the meantime. We were eager to start getting the index into galley form for another reason. Although we had made several trial runs for the computer conversion of code-numbers and for the layout of the pages we were still apprehensive about the final result; every system needs to be 'debugged' and we were not sure just how stubborn the final bugs would prove to be. Furthermore, any mistake in control cards for the programme or in punching the tapes might take a great deal of time to trace and correct and we knew that in the very final stages the time margin available to us would have to be measured in days and hours and not in weeks. There was always the possibility that we would have to do the conversions by hand, and to this end we had prepared a back-up programme. We had ordered from the computer a print-out of all the index numbers in the text according to volume and this we received as soon as each volume was transferred on to one tape. We had also ordered a completed conversion of all those numbers, which we would get as soon as the pagination of the entire encyclopaedia was registered in the computer. We could have ordered this second print-out for each individual volume but the cost was prohibitive. Should the programme collapse entirely, the first print-out, which indicated those numbers that had for one reason or other been rejected, would be of some help; should the conversion programme work but the matching up part of it fail, the second print-out would be invaluable.

As each volume was paginated the pagination was registered into the computer. Because of the illustrations it was impossible to use the computer to make-up the encyclopaedia pages as we did for the index (more on this later). The film of the text was produced by the Photon and the pages were made up by hand, incorporating the illustration material. It was necessary, therefore, to 'inform' the computer of the make-up, i.e. what articles appeared on which pages. When this process was completed the computer would convert all the code numbers in the order in which they appeared in the text into their corresponding real number and then it would take the index in which the code numbers appeared in random order and substitute the correct volume and page numbers for the code numbers. By this stage the index cards had already been edited thoroughly. The entries had been built and all the cards had been checked for the proper use of the conventions decided upon with the type-setting department. The illustration cards were now merged with the text index cards and the boxes were given a final editorial review. All in all there were more than 200,000 index cards.

Galleys and Updating

The boxes were divided so that each contained approximately 350 cards, and from now on each such box was treated as a galley. Each box was given a distinctive computer number made up of the four letters INDE and six digits arranged so that the third, fourth and fifth were in running order;

this was for easy internal identification—the other digits were according to the computer logic. The boxes of cards were sent for typesetting and we received back hard-copy typed sheets; the punched tapes were not yet sent to the computer. The hard-copy was proof-read against the boxes of cards (a difficult job since indentations were indicated on those sheets by computer code signs) and the cards which had come in since the boxes were sent for setting were integrated into the sheets as corrections.

The corrected sheets were then returned to setting, the corrections made and the tapes sent to the computer. Electronic tape was received back which activated the Photon electronic typesetter which produced film galleys of the index. These galleys were proof-read and corrected, and the index-cards which had accumulated were added as corrections. The galleys were returned and corrected, and another round produced for which we followed the same procedure. On the second galley we succeeded in integrating nearly all the outstanding cards since by that time nearly all the encyclopaedia articles had reached us.

Computer Problems

The major problem during this stage was mechanical in origin. If there was the slightest mistake or abnormality in the punching of the galley header (i.e. the number) when the correction was typed in for integration by the computer, there was the possibility that those corrections might find their way into another galley and even displace material which rightfully belonged there. It is not difficult to imagine the chaos that this created. We made very serious efforts to eliminate such errors; the corrections were proof-read before sending the tape to the computer and the punched paper tape itself was examined. Notwithstanding our best efforts, some mistakes did occur. When the correction involved was minor we preferred to correct it on the galley and send that back as a correction; when, however, it was major we sent the galley back for retyping from the original until an acceptable result was achieved.

By this time the registration of the pages into the computer was complete and we received a print-out listing every index code number and the page on which it appeared. The print-out also indicated those numbers which, for one reason or other, no page number had been found. There had been several articles which had not been set through the computer or which had been so drastically re-edited at the film stage after the computer, that the computer record was to all intents and purposes useless. For these articles, of which we had been kept informed, we prepared conversion tables of our own. These were now used to supplement the computer sheets.

Lay-out

The instruction was now given to the computer to prepare justified, converted galleys. The earlier galley rounds had been in specially large type and with a great deal of space between the lines (the Photon machine is capable of producing innumerable variations) to facilitate proof-reading and correcting. This converted justified galley was produced in the exact size in which it would be printed and the length of the lines was justified. All the code numbers were now replaced by volume and page numbers and those for which the computer had not found the page number appeared on separate lines and were easily spotted. These were now inserted manually. The conversion was better than we had imagined it even in our rosiest dreams; immediate checks were made in large samplings and the margin of error was negligible. We did discover that occasionally a code number that appeared on the last line of one column was converted as though it was on the next column but in a very large sampling this happened in only a very few cases. This round of galleys was proof-read and final additions were made. The following and final computer stage was the page make-up. The programming called for the lay-out of the index to be done automati-

cally; this meant that the Photon would produce a film of each page laid-out in four columns and that each page would have two running headers, one in the top left-hand corner and one in the top right-hand corner, indicating the scope of the index for that page. These headers would indicate the first and last title or main entry on the page but not a sub-entry and they would appear in the same type face as the entry they represented but in a larger size. We had also decided to start every letter of the alphabet on a new page so that if there were any complications in a specific letter of the alphabet they would affect only that letter and not everything after it. This decision, as it turned out, was a most important one. The page make-up programme worked well except for a few of the smaller letters of the alphabet which had to be cut up into columns and made up by hand. However for the major bulk of the index we received perfectly good film from the Photon. This was proof-read and the corrections were stripped in. The index then went to press. Since the pagination of the encyclopaedia was done on the first justified galley proofs, we were able to achieve what I think must be a 'first': the index was printed and bound while there were still two volumes of the encyclopaedia which had not yet been printed.

Evaluation

When reviewing the whole programme it is clear that the use of the computer did save us a great deal of time. The programme was, in fact, a straightforward one in its conception but rather complicated in its operation. It was not sophisticated but, because of the many stages involved and the huge numbers of items, complex. We would certainly not have been able to produce the index together with the encyclopaedia had we not used such a programme. However, the computer had no effect on the actual index itself; here there can be, happily, no substitute for the intelligent, informed and educated human being, since the discretion required is entirely beyond the computer. Our evaluation of the programme indicates that the use of the computer is only justified (from a financial point of view) if: (1) the text to be indexed is, anyway, going to be set by computer; (2) the size of that text is so large as to be unwieldy, and (3) if great speed of production is required. Should any of these three conditions be lacking it is our feeling that as good a job can be done manually and probably at less cost.

Pages 467 and 697 of the Index are reproduced to illustrate the article. The entries Ghriba (syn., Tun) 15:1430 on page 467, and PRIESTS AND PRIESTHOOD, in the 'General' sub-division the sub-entry Tunisia legend 15:1430 on page 697 show the final appearance in the Index of points made in the article.

Three Encyclopaedia Indexes

Delight Ansley

Does an encyclopaedia need an index? A small encyclopaedia in one or two volumes has short articles in alphabetical order, and it is usually well provided with cross-references to related articles. For such a work an index is as superfluous as it would be for a dictionary. But in an encyclopaedia as large as the *Britannica,* or even half as large, it is almost impossible to locate small details of information without a complete and well organized index.

From personal experience with two encyclopaedia indexes and some knowledge of a third, I can present some ideas that may be useful to other indexers who have the privilege of doing similar work.

The *Encyclopedia of science and technology,* published by the McGraw-Hill Book Company, is a work in fourteen volumes with volume fifteen as the index. There are approximately 700 pages in each volume. All volumes were in proof before the index was made, and the schedule called for the index to be completed in three months. That seemed impossible, but it was done.

The work was organized in this way. As supervisor of indexing for the McGraw-Hill Book Company, I had the opportunity to examine a few samples of the text and to consult the editors in order to make some general plans and recommendations in advance. Then I spent a week in the editorial offices of the encyclopaedia.

There were about half a dozen supervising editors, each one responsible for the articles in a certain category—electrical engineering, physics, biological sciences, and so forth. They were asked to mark the index entries on page-proof of the articles, and they had been thinking about their problems before I came.

The editors and I met together for two days to discuss the typographical style, the system of marking pages, and particularly the choice and arrangement of index entries. Everyone had a chance to express his opinions and to ask questions. When we reached a decision on anything I wrote it down and read it for the approval of the group. (This is the customary procedure of a Quaker business meeting, and it works admirably with people who want to reach a common understanding.) At the end of two days we had a complete set of written instructions, and each editor received a copy.

Reprinted from *The Indexer* 5, no. 1 (Spring 1966): 16–22.

The same thing was done with the typists who were to copy the entries on cards and with the clerical workers who were responsible for alphabetising. The whole staff worked for a few days under my direction, and when the work was finished I spent three weeks on the final revision.

In editing the cards we found a large number of duplicate entries for subjects mentioned in more than one article. All volume and page numbers were placed in sequence on one card, but the duplicates were kept. When the index was revised a few years later they were arranged with volume and page numbers in numerical order so that all transpositions and changes in the text could be noted.

The index has proved to be so satisfactory that no fundamental changes were needed for the revised edition of the encyclopaedia. It may seem odd that the index for a work of this kind was not prepared by a more advanced technique of data processing. Electronic methods were considered, but at the time they seemed prohibitively expensive and the copy that they produced was not suitable for our material. More than five years later the methods have been so much improved that if we were planning the index now we would probably make a different decision.

The *Encyclopedia of world art*, on which I am working at the time this article is written, requires an intricate and flexible type of indexing that could hardly be done by mechanical methods. We have begun our work in time to give the material as much care as it deserves.

The first volume of this encyclopaedia was published in 1959 and the last one should be finished in 1967. There will be fourteen volumes with volume fifteen as the index. Each volume contains approximately 900 to 950 numbered columns and 500 plates.

Because time is not severely limited we are using a very small staff. I have one assistant, a highly intelligent young woman who has done a great deal of research and editorial work on the text. We are lucky to have a capable, accurate typist. We work together intimately; we agree on what we are doing and how we are doing it. With a larger group such understanding would be possible but more difficult.

The routine of indexing is exactly as it would be for a small book. We select the entries and mark them in the text or write them on fliers attached to the pages. The typist copies the entries on cards. As soon as cards for one article are finished we proof-read them, alphabetize them, and file them with the cards that have been made before, all in one alphabet. When we find a duplication we add the new volume and column number to the card in the file. We do not keep duplicate cards because it is unlikely that a full revision of the encyclopaedia will ever be made.

The form of our entries has been planned to make the index useful as a reference tool, and the information is useful to us as the index grows. Every personal name is followed by a brief identification such as (Gr. sculp., 5th cent. B.C.) or (It. ptr., 1452-1519). Towns and archaeological sites are identified by country; historical periods such as dynasties have dates whenever this is practical.

Most of the encyclopaedia articles are long essays, some as large as fair-sized books. The articles were written by authorities in various countries who had no way of knowing what was in other articles, so there is a certain amount of overlapping of subject matter.

Every article title is indexed, but some article titles are not suitable as main entries. Some contain more than one subject, for example, 'Flemish and Dutch art' or 'cubism and futurism'. Others, such as 'European modern movements', are full of important information which no one would expect to find by looking for sub-entries under that title.

The solution of this problem is obvious. We treat 'cubism' and 'futurism' as separate entries. To each one we add the information on the subject which we find in the article 'European modern movements' or anywhere else. An artist, Picasso for example, may be discussed at some length in both articles as well as in several others, including a relatively short article under his own name. Plates illustrating his work may appear with a dozen articles. (Plates are indexed at the same time as the articles, not separately.) Our idea is to collect all information about a person, a place, an idea, or any other subject and put it together in a logical form.

The typographical arrangement of the index is simplified as far as possible, but it is complicated enough. We use italics for titles of works of art. We do not use bold face or capitals to emphasize article titles or important main entries. (If one starts doing that, what is an 'important' entry?) We give inclusive column numbers to show the length of a discussion. Column numbers for an article are marked with an asterisk. Volume numbers are in bold face: **7** 248-310*.

The most serious typographical problem is the immense number of accents and other diacritical marks in foreign names, including Arabic, Chinese, and others which will be a printer's nightmare. We have a special typewriter which can give many unusual marks, but the rest have to be inserted by hand. Our typist deserves a vote of thanks for her patience and skill.

Many of the names which are not fully identified in the text have to be looked up in other sources, and my assistant often spends a day in library research. If we do this gradually, settling small problems as we come to them, we will have less time-consuming work at the end of our project.

As we work our way through the text we know how valuable a good index will be, and we are doing our best to make one.

The *New Catholic encyclopaedia*, also published by McGraw-Hill, has a totally different indexing situation. Like the other encyclopaedias I have mentioned, it is in fourteen volumes with volume fifteen as the index. All volumes will be published at the same time. According to the schedule the index should be finished approximately six months after the first page proofs are received.

The impossibility of meeting such a schedule with any conventional method of indexing made it necessary to use an electronic data-processing system. A survey of costs showed that this would not be much more expensive than hiring the large staff that would be needed to do the work by hand in such a short time. The data-processing firm regarded this project as a valuable experience for them, and they agreed to share the cost.

The indexing procedure was explained to me by Sister Claudia, the index editor, and I am most grateful for her co-operation.

The first step was the preparation of a list of article titles in the encyclopaedia. (Most of the articles are fairly short, although some have as many as 30,000 words, and their titles are specific.) Each article was given a code number, and the article titles formed a starting point for the structural basis of the index.

The text of the encyclopaedia is being printed in galleys, one article at a time, not in consecutive order. Galley proof for indexing is mounted on paper of the standard typewriting size, which allows plenty of room for writing entries on margins. When galleys for an article are received, an indexer marks or writes the entries. About half a dozen indexers are working together. They have a full understanding of the principles governing the choice of entries, and all their work is revised by the index editor.

To locate the position corresponding to a page number, the index uses the code number of the article and the line number in the text. In the finished index this will be converted to volume number, page number, and quadrant or quarter-page location. Only the first page number of an article will be given, not inclusive pages.

Entries within an article are related as closely as possible to other article titles, and the index editor watches for this in her revision. She writes the code numbers of the article titles beside the entries or sub-entries on the galleys. Cross-references have a special identifying number.

When the entries are ready a typist copies them as a list, with entries for each article on a separate sheet of paper. Sub-entries are indicated by their position and by a number (1, 2 or 3) showing the degree of indention. An additional citation of an entry that has been used before is simply the number of that entry followed by a new location number.

The list is sent to the data-processing firm. There the entries are copied on punched cards, automatically sorted for alphabetization, and transferred to tape from which a printed copy is made.

Approximately once a month the index editor receives several copies of a cumulative printed list containing all entries which have been received at that time. The list is on large sheets in a flexible binder. A sample of the items in this list is shown below.

```
026524      TARTAGLIA, NICCOL6O                    15389 0000
  01    1     cubic equations                      10248 0404
  02    1     projectile motion                    14367 0124
  03    1     x Fontana, Nicola/ Tartalea,
                Niccol6o                            75389 0001
026525      Tartalea, Niccol6o, <see> Tart
              aglia, Niccol6o                       60002 0206
026526      TARTARUS                                15390 0000
  01          chthonic divinities                  03397 0044
026527      TARTE, JOSEPH ISRAEL                    15391 0000
026528      TARTINI, GIUSEPPE                       15392 0000
026529      <Tartuffe> (Moli6ere)                  10737 0127
```

On the left are the alphabetical sequence numbers; on the right are the article and line numbers. Alphabetization is word by word, coded for such details as stopping for a comma or ignoring a preposition. When several names have the same spelling, the sequence is coded according to the accepted rules for saints, popes, kings, etc.

Article titles are in full capitals; other entries are capital and lower case. No italics are available, but words to be italicised are enclosed in angular brackets. Diacritical marks and accents are not available; they are indicated by superscript or subscript numbers. (Notice the entry ' Tartuffe '.) An item preceded by lower case x indicates that a cross-reference has been made. It is only for the convenience of the indexer, and it will be dropped from the printed version. Division of a word at the end of a line is purely mechanical, and it will be corrected in printing. Indention of turnover lines will also be corrected; they are now aligned with the entries.

When the indexers receive the printed list they do the revision and editing that would normally be done on cards—correcting mechanical or typographical errors, co-ordinating entries, and so on. This is easier to do on a page than on cards.

In the final stage the electronic processing will supply the page numbers and the index will receive a final copy-editing before it goes to the printer. The printing process has not yet been determined, but if possible the index will be set from tape or photographic copy.

The indexers are happy with the data-processing system, but they know that a computer cannot make an index. It can only perform certain mechanical operations which are directed by human intelligence. After all, who makes the computer?

A good index of any size, made by any method, is the work of a skilful and intelligent human being. A simple index for a small book is a test of his ability, and the most complicated encyclopaedia index is the same thing on a larger scale.

No index can be of any use without a planned structure of some kind. The indexer must decide what should be indexed and in what form. No one will tell him; there are no rules, and every book has its own problems.

Amateur indexers often begin with the idea that they should include everything, every time it is mentioned, in any form in which any reader might look for it. This noble ambition is usually given up after the first twenty pages.

When we discussed the choice of entries for the *Encyclopedia of science and technology* index we chose an example, ' three-phase alternating-current squirrel-cage electric motors '. This item could be indexed in at least five forms. How many kinds of motors would be mentioned in the encyclopaedia, and in how many forms could each of them be indexed? We decided on ' motors ' for general discussion of all types, ' alternating-current motors ' with inclusive page numbers for the description of that type, and separate entries for specific motors.

The index of the *New Catholic encyclopaedia* seems somewhat limited by dependence on article titles, but the indexers are free to add any other entries that seem necessary, and they can use their imagination by fitting new material into the general pattern.

The choice of entries for the *Encyclopedia of world art* index was considered long before the work began. The most obvious question was this : should paintings be indexed under their titles, under the artists' names, or in both places? We decided to list them only under the artists' names, and every day we are thankful for that decision. The number of paintings with the same title is astonishing. If we had a sequence of more than a thousand titles beginning with the word ' Madonna ' or ' Virgin ' we would have a longer index but not necessarily a more useful one.

We also considered the problem of churches. Innumerable churches have names beginning with Saint, San, or Santa. Even if ' Saint ' or its equivalent were ignored, how many would we have under John, Jean, Juan, or Giovanni? We decided that churches and other buildings should be indexed by the places where they are located. Under the name of a church we can have sub-entries for architecture, sculpture, and painting, with the names of the artists. (This information is also given under the artists' names.) So the sub-entries under ' Florence ', for example, will be almost a guide-book to the works of art in that city.

Indexers who are responsible for large projects may try to establish some rule for selection of items according to the length of discussion in the text. Listing a word every time it appears, whether anything is said about the subject or not, can produce a solid block of undifferentiated page numbers, all of which the reader has to look up before he finds what he wants. Should indexers make an arbitrary rule such as ' nothing less than five lines '?

No rule of this kind was made in any of the encyclopaedia indexes I have known. In the *Encyclopedia of science and technology* an important equation or chemical formula can be in one line. In the *New Catholic encyclopaedia* or the *Encyclopedia of world art,* two lines may give a man's name, his nationality or

field of work, and the dates of his birth and death. It is impossible to determine the importance of an item by measuring the number of lines, and no rule is needed.

An encyclopaedia index may be made by two women with lead pencils and one woman with a typewriter, or it may use all the resources of an electronic system, but the human qualities it needs are those that every good indexer must have. These qualities may be defined as infinite patience with small details, a trained and disciplined imagination, and the pride of craftsmanship.

*   *   *

The Society's Chairman comments:

Having been privileged to have a preview of the above interesting article based upon Miss Delight Ansley's important work as indexer-in-chief for two large encyclopaedias, one or two observations occur to me.

In her first paragraph Miss Ansley appears to deem an index superfluous in the case of ' a small encyclopaedia in one or two volumes '. To my way of thinking, because of the multitude of names and subjects necessarily referred to in more than one alphabetically headlined article (only a tiny fraction of which can be adequately treated by means of cross-references), an encyclopaedia index can never be considered superfluous. I would grant, however, that it might be difficult to provide one for a pocket encyclopaedia! Perhaps I may best illustrate my theme by citing the two-volume *Focal encyclopedia of photography* (Caxton, 1958), which contains an excellent index, without which the usefulness of the work as a whole would be reduced by half.

Secondly, I am sorry to note that Miss Ansley has dispensed with bold face type for the reference numbers to article titles, as this practice always seems to me of the greatest assistance to index-users. On the subject of typography, I would also mention that to use italics for titles of works of art seems contrary to English custom; the Oxford *Authors & printers' dictionary* expressly lays down that titles of pictures and sculptures should be in quotation marks.

Again, it is noticed that Miss Ansley has helpfully differentiated between the two-a-page columns in her indexes. It might have been even more advantageous to have adopted the *Britannica* method of dividing up each of its large pages into four sections (a, b, c, d) for the purposes of the index. I have inspected some very ancient works in which the index-maker, in his anxiety to please, indicates not only the page number but also the actual *line number* on the page on which each entry appears in the text. But possibly such meticulousness is beyond the capacity or patience of the modern index-maker!

G. N. K.

*   *   *

Miss Ansley explains as follows: Mr. Knight's comments are interesting. Italics for titles of works of art may be contrary to English usage, but it is the style used in the encyclopaedia we are indexing; that's why we have to use it in the index. And ' bold face type for the reference numbers to article titles ' wouldn't be possible since the volume numbers are always in bold face. We use an asterisk instead.

V. Indexing Scientific and Technical Literature

Scientific and Technical Indexing*

E. J. Coates

In case the title of this paper carries the implication that there is something peculiar or fundamentally different about scientific and technical indexing which marks them off from other kinds of indexing, I should make it clear that I do not think this is so. Very few of the points with which I shall deal will have no application to indexing in other subject fields. The main factors which from the indexer's viewpoint distinguish science from non-science material are questions of degree only. Scientific literature contains a greater number of concepts *in toto* and a far higher proportion of precisely defined concepts than does the literature of the humanities, so that from the point of view of the multiplicity of concepts scientific indexing looks at first glance formidable, but from the point of view of the battle between words and meanings, the scientific indexer gets off relatively lightly, I say relatively because, despite all essays at standardised nomenclature, there is plenty of ambiguity in scientific, and more particularly technological, terminology. But at least, despite all that is justifiably said about the sheer incompetence of much scientific writing as communication, the scientific author usually does manage to convey the definite topic about which he is writing. The same cannot be said in all fields.

The second difference of degree concerns the consumer side of scientific index-ing. Scientific activity, as you know, has an increasingly serious information problem upon its hands, and a great deal of attention is at the moment being focused upon scientific indexes. Some elaborate experiments are being carried out on the efficiency of scientific indexes, at Cranfield in this country, and elsewhere. Taken all in all it would be fair to say that scientific indexes are under particularly close scrutiny and at the present moment rather more is being expected of them than is the case with other types of indexes.

Some of the interesting things that are being done in connection with scientific indexing are worth considering for the light they throw on the basic purposes and aims of indexing generally. There is, for instance, the KWIC indexing system, a not too distant variant of which is now being used to provide a current subject approach to chemical literature. KWIC was invented by one of the giant computer-manufacturing concerns seeking to develop fresh uses for computers. It is meant for the indexing of scientific papers, though it is possible to conceive how it might be used for book indexing. Briefly, the computer is programmed to take each word in the title, with some exceptions which I will mention shortly, and to print out the title repetitively under each selected word. This is achieved, without disturbing the word order, in this fashion: For the given title 'Efficiency and transparency of cheap liquid scintillators' the following is produced:

* A talk given in the Society's Fourth Training Course.

Reprinted from *The Indexer* 5, no. 1 (Spring 1966): 27–34.

AND TRANSPARENCY OF   CHEAP LIQUID SCINTILLATORS. EFFICIENCY
LIQUID SCINTILLATORS   EFFICIENCY AND TRANSPARENCY OF CHEAP
TRANSPARENCY OF CHEAP   LIQUID SCINTILLATORS. EFFICIENCY AND
OF CHEAP LIQUID   SCINTILLATORS. EFFICIENCY AND TRANSPARENCY
EFFICIENCY AND   TRANSPARENCY OF CHEAP LIQUID SCINTILLATORS

Now you will see that you get an entry under all words in the title except articles, prepositions and conjunctions. It is of course quite easy to give the computer a list of articles, prepositions and conjunctions and instruct it to ignore these; not so easy, and indeed not attempted, to give it a formula enabling it to reject the value-less entry under CHEAP.

I mention KWIC because it is an outstanding demonstration of indexing at its lowest level of sophistication. All that it requires is that words given in the text (or title, for a bibliographical index) should be picked up and manipulated into alphabetical order. Even at this low level a certain discrimination is needed to reject non-significant words, which no one will ever want to look up. We see that the computer can only discriminate to the extent of rejecting a predetermined list of non-significant words, and that usually this list comprises only articles, prepositions and conjunctions. This question of deciding what is or is not significant is the most pervasive unsolved problem of indexing at every level. When we ask ourselves about significance, we should ask 'significant to whom?' It is a fact that the significance problem is in inverse proportion to the extent that we can visualise the needs of the person who is going to consult the index, and in general this means that it is an acute problem for an index covering a wide subject field of interest to many different kinds of specialist interest, and less acute for indexes covering narrow subject fields. Even the word CHEAP might be significant in a bibliography or book on ' How to sell scientific instruments '. We cannot easily overcome the significance problem, which exists in scientific indexing as in other indexing,

though we may be able, as in the KWIC system, to whittle it down just a little.

I pass now to what can be regarded as indexing of the middle or second degree of sophistication. Before leaving KWIC behind, I should like to say that for all its wide-open loopholes which will be obvious to all of you, it is doing a job which at the moment is too big for human indexers, or what is more important, needs to be done more rapidly than can be carried out by human indexers. It has the virtue of its name. It *is* quick, and speed is of paramount importance in scientific literature indexing. The scientist, particularly the applied scientist, just cannot afford to wait for the leisurely index which comes months or years after the event to which it refers.

The second level of indexing to which I now wish to turn is distinguished from the first in that the indexer is no longer simply a manipulator of words, but someone who tries to isolate the concepts signified by the words. His task is to utilise words to indicate the concepts lying behind the author's words—an invidious task, and perhaps logically doomed to fall short of 100 per cent. success. For this process of signposting the concept behind the word, conventional jargon has given the name of ' vocabulary control '. Vocabulary control means nothing more than that one identifies synonyms, or phrases of equivalent meaning among the index words which one has collected from the text, and having identified a pair of synonyms, one either lists under each all the references already given under the other member of the pair, or alternatively one assembles all the references at one term only and makes a cross-reference from the other.

Of the various features which contribute to the practical utility of a book index, none is more important than synonym control. Two questions arise in this connection to which no easy answers can be given. The first is, how does one spot synonyms, or what can one do to ensure that synonyms are not missed and entered as if they stood for different concepts. The rule of thumb method is that one notices or remembers that there was another word which meant the same thing, but the larger the index the greater the load placed on memory and the more synonyms will slip through the net. The only device for checking synonymy of terms is classification. Classification is simply the ordering of terms into a systematic pattern of likeness of meaning, so that terms that mean nearly the same thing are close together. Each term in the index is assigned to its proper place in the classification and when one finds oneself wanting to put a term into a position already occupied by another term here is the evidence of likely synonymy. It is a formidable task to have to make one's classification and then, as it were, to fit every index term into it—there is however no other way of systematic checking for synonymy. The making of classifications is of course a matter about which librarians have been heavily exercised for a long time, but I do not think that any existing ready-made classification is ideal as it stands, for the purpose of synonym control. The basic technique for constructing classifications is not difficult to acquire, and becomes easier with practice: I suggest that anyone interested would do worse than to read *Faceted classification* by B. C. Vickery, in which the author explains very clearly how to approach the classification-making problem.

The second question which arises in synonym control is this: if I decide to prefer one term and make cross-references from the others, which do I prefer? If you are indexing the work of a single author, the author's preference will surely determine yours, but if you are indexing a composite work of multiple authorship, or if you are doing bibliographical indexing, the problem is not always so simply resolved. Attempts have been made in some scientific fields to standardise terminology, but these standards often go against strong conventional preferences. This is particularly the case in chemistry where considerable steps towards systematisation of nomenclature have been made, but where also the briefer so-called trivial names strongly persist in the literature. The names of technical processes often take a long time to settle, and the indexer is frequently called on to take a decision long in advance of a conventional preference. An example which comes to mind is the bulking process applied to yarns to give them softness to the touch, apparent elasticity, and varied thermal insulation properties. The process is variously called bulking, crimping, false twisting, texturing. It recently appeared that texturing was winning the day, but there is now a new variant ' texturising '.

It is not always the logical names which prevail against the more superficial ones. 'Hovercraft' is firmly ascendant in Britain for a certain novel type of vehicle, despite the existence of two other names which refer to more fundamental properties. 'Air cushion vehicle' is logically preferable, because it refers to a more concrete attribute of the vehicle, and anyway there are other vehicles which are not hovercraft which nevertheless hover. Perhaps even more to be preferred is ' ground effect machine', which had a good start in the literature, and formed a pleasant little acronym GEM, but which is rapidly falling out. The direction in which technical advances are made does itself help to establish a conventionally preferred name. I would guess that Hovercraft will eventually give way to Air Cushion Vehicle because the same air cushion principle is now finding applications elsewhere, for instance in the handling of delicate strip material at the strip mills. It is not possible to bring the word Hovercraft into a name for these air cushion bearings, though they have been called Hover Pulleys. There is little more that can be said about correct choice of synonym except that, like nearly every other indexing problem, it becomes harder in proportion to the width of subject field being covered.

I have dealt so far with two levels of sophistication in indexing. At the first level, the essential operation was one of manipulating given words, and at the second the concern has moved on to the listing of concepts, by means of words it is true, but by means of words to which synonym control has been applied, so that the index user's luck no longer depends upon the particular term under which he first thinks of looking. At both of these levels there is also the common underlying question of what is a significant term and what is not.

Both of these levels in various admixtures are the common characteristic of indexes to books by individual authors, and I think we can say that the better sort of book index is normally the one operating on level two. The third level is normally appropriate to indexes to compilative or collective works with contributions from various authors, and to bibliographical subject indexes. It is distinguished from level two in that it includes connective references between related terms in the index.

It is easy to see why this is generally only appropriate to the indexing of material of heterogeneous origin. In the text by an individual author, the arrangement of the material itself is determined by the relationships between the various parts of the subject that the author thinks important. I doubt if it is part of the indexer's job to indicate other relationships, or even to reproduce those implicit in the arrange-

ment of the text. But you will see that different considerations apply in the case of indexes to heterogeneous material or to the contents of large numbers of individual items such as scientific papers.

Now anyone who sets about constructing a network of relational cross-references quickly realises that there is no end to this process, and the network very quickly becomes a maze. The problem is how to put a limit on the process, and the general answer is to confine oneself to showing one type of relationship only. For most purposes the most useful relationship is that of inclusion. Make connective references from a term to others included within its meaning as from INTERNAL COMBUSTION ENGINE to DIESEL ENGINE and GAS TURBINE or from FISHING VESSEL to TRAWLER, from POLYAMIDE FIBRE to NYLON. But here again we do not go very far before being beset by difficulties. For any given term, there are usually a number of possible including terms. For instance, we might legitimately insist that GAS TURBINE should have a cross-reference from the inclusive term TURBINE, and NYLON might equally well be regarded as coming under THERMOPLASTICS, as under POLYAMIDE FIBRES. So we need not only to limit ourselves to inclusion relationships but we also need a device to help us sort out the inclusion relationships themselves. We find such a device in classification schemes, for these are essentially attempts to lay out multidimensional relationships in linear form.

So we see that classification is relevant to indexing in two ways. First of all on what I called level two as a helpful means of detecting synonyms, and now also as providing a basis for a network of relational references. Once again I have to repeat what I have said in other connections, this particular aspect of the indexing task, like most others, is easier in proportion to the narrowness of the subject field being covered. The wider the harder.

I want now to turn to another aspect of indexing work which in some degree applies to all fields but is especially prominent in indexing scientific and technical material. Most of the concepts which we wish to index are composite in character, that is to say they cannot be expressed in a single word, but require a phrase, sometimes something almost approaching a sentence. For example, DROP FORGING. DROP FORGING HAMMERS. VIBRATIONS OF DROP FORGING HAMMERS. DAMPING THE VIBRATIONS OF DROP FORGING HAMMERS. Let us concentrate on the most complex example:

DAMPING VIBRATIONS OF
    HAMMERS FOR DROP FORGING

Why don't we index the subject just in that form? The answer is not that the subject is too long to express—we have to accept that subjects of that degree of complexity are sought by people who consult indexes, though they may not start with exactly those words or that order of words in mind. The phrase as it stands is unacceptable for indexing purposes because it contains prepositions which are always non-significant words. So let us then take out the prepositions: We are left with

DAMPING, VIBRATIONS,
    HAMMERS, DROP FORGING

This composite term entry remains intelligible even when the prepositions are dropped because the order in which the five significant terms appeared in the natural language phrase is still retained. If we start shifting the five terms round very much, we soon begin to lose the sense, for very good logical reasons. The damping is directly related to the vibrations and only related to the hammer through vibrations, so that we have a linear chain of relationships. If we start to tangle up the straight chain, then in-

telligibility suffers. But you will quite rightly insist that the index should provide a lead-in to this composite concept from each of the significant terms, VIBRATIONS, HAMMERS, DROP and FORGING. How does one manage this and yet at the same time avoid the chain-tangling that I have mentioned? There are two (and perhaps more than two) fairly simple ways of doing this. Can I recall the technique of the KWIC index, and rotate the terms as follows:

Entry 1
    DAMPING, VIBRATIONS, HAMMERS,
                        DROP FORGING
Entry 2
    VIBRATIONS, HAMMERS,
                        DROP FORGING/DAMPING
Entry 3
    HAMMERS, DROP FORGING/DAMPING,
                        VIBRATIONS
Entry 4
    DROP FORGING/DAMPING,
                        VIBRATIONS, HAMMERS
Entry 5
    FORGING/DAMPING, VIBRATIONS,
                        HAMMERS, DROP

The sense in these cases remains reasonably clear because the linear chain has been broken once only, though I think that entry 5 suggests that breaking between a term and a qualifiying epithet may never be justified. A variant of this method that is sometimes used is the following:

DAMPING	Damping, Vibrations, Hammers, Drop forging
VIBRATIONS	Damping, Vibrations, Hammers, Drop forging
HAMMERS	Damping, Vibrations, Hammers, Drop forging
DROP	Damping, Vibrations, Hammers, Drop forging
FORGING	Damping, Vibrations, Hammers, Drop forging

One point to be noticed is that the linear chain may be used equally well in either direction:

FORGING, Drop, Hammers, Vibrations,
                        Damping

In this case to translate the index entry into natural language, one reads the elements backwards, Damping *of* Vibrations *of* Hammers *for* Drop forging. The backwards form is in fact used in the *British Technology Index*. Where it is an economy to use references in the index instead of direct entries, the problem can be approached in another way. In this illustration I will use the reversed form just mentioned, though the forward form will do equally well. We start off with a full entry:

FORGING, Drop, Hammers, Vibrations,
                                    Damping

Next we make references as follows from each of the other four significant terms:

DAMPING, Vibrations, Hammers, Drop forging. See FORGING, Drop Hammers, Vibrations, Damping.
VIBRATIONS, Hammers, Drop forging. See FORGING, Drop Hammers, Vibrations
HAMMERS, Drop forging. See FORGING, Drop, Hammers
DROP FORGING. See FORGING, Drop.

The point to notice here is that only the first of the above references details the complete concept. The others are generic references, the import of which is for instance that *something* on DROP FORGING, not necessarily a comprehensive account, is recorded in the index.

This is a very sketchy glance at the problem of ordering the elements of composite concepts which require to be cited in indexes. The practical solution is not always as simple and straightforward as in the illustration given, but on the other hand it is not impossibly complex once its measure has been taken. The indexing in the *British Technology Index* is fairly sophisticated as indexing goes, yet we have been able to reduce most of our problems to a dozen basic situations. I would add, however, that the residual issues are often of very considerable difficulty.

Perhaps I may end with a mention of three persistent danger points which call for the utmost watchfulness.

The first of these relates to homonyms, which abound in technical literature, because of the engrained habit of electrical,

electronic, nuclear and even, I think, chemical engineers, of borrowing words from the field of mechanical engineering and assigning them by analogy to new objects and processes. Thus the electrical engineer has taken over FILTER and BRIDGE to mean a particular circuit, the electronic engineer has, of course, TUBES or VALVES only very tenuously related to the tubes and valves met in mechanical engineering. The chemical engineer 'cracks' hydrocarbons, and the nuclear engineer contemplates the 'burn up' of uranium, though the process is fundamentally different from what is meant by burning in other contexts. The practical problem is to avoid alphabetical interspersion of homonyms of this kind:

BRIDGES, A. C.
BRIDGES, Arch
BRIDGES, Bascule
BRIDGES, Decks
BRIDGES, Electrical
BRIDGES, Girders

We can improve this by inserting a qualifier:

BRIDGES, Arch
BRIDGES, Bascule
BRIDGES, Decks
BRIDGES, Electrical
BRIDGES, Electrical, A.C.
BRIDGES, Girders

However, we still have blocks of material on structural bridges sandwiching the electrical ones. We can further improve matters by attaching to the introduced qualifier term some punctuation device with an arbitrarily assigned ordinal value greater than Z. But we lose in other directions. Arbitrarily assigned order, even of the simplest kind, leaves wideopen pitfalls to the user who is usually prepared to accept the burden of knowing A to Z order, but not one jot or tittle more. We try to meet the more difficult homonym problems in *BTI* in this way:

BRIDGES, Decks
BRIDGES, Electrical. See after the last subheading on structural bridges
BRIDGES, Girder

BRIDGES, Zurich
BRIDGES, Electrical
BRIDGES, Structural See subheadings preceding BRIDGES, Electrical

The second general difficulty to which I should like to refer is that connected with the subject naming of pieces of equipment which are so novel in character that at the time of indexing they have no settled name. It is instructive to consider generally how objects are named. Any object has the basic properties of shape, material function, and sometimes method of working. If you consider established names of man-made articles you will find that usually the name refers to function. As an example, a familiar object comprising a thread of mercury in a graduated capillary tube is called a thermometer in reference to its function. It is not called a mercury capillary, or a mercury expansion column or anything of that sort. The moral for indexers is fairly clear. A new, as yet unnamed object is to be described primarily by its function, or by its shape if its function is multifarious. Thus a new textile fabric would be designated in *BTI* as

CLOTHING (Function)   Fabrics (form)
                               Polyester fibre (Material)

If it is used for a variety of purposes beside clothing it will be entered as

FABRICS (Form)   Polyester fibre (Material)

If it is a question of a new material only, which might be made in the form of either yarns, cords, or fabrics, then we enter simply under the chemical name of the material:

POLYESTER FIBRE

The third problem is the most intractable of all. Many technical objects and processes possess properties which are nearly always applicable, taken for granted and therefore not mentioned, until a new development arises in which the object or process turns up with this normally taken for granted property absent. For example, nearly all the literature on welding is actually on fusion welding, that is to say on welding in which solid metal is converted to the liquid state by heating. Unfortunately this fusion property is taken for granted until a new technique is devised which does not involve actual melting of metal. At some stage we have to go back and amend our material under WELDING to WELDING, Fusion. The difficulty is to know how soon, after what delay, to do this. Another concept in technical literature which often illustrates the same difficulty, is that of METAL. There are many names of processes which imply metal nearly but not quite all the time. MACHINING as used in the technical literature nearly always means the machine forming of metal, but it can be extended to wood, glass, and plastics. WELDING and CASTING usually, but again not quite always, imply metal. The printing trade journals often talk of PRINTING when they actually mean letterpress printing, and if one follows this in indexing one is never sure whether material under PRINTING is about printing generally (letterpress, lithography, gravure and so on) or about letterpress alone. Perhaps as a general rule it is preferable in the long run to err on the side of pedantry.

The stratum of snags and difficulties I have attempted very sketchily to explore, is that which arises once you have cleared essential questions of definition, of the meaning of words, out of the way. Because science and technology deal proportionately with more concrete and definite topics than do other fields, this layer of difficulty is reached earlier in scientific and technical indexing than in indexing in the humanities field. I think, however, that it is to be found in indexing of all kinds.

The Indexing of Scientific Books

J. Edwin Holmstrom

I want to explain straight away that in talking to you for about thirty minutes on the indexing of scientific books I am not giving a formal lecture and am not intending to be in any way dogmatic. By this I mean that I am not claiming the opinions I shall express are necessarily right or the methods I shall describe are necessarily the best ones, but am putting them forward simply as something for you to shoot at, in order to start a discussion on some moot points which ought to be raised and discussed.

In one of the early numbers of *The Indexer,* to be precise in Vol. I, No. 4, Autumn 1959, I contributed an article entitled ' Some ideas on indexing ' which began with the definition that indexing in the wider sense of the word includes ' any device for discovering *or rediscovering* in a book, or in a collection of papers or notes, such items of information or passages of text as have *a wanted relevance* '. By the words italicised here I meant that the purpose of an index is to supply an answer to either or both of two questions :

(1) Does this book (or this file or collection of papers) contain anything that might be useful for me as regards the topic I am now thinking about or wanting to know about?

(2) Knowing or already having reason to believe it contains something I want, on what particular page (or on

what particular bit of paper) shall I find that?

I went on to examine the fundamental principles by which provision can be made for answering these two questions, pointing out that essentially an index has to be some kind of classification of symbols which serve to characterise individual items of information contained in the book or file. What the user of an index has to do is first of all to decide which symbol would correspond with what he is looking for, then to locate that symbol by searching in the index. If it is there, he will find after the symbol the page number or the reference number which he should turn up in the text itself. I further pointed out that in principle there are two fundamentally different kinds of classification symbols that can be adopted for this purpose. One principle is to use symbols listed in numerical order (like those of the Universal Decimal Classification) or in a mixed numerical and alphabetical order (as in certain library systems for classifying books) wherein the symbols represent places in a systematic or hierarchical scheme—as it were co-ordinates in a sort of map of the field of knowledge with which the searcher is concerned. The other principle is that which is nearly always adopted for making indexes to individual books, which is what concerns us here tonight. This principle, when you come to think of it, is really a very odd sort of classification : the symbols adopted are descriptive catchwords, and the order in which they are arranged in the index

Adapted from an introductory talk at a discussion meeting of the Society of Indexers on March 25th, 1965.

Reprinted from *The Indexer* 4, no. 4 (Autumn 1965): 123–131.

has nothing to do with the logical inter-relationships of the concepts themselves but represents merely the sounds which people utter—the noises they make—each in his own language when they think about them. They are arranged in an arbitrary but conventional order which everyone learns in childhood, known as the alphabet. That is what we mean by alphabetical indexing.

From a practical point of view this has certain advantages and also certain disadvantages as compared with systematic classification. Sometimes, for instance, it is a disadvantage that logically contiguous items are distributed haphazardly from beginning to end of the index according to the letters of the alphabet with which their names happen to begin. I think myself that nevertheless this will continue to be the normal form of indexing within individual books, but it would be interesting to hear if anyone differs from this view. This is a question which depends on what answer is given to the first two of those I have put down in the notice of the discussion we are now going to have, namely the fundamental question, 'For what purposes do readers of scientific books need indexes in them?'—a question we certainly ought to ask ourselves if there is to be any rational basis for deciding how much time and thought and money ought to be spent on the provision of indexes in books—and, closely linked with it, the further question whether indexes in scientific books need to have any different characteristics from those in other books. As I see it myself—but here again I should be interested to hear if other indexers think otherwise—the answers to these two related questions depend on what sort of scientific books we have in mind. To explain what I mean I must make a short digression. The best defini-

tion of science I know is taken from a book by T. H. Savory, a biologist schoolmaster. 'Science,' he says, 'consists of organised knowledge in which the facts have been obtained by observation and progress has been directed by hypothesis.' The aim pursued by pure scientists is to clarify and amplify our understanding of phenomena by arranging observed and recorded facts in patterns and trying to discern recurrent relationships among them: when they think they have discerned such a theme they call it a hypothesis and test it by experiment; if the experiment is found to confirm the hypothesis (both qualitatively and quantitatively) however many times it is repeated, the relationship discovered is put forward as a scientific law. What applied scientists do is to look for ways of turning the world's accumulated knowledge of such laws to economic and social advantage in technology, medicine, agriculture, and so on. What makes it possible by these means to deepen and widen our understanding for the purpose of improving our material environment is an interplay between purposefully directed experimental research and efficiently exploitable records of already established data and knowledge. Those two things, original research and the study of existing records, are interdependent necessities for progress. They form a cycle.

Therefore, what makes it necessary for scientists to read books is not so much reading as an end in itself but the possibility of finding data, bits of knowledge, in those books which they in turn can utilise as a basis either for further hypotheses and experiments of their own if they are pure scientists or for practical ends if they are applied scientists. This is quite a different motive from the one that animates the reader of a literary work, for instance a novel or a biography. He reads the latter as an end in itself—for enjoyment, for education, for culture—because he is interested in the theme of that particular book *as a whole* and its manifestation of its author's personality, whereas a scientist reading a scientific book is relatively disinterested in the arrangement of character or authorship of the book as such. He regards it rather as a kind of quarry from which he may be able to extract useful raw material for his own work of processing and integrating that material with other material in order to reach a higher stage of development.

This difference in outlook and purpose is, or ought to be, reflected in differences between the types of indexing proper to 'literary' and 'scientific' works. One can arrange varieties of scientific books, somewhat arbitrarily, in a sort of spectrum having those that are most akin to 'literary' on the left and those whose purpose is most exclusively and directly 'scientific' in the sense explained on the right:

Science fiction and popular science	School text-books	More advanced textbooks intro-ducing students to the methods of science and leading them up to its frontiers	Progress reviews of particular fields, serving as frame-works for biblio-graphical references to the original sources of data	Reference books, collections of abstracts, and compendia of established data including citations of their original sources

The further you go to the right in this spectrum the more essential is the indexing. Indeed, on the extreme right the indexing may be as important as the text. This is because the original sources of scientific data—the 'papers' and articles currently appearing in the world's 50,000 or more scientific periodicals (including notably the proceedings of learned societies and technical institutions) which report the results of new research and describe new applications—run into millions every year, so that nobody has time even to scan, let alone to digest, more than a minute fraction of them for himself. It has to be done vicariously. (Professor J. D. Bernal has estimated that if a chemist were fluent in 30 languages and started on January 1st to read all the papers in his particular field of chemistry, keeping it up for forty hours a week at a rate of four an hour, then by December 31st he would have read not more than one-tenth of the material published during that year, from which the benefit would be nil as he would have had no time to do anything with the knowledge he gained). In order to cope with this situation a vast apparatus of abstracting and bibliographical publications has grown up for the purpose of supplying scientists and technologists with at any rate an indirect awareness of what has been published in the fields that concern them, and of making it possible for the original sources of the items that have the relevance they want to be 'retrieved' (to use the now fashionable word) for them from among all the millions upon millions stored up in the world's libraries. To assist in this process it is important that the indexes to particular books should cover not only items in those books themselves but also bibliographical references cited incidentally in them.

So the answer to our question whether indexes in scientific books need to have different characteristics from those of other books is 'yes', to an extent governed by how closely the book in question comes to the scientific end of the 'spectrum'. Indeed one might go further and argue that it would be a good thing—though difficult to carry out—if the systematics of the internal indexing within particular books could be directly correlated with the external indexing of all books in the shape of library cataloguing and bibliographical controls. (If you like using bastard Greek words, you could call these two things 'microindexing' and 'macroindexing', both ideally forming part of one integrated system).

All this is rather abstract, so let us now consider a few practical examples of what it implies. First, the arrangement of subheads under a main heading in an index entry. In a narrative literary work the plan which is easiest for the indexer to follow, and which also is convenient to the user of the index, is to put the subheadings in the same sequence as they occur in the text. For instance, in the index to Sir Winston Churchill's book *The Second World War* you will find this example:

War Cabinet—Sir Archibald Sinclair and, 11; composition of, 13; meetings of, 15, 18; on need to retain air defences, 40; prepared for evacuation of army, 52-3; determined to fight on, 80-157; and Italian appeasement, 190-191; in consultation on fall of France, 175-176, 180-1; etc., etc.

This is a satisfactory arrangement for the purpose, because in a narrative work the order of the page numbers will generally correspond with the time order of the events reported and this is as helpful an order as any for the reader to follow when searching for whichever items having a 'wanted relevance' he requires. But in a scientific work the historical sequence in which data were established is of little or no importance so the sub-heads are usually, and more conveniently, catchwords or phrases denoting particularisations of what the main heads denote, arranged in alphabetical order under those, like:

Cell division, 73
   activation energy, 148
   clock models for, 470 ff, 477 ff
   doubling time, 528
   isochronous, 284
   kinetics of, 442
   non-clock model for, 482
   normalized rate of, 498
   partial synchrony of, 307
   phased, in marine dinoflagellates, 307
   sequence finite number, steps, 478

(As explained in a note at the beginning of the subject index to the book from which this is taken, the letters ff indicate that the stated subject is mentioned again on one or both of the next two following pages'. Personally I see no objection to this device, which saves quite a lot of printing.)

Another question that arises in making the subject index to a book of this kind is how far you should go, and what principle you can follow, in deciding whether to group many sub-headings under one main heading; because if you overdo this you are apt to get what has been called 'concealed classification' of subject matter introduced haphazardly into the middle of what purports to be a straight alphabetical index. That is a bad thing because, to give a very simple example, somebody wanting to turn up 'Electron microscope' has no means of knowing whether he should look under 'E' or for a sub-item under 'Microscope'. It is rather difficult to arrive at a principle for deciding this and I should be glad to hear what others think of it. My own feeling is that the principle should be not to introduce subheadings unless they can be read joined on to the main headings (the entry phrases) without involving a reversal of the ordinary sequence of words in the English language. For instance, in the example I gave just now I think it better to put 'Electron microscope' under 'e' than to enter it as 'Microscope, electron'. Certainly I prefer 'Mass spectrograph' to 'Spectrograph, mass' as this is a fundamentally different instrument serving a different purpose from an ordinary optical spectrograph. Sometimes the principle I advocate involves using adjectives or adverbs, or present participles of verbs, as entry terms in an index; I see no objection to this if it makes for consistency.

The disadvantages, of course, of generally preferring to make each item a main head of its own rather than enter it as a sub-head under another item in cases of doubt is that if you do that it will inevitably lead to related concepts being spread at random all over the index according to the letters with which their names happen to begin. But you cannot have it both ways. Either you must classify concepts systematically or you must classify their names alphabetically. If you forget which you are doing and sometimes introduce 'concealed classifications' into an alphabetical index, the user of the index is never sure where he is to look and the index is not an efficient one. The proper place to perform systematic classification is not in the index appended to the book but in the list of contents printed at its beginning—or better still in a more detailed list of contents printed at the beginning of each chapter, wherein the sub-divisions of that chapter are listed in the order they occur in the text, giving the page numbers where they begin.

These sequential lists of sub-divisions of chapters can be extremely valuable. In effect they constitute a third sort of indexing principle: neither an impersonal 'map of knowledge' like a systematic classification such as the U.D.C., nor, so to speak, an alphabetical gazetteer listing the place names in the map and telling you the map squares in which those places are marked. Instead, they are an itinerary of the route that the author of the book, who presumably is an expert on its subject field, has chosen for guiding the reader through it. If each chapter, or section of the book, is preceded by a list of the sub-section headings or cross headings in the text in this 'itinerary' form, the alphabet indexing at the end can be economised, for if you put a note calling the reader's attention to the fact that the sub-divisions of chapters are listed at the beginnings of the chapters there is no need to include the headings of those sub-divisions over again in the alphabetical index appended to the book as a whole. In that way you can save space and effort, and therefore money, which if desired may be used for indexing additional items which otherwise would have been crowded out. The note can suggest that where a single index entry (such as a geographical name) is followed by a long string of page numbers the reader should consult the list of contents at the beginning of the book in order to differentiate them according to the contents of the successive chapters. This applies to the 'author index' as well as to the 'subject index'. The provision of a separate index to the names of authors whose works are cited in bibliographical references included in the book is another feature typical of scientific books. Commonly each chapter of the text is followed by a bibliography of the papers and articles cited in it. In some subject fields there is need for yet other indexes, as in the case of *Chemical Abstracts* mentioned later.

In the example here reproduced as Fig. 1, taken from a collective work in which each chapter is by a different author, some typographical distinctions are introduced which may appear complicated but which are useful.

Authors' and joint authors' names of Chapters in this book and the page numbers at which these Chapters begin are printed in heavy type, page numbers of citations in the text are in ordinary type and those of bibliographical references listed at the ends of the chapters are in italics.

Abe, Y., *114, 118*
Abhyankar, S. M., *116*
Abu-Nasr, A. M., *114*
Achaya, K. T., *114*
Adams, B. A., *394*
Aggarwal, J. S., *115*
Ahn, P., *92*
Ahrens, E. H., Jr., 72, *92, 94*
Akahori, S., *328*
Akai, Y., *114*
Alais, C., *227*
Alase, B. H., *116*
Alelios, G. F. d', *394*
Alifax, R., *228*
Allen, C. F., *115*
Alonso, L., *115*
American Oil Chemists' Society, 4, 77, 149, 170, 171, 172
André, E., 47, *55*
Andrew, E. R., 327
Angla, B., 98, *115*
Arata, Y., 328
Bannerot, R. A., *115*
Barford, R. A., *230*
Barker, G. E., *115*
Bauman, W. C., 368, *394, 395*
Bauschinger, C., 12, *55*
Beadle, B. W., 65, *92*
Beavers, E. M., 86, *93*
Becker, F., 181
Bedford, F., 35, *55*
Beers, G. J. van, 63, 76, *94*, 216, *228*
Beerthuis, R. K., *92, 228*
Béjambes, M., *228*
Belcher, R., *228*
Benedikt, R., *47, 55*
Bengen, M. F., 95, 103, *115*
Benham, G. H., 35, *55*
Bernstein, H. J., 319, 320, *328*
Berntrop, J. C., 206, *228*
Beroza, M., *55*
Bertrand, J. E., 281, *307*
Bertram, S. H., 16, 29, 130, 305, *307*
Beveridge, J. M. R., *55*

FIG. 1. Sample of an author index.

The third of the questions suggested for discussion, in the programme for this meeting, is whether it is possible to formulate any general objective criterion for deciding upon the density of indexing, the average number of index entries per page of text. It would be very valuable to authors and still more to publishers, when planning a new publication, if this question could be answered 'Yes', but that, it seems to me, is very difficult. We can assume, I think, that the needed density of indexing increases as you proceed from left to right in the 'spectrum' aforementioned, for even if in popular science books or school textbooks the indexing may be *relatively* unimportant, in reference books it may be as important as the text. It might be interesting, and perhaps worth while, for this Society to sponsor a survey of successful scientific books for the purpose of establishing what density is typical in each category.

The most densely indexed publication I know is the American *Chemical Abstracts*, which provides an example of the art of alphabetical indexing brought to its highest perfection in a field where particularly difficult questions of nomenclature continually arise. In that publication there are 650 words of indexing for every 1,000 words of text. The abstracts appear fortnightly and they cover some tens of thousands of articles contained each year in some thousands of journals all over the world, as well as about 12,000 chemical patents every year. Each fortnightly issue of the abstracts has indexes to its contents and on the conclusion of the annual volume these are cumulated in a large separate volume containing nothing but the indexes; also every ten years they are cumulated to make a decennial index. Covering the year 1952, for instance, the subject index alone totalled 1,586 pages, the author index another 625 pages, the empirical formula index 347 pages, and the patent index 16 pages.

Having now, I hope, been sufficiently provocative in raising moot points of principle in the indexing of scientific books I want to use the remaining few minutes, before inviting discussion, by setting up targets for your criticisms in the field of indexing procedures. In particular it would be helpful to myself to hear the reactions of other indexers if I described the methods I have gradually been developing and improving since I first took up the indexing of scientific books as a sideline to other work.

At first I followed perhaps the most usual method, that of writing each proposed index entry on a separate slip of paper or card and filing these in alphabetical order as I went along. I found however that even with a great many projecting tabs to mark where each sub-section of the alphabet begins much time is wasted fumbling among the slips already inserted in order to make additional entries on them, so I hit on the 'shingled sheets' method illustrated in my second article in *The Indexer* (Vol II, No. 1, Spring 1960). Using this method the entries are written in alphabetical order but leaving gaps between them for later additions, on foolscap sheets stapled together in batches of ten so that the bottom edge of each sheet projects below the previous sheet ¼ inch, making it very much quicker to find the correct alphabetical positions than when each entry is written on a separate slip. The secret for not getting some of the sheets overcrowded (such as those for the unexpectedly prolific letter C) is threefold: allow plenty of space and do not be afraid of wasting some paper; mark the bottom right corners of the suc-

cessive overlapping sheets with beginnings of words like Bro-Car-Cer-Cey-Cha- . . . copied from the entry words that occur at successive regular intervals in going through an existing large index or dictionary so as to ensure that roughly the same number of entries may be expected between, for instance, ' Bro ' and ' Car ' as between ' Car ' and ' Cer '; and, to provide for the eventuality that however much foresight you exercise there may be cases where you will need to add another entry between two already written on successive lines, use at first only the right hand half of each sheet and leave the left half free for interpolations.

Except for the practical point that constant lifting of the corners of the sheets tends to make them excessively dog-eared this procedure works well. It does not, however, remove certain disadvantages which are inherent in any system where everything has to be done by one person:

(1) It is not realistic to expect that one person copying out many hundreds of technical expressions and personal names of mixed national origins in alphabetical order, followed by page numbers, will never make a mistake.

(2) Ability to decide what to include in a subject index requires appropriate technical education and informed judgment, but indexing is not well paid and an indexer having these qualifications is not using his time to economic advantage if most of it is absorbed in the purely clerical part of the task and in checking.

(3) Not every indexer's handwriting is disciplined enough to be acceptable by printers, but retyping from a hand written draft involves additional work and risk of error.

13. Cumulenes   1027

mixture of C_5 hydrocarbons, he was apparently the first one to contrive the formula of an allene.   In 1875, Henry[3] proposed the trivial name 'allene' for propadienes in connexion with his alleged synthesis of tetramethylpropadiene which again seems to have been only a mixture[4]. Curiously enough, Burton and Pechmann synthesized glutinic acid in 1887[5], and assigned to it the structure **2**, discarding the allenic formula **3** on the grounds that the new compound reacted in an analogous way to acetylenedicarboxylic acid.   They even went so far as to claim that this demonstrated the impossibility of a single

$$HOOCC{\equiv}C{-}CH_2COOH \qquad\qquad HOOCCH{=}C{=}CHCOOH$$
(**2**)   (**3**)

carbon atom forming two double bonds.   Yet these investigators were the first to have a pure cumulene in their hands!   This was revealed 67 years later when Jones and coworkers[6] showed that 'glutinic acid' had the allenic structure **3**.   Burton and Pechmann's pessimistic view was proved to be unfounded only one year later when, in 1888, both Russian and American investigators succeeded in synthesizing allene itself and several alkyl-substituted propadienes, whose structures were proved conclusively[7,8,9].

There seems to have been the general belief that compounds with more than two consecutive cumulated double bonds would be unstable, and it was only in 1921 that Brand[10] obtained the next higher homolog of allene, namely a butatriene.   Even this appears to have been more of an accidental discovery than the result of a systematic search in this field.   It took another 17 years to extend the series of cumulenes still further.   This was done by Kuhn and coworkers[1] who synthesized tetraphenylhexapentaene, which turned out to be almost as stable as its forerunner.   However, an accumulation of more than five double bonds proved to be difficult.   Such compounds can so far only be obtained in solution.

B. Naturally Occurring Cumulenes

Although the history of cumulenes begins as early as 1864, the right of priority has to be given to nature.   In 1906, Semmler[11] had already suggested that carlina oxide, which he had obtained from the essential oil of *Carlina acaulis*, should have an allenic formula.   However, this was later shown to be the isomeric acetylene[12].   In 1924, Staudinger and Ruzicka[13] proposed formula **4** for pyrethrolone, a component of

FIG. 2. A page of text marked up by indexer as guide to assistant, showing subject index entries on left and authors' names index entries on right.

Reproduced by courtesy of John Wiley & Sons Ltd.

Therefore I am now trying out and improving a more radically different procedure, wherein the work and the payment for it are shared between two people—a qualified indexer and an assistant who needs merely to be able to write and type accurately—each of whom automatically checks the previous operation performed by the other. This new method, although simple in practice, would take too much space to describe in detail here but its principle is as follows (Fig. 2): after the indexer has underlined in the text the names to be indexed and made a mark in the margin against each name the assistant writes abbreviations of these (normally the first two letters and the last letter of each name) followed by the page number on very small gummed labels, which, after the indexer has checked them, she sorts into alphabetical order and sticks into place following the full surnames and initials which she has copied from the lists of references at the end of the chapters, as illustrated in Fig. 3. (The printer is instructed to print the underlined numbers, in italics, after the other numbers.) Self-sticking 'tacky' labels are more convenient to use (but more expensive) than labels that have to be moistened, and it is easy to type on them without stripping them off the backing sheets on which they are supplied, so they can be kept in page-number order until the indexer has checked them at a glance

The entries to be made in the subject index are underlined in the text and marked in the other margin, or written in that margin, to be treated in a somewhat similar manner, using larger labels.

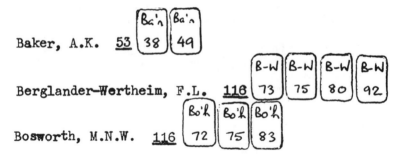

FIG. 3. Self-sticking labels stuck against index entry headings.

User Preferences in Technical Indexes*

John F. Drage

I felt very honoured to be asked to take part in the above meeting, and was particularly pleased to do so because I feel that information scientists like myself and professional indexers can both benefit from closer contact with each other.

Information scientists have tended to concentrate on developing information retrieval systems which in theory have a good performance (recall and precision), and have paid less attention to such factors as the general appearance of an index, and its consequent psychological impact on the user.

However, recall and precision are very important as measures of how well an index is doing its job, and I feel that familiarity with these concepts should be of value to all who are concerned with indexing. They represent the two main aspects of the function of an index: its ability to lead the user to look at as many as possible of the relevant parts of the document(s) indexed (recall), and its ability to lead him to look at as few as possible of the non-relevant parts (precision).

I think it is reasonable to suppose that all users of indexes would prefer them to have the highest possible capacities for recall and precision. However, it has been shown that indexes with high capacities for recall tend to give poor precision, and *vice versa*. (Aslib Cranfield Research Projects.) So it is important to find out what balance between these two qualities our users prefer.

We made a preliminary attempt to do this by asking a few important users of *Sugar*

Industry Abstracts to state their preferences for either the 1955 or 1966 index to that journal (*The Information Scientist*, 1968, Nov., 111-114).

The former index has more detailed, phrase-type entries, which would be expected to specify the subjects more clearly and unambiguously, and therefore make for greater precision. But because of this greater detail within entries the index becomes more difficult to scan rapidly. The user would therefore be more likely to give up a search before finding all the relevant material which was retrievable in theory, making for lower recall.

In the 1966 index the relational words were omitted, and were replaced by punctuation marks. This index should therefore be easier to scan rapidly, making for higher recall in equal times. But the individual entries lose something in clarity, and therefore the user might have to look at a greater number of non-relevant abstracts (lower precision).

The users' comments showed that their immediate preferences were less influenced by the above factors than by the improved general layout and typography of the 1966 index. So it is important to pay careful attention to the effects of 'presentation' on the user, and we can only measure these effects by seeking some reactions from the users themselves. However, when we have achieved an acceptable presentation it is then pertinent to ask how effective our indexes are in terms of recall and precision.

*   *   *

In the discussion there was general agreement that the most obvious improvement in

* *Based on an informal talk and discussion at a meeting of the Society on 15th April, 1969.*

Reprinted from The Indexer 6, no. 4 (Autumn 1969): 151–155.

the 1966 index had been the clearer indentations (3 instead of 1 en spaces at a time).

Some members said that a large proportion of the entries in the 1966 index seemed very unclear in meaning, and would seem so to many users who were unfamiliar with the subject matter and terminology of the journal. They thought that the index should be made simpler still. I feel this may be true, but it is certainly true that a specialist abstracts journal is intended primarily for specialists in the field, and so one could assume that its users had some greater degree of familiarity with the terminology than had the users of more general, educational publications.

Some thought that the lack of relational words in the 1966 index, and the abbreviations used, also seriously hindered clarity of meaning. This must indeed be the case for a user who is unfamiliar with the subjects and the abbreviated terms. However, the abbreviations used were restricted to only half a dozen which, it was felt, would be very familiar to nearly all users of the index. As to the lack of relational words, it is surprising how few of the entries in the 1966 index are in fact ambiguous—to a sugar technologist, we judged, only about 1 per cent. Given that one understands the terms in the entry, one tends to 'read in' the implied relations automatically. This is possibly why none of the users we questioned in our test commented upon the presence or absence of relational words in the two indexes.

Several members pointed out improvements which could be made to individual entries in both indexes. Most of these faults should be acknowledged, but it should be pointed out that, in the production of this type of index, the cost factor comes very much to the fore, and a certain departure from perfection may be justified by a considerable saving in cost. In this connection we should distinguish between two different types of fault. There is the fault which directly reduces the performance of the index, such as an omitted entry, a badly placed entry, or an ambiguous entry. This is the more serious kind. Then there is also the type of fault which does not directly affect the performance, but which simply 'looks bad', such as when two entries referring to the same abstract appear next to each other, so that a single entry would have been sufficient. It is important to eliminate this kind of fault as well, because it adversely affects the 'psychological impact on the user', but I think such faults are less serious than the former kind, and may be tolerable in some cases in exchange for reduced costs.

It was agreed that in indexing a serial publication, particularly an abstracts journal, continuity of form from year to year is an important consideration. As a professional user of indexes, carrying out frequent retrospective searches for information in abstracts journals, I find it a pleasure to use the occasional journal in which the annual indexes have been kept in the same well-ordered form for decades. For in using any such set of indexes in a particular search a considerable amount of effort is involved in getting familiar with the characteristics of the particular index, and in deciding which headings and sub-headings are to be used in the search. It can therefore considerably delay the search whenever one comes upon a year in which the system was changed, and one has to repeat the process of familiarisation.

It does not, of course, follow that a journal's indexing system should never be improved, but one should always carefully weigh the advantages of a proposed new system against the above consideration.

Conclusion

In further tests of this type, we consider that the significant advantages of each index should be explained to the user beforehand, to enable him to attach due weight to each of them in forming his possibly 'modified' judgement.

It is planned to conduct further user tests, comparing conventional and computer-produced indexes, in which the contrasts would be greater than in the case described.

Acknowledgement

I gratefully acknowledge the help of the users who co-operated in this test, of Mr. J. Farradane, under whom the 1955 index was produced, of Dr. A. H. Hyde (a past Editor of *Sugar Industry Abstracts,* Tate and Lyle, Ltd.) and of members of the Information Science Discussion Group.

Extracts on the next two pages by courtesy of Tate & Lyle Ltd.

S.I.A. Subject Index User Preference Test

We have some doubts about the present trend towards simplification of our indexes, and would be grateful if you would tell us which of the enclosed two types you would find the more useful *to yourself*. Please tick the appropriate column and pass to the next person on the list. If you do not have time to do this at present but would like to later, please tick 'to see again' on the envelope. Please do not be influenced by other peoples' choices, because your needs may differ and a compromise might be the ideal.

User	1955	1966	Comments?
A			in my opinion no major difference
B	√		
C		√	greater difference in type makes clearer presentation
D			
E		√	contrast of headings aids rapid location
F		√	clearer presentation makes more rapid location of headings
G		√	
H		√	neater; no less useful as index
I		√	Clearer
J		√	because fount is more compact
K	√		thinner pages—otherwise no improvement
L		√	clearer headings
M		√	
N		√	clearer headings '66 better
O		√	prefer latter type-face

(*Reprinted by permission from* **The Information** *Scientist, November, 1968.*)

SUGAR INDUSTRY ABSTRACTS

published by

Tate & Lyle Refineries, Ltd.

Vol. 17   **SUBJECT INDEX**   **1955**

The reference numbers are the abstract serial numbers, unless noted otherwise.

Patents are indicated by (P).

SUGAR INDUSTRY ABSTRACTS

published by

Tate & Lyle, Ltd.

Vol. 28	SUBJECT INDEX	1966

The reference numbers are the abstract serial numbers, unless noted otherwise. Patents are indicated by (P). Short relational words have been omitted or replaced by symbols to increase conciseness. The symbols '–' and '/' respectively denote 'and' (in combination with) and 'or' (alternatively). A full stop denotes a break in the chain of related terms. In order to limit the number of alternative entries, sub-headings in small capitals (e.g. **Bagasse**, PAPER) have been introduced: these signify that the corresponding entries will be found only under the word in small capitals as the main heading (e.g. **Paper**, bagasse).

Aims and Methods of the *British Technology Index**

E. J. Coates

This paper deals with an index which has been in existence for less than two years, but the wider problem to which the B.T.I. is intended to be a very partial and limited answer has grown upon us rather insidiously over the past thirty or forty years. This is the problem of communication in science, pure and applied, which has arisen partly because of the volume of scientific literature, which is now so great that the individual specialist is less and less able to keep up with the writing on his own subject, and secondly because of the steady melting away of the hard-and-fast boundary walls which formerly separated one scientific or technical specialty from another. Fundamental advances in knowledge and innovations in the application of knowledge have exposed connections not hitherto suspected, and so we are approaching the situation in which a really up-to-the-moment awareness in one's special field calls for a simultaneous knowledge of what is going on in several other fields. Thus for instance the petroleum chemist working in lubricating oils may find it essential to keep abreast of the latest developments in the design of mechanical bearings, the food processor may be deeply interested in the development of plastic films for packaging, and the plastics specialist may have a considerable preoccupation with the problems of corrosion. There is therefore a great need for indexes and other information-processing compilations which will enable pure and applied scientists to survey not only what is going on in their own field but in marginal fields as well. The problem is, as you can imagine, no easy one and it is made even more intractable by the fact that the literature concerned is written in a variety of languages.

The British Technology Index confines itself to applied science, interpreting that term fairly broadly, though excluding medicine and agriculture. Its source coverage consists of 400 British technical journals. There must be very few British technical journals of importance not covered by this list, but we have to remember that it is still a fraction of the world's output of technical periodical literature. However, it is a sufficiently large fraction to be worth recording. The *Index* is published monthly and comprises a subject-index to between 2,000 and 3,000 articles per issue, and the articles thus indexed will in most cases have appeared within the preceding seven weeks. This is an extremely short time lag as indexes go, and currency occupies first place in the *Index*'s priorities.

The *Index* has a counterpart in the United States, but no competitors. Indeed, two earlier attempts to provide a current guide to British technical periodical literature failed for inadequate support. The reasons for these failures are not very clear, but it might not be too far-fetched to suggest that to some extent they are attributable to the arrangement of the entries. These were grouped under broad subject headings corresponding to the organisational diversification of industry, and

---

* Paper read to the Society on February 28th, 1963.

Reprinted from *The Indexer* 3, no. 4 (Autumn 1963): 146–152.

it was not usually easy to trace highly specific information. It was there, but was not signposted in detail and had to be searched for without the assurance that it was there. Periodical articles are, of course, not the only form in which technological developments are reported, but they are by far the most important form. One kind of guide to this periodical literature which is perused by many engineers and technologists is the abstracting service. These services provide a digest of each article they record. They cover many, though not all, of the branches of technology. The material they contain is usually broadly grouped by subject, sometimes placed in systematic classified arrangement, and sometimes bear significant catchwords in the margins of each page. The time lag between the publication of an article and its appearance in abstracts is usually three months or longer, but with one or two exceptions detailed subject indexes to the abstracts are published only annually, if at all. Though I emphasise that indexes and abstracts have quite separate rôles, I have probably said enough to indicate the gap that B.T.I. is intended to fill, namely the three months immediately following the publication of the articles when there is no record of them at all, and the longer period before annual subject indexes to abstracts make their appearance. Our purpose is therefore to provide a guide to very recently published technical articles which will signpost specific subject information, without asking the user to read through broadly grouped headings on the chance that what he requires may prove to be there. Values of any index include not only the fact that it tells you what is available, but also that it tells you at once, by implication, what is not there.

To secure the result desired, alphabetical specific subject arrangement is followed. By this I mean that any subject which can be fully described in a single word or phrase is entered directly under the word. Thus an article on the new printing technique FILMSETTING is entered directly under that term and not under COMPOSING or PRINTING. However, there are not many subjects found in the technical literature which can be covered unequivocally by a single word. Most require a combination of words. Composing—the assembly of type in printing —is a case in point. We cannot just use " Composing " alone, because in isolation it is ambiguous, even in an index limited to technology: it could mean composing in industrial design, in photography and possibly in other spheres. We need to add a further word or words to make clear what we mean. We can say either Composing, Printing, or Printing, Composing, and here we run straight into the problem —the primary problem in all subject indexing, namely, the order in which we should cite the various words in such a composite heading. With a two-element heading such as Composing, Printing, there are two alternatives only. But a three-element heading faces us with six alternatives, and there are 24 ways of arranging the individual terms in a four-element heading, of which we find ourselves creating a great number in specifying the subjects of technical articles. So you see that we have a situation which calls for some rigour in deciding element order if we are not going to find ourselves overwhelmed with permutations.

Before going into this further, I should like to draw your attention to one or two points on the general structure of the *Index*, particularly to the cross-reference structure. Two kinds of cross-references are employed. When we have a subject heading consisting, say, of three elements we do not produce entries under each of the six possible permutations. We choose one, in most cases, on principles which

I shall explain shortly, and we refer from each of the terms used as a sub-heading if we think it is likely to be a sought term at any time. Most of these sub-heading terms are sought terms, but there are some very general ones such as "Manufacture", "Measurement", "Research", "Equipment" which we think will never be used as approach terms. These references from sub-headings are made almost mechanically by reciting the terms of the heading from right to left, inserting the word "see" and then giving the same terms in their left to right order. Thus if we have an article on the Transport of molten aluminium by road, the entry will take the heading:

ALUMINIUM, Molten, Transport, Road

The references will be:

(1) ROADS, Transport, Molten aluminium. See ALUMINIUM, Molten, Transport, Road

Notice that we use the plural form when we place ROADS in the first position in the reference:

(2) TRANSPORT, Molten aluminium. See ALUMINIUM, Molten, Transport

(3) MOLTEN ALUMINIUM. See ALUMINIUM, Molten

You will note that the reference (1) tells the searcher for road transport of molten aluminium that the subject is in the index *at once*. Whereas (2) and (3) tell the person who comes in at Transport or Molten that it may be worth his while to proceed as directed to the actual entry under Aluminium, where he will see whether the subject required is present. Quite a number of enquirers wanting road transport of molten aluminium specifically will in fact try first Transport or Molten and (2) and (3) represent the provision made for them. Now this method of carrying molten aluminium around in a trailer is, I think, the first attempt of its kind. The idea may catch on, in a few months there may be another article, this time upon transporting molten lead by road. The entry heading will read:

LEAD, Molten, Transport, Road

Now an index of this kind ought to indicate in some way to the searcher when he comes in at LEAD, Molten, Transport, Road, that the earlier material exists. To make a direct reference to it would, if it were the general practice in all such cases, swell the index perhaps four or fivefold and would raise very awkward problems in production. Fortunately such provision is not essential, for we also make the routine references:

ROADS, Transport, Lead. See LEAD, Transport, Road

TRANSPORT, Molten lead. See LEAD, Molten, Transport

MOLTEN LEAD. See LEAD, Molten.

The point is that these references fall next to or very close to the similar set of references for the case of the aluminium, so that the enquirer interested in the road transport of molten lead who is also interested in similar handling procedures for other molten metals, can discover whether the index contains anything about them by looking up in the main sequence the subheading terms MOLTEN, TRANSPORT, Molten and ROADS, Transport, Molten. The alphabetical index can be made to disclose the presence of such related material, provided that the entry heading is sufficiently specific in the first place and that systematic referencing is carried out.

This is the general picture of the inversion references in B.T.I. In fact the close-up picture is a little more elaborate than that. When we have an element in a sub-heading which specifies the type or kind of the preceding element, our procedure includes a permutation. I give an example:

ALUMINIUM, Molten, Transport, Motor vehicles, Articulated

Articulated specifies a type or kind of motor vehicle and the scheme of references in this case is:

ARTICULATED MOTOR VEHICLES, Transport, Molten aluminium

MOTOR VEHICLES, Articulated, Transport, Molten aluminium

TRANSPORT, Molten aluminium

MOLTEN ALUMINIUM

You will see that in reference (2) here we go first left to right, and then right to left, leaping over the starting term. The second complication is that in a certain limited number of cases we give two entries instead of an entry and a reference. We do this when the entry heading and first sub-heading are in the relation of the whole to part. The point here is that an engineer's interest in a component as such, without regard to its particular application, may be very great indeed. Thus you will find in the *Index* identical entries under:

SHIPS, Diesel engines

and

DIESEL ENGINES, Ships

We have one other occasion when we use plural entry in the *Index*. This is when the subject of the article is a proper name, such as the BUILDING CENTRE or DEPARTMENT OF TECHNICAL CO-OPERATION. We give here an entry under the proper name and a further entry under the subject which the proper name entity illustrates.

The second type of reference which we have in the B.T.I. is not derived from the sub-headings, but from library classification. These references direct the enquirer from a general to a more restricted heading. This is a necessary facility in any index of this kind, because quite a high proportion of index users begin by looking up a term with a broader meaning than the topic on which they actually need information. So we need a chain of references modulated step by step down from the broadest to the narrowest headings. The classification scheme from which this system of reference is derived is mainly the Universal Decimal Classification, chosen because it was the scheme most familiar to most of the indexers. It is not entirely satisfactory for our purpose, and our reference structure is bolstered up at particular points on the technological map by other more recently produced special schemes. Improvement in this reference structure probably awaits further fundamental work in library classification. In the meantime it must depend on such classifications as we have, if it is not to proliferate beyond controllable limits. All knowledge is multidimensional in the manner in which the various parts are related. A classification scheme is simply an attempt to plot these multidimensional relationships upon a two-dimensional page.

This question of the citation order of the elements in composite headings on which I have already touched is of importance, because we want our indexing habits to be predictable to users. I refer here not only to consistency in assigning headings to the same subject but also consistency in overall pattern which regulates the analogous treatment of unconnected or remotely connected subjects. While we should not *require* our users to know what our indexing rules are, they can be expected to absorb unconsciously a pattern that is consistently offered to them, and this is of considerable utility because it enables them to anticipate how the index will handle a new subject. You will appreciate that every month we index such a high proportion of new developments that there is no authoritative list to which we can turn and hope to find answers. We have to construct these headings as we go and it is essential both from the point of view of the indexers, who should know clearly what they are doing, and also of the users, that we construct them according to reasonably definite rules.

In general we arrange our composite headings in order of decreasing concreteness—so that the most concrete term in the compound takes the leading position. However, in technology we frequently require composite headings in which there are two or more elements of equal concreteness, e.g. Corrosion of iron, by wood acids, To meet this situation we have been obliged to go into the question of relationships between the individual terms in the compound. Some of you will remember the highly original paper given to your Society in 1961 by Farradane on Relational Indexing.* Though I do not fully understand all of Farradane's views, nor agree with all that I think I do understand, some of his ideas have helped us a very great deal to formulate systematic rules of attack on subject-heading problems: We think we have isolated 15 distinct varieties of composite headings, of which 10 are proving to be important. In the first five of these ten, one term is a Thing and the other specifies a particular kind or variety of the Thing. I give some examples:

(1) FABRICS, Foamback   Fabrics *with* foamback
    (Thing₁, Thing₂)

(2) TRIMMING, Presses   Presses *for* trimming
    (Function, Thing)

(3) BUSES, Garages   Garages *for* Buses
    (Thing₂, Thing₁)

(4) FABRICS, Elastic   Fabrics *with* elastic property
    (Thing, Property)

(5) BUSES, Bodies   Bodies *of* Buses
    (Thing₂, Thing₁)
    BODIES, Buses
    (Thing₁, Thing₂)

The other five important types of headings are concerned with properties and actions upon things and by things. Some examples follow:

(6) BEAMS, Strength   Strength *of* beams
    (Thing, Property)

* See *The Indexer,* Vol. 2, pp. 127-133.

(7) GRAIN, Drying   Drying *of* grain
     (Thing, Action upon it)
(8) WOOL, Scouring,   Scouring *of* Wool *by* Compression jets
          Compression jets
     (Thing₁, Action upon it,
               Thing₂)
(9) NITRIC ACID, Production,   Tail gases *byproduct of* Production *of*
          Tail gases   Nitric acid
     (Thing, Action upon it,
               Byproduct)
(10) BARREL FINISHING   Finishing *by means of* barrels
     (Thing, Its Action)

These rules take care of most of the problems of term-order in compound headings, though there are some residual points awaiting further experience. As practical indexers you will not need to be told that this is not the end of indexing problems. B.T.I. is fully exercised on the pitfalls in synonym control. This is in one respect made relatively easy (I stress 'relatively') for us, because technical writers have the habit of definition better ingrained than writers in most other fields. On the other hand, B.T.I. covers about 50 recognisably distinct subject specialties, and quite often different specialties use different terms to mean the same thing or action. We take two precautions. We are as generous as possible in referencing from synonyms—for it is the arrival of the previously unreferenced synonym which is liable to trip up an indexer. Secondly we do refer all new concepts to their context in library classification schemes. There is a presumption that two terms which classify in the same place in the scheme may be synonyms.

Homonyms abound in the technical literature, because in applied science new concepts are often named by appropriating a term from someone else's field (usually the mechanical engineers') and investing it with a new meaning. We have not yet found a fully satisfactory solution to this problem which is consistent with mechanical alphabetical order.

Yet another awkward problem which easily produces errors is concerned with what may be called "nearly universal properties". Nearly all tyres today are made of rubber, nearly all workshop practice concerns the making of shapes in *metal*, nearly all welding is *fusion* welding. Our policy to date has been to omit what we call "nearly universal" property terms as a contribution to brevity and avoidance of pedantry.

A brief account of the way in which the indexing is organised may be of interest. We have a staff of four library qualified indexers and two clerical workers, and the transcription of titles, author, journal, date and page details is done by the clerks by typewriter on continuous stationery. The actual clerical effort required from indexers at this stage is limited simply to writing the appropriate subject headings on the entry. If the indexer decides that it is a subject which we have not handled before, then he also has the task of setting up the new piece of reference structure. At a later stage there is however a considerable amount of what could be considered high-grade clerical work which falls upon the indexers rather than upon clerks. Generally these jobs are of the sort in which errors must be kept to the absolute minimum if the indexing routine is to function at all satisfactorily. All in all, each indexer spends about half his or her time actually on indexing ; the other half is spent on such tasks as reading the master copy, which is prepared on cards for litho reproduction, and maintaining the authority file of all our decisions. I should mention that the master copy is typed by Varityper (by a contractor) on cards each of which contain one line only of copy. The principle is that the cards thus typed are passed at high speed through a special camera which photographs each line on a film one below the other. If one card gets out of order you get a printer's error of a fairly common kind, but if it is a heading which comes adrift and finally rests upon an entry to which it does not belong then we have the serious matter of the *Index* giving wrong information. About 18,000 of these cards have to be sorted into as nearly as we can make it perfect order for each monthly issue. When the set of 18,000 have been through the camera for the month's issue they then have to be interfiled with the cards for earlier months of the year to form the annual volume. This interfiling calls for the sorting of about 160,000 cards, and when this is complete they all go through the camera again to form the Annual Volume of about 900 pages.

In the context of this considerable load of clerical work, one naturally thinks of the possibility of further mechanisation of production processes. B.T.I. operates in a half-way house on the road to mechanisation, with advantages in speed of production, but with some slightly bizarre results relative to the division between indexing and clerical labour. Computers can, of course, be used to perform some of the purely clerical operations. Indeed, in America some very large scientific literature indexes are being produced by computer. These rely for their effectiveness upon the appearance of sought subject terms in the title. There is, however, no machine which will, as it were, go behind the title and summarise the actual subject content. We have not yet discovered how to break down the summarising process into the series of simple instructions which a machine can handle. I will not say that no research is being done in this direction, but it is scarcely beyond the stage of experimentation based on word-frequency counts. At the moment, therefore, the essential indexing operation can be carried out only by human beings—and I think can be carried out well only by human beings with the requisite qualities of temperament, such as a methodical mind, coolness and reflection in facing what is initially incomprehensible, interest in the subject matter *in breadth,* and the ability to remain open to fresh knowledge. These qualities are not very frequently found in combination and their comparative rarity is a little discussed but real issue in the information-retrieval problem.

" The lack of an index completely destroys what little value the book might have had "—John Bulloch, reviewing *They call it intelligence : spies and spy techniques since World War II,* by Joachim Joesten (Abelard-Schuman) in *The Daily Telegraph,* August 23rd, 1963.

Technical Indexing at *B.T.I.*

Alan Singleton

This is a description and personal view of the British Technology Index. The historical development of indexing and classification thought provides a framework for description, and emphasis is laid on the debt to Ranganathan's ideas of synthesis, facet analysis and chain indexing. Although an analytically derived index, B.T.I. has, as an authority file, many points of similarity with the thesaurus of co-ordinate indexing, and these are illustrated. The use of the computer both for typesetting and as an aid to compilation is considered. Some difficulties that users are likely to experience are explained since these, once appreciated, may be overcome. Some suggestions for further development are made. Finally, a brief analysis of six months of an indexer's time is given.

"An alphabetical index might be described as a phonetic classification; the references in it are classified, not according to their own logical interrelationship, but according to the noises people make when they talk about them". So said J. E. Holmstrom[1]. This article is a general discussion and personal view of one "alphabetical" index, the *British Technology Index*, a now widely used and respected index to the British technical literature. However, it is hoped that a description of its structure will show that *B.T.I.* has developed a sophistication and depth which make it a successful retrieval tool on highly specific topics, without being difficult to use, even though "phonetic".

We may also hope that readers will be interested to know something of the actual working day of a technical indexer, and the last part of the article describes the process of construction of the index, together with a statistical breakdown of six months' activities of a new indexer.

The *British Technology Index* is a publication of the Library Association. First published in 1962 under the editorship of E. J. Coates, it is a monthly subject index, with annual cumulations, and it aims to provide access to technical papers in over three hundred British journals. Since January 1972 an author index has been included.

The journal coverage has wide scope in its range of subject fields, and, it should be admitted, in the quality of journals scanned, although the latter is to some extent a function of the former. This subject range enables the index to claim that it is truly interdisciplinary in nature, and it may bring to the attention of the user interesting and useful articles from fields outside his own. Another justifiable claim refers to the good "currency" of the publication, i.e. around seventy to eighty per cent of journal articles should be found in *B.T.I.* between three and seven weeks after the date of original publication.

Reprinted from *The Indexer* 9, no. 2 (October 1974): 37–49.

Helped by an Office for Scientific and Technical Information (OSTI) grant, *B.T.I.* was one of the first publications of its kind to make use of the computer, both as an aid to compilation and for typesetting. This was orginally carried out using a KDF 9 computer, and a Digiset for the typesetting. Since 1972, an ICL 470 has been used together with a Fototronic. One 'spin off' from this has been the production of magnetic tapes containing *B.T.I.* on file.

Previous articles by Coates in this journal [2,3,4] have over the years outlined some features of the index structure and production, and it will be noticed how these have not remained static. In *B.T.I.* as it is now, can be detected the incorporation of several features of many of the major developments of classification and indexing thought over the last forty or fifty years.

These developments, in as much as they are apparent in *B.T.I.* structure, may provide a logical framework for description.

Let us take as a starting point those two classifications from the last century, which, for all their much criticised imperfections, are still in considerable use, i.e. the Dewey Decimal Classification and the Universal Decimal Classification. As with many other traditional classifications, these took an "Aristotelian" view of human knowledge. That is, to put it crudely, there is the sum total of knowledge, and all that is necessary is to carve it up into suitable sections or subjects and place incoming material into those sections.

With the increasing growth of technology and its associated terminology, the major faults in this approach became apparent. These can be roughly summarised by referring to the inflexibility of such classifications, both in their failure to have sufficient appropriate spaces for the accommodation of new subjects, and in the lack of provision for combination of terms from the classification, respectively their poor "hospitality" and lack of "synthesis".

The mathematician Ranganathan was one of the major proponents of a flexible and synthetic system, as outlined by his famous Colon Classification. [5,6,7] Basically, this suggested that any subject was in fact a combination of one or more of five basic "concepts" or "fundamental categories". These are: Personality, Material,

Energy, Space and Time and are referred to generally as

PMEST   – (1)

The most difficult of these to grasp is "Personality" and it is perhaps worth quoting Ranganathan's own explanation of this [5] "not only human personality but everything – human, animal, vegetable or other category like language, religion, social group and legal system, which have an individuality, unity, and aroma of their own".

Thus, for any subject, from those five fundamental categories were derived the relevant characteristics to describe it, e.g. "Medicine" required two of these categories represented thus:

L [O] : [P]

where [O] refers to the "Organ" which is considered as the "Personality" concept, and the [P] refers to "Problems" (i.e. methods of study, treatment, etc.) as part of the "Energy" concept, and L refers to the class "Medicine". For each class there are such "facets" corresponding to some of the five categories. These "facets" have schedules of their own.

This technique of analysing a subject is known as "facet analysis". From this grew the idea of "faceted classification" which depended on defining sets of "facets" for subjects, which might differ markedly from Ranganathan's concepts, each facet having a "schedule" listing all the terms within that facet. A subject was then classified by bringing together terms from all relevant facets. [8]

Let us imagine a faceted classification for "Workshop practice". This might have several facets, and among them, perhaps:

A—Workpieces
C—Materials   – (2)
F—Processes
H—Tools

Let us suppose that we now have to classify an article on the use of lasers for the machining of steel sheets. We would find each of these terms in the schedules of the above facets. Each term would have its own code, and the final classification would be achieved by bringing these together, e.g.

AabCsFdfHi   – (3)

British Technology Index follows this synthetic approach very closely. However, since it is an index and not a classification, it retains the words for direct access, and would have as a heading:

SHEETS ; Steel : Machining : Lasers   – (4)

As with faceted analysis, the rough criterion can be used that a "good" heading will make sense when read from right to left with the insertion of suitable prepositions.

In *B.T.I.* there are no fixed facets as in faceted classification, and terms are not defined in terms of Ranganathan's fundamental categories. Nevertheless the debt can already be seen to be fairly large, and will increase a little more as we progress.

We might well now ask: what is the significance of the order of terms in (4), and how is it arrived at? The significance for the user is that, on the printed page of *B.T.I.*, under the list of terms arranged in that order, called the "entry" order, will be found the bibliographic reference to the article in question, i.e.

SHEETS ; Steel : Machining : Lasers
How you can cut up your sheets with light. J. Askew   – (5)
Machining, 54 (8 Jul. 74) p.112-21.

As far as order is concerned, we may once more turn to Ranganathan for a clue [5] to Coates' eventual conclusions on this point: "shelf-arrangement of entries in the catalogue should be in order of increasing concreteness and decreasing abstraction. To achieve this, the facets in the facet formula of a subject have to be arranged in just the reverse order, i.e. in the order of decreasing concreteness and increasing abstraction".

The order of decreasing concreteness is the basic one followed in *B.T.I.* In our example this is taken to be 'sheets,' i.e. the term to which all the others are ultimately directed. However, if the article had given us more information, e.g. that the sheets were to be used in car bodywork, we would then have a more concrete term and this would then take precedence:

MOTOR CARS : Bodies : Sheets ; Steel : Machining : Lasers   – (6)

We should note also that strict adherence to this principle can, on rare occasions, lead to reversal of order of what we might expect from the above. Thus if our specimen article had been concerned solely with the use of lasers for machining purposes generally, then "lasers" would be considered the more "concrete" and the entry order would become:

LASERS : Machining   – (7)

We will see later how this last situation may be confusing to a searcher.

Although "concreteness "may be the guiding principle on term order, Coates has been at pains to point out that it is not an ideal solution and cannot hope to be the best order in all circumstances or for all points of view, e.g. the laser expert may not consider the orders (5) and (6) the most helpful to a search concerning all the different applications of lasers. Indeed, without further guides, he would have difficulty finding any information at all. This brings us to the next and very important feature of the *British Technology Index*—the cross-reference.

What is the most appropriate form for the cross-reference? Ranganathan pondered this problem in connection with a catalogue or "index" to his classification. He came up (in 1938) with a form of permutation, called "chain indexing" (fairly thoroughly discussed in Coates's book). [9]

This procedure, which in the main is followed in *B.T.I.*, consists of providing cross-references from each significant term in the heading, in the manner illustrated below.

Let us consider one of Ranganathan's own examples [5] for a document dealing with "Systematic study of the teak-wood forest in Burma". He performs a facet analysis leading to a "colon" coding as follows:

(Forestry) (Teak-wood) : (Diseases) (Entomological) : (Biology) : (Systematic Study) : (Burma), coded as
JAT : 4K83 : G : 12 : 438

A comparison of Ranganathan's treatment of cross-references with that for a typical heading in *B.T.I.* is given in Table 1.

Ranganathan	B.T.I.
Heading : JAT : 4K83 : G : 12 : 438	*Heading* : SHEETS ; Steel : Machining : Lasers, Pulsed : Design : Manuals
Cross-references BURMA. Entomology. Teak-wood. see JAT : 4K83 : G : 12 : 438	*Cross-references* MANUALS : Pulsed Laser design : Machining : Steel sheets see SHEETS ; Steel : Machining : Lasers, Pulsed : Design : Manuals.
SOUTH-EASTERN ASIA. Entomology. Teak-wood. see JAT : 4K83 : G : 12 : 43	PULSED LASERS : Machining : Steel Sheets see SHEETS ; Steel : Machining : Lasers, Pulsed
ASIA. Entomology. Teak-wood. see JAT : 4K83 : G : 12 : 4	LASERS, Pulsed : Machining : Steel Sheets see SHEETS ; Steel : Machining : Lasers, Pulsed
SYSTEMATIC STUDY. Entomology. Teak-wood. see JAT : 4K83 : G : 12	MACHINING : Steel Sheets see SHEETS ; Steel : Machining
ENTOMOLOGY. Teak-wood. see JAT : 4K83 : G	STEEL SHEETS see SHEETS ; Steel
INSECT. Disease. Teak-wood. see JAT : 4K83	
DISEASE. Teak-wood see JAT : 4	
TEAK-WOOD. Forestry see JAT	
FORESTRY see JA	

Table 1—Two methods of treating cross-references

The similarity of the two methods is evident. So also are some differences. In Ranganathan's system

(i) a cross-reference is made from each higher hierarchical term in a facet, e.g. from Burma, from South-Eastern Asia and also from Asia.

(ii) the abstract term "systematic study" is only included for a reference from that term. Otherwise it is not included. Contrast this with the *B.T.I.* treatment of the term "Design", which, since considered an unsought term, is not provided with its own cross-reference, but is present in the reference from "Manuals". Note also the change in order to produce "pulsed laser design".

In the *B.T.I.* system an important modification is shown by the treatment of "Lasers, pulsed" where the qualifying adjective is never separated from its noun, as it would be in a "pure" chain index.

The production of the cross-references in *B.T.I.* is almost totally carried out by computer, which also, for each issue, takes all other entries and cross-references for other indexed articles and merges them into one alphabetical, word-by-word sequence. Computer typesetting is used to produce the printed page, and special programs are required to look after typographical details, e.g. headings are printed in bold type, cross-references are not. Fig. 1 illustrates a page of *B.T.I.* as it is when published.

The word-by-word sequence is affected by the punctuation system, in that the space between words has a different sort value from the punctuation as in (8). In addition, a convention for certain chemical compounds breaks the rule (9):

AIR TRANSPORT precedes AIRCRAFT
but FOIL ELECTRODE BATTERIES *follows* FOIL ; Silicon   – (8)

SULPHURIC ACID   *follows* SULPHUR TRIOXIDE
but METHYLENE BLUE   *precedes* METHYL ETHYL KETONE   – (9)

From our considerations of the permutations and the merging for the printed product, we can now see how a heading of LASERS : Machining can be a little confusing. We might have together on the page

LASERS : Machining

in bold type with its associated bibliographic reference, filed next to

LASERS : Machining : Steel Sheets see

SHEETS; Steel : Machining : Lasers   – (10)

as a cross-reference.

This may give the user a feeling of insecurity in his understanding of the index and little would be lost if – (10) were changed to

LASERS : Machining

see MACHINING : Lasers

This example may also be used to illustrate another difficulty which in some cases is unavoidable in this type of index, i.e. where the index terms themselves are arranged in a linear sequence. If the article on lasers was concerned with the design of their plastic casings, at present we would need to have a heading along the lines of:

LASERS : Machining : Housings ; Plastics : Design : Specifications   – (11)

where the Housings refer to the lasers and not the machining. The one-dimensional limitation is also illustrated in (11) by the term 'Design' which is somewhat ambiguous in its application, i.e. one might need:

LASERS : Machining : Housing ; Plastics
$$| \atop V \qquad – (12)$$
Design

to make the meaning clear.

It may be noticed that the permutation is related to the punctuation symbol used between terms. For the first six years of *B.T.I.*, when the cross-references were produced manually, similar permutation was used although only one punctuation symbol, the comma, was in evidence. With the change to mechanisation, the necessity and opportunity arose of making explicit relationships between terms; necessity, since the computer needed to be instructed in how to perform the permutation, and opportunity, in that some part of that instruction could be used in the printed index to display relationships.

It is here that we have a reflection of another significant development in classification and indexing thought. The idea of formalising relationships between terms was a fairly popular post-war one, including developments of Ranganathan's phase relations and also the work of Farradane. Coates himself has spoken of his debt to Farradane's relational methods: "Though I

LAMPS : Electroluminescence. See ELECTROLUMINESCENCE : Lamps

LAMPS : Time marking : Film : Cinematography. See CINEMATOGRAPHY : Film : Time marking : Lamps

LANCIA MOTOR CARS. See MOTOR CARS, Types, Lancia

LAND : Reclamation : Estuaries
New airport or new county? *Consult. Engr.,* 37 (Sep 73) p.17. *il.*

LANDING : Instruments
Battle for the new airport landing aid. R. Brown. *New Scientist,* 60 (4 Oct 73) p.44-6. *il.*

LANDING GEAR : Military aircraft. See AIRCRAFT, Military : Landing gear

LANDSCAPE : Preservation
Related Headings:
PARKS, National

LANDSCAPING
Landscape and the environment. Pt.2: application of design ideas. *Master Bldr.,* 18 (Oct 73) p.15-17. *il.*

LANGMUIR PROBES : Reference electrodes
Inadequate reference electrode, a widespread source of error in plasma probe measurements. J.S. Chang. *J. Phys. D: Appl. Phys.,* 6 (18 Sep 73) p.1674-83. *il.refs.*

LANTERNS : Lighting : Streets. See STREETS : Lighting : Lanterns

LAPLACE EQUATION : Robin problem : Solution : Alternating direction implicit method
Numerical solution of the Robin problem by extrapolated A.D.I. methods. K.I. Iordanidis. *J. Inst. Math. Applic.,* 12 (Aug 73) p.91-6. *refs.*

LAPPING
Related Headings:
DIAMOND LAPPING

LASERS; Argon : Tubes, Segmented; Aluminium : Cathodes, Plasma jet
Demountable argon ion laser of 'all-metal' construction. J.C.L. Cornish & A. Maitland. *J. Phys. E: Sci. Instrum.,* 6 (Sep 73) p.880-4. *il.refs.*

LASERS; Carbon dioxide : Machining : Analysis specimens : Ribs : Bones. See RIBS : Bones : Analysis : Specimens : Machining : Lasers; Carbon dioxide

LASERS, Carbon dioxide,, Pulsed, Picosecond,, Transversely excited : Line broadening : Collisions : High pressure
Rotational line overlap in CO_2 laser transitions. B.S. Patel & P. Swarup. *J. Phys. D: Appl. Phys.,* 6 (18 Sep 73) p.1670-3. *refs.*

LASERS, Carbon dioxide,, Pulsed,, Transversely excited
Parametric study of the performance of a TEA CO_2 laser. M.S. White & A.E. Dangor. *J. Phys. E: Sci. Instrum.,* 6 (Sep 73) p.891-4. *il.refs.*

LASERS; Carbon dioxide—Helium—Nitrogen : Machining
High power laser cutting of metals. M.J. Fletcher. *Weld. Metal Fabric.,* 41 (Sep 73) p.308-11. *il.*

LASERS; Carbon dioxide—Nitrous oxide,, Chemically driven : Nitrous oxide : Reaction with sodium vapour
Reaction between Na vapor and N_2O at room temperature. R.E. Walker & J.E. Creeden. *Combust. Flame,* 21 (Aug 73) p.39-43. *il.refs.*

LASERS : Doppler effect optical flowmeters : Turbulent flow : Fluids. See FLUIDS : Flow, Turbulent : Flowmeters, Optical,, Doppler effect : Lasers

LASERS, Gas : Frequency : Stabilisation
Frequency stabilization of gas lasers. A.J. Wallard. *J. Phys. E: Sci. Instrum.,* 6 (Sep 73) p.793-807. *il.refs.*

LASERS : Machining : Electronic component manufactures. See ELECTRONICS : Components : Manufactures : Machining : Lasers

LASERS : Michelson interferometers : Ellipsometry. See ELLIPSOMETRY : Interferometers, Michelson : Lasers

LASERS, Pulsed : Photolysis : Anthraquinone dyes. See ANTHRAQUINONE DYES : Photolysis : Lasers, Pulsed

LASERS : Pulses : Measurement : Photodiodes; Silicon : Performance : Monitoring
Analysis and measurement of the speed and linearity of silicon photodiodes for measuring short laser pulses. J.G. Edwards & R. Jefferies. *J. Phys. E: Sci. Instrum.,* 6 (Sep 73) p.841-53. *il.refs.*

LASERS : Spherical detonation excitation : Acetylene—Oxygen. See ACETYLENE—OXYGEN : Detonation, Spherical : Excitation : Lasers

LASERS : Thermal decomposition : Indian coal. See COAL, Indian : Thermal decomposition : Lasers

LASIOCEPHALIN
Revised structure of lasiocephalin: a new coumarin from *Lasiosiphon eriocephalus* Decne. S.C. Das, S. Sengupta & W. Herz. *Chem. Ind.* (18 Aug 73) p.792-3. *refs.*

LASTING : Shoes. See SHOES : Lasting

LATERAL PRESSURE : Twisted filament yarns. See YARNS, Filament,, Twisted : Lateral pressure

LATHES, Centre : Control systems
New DSG type 500TC n.c. lathe. J.J. Marklew. *Machinery,* 123 (12 Sep 73) p.366-8. *il.*

LAURYL SULPHATE—HYDROCHLORIC ACID : Solutions : Platinum; Cathodes. See CATHODES; Platinum : Hydrochloric acid—Lauryl sulphate solutions

LAVERDA 750 MOTOR CYCLES. See MOTOR CYCLES, Types, Laverda 750

LAYING : Submarine pipelines : Natural gas. See GAS, Natural : Pipelines, Submarine : Laying

LAYING : Submarine pipelines : Petroleum. See PETROLEUM : Pipelines, Submarine : Laying

LAYING : Underground coaxial cables : Frequency division multiplex telephony. See TELEPHONY, Frequency division multiplex : Cables, Coaxial,, Underground : Laying

LAYOUT : Plant : Wood manufactures. See WOOD : Manufactures : Plant layout

LAYOUT : Steel; Pipework : Compressed air. See AIR, Compressed : Pipework; Steel : Layout

LEACHING : Cuprous oxide : Anti-fouling compositions. See ANTI-FOULING COMPOSITIONS : Cuprous oxide : Leaching

LEAD
Future of metals. Pt.10: lead. L. Sanderson. *Tooling,* 27 (Oct 73) p.25-7. *refs.*

LEAD : Alloys—Stainless steel-wires : Fibre—Matrix bonds : Shear strength : Pull out tests
Improved test for interfacial shear strength. J.C. Swearengen & T.F. Covert. *Composites,* 4 (Sep 73) p.203-7. *il.refs.*

LEAD; Priming paint : Steel : Structures. See STRUCTURES : Steel : Paint, Priming; Lead

LEAD : Smelting : Metal—Slag reactions
Mass transfer between molten lead and a fused salt with bubble stirring. J.K. Brimacombe & F.D. Richardson. *Trans. Instn. Min. Metall.,* 82 (Jun 73) p.C63-72. *il.refs.*

LEAD—ACID BATTERIES. See BATTERIES, Lead—Acid

LEAD DIOXIDE; Anodes. See ANODES; Lead dioxide

LEAD—INDIUM; Foil. See FOIL; Indium—Lead

LEAD IODIDE PHOTOGRAPHY. See PHOTOGRAPHY, Lead iodide

LEAD—LITHIUM CHLORIDE—POTASSIUM CHLORIDE, Molten : Interfaces, Stirred : Bubbles; Argon : Mass transfer
Mass transfer between molten lead and a fused salt with bubble stirring. J.K. Brimacombe & F.D. Richardson. *Trans. Instn. Min. Metall.,* 82 (Jun 73) p.C63-72. *il.refs.*

LEAD PHOSPHATE GLASS. See GLASS, Lead phosphate

LEAD SELENIDE—CADMIUM SELENIDE
Some physical properties of the systems Pb_{1-x} Mg_xSe and Pb_{1-x} Cd_xSe. B.J. Sealy & A.J. Crocker. *J. Mater Sci.,* 8 (Sep 73) p.1247-52. *refs.*

LEAD SELENIDE—MAGNESIUM SELENIDE
Some physical properties of the systems Pb_{1-x} Mg_xSe and Pb_{1-x} Cd_xSe. B.J. Sealy & A.J. Crocker. *J. Mater Sci.,* 8 (Sep 73) p.1247-52. *refs.*

LEAD—TIN; Foil. See FOIL; Lead—Tin

LEAKS : Flow : Measurement
Leaks. R.N. Bloomer. *Vacuum,* 23 (Jul 73) p.231-8. *il.refs.*

LEAKS : Vacuum bubblers
Leak detection and measurements by vacuum bubblers. R.N. Bloomer. *Vacuum,* 23 (Jul 73) p.239-44. *il.refs.*

LEAST SQUARES : Function approximation. See FUNCTIONS : Approximation : Least squares

LEATHER
Related Headings:
SHEEPSKINS

LEATHER : Mechanical properties : Correlation with anatomical topography
Topographic differences in physical properties. A. Vos & P.J. van Vlimmeren. *J. Soc. Leath. Technol. Chem.,* 57 (Jul-Aug 73) p.93-8. *refs.*

LEATHER : Production
Related Headings:
TANNING

LEATHER, Tanned, Chrome : Drying
Drying characteristics of chrome-tanned leather. E.P. Lhuede. *J. Soc. Leath. Technol. Chem.,* 57 (Jul-Aug 73) p.99-106. *refs.*

LEATHER : Testing
International Union of Leather Chemists Societies: Report of the Physical Testing Commission 1971-2. *J. Soc. Leath. Technol. Chem.,* 57 (Jul-Aug 73) p.107-8

LEEDS
See
PEDESTRIANS : Access : Town planning.. Leeds
TRAMWAYS.. Leeds

LEVEL CONTROL, Two level : Dewar vessels : Liquid nitrogen. See NITROGEN, Liquid : Dewar vessels : Level control, Two level

LEVEL INDICATORS
What's the position on levelling? R. Robinson. *Mech. Handl.,* 60 (Oct 73) p.45-8. *il.*

LEVITT, B.P.
Findlay's practical physical chemistry. 9th ed. rev.: reviewed by A.J.B. Spaull. *Chem. Ind.* (1 Sep 73) p.853-4

LIFT : Flight : Chalcid wasps. See CHALCID WASPS : Flight : Lift

LIFT TRUCKS, Fork. See FORK TRUCKS

LIFTS, Tail : Unloading : Commercial vehicles. See VEHICLES, Commercial : Unloading : Lifts, Tail

LIGHT
Related Headings:
COLOUR
LUMINESCENCE
OPTICAL
PHOTOMETERS
SUNLIGHT
TRANSMITTANCE

LIGHT : Distribution : Lanterns : Lighting : Streets. See STREETS : Lighting : Lanterns : Light distribution

LIGHT : Effect on matter. See OPTICAL PROPERTIES

LIGHT : Fastness : Benzanthrone dyed polyester fibre fabrics. See FABRICS; Polyester fibres,, Dyed : Benzanthrone : Light fastness

Fig. 1.   A page from the *British Technology Index.*

do not fully understand all of Farradane's ideas, nor agree with all I think I do understand, some of his ideas have helped us a very great deal to formulate systematic rules of attack on subject-heading problems".[2] Farradane's approach is to consider the psychology of learning and subject identification, and develops into a fairly sophisticated form of indexing. *B.T.I.*'s approach is, of necessity, more simple and immediately pragmatic. Having isolated about fifteen distinct types of relation, these were pruned and merged, at the same time considering their importance and how they could best fit into the permutation system.

The major relational punctuation symbols used in *B.T.I.* are as follows.

(i) The colon, the most common, used to denote the relation between subject and verbal form or verbal form and object. When reading the heading from right to left, the prepositions 'for' and 'of' can usually be inserted, e.g.

SHEETS : Machining : Lasers

i.e. Lasers *for* the machining *of* sheets.

(ii) The semicolon. This is used to express the relationship between an object and the material from which it is made. From right to left, no preposition is required, e.g.

SHEETS ; Steel : Machining.

(iii) The comma. This is used for the relationship between a noun or entity and an attribute or qualifying adjective, e.g. colour, type, etc.

(iv) The dash or hyphen. This is used to denote a combination or compound term, where each term is of equal status, e.g.

BATTERIES ; Lead—Acid.

Other symbols are used to denote places, named types of cars, ships, etc. The indexer uses these to indicate the relationship between terms, and then inserts a second punctuation symbol which does not appear in the printed index; these together instruct the computer in its permutation procedure, e.g.

(a) STREETS : . Lighting

The full stop instructs the computer to provide a reference:

LIGHTING : STREETS see STREETS : Lighting

(b) LAMPS : < Testing : . Instruments.

Here the < suppresses a cross-reference from the word testing, considered an 'unsought term'. Not only that, but the system is sophisticated to the extent that for the reference from "Instruments" the "s" is automatically removed from 'Lamp' and the order of terms changed to give

INSTRUMENTS : Lamp testing see

LAMPS : Testing : Instruments.

This device was also illustrated in Table 1 with "pulsed laser design".

(c) Special symbols are used for a limited number of common relations, e.g., "effect of" is treated thus:

POLYTHENE : . Creep]. Temperature

produces automatically a reference from Temperature as follows:

TEMPERATURE : Effect on creep : Polythene see

POLYTHENE : Creep : effect of temperature.

A more comprehensive list of symbols and their effects is found in Coates and Nicholson[10].

This system copes well and unambiguously with the majority of situations. However, problems of several sorts can occur, many of which are well-known and common to several systems, for example, where usage has made popular an adjectival noun. Here there may be some difficulty as to whether to use a colon or a comma as the relationship symbol, for example, let us consider "radio frequency", already a compound term, in its application to Sputtering. In *B.T.I.* this is indexed as

R.F. : Sputtering.

whereas for Heating, we have

HEATING, R.F.

Amongst the many types of welding we have Inert gas welding, indexed as

WELDING, Gas, Inert.

but Electron beam welding, indexed as

ELECTRON BEAMS : Welding

One can see that this problem is partly caused because many of the terms, for example, Electron beams, will exist in contexts where they are not combined in this way, and a consistent filing sequence is required at the term "Electron beams".

A very similar problem sometimes results in *B.T.I.* using combination of terms which appear slightly awkward compared with everyday language, e.g. *B.T.I.* has the heading

FIRES : Control   – (13)

which is clear enough.

What about methods or equipment to control fires, e.g. a fire extinguisher? "FIRE EX-TINGUISHERS" would seem straightforward, but we then have the problem that FIRE EX-TINGUISHER as a heading in a long sequence might well file some distance from (13).

"FIRES : Control : Extinguishers"

could be used but the compromise is

"FIRES : Extinguishers".

It seems to me that this situation only becomes serious when the terms used are not in first place in the heading. In this case the searcher *will* need some knowledge of how the permutation system works, for example if the article indexed may be particularly concerned with office fire extinguishers.

This may be indexed as

OFFICE BUILDINGS : Fires : Extinguishers – (14)

The cross-references from this are as follows:

FIRES : Office buildings see

OFFICE BUILDINGS : Fires   – (15)

EXTINGUISHERS : Fires : Office buildings see

OFFICE BUILDINGS : Fires : Extinguishers – (16)

Thus the searcher will find no direct reference from

FIRES : Extinguishers

to such an item.

The procedure is entirely logical, but my guess would be that difficulties of this type account for a substantial proportion of non-retrieved items in *B.T.I.* Interested readers might like to search *B.T.I.* for articles on "Traffic lights" and "Petrol pumps" for further examples. Any incomplete permutation system will have difficulties of this type, though there may be a case for extra cross-references where certain of these combination terms are involved.

We now pass on to consider the major lines of development in post-war indexing. The major influence here has, of course, been the computer. As far as *B.T.I.* is concerned, we should give a passing nod to the KWIC index of H. P. Luhn [11] which has a superficial resemblance to *B.T.I.* and in some ways could be a *B.T.I.* without the intellectual effort and therefore without the control, though also without the same expense. It and its relations KWOC and KWAC are still much in evidence, as was indicated by the recent article in this journal on an index for the proceedings of a public inquiry [12].

It is perhaps more interesting to consider the relationship between *B.T.I.* and co-ordinate indexing. Although the co-ordinate index is not confined to the computer, nearly all large machine-based systems rely on it. One of the early developments of getting the computer into the act was Mortimer Taube's idea of "freeing the index language" by using "uniterms". [13]

This consisted essentially of selecting terms from an article on the basis of frequency only, assuming that the most frequently occurring terms were in fact the most significant. These words were then stored in the computer as "labels" for each document, retrieval to be effected by matching search words with these stored "uniterms".

Gradually more control was considered desirable, and this was attempted by the introduction of the now familiar concept of the thesaurus. This tool acted as an "authority file" and "memory jogger" for searchers and indexers for the control of synonyms, etc., and gradually became more complex with the indication of relationships between terms in the thesaurus. Indexing terms often included groups of words to be used together (i.e. preco-ordination) and these also were often called, incorrectly, "uniterms". In this way the language became markedly less free, but it is still very different in its overall approach from the highly controlled *B.T.I.*

Nevertheless, there. are several points of similarity between the internal structure of *B.T.I.* and a conventional thesaurus and the relationship may have some implications for possible future developments.

(i) *Authority file.* Just as in most indexing systems based on a thesaurus, indexers at *B.T.I.*

are not free to choose any term they wish, but are obliged to consult an authority file which is a list of all terms and headings that have previously been used. Thus great store is set by precedent. The finished printed index can be used for this purpose, but, until computerisation, a large cumulated manual file in card form was maintained. This file, which is still in use although not now updated, covers a whole wall of the *B.T.I.* office and contains some 200,000 items. Latest precedents on the whole tend to hold sway and where they differ from older versions usually indicate a change of policy.

Therefore an indexer will first consult the latest volumes of the published indexes together with the most recent monthly issues (these are cumulated each month by the computer and issued as a print-out to each indexer) to establish a heading.

Consistency of indexing over several years is a considerable problem in technical indexing, dealing as it often does with areas of rapid technological advance, with accompanying terminological change. Not least is the difficulty of distinguishing a passing fashion from a genuine change or new term, e.g. the word "thyristor" has been well established for some time, in preference to "silicon controlled rectifier", whereas the fairly new word "terotechnology" has only just been admitted since presumably the distinction between it and "plant maintenance" is now sufficiently defined. Thus the policy of *B.T.I.* is continuous, but cautious, updating.

(ii) *Internal structure*. The other main point of similarity between the thesaurus or co-ordinate index and *B.T.I.* is the internal classifi-

catory structure which has grown up in each. The thesaurus entries of "broader", "narrower", "related" term, etc., are now well known. In *B.T.I.*, in addition to the permutation cross-references, there are two other sorts, the simplest of which is the control of synonyms; this is accomplished by a "see" reference, e.g.

OPTICAL MASERS see LASERS

The other form is called a "related heading" reference, e.g.

FURNITURE
Related Headings
CHAIRS
SEATS
TABLES

We can see that "related headings" in fact refer one from a broader or more general term to narrower or more specific terms. Almost all terms in the index are incorporated into this related heading structure, forming a comprehensive internal network. One could extract this network and display it in a conventional hierarchical or "tree" format. In fact, if we do this, we may see how *B.T.I.* has not escaped some of the traditional classification problems, e.g. if we take the subject of "Electrical Engineering" and extract the related heading structure from the index, we find [see diagram].

Thus a searcher will not be led from either "Electrical Measurement" or "Electric Meters" as might reasonably be expected. This is a common problem of classification where one has to decide to divide a term arbitrarily by a property or attribute. We can see that, for our example,

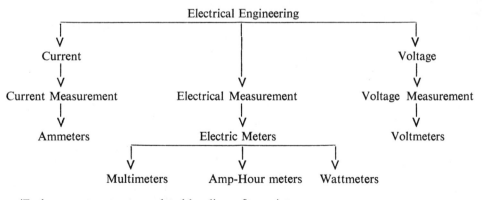

(Each arrow represents a related heading reference)

we could only reduce the problem by not considering "measurement" as a legitimate dividing term (though this, in its wake, creates other difficulties) i.e.

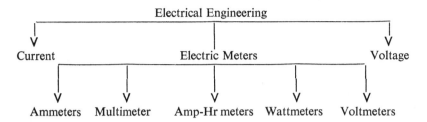

This is exactly the sort of difficulty that many modern thesauri increasingly experience, as they depart more and more from Taube's original uniterms and plump more and more for preco-ordinated phrases.

The major points of similarity between thesaurus and *B.T.I.* structure are listed below:—

B.T.I.	*Co-ordinate Index (Thesaurus)*
Authority file	Thesaurus
Heading/Terms	Index terms/Keywords/Uniterms, etc.
Related Heading	Narrower term
Reverse related heading	Broader term
"See" or synonym reference	"see" or "use" reference
Reverse synonym reference	"used for" reference
No equivalent	related term or "see also"

Reverse related and reverse synonym references do not appear in the printed form of *B.T.I.* but are incorporated into the indexer's authority file, as well as the magnetic tape files.

The differences between *B.T.I.* and the co-ordinate index are readily apparent. *B.T.I.* goes further by arranging its "keywords" in a logical and related framework, even though "phonetic", thereby enhancing their meaning. It has the constraint of having to be visibly accessible, i.e. produced in printed form, for which the system of permutations for cross-references makes suitable provision. The co-ordinate index has some advantages in its freedom from these limitations.

For example, it would often be easier to use a co-ordinate index for broad subject searches. One reason for this is that although many keywords may be used to describe a document, a searcher may only use one or two if he requires, thus keeping the search vague. But, on looking through an index such as *B.T.I.*, this is not so easy, since the two terms chosen may be separated along a chain by several others, all of which will have to be scanned. Another simple reason is the fact that in the printed index *B.T.I.* does not indicate broader headings, thus handicapping the searcher.

However, from our considerations we can see that *B.T.I.* could be used as an authority file for co-ordinate indexing, particularly in a form where reverse-related and reverse-synonym references are displayed. Again it would seem possible that the *B.T.I.* tapes could be searched in a purely co-ordinate way, even though this method would not avail itself of the presumed advantages of the relational and logical order aspects of the indexing.

B.T.I. has also potential, and has been used as a classification system for documents, where they can be arranged in *B.T.I.* order, with the possibilities of a "merged" or separate index, or even *B.T.I.* itself, as an access tool.

Perhaps the most obvious way of development for *B.T.I.* is in expansion of its coverage. Perhaps it could become a European Technology Index, or instead look across the Atlantic and try to cope with some of the enormous American literature. Financial and indexing supervision problems would likely be large if this course of action were decided on.

Since *B.T.I.* already annotates many of its bibliographical references with firm organisation or even product information, it would seem possible to produce a separate index listing this type of useful data.

One other area in which work could be usefully done is in direct or comparative evaluation testing of *B.T.I.* Little has been done, and, particularly when comparing with other printed indexes, the enormous varieties in structure make life very difficult, as the recent INSPEC studies indicate[14]. In fact, even a large scale *subjective* evaluation (e.g. a questionnaire survey) remains to be done.

It is to be hoped that the apparently considerable potential of the *B.T.I.* system and product will be investigated and exploited in the future, thus building on the sound basis which I have tried to outline.

Index Production.

A flow diagram of the main processes involved in production is given in Fig. 2. The first stage takes place when the indexer scans the journals and marks those articles to be indexed. On the whole he follows fairly simple criteria for inclusion, i.e. that the article should be technical within the scope of *B.T.I.* (outlined in the annual volume introduction) and of at least one page in length, not including half-tones. There is usually little difficulty in establishing subject suitability, though when we consider the variations in journal size some anomalies are inevitable. At this stage also, the indexer annotates or expands titles, perhaps by including subheadings or by indicating the topic or place discussed. This occurs most frequently with trade journals where a title itself may often contain no subject information at all.

A typist then transfers the full bibliographic details of each article on to indexing forms of a fairly simple format which allows space for entry of indexing terms as well as indications of what precedents have been found and other explanatory notes for the editor. He, incidentally, sees every heading before its input to the computer.

Broadly speaking, each indexer has to index regularly a set of journals covering a fairly broad subject area, e.g. chemical sciences, engineering, etc.

After indexing, the headings and article details are transferred to punched tape for input to the computer and this input is checked by the indexer by means of the typed copy from the tape typewriter used to punch the paper tape. After computer processing each month, a sorted print-out is produced containing all the permutations and references. The indexer is also required for this task since this is a stage where the results of the month's work are manifest and items are brought together, thus giving an opportunity for checking consistency of indexing, notation and any special or new permutation difficulties that are thrown up. It will be appreciated how the indexer's knowledge of the system and indexing methods is required here, although understandable that as he becomes more experienced, this operation will feel more routine. However, new and unexpected problems never fail to arise.

Finally, after computer typesetting, the page proof of the finished index must be corrected. This, together with clerical tasks such as booking in of journals and filing of indexing sheets (kept for one year) make up the indexer's job. While working as a technical indexer at *B.T.I.* I kept a record of how my time was spent, how many articles I indexed, etc. Some of the main statistics, covering the first six months, are now presented.

The indexing staff consists of four full-time indexers and an editor/indexer. Each year *B.T.I.* produces about 25,000 entries. In the first six months I indexed a total of 1,800 articles somewhat below the average. From the details given in Table 2 we can see that new indexers can expect to spend over sixty per cent of their time indexing, and during that time index an article correctly every nineteen to twenty minutes. The number of articles indexed per week over the first 26 weeks varied from 21 in week 24 to 133 in week 6. The number of articles indexed per indexing hour also has its maximum variation at weeks 24 and 6. A plot of production per indexing hour against indexing time per week (not shown) shows wide scatter and little relation, with perhaps a slight suggestion that more lengthy periods devoted to indexing are more productive than a sequence of short periods as would be expected. The lack of a steady increase in rate of indexing may in part be attributed to the fact that as an indexer gains in experience he naturally progresses to more difficult journals.

The computer problems referred to were those associated with the changeover to the ICL 470. These problems, the editor believes, were in part responsible for what he considers the low figure

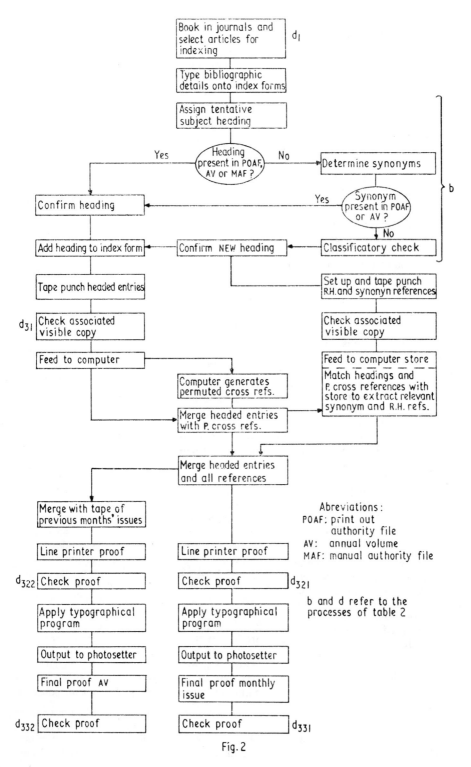

Book in journals and select articles for indexing — d_1

Type bibliographic details onto index forms

Assign tentative subject heading

Heading present in POAF, AV or MAF ? — Yes / No

No → Determine synonyms

Synonym present in POAF or AV ? — Yes / No

Yes → Confirm heading

No ↓ Classificatory check

Confirm heading

Add heading to index form ← Confirm NEW heading ← Classificatory check

Tape punch headed entries

Set up and tape punch R.H. and synonyn references

d_{31} Check associated visible copy

Check associated visible copy

Feed to computer

Feed to computer store

Computer generates permuted cross refs.

Match headings and P. cross references with store to extract relevant synonym and R.H. refs.

Merge headed entries with P. cross refs.

Merge headed entries and all references

Merge with tape of previous months' issues

Line printer proof

Line printer proof

d_{322} Check proof

Check proof d_{321}

Apply typographical program

Apply typographical program

Output to photosetter

Output to photosetter

Final proof AV

Final proof monthly issue

d_{332} Check proof

Check proof d_{331}

Abreviations:
POAF: print out authority file
AV: annual volume
MAF: manual authority file

b and d refer to the processes of table 2

b

Fig. 2

of 48 hours for indexing discussion. These periods spent on discussing particular indexing problems and procedures are among the most important, interesting and profitable spent in this particular job. The most-experienced indexers still have such regular sessions of discussion.

When considering these statistics, it should be borne in mind, particularly if comparison is to be made with other systems, that indexing time can legitimately vary from one or two minutes to one or two hours. A complex paper will naturally take longer to analyse and as we have said, considerable time may be spent checking the accuracy and consistency of terminology and headings.

Number of articles indexed	a	= 1801
Number of hours indexing	b	= 581
No. hours indexing new articles	b_1	= 491
„ „ indexing discussion	b_2	= 48
„ „ indexing correction	b_3	= 42

Rate of indexing : $c = \dfrac{a}{b} = 3 \cdot 1$ articles/indexing hour

Hours on other activities	d	= 384
Marking-up & booking-in journals	d_1	= 71
Filing (indexing sheets & journals)	d_2	= 44
Proof reading (including indexing check)	d_3	= 180
„ „ (tape typewriter copy)	d_{31}	= 44
„ „ computer print out	d_{32}	= 85
„ „ „ „ „ (monthly issue)	d_{321}	= 36
„ „ „ „ „ (annual volume)	d_{322}	= 49
„ „ final copy	d_{33}	= 51
„ „ „ „ (monthly issue)	d_{331}	= 27
„ „ „ „ (annual volume)	d_{332}	= 24
Identifiable with computer problems	d_4	= 38
Other (including errands, subject investigation, etc.)	d_5	= 51

(Note: Unquantifiable parts of d_2 & d_3 are also related to the indexing process)

TABLE 2—Indexing Statistics

References.
1. Holmstrom, J. E. *Records and research in engineering and industrial science*. 3rd Edition. Chapman & Hall. 1956.
2. Coates, E. J. Aims and methods of the *British Technology Index. The Indexer*. 3 (4). Autumn 1963. pp. 146-52.
3. Coates, E. J. Scientific and Technical Indexing. *The Indexer*. 5 (1). Spring 1966. pp. 27-34.
4. Coates, E. J. Computerised data processing for *British Technology Index. The Indexer*. 6 (3). Spring 1969. pp. 97-101.
5. Ranganathan. S. R. Self-Perpetuating Scheme of Classification. *Journal of Documentation* 4 (4). March 1949. pp. 223-44.
6. Wells, A. J. The Colon Classification, *Aslib Proceedings*. 2 (2). Feb. 1950. pp. 14-22.
7. Ranganathan, S. R. *Prolegomena to library classification*. 2nd Edition. Library Association. 1957.
8. Vickery, B. C. *Faceted classification : a guide to the construction and use of special schemes*. Aslib. 1960.
9. Coates, E. J. *Subject catalogues : headings and structure*. Library Association. 1960.
10. Coates, E. J. & Nicholson, I. *British Technology Index*—a study of the application of computer processing to index production. In *Organisation and handling of bibliographic records by computer held at Newcastle Upon Tyne, July, 1967* (Ed. by N. S. M. Cox and M. W. Grose). Oriel Press. 1967. pp. 168-78.
11. Luhn, H. P. Keyword – in – context index for technical literature. I.B.M. Report 1959 and American Documentation. 11 (4). Oct. 1970. pp. 288-95.
12. Thomas, P. A. The use of KWIC to index the proceedings of a public inquiry. *The Indexer*. 8 (3). April 1973. pp. 145-52.
13. Taube, M., Gull, C. D. and Wachtel, I. S. Unit terms in Coordinate indexing. *American Documentation*. 3 (4). Fall 1952. pp. 213-18.
14. Aitchison, T. M., Hall, A. M. and Broadbent M. *Laboratory evaluation of printed subject headings*. INSPEC report R73/17. 1973.

Citation Indexing*

John Martyn

American law, like English law, is to a large extent based on precedent. Since 1873 the American legal profession has enjoyed the use of a publication called Shepard's Citations, which has to a very great extent facilitated the location of legal precedents relevant to a particular case in law. It consists of a listing of individual American court cases accompanied by a note of all subsequent cases which have cited it as authority and whether subsequent cases have reversed or overruled or in any way modified the authority of the decision in the original case.

In 1949 a note in the *Journal of the Patent Office Society* by Arthur H. Seidal referred to Shepard's Citations and suggested that something of the same system might be applied in the American Patent Office. ' Thus every patent could be given a separate index card and a notation made upon this index card whenever it was cited by the Patent Office as a reference against a later issued patent. Through the use of this card one could readily ascertain later correlated patents . . . By the use of this method a searcher, who had found a patent closely paralleling the disclosure which he was searching, could rapidly determine the state of the art both before and *after* the patent, and thereby accelerate his search.'

In 1955 a short article by W. C. Adair, a former executive vice-president of the publishers of Shepard's Citations, appeared in *American Documentation*. Adair suggested that the principle of Shepard's Citations might be applied to other fields, notably to scientific literature. This paper was written at the suggestion of Eugene Garfield who was at the time an associate editor of *American Documentation*.

A little later in the same year Garfield published a paper called ' Citation Indexes for Science ' in which he proposed an index which would have the following characteristics: First there would be a complete alphabetical listing of all periodicals covered . . . similar to the *World list* but without the library holdings information. The main portion of the Citation Index would list all the articles in these periodicals which were covered by the index and with the details of each article would appear a note of other articles that had referred to the article in question, together with an indication of whether the citing source was an original article, review, abstract, patent and so on. In effect, the system would provide a complete listing, for the publications covered, of all the original articles which had referred to the article in question. Several other papers by Garfield and others followed in various journals, and in 1961, with support from the National Science Foundation, the National Institute for Health and

* A paper read at a Discussion Meeting on January 20th, 1966.

Reprinted from *The Indexer* 5, no. 1 (Spring 1966): 5–15.

the Institute for Scientific Information in Philadelphia, an organisation directed by Dr. Garfield, began the work which led to the publication in 1963 of the first issue of the *Science Citation Index*.

Now, as to what a Citation Index actually is. This can perhaps be best explained by showing you how the *Science Citation Index,* to take the biggest and best-known example, is compiled. A large number of journal titles (more than eleven hundred in 1965) is taken by the Institute for Scientific Information and an entry prepared for every paper, editorial letter, communication, review, report and so on —in fact everything except advertisements and announcements appearing in these journals. These entries are ordered alphabetically by the author, with 'See' entries for co-authors, and form the Source Index part of the Citation Index. The characteristic entry will look like this:

SNAPE F
PROC PICK C   93   129   64   6R   21246
FURTHER STUDIES OF THE ECOLOGY
OF THE HAMPSTEAD PONDS

Snape F. was the author, we will imagine, of a paper called ' Further studies of the ecology of the Hampstead Ponds ' which appeared in 1964 in the Proceedings of the Pickwick Club, volume 93, page 129. It carried six references in its bibliography. 21246 is the accession number assigned by the Institute for Scientific Information to this issue of this particular **journal**.

The six references cited in this paper by Snape, together with all the references in all of the other papers listed in the Source Index, are taken, and sorted, and listed by cited author and cited reference to produce the Citation Index proper. Let us suppose one of Snape's six references was to an earlier paper in *Transactions of the Pickwick Club,* vol. 1, page 14, by Pickwick, S., in 1827. In the Citation Index we will therefore find this entry:

PICKWICK S...27. TRANS PICK C...1...14
    SNAPE F   PROC PICK C....64....93....129

Should other authors have cited **Pickwick's** paper, then they will be listed alphabetically in the same way as Snape under the entry for this paper by Pickwick.

Now let us look at a real entry:

JAN 14
ITCH

JAN 28
STING YARN

S
EM 239   43
S
YC   28   23

N1   50389
RANDS IN

N7323 49339
IES

SYLV EL PRO
FEB 25

ON 170 195

JAN 28
IT FOR

      154 197

N1   49908
EXOSES TO
ODIUM IN

      23 T 17

N1   50319

N1   50319

/   43   32
ED 60 320

N1   52239
MPOSITION OF

IT 87 49

N1 51248
NSILLECTOMY

JAN 14
JCTION

      51   71
      26   47

MAR 3
NL FLANGE ON

S
JR 16 312
NE 144 299
      17 185

BECK JC
I7   50884
UPON
NANSPORT

N493P1 51025
E & N-BUTANE

-

SMITH S
N4914 49368
NRIANT OF
EGG

N1   50000

      90   12

DAYAL HM   SAXENA BN   NIGAM SS
  I J EX BIOL   2   62 64   N   2R   N1   49991
  ERADICATION OF MITES FROM FUNGAL CULTURE
  COLLECTION

DAYES L   SEE DOSSETOR JB CAN MED A J   90 471

DAYKIN DR   INT BUS MAC
  3121800 US   64   P   2R   FEB 18
  CL307/88 PULSE GENERATING CIRCUIT

DAYKIN PN   SEE BLOOR JE   CAN J CHEM   42 121
DAYSTR INC SEE BLANCO E   3120650 US
DAYSTR INC SEE FREEMAN RW 3122018 US
DAYSTR INC SEE LENDER RJ   3119962 US
DAYSTR INC SEE PRATT WW   3119919 US
DAYT PERF I SEE BLEICHER RL 3118260 US
DAYTON PG   SEE FINSTER M   ANESTHESIOL 25   94
DAYTON PG   SEE WEINER M   AM J MED SC 247 75
DCRUZ IA   SEE NAMIN EP   AM J CARD   13 124
DCRUZ IA   SEE NAMIN EP   AM J CARD   13 124
DCRUZ IA   SEE WEINBERG M J THOR SURG 47   40

DEACON GER
  NATURE   201 561 64   E NO R   N4919 50438
  INTERNATIONAL INDIAN OCEAN EXPEDITION

DEAKIN ST   SEAL CORP
  3120418 US   64   P   8R   FEB 4
  CL339/126 ELECTRIC SOCKET CONTACTS

DEAL LA
  3119321 US   64   P   2R   JAN 28
  CL99/277.1 APPARATUS FOR AGING ALCOHOLIC
  SPIRITS

DEALFARO V PREDAZZI E   ROSSETTI C
  NUOV CIMENT   31   42 64   25R   N1   50607
  ANALYTICITY IN ANGULAR MOMENTUM IN POTENTIAL
  SCATTERING

DEALY JM   GREEN AA   ALB PIP SUP
  3119635 US   64   P   6R   JAN 28
  CL287/108 H-BEAM PILE CONNECTORS

DEAN ACB   MASON MK
  GUT   5   64 64   12R   N1   51679
  DISTRIBUTION OF PYLORIC MUCOSA IN PARTIAL
  GASTRECTOMY SPECIMENS

DEAN ACR   HINSHELW.C
  NATURE   201 232 64   96R N4916 49833
  SOME BASIC ASPECTS OF CELL REGULATION

DEAN DC   SEE DESANCTI.RW CIRCULATION 29 14

DEAN DJ   LIEBERMA.J ALBRECHT RM ARNSTEIN P
           BAER GM   GOODRICH WB
  PUBL HEALTH 79 101 64   25R   N2   51186
  PSITTACOSIS IN MAN & BIRDS

DEAN FN   JONES PG   MORTON RB   SIDISUNT.P
  J CHEM SOC   411 64   10R   JAN   51086
  ADDUCTS FROM QUINONES & DIAZOALKANES .4.
  TROPONES FROM ACETYLQUINONES

DEAN RA
  CAN J MATH   16 136 64   8R   N1   49515
  FREE LATTICES GENERATED BY PARTIALLY ORDERED
  SETS & PRESERVING BOUNDS

DEAN RE   ANDREW JH   READ RC
  J AM MED A 187   27 64   15R   N1   49430
  RED CELL FACTOR IN RENAL DAMAGE FROM
  ANGIOGRAPHIC MEDIA - PERFUSION STUDIES OF IN
  SITU CANINE KIDNEY WITH CELLULAR & ACELLULAR
  PERFUSATES

DEAN RL   SEE ALBRONDA HF ARCH G PSYC 10 276
DEAN WV   SEE TOWELL BH   3123141 US
DEANE   SEE ZIMMERMA. J HIST CYTO 12   6

DEANE EH   WILSON RJ   EASTM KOD C
  3117508 US   64   P   4R   JAN 14
  CL95/89 VISCOUS SOLUTION PROCESSING DEVICE

DEANE GE
  J EXP PSYCH 67 193 64   3R   N2   50762
  HUMAN HEART RATE RESPONSES DURING
  EXPERIMENTALLY INDUCED ANXIETY - FOLLOW UP
  WITH CONTROLLED RESPIRATION

DEANE P
  J AM STAT A 59 278 64   B   1R   N305 51382
  ECONOMIC TRENDS IN SOVIET UNION

DEANGELI.A AM OPT COMP
  3122962 US   64   P 16R   MAR 3
  CL85/1 RING-LIKE RETAINING DEVICES

DEANS T
  NATURE   201 599 64   L NO R   N4919 50438
  ISOTOPIC COMPOSITION OF STRONTIUM IN

DEBONO AHC
  BR J SURG
  LUNG TRA

DEBORGER L
  B S CHIM B
  1.2-CYCL

DEBRAY C

DEBRIE AVL
  3119319 US
  CL95/89
  MACHINES

DEBROW PL

DEBRUIN HJ
  REV SCI IN
  PRECISIO
  DIFFUSIO

DEBRUIN HJ
  3120776 US
  CL82/33

DEBRUIN HJ
  3122037 US
  CL81/9.5

DEBRUYN WT
  3121923 US
  CL20/52.

DEC NV
DECASTRO

DECATUR PS
  3116984 US
  CL34/79

DECC LIM
DECENCIO D
DECHAMPL.J
DECHAMPL.J
DECHAMPL.J
DECIUS JC
DECKEL FW
DECKEL FW
DECKEL FW
DECKEL H
DECKEL H
DECKEL H
DECKER DG

DECKER HL
  3121260 US
  CL20/22

DECKER K
  B S CHIM B
  SUR LA B
  CLOSTRID

DECKX R
  CLIN CHIN
  MODIFIED
  SUITABLE
  METABOLI

DECORDOV.SF
  3120871 US
  CL166/55

DECOSTAN.PF
  3120672 US
  CL15/250

DECRAENE EP
DECROLY P

DECROOCO D
  B S CHIM F
  LA CONST
  MELANGES

DEDEN C
DEDERICK MM

DEDEURWA.R
  J POL SCI
  VISCOMET
  TEMPERAT

DEDIC AM
  3117689 US
  CL217/60

DEDINSKY JP
  3116497 US
  CL9/6 CO

FIG. 1.

```
WAVES THEIR USE¤            159
 J PHYS         64    32     16
TROPHYS J---------    61    140
OPT SOC         64    54    147
UDIES OPTICS U CHI¤          11
OPT SOC         64    54      1
UDIES OPTICS-------¤         21
 J PHYS         64    32     16
TURE--------------    18    195
 J PHYS         64    32     16
TURE--------------    21     94
 J PHYS         64    32     16
TURE--------------    21    120
 J PHYS         64    32     16
TURE--------------    21    226
 J PHYS         64    32     16
 J SCI------------    22    120
 J PHYS         64    32     16
TURE--------------    24    460
 J PHYS         64    32     16
 J SCI------------    23    395
 J PHYS         64    32     16
 J SCI------------    24     92
 J PHYS         64    32     16
MPT REND----------    94    520
 J PHYS         64    32     16
PHYS PARIS--------     1    183
 J PHYS         64    32     16
IL MAG------------    13    236
 J PHYS         64    32     16
RSONAL COMMUNICATI¤
 J PHYS         64    32     16
RSONAL COMMUNICATI¤
 J PHYS         64    32     16
 J SCI------------    31    377
OPT SOC         64    54    147
 J PHYS         64    32     16
 J SI-------------    34   C333
 J PHYS         64    32     16
IL MAG------------    24    449
 J PHYS         64    32     16
DEREAL MESSENGER--     6    306
 J PHYS         64    32     16
ASSN ENGRG SOC----
 J PHYS         64    32     16
PHYS PARIS--------     1    444
 J PHYS         64    32     16
AAAS--------------    37      3
 J PHYS         64    32     16
 J SCI------------    38    184
 J PHYS         64    32     16
NATL ACAD SCI US--    41   1079
 J PHYSL        64   206    338
CH PATH         64    77     64
TURE--------------   182   1502
THEOR BIO       64     6     26
CHEM SOC----------         1371
AM CHEM S       64    86    111
CHEM SOC----------         3655
N J BIOCH       64    42     87
EMISTRY INDUSTRY--         1267
S CHIM BI       64    46     71
AEPELIN PSYCHOL AR¤    2     84
YCH NEUR        64   147     30
AM MICROSCOPICAL S    78    256
P PARASIT       64    15      7
A ARCH DERM-------    71    628
CH DERMAT       64    89    104
ER J PHYS ANTHROP-     2    151
T PAED U        64    53     79
PL MICROBIOL------     7    166
FOOD SCI        64    29     80
W ENG J MED-------   265   1075
 J DIS CH       64   107    131
T               64     5      1
CH IN MED       64   113    153
ESTHESIOLOGY------
ESTH ANAL     D 64    43    102
ESTHESIOLOGY------    24    177
ESTH ANAL     D 64    43    102
N SURG          64   159    125
N SURG------------   159    125
AM MED A      A 64   187    164
AMER MED ASS------   179    854
UT MED WO       64    89    313
ER J MED----------    28     77
SW MED WO       64    94     79
TURE LOND---------   171     26
IET RES         64     5     20
ROY SOC          B   144    241
IET RES         64     5     20
N NEW YORK ACAD SC    99    670
OOD             64    23    117
POLYMER SCI-------    51     85
POL SCI A       64     2    225
LYMER-------------     2    447
POL SCI A       64     2    225
TEXTILE I---------    53   T493
POL SCI A       64     2    225
 CHEM-------------    62    489
IT J BIOL       64    17    271
NATSSCHR CHEM-----    82    944
VELOP BIO       64     9     56
HROMATOG----------     1     93
A CL MED        64    63    306
HROMATOG----------     1     93
 J BIOCH        64    42    219
 CELL RES---------    26    129
URE             64   201    375
------------------    14   2177
OL SCI A        64     2    181
 PHAMPHL----------¤           3
8531 US       P 64
 PHAMPHL----------¤          11
.8531 US      P 64
INTA--------------    58    549
IT J BIOL       64    17     10
 BOTANY         64    28    137
URE           L 64   201     98
SSE MED-----------    61   1419
H RHEUM         64     7     87
H FRANC PEDIAT----    16    695
MED J         L 64     1    486
TET GYN         64    23     21
IG----------------     5     31
 J MED          64    36    151
IG----------------     5    381
 J MED          64    36    151
ICEPTION CAUSALITY¤
 J PSYCHI     B 64   110    142
URE           B 64   201    115
 J MED PS     B 64    37     84
A RHEUM SCAND-----     5    148
H RHEUM         64     7      8
IN CHIR-----------    55    565
IT MED WO       64    89     30
IERV MENT DIS-----   125    478
H G PSYC        64    10     47
A STATE J SCI-----    36    349
IENCE           64   143    373
```

```
        LIN YK            J ACOUST SO        64   36    82
      ---------------60-STATISTICAL COMMUNIC¤          141
        BARNARD RD        BELL SYST T        64   43   233
MIDDLETON DC-------*63*THESIS U CALIFORNIA-¤
        MIDDLETO.JT       ARCH ENV HE      M 64    8    19
MIDDLETON GS-------*11*GLASGOW MED J--------      76     1
        WILKINS RH        J NEUROSURG        64   21    73
      ---------------11-GLASGOW MJ-----------     76   139
        MIXTER WJ         J NEUROSURG        64   21    74
MIDDLETON JT-------*50*PLANT DIS REP--------      34   245
        MIDDLETO.JT       ARCH ENV HE      M 64    8    19
      ---------------55-3 P NAT AIR POLL S S¤      3   191
        MIDDLETO.JT       ARCH ENV HE      M 64    8    19
      ---------------56-AMA ARCH INDUSTR HEA      14   526
        MIDDLETO.JT       ARCH ENV HE      M 64    8    19
      ---------------56-CALIF AGRICULTURE---      10     9
        MIDDLETO.JT       ARCH ENV HE      M 64    8    19
      ---------------58-J AIR POLLUT CONTR A       8     9
        MIDDLETO.JT       ARCH ENV HE      M 64    8    19
      ---------------61-ANN REV PLANT PHYSIO      12   431
        MIDDLETO.JT       ARCH ENV HE      M 64    8    19
      ---------------61-J AIR POLLUT CONTR A      11   129
        MIDDLETO.JT       ARCH ENV HE      M 64    8    19
      ---------------63-1022 P NAT C AIR POL¤          166
        MIDDLETO.JT       ARCH ENV HE      M 64    8    19
MIDDLETON KR-------*60*J RUBB RES I MALAYA-       16   139
        BOLTON J          J SCI FOOD         64   15     1
MIDDLETON LJ-------*55*J EXPTL BOT----------       6   422
        TROJANOW.J        POST BIOCH       M 64   10    93
      ---------------60-PLANT PHYSIOL-------      35   913
        BOSZORME.Z        PHYSL PLANT        64   17    81
MIDDLETON R--------*52*P PHYS SOC-----------A     65   752
        HAMBURGE.EW       NUCL PHYS          64   50    66
MIDDLETON W--------*51*J OPT SOC AMER-------      41   419
        KORTUM G          Z N 'URFO A        64 A 19    28
        MCINTYRE D        J RES NBS A        64 A 68    87
MIDDLETON WEK------*52*J OPT SOC AM---------      42   572
        AROYAN GF         J OPT SOC        L 64   54   130
      ---------------52-VISION THROUGH ATMOS¤
        AROYAN GF         J OPT SOC        L 64   54   130
      ---------------52-VISION THROUGH ATMOS¤          104
        FRASER RS         J OPT SOC          64   54   157
      ---------------53-ECOLOGY-------------      34   416
        ADHAV RS          J SCI INSTR      N 64   41    50
MIDDLETON WJ-------*58*J AM CHEM SOC--------      80  2788
        DITTMER DC        J ORG CHEM       N 64   29   497
MIDDLETON WS-------*39*AM JM SC-------------     198   301
        BURCH GE          AM HEART J         64   67    99
      ---------------47-AM HEART J----------      33   250
        BURCH GE          AM J MED           64   36    54
MIDELFORT CF-------*57*FAMILY PSYCHOTHERAPY¤
        HARMS E           ACT PSYTHER        64   12    53
      ---------------62-FAMILY PROCESS------       1   114
        GREENBER.IM       ARCH G PSYC        64   10     7
MIDENET M----------*62*ANN MEDICOPSYCHOL---      120   268
        WORTIS J          AM J PSYCHI      R 64  120   643
MIDER GB-----------*47*ARCH PATH------------      43   102
        MORRIS JH         NEUROLOGY          64   14   147
      ---------------52-CANCER--------------       5  1104
        WOODRUFF JD       J LANCET           64   84    11
      ---------------53-ANN REV MED---------       4   187
        COSTA G           J AM DIET A        64   44    15
      ---------------55-2 P CAN CANC C-------¤         120
        TELLER MN         CANCER RES         64   24   114
MIDGELEY AR--------*61*P SOC EXP BIOL MED--      108    85
        LEWIS J           J CLIN END         64   24   197
MIDGLEY------------*23*J AMER CHEM SOC-----       45  1821
        EMELEUS HJ        J CHEM SOC       N 64        511
MIDGLEY JEM--------*62*BIOCHIM BIOPHYS ACTA       61   513
        BROWN DD          P NAS US           64   51   139
        DEAN ACR          NATURE             64  201   232
        DOI RH            J BACT             64   87   323
        MOYER RC          ARCH BIOCH         64  104   193
MIDLO C------------*38*P LOUISIANA ACAD SCI        4   136
        TIPS RL           HUMAN BIOL         64   36     1
      ---------------42-20 AM AN ASS MEM PAL¤
        TIPS RL           HUMAN BIOL         64   36     1
MIE G--------------*03*ANN PHYSIK-----------      11   657
        NEGRETE P         J CHEM PHYS        64   40   255
      ---------------08-ANN PHYS LPZ--------      25   377
        KORTUM G          Z NATURFO A        64 A 19    28
        NAPPER DH         J COLL SCI         64   19    72
MIEHER RL----------*60*PHYS REV LETTERS----        4    57
        EISENSTA.M        PHYS REV A         64  133  A191
      ---------------62-PHYS REV------------     125  1537
        EISENSTA.M        PHYS REV A         64  133  A191
MIEHER WC----------*62*JAMA-----------------     179   854
        DELEU J           AM J DIG DI        64    9    97
MIEHTTINEN T-------*59*ACTA CHIM SCAND-----       13   856
        HASHIMOT.Y        ARCH BIOCH         64  104   282
MIELE AJ-----------*63*RADIOLOGY------------      80   779
        FRED HL           AM J ROENTG      R 64   91   138
MIER M-------------*60*BLOOD----------------      16  1586
        HARDERS H         DEUT MED WO        64   89   248
        INGRAM M          ANN NY ACAD        64  113  1066
MIESCHER G---------*21*DERM Z---------------      32   276
        AKESSON HO        ACT MED SC         64  175   115
      ---------------29-HANDBUCH HAUT GESCHL¤     11   441
        LUSCOMBE HA       ARCH DERMAT        64   89   274
      ---------------46-DERMATOLOGICA-------      92   225
        WINKELMA.RK       MEDICINE         R 64   43    59
MIESCHER K---------*32*HELV CHIM ACTA------       15   168
        ECKERT T          ARCH PHARM         64  297    31
      ---------------37-BIOCHEM Z-----------     294    39
        RUBIN M           J ORG CHEM         64   29    68
      ---------------39-HELV CHIM ACTA------      22   962
        UENO K            CHEM PHARM         64   12    92
MIESCHER P---------*  *RETICULOENDOTHELIAL-¤           149
        AZEN EA           J LA CL MED        64   63   122
      ---------------54-ACTA HAEMAT---------      11   152
        PAYNE R           PEDIATRICS         64   33   194
      ---------------55-SANG----------------      26    71
        HARTL W           DEUT MED WO        64   89    81
      ---------------56-ERGEBN INN MED KINDE       7   170
        HARTL W           DEUT MED WO        64   89    81
      ---------------56-SCHWEIZ MED WCHNSCHR      86   799
        WINKELMA.RK       MEDICINE         R 64   43    59
      ---------------56-SCHWEIZ MED WSCHR---      86  1461
        HARTL W           DEUT MED WO        64   89    81
      ---------------56-VOX SANG BASEL------       1    83
        DUESBERG R        DEUT MED WO        64   89   153
      ---------------57-SCHWEIZ   ) WCHNSCHR      87  1339
        WINKELMA.RK       MEDICIN          R 64   43    59
      ---------------57-VOX SANGUINIS-------       2   283
        STURGILL BC       P SOC EXP M        64  115   246
      ---------------58-SCHWEIZ MED WCHNSCHR      88   432
        GILMAN A          AM J MED         E 64   36   167
        URBAN H           DEUT MED WO        64   89   223
      ---------------61-IMMUNOPATH KLINIK FO¤
        DUESBERG R        DEUT MED WO        64   89   153
      ---------------61-IMMUNOPATHOLOGIE KLI¤
        HARTL W           DEUT MED WO        64   89    81
        VODRAZKA Z        CHEM LISTY       B 64   58    34
      ---------------61-P SOC EXP BIOL MED--     107    12
        LERNER EM         J EXP MED          64  119   327
      ---------------61-SCHWEIZ MED WCHNSCHR      91   939
        GILMAN A          AM J MED         E 64   36   167
        URBAN H           DEUT MED WO        64   89   223
MIESCHER PA--------*58*IMMUNPATHOLOGIE KLIN¤           178
        WIEDERMA.G        SCHW MED WO        64   94   257
```

```
        GROSS D           J CLI
        SOLOMON A         J CLI
        TAKATSUK.K        J IMM
MIGLIACCIO AV------*62*RHODE
                          AM J
MIGLIORINI RH------*62*AMER
        WALKER DG         BIOCH
MIGNOLET JCP-------*55*REC T
        OGURI T           J PHY
MIGONE L-----------*62*METAB
        TRINER L          PHYSL
      ---------------62-SHOCK
        DRUCKER WR        AM J
MIGRDICHIAN--------*57*ORGAN
        VONSCHIC.O        31217
      ---------------57-ORGAN
        VONSCHIC.O        31217
MIGRDICHIAN V------*57*ORGAN
        KAMAL MR          J ORG
MIGULA W-----------*97*SYSTE
        STURDZA SA        ARCH
MIHALKOVICS--------*85*CITED
        MARINPAD.M        ANAT
MIHALYI E----------*53*J BIO
        KHAN AW           J FOO
      ---------------54-J BIO
        WINZOR DJ         ARCH
MIHELICH JW--------*57*PHYS
        FUJIWARA I        NUCL
MIHICH E-----------*60*FED P
        SCHUBERT M        BIOPH
      ---------------61-P SOC
        RASKOVA H         PHARM
      ---------------61-P SOC
        RASKOVA H         PHARM
      ---------------62-CANCE
        BLOCK JB          J NAT
      ---------------62-CANCE
        BLOCK JB          J NAT
MIHINA JS----------*62*J ORG
        ROWLAND AT        J ORG
MIHRAN TG----------*62*62RL3
        BRADSHAW JA       AM J
MIILLER HS---------*62*IRE T
        AMAREL S          IEEE
MIJNLIEFF PF-------*58*THESI
        ANACKER EW        J PHY
      ---------------62-KONIN
        ANACKER EW        J PHY
      ---------------62-KONIN
        ANACKER EW        J PHY
MIJOVIC MPV--------*60*J CHE
        MALINOWS.T        POST
MIJOVIC MV---------*52*HELV
        CHANLEY JD        J ORG
MIKA---------------*60*J BAC
        MCCONNEL.SJ       J BAC
MIKAILOV NV--------*61*J POL
        TYUZYO K          J POL
MIKAMI S-----------*58*J FAC
        FARNER DS         AM SC
MIKAMI SI----------*62*ENDOC
        MIRSKY IA         AM J
MIKASA A-----------*61*P SOC
        TAQUINI AC        CAN M
MIKAT KW-----------*64*ARCH
                          J AM
MIKATA I-----------*59*KEIO
        RITZEL G          SCHW
      ---------------59-KEIO
        RITZEL G          SCHW
MIKELS E-----------*63*J REH
        MANN WA           AM J
MIKES O------------*57*2 VSE
        MIKES O           CHEM
      ---------------58-4 INT
        MIKES O           CHEM
      ---------------60-P S A
        MIKES O           CHEM
      ---------------61-COLLE
        WALSH KA          P NAS
      ---------------62-COLL
        MIKES O           CHEM
      ---------------62-COLLE
        WALSH KA          P NAS
      ---------------62-Z OBS
        MIKES O           CHEM
      ---------------63-COLL
        MIKES O           CHEM
MIKHAIL G----------*63*ACTA
        HAYNES RC         ACT E
      ---------------63-ACTA
        HAYNES RC         ACT E
MIKHAILOV----------*54*DOKLA
        YATES J           31198
      ---------------55-CA131
        YATES J           31198
MIKHAILOV BM-------*49*IZVES
        DAVIS MA          J MED
      ---------------50-CA296
        DAVIS MA          J MED
      ---------------52-DOKLA
        GARST JF          J AM
      ---------------53-IZVES
        BECKWITH AL       AUST
      ---------------59-IZV A
        ARZOUMAN.H        J AM
MIKHAILOV G--------*  *EM420
        POST C            ARCH
      ---------------59-ARKH
        POST C            ARCH
MIKHAILOV IG-------*53*DOKL
        GRUBER GJ         J CHE
      ---------------57-VESTN
        PADOVA J          J CHE
MIKHAILOV IN-------*63*ACTA
        MIKHAILO.IN       DAN S
      ---------------63-ZHETF
        MIKHAILO.IN       DAN S
MIKHAILOV V--------*54*KLIN
        PORTNOY LM        AM J
MIKHAILOVA IG------*58*SBORN
        TOKIN BP          FOL B
      ---------------58-6 CBL
        TOKIN BP          FOL B
      ---------------59-VESTN
        TOKIN BP          FOL B
      ---------------60-ARKHI
        TOKIN BP          FOL B
      ---------------60-NAUCH
        TOKIN BP          FOL B
      ---------------60-SBORN
        TOKIN BP          FOL B
      ---------------60-TRUDY
        TOKIN BP          FOL B
      ---------------60-VESTN
        TOKIN BP          FOL B
      ---------------61-DAN S
        TOKIN BP          FOL B
      ---------------61-TRUDY
```

FIG. 2.

Figure 1 is part of a page from the Source Index for the first quarter of 1964 and here you will see we have a paper which has two authors: A. C. R. Dean and Sir Cyril Hinshelwood. You will see that the second author has had his name truncated. They published a paper called 'Some basic aspects to cell regulation' in *Nature,* volume 201, page 232, in 1964 which had 96 references. The issue number of *Nature* was 4916 and the ISI accession number was 49833. Now these 96 references have been taken and distributed to form the Citation Index, and this is the relevant extract from the Citation Index. One of the references (See Figure 2) was to a paper by Midgley in *Biochim. Biophys. Acta* in 1962, volume 61, page 513. Here you see beneath the reference of this paper a reference to the paper by Dean and Hinshelwood in *Nature.* You will also observe that Midgley's paper has been cited in the same period by Brown, in the *Proceedings of the National Academy of Science* in the United States, by Doi in the *Journal of Bacteriology* and by Moyer in *Archives of Biochemistry.* You can see that the citations given in the papers by these authors have been sorted alphabetically by the cited author, thus bringing these four references to Midgley's paper together. If you like to think of all the citations used in writing a scientific paper as being to some extent the ancestors of that paper, then we may think of the Citation Index as being a list of ancestors with their associated descendants.

The *Science Citation Index,* from which I have drawn this illustration, is a multi-disciplinary service, including all scientific disciplines in its journal coverage. Other citation indexes have been confined to one subject area, such as the *Genetics Citation Index,* also produced by the Institute for Scientific Information, in 1963, and the index to statistics which is being produced by Dr. John W. Tukey. Some have been produced as indexes to the material appearing in one journal, the outstanding example being the index to volumes 1-31 of the *Annals of Mathematical Statistics.* This has a citation index to papers appearing in the *Annals,* arranged by author, which gives the reference to the paper, a reference to the abstract or abstracts of the paper (eight abstracting journals were searched to provide this), references to papers in the *Annals* citing the original, and references to papers in *other* journals citing the original, these last being produced by searching 37 journals in the statistical field, the proceedings of three Symposia, and three presentation volumes. In addition a subject index in great depth to papers and often to the content of specific pages is given, and, a most interesting feature, a 'forwards' citation index, collecting and listing the citations *to* other journals by authors of papers appearing in the *Annals.* This index was produced without the aid of a computer. The index to the *Journal of the American Statistical Association,* vols. 35-50, also includes in its author index a note of subsequent citing papers in the *Journal,* but in no other journal, and so is on rather a small scale. It also was hand-prepared. Tukey reports two other citation indexes, one a *Bibliography of non-parametric statistics,* by I. R. Savage, Harvard University Press, containing 'for each item indications of the other items in the bibliography which were known to refer to or, in the compiler's judgment, should have referred to the item in question'; the other is the annual index to *IRE Trans. of the Professional Group on Information Theory,* 1958 to date, which contains, as an 'Index to Footnote References', an author-ordered list of footnote citations from that volume to all items. A citation index appears in the *Bibliography of aquatic sciences,* compiled by the Food and Agriculture Organisation. A citation index to the published proceedings of the two UN International Conferences in Peaceful Uses of Atomic Energy was compiled by Itek Laboratories for experimental purposes, and work involved has been reported by Ben-Ami Lipetz. The index is not publicly available. Another index was also prepared by Lipetz in a limited part of the field of physics, in connection with an experimental evaluation of the impact of a citation index.

Finally, the Short Papers contributed to the Theme Sessions of the 26th annual meeting of the American Documentation Institute, in December 1963, published in two volumes under the title *Automation and scientific communication* contains a citation index to all the references cited in the papers arranged by author and giving the full bibliographic details, including titles, of all citations, and additionally a KWIC index to these references. This was prepared on an IBM 1401.

We have seen that citation indexes can be prepared covering a large part of the field of science and technology, or specific areas, or to one journal-series, or indeed to any body of literature. They can be annual, cumulative or 'once-for-all' jobs, depending on the nature of the subject and the material. They can be arranged by author, by journal, or even, if specific to a particular journal, by initial page of the cited item, as has been suggested. They are flexible devices and can be arranged in whatever form is most suited to the needs and convenience of the user. They *can* be prepared by hand, but if they are to be of any size or cover more than a very small body of literature, or if speed of production is important then computer processing is essential.

To demonstrate this last point, we may note that the 1964 *Science Citation Index* has 151,639 source journal articles from 700 journals, carrying a total of 1,789,753 citations, which when sorted and arranged give references to 1,092,384 unique authored items by 323,889 authors.

Machine processing, however, does not solve all the problems, one such problem being that of inaccurate citation by authors. Different journals have different policies regarding references, and where one journal may encourage authors to give full references, showing the cited author's name and initials, journal, volume, page-numbers, date and full title of cited work, others may drop the initials, title of cited work and journal page-numbers, and of course may very often produce their own version of abbreviated journal title. A surprising number of authors think it adequate to refer to ' Berichte ', without stating whether *Chemische Berichte* or *Physikalische Berichte,* is meant, or to Ann., meaning Annalen or Annals, without specifying which of the seventy-odd journals, to which the abbreviation could be applied, is meant. Something can often be done by skilful programming to offset the source author's varied citation habits; if one has three references, one to a paper by SNAPE, *tout court,* one to SNAPE F and one to SNAPE F H, then if the page, journal and year are the same for the three references, all three will be brought together under the longest entry. But, of course, if an author has used an incorrect citation, citing, for example, a non-existent journal, then this error cannot always be corrected.

Citation indexes have had a mixed reception. My own opinion, based largely on personal contacts, is that scientists are on the whole rather in favour of them, while librarians are much more cautious.

As an illustration of the scientist's view—perhaps an extreme view—Dr. J. M. Hammersley, reviewing the index to the *Annals of Mathematical Statistics* in *Nature*, said, 'Librarianship in the future will become a task less for the bibliophile and more for the electronic engineer. With the publication of these indexes . . . the writing is already on the library wall'. Examples of the librarian's view are harder to come by, but a representative view is expressed by E. M. Keen, who wondered '. . whether the citation index would look so attractive if similar effort were being expended on conventional indexes'.

We know that following up references cited in relevant papers is the scientist's most favoured method of obtaining information; it is not therefore very surprising that a device which allows them to follow references in time as well as backwards is greeted with enthusiasm. I suspect that there is another attraction for the scientist. We know too that using a library card index to gain information is second in unpopularity among scientists only to asking a librarian for assistance. (We do not know why this antipathy exists, we only know at present that it does—and deploring the fact does not change it.) A citation index allows them to attack the literature directly, in a way to which they are accustomed, without benefit of intermediaries, and I believe that this is a factor which possibly influences many scientists' initial acceptance of the Citation Index.

Before we discuss specific methods of using it we must be clear on one point. The Source Index is in effect an author index to all items published in the titles covered by the *Science Citation Index* in the particular year for which the index is issued, but the Citation Index itself is *not* an author index, and should not be used as such. It is an index to specific documents which are cited by those other documents which form the Source Index, and is arranged by first author purely for the convenience of the user. It should not be used for compiling author bibliographies, firstly because it lists first authors only, and secondly because a first author's paper will only form an entry *if* it has been cited by one of the items in the Source Index.

The basic assumption upon which citation indexing rests is that there is some connection between a scientific paper and those other papers which it cites. That is to say, we assume a cited paper and the paper which cites it are roughly dealing with the same subject. This is a considerable over-statement which I shall now qualify.

The author may cite because his paper is a continuation of previous work by himself or by another, or to substantiate or refute previous work, or to compare or contrast the previous work with his own or because he is questioning previous work or applying previous work. He may in the introduction to his own paper be summarising or referring to a large body of previous work—in a sense performing the ritual obeisances to the father figures of his particular sub-discipline. Very often he will be citing previous work as a sort of shorthand to save himself the necessity of adducing proof of a particular point at length. He may, indeed, if not over-scrupulous in these matters, be merely interested in dazzling the bystanders with a display of his own erudition or adding corroborative detail, intended to give artistic verisimilitude to an otherwise bald and unconvincing narrative—but in general a citation implies a relationship between a part or the whole of the cited paper and a part or the whole of the citing paper. By following the subsequent citations of a paper one is tracing the history of an idea, discovering where and how it has been used or applied and whether it is sustained or refuted or absorbed into later work.

How then is a Citation Index used? The normal approach would be to take a paper which you know to be relevant to your needs and interests and to turn to the Citation Index to discover in what subsequent publications this paper has been cited. If you find it has been cited in later papers you may then turn to the Source Index and look at the titles of these later papers and decide from the titles which of these papers you wish to see. Then you may 'cycle'. You collect those papers whose references you have discovered, select those which are relevant and look at their bibliographies to find further relevant references. You would look at these further references and select the most appropriate as further entry points to the Citation Index. Thus you will speedily collect a body of literature, which is relevant to your immediate need, by moving from Citation Index to Source Index and back again as many times as need be, at each stage sifting the discovered material for relevance either by scanning titles or the discovered papers themselves.

Human nature being what it is, at this point two questions usually spring to mind. The first question is: 'Suppose I do not find that my original paper is cited at all. Does this mean that I will find nothing?' And the second is: 'If my first paper is cited and I am able to start cycling, does this mean that I am going to find too much?' To answer the first question it is quite possible that your entry paper has not been cited, although if it were not cited in 1961, 1964 or 1965 (the

three years for which the *Science Citation Index* has so far been published) then this suggests either that your paper is on such a specialised topic that no one else has done any subsequent work upon its theme—which is worth knowing anyway—or that it was not a particularly good paper in the first place. However, all is not lost. Your entry paper itself probably has some references appended to it and these themselves may be used as entry points to the Citation Index. You may find on looking at the Index that the particular paper you have in mind has not been cited but that some other papers by the same author have been, and you may be able to decide that one or more of these will serve as a suitable starting point. Generally though, if you are beginning a search on a specific subject it is unlikely that you have only been able to find one key reference as an entry to the index.

On the second point, that of finding too many references of varying degrees of relevance, we must not forget the ability to filter the returns according to our particular needs by using either the discovered titles or the discovered papers themselves. The fact that a fairly large number of references may be discovered is not in itself a bad thing. All we are doing when we are using a published index is to select from the enormous library gathered by the whole index, a sub-library of material of greater specificity to our needs than the whole, which in almost all cases must be subject to some evaluatory process carried out by the person whose information need is the subject of search. For example, if we enter the Citation Index with a paper dealing with a certain experimental technique, we would expect to find a number of papers concerned with the applications of that technique, some concerned perhaps with modifications of it, some with further associated techniques, one or two perhaps refuting its validity. A manufacturer of apparatus might be more concerned with different applications, an experimentalist with allied techniques, other research workers and naturally the original worker himself with modifications of the technique, and presumably everybody in possible refutations. The point I am trying to make is that having gathered a body of literature, which is in a broad sense about the specific topic, then part of that body will be relevant to some enquirer, other parts to other enquirers, and however refined the type of indexing applied it seems to me over-idealistic to expect to be able to present a seeker after information not only with *all* the information he requires but also with *only* the information he requires. What is noise to some is very relevant to others.

I have reported elsewhere the results of some small-scale tests of the performance of the *Science Citation Index*, and I shall not this evening repeat the figures I obtained. Instead, I shall give you some opinions, based on studies made by myself and others. In terms of information retrieval on a specific subject, whether the subject is defined in words (as it must be to approach the subject index of an abstracting service) or in citations, the *Science Citation Index* performance is comparable to that of one of the larger abstracts journals; a real comparison is not strictly practicable, because citation indexing is more flexible than a formal subject index, and because the types of information produced by the two sorts of index are not the same—it is rather like trying to compare kippers with bananas, but to pursue this analogy, kippers and bananas are both foods, and it is possible to say to what extent one finds each satisfying. I think I have already demonstrated, in reporting on some tests of

abstracts services carried out at Aslib, that no abstracts service is comprehensive, and that to approach even 90% coverage of a topic it is necessary to use a number of services, each of which adds a little more to the total. Similarly, some unique items would always be added to your search product by using the *Science Citation Index,* and taken on its own, one could expect to find a satisfactory proportion of the total sought.

Where the Citation Index scores over an abstracts service is in its interdisciplinary nature. Because its source journals cover the whole field of science, it is not bound as are most abstracts services to one discipline, and consequently may not only be expected to provide a reasonable coverage of many disciplines but also can indicate the links between disciplines, the ' cross-fertilisation ' effect of an idea originating in one branch of science which is applicable or useful to another.

It must be remembered, though, that a Citation Index is essentially only a guide to the existence of information and not a container of information in itself, in the sense that an abstracting service is. Whereas a volume of abstracts may serve in some cases as a substitute for original documents, this is practically never true of a Citation Index. The Citation Index is a tool which can only be exploited to the full in a large library, or in a situation where the user has access to a large library. Ideal situations in which one might hope to find a Citation Index are the Patent Office Library and the Science Library—neither of which has one—or in a university library. However, as the existence of the National Lending Library makes an extremely large collection available to all, there is no reason why a Citation Index should not be useful in smaller libraries.

I am sure that I could not find a better audience to which to express the view that normal subject indexing is an intellectual process, and I hope I shall not be misunderstood when I say that to me one of the attractions of citation indexing is that it is *not*. What I mean by this is that citation indexing of documents does not require the same analytical effort as normal indexing. If citation practice and journal title abbreviations were standardised, citation indexing would be an essentially clerical process, and if, as Tukey and Waldhart suggest, a Permuted Title Index to the source citations were added, it would still remain a clerical job. Given the computer programmes, and some high grade clerical effort in the initial preparation of the input data, very large numbers of documents can be indexed by machine methods, very quickly. If this discourages you, remember that citation indexing is not a substitute or replacement for conventional indexing; it is a new form of indexing in its own right, and is an *additional* and parallel means of access to the literature. And as one can only apply it to material which carries citations, it will not be applicable to a large proportion of published books.

What will be the future of Citation Indexing?

One recent development is that the Institute for Scientific Information is offering an Automatic Subject Citation Alert service, ASCA. Subscribers to the service submit a 'profile' of bibliographic citations reflecting their subject interests—they pick, say, fifty papers in their own field which they consider to be very much on their principal subject interests—and they receive every week a computer printout describing every current item in the ISI coverage that cites any of the question-citations in their 'profile'. (They may also use as profile items the name of an author, whether first author or no, the name of an organisation, the name of a patent assignee, or a US Patent Class.) This is considerably cheaper than a subscription to the *Science Citation Index*, and being a weekly service, more up-to-date. As the ASCA service and the *Science Citation Index* are produced from the same data, the one may be considered as an extract from the other, tailored to the individual user.

Another interesting use of citations has been their use as one of the means of access to the literature store of the Massachusetts Institute of Technology Technical Information Project, under the direction of Dr. M. M. Kessler. Very briefly, this is a computer-stored collection compiled largely from the periodic physics literature. 'For each of the articles in each of the twenty-one journals the location of the article (journal, volume, page) is recorded, the title, authors, the institutional affiliation of the authors, the citations (journal, volume, page), the location of the article in *Physics Abstracts* (when this information becomes available), and subject-index information if the latter is available from a published source. The above information is punched on cards, verified, edited, and transferred to magnetic tape for permanent storage. This tape is then edited by the computer to detect clerical errors and transferred to an assigned location on the computer disc memory where it is immediately available for manipulation or search.'

'The computer facility at the project's disposal is an IBM 7094 operating in remote, time-sharing fashion. This facility is itself an experimental project (Project MAC). It consists of a central computer with 100 remote consoles having access to its facilities. The consoles are standard teletype machines presently distributed at various locations around the MIT campus. Contact with the computer is by means of ordinary telephone connections. The 100 consoles are available to perhaps 400 people who can at any time try to use the computer on a time-sharing basis. As many as thirty people may use the computer at the same time.'

By making requests to the store via one of the consoles, access may be had to the literature, using authors' names, words in titles, journal volumes and so on, or by using a citation to demand all papers in the store which cite a specified document. The response to this last query will be a list of journal papers, so that the output from the console looks very much like an entry in the citation index. Further description of this system can be found in the various published papers of Dr. Kessler.

This evening I have told you what a Citation Index is and a little about its performance characteristics. I have not said much about how it will be used in practice, because citation indexes have not yet been available for long enough to enable us to assess their impact on literature-use habits of scientists and information workers. There is another aspect of citation data which I have not touched on at all; this is their use in historical and sociological studies of science itself. It will be obvious to you that citations provide a powerful tool in the study of networks of scientific papers, and consequently in the study of the development and ramification of scientific thought and progress. I feel that its possibilities in this direction, discussed by Dr. Garfield in a recent report, ' The Use of Citation Data in writing the history of Science ', and by Professor Derek de Solla Price in several papers notably ' Networks of Scientific Papers '

in the journal *Science* last year, have still barely been explored, and many uses remain to be found for this fascinating and valuable source of data. But this is to touch on a hobby-horse of my own, and a hobby-horse which I shall not ride tonight.

A Short Reading List on Citation Indexing and its Uses

Garfield, E. 'Citation indexing : a natural science literature retrieval system for the social sciences.' *American Behavioural Scientist.* VIII, June 10th, 1964, 58-61.

Garfield, E. 'Science Citation Index—a new dimension in indexing.' *Science,* 144, 3619, May, 1964, 649-654.

Garfield, E., Sher, I. H. 'New factors in the evaluation of scientific literature through citation indexing.' *American Documentation,* 54, July, 1963, 195-201.

Garfield, E., Sher, I. H., Torpie, R. J. *The use of citation data in writing the history of science.* Philadelphia, Institute for Scientific Information, 1964.

Kessler, M. M. 'The MIT Technical Information Project.' *Physics Today,* 16, March 3rd, 1965, 28-36.

Kessler, M. M., Heart, F. E. *Concerning the probability that a given paper will be cited.* Massachusetts Institute of Technology, November, 1962.

Martyn, J. 'An examination of citation indexes.' *Aslib Proceedings,* 17, June 6th, 1965, 184-196.

Pipetz, Ben-Ami. 'Evaluation of the impact of a citation index in physics.' *American Institute of Physics,* September, 1964.

Price, D. J. de S. 'Networks of scientific papers.' *Science,* 149, July 30th, 1965, 510-515.

Waldhart, T. J. *A preliminary analysis of the Science Citation Index.* Thesis on microfilm, University of Wisconsin, 1964.

Tukey, J. W. 'Keeping research in contact with the literature : citation indices and beyond. *Journal of Chemical Documentation,* 2, January 1st, 1962, 34-37.

Genetics Citation Index. Evaluation Survey. Washington, D.C., Science Communication, Inc., April, 1964. Contract NSF C—330.

Effective use of the Science Citation Index. A programmed text. Philadelphia, Institute for Scientific Information, 1964.

Subject Bibliographies in Information Work

K. Boodson

The purpose of bibliographies and their use in information retrieval; notes on history and development, types of bibliography, and the components and features of a subject bibliography; the function of abstracts and the importance of effective indexing; concludes with a section on the Bibliographical Guide as a literature searching tool.

Introduction

Heard less now, threadbare in impact through repetition, the phrase "information explosion" was for many years in constant use in the information world. Certainly the reference to an explosion was justified, represented by a phenomenal growth in the number of published works, largely periodicals of great diversity containing a mass of contributed articles of equally diverse variety and merit. But how justified was it to refer to this as an "information explosion"; would the description "publication explosion" be less of a misnomer? The scientist would relate this growth to a vast increase in scientific research in new and expanding fields; the economist would study the economics of publishing; and possibly the sociologist might concern himself with prestige, personal and national, as a force behind publishing. But might it not be postulated that an exponential growth in the number of published articles would be complemented by a lineal growth in the sum total of information?

Whatever the factors behind the explosion, scientists, research workers and information workers needed to know what had been published, to sift and sieve the mass and retrieve that information relevant to their own work and interests. To this end, and parallel with the growth in primary publications, there was an increase in secondary sources, the information tools used in searching the literature for profiled information. Pending some expansion and definition later in the article, it will be convenient to think of these secondary sources as having the same form and function as bibliographies, particularly the subject bibliography. It is this type that I shall be concerned with, against a more general and perhaps scanty survey of bibliographies and their place in the information world.

The librarian and information officer, each working with facts and data in his particular hall of knowledge, is regularly surprised by the unfamiliarity shown by scientists, students and research workers towards bibliographies and other sources of information. In his searching,

Reprinted from *The Indexer* 10, no. 1 (April 1976): 15–23.

the librarian may use personal contacts with specialists, reference and data handbooks, text-books, encyclopaedias, periodicals and scientific journals, monographs and reviews, research reports, conference reports, catalogues, standard specifications, patent specifications, theses, citation indexes, and bibliographies.

The science (and art) of finding facts from these sources is known professionally as "information retrieval". It is a less absolute science than most, and the professional worker comes to recognise and accept its restrictions and limitations, these deriving largely from the economics of information handling, the effectiveness of systems, and the mass to be handled. Estimates of the number of articles published throughout the world each year now reach seven figures, and a recent cumulative total for the last 20 years was 30m. Repetitive publication, summary and digest articles, open plagiarism, may reduce this by a significant factor, but the mass remaining forces an information service to operate within two precepts: (a) that economic factors will impose limits on the effectiveness of the service in supplying information from its own resources, and (b) that no means exist by which the full information on a subject can be produced. It is often the subject bibliography in its various forms that enables the individual information worker to operate as effectively as possible within these precepts.

Definitions

Politicians and scientists abuse language equally, enclosing words either into strait-jackets or into off-the-peg portmanteau suits to accommodate the meaning they wish. In our own science of information there is sometimes a tendency to this, and it is likely that my own connotation of the word bibliography will differ from that of the antiquarian or the bookseller. There is the further difference between bibliography and *a* bibliography, between systematic and critical bibliography; the study of books, book-making and book usage, the world of the bibliophile on the one hand, and the compiled guide to literature on the other. Looking at *O.E.D.* we have

"a list of the books of a particular author, printer or country, or of those dealing with any particular theme; the literature of a subject."

What we are now concerned with is mainly the scientific information bibliography, used to locate published knowledge on a subject. For these one

might hope for a further expansion in the next edition of *O.E.D.*, to cover the current usage by the professional:

" a guide, annotated or otherwise, to the book, periodical, report, and other primary source literature of a subject', often referred to as a 'secondary source'."

History and development of bibliographies

Against the more precise definition, bibliographies are comparatively recent, but in the wider sense they have a long history. The scholarly text by Theodore Besterman[1] describes the history of bibliographies from the earliest times; I am indebted to this work for the following notes on some of the outstanding developments.

The earliest bibliographies were the lists of an author's works, usually included by the author in one of his later volumes. A list of this type appeared in a collection of Galen's works, printed in Venice in 1525 from a 2nd century MS.; it gave about five hundred titles in a classified arrangement. A number of early MS. works had similar lists, or were in the form of compiled histories of the lives of various writers and included lists of the works of each. In general, the invention of printing did little to advance the development of bibliography, and early printed books continued the form of listing found in MSS. J. Tritheim, however, issued a number of bibliographical works with new features. His *History of ecclesiastical writers*[2], 1494, gave a chronological arrangement of about 1,000 authors, with brief biographical notes and a list of works by each one, with a total of some 7,000 titles.

What may be considered as the earliest subject bibliography appeared between 1545 and 1555. This was Gesner's *Universal bibliography*[3-5], with a subject index and appendix. The main volume with the appendix reported some 15,000 titles of 3,000 authors. These were complemented by the *Pandectarum*, in which the items were indexed under twenty-one main classes, each sub-divided, followed by a detailed subject index to the class headings: Gesner made various contributions to bibliography, and is perhaps the first writer to approach bibliography as a science and to introduce logical methods.

A major national bibliography which appeared towards the end of the 16th century was Maunsell's *Catalogue of English printed books*[6]; this also introduced important developments in bibliographical science. The Catalogue took the form of an alphabetically arranged subject bibliography, the more important subject groups being sub-divided. In each group, the titles were also in alphabetical order; authors' surnames were used throughout. The bibliographic description used by Maunsell was comparable to the modern bibliographic form.

With these and other works, the foundations of bibliographical science had been prepared by the 17th century, but the importance of bibliography was not recognised until later, and its development as a science did not take place until late in the 18th century, when the first analytical guides to literature began to appear.

A brief history of indexing[7] refers to subject indexes in 16th century printed works; the earliest, however, in 1525, omitted page references, becoming just an alphabetical list of contents. Two editions of *Urbinatis Anglicae historicae*, by Polydor Virgil, 1546 and 1555, had quite detailed subject indexes, the later one with page and line references. The earliest indexed work which the author found in English was *The naturelle history* of C. Plinius Secundus, translated by Philemus Holland in 1601. Thus recognition of the need for some guidance to the subject matter of a book appeared quite early; in the 20th century demand for effective indexing, parallel with the increasing complexity of information retrieval and the growing use of subject bibliographies, has given rise to intensive study of indexing techniques and methodology.

Types of bibliographies

Regarding bibliographies in their basic form as a listing of information sources, there are five main features which put them into various categories:

(a) Data: the form in which information is given in the entry. It may vary from merely author, title and date for a simple reading list, to full details of article title, author, periodical source, place of publication etc. in a subject bibliography.

(b) Annotations: whether annotated or not. The annotation may vary from a brief explanatory sentence to a detailed summary of the subject matter of a scientific article or report.

(c) Format: overall presentation of material. The arrangement of the entries will depend on the needs of the user and the intention of the compiler, and may be by date, by author, in subject groups, by title, or possibly by some special feature such as place of origin.

(d) Indexing: inclusion of author and subject indexes. There are few bibliographies whose value is not enhanced by some form of indexing, and in subject lists it should be considered essential.

(e) Form of publication: single document or periodical publication.

With the bibliography in information work, there is a further natural distinction between those concerned with book and report literature, single complete documents on the one hand, and those dealing with periodical literature on the other. Very broadly, new knowledge and developments are reported in periodicals, digested, and become established to appear in the contents of books. Searching for established information thus starts with the book index and contents list. In some searches this may give the full answer required. But to cover not only established book information, but to check also what has been published in scientific journals in the past and what is currently being reported, the book search must be followed by reference to suitable bibliographies as secondary sources and possibly issues of recent current journals.

The results of an information search will probably be in one of three forms: (a) specific data, e.g. vapour pressure of methyl chloride at room temperature, coefficient of friction of bronze against nickel-steel, etc., (b) a list of source publications where information on the subject can be found, or (c) a digest of published information relevant to the enquiry, with summaries (abstracts) of each article or source, and full details of the original reference. This means that there is a growing degree of complexity, effort required and cost, between the simple search and the extended digest bibliography.

Possibly the most elementary form of subject bibliography is the un-annotated list of main texts on a topic, with subject indexing for more extensive ones. The introduction of annotations should increase the value of any such list, at the same time, however, multiplying the cost and raising the level of experience required to do the work involved. A large number of guides of this kind are published, or are produced internally by information units of various organizations. A more sophisticated approach which has become popular in recent years is the "Guide to the literature of . . ." or "How to find out about . . .". These take the form of written texts on the literature of a subject, describing and assessing main and auxiliary works. Schutze[8] lists over 1,000 in his main work and supplements. The sources covered are generally books and reports, with notes of the titles of periodicals which deal with the subject in question.

The worker with scientific literature is very largely concerned with information in the separate contributions to the periodicals, and among his major working tools will be the different guides to this information. The most prolific is the abstract journal, published at regular intervals, and carrying digests of the information contained in current issues of periodicals within a determined subject field. This may be confined as with *Rare Earth Metals*, or quite comprehensive as with *Chemical Abstracts* (which includes information in ancillary fields well outside the conventional connotation of chemistry) or the Russian *Referativnyi Zhurnal*. Nearly every branch of science and technology is represented by one or more of these abstract journals, a number produced by institutional organizations or commercially, and available against an annual subscription, others prepared as "in-house" publications by individual companies. In compiling the "in-house" journal, the information staff have the great advantage in abstracting of highlighting matters of specific company interest which could be passed over in a more general summary; there is also, in general, a significant gain in reducing delay between the date of publication of the original and the appearance of the abstract. In addition to the periodical devoted solely to abstracts, there are a number of commercial and institutional publications which include a section of abstracts in each issue.

Whereas the abstract journal is designed for awareness of current information and for literature searching, a parallel series of compilations can be used for guidance to literature over a set period. These are in the form of narrative and evaluative reviews, bringing together in a single text an assessment of knowledge and developments reported in a subject, the text being accompanied by a full bibliography and usually having subject and author indexes. Some are

in the form of monographs, supplemented and brought up-to-date at intervals, while a number appear as "Annual reviews of . . ." or "Reviews of progress in . . .". It is unfortunate that, in recent years, various factors have resulted in the disappearance or less frequent issue of a number of these most useful guides.

The citation index, a fairly recent advent to the information field, has a function similar to that of the abstract journal, but is based on a quite different approach. It consists basically of a list of source references arranged alphabetically by the names of authors cited in the literature, with entries chronologically under each cited author. Following the citation reference there are the details of the source article in which the citation is given. Citation indexes, of which perhaps *Science Citation Index* is the best known, are designed for computer operation, and are brought up-to-date at regular intervals. The subject index is likely to be of the "Key-word-in-context" (KWIC), "Key-word-out-of-context" (KWOC), or Permuterm type. The idea behind a citation index is that an initial check of one entry will lead by a chain reaction to all quoted and relevant work in that and related fields, to give a more comprehensive picture than might be obtained from a search of abstract journals using conventional subject indexing.

Elements and characteristics of a bibliography

Bibliographies, as with library catalogues, have a general function to retrieve information from a mass of documents; but the specific function may vary from locating and identifying a single document, to a detailed study and assessment of what is available on a subject. The compiler will determine the format and contents accordingly, and should then consider:

(a) definition of the subject scope
(b) period to be covered in the search
(c) sources to be searched for references
(d) basis of selection and inclusion of material
(e) arrangement and presentation of material
(f) format for entries
(g) abstracts and abstracting policy
(h) extent and lay-out of indexes.

As far as practicable, consideration of the user and his needs should be paramount, but economic and labour factors are likely to exert dominant influences on the form which the final product takes; overall time devoted to the work, level of abstracting and indexing, format and appearance are more likely to be related to cost than to ideal requirements.

Two features of the bibliography do not affect the general user, but are of some concern to the librarian. These are the form of the source reference, and the abbreviation used if any for the periodical title. Details which should be provided in the reference and the form of printing are specified in BS 1629 *Bibliographical references*, with permissible variations. When these are followed, the particulars of the article required are clearly set out, and there is no confusion between volume numbers, part numbers, dates and pages, as is often the case. I have met, for example, the form *in extremis*

Iron Age, 73; 66.

with no further guidance as to whether it is vol. 73, p.66; p.73, vol. 66; p.73, 1966; or p.66, 1973. These are in practice possibly librarians' matters, but in present circumstances, particularly where photocopying of periodical articles has to a great extent become standard procedure in borrowing and lending, accuracy and precision of a source reference is important, and will of course be of benefit to the library user in reducing the number of queries. There is, however, still great diversity in the styles used in periodical reference lists, although BS 1629 has been available since 1950.

There are also wide variations in the abbreviated form used for the periodical title. It is normal in a reference list to shorten the title for most periodicals, certainly desirable, for example, with *Transactions of the American Society of Mechanical Engineers; (A) Journal of Engineering for Power*, if not necessarily for *Journals of Metals* or *Library World*. Some organizations have developed their own guide rules and standard conventions for abbreviating, but there is a tendency now to follow the contracted forms used either by the American Chemical Society in *Chemical Abstracts* (a list of periodicals abstracted with their contractions is issued by A.C.S.) or those of the *World List of Scientific Periodicals* (the *British Union Catalogue of Periodicals incorporating World List of Scientific Periodicals*).

As with the details of the reference, confusion over titles can be avoided by following a standard and recognised form. Both the A.C.S. list and the

World List, for example, have prescribed forms for *Metall, Metallurg, Metallurgia, Metallurgie* and *Metallurgist*, but these titles may be found in non-standard bibliographies with the abbreviation "Metall." or even "Met.", indiscriminately. It is helpful, especially in an extensive bibliography, to indicate whether one of the standard lists has been followed.

Abstracts and abstracting

There has been much debate on the justification and need for annotations, summaries and abstracts in bibliographies generally and in scientific subject bibliographies in particular. It is mostly accepted that they add value to a list, to give details of the physical features and special characteristics of an item in a bookseller's list perhaps, to indicate the trend of a scientific article, or at the highest level to provide a reader with the essential facts from an article so that he need not necessarily refer to the original from which the abstract has been prepared. It is this third function, often in relation to limited distribution sources and foreign periodicals which are difficult of access, that is most significant. It is also the most debated, the arguments centring on whether it is possible to satisfy the scientist or research worker with information in an abstract however detailed, or whether he will still need to see the original text. The preparation of abstracts at this level is expensive in any case, and requires staff with good qualifications and experience; it can generally only be undertaken by large organizations on a cooperative or subscription basis.

A relevant and classic comment, valid at the time although less so since computerization, was that of F. T. Sisco[9] about 18 years ago:

"If a research job in the U.S.A. costs less than $100,000, it is cheaper to do it than to find out if it has been done before and reported in the literature."

This referred to the situation in metallurgical literature, a field in which there have since been major improvements and developments in the source guides, in addition to the significant advances in indexing techniques generally.

Cost aspects and divergency of views on their value have led to two accepted forms of abstract, the indicative and the informative. The former is intended to give the reader guidance to decide for himself whether he should see the original; it indicates the type of article, level of treatment and author's approach, but does not generally include specific data. The second sets out in summary the main data, author's aim, equipment and methods used, main findings, and conclusions. The object here is to relieve the reader of the necessity to see the original article.

An abstractor is not called upon to make critical assessment of any aspect of an article or reported work, although some information workers have suggested this responsibility. My own opinion is that any form of criticism by an abstractor is wrong, other than that which rests with him in the selection or exclusion of material for abstracting. His job is to present a summary of the factual content of the article; it would seem unlikely that he would often be in a position to evaluate those facts.

As a working tool in information services, abstracts may be used in a current or retrospective function. Individuals in an organization must be fed promptly and regularly with selections from currently published literature. This may be done by some form of "current awareness" bulletin, a periodical listing of abstracts covering the interests of and distributed throughout the whole organization; or it may be by some system of "selective dissemination of information", whereby individuals receive only abstracts of direct interest to them. Retrospective use of abstracts, part of the business of information retrieval, is usually in the production of a bibliographic list of summaries, to give information from source articles relevant to a particular subject enquiry. The data base searched in the preparation of a list will often be the files of the library's "current awareness" bulletin; where fuller information and a wider search is needed, or where the enquiry is outside the subject scope of the bulletin, other suitable abstract journals will be used for the search.

The high cost of producing abstracts, which has led many libraries to rely on subscription abstract journals rather than produce their own "in-house" bulletin, has also resulted in some experimental work in auto-abstracting by computer. Word frequency and usage in an article form the basis of the approach, the assumption being that an author will use constantly the established terms and pertinent expressions of his subject. Computer scanning of the text against prepared "significance factors" results in the selection and print-out of regularly repeated phrases in order of significance factor, to produce the abstract. Developments of this kind are certain to progress as O.C.R. and text scanning techniques develop; but how far computer technology may effectively take the place of creative and evaluative mental effort remains debatable.

Another novel approach which combines abstracting and indexing has also been suggested. With this, a prepared "summary" of the contents of an article is reduced to significant "data lines", which are converted to key-word chains to be used as index entries. For example, a summary:

> "Titanium, added to high-tensile steel with C content between 0.5 and 1.5%, gave fine grain structure, superior to that obtained with established additives"

would give key-word chains:

(1) Titanium — additive — high-tensile steel — grain structure
(2) Steel, high-tensile — grain structure — additives — titanium
(3) Steel, high-tensile — C content — grain structure — additives — titanium
(4) Steel, high-tensile — additives — titanium — grain structure
(5) Grain structure — fineness — steels — additives — titanium.

The key-words must be from an established thesaurus, to enable programmed co-ordination to retrieve effectively from the data base. It is unlikely that a system of this nature could form the basis of an informative abstract system, but it has possibilities at the indicative level.

Indexing

The value and effectiveness of a collection of abstracts will be determined by the quality of the indexing, and the index must be both efficient as a retrieval tool and acceptable from the searcher's point of view. The importance of acceptance by users should not be minimised. One has only to think of microfiche in information work generally to suggest that techniques dictated too largely by economic considerations, or theoretically cost-saving advances in information processing, are in practice self-defeating where the end-product is likely to be rejected by the user. There is also evidence of this situation with some forms of computer print-out indexes. Information workers become familiar with and accept unconventional forms; the scientist and general reader, using information and indexes as an adjunct to their main job, should not be expected to read extensive explanatory notes or have detailed instruction before being able to understand how an index works. In 1972 I.E.E. issued two parallel documents[10-11] on users' attitudes to indexes. The first was based on a study of reactions to various indexes in scientific abstract journals. Among the preferences shown by users were:

(a) accuracy
(b) ease of use
(c) lay-out and presentation
(d) choice of subject index headings
(e) optimum use of cross references
(f) overall effectiveness in practical use
(g) minimum amount of "noise".

The second report was concerned with the procedures used by scientific workers and information officers in making searches from *Seience Abstracts*. One conclusion was that users generally expected a high pre-coordination of index terms; most made a practice of going straight to the index for a pre-conceived concept of their own, and proceeded from there to more standard thesaurus-type descriptors if the first step was unfruitful. Information workers pondered and searched for alternative terms to a greater extent than did scientific workers. The need for a "lead-in" vocabulary, to take the user from his initial mental image concept to the correct descriptor used in the index, was apparent. Users without the specific subject knowledge found difficulty with some of the more specialised indexes and needed assistance.

The truism that only a participant can know the real effort involved in any activity certainly applies to indexing and the production of an effective index; in an extensive collection of abstracts the work may equate to that in the compilation and production of the abstracts. In 1958 (pre-computer days) one half of the total effort in producing *Chemical Abstracts* was devoted to the indexing; it took between two and five years to train an indexer from Ph.D. to the required level.

One attempt to reduce the total effort in indexing followed the principles used in auto-abstracting methods, mentioned earlier. An extension of this is the Permuterm index, in which all significant words in a title, excluding articles etc., are used as main descriptors in the index; under each, in alphabetical order, are put as subterms all other main words of the title. Another

suggestion has been to eliminate both abstracting and indexing by putting into computer store the whole unprocessed text of documents. Natural language questions put to the computer are converted against a thesaurus to give suitable matching words, and the stored data base is searched for relevancy.

Advances in computer technology will tend to lower the level at which computerisation of information work becomes economically justified and, correspondingly, the proportion of mental to machine activity in the system. But at basis in this field the computer remains, and is likely to remain, a sophisticated machine whose operational efficiency is determined by the intellectual direction it receives.

Nevertheless, computers may be programmed to reduce if not eliminate the results of personal idiosyncrasies in the input. Indexing particularly will reflect strongly the personal approach and mental images of the compiler. C. L. Bernier[12] suggested the introduction of indexing specifications, on a par with engineering specifications.* These might cover the kind of index required, size, accuracy, terms and concepts, and format and typography. This is parallel to the ASI Guideline reported in the April 1975 issue; the forthcoming revision of BS 3700 on indexes for books, periodicals and other publications, was noted in this number, which also carried an article by F. Blum on the work of Committee Z39 of the American National Standards Institution. This committee is concerned with library work, documentation, and related publishing practices; among its current standards are:

Z39.4—1968: Basic criteria for indexes.

Z39.19—1974: Guidelines for thesaurus structure, construction and use.

It is desirable that codes and guidance should be available for indexing and indexes, and some aspects could no doubt be covered effectively by specifications. But there must be inherent difficulties in thinking of these along the lines of engineering specifications. Hardness, composition, heat treatment of a bolt may perhaps be comparable to such requirements as type-size, paper quality, number of entries per page, in an index. But specifying and achieving dimensional tolerance and overall dimensions in engineering bears little relationship to specifying

---

*Specifications prepared by the American Society of Indexers appear in our last issue.

and achieving accuracy and size in an index. How does an indexer, prior to commencing the index to a reasonably complicated text, organise his work to meet a specification, for example, for x total entries, y total subject headings, 2.9 mean terms per item, and an accuracy of 5 errors per 1,000 terms?

Another aspect of standardisation where some uniformity would be desirable, and with much wider implications than in indexing, is that of technological terms. One has only to compare various standard thesauri to see the wide diversity in selection of concepts in the same subject area. Recommendations for the general acceptance of a major and standard published thesaurus as a guide to preferred descriptors in a specific field might be an initial step in this direction.

Bibliographical guides

Abstracts and indexes loom large in the life of a librarian or information worker, concerned as he is with the retrieval and assessment of published material. But literature searches can be erratic in their results and sometimes extremely frustrating. Guides to literature and other sources of data have their inadequacies and limitations, both in compilation and in coverage of the subject, and their effectiveness in use is determined by indexing efficiency. The searcher must be alert to the existence of sources untapped by the retrieval tools which he is using, and to the overriding impact of his own searching efficiency, his understanding and use of the retrieval systems. It has been estimated, in this context, that searchers using only one abstract journal for a literature search could miss as much as one half of relevant published references in a specific subject field. A sobering thought for any information worker!

It seems logical to conclude that, all-in-all, there are no present means whereby information searching and retrieval can ensure that all the possible documents which might be relevant to an enquiry will be produced as a result of the search. Is it feasible to devise and operate any system which could achieve this? Major considerations are availability of material, effectiveness of worldwide co-operation, and the development of input and retrieval systems independent of human individuality. It is probable that both the practicalities and cost would be insurpassable barriers to any such scheme.

One must consider at what stage cost of searching for knowledge exceeds the benefit of having found it. Sisco's comment, quoted above, is applicable at various levels of searching. A research worker, for whom hardness data he needed had been found from standard sources for all except one of a number of alloys, would probably agree that it was preferable to establish the missing one in the laboratory, rather than search extensively in the literature.

One of the available types of guide to literature perhaps offers, by the nature of its approach, a higher benefit in access to literature in return for cost of effort than is general. This is the Bibliographical Guide, designed for retrospective searching, and offering selective access to published literature in a specific subject field. Important survey and review literature in the area, each item having its own list of references to related published work, is collected into one compilation, with detailed author and subject indexes. Typical are the works in a series published by MacDonald Scientific and Technical over a period of years from 1961. The indexing approach to one of these, on *Non-ferrous metals*, was described in the April 1975 issue of *The Indexer*.

The Bibliographical Guide does not attempt an exhaustive or comprehensive listing of all known references on the subject, but is regarded as a key reference work from which to start a survey. As with citation indexes, the searcher would, through the bibliographies and reference lists of items in the Guide, be provided with a conspectus of the whole subject literature. Since a variety of abstract journals, monographs and reviews, bibliographies, and original literature is consulted in the compilation of the text, it offers access to a much wider range of source literature in a more concise form than is generally possible.

Conclusion

Information handling, as the concern of the librarian and information officer, requires varied and diverse techniques in both data storage and retrieval. Equally, on the retrieval side, there is a wide variety of searching tools available, each suitable for a different type of data base or a specific form of information activity.

It should not be expected that one searching tool, a subject bibliography or a citation index or a KWIC index, could be used equally well for all types of retrieval search; this is as facile as thinking that all machining requirements in an engineering workshop might be met by one machine tool. The tool must be designed for the kind of work and adjusted by the operator for the

job in hand. Thus in information work bibliographies, as the most important class of retrieval
tool, are in many diverse forms, and the user
must understand the function and purpose of
each in relation to the retrieval job he is doing.
The parallel can, in fact, be taken further with
one of those oddities of terminology, the term
"indexing"; accuracy and effectiveness of indexing in a machine tool will determine the quality
of the end-product, and how true this will also
be of the bibliography.

References.

1. Besterman, T. *The beginnings of systematic bibliography*. O.U.P. 1935. pp.xii, 81.

2. Tritheim, J. *Liber de scriptoribus ecclesiasticis*. Basileae. 1494. ff. [vi], 140.

3. Gesner, C. *Bibliotheca universalis*. Tiguri. 1545. pp.[xviii], 631.

4. Gesner, C. *Pandectarum sive partitionum universalium . . . libri XXI*. Tiguri. 1548. pp.[vi], 374.

5. Gesner, C. *Appendix bibliothecae Conradi Gesneri*. Tiguri. 1555. pp. [xvi], 105.

6. Maunsell, A. *Catalogue of English printed books*. London. 1595. [2 vols].

7. Knight, G. Norman. "Book indexing in Great Britain: a brief history". *The Indexer* 6 (1) Spring 1968. pp.14-18. also in: *Jnl. Library History* 3 (2) April 1968. pp.166-172.

8. Schutze, G. *Bibliography of guides to the S-T-M literature: scientific, technical, medical*. New York. 1958. Suppts. 1958-1962, 1963.

9. Sisco, F. T. "What's in the literature". *Metal Progress* 72 (10) Oct. 1957. pp.122-124.

10. Hall, A. M. *User preference in printed indexes*. Inspec rept. R/72/7. I.E.E. July 1972. pp. 86.

11. Hall, A. M. *Case studies of the use of subject indexes*. Inspec rept. R/72/8. I.E.E. July 1972. pp.[vi], 15.

12. Bernier, C. L. "Index specifications". *The Indexer*, 9 (1) April 1974. pp.9-12.

Indexing a Bibliographical Guide

K. Boodson

Indexing of a large collection of scientific literature abstracts differs from that of a complete volume of uniform textual matter. The approach to the indexing of a collection of over 4,000 abstracts from the literature on non-ferrous metals is discussed, and special features of author and subject indexes are given, with some observations on the use of "see" and "see also" references. Pros and cons of continuous progressive, as opposed to terminal, indexing are examined.

Included are calculations and formulae, based on these indexes, which may be used to estimate the number of author entries and subject index terms in a comparable index to a volume of scientific abstracts, related to a postulated number of abstracts. The contribution concludes with notes on the records used and procedure followed in compiling the index.

The bibliography.

A bibliographical guide is one form of a diverse family of guides to literature under the general description of "bibliographies". All are intended to survey the literature of a subject; some bibliographies will do this extensively to cover all possible references, others selectively to provide only references to major contributions to the literature. *Non-ferrous metals—a bibliographical guide* (referred to subsequently as The Guide) is one of a series produced by Macdonald Scientific and Technical, and follows the pattern and intention of the others in the series. The aim was to

present a critical assessment of the literature through selection of important reviews and similar literature of a subject. Its main expected users, librarians, information workers, metallurgists, research workers and students, would be used to handling such bibliographies, and would, it was hoped, readily accept the form in which the text was presented; they would require a detailed and effective index.

Initially a publication date of August 1971 was agreed. Copy was due at the end of 1970, but actually delivered in February 1971. Some delays were experienced in proofing and galley alterations, and publication was late in 1972. Compilation started in April 1968, and abstracting finished at the end of 1970. The index was completed in April 1971, so that the work took just over three years in all.

The literature period covered by the abstracts was 1955 to 1970, with some earlier references where justified. Source literature was identified by studying *Metallurgical Abstracts* and the *A.S.M. Review of Metals Literature* (later combined as *Metals Abstracts*) and a selection of specialized abstract journals such as the *B.N.F.M.R.A. Bulletin* (under various titles), *Z.D.A. Abstracts*, etc. Reference lists in original source material were also checked. In the later stages of the project, scanning of current technical and scien-

280

Reprinted from *The Indexer* 9, no. 3 (April 1975): 93–100.

tific periodicals was done to supplement the other searching activities. The sources abstracted included a proportion of U.K. and other government reports. Abstracts, sequentially numbered throughout, were classified and arranged in main subject groups, divided into sub-groups where required, and by date order in each main or sub-group. It was often found that an abstract had some interest for two or perhaps three groups; extra copies were then prepared and filed in each relevant group.

The index.

The indexer of a completed collection of abstracts is in a position, as is the indexer of a published book text, to assimilate and (one hopes) generally comprehend the total content before he starts indexing. But with a progressive cumulation of abstracts, an annual volume of *Metals Abstracts*, for example, indexing may be done when the volume is completed or on a continuing basis as the collection of abstracts grows. Computerisation has enabled progressive indexing of a large body of abstracts to be done satisfactorily, with subject and author indexes to each monthly issue and in some cases periodic accumulations through the year. Although there is still a time lag before the appearance of the annual index volume, it compares favourably with the delays generally found in pre-computer days, particularly with complete volume indexing.

The compilation and indexing of The Guide suggested a parallel situation although on a smaller scale, certainly below computer level. The indexing could be left until abstracting was finished, and then tackled as a whole; this would certainly have eliminated some difficulties. Or it could be done continuously, with the expectation that delay between completion of the text and finalisation of the index would be reduced. After an intensive method study, it was decided to follow the second course; each approach had strong advantages and disadvantages, but the major deciding factors were the expected reduction in delay, and the value of having the growing index continually available for reference.

Another decision was to use a completely free vocabulary in the subject index, rather than a set thesaurus. It was still found useful to prepare a skeleton thesaurus on which the index could be built. Three standard thesauri were used for this, those published by the E.J.C.[1], the A.S.M.[2], and the English Electric Co. Ltd.[3]. These documents also proved valuable in checking term connotations during the exercise, and in selecting preferable terms.

Author index details.

The subject index was obviously going to require the major effort, but the author index produced its own trail of problems and queries; possibly professional library training tended to highlight some of these. A librarian cataloguing library accessions is building a catalogue which should be regarded not only as a guide to the collection but also as a reference tool, an authority to which reference may be made in dealing with bibliographic queries. The cataloguer, with this in mind, must check pseudonymous works to see if the original author can be established, must identify the correct forms of patronymics and complex oriental names, transliterate where necessary and relate transliterated variants of authors' names, and so on. I was concerned as to how far the bibliographer/indexer should accept similar responsibility, so that on completion his index might also be used as a reference authority, approaching the standard of an effective library catalogue. As an indexer (and not conditioned too strongly, I hope, by the body of work before me) I concluded that he did not have this responsibility. His was to index effectively the subject material in the form as presented, correcting patently obvious typographical errors, and perhaps drawing attention to suspected errors and suspect facts by the discreet use of *sic*.

The sort of oddity I have in mind is exemplified by two articles from German periodicals, both writers dealing with the quite specialised field of nuclear resonance spectroscopic analysis. In one case the author was given as *H. Pfister*, and in the second as *H. Pfisterer*. Coincidence of two authors of similar names, with the same initial and writing in the same highly specialised field, or an overlooked typing error? Here I did spend time trying to find an answer, but without success. The answer to the general question of the indexer's responsibility may lie with this example, of course, since the article would be referenced and sought for bibliographically under the separate forms of the names; the coincidence of their juxtaposition in an index merely reveals the oddity.

It was decided to put multiple entries for complex, hyphenated and prefixed names under the relevant components of the name, thus:

a. Nguyen-Quy-Dao *also under*
    Dao, Nguyen-Quy-

b. S. M. de De Micheli   under
    Micheli, S. M. de De   *and*
    de De Micheli, S. M.

The B.S. specification for transliteration[4] was used where required, the printed form given being followed otherwise. Obviously suspect variations were altered to avoid confusion, with a *see* reference from the original form. Thus a German transliteration to *Beljajew, A. I.*, was amended to *Belyaev, A. I.*, to correspond with an entry already established in this form. The author index included corporate body entries where an organization sponsored reported work or a series of reports, but not for the organization solely as publisher or where it was mentioned only as the location of research work reported in the document.

Subject index details.

As noted earlier, some published thesauri were used regularly in the selection of terms for the subject index. It was found that a close association with the non-ferrous metal industry was valuable in recognising such terms as "hot short cracking", "cold shuts", "massive structures", etc., which did not appear in the thesauri (meat for the lions in the "subject specialization is vital/doesn't matter" arena?). The skeleton thesaurus which was produced initially before full indexing started listed some 300 terms, which were checked against a selection of abstracts in various subject fields within the scope of The Guide. This proved useful in crystallizing some ideas about the indexing approach, and enabled general working rules to be formulated before the major work went ahead.

A normal concept and facet principle was used for descriptors, single word and natural language phrases being selected primarily for searching efficiency,

e.g.   Yttrium
              as alloying addition in refractory metals
or   Snoek relaxation activation energy

Inversion was used but rarely, and then generally where an uninverted term was in common usage, but its inversion brought together related subjects, as in:

Continuous casting   *inverted to relate*
                            to casting

Casting
    hot short cracking in
    solidification in
Casting, continuous

It was expected that this type of bibliographical guide would be used both by searchers for information on a precise topic and by "browsers" reading through a collection of abstracts in a group. The latter were catered for mainly in the subject classification of the text, but a further form of "index browsing" was provided by a dual approach to the subject indexing. This was done by including the schedule headings for all groups and sub-groups as descriptors in the alphabetical arrangement of terms; all entries would then appear under the relevant class heading as well as in the normal alphabetical arrangement.

Thus
    photo-emission in copper
would be in the normal sequence under photo-emission, and would be repeated as a term under the section heading:
    Copper: structural metallurgy : Section 20.2
    photo-emission

The use of chemical element symbols was desirable in order to reduce the length of the descriptors in the short column space available at three columns of index to the page. But to avoid possible confusion to the user (arising e.g. from Ag/silver, Pb/lead, W/tungsten) the element was used in full where it formed the primary concept term.

Metal alloys prove tricky customers in any kind of catalogue, index or bibliography. Different combinations of copper, nickel and zinc as Cu-Zn-Ni alloys might be termed German Silver, Nickel Silver, Gun-metal, Admiralty metal, condenser alloy, and so on; Naval Brass on one side of the Atlantic may have a different composition from Naval Brass on the other side. A workable method is to identify alloys by their chemical element symbols arranged in order of importance in the composition, and then arrange them under *Alloys* as a subsection or facet of the base metal.

This would give, for example:
    Titanium alloys: Section 50.11
        Ti-Al
            emission spectra
            phase diagrams
            slip planes

Ti-Al-Mn
    oxidation
    powder metallurgy

Ti-Al-Mo-V
    embrittlement by

Ti-Al-Sn
    oxidation
    recrystallization

Ti-Al-Sn-Zr-Mo
    weld properties

                    etc.

This should be supplemented by generic terms for special groups of alloys such as bronzes; these, though generally copper base alloys, may have a variety of alloying elements in them.

Indexed notes of all decisions made, major and minor, with working examples where necessary, were kept in a log book.

Use of references.

At the outset it was decided to reduce the use of "*see*" and "*see also*" references to a minimum. I now find myself at variance with John Eyre, writing in the October 1974 issue of *The Indexer*. In his study of computer-based indexing he writes:

"Use of '*See*' and '*See also*' references increases the power of the index while keeping down the number of main entries".

While one would not dispute this as a statement of fact, and applaud the indexing economy which should derive from it, the convenience of the user seems ("as usual" hesitates at the end of my pen) to have taken second place. Following this comment Eyre gives an example from *BTI:*

"*PLATFORMS:* Offshore drilling. Natural gas. See Gas, Natural : Drilling, Off shore : Platform . . . There will also of course be reference from NATURAL GAS to GAS, natural."

I have not checked this reference, but it would seem that the searcher for information on off shore drilling platforms in natural gas exploration might have a one-in-five chance of locating his source reference at first try. Are there further complications with "*See also*" references:

Oil, Drilling, Off shore : Platforms

See also Gas, Natural : Drilling, Off shore :
    Platforms.

More power to the index's elbow possibly, but what about the customer?

A basic step in reducing the number of "*see*" references in the author index to The Guide was the above decision to enter different types of complex names under each of the variants. Apart from special complications of the Beljajew/ Belyaev kind, the only remaining use of "*see*" references in the author index was from initials and acronyms to the full styles.

There were four general types of "*see*" references in the subject index, of which the following are examples:

1. Columbium *see* Niobium
    Wolfram *see* Tungsten
i.e. synonymous terms, perhaps transatlantic variants or one gone into disuse.

2. SAP *see* Sintered aluminium powder
i.e. typical reference from initials to the full descriptor.

3. Anisotropy *see* Boundary phenomena:
        anisotropy : Section 3.5.
    here a subject forms part of the total content of a wider section group under another filing descriptor.

4. Barium *see* Minor metals: Section 59.
    review literature on some of the less used metals was not sufficient to justify a separate section for each. These were collected in a single group, Minor metals.

"*See also*" references appeared in the subject index only, generally of the following three types:

1. Liquid metals *see also* Molten metals
i.e. normal linking between parallel but discrete terms.

2. Bronzes *see also* specific materials
    to link a generic descriptor with descriptors for components of the family.

3. Composite materials *see also* Reinforced
        metals; Cermets : Section 9.2.
    comparable to example 3 of the "*see*" references, but with the concept outside the scope of the section descriptor although allied to the section subject.

Index size calculations.

No size limit was set for the indexes, but it was accepted that they should be full and detailed, with a comprehensive in-depth subject index. It was desirable initially to have some idea of an overall target size, both from the general point of view and in relation to a working procedure.

Three variables had to be considered in making an estimate:

(a) the number of abstracts in the completed text.

(b) a figure representing, in the author index, the mean relation between the number of multiple authors and the number of single authors of articles, and in the subject index the mean number of terms per abstract.

(c) a figure showing the mean frequency of repeated citations of one author in the case of the author index, and of recurrent usage of terms in the subject index.

If these three were available, it would be possible to deduce the number of entries in the final index. At least it was possible to estimate the first and to adhere reasonably to the estimate by strict selection of material. But in practice considerations of completeness overrode strictness of selection, and an original estimate of 3550 expanded to 4335 in the final text. I felt that there was no way of calculating b or c. There could be a solution in a random count of a volume such as *Metals Abstracts* or similar abstracts journal, but the expectation that differing indexing approaches and systems would lead to wide variation in results led to a decision instead to use my own experience in establishing quite arbitrary figures. At the completion of the work, very much as a matter of interest only, a rough count was made to check these. More recently, in view of the interest in index size estimation apparent in *The Indexer*, I thought it worth while to do a more precise check, using random sampling counts on the printed author and subject indexes. The estimated and deduced results for both indexes follow.

AUTHOR INDEX
PRELIMINARY ESTIMATE
(checked figures in brackets)

(a)	Estimated number of abstracts	3,500	(4,335)
(b)	Estimated mean relationship single/multiple author articles	1.50	(1.70)
(c)	Overall number of author references (a x b)	5,250	
(d)	Estimated mean frequency of multiple citations of same name	1.4	(1.47)
(e)	Final expected number of author entries (c ÷ d)	3,750	(5,000)

AUTHOR INDEX
CHECK ON COMPLETION

(f)	Number of columns of index	85	
(g)	Average number of name entries per column	59	(random count)
(h)	Average number of source references per column	87	(random count)
(i)	Total number of name entries (f × g)	5,015	
(j)	*Apparent mean frequency of multiple citation of same name* (h ÷ g)	1.47	
(k)	Overall number of source references quoted (f × h)	7,395	
(l)	Number of abstracts	4,335	
(m)	*Mean relationship single/multiple author articles* (k ÷ l)	1.70	

SUBJECT INDEX
PRELIMINARY ESTIMATES
(checked figures in brackets)

(a)	Estimated number of abstracts	3,500	(4,335)
(b)	Estimated mean number of entries per abstract	3.5	(3.46)
(c)	Hypothetical total subject index references (a x b)	12,250	
(d)	Estimated mean frequency of individual term usage	2.5	(2.25)
(e)	Resultant estimated number of subject index terms (c ÷ d)	4,900	

SUBJECT INDEX
CHECK ON COMPLETION

(f)	Number of columns of index	142	
(g)	Average number of terms per column	47	(random count)
(h)	Average number of source references per column	106	(random count)
(i)	Overall number of subject term entries (f x g)	6,674	
(j)	*Apparent mean frequency of multiple usage of same term* (h ÷ g)..	2.25	
(k)	Total number of source references quoted (f x h)	15,000	
(l)	Number of abstracts..	4,335	
(m)	*Average number of subject term entries per abstract* (k ÷ l).. ..	3.46	

From these data it is possible to deduce the number of author name and subject term entries in an index from a specific number of abstracts, using in each case the formula:

Number of entries $\quad = \quad \dfrac{l \times m}{j}$

or simply

                        1.15 l   in the case of author index,

and   *1.54 l*   with the subject index.

But, as I have said, variations in personal approach and system used will cause considerable differences, and this must be borne in mind in making any estimate.

Method study and procedure.

In considering working routines it had to be remembered that

(a) the whole exercise was expected to take some three years or more.

(b) the routines had to cover acquisition, abstracting, indexing, recording and preparing copy for (initially) 3,500 abstracts.

(c) the index was to cumulate progressively with the abstracts.

(d) both working copy and printer's copy would be desirable.

(e) abstracting of source material would be done on a broad chronological basis, related to the progressive coverage of source guides; this meant that abstracts would not cumulate in group order or final text sequence. This required a system of temporary numbering for processing and recording, to be related finally to the permanent sequential numbers of abstracts in their classified groups and in date order.

The procedure should thus enable

(a) general progress to be logged and steps recorded.

(b) a check to be made of cases of repetition of the same or closely parallel articles by the same author (or perhaps plagiarized) and appearing in different journals.

(c) continuous adjustment and modification to the index.

(d) copy to go to the printer with minimum delay after completion of the abstracting. It was expected and had been agreed that copy for the index would follow the main text.

To cater for these requirements, the following records etc. were used:

(a) Log book. This carried details of all source material, date abstracted, the temporary number and group code of the abstract, and the date typed. A tick was made in the final column when index slips had been typed and all slips and copy filed.

(b) Manuscript copy of abstract. This was written at the time the original source became available, and was the authority from which all typing was done. Temporary identity number and group code were put on the front and index data on the back. MS copy was filed in subject group/date order, i.e. in the final order of the text when printed. As well as showing the build-up in each section, this facilitated indexing of parallel articles to give a uniform approach.

(c) Typed copies. Two typed copies were made, the top one being printer's copy and the carbon for a working reference copy;

additional carbon copies were done for abstracts with duplicate or triplicate subject interest, which would appear in different sections.

(d) Number register. This was a record kept for use in transferring temporary to final numbers at the end of the exercise.

(e) Index slips. In view of the overall number of index entries, the use of cards was dismissed on grounds of cost and bulk. The slips used measured 6″ x 3″, and were guillotined by a printer from heavy quality bond off-cuts. The collection of slips was accommodated in stout cut-down envelope boxes.

Having established procedures and records, the working routine to be followed was:

(a) Search source guides and identify required material.
(b) Enter bibliographic details in log book.
(c) Obtain original or copy of article.
(d) Abstract and prepare MS copy. Enter date in log.
(e) Add temporary subject index 'indicators' on back, while original was still available.
(f) Put temporary numbers and group code on MS copy and in log.
(g) Type, check and file printer's and working copy. Enter date in log.
(h) Enter number and code of abstract in Number Register.
(i) Index abstract, putting author and subject index entries on back of MS copy.
(j) Type, check and file index slips.
(k) File MS copy.
(l) Add tick in final column of Log book.

Thus, when all abstracting had been completed there were:

(a) Printer's copy in temporary number sequence.
(b) MS copy in correct text order, but carrying temporary numbers.
(c) Working copies in temporary number sequence.
(d) Completed Log book.
(e) Number register, with completed sequence of temporary numbers, and blank column for final numbers.
(f) Completed file of author and subject index slips, carrying temporary numbers.

The remaining stages, each certainly tedious and time consuming, were:

(a) Number the sequence of MS abstracts to give the final text order and final numbering

sequence; leave the temporary numbers on each abstract.
(b) Enter final numbers in the blank column of the Number Register, using the MS abstracts as authority.
(c) Using the completed Register, erase the temporary numbers from printer's copy and add final numbers. (The working copies were kept in temporary number sequence, to retain a direct link with the Log book.)
(d) Put printer's copy in final order.
(e) Type caption sheets for each group and sub-group section. These were put before the appropriate abstracts as guidance to the printer, and indicated the sequential numbers in each group.
(f) Prepare and type copy for preliminary pages.
(g) Edit index, and transfer temporary numbers on slips to final numbers.
(h) Type printer's copy of index.

And that, so far, was that. Between completion of the copy and publication lay a devious, tortuous pilgrim's progress of proof checking...

Conclusion.

A library catalogue and an index are both condensed guides to collections of information. But whereas in the catalogue there is the need to eliminate variations due to personal and individual approach, this cannot readily be done with indexing. The qualified professional cataloguer uses precise codes to cover every aspect of document recording in a library catalogue. The indexer, within broad limits of systems and indexing conventions, makes his own decisions. It is difficult to think of two indexes (excluding with some reservations computerised indexes using the same programme) produced independently and having the same uniformity that qualified cataloguers using the same codes should achieve.

In this article I have discussed some aspects of indexing a volume of technical abstracts, and have described how it was tackled. I mention this question of personal approach but to emphasize that this was just one way of doing the job. Nor would I pretend to any authority, of experience or other, in thinking the approach was the right one or necessarily the best. Less than a quarter of the way through the business of transferring temporary to permanent numbers, I cursed myself for having decided on a continuous indexing system rather than a final total effort at the end of abstracting. But looking back later, both the time and effort which would then have been required (and without access to the originals to supplement the abstract) and the usefulness of the index as it built up during the course of the work, confirmed in my own mind that it was the right decision. And at least the procedures and records worked and achieved what they were intended to. My hope is that an indexer faced with a similar project may find some part of the article of help in deciding his own *modus operandi*.

References

1. *A thesaurus of engineering and scientific terms.* Engineers Joint Council. (U.S.A.) 1967.
2. *Thesaurus of metallurgical terms.* American Society for Metals. 1968.
3. *A thesaurus and faceted classification for engineering and related subjects.* English Electric Company Ltd. 1969.
4. BS 2979. *Transliteration of Cyrillic and Greek characters.* 1958.

VI. A Selection of Indexing Systems and Methods

The PRECIS Indexing System

K. G. B. Bakewell

The development and current application of the subject indexing system used by The British National Bibliography *is described. This system allows the user to enter the index at any one of the significant terms which together make up a compound subject statement and there find entries for every subject statement in the index which contains this term, the proper context of the term being preserved in each case. Reference is made to a manual providing guidance in the construction of these index entries. Details are given of a small evaluation study carried out at Liverpool Polytechnic's Department of Library and Information Studies on an experimental index covering 584 periodical articles on management. Finally the future of the system is briefly considered.*

The Development of PRECIS

When the *British National Bibliography (BNB)* began in 1950, it used a system of subject indexing introduced by the distinguished Indian librarian S. R. Ranganathan and known as chain indexing.[1] The system was at first viewed with some scepticism by a number of more conservative librarians, but it quickly became established as the accepted method of producing a subject index to a classified catalogue. However it was not, for various reasons, ideal for a computerized system, and in 1971, when BNB had developed the MARC system in the United Kingdom and was also using computers for the production of BNB itself, chain indexing was replaced by a new system known as PRECIS.

PRECIS is an acronym for *PRE*served *C*ontext *I*ndex *S*ystem, conveying the intention of allowing the user of an alphabetical subject index to enter the index at any one of the significant terms which together make up a compound subject statement and there establish the full context in which his chosen term has been considered. A full statement—a kind of précis—is therefore offered to the user under every term in the subject which the indexer considers significant enough to be used as an entry word.

The PRECIS system had its roots in reactions by the Classification Research Group (CRG) and others against traditional library classification schemes for a number of reasons, including their inability to cope with compound subjects and their unsuitability for machine retrieval. The North Atlantic Treaty Organization financed a CRG project for the development of a faceted classification, and by the end of the project (1969) three main components of a freely faceted scheme had been established:

1. An outline thesaurus with experimental hierarchical notation.
2. A set of relational operators with an inbuilt filing order.
3. Provisional rules for classing.

A feature of the scheme was the use of a unique notation for every concept, making it attractive for machine retrieval but producing quite formidable notations for the expression of compound subjects. For example, the notation for "Energy balance in the turbulent mixing layers of a gas" would be C35(5)q24(59)x75(599)v6(54)B27(546)r2.

PRECIS Today

The PRECIS system as used today retains all the essential features of this classification system apart from the notation:

1. The thesaurus consists of an authority file of terms, ensuring that the same subject is consistently indexed under the same form of words whenever it occurs. This thesaurus is "open-ended", new terms being admissible at any time once they have been encountered in the literature.
2. The relational operators (called role operators) indicate the function of the indexed term and determine its position in the string of terms representing the subject of the document. They are for the guidance of the indexer only and do not appear in the index entry. (See Figure 1.)
3. The rules for classing are embodied in the rules of English grammar. (It is interesting to note that, although the rules were based on the rules of *English* grammar, the system has since been applied successfully in a number of other languages including French, German and Danish.) The first process is to seek a term denoting *action*, then to look for the *object* of the action (or *key system*), which may be accompanied by a number of *dependent*

Reprinted from *The Indexer* 9, no. 4 (October 1975): 160–166.

Main line operators

Environment of observed system	o	Location
Observed system (Core operators)	1	Key system: *object of transitive action; agent of intransitive action*
	2	Action/Effect ·
	3	Agent of transitive action; Aspects; Factors

A ————————————————————

Data relating to observer	4	Viewpoint-as-form
Selected instance	5	Sample population/Study region
Presentation of data	6	Target/Form

Interposed operators

Dependent elements	p	Part/Property
	q	Member of quasi-generic group
	r	Aggregate
Concept interlinks	s	Role definer
	t	Author attributed association
Coordinate concepts	g	Coordinate concept

B ————————————————————

Differencing operators (*prefixed by $*)	h	Non-lead direct difference
	i	Lead direct difference
	j	Salient difference
	k	Non-lead indirect difference
	m	Lead indirect difference
	n	Non-lead parenthetical difference
	o	Lead parenthetical difference
	d	Date as a difference

Connectives

(*Components of linking phrases; prefixed by $*)	v	Downward reading component
	w	Upward reading component

C ————————————————————

Theme interlinks	x	First element in coordinate theme
	y	Subsequent element in coordinate theme
	z	Element of common theme

Fig. 1.—Role Operators used in PRECIS

elements. The order of terms achieved by the operators is based on the principle of *context dependency*, each term setting the next term into its obvious context.

For example, the subject "The assessment of library school students in polytechnics" would be written by the indexer as

(1) polytechnics (representing the key system)
(p) library schools (representing a part of the key system)
(p) students (representing a further part)
(2) assessment (representing the action)

Computer instruction codes are then added to the string and the computer "shunts" each term through the following three basic positions in the index:

giving the following entries for the example quoted above:

Polytechnics
    Library schools. Students. Assessment

Library schools. Polytechnics
    Students. Assessment

Students. Library schools. Polytechnics
    Assessment

Assessment. Students. Library schools. Polytechnics

Two terms are not written as adjacent components of a string if the first serves only to establish the class of concept to which the second belongs (for example, Birds. Penguins). In such a case only the second, more specific, term is included in the string, a *see also* reference being made to this term from the first. The terms which are semantically related to a newly admitted term (such as synonyms, superordinate terms, etc.) are determined from dictionaries, thesauri, etc., and a number is assigned to such terms in a machine-held file so that the computer can automatically extract and manipulate them as required. Cross-references are made in the traditional manner—*see* references from synonymous terms and *see also* references from superordinate to subordinate terms, for example:

Swine *see* Pigs
Mammals
    see also
        Pigs
Animals
    see also
        Mammals

The PRECIS Manual

The description above is just the bare bones of the PRECIS system. There is a great deal more to it than that, as can be seen by reading a very full article by the man primarily responsible for the development of the system, Derek Austin.[2] More recently Austin has followed up this excellent article with a comprehensive manual which makes the construction of PRECIS indexes within the capabilities of every indexer in the country.[3]

At first sight the 551 pages of this manual might be off-putting. It does, however, provide a very clear and thorough survey of the development of PRECIS, the construction of PRECIS entries, computer manipulation of PRECIS strings, and the construction of *see* and *see also* references. There are useful sections on the automatic construction of feature headings, some management aspects of PRECIS, and problems requiring further investigation. The appendices include some foreign-language examples, a useful feature in view of the interest shown in PRECIS by indexers from a number of overseas countries.

The manual's guidance is provided in thirty-nine steps and the would-be indexer can work through these at his own speed. At various intervals the text is broken up with a series of exercises allowing the reader to test his understanding of the instruction given and his ability to write PRECIS entries. Fortunately, answers are provided at the end!

The reader of *The Indexer* may well ask whether the PRECIS system has any relevance to book-indexing. The answer is provided in the manual, which contains two PRECIS-style indexes, one covering the examples used and the other covering the text. The indexes are not perfect—I detected a number of omissions—but they are very good and do illustrate the feasibility of PRECIS as a system for producing book indexes—provided enough space has been allotted to the index!

Evaluating PRECIS

We may, after reading the manual, be able to construct PRECIS entries but we do not know enough about user reactions to PRECIS indexes. At Liverpool we have always paid a great deal of attention to the PRECIS system and our teaching methodology has been explained elsewhere.[4] For their final project in the practical indexing session of the B.A. course we ask students to produce a "mini-catalogue" using any recognized system of subject indexing, and it is interesting that 11 of the 24 students graduating in 1975 chose to use PRECIS.

In 1973 a number of Liverpool students participated in a small evaluation study, carried out with the cooperation of the PRECIS team of investigators at the British Library Bibliographic Services Division's Subject Systems Office. This team had indexed in depth a number of periodical articles on management, the articles concerned being those covered by *Anbar Management Services Abstracts*, vol. 10, nos. 11 and 12 (July/ August 1971), and *Personnel + Training Abstracts*, new series, vol. 1 no. 1, October 1971. Thirty copies of the index, covering 584 journal articles, were kindly supplied to us, and this enabled us to give one copy to each student participating in the exercise. These students consisted of 20 second-year students for the Library Association General Professional Examinations, specializing in indexing, and five postgraduate students. Three members of staff also took part in the exercise.

The procedure adopted in the experiment was that two members of staff (myself and the departmental research assistant, Mrs. D. M. Allchin) produced 100 questions from the data base, which it was felt represented "typical" enquiries handled by a management information service. Each searcher was asked to attempt to answer four questions via the PRECIS index, indicating the results and the time taken on a special form (see Figure 2).

The following were the results obtained:

Number of questions	100
Number of items located	83
Search times	
Less than 1 minute	34
1-2 minutes	28
2-3 minutes	8
3-4 minutes	6
4-5 minutes	5
more than 5 minutes	2

The important question is why were seventeen items not located? Seven failures were due to inadequate searching and two could be blamed on ambiguity in the formulation of the question. This leaves the following eight which are attributed to inaccurate or incomplete indexing:

1. "The use of exhibitions to promote sales."

   Indexed as
   Exhibitions
   Planning

but the searcher ignored this entry because "sales promotion" was missing from the string.

2. "Creativity in management."

   Indexed as
   Lateral thinking
   Applications

without reference from "creativity". (The term "lateral thinking" was used in the title of the article.)

3. "The problem of management terminology."

   An article entitled "Clearing the jungle of management obscurity" was not located at all.

4. "Sensitivity training."

   An article entitled "Human relations: lessons learned" was indexed as

   Canada
   Accounting firms. Inter-partner relationships. Improvement. Role of psychologists

Sensitivity training was specifically mentioned in the abstract and should have had an entry in the index.

5. "The reason for the breakdown of contractual joint ventures."

   An article entitled "Joint ventures in the multinational company" was indexed as

   Firms
   American-owned firms. Partnerships with foreign firms

A reference from "Joint ventures" to "Partnerships" would have assisted location, since there was, of course, also an entry under "Partnerships". The absence of an entry under "Multinational firms" is unfortunate, although not relevant to this particular enquiry.

6. "The one-way and two-way appraisal process."

   An article entitled "Power networks in the appraisal process" was indexed as

   Managers
   Performance appraisal

No.

LIVERPOOL POLYTECHNIC

DEPARTMENT OF LIBRARY AND INFORMATION STUDIES

SUBJECT

SEARCH STRATEGIES (please state briefly and continue on another sheet if necessary)

RESULT (Abstract nos. and keywords etc. found)

TIME TAKEN (in minutes)

COMMENTS

SIGNATURE ....

Fig 2. Search sheet for PRECIS evaluation study

A reference from "Appraisal" to "Performance appraisal" would have assisted location.

7. "The development of interactive skills."

An article entitled "Developing interactive skills" was indexed as

> Managers
>> Training: T-group method—*Study examples: British Overseas Airways Corporation & International Computers Ltd.*

The inclusion of "interactive skills techniques" in the string might have been useful.

8. "The role of the professions in management."

An article entitled "Industry, society and the professions" was indexed as

> Accounting as a profession
> Social responsibility

An entry under "Professions" seems to have been called for as the article dealt with "the Professions generally and the accounting profession in particular." Even if the article had dealt solely with the accounting profession, a general reference from "Professions" would have been helpful.

Some students also commented on the absence of expected entry terms in the case of successful searches. For example:

1. An article on "EDP security arrangements" was traced under

> Security measures. Computer systems

but the expected entry or reference under "EDP" was missing.

2. An article on "estimating the size of markets" was indexed as

> Industrial markets
> Size. Estimating. Lorenz distribution

but, as the searcher commented, there should surely have been an entry under "market research".

3. The student who found an article on "the influence of the Fulton Report on the attitudes of civil servants to their work" under

> Civil Service. Great Britain
> Personnel. Young persons. Attitudes to workings conditions.—
>> *Surveys*

said "As a result of the PRECIS indexing method the above abstract is indexed under 'attitudes', 'personnel' and 'young persons'. It seems debatable whether anyone would look under these headings for material on this subject, whereas they would be very likely to look under 'Fulton' or 'Fulton Report'." (The title of the article was "Fulton and morale".)

What did the experiment achieve? It ensured that students used the PRECIS index, and there is no better way of becoming acquainted with the system. It indicated that some students need more guidance from their tutors in the formulation of search strategies. And it provided feedback for the PRECIS team, the most obvious lessons being the need for adequate cross-references and the danger of being over-influenced by the wording of the title when making index entries.

Last but by no means least, it gave some indication of the reactions of students to the subject indexing system used in our national bibliography. Not all students completed the "comments" section on the search form, but the fact that 81% of the questions were answered satisfactorily in less than five minutes is a clear indication that their reaction was generally favourable. The following are among the comments which were made:

"No trouble". (This comment, or something similar like "Simple" or "Marvellous", occurred a number of times.)
"Indexing is perhaps a little too deep."
"Simple when best lead term found, but long series of entries at 'computer systems' is not helpful." (This comment came from a student searching for material on the use of computers to design office layouts.)
"This method appeals to me more with each example."
"Has a lot of keywords for which a searcher might look and enough references to guide the searcher to entries."
"Time was mostly consumed thinking of keywords to look up rather than searching, where entries were reasonably clear."

The Future of PRECIS

PRECIS has been successfully used in *The British National Bibliography* for more than four years and has also been adopted for *The Australian National Bibliography* and *The British National Film Catalogue*. It is anticipated that it will be used for *British Education Index* from January 1976.[5] One would expect that it will be adopted as the method of compiling the

British Museum Subject Index, especially now that the BNB has been absorbed into the British Library as the Bibliographic Services Division. Its future looks rosy indeed, but we do need to know more about the reactions of users to the system: so often they are ignored while we indexers happily experiment!

Acknowledgement

I am grateful to Derek Austin and Jeremy Digger for advice given during the preparation of this article.

References.

1. There are several good accounts of chain indexing, the best being Mills, Jack, "Chain indexing and the classified catalogue", *Library Association Record* **57** (4) April 1955, pp.141-148. A briefer summary appears in Bakewell, K. G. B., *A manual of cataloguing practice*, pp.84-88. Pergamon Press, 1972.

2. Austin, Derek, "The development of PRECIS: a theoretical and technical history", *Journal of Documentation* **30** (1) March 1974, pp.47-102.

3. Austin, Derek, *PRECIS: a manual of concept analysis and subject indexing*. Council of the British National Bibliography, 1974.

4. Bakewell, Ken, and Hunter, Eric, "Teaching PRECIS at Liverpool", *Catalogue and Index* (36), Spring 1975, pp.3-6.

5. Personal communication from Derek Austin and Christine Shaw.

Syntactic and Semantic Relationships —

or: A review of *PRECIS: a manual of concept analysis and subject indexing,* by D. Austin

P. F. Broxis

PRECIS[1] is probably one of the most important projects in subject indication undertaken
during recent years and one which could well
influence the future course of librarianship and
information science. The background to PRECIS
has already been outlined by Austin[2] and it should
be sufficient to say here that it was developed at
the time when the *British National Bibliography*
started to co-operate with the MARC project
and decided that the combination of the chain-
indexing procedure with the Dewey Decimal
Classification used for the main subject sequence
did not lend itself to satisfactory computerisation.
However, it should be mentioned that chain-
indexing does not necessarily have to be tied to
a classification scheme and can be used with
alphabetical subject-headings as is the practice
for the *British Technology Index*, where a slightly
modified form of chain-indexing is used. The
British Technology Index was in fact computerised before the MARC project began.

PRECIS stands for *Pre*served *C*ontext *I*ndex
*S*ystem and is an attempt to bridge the syntactic
and semantic aspects of indexing through natural
language as used in everyday speech. It should
be stressed that, despite claims to the contrary
which have been made, PRECIS is a system of
classification. Confusion arises because we are
conditioned to thinking of a classification scheme
as being a predetermined notated system, rather
than one which exhibits syntactic and semantic
relationships in a logical order, be that in the
form of a printed classification scheme such as
Dewey, or as alphabetical subject-headings. In
PRECIS, subject-heading strings are manipulated so as to preserve the full connotation of the

main string in each of the references made. This
differs from chain-indexing in that successive
terms of a heading are not truncated in making
references to the next highest term in the string.
An example of the way in which this is achieved
in PRECIS is:

(0) Canada
(1) paper industries
(2) management

(0), (1) and (2) being role operators used both to
determine facet order and to instruct the computer as to the necessary manipulations required
to produce the required references as follows:

CANADA
 Paper industries. Management

PAPER INDUSTRIES. Canada
 Management

and

MANAGEMENT. Paper industries. Canada.

This technique has been termed 'shunting' and
the basic mechanism can be represented as:

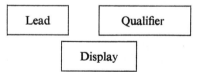

and is known as the standard format. Occasionally more than two lines are used to display a
complete reference string.

The following table shows the extent of the
role operators used in PRECIS:

Reprinted from *The Indexer* 10, no. 2 (October 1976): 54–59.

Main line operators

Environment of observed system	o	Location
Observed system (Core operators)	1	Key system: *object of transitive action; agent of intransitive action*
	2	Action/Effect
	3	Agent of transitive action; Aspects; Factors

A ─────────────────────────────

Data relating to observer	4	Viewpoint-as-form
Selected instance	5	Sample population/Study region
Presentation of data	6	Target/Form

Interposed operators

Dependent elements	p	Part/Property
	q	Member of quasi-generic group
	r	Aggregate
Concept interlinks	s	Role definer
	t	Author attributed association
Coordinate concepts	g	Coordinate concept

B ─────────────────────────────

Differencing operators *(prefixed by $)*	h	Non-lead direct difference
	i	Lead direct difference
	j	Salient difference
	k	Non-lead indirect difference
	m	Lead indirect difference
	n	Non-lead parenthetical difference
	o	Lead parenthetical difference
	d	Date as a difference

Connectives

(Components of linking phrases; prefixed by $)	v	Downward reading component
	w	Upward reading component

C ─────────────────────────────

Theme interlinks	x	First element in coordinate theme
	y	Subsequent element in coordinate theme
	z	Element of common theme

Role Operators used in PRECIS

This certainly reveals the thoroughness and care with which Austin has pursued his researches. The use of natural language for subject-headings is not entirely new; what is new, however, is the linking of terms by prepositions and various other parts of speech in such a way that references read almost as sentences:

(1)   buildings
(2)   damage $v by $w to
(3)   frost

which gives the following references:

BUILDINGS
    Damage by frost

DAMAGE. Buildings
    By frost

and

FROST
    Damage to buildings.

One of the omissions from the discussion in this Manual is the extent to which an indexing language should verge into the realms of natural language usage and the extent to which it should go to the degree of refinement found in PRECIS. The *British Technology Index*, for example, relies on the use of, first, a consistent facet order, and, second, a very restricted number of operators, or role indicators, to express the meaning of both heading and reference relationships. It has to be admitted, however, that the problems of producing a national bibliography covering the entire field of knowledge is rather different from that of an index restricted to a particular subject field. It has already been accepted that the system as used by the *British Technology Index* would be inadequate for the social sciences, and Coates[3] has already suggested the likely modifications which would be necessary. Nevertheless, Austin's analysis does make a valuable contribution to our understanding of various indexing problems which have not previously been mooted. This, indeed, makes the Manual essential reading for the serious student of indexing methodology.

One of the more controversial aspects of PRECIS is Austin's treatment of phrases. Any compound term can be analysed into a focus and a difference, so that the phrase *turbulent flow in pipes* is treated as:

Turbulent flow in pipes

/ | \

Difference   Focus   Difference

in pipes being a prepositional phrase. In PRECIS, phrases are always kept as a unit and never factorised as:

pipes — flow — turbulent

where pipes are regarded as the subject of the action flow which is in the turbulent mode.

Differencing operators are outside the main group of operators in that they function semantically rather than syntactically. *Lightweight concrete reinforced foot bridges* could be coded:

(1)   bridges $i foot $i concrete $m reinforced
       $m lightweight

and would produce entries:

Bridges
Foot bridges
Concrete bridges
Reinforced concrete bridges
Lightweight concrete bridges

with the whole term in its natural language order appearing as a display. It is recommended, however, that consideration should be given to making *see also* references from one part of a compound to another:

Bridges
    See also
        Concrete bridges.

It is argued that this will be more economic and make the index easier to consult, especially if there is a likelihood of there being more than twenty-five or thirty displays under a given heading. The disadvantage of such a permissive policy is twofold; first, it can lead to inconsistent indexing decisions unless very great care is taken in checking precedents; and, second, the user is faced with the problem of a variable indexing policy to grapple with when undertaking a search under a number of different topics.

The example on *frost damage to buildings* already quoted earlier serves to illustrate another feature used in PRECIS known as the predicate transformation. This transformation occurs when an action, operator 3, comes into the lead and the next highest term in the string is coded 2. Operators s and t also produce this format. It is so named because the object upon which an agent is performed is regarded as a predicate.

This results in a turntable effect, to use another of Austin's railway metaphors. This can be illustrated graphically as:

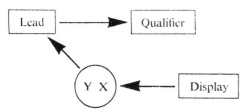

which corresponds to what happened in the example.

Care has to be taken not to confuse whole—part relationships with difference relationships. *Managagement decision making* should be treated as:

(2) management   = Action
(p) decision making = Part of action

which illustrates the extent of the whole—part relationship in PRECIS; it is used not only of things and their parts but also of actions and their parts or properties. This mechanism is also used for places: Paris being a part of France. Rather more unexpected, however, is the extension of this principle to topics such as:

(1) Great Britain
(p) law

on the grounds that there is a whole—part relationship between a social system and an abstract concept which should be treated as a subsystem. To have regarded law as an agent would be incorrect in this case:

(1) Great Britain
(3) law

although this would be the correct analysis in indexing the topic *law relating to libraries in Great Britain*, which would be coded:

(0) Great Britain
(1) libraries
(3) law.

The logic behind this strategy shows the meticulous attention given to the syntactic side of PRECIS. The corollary of this is the fine distinction made in deriving indexing strings.

Place and location in PRECIS can occur at a number of points in a string and can be introduced by the operators 0, 1, 3, or 5. The following is a brief account of the use of these operators:

0 — used in cases where the relation between locality and the following concept is one of geography
1 — used where locality is the principal or only entity in the subject
3 — used where a place name represents a social entity in the role of an agent:
    (1)   Vietnam
    (2)   war $d 1961—
(sub 2) (2)   Vietnam war $ 1961—
    (s)   role $v of $w in
    (3)   United States
This is the least common mechanism for introducing a country.
5 — used when place is used as a study region with the subject *per se* having a wider application:
    (1)   book trade
    (2)   management
    (5)   study regions
    (q)   Germany
which represents a general study of the book trade based on the author's experience of that in Germany—it is not about the management of the book trade in Germany.

While these various roles of place and location have always existed, little attempt has previously been made to identify them systematically and to distinguish between them in practical indexing.

This survey of some of the more important aspects of the syntactic side of PRECIS cannot be left without mentioning that there are a number of devices available for varying a term when it appears as a lead term and for achieving the desired typographical form of the entry. The string already used concerning the book trade will produce entries like:

Book trade
   Management—*Study regions: Germany*

where the typographical program automatically selects the required type-face and inserts the correct punctuation between terms as required.

Once a string has been established it is allocated a SIN (subject indication number) and this is entered into the computer store. Should the identical string be required for another document, the indexer merely cites the SIN number.

When discussing the difference operators it was shown how *see also* references were created for terms such as concrete bridges. This is one of the ways in which the syntactic side of PRECIS is interrelated with the semantic side of the system. Another way in which this is achieved is by what is termed the quasi-generic member, the operator q. Consider:

(1)   pests
(q)   aphids

aphids are a species of homoptera which in turn is a species of insects. These and other intermediate terms are not included in the main string. Reliance is placed on the semantic side of PRECIS, using q, to display such relationships. There is also a mechanism designed to by-pass an intermediate term should there be no other function for the term than that of a connection link, producing the direct reference:

Insects
    See also
    Aphids.

The semantic aspects of PRECIS are, in the main, fairly conventional. An attempt is made to relate collateral (or sibling) terms—those having one ancestor in common—as, for example, carpets and rugs, both being floor coverings; but they also share many common attributes and tend to quasi-synonymity. The danger of this kind of relationship is the problem of deciding the bases for establishing collateral terms such as these as there is a large grey area where the views of indexers are bound to differ, making consistency of the semantic structure difficult to achieve.

Two-way relationships, welds/welding and welding/welds, are also displayed in PRECIS. Whilst not doubting the value of such collocation in theory, these particular terms will always file close to each other. Again, there is the problem of control in relating such root words. One solution would be to make such references only where unrelated words file between variants of the same root, as arc and arcs or electron and electronics, which are separated by architecture and electronic respectively, due to alphabetisation.

A feature which has always been a problem in indexing is that of polyhierarchical relationships, terms belonging to more than one class. Austin seems to have extended the meaning of polyhierarchical to include terms having more than one synonym (paragraph 31.20), but this is an incorrect use of the term. PRECIS attempts to make all possible links, so that pianos will be related to stringed instruments, keyboard instruments, and percussion instruments—all of which will be related to musical instruments.

In the same way as a SIN is assigned for the syntactic strings, a RIN (reference indicator number) is assigned to the strings required for the semantic structure.

The overriding consideration which the syntactical side of PRECIS, and indeed the system as a whole, brings to mind is that of its economics. No information has yet been released on this aspect of the scheme, with the result that we are without knowledge of its true costs as compared with other possible methods.

The final part of the Manual demonstrates the application of PRECIS to languages other than English, with examples in French and German. Various algorithms of the operators are also given, together with answers to the exercises set at stages throughout the text. Finally, there is an index derived from the numerous examples used throughout the text, but unfortunately this does not extend to include the semantic structure.

In the following paragraphs an attempt will be made to make some general observations. It should be appreciated that any review of a work as important as this Manual can only scrape the surface, with the comment which could be made on many points of detail having to be omitted. For the same reason detailed consideration of the computer coding and operation has been avoided.

An important consideration of PRECIS is that, in its present form, it is designed as a two-sequence system consisting of a sequence of entries, arranged by the Dewey Decimal Classification in the case of the *British National Bibliography*, or by any other means, as, for example, an arbitrary running number, and a separate sequence of references produced by PRECIS. No facility has so far been provided to permit entries and references to be organised into a single sequence index. There are two probable reasons for this. The first is that the length and structure of the strings produced from the coded instructions would make direct references unwieldy. The second is that the primary string produced would prove unsuitable for use as a main heading and, if so used, would result in very poor collocation of entries arising from the rules of differencing and the effect of having subject-headings presented in a display form.

Although described as one of *concept analysis and subject indexing*, the PRECIS Manual goes beyond this remit in that it is also concerned with the mechanics of computer assistance in manipulating the syntactical and semantic aspects of the scheme. The typographical details are also dealt with in depth. These various aspects of the scheme are considered in relation to each other, with the result that the student of this work needs to pause from time to time in order to isolate the different strands which constitute the system. It should be emphasised that, whilst PRECIS is basically designed for computer assisted production, it can nevertheless be produced by manual methods.

Austin sometimes falls into the trap of making claims which are not unique to PRECIS. On page 5 (0.8), for example, in discussing the inconsistencies which can arise between indexers, Austin claims that, 'To a certain extent, however, PRECIS guards against inter-indexer inconsistency by requiring all indexers to test a subject systematically for the presence or otherwise of certain concepts which have known syntactical roles. A subject containing an action, for example, must be tested for the object of the action, since this often determines how the rest of the subject should be handled'. Such a procedure should be routine in any indexing service where, in addition, indexers should continually be consulting their authority files, whatever form these may take. Reliance is also placed on the order of operators for crystallising facet order. There are also elaborate rules for deciding the order of adverbs and adjectives. In practical indexing, however, the order of such terms can sometimes vary, especially when describing an experimental situation where, for example, a steel specimen may either be annealed and then quenched, or quenched and then annealed. At this level of indexing, rules which are too rigid in detail may well prove to militate against the accurate description of a subject. Procedures of this kind do not automatically lead to two indexers reaching identical decisions. A document, for example, may contain a number of action terms, all equally important; one indexer may decide to state all these actions, whereas the other may decide to state only the final action involved. What is a paramount requirement for consistent indexing is a combination of rules for formulating subject-headings, together with a policy relating to the degree of exhaustivity and specificity which the index aims to achieve.

One of the problems Austin had to reconcile in devising PRECIS, and one which could affect its application in practice, is the number of alternatives which appeared possible. The result of this has been that an appreciable amount of space has been devoted to discussing these possibilities and to justifying why only the standard routine should be adopted. The criterion for a good indexing system ought to be how well the principles can stand by themselves with as few exceptions as possible to the general rules. The passage of time will undoubtedly show how well or otherwise PRECIS attains this measure.

References

1. Austin, D. *PRECIS: a manual of concept analysis and subject indexing.* Council of the British National Bibliography Ltd, 1974.
2. Austin, D. The development of PRECIS: a theoretical and technical history. *Journal of Documentation* 30 (1) March 1974. pp. 47-102.
3. Coates, E. J. Computer handling of social science terms and their relations. In: *European Documentation and information system for education, Vol. 3: Technical studies.* Strasbourg, Council of Europe, 1969.

Indexing *LISA:*

Chains, KISS and the Bold Approach*

Tom Edwards

Describes chain indexing in LISA and the modifications to the technique made necessary by a practical working situation. The method was adopted on a "Keep it Simple and Stupid" basis. However, some permutation and a number of qualifying words have been introduced in order to make entries more understandable. Other difficulties have emerged because the subject field of LISA is connected so closely with social institutions and human relationships. There is also the problem of certain foreign language terms which are virtually meaningless when translated into English. A retrieval test carried out by E. M. Keen had a useful by-product in showing that the layout of the LISA indexes could be improved and the use of bold lead terms is now under consideration.

Mr. Chairman, Ladies and Gentlemen. It is a great pleasure to be here tonight for several reasons. Naturally, I am flattered that Mr. Harrod and Mr. Menzies felt you would be interested in what I have to say about the problems of indexing for an abstracting service; in addition, it is always pleasant to talk to other people about one's work rather than to oneself, which I certainly do when indexing and I suspect is a common habit of indexers; and, perhaps most importantly, there is the further evidence of the cordial relationship that exists between your Society and my employers, the Library Association. Some mysterious meetings take place within this building—when the Society of Indexers is here the LA staff does feel that friendly Injuns are occupying the premises. On the many occasions over the past few years when it has been necessary to burn the midnight oil I have been caught up with some pretty hair-raising people. A few months ago I was quite looking forward

to the Ridgmount Gardens Association gathering because I thought this room would hold some splendid examples of pot plants and flowers and I might pick up a few cheaply. The meeting turned out to be an extremely militant protest about rents by a local residents' association. I think this experience shows the pitfalls that natural language holds for the indexer and it also demonstrates my lack of subject knowledge concerning the names of the streets around this building. I do sincerely hope that tonight's meeting will not be so militant, even if my paper does not meet with your approval.

Mr. Chairman, I do not know how your meetings are usually conducted. I would like to try to overcome that languid atmosphere which often develops after about twenty minutes, when the speaker's voice has not shown one variation in pitch over ten sentences and the audience's eyes are beginning to look glazed. No doubt, this does not happen at your meetings. Anyway, participation from the floor, under your direction, Mr. Chairman, would be welcome. In other words, ladies and gentlemen, please interrupt if anything is unclear and also if you feel that something I say simply cannot be allowed to pass without comment. The material distributed to you is for information, but may be rustled if you wish.

Origins of LISA

LISA may be unfamiliar to some of you and a brief background will set the scene against which indexing is carried out. Organised abstracting in this country for the subject field of librarianship was pioneered by R. N. Lock and his wife, C. Muriel Lock. In the late 1940s the Locks devised the idea of circulating abstracts in typescript form for current literature about librarianship. The main audience they had in mind was the

*A paper given after the Annual General Meeting of the Society, 29th May 1975.

Reprinted from *The Indexer* 9, no. 4 (October 1975): 133–146.

library student, but it quickly became obvious that the practising librarian could find such a service just as valuable as the student. As a result, in 1950 the Library Association was persuaded to take over the abstracts and to produce them as a printed, quarterly publication entitled *Library Science Abstracts* (*LSA*), with the Locks as editors. In 1951, they were succeeded by H. Allan Whatley, who was responsible for the service until 1968. The abstracts were compiled by a team of librarian/abstractors working at home in their spare time. Editing and indexing were also carried out on a "private-time" basis by Whatley.

It became increasingly clear during the late 1960s that these arrangements were not able to reflect adequately the turmoil of activity that the subject field had become and it was decided to bring the work, or as much of it as possible, in-house to Library Association headquarters with full-time staff. Talks with Aslib resulted in an agreement to expand the publication with abstracts for the information science wing of the subject area to be provided by Aslib Library Staff.

Library & Information Science Abstracts, which produces the pretty acronym *LISA*, began publication with the January-February 1969 issue and I have been its editor since the beginning. The prime object of the service is to provide abstracts of about 120-150 words each concerning the subject field of librarianship and information work and also "fringe" areas such as publishing, bookselling and reprography. The primary material covered includes periodical articles, conference papers, monographs, reports and so on. *LISA* is published once every two months and at present about 4,000 abstracts are published each year. Author and subject indexes are compiled for each issue and these are cumulated annually and published as a separate issue. A brief word about *LISA's* editor. By occupation, I am a professional librarian, and my experience of indexing centres within this field, i.e., I have been a cataloguer in public libraries and the old National Central Library, which used to occupy the British Library's premises next door, and I spent three years as an indexer at the *British Technology Index*. I have never undertaken the indexing of a book.

Subject work in LISA

It is likely that the indexer *qua* indexer would produce a rather different kind of subject index to *LISA* than the ones now compiled. An abstracting service, when you think about it, is a rather strange publication, a hybrid with part intellectual content of its own, but always dependent for real, meaningful knowledge transfer on the original material. Each comparatively brief entry in *LISA* potentially contains a wealth of index matter and it would be perfectly possible for the indexer to scan each section of an abstract, perhaps each line, for significant phrases and terms. Not only possible but, I can almost hear you saying, obvious and also desirable. Perversely, I have to tell you that this is *not* the method used in *LISA*.

The strangeness of the abstracting service as a publication is probably matched, in the non-librarian's eyes, by the way in which librarians or information workers approach subject indexing—I have little doubt that Society members have found this diversity of views to be true over the years. Part of the core of the librarian and information worker's mystique is the use of controlled lists of terms, e.g., classification schemes and thesauri, on which to base the subject arrangement of material. Books on the local library's shelves arranged by the Dewey Decimal Classification are an obvious example, together with their back-up alphabetical subject indexes in card, sheaf or printed form.

The result of this close attention by the profession to subject work is that anyone rash enough to compile the indexes for an abstracting service in the field has a double burden. Not just the usual difficulties of index compilation, which are severe enough, but also the problem of knowing that each user is, potentially, an expert in the art of indexing as well as on the subject discipline itself. A similar experience must be had by the member of the Society of Indexers who indexes your journal. He has my sympathy.

I think it would be fair to say that when I arrived at the Library Association in late 1968 some confusion existed over the methods to be adopted for indexing the new service. The situation was that the indexes to the old *Library Science Abstracts*, compiled like back-of-the-book indexes, had received some criticism during the 1960s. The general feeling appeared to be that efforts should be made by *LISA* to meet the user-expressed demands for change. On the other hand, it was not all that easy to see how an alternative means of indexing could be offered, particularly with the very small number of staff employed. The *LSA* indexing had been attacked on several grounds, but one main aspect was the lack of a thesaurus to control the terms entered in the index.

Incidentally, I personally do not think that all the criticisms of the *LSA* indexing were justified and it is interesting that one or two practices which I felt to be perfectly acceptable and simply transferred to the *LISA* indexes have never been criticised in their new format. Of course, as soon as this paper becomes known, ten letters of criticism will arrive on my desk.

So, well on into 1968—and remember the service was due to start with an issue published in March 1969—no decision had been taken on indexing methods for the new publication. We had a very short time in which to think about the problem. Consider for a moment an actual abstract published in *LISA* this year; it is number 75/94 and gives a good idea of the difficulties of methodology to be faced when indexing an abstracting service. The title of the original article is "The curriculum in Australian library schools" and the opening lines of the abstract read:

"Outlines the curricula at the University of New South Wales School of Librarianship; the Royal Melbourne Institute of Technology; the Canberra College of Advanced Education; the Western Australian Institute of Technology; the Tasmanian College of Advanced Education; and the State College of Victoria at Melbourne. Curricula at the South Australian Institute of Technology are referred to but are not quoted in detail because they are under review".

Perhaps you would like to place yourselves in the position of an indexer having to index this passage in the context of a publication which prints 650-700 abstracts every two months, many of them with a similar cramming of material. Further, the service is subject to quite rigorous cost control—in fact, *LISA* is expected to make a surplus on each year's trading activity. I will come back to this example later, but first of all let us return to the situation in 1969.

As a result of the criticism of the *LSA* subject indexes and after as much consideration as possible in the time available, it was decided to adopt a controlled list of terms for *LISA* on which to base the arrangement of abstracts and

the alphabetical subject indexing. The advantages would include: (1) the possibilities for detailed subdivision of the abstracts suitable for browsing-type searches; and (2) a subject index could be compiled for each issue as well as annually, even though the staff initially consisted of just the editor and a typist. The only suitable scheme available was that of the Classification Research Group, which was at that time called *A classification of library science*, and so this was adopted. For reasons of economy it was decided to utilise the chain indexing technique for compiling the alphabetical subject index entries, but it must be emphasised that this method is not a necessary part of the CRG scheme.

Chain indexing

Indexing in *LISA* cannot be discussed without referring to the *whole* subject arrangement, i.e., the classified arrangement of the abstracts themselves and the alphabetical subject index entries. In order to be fully effective, chain indexing should be based on a faceted classification scheme and this is what the CRG Classification is. In such a scheme, only terms for "elementary" subjects are listed in the schedules; "compound" subjects are classified by synthesising, or number building, the notations from the appropriate parts of the schedules. For example, the elementary terms "university libraries" (Gd) and "buildings" (Qi) are listed in their appropriate facets in the schedules of the classification. In order to classify the compound subject "university library buildings" the two notations are combined by the classifier/indexer in accordance with definite rules—in librarian's jargon, the citation order. In the CRG scheme these terms are combined in the following way:

QiGd—Buildings.   University libraries

The letter notations in the example above are taken from the 1971 version of the scheme— a definitive version, with different notation, has recently been published by the Library Association on behalf of the CRG.[1]

What index entries does the application of chain procedure produce for this example? Before answering that, ladies and gentlemen, and in the way of light relief, I should like to tell you about my experiences before writing this paper of trying to find a simple definition of chain indexing and also searching through *The Indexer* to discover whether your Society had ever been addressed on the subject of chain indexing.

I was not very successful in my search for a brief, succinct definition. In its article on chain indexing, the Marcel Dekker *Encyclopedia of library and information science* is, I think, a little too deep for our purposes. Among other things, it talks of:

". . .a method of deriving alphabetical subject index entries in a semiautomatic fashion from the chain of successive subdivision that leads from a general level to the most specific level needed to be indexed."[2]

Your Mr. L. M. Harrod's *Librarians' glossary* is more helpful for our purposes:

"An alphabetic index wherein a heading is provided for each term, or link for all the terms used in a subject heading or classification. Each term represented by a given part of the classification symbol, followed by the term for each other part, appears as a heading in the reverse order of the symbol, so that the last term in the symbol becomes the first. If the symbol is comprised of four parts, there will be four entries: the first consisting of four terms; the second of three after the first term of the previous entry has been omitted; the third, of two, and so on."[3]

The important aspects of chain indexing, brought out in this definition, are the conception of each term or group of terms as a link, the fact that index entries are made in the *reverse* order of the main file and the idea of dropping links of the chain for the more generic entries.

My search of *The Indexer* showed that you have indeed been addressed on the subject of chain indexing—by Jack Mills in 1960. I know your delight for the odd juxtapositions often thrown up by indexes, and the entry for "chain indexing" in the index to volume 2 of your journal provides a nice example. The entry files next to one for Lewis Carroll. The Carroll entry leads to an item reprinted from the *Buenos Aires Herald* under the title "Indexing Gone Mad!" (according to this, the Reverend Mr. Dodgson insisted that his novels should have indexes with cross-references to the author's favourite jokes). After my account of chain indexing in *LISA* I hope that this meeting will not feel the same way about the technique.

Jack Mills's 1960 paper gave a full explanation of the chain indexing method and also discussed the possibilities of using it for back-of-the-book indexing:

"But the central principle is undoubtedly relevant when deciding the degree and manner of permutating the terms of compound headings (e.g. Electronic Indexing of the Dead Sea Scrolls). This principle is that the alphabetical index need not attempt to duplicate the grouping and association of one topic with another which is found in the text of the book itself."[4]

This is one of the basic principles of indexing in *LISA*. The chain index provides term associations and word orders that are different from those of the classified arrangement of abstracts. Developing the example just mentioned, an abstract entered under the following heading in *LISA's* abstract file:

QiGdD71—Buildings. University libraries. Canada

receives these alphabetical index entries compiled by the chain method:

Canada : University libraries : Buildings
University libraries : Buildings
Buildings : Libraries

A specific entry for each abstract in *LISA* is, therefore, made at only *one* point in the index, i.e., a full entry is only made from the term mentioned last in the abstract file. For each succeeding entry, the right-hand term, or link, from the abstract file is dropped. The result is a highly economic index for two reasons: (1) less page space is taken up because the higher terms in the chain (University libraries, Buildings) stand for all other entries in the file on university library buildings and for buildings as well as the one on Canadian university library buildings; and (2) after the indexer has written the basic subject string, a good, experienced typist can construct the index entries by herself without necessarily understanding all the ramifications of the method.

It should be noted that provision is required for alternative means of entry by the user. In the example above, additional entries must be made for

Library buildings
Architecture : Library buildings

Subject analysis in LISA

There is a further question to be considered in *LISA* indexing, and in the indexer's work it comes *before* the application of the chain technique outlined above. In librarian's terminology, it is necessary to perform a subject analysis or concept analysis of the abstract. For a demonstration of how this is carried out, we can return to the example I asked you to consider a short while ago concerning the curricula offered in Australian library schools. It will be remembered that several schools were mentioned in the abstract and I asked you to consider how this could be indexed in an economical way. The point I wished to implant in your minds was that in the commercial situation within which *LISA* operates it would be hopelessly uneconomic to index each library school named in the abstract. In addition, it is not at all certain that users are well served by over-detailed indexing. In this example, very little further information is given in the abstract for each institution. The user must go back to the original article for the detailed accounts of the courses.

The method employed in *LISA* indexing is as follows. Each abstract is read by the indexer so that it is fully understood. Sometimes, it is necessary to go back to the original paper for clarification and this might, in turn, lead to a re-written or amended abstract. The indexer then compiles a specific subject phrase in words that are tailor-made to fit the abstract. Although specific, this phrase is general enough to include all aspects of the topics that are mentioned. So the specific subject phrase for the Australian example is, "The curricula in Australian library schools" which, translated into CRG scheme citation order, results in:

Bvruf—Curricula. Library schools. Australia

The phrase is also the title of the article, but this is merely coincidental for this relatively simple example. *LISA* indexing is not title indexing. The chain index entries for this article are:

Australia: Library schools: Curricula
Library schools: Curricula
Curricula: Education: (Professional): Librarianship
Education: (Professional): Librarianship

and *see* references are made from:

Schools of librarianship. *See* Library schools
Courses. *See* Curricula

Library education. *See* Education: (Professional): Librarianship
Professional education: Librarianship. *See* Education: (Professional): Librarianship

A more complicated example is provided by abstract number 75/358, which has the uninformative title "Library planning and design, I". Subject analysis by the indexer of the abstract produced the phrase, "Planning the building of the teacher college library at Cardiff College of Education". In CRG classification order this leads to:

QiNbmGkD29—Buildings. Planning. Teacher college libraries. Cardiff College of Education (UK)

with alphabetical subject index entries under:

Cardiff College of Education (UK): Teacher college libraries: Planning: Buildings
Teacher college libraries: Planning: Buildings
Planning: Buildings: Libraries
Buildings: Libraries
Library buildings
Architecture: Library buildings

and a *see* reference from the following, leading to Teacher college libraries,

College of education libraries. *See* Teacher college libraries

Additional entries are made for the annual cumulation of the subject index under,

Wales: Teacher college libraries: Planning: Buildings
U.K. Teacher college libraries: Planning: Buildings

Reference Structure

The examples already mentioned have indicated that, added on to the basic chain indexing, there is a further level of indexing procedure in *LISA*. References are made for synonyms; for the unused forms of terms containing several words; for related entry points, particularly in the annual index; for the initials of the names of organizations; and for the full forms of commonly recognised acronyms. The following are a few examples.

Synonym references

Bibliobuses. *See* Mobile libraries
Bookmobiles. *See* Mobile libraries
Travelling libraries. *See* Mobile libraries

Compound terms
   Indexing: Subject. *See* Subject indexing
   Librarianship: Comparative. *See* Comparative librarianship
Related entry points
   Public libraries. *See also* County libraries, District libraries, Municipal libraries, Rural libraries
Initials of organisations
   A.L.A. *See* American Library Association
   A.L.A. *See* Associates of the Library Association
Full forms of acronyms
   Information Services in Physics, Electrotechnology, Computers and Control. *See* INSPEC

Advantages of chain indexing

For most of the remainder of this paper I should like to concentrate on the difficulties posed by indexing *LISA*, because the problems presented by indexes are always more interesting than the success-side and also because talking about the difficulties might lead to solutions. Perhaps, however, before doing this, it is worth emphasizing that chain indexing in *LISA* over the past six years has shown the following advantages: (1) it is a systematized procedure which is semi-mechanical, thus making it possible for a very small staff to produce indexes regularly to the bi-monthly issues as well as an annual index; (2) the method is predictable and so it is possible for the regular user to learn and understand it—some effort is necessary, of course, but the users are librarians and information workers who are likely to have come across the technique in their day-to-day work; and (3) chain indexing is extremely economical both in terms of page space occupied (particularly important in the context of today's high prices for paper) and in terms of the indexer's time.

Keeping it simple

The point in number (2) above concerning the predictability of chain indexing and the possibility presented to the user of learning the method is, in fact, a springboard for discussing some of the difficulties that occur with the technique.

The phrase "regular user" should be emphasized when the method's predictability is mentioned. Originally, the basic aim for the subject work in *LISA* was to keep it as simple as possible. In modern acronymic terms, the philosophy of the service can be summarised as KISS—Keep

It Simple and Stupid. Six years ago, I would have defended the philosophy of indexing in *LISA* on the grounds that its relative simplicity made the user's task of locating entries that much less difficult. Perhaps I should have read the pages of *The Indexer*. Jack Mills's article, which I mentioned previously, resulted in a comment in your correspondence columns from a writer who called herself the "unsophisticated reader". Ruth Archibald wrote, addressing herself directly to Jack, on a number of points and concluded:

> "If you could put yourself in the state of mind of an unsophisticated (classification- and indexing-wise) reader I should value your comments on these points. [1 sentence omitted.] I still grope after a solution which requires less training of the *user* than does chain indexing."[5] [emphasis added.]

It must be admitted that the sophisticated users of *LISA* have also discovered some difficulties with the chain index approach and, over the years, modifications have been made to the method to try to produce a more acceptable representation of subjects. One of the main difficulties is that the user, particularly one who consults the service only a few times a year, is likely to adopt the order of natural language at the commencement of a search. Because chain indexing is based on the *reversal* of the term order used in the main file, natural language is not always the order produced in the alphabetical index entries. For example, abstracts concerning public library conferences are entered in the classified sequence under

FvAg—Public libraries. Conferences

The application of chain indexing results in alphabetical index entries for

   Conferences: Public libraries
   Public libraries

and so the user looking for this subject under "public libraries" would find no entry. With the CRG scheme's citation order, many entries do, in fact, file under public libraries and it is likely that the unwary searcher would conclude that there were no abstracts on conferences if the chain technique were rigidly applied. Accordingly, in the *LISA* indexes, for two-element cases like this, rotated indexing is adopted and an entry for

   Public libraries: Conferences

is made. This has led to comments from some users that they do not now understand what indexing method is being employed. Clearly, *all* indexes can be criticised!

There is a more serious difficulty with chain indexing, which again is caused by the order of the classification scheme and the rules for making up compound subject representation. Entries for some subjects which might well be sought by the user in a directly linked manner are separated in *LISA*, both in the sequence of abstracts and in the alphabetical subject indexes. This can happen in what must be fairly common searching situations. For example, the user requiring all the abstracts on the application of computers in a particular country, say West German library and information work, is not served very well by *LISA's* displays of subjects. The abstracts are scattered in the classified file under the different main classes such as Computers, Information work and Cataloguing. Unfortunately, they are also scattered in the subject index among other entries for West Germany which, in the cumulated annual index, extend to over a column in length. It would be perfectly possible to find relevant entries at the following points:

West Germany:
    Computerised cataloguing
    Computerised information work
    Computers: Library equipment
    Public libraries: Computers
    Science and technology: Computerised
        information work
    University libraries: Computers

In other words, *all* the entries under West Germany must be scanned in order to ensure the retrieval of every relevant entry. There is no doubt that this must lead to some frustration for the user.

Problems of language and terminology

Another great range of problems in the indexing of *LISA* derives from language—ambiguity of terms as well as the problem of translating foreign languages—and the difficulties of terminology in a rapidly developing subject field. *LISA* is an international abstracting service in two senses: it covers the primary material on a world-wide basis, including abstracts for original material in some twenty languages; and about 80% of the subscription income comes from outside the United Kingdom, so that the needs of overseas users must be constantly borne in mind.

The service covers a subject field which holds a position that Dr. Coblans has compared with that of alchemy at the time of the Renaissance.[6] Library and information work is an emerging social science and its developing situation causes many terminological difficulties. It also suffers from all the traps of terminology that human organizations and relationships hold.

At a relatively simple level of language and terminology it is very easy to introduce problems into the indexes. The possibilities that are open for making ambiguous entries are numerous. I was quite happy for several issues to make an entry for "library staff" in the following form,

Staff: Libraries

until an article turned up on the staff library at the old National Lending Library for Science and Technology at Boston Spa. So we now use qualifying phrases,

Staff: Libraries: (Type of library)
Staff: Library staff

A number of words can lead to this problem of ambiguity, including "education", "law" and "statistics". They might stand as the lead term in entries for types of libraries, subject disciplines and for operations and techniques that are special to librarianship and information work. "Statistics", for example, serves to introduce entries concerning statistics libraries, library statistics and statistics as a subject field. Qualifying phrases and the use of prepositions and conjunctions are necessary so that each entry is unambiguous by itself. The reason is that in any one bi-monthly issue there might not be sufficient surrounding entries to give the correct context. The following is an example of these structured entry terms,

Statistics: *About* Bibliographies: (Fringe
    subject)
Statistics: Information work by subject
    interest
Statistics: Libraries: (Type of library)
Statistics: (Library statistics)
Statistics: (Library statistics): *Of* Library
    stock
Statistics: Library stock by type of material
    published

There are many examples from the world outside librarianship of the difficulties of language and terminology in *LISA*. For instance, a good deal of material is published on librarianship in the Third World countries. In 1969, these areas were almost invariably known as the "developing countries", reflecting the optimism of the 1960s. There now appears to some reaction against this term, perhaps because of its overtones of the Western liberal's unwillingness to face reality. It may be that the older term "underdeveloped countries" will make a comeback and "emerging countries" is yet another candidate.

The volatile American language also raises problems for the indexer with its constant and subtle changes of meaning. There is a substantial body of library literature on racial and ethnic groups as users of libraries and as library staff members. This area is charged with booby traps for the unwary indexer, as the Library of Congress has recently found—subject staff at LC have been unwise enough to introduce the heading "Mammies". Use of the term "Blacks" in the *LISA* indexes still seems to be all right, though to me "Afro-Americans" seems much more correct and also more neutral (those liberal overtones again!). "Mexican-Americans", however, is out in favour of "Chicanos". "Blacks" may pass, but it is absolutely impossible to use the term "Red Indians"; "Native Americans" does not seem to have caught on, although I used it for one year in *LISA*, largely on the strength of articles in a single issue of *Library Journal*. The preferred term now is "American Indians".

The *LISA* indexes must also reflect the fact that the subject field of librarianship and information science is based firmly on organizational and social structures which differ in the various parts of the world. So it is necessary to use some terms which look unfamiliar to British eyes— community college libraries (USA), prefectural libraries (Japan), republican libraries (USSR), and commune libraries (Italy) are a few that spring to mind. In effect, the language base of the *LISA* indexes has now settled down to a 5-level system which includes British English, American English, Commonwealth English, English translations of foreign language terms, and some non-English terms, entered in their foreign language form because they are simply untranslatable or, at least, have no real meaning in English.

Tremendous difficulties arise when an English translation of a non-English term has not gained common recognition and also when the overseas social or institutional structure has no acceptable equivalent in the English-speaking world. There are many examples, including the following— the English translations are those suggested by *LISA* abstractors:

> the West German "Gesamthochschulbibliotheken" ("Collective college" or "Comprehensive college" libraries)
> the East German "Wissenschaftliche Allgemeinbibliotheken" ("Public research" libraries)
> the French "Bibliothèques centrales de prêt" ("Central lending" libraries)
> the Japanese "Katei Bunko" ("Home" libraries for children)

The indexer's dilemma is this: do the English translations of these terms hold any information transfer meaning at all for *LISA*'s users? In a number of cases it seems extremely unlikely that they do and the solution adopted to date has been to index the term in the original language and to make additional entries or references under the suggested English language translation.

Typographical layout of the indexes

A further area of concern in *LISA* indexing, particularly in view of the need to avoid unnecessary costs, is the presentation of the index on the printed page. However good an indexing method is, whatever thought is expended on its detailed structure and terminology, poor layout will affect the searcher's ability to make good use of the index. The subject indexes to the bi-monthly copies of *LISA* are set directly from 5in. x 3in. cards and simply reproduce the entry—little attention is paid to layout apart from the indenting of run-over lines for a long entry and a space left between each letter grouping. For the annual cumulation slightly more effort is made to present the subject index in an inviting manner. Entries with the same lead term are indented under that term in a display style,

> University libraries:
>   Academic status: Staff
>   Annual reports
>   Book selection
>   Cataloguing

User opinions

Having produced a chain index for some years, what evidence is there to suggest that the method

County libraries:Assessment forms:Use for Promotion and Deployment:Professional staff Pjce
County libraries:Buildings QiFw
County libraries:Computer-output-Microfilm (COM) catalogues and Computerised acquisitions SbOq+Uehyh
County libraries:Microfiches:Computer-Output-Microfilm (COM) catalogues UehyhbFw
County libraries. See also Rural libraries
County Libraries Group:Library Association:Week-end School on Design for Cooperation—Building on Strengths (1973) AgD1(LA)
Courses. See Curricula
Coverage:Science and technology:Information services RnM(5/6)
Coward, Bruce:Viewpoint on Library Association Publications Department Ac/vD1
Crops:Agricultural:Optical coincidence punched cards:Coordinate subject indexing ZkhfM(633.003.1)
Cuba:Librarianship AD792
Cuba:Medicine:Information work RmM(61)D79
Cultural activities:Libraries Ry
Cultural centres:Public libraries RyFv/x
Cultural Council (Sweden):Organisations:Connected with Libraries Bjm(KUL)
Culturally handicapped:Reading promotion:Use:Library materials JjHx
Culture:Information work RmM(008)
Curricula:Education:(Professional):Librarianship Bvr/Bx
Curricula materials:Classification schemes (Special) Xsk(371.214)
Cutter's Rules:Subject heading schemes:Alphabetical subject indexing: Dictionary catalogues Yxypd
Czechoslovakia:Commercial and economic aspects:Chemistry:Information work RmM(54:38)
Czechoslovakia:Cooperation:Culture:Information work RmM(008)
Czechoslovakia:Economics:Information work by subject interest RmM(33)D437
Czechoslovakia:Nuclear energy:Information work RmM(539.1)
Czechoslovakia:Political party libraries HjD437
Czechoslovakia:Research:(Library research):Into Use instructions: Libraries and library materials RmiBge
Czechoslovakia:School libraries HykGpD437
Czěchoslovakia:Trade and commerce:Information work RmM(38)D437

Damage:Library stock Sf
Danish Library Association Bko(DAN)
Danish. See also Denmark
Danmarks Biblioteksforening. See Danish Library Association
Data:Bibliographic. See Bibliographic records
Data:Chemistry:Information work RmM(54:083)
Data banks RmOqAid
Data files:Machine-readable. See Computerised bibliographic records
Data processing O
Data processing:Computers. See Computerised, Computers
Decentralisation:Comparison with Centralisation:Administration: Librarianship NjrAx
Decimal Classification:Dewey. See Dewey DC
Decimal Classification:UDC. See U.D.C.
Delays:Time:Abstracting and indexing services:For Library profession Avc
Delhi Public Library FxD54
Denmark:Computers:Library equipment OqD485
Denmark:Foreign materials:Printed union catalogues Uzheb(-87)
Denmark:Research libraries:Relationship with External organisations Nbz&Eqr
Denmark:Viewpoint:On Phuket (Thailand):Public libraries FvD593
Denmark. See also Danish
Department of Education and Science (UK):And Association of Teachers in Colleges and Departments of Education, Library Section:And Library Association Colleges, Institutes and Schools of Education Group:Joint Conference on College of Education Libraries and Higher Education (1973) GcAg
Department of Education and Science (UK):College of Education Libraries Research Project Report GkD1
Department of Education and Science (UK):Viewpoint on Local government reorganisation:Influence on UK:Public libraries FvD1Az
Department of State. See United States Department of State
Departmental libraries:Polytechnic libraries:Optimum allocation of funds:Budgets:Purchasing:Acquisitions SccNtt
Departmental libraries:University libraries:Entries for:Accessions-katalogen:Foreign materials in Denmark:Printed union catalogues Uzheb(-87)
Deployment and Promotion:Professional staff:Library staff Pjce
Depositories:Storage. See entries under Storage
Depth of indexing:Subject indexing Vqi
D.E.S. See Department of Education and Science (UK)
Descriptive cataloguing Ts
Descriptor languages. See Index languages
Descriptor terms. See entries under Term
Design:Interior design:Buildings:Libraries Qine
Design for Cooperation—Building on Strengths (1973):Weekend School: Library Association County Libraries Group AgD1(LA)

Design of Information Systems in the Social Sciences:Bath University Library (UK). See DISISS
Detection systems:Theft prevention:Library stock Sft&
Deutsche Bibliothekskonferenz (German Library Conference 1973): Arbeitsgemeinschaft der Spezialbibliotheken papers HbAgD43
Deutsche Staatsbibliothek (German State Library):East Germany: National libraries:Incunabula and Manuscripts:Stock Lv
Developing countries:Education:(Professional):Librarianship BmDr
Developing countries:Librarianship ADr
Development of Documentation and Information Networks in Eastern Africa:Unesco International Conference (1973) AgD6
Dewey DC Xsi(DEW)
Diachronous data:Comparison with Synchronous data:Obsolescence: Bibliometrics:Periodical articles:Sociology M(301)
Dial-A-Story:Fon du Lac District Library, East Peoria (Illinois): Children's libraries:Extension work RytHykFxAw
Dice's Similarity Coefficient:Use for Word stems:Clustering:Associative indexing:Automatic subject indexing Ztirf
Dictionaries:Terminology of Librarianship Abtc
Dictionary catalogues Yx
Digital computers. See Computerised, Computers
Diplomates in Librarianship:Colleges of Advanced Education (Australia):Surveys:Employment prospects and salaries Pcd+PfD94
Directories:Of Information services RnM(5/6)Aj
Directories:Of Manufacturers and Suppliers:Readers and Reader-printers:Microforms 87&
Directories:Of Periodicals 773-4442&Aj
Disabled. See Handicapped
Disadvantaged:Reading promotion:Use:Library materials JjHx
DISISS (Design of Information Systems in the Social Sciences):Bath University Library (UK):And Geo Abstracts:Survey:Style of publication:Influence on User satisfaction:Physical planning: Abstracting and indexing services by subject interest Rr/sM(309.2)
Displays and Exhibitions:Publicity:(Library publicity) Rkq
Dissemination:Selective. See S.D.I.
Dissemination Center for Bilingual Bicultural Education, Austin, Texas RmM(37=00)
Dissertations:Assessment methods:Library students Bvq
Distributions:Frequency:Bradford's Law. See Bradford's Law of Scatter
Distributions:Frequency:Character strings:Influence on Natural language:Searching:Strategies:Computerised subject indexing ZkjVsq&
Distributions:Frequency:Depth of indexing:Subject indexing Vqi
Distributions:Frequency:Lotka distributions:Author productivity: Bibliometrics:Periodical studies:(Library periodicals) Aokb
Distributions:Frequency:Use for Computerised bibliographic records: Searching:Personal authors UpTi
District libraries:Metropolitan district libraries Fzm
District libraries:Metropolitan district libraries:Metallurgy:Card catalogues UedM(669)
Djakarta. See Jakarta
Document analysis:Subject indexing Vqf
Document delivery:Evaluation:(Performance measurement):Libraries Nhrx
Documentalists Pyd
Documentalists:Curricula:Education:(Professional) Bxrm
Documentary reproduction: Library services. See Copying services
Documentary reproduction:Microforms. See Microforms
Documentation. See Information science, Information work
Documentation centres:Cable television RmM(621.397.5)
Documentation centres:In-service training:Staff PgHb
Documentation centres:Science and technology RmM(5/6)Eqv
Documentation centres:Science and technology:Comparison with Technological university libraries:Policies:Periodicals:Acquisitions SbLmNbc
Drawings. See Pictures
Drenthe (Netherlands):Central libraries:Provincial libraries:Public libraries:Modern literature:Literary activities:Extension work Ryr
Drexel Institute of Technology, Pennsylvania (now Drexel University) Library:Comparison with Iranian Documentation Centre (IRANDOC): Policies:Periodicals:Acquisitions SbLmNbc
Drugs:Pharmaceutics. See Pharmaceutics
Duplicate lists:Selection aids:Acquisitions Sbg&
Dutch Association of Librarians:Bibliotheekdag (Library Day, 1974) AgD492
Dutch Library and Literature Centre:Bibliotheekdag (Library Day, 1974) AgD492
Dutch literature:Library materials M(839.3)
Dutch. See also Netherlands

EALS (East African Literature Service) StD67
Early books:Computerised printed union catalogues UzhebOqKx
Early books. See also Incunabula
Earth sciences. See Geology
East Africa:Librarianship AD67
East African Literature Service StD67
East Central European materials:Union catalogues UzhKz

JANUARY-FEBRUARY xi

Fig. 1—Subject index to individual issue

University libraries:(Continued)

Departmental libraries:Linear programming:Optimum allocation of funds:Budgets 2326
Departmentalisation:Administration 785
Discounts:Costs:Acquisitions 915
Displays and Exhibitions 1858
Document delivery:Reader services 1441
East European and Slavonic materials:Stock 1747-1749
Economic aspects:Periodicals:Exchange 922
English literature:Modifications:UDC 1515
Exhibitions and Displays 1858
Expansion:Card catalogues 961
Extensions:Buildings 1848
Failures:Searching:Author cataloguing 1987
Failures:Searching:Card catalogues 2477
Flood damage salvage methods 2957
Foreign materials:Acquisitions in UK 908
French language and literature materials:Use instructions 2411
Government planning 763
Guides and Handbooks:Promotion:Use 2844
IBM Administrative Terminal System:Computerised cataloguing: Use for Reclassification:Dewey DC to Library of Congress Classification 2008, 2502
IBM TEXTPAC:Programs:Computers:Use for SDI 341
In-service training:Of Supervisory assistants 1352
Index Medicus:Comparison with Current Contents:Life Sciences and Current Contents:Behavioral, Social and Educational Sciences:Behavioural scientists:Use of SDI 1428
Interior design:Buildings 254
Interloans 1958
Japanese area materials:And Government publications: Acquisitions 907
Japanese area materials:And Government publications: International exchange 921
KWOC indexing 2018
Legal deposit:Acquisitions 1465
Library committees 189, 1292
Library of Congress Classification:Modifications 415
Location theory:Use for Maps:Collections:Centralisation: Comparison with Decentralisation 1315
Map rooms:Buildings 2349
Maps:Stock 727, 1270, 2276-2277, 2754
MARC:Retrospective conversion of Card catalogues to Computerised catalogues 1491
Mexican-Americans:Users 700
Microfiches:Loans 2959
Microforms:Stock 164
Modular construction:Buildings 2840
Monastic manuscripts:Microfilms:Stock 733
Old and Rare books:Preservation 1960
Opening hours 1371
Organisation:Relationship with Higher internal organisation 1293
Out-of-print books:Acquisitions 2942
Participative management:Decision making:Administration 2802
Periodicals:Document delivery failures:Evaluation:(Performance measurement) 202
Planning:Administration 750
Politics:Library materials:Use instructions 2411
Professional staff 1344, 2827-2828
Public relations 197
Rare books:Preservation 1960
Reader services 835
Reading surveys 2734
Reports on 1163-1164
Reserve book systems 155, 2745
Role as Information centres 1677
Role as National reference libraries 2187
Role in Data banks:Social sciences 303
Salaries:Staff 223
Science and technology:Information work 2380
Science and technology:Library materials:Use instructions 2901
Science and technology:Magnetic tape:Computerised information services:Use for SDI 2425
Screenplays:Films (Cinematography):Classification and cataloguing 2967
Series publications:Microforms:Author and Title entries: Analytical entries:Card catalogues 2478
Simplified cataloguing 959
Slavonic and East European materials:Stock 1747-1749
Social class:Influence on Higher education students:Use of materials 2728
Social context 1298
Special collections:And Antiquarian materials:Stock 1743-1744
Special collections:Literature and Religion 1289
Staff:Curricula by library occupation:Education:(Professional) 582
Standards 658-659

University libraries:(Continued)

Statistics 96
Stock 718
Stock revision 930
Subject specialists:Staff 233
Successive entry principle:Periodicals:Title cataloguing and Corporate author cataloguing 1990
Summer school students:Open University Students:Use 138, 2727
Tagging:MARC:Computerised cataloguing 388
Technological. See Technological university libraries
Telefacsimile:And National Lending Library for Science and Technology (UK):Use for Periodical articles:Interloans 927
Teleprinters:Interloans 2452
Theses:Legal deposit:Acquisitions 363
Theses:Stock 152-153
Time study of Subject specialists:Staff 814
Times and Costs:Interloans 2450-2451
Tobacco and Health:Information work 2887
Truncation:Coding:Searching:Computerised circulation control:Stock 2459
US Superintendent of Documents System:Classification schemes: Use for Government publications:Shelf arrangement 997
USA area materials:And Government publications: Acquisitions 907
USA area materials:And Government publications:International exchange 921
Use 136, 705-706, 2725
Use instructions 871-872, 1414
Use of External magnetic tape information services 336, 1426, 1917-1918
Use of Library of Congress:Centralised cataloguing 1977
Use of Ohio College Library Center:Centralisation:Computerised cataloguing 1484, 2467, 2972
User needs:Influence on Card catalogues:Retrospective conversion to Computerised catalogues 1489
User suggestions:Staff-User interaction 1231
Working papers:Unpublished materials:Economics:Library materials by subject interest 2285

University Library Management Studies, Office of:(ULMS):Association of Research Libraries (USA) 2311
University of California Union Catalog Supplement:Use for Higher education libraries:Card catalogues:Retrospective conversion to Computerised catalogues 1490
University of [Name]. See significant part of name, e.g., California, Sheffield
University research workers:Information communication:Science and technology 291
University undergraduates. See Undergraduates
"Unofficial" library copyright:Influence on Microforms:(Fringe subject) 2562
Unpublished materials:Economics:Library materials by subject interest 2285
Up-dating:Thesauri 2022
Upper House libraries:Parliamentary libraries 2158
Upplands Väsby (Sweden):Municipal libraries:Cultural activities 1446
Uppsala University Data Centre/Pharmacia AB (Sweden):INTEREST II-DOC-System:Pharmaceutics:Searching:Computerised subject indexing 450
Upsala College, East Orange (New Jersey):College libraries:3M Tattle-Tape:Theft prevention:Stock 1963
Urban information. See Social services:Information work
Urban Information Interpreters Inc., College Park, Maryland (USA): Social services:Information work 2360
Urban Information Specialist Program:Maryland University School of Library and Information Services (USA):Educational Change Game 34
Urban libraries. See Municipal libraries
Urban planning:

And Construction industries:Information work 1404
Information work 2857
Libraries by subject interest 1124, 1646, 2644

Urbana:Champaign-Urbana (Illinois):

Municipal libraries:Black users 130
Municipal libraries:Browsing displays:Shelf arrangement: Influence on Borrowing:Use:Library materials 141

Urdu:

Personal authors:Form of heading:Author cataloguing 1988
See also Hindi

U.S.A.:

Academic libraries:Audio-visual materials:Stock 1262
Aerospace engineering:Libraries:Commercial firm libraries: Computerised periodicals control 1454
Affirmative action:Equal employment opportunities:Career prospects:Administrative staff:Women:Library staff 2344
Aims and Objectives:Public libraries 2663-2664
Alternative press:Periodicals:Socially unacceptable stock: Library stock 1255
And Japan:Exchanges:Staff:Library staff 803
Annual reports:Public libraries 70

ANNUAL INDEXES 1973

xci

Fig. 2—Cumulated subject index

Bki/o—LIBRARY ASSOCIATIONS (Continued)

desirability of seeking closer links with the South African Library
Association. This reminds the author of the Central African Branch
of the SALA, embracing Southern Rhodesia, Northern Rhodesia, and
Nyasaland, which was founded in 1947, flourished in 1948-53, and then
slowly died. Its work and achievements are outlined. (S. D.)

**Bko(DAN)—Danmarks Biblioteksforening (Danish Library
Association)**   75/75
    Danmarks Biblioteksforening: Virksomhedsberetning 1973-74.
[The Danish Library Association: Annual Report for 1973-74.]
Bogens Verden, 56 (8) 1974, 247-258.
    A report on the activities of the Association, 1973-74. Describes
the annual general meeting 1973 and the work of the executive committee during the year. Lists the bodies on which the Association is
represented. As national secretariat for libraries it organises conferences, exhibitions and other public relations work, e.g. distribution
of documentary films, and these are described. The work of the
district branches and the groups (A—E), including their balance sheets,
are also discussed. (E. L. D.)

Bko(HLA)C—Hawaii Library Association. History   75/76
    A history of the Hawaii Library Association, 1921-1974. Jean
Dabagh. HLA Journal (Hawaii Library Association), 31 (1) June 74,
11-13.
    Outlines the Association's development, mentions some of its
publications, and lists its presidents. (S. D.)

Bm/z— EDUCATION (PROFESSIONAL)
                                                           75/77
    Education for librarianship: future needs and prospects. Alan
Horton. In: Curriculum Design in Librarianship—an International
Approach: Proceedings of the Colloquium on Education for Librarianship held at the Western Australian Institute of Technology, August
28-30, 1973; edited by Edward A. Parr & Eric J. Wainwright. Perth,
WAIT Aid Inc., 1974, 139-159. 30 refs.
    Emphasises 3 critical elements in library education: the people
who are recruited to the profession must be quality people, highly
motivated to becoming librarians; the library schools should not
inhibit their enthusiasm; students should receive a largely self-
motivated education which should follow their interests. The following further points are elaborated: the schools should leave something
for their students to learn later on; education should be carried out
in cooperation with the profession and not be primarily related to
its existing needs; the cultural elements in society should not be
neglected; library education should include a general education,
specialisation in a discipline, a professional core and practical experience; students should learn and not be taught; emphasis should be
placed on oral and written communication; the behavioural sciences
should not be neglected; there is an advantage if the person becoming
a librarian can see that education is relevant to this. (N. J.)

Bm+BgebgpdD73—And Research. Finance. Grants. USA   75/78
    Getting on with Uncle $am... where the action (money) is.
Ruth M. Katz. Bulletin of the American Society for Information
Science, 1 (1) June-July 74, 14-15, 33-34.
    Government and quasi-government agencies continue to offer the
main support for university-based programs of information science
education, training and research. However, multiple fund sources are
available: (1) the National Science Foundation provides support for
proposals related to technology and systems, their applications and
courseware, as well as special projects; (2) the National Bureau of
Standards has an Experimental Technology Incentives Program; (3)
other funding sources include the National Endowment for the Humanities which attributes grants for humanities programs, projects, planning and for institutional developments. Colleges and universities are
eligible for funding of special programs and projects within the US
Office for Education. The proposed Information Partnership Act
should be supported by state and local funds. (Aslib)

**BmAgD669—Conferences. Nigeria. University of Ibadan
    Department of Library Studies Colloquium on Educa-
    tion and Training for Librarianship in Nigeria (1974)**   75/79
    Colloquium on Education and Training for.Librarianship in
Nigeria. E. Bejide Bankole. Nigerian Libr., 9 (3) Dec 73, 169-171.
    Report of a colloquium held in Mar 74 (sic). A list of the papers
delivered is given together with the recommendations accepted. The
proceedings are to be published by the Department of Library
Studies, University of Ibadan. (T. E.)

**BmAgD94—Conferences. Australia. Western Australian
    Institute of Technology Colloquium on Education for
    Librarianship (1973)**   75/80
    Curriculum design in librarianship—an international approach:
proceedings of the Colloquium on Education for Librarianship held
at the Western Australian Institute of Technology, August 28-30, 1973.
Edward A. Parr & Eric J. Wainwright, eds. Perth, WAIT Aid Inc.,
1974, 162p. illus. refs. (ISBN 0 909848 09 2)
    For abstracts see the following serial numbers:-

77	£1	82	83
85	86	87	89
92	94	97	113

The Introduction, by John Dean, has not been abstracted. (S. D.)

Bm/z—EDUCATION (PROFESSIONAL) (Continued)

BmBba—Aims and Objectives   75/81
    Affective objectives for education in librarianship. A. J. Lons-
dale. In: Curriculum Design in Librarianship—an International
Approach: Proceedings of the Colloquium on Education for Librarianship held at the Western Australian Institute of Technology, August
28-30, 1973; edited by Edward A. Parr & Eric J. Wainwright. Perth,
WAIT Aid Inc., 1974, 23-29. 3 refs.
    Discusses the results of a group exercise in which the Collo-
quium participants were asked to suggest the objectives (attitudes,
values, appreciations, or feelings) which should be developed in a
librarianship course. Each objective was rated according.to its
degree of importance (based on the number of times it was mentioned
and the importance attached to it by participants) and level of commit-
ment (a guide to the objective's intensity). Objectives relating to
the librarian/library user relationship and the manner in which a
librarian approaches and solves problems were considered to be of
prime importance. It is hoped that these results will serve as a
basis for further discussion despite the following qualifications: they
relate only to those objectives which were explicit enough to be
interpreted and which had a reasonable amount of support; they provide no information on the relative importance of affective objectives
and objectives involving knowledge and intellectual skills; and participants felt there was insufficient time to consider potential objectives, clarify meanings and debate desirability. (S. D.)

BmDr—Developing countries   75/82
    Library education and curriculum problems in the developing
countries. John Dean. In: Curriculum Design in Librarianship—an
International Approach: Proceedings of the Colloquium on Education
for Librarianship held at the Western Australian Institute of Technology, August 28-30, 1973; edited by Edward A. Parr & Eric J. Wainwright. Perth, WAIT Aid Inc., 1974, 89-98. 6 refs.
    Among the library education planning problems faced by emer-
gent countries are an inability to identify or successfully implement
curriculum objectives; limited personnel, equipment, and accommodation; inadequate educational backgrounds of some students; a lack of
curriculum dynamism and rethinking; and the misuse of library tech-
nicians. Australia can help by relieving the isolation of professional
librarians in these countries and by sending them teachers to
strengthen their library schools. IFLA or Unesco should convene a
conference of library educators and senior librarians in SE Asia and
the Pacific to discuss cooperation. (S. D.)

BmD1AxD94—UK. Comparison with Australia   75/83
    The curriculum in Britain. John Horner. In: Curriculum Design
in Librarianship—an International Approach: Proceedings of the
Colloquium on Education for Librarianship held at the Western
Australian Institute of Technology, August 28-30, 1973; edited by
Edward A. Parr & Eric J. Wainwright. Perth, WAIT Aid Inc., 1974,
82-88.
    An account of the professional librarianship qualifications and
awards available in Britain and the difference between British and
Australian library training. (S. D.)

BmD431—East Germany   75/84
    Stand und Entwicklungstendenzen der bibliothekarischen Fach-
schulausbildung in der DDR. [State and development tendencies of
library school education in the GDR.] Rosemarie Werner. Zentbl.
Biblioth., 88 (9) Sept 74, 587-591. 2 refs.
    The standardisation of the library profession in terms of quali-
fications and training requires the establishment of a basic educational course which simultaneously permits a subject specialisation
appropriate to a particular kind of library. Organisations responsible
for the training of librarians are the Erich Weinert Library School,
Leipzig (Ministry of Culture), the School for Academic Librarianship,
Leipzig, and the School for Scientific Information and Academic
Librarianship, Berlin (Ministry of Higher Education). (C. P. A.)

BmD595AwD94—Malaysia. Australian viewpoint   75/85
    Education for librarianship in Malaysia. Ken C. Gilmour. In:
Curriculum Design in Librarianship—an International Approach:
Proceedings of the Colloquium on Education for Librarianship held
at the Western Australian Institute of Technology, August 28-30, 1973;
edited by Edward A. Parr & Eric J. Wainwright. Perth, WAIT Aid Inc.,
1974, 99-110. 18 refs.
    The unplanned growth of libraries and library services in
Malaysia since the late 1960s has created a manpower problem of unknown dimensions. Despite calls for a national library school since
1955, there is still only one school of library science; this accepts
Malay students only. It is at the Mara Institute of Technology and was
founded in 1968; its curriculum and problems (recruitment of suitably
qualified teaching staff, limited resources resulting from limited
funds, recognition of the School's awards by employers) are discussed.
Ways in which Australia can help are outlined. (S. D.)

BmD73C—USA. History   75/86
    Problems associated in the coordination of library education
programmes at the national level. Harold Lancour. In: Curriculum
Design in Librarianship—an International Approach: Proceedings of
the Colloquium on Education for Librarianship held at the Western
Australian Institute of Technology, August 28-30, 1973; edited by

Fig. 3—Abstract file

MARC format
  Role in standardisation of data bases for National Science Library of Canada CAN/SDI system 1069
MARC records. Data base. Computer systems. Georgia Institute of Technology. Price Gilbert Memorial Library
  Cumulative files. Searching. Costs. Effects of file size 1138
MARC records. Data base. Computer systems. University of Saskatchewan. Saskatoon. Library. Canada 1137
MARC records. Data base. Computerised subject indexing systems. Documents on geographical areas
  Fields: Decimal Classification classmarks. Library of Congress Classification classmarks. Library of Congress subject headings & titles. Retrieval performance — *Study examples: Documents on Latin America & Middle East — Comparative studies* 1213
Marketing
  See also
    Commodities
    Exports
    Information services for marketing personnel
    Trade
Marxism-Leninism. Socialist countries
  Role in architectural design of libraries 981
  Role in library development — *Summaries of conference proceedings* 752
Maryland
  University of Maryland. School of Library and Information Services. Urban Information Specialist Project 803
Massey University. Library. New Zealand
  Buildings. Architectural features 994
Materials
  See also
    Metals
    Plastics
    Polymers
    Raw materials
Mathematical models. Library management 946
Mathematical models. SLIC indexing system 1191
Mathematical techniques
  See also
    Algebraic techniques
    Statistical techniques
Mathematical techniques. On line searching. United States. Army. Chemical Information and Data System 1205
Mathematics
  See also
    Bibliometrics
Matica Slovenska. Czechoslovakia
  Services 819
Meaning
  See also
    Semantics
Mechanisation
  See also
    Computer systems
    Data processing equipment
    Data processing systems
    Punched card systems
Mechanised indexing *See* Machine indexing
Mechanised information retrieval services
  Planning. Influence of users' information requirements 1043
Mechanised information services
  Management 1038
Mechanised retrieval devices. Books. Stock. Libraries 1118
Mechanised storage devices. Books. Stock, Libraries
  Mechanised compact storage devices 1118
Media
  See also
    Information sources
    Records
    Regional libraries on medicine
    Reports on medicine
MEDLARS. *Study example*
  Information services on medicine 1029
Meetings
  See also
    Committees
    Conferences
Membership. Library Association of Australia
  Activities promoting membership 789
Metallurgy
  See also
    Documents on metallurgy
Metals
  See also
    Iron & steel
Michigan
  South-east Michigan. Libraries on medicine. Inter-library loan services — *Surveys* 815
  South-east Michigan. Libraries on medicine. Resources & services — *Surveys* 815
Microfiches
  See also
    PCMI
Microfilm equipment. Libraries
  — *Surveys* 1125
Microfilming. Newspapers. Stock. Biblioteca Nazionale Centrale'Vittorio Emanuele II'. Rome 906
Microfilms
  See also
    Aperture card systems
    COM
Microforms
  See also
    Microfiches
    Microfilms
Microforms
  Computer-stored indexes. Searching. Applications of electron microscopes 1160
Microforms. Stock. Libraries 905
Microreduction
  See also
    Microfilming
Microscopes
  See also
    Electron microscopes
Middle East
  See also
    Documents on Middle East
Military forces
  See also
    Armies
Military forces. Yugoslavia
  Libraries 818
Mining
  See also
    Bergakademie Freiburg i. Sachsen
    Documents on mining
    Libraries on mining
Ministry of Information/Directorate for Propaganda *See* Directorate for Propaganda/Ministry of Information
Mobile libraries. Public libraries. Great Britain
  Motor vehicles. Design — *Surveys* 843
Mobile libraries. Public libraries. Japan
  — *Proposals* 841
Mobile libraries. Public libraries. Leskovac. Yugoslavia 840
Models
  See also
    Mathematical models
Models. Storage. Stock. Libraries 1107
Molecular structure
  See also
    Data files on molecular structure
    Data on molecular structure

Fig. 4—Experimental PRECIS index (1971 version)

is helpful to the user as well as proving acceptable on the input side in terms of cost and time? A test was completed in April of this year by Michael Keen of the College of Librarianship Wales, on behalf of Unesco, which compared the retrieval performances of six published indexes in the field of library and information work. Those of *LISA;* the American services *Information Science Abstracts* and *Library Literature; Computer and Control Abstracts*, Chapter 8.5 entitled Information Science; and the relevant sections of the big multi-disciplinary abstracting services, the French *Bulletin Signalétique* and the Russian *Referativnyi Zhurnal.* I will not say anything about the detailed retrieval tests because the results have not yet been published, but Mr. Keen has kindly allowed me to pass on to you my own remarks concerning some of the *subjective* comments made by the searching team. The searchers used to obtain the test results were asked, at the end of their work, a series of questions and in their replies ranked the six services in a kind of merit order. It must be emphasized that these were entirely subjective reactions. In the ranking lists which resulted the *LISA* indexes did very well in answers to the following questions: Which gives most help in the initial stages of a search; Which provides index words that match most closely with request words; Which provides the most usable set of index terms for use throughout the search; Which has the most adequate set of "see" references; and Which has the most adequate set of "see also" references.

Keen's test does give some sign that chain indexing can work for the user, perhaps in the sense that the adoption of a technique enables the indexer to work within a highly controlled atmosphere, ensuring that entries are made consistently and that appropriate references are made.

LISA did not do so well in the CLW test in answer to the question, "Which had the best layout and typography in its index" and it is clear that efforts must be made to improve this aspect of the service.

Bold lead terms

In this connection, I must mention an experimental index produced by Derek Austin and Jeremy Digger for the May-June 1971 issue of *LISA* using the British National Bibliography's Preserved Context Index System (PRECIS). The index contains one or two strange entries (e.g. "Medical libraries *See* Libraries on medicine") but the reason for this is that an early version of PRECIS was used in order to test the application of the system in a special subject field. Modifications to the system have now been made. But the important point from *LISA's* view is the great improvement that this index shows over the normal indexes on the grounds of layout and typography. The PRECIS index does show, I think, how much more inviting an index can look with bold lead terms and suitable displays of subordinate terms. Interestingly, despite the triple-column setting, the PRECIS index takes up twice the number of pages occupied by the published chain index for that particular issue of *LISA.* Of course, bold lead terms could be introduced to the chain index entries and this is now under active consideration.

Conclusion

Ladies and gentlemen, I am drawing to the end of my paper. It is my experience that indexers do not enjoy a carefree life in their endeavours to make the contents of works available. However, there are occasions for the odd flash of merriment, as the examples of humorous entries discovered by Society members over the years show. I have received a quatrain about *LISA* indexing, obviously by a London-based information worker and equally clearly owing some debt to the rather better poem by the much missed Barbara Kyle on roles and "terms tied and free".[7] Nevertheless, I should like to read you my verse as a salutary reminder of the barriers we face as indexers. The author prefers to remain anonymous.

I sought it by class, I sought it by chain,
I tracked it through link after link;
But all my endeavours proved totally vain,
'Cos you don't index like wot I fink.

References.
1. Daniel, R., Mills, J., Selwood, R., *and* Elliott, P. *A classification of library and information science.* The Library Association. 1975.
2. Kent, A. *and* Lancour, H., editors. *Encyclopedia of library and information science*, Volume 4. New York, Marcel Dekker, 1970. Article on 'Chain indexing', p.423.
3. Harrod, L. M. *The librarians' glossary*, 3rd (revised) edition. André Deutsch. 1971. Entry on 'Chain index'.
4. Mills, J. 'Indexing a classification scheme.' *The Indexer,* 2 (2) Autumn 1960. p.46.
5. Archibald, Ruth. Letter in correspondence columns. *The Indexer,* 2 (3) Spring 1961, pp.103-104.
6. Coblans, H. Background paper, *Symposium of editors of documentation, library and archives journals*, Paris. Unesco House, 16-18 May 1972 (Com-72/CONF. 11/3), section 1.1.
7. Quoted on p. viii of Gilchrist, A. *The thesaurus in retrieval.* Aslib, 1971.

Indexing Methods Used by Some Abstracting and Indexing Services

K. G. B. Bakewell

Various methods used for compiling the subject indexes of abstracting and indexing services are described, with particular reference to Applied Science and Technology Index, British Technology Index, Education Index, Current Journals in Education, World Textile Abstracts, Library and Information Science Abstracts, *the abstracting journals issued by Anbar Publications Ltd., and* Sociology of Education Abstracts. *The possibilities of a standardised system are considered, and the importance of a good alphabetical index is stressed if the arrangement of the abstracting or indexing service is a systematic one.*

The idea for this article came when the editor sent me an index to an abstracting journal with a request that I either submit a review of it or use it as a 'peg' on which to base an article on indexing methods used by abstracting and indexing services. I chose the second alternative since I have long felt, after several years of lecturing on this topic, the need for a comparative study of such indexes. The article is only concerned with indexes to groups of periodicals, not with indexes to specific periodicals. I am, of course, making no attempt to be comprehensive and I would welcome the views of readers not only on this article but also on their experiences of other indexes.

There are several different methods of arranging abstracting and indexing services but most are arranged alphabetically by subject or in some sort of systematic or classified order. Exceptions include *Sociology of Education Abstracts*, which is arranged alphabetically by author or title and supported by a classified index, and the five abstracting journals on management published by Anbar Publications Ltd., which are arranged alphabetically by journal title and supported by classified and alphabetical subject indexes.

The alphabetical approach

The two main groups—alphabetical and systematic—have several subgroups. There are many different classification systems and, contrary to popular belief but well known to indexers, there is more than one method of alphabetical arrangement. One can see this clearly by comparing *Applied Science and Technology Index* (*ASTI*), one of the many indexes published by the H. W. Wilson Company of New York, and *British Technology Index* (*BTI*), published by the Library Association. *BTI* is certainly an alphabetical index, but it has a built-in classified structure. Its indexing principles have been clearly explained in a number of articles, many of them in this journal.[1/4] Briefly, documents dealing with complex subjects are indexed as

Reprinted from *The Indexer* 10, no. 1 (April 1976): 3–8.

specifically as possible according to a pre-determined formula which owes a great deal to the classification formula developed by S. R. Ranganathan for his Colon Classification:

THING; Material: Operation: Instrument

and cross-references are provided from 'hidden' terms reading from right to left:

MATERIAL. See THING; Material
OPERATION: Material; Thing. See THING;
Material: Operation
INSTRUMENT: Operation: Material; Thing. See
THING; Material: Operation: Instrument

The resulting heading can be quite formidable and the system also means that a large number of cross-references are necessary. For this reason many people find *BTI* difficult to use, preferring the 'broad headings' and 'multiple entry' approach of *ASTI* and the other Wilson indexes. But is this so helpful to the person searching for information on a specific topic? I think not and shall try to demonstrate why with just one example.

On pages 1322-8 of volume 3 of *Applied Physics* (September 1970) there appeared an article entitled 'Applications of photoluminescence excitation spectroscopy to the study of indium gallium phosphide alloys'. Specifically the article dealt with indium gallium phosphide lamps, though this is not clear from the title. It was indexed in the September 1970 issue of *BTI* under the following heading:

LAMPS; Gallium phosphide-Indium phosphide:
Photoluminescence excitation spectroscopy

with cross-references as follows:

GALLIUM PHOSPHIDE-INDIUM PHOSPHIDE; Lamps.
See LAMPS; Gallium phosphide-Indium phosphide
INDIUM PHOSPHIDE-GALLIUM PHOSPHIDE; Lamps.
See LAMPS; Gallium phosphide-Indium phosphide
PHOTOLUMINESCENCE EXCITATION SPECTROSCOPY:
Gallium phosphide-Indium phosphide; Lamps.
See LAMPS; Gallium phosphide-Indium phosphide:
Photoluminescence excitation spectroscopy
LUMINESCENCE
Related headings:
ELECTROLUMINESCENCE
PHOTOLUMINESCENCE
SPECTROSCOPY, Photoluminescence excitation:
Gallium phosphide-Indium phosphide; Lamps.
See LAMPS; Gallium phosphide-Indium phosphide:
Photoluminescence excitation spectroscopy

It will be seen that, at whatever term the user chooses to enter the index, he will be led to a statement which correctly identifies the subject of the article he is seeking, though unless he regards 'lamps' as the major subject he will be forced to make at least two consultations of the index. In contrast *ASTI* (1971) makes four separate entries for this article under the following headings:—

GALLIUM PHOSPHIDE
INDIUM PHOSPHIDE
LUMINESCENCE—Photoluminescence
SPECTROSCOPY

with a cross-reference:

PHOTOLUMINESCENCE *see* LUMINESCENCE—Photoluminescence

Surprisingly, no entry is provided under ELECTRIC LAMPS (the heading to which we are referred from LAMPS), perhaps because lamps are not mentioned in the title.

It might be argued that, because *ASTI* provides entries under many headings, it is being more helpful to the user, but is this really the case? None of the four headings accurately identifies the subject of the article, as does the *BTI* heading. If the user consults INDIUM PHOSPHIDE or LUMINESCENCE—Photoluminescence this is of little consequence: there are only nine and fifteen entries respectively under these two headings, so that there is little difficulty in scanning all the titles and little chance that the user will miss the desired article. There are, however, two columns of entries under GALLIUM PHOSPHIDE and five columns of entries under SPECTROSCOPY, so the user might well give up the search or overlook the title.

The *BTI* system also provides a systematic approach to the construction of subject headings which appears to be lacking in so many other methods. For example, an article on the evaluation of mathematics instruction in the elementary classroom was indexed in *Education Index* (1973/74), another Wilson index, under

MATHEMATICS—Teaching—Elementary schools

but not under

MATHEMATICS—Teaching methods—Evaluation

or

ELEMENTARY SCHOOLS

In contrast *Current Index to Journals in Education* (May 1974), produced by the American Educational Resources Information Centre (ERIC), indexed the same article under

ELEMENTARY SCHOOL MATHEMATICS
EVALUATION
TEACHING METHODS

but not under

MATHEMATICS
MATHEMATICS EDUCATION
MATHEMATICS INSTRUCTION

Another indexing method which provides a precision lacking from these two examples is PRECIS (Preserved Context Index System),[5/6] which has been used for *British Education Index* since January 1976. The following are the kinds of entry one might expect to find for the above title in *British Education Index:*

ELEMENTARY SCHOOLS
Curriculum subjects: Mathematics. Teaching
methods. Evaluation
CURRICULUM *see also* Curriculum under names of
subjects
MATHEMATICS. Curriculum subjects. Elementary schools
Teaching methods. Evaluation
TEACHING METHODS *see also* Teaching methods under
names of subjects
EVALUATION. Teaching methods. Mathematics.
Curriculum subjects. Elementary schools

(The above examples were constructed before the appearance of an issue of *British Education Index* constructed according to PRECIS principles. I understand that the term ELEMENTARY SCHOOLS will be replaced by the more usual British term PRIMARY SCHOOLS and also that, for reasons of economy, curriculum subjects are not likely to be listed under type of school, a general cross-reference being provided instead).[7]

In the new-style *British Education Index* all entries are numbered consecutively and arranged alphabetically according to the heading regarded as the most significant for the particular article. The other entries, as well as the principal entry, are listed alphabetically at the front of each issue of the index, each entry (apart, of course, from general cross-references) referring to the appropriate number. The rules for the construction of PRECIS entries should ensure that the user of the index will locate the required article whatever term he consults, which is certainly not the case with *Current Index to Journals in Education* or *Education Index*.

Another method used for the construction of alphabetical subject indexes is the articulated subject index. This is a type well known to and commonly used by book indexers, consisting (in its simplest form) of a lead term followed by some modifying phrase to which it is linked by a structure word such as a preposition—for example:

abstracting journals, indexes to, characteristics of
indexes to abstracting journals, characteristics of

Professor Michael Lynch, of the University of Sheffield Postgraduate School of Library and Information Science, has developed a computerised system of articulated subject indexing[8]/[9] and this is used in *World Textile Abstracts*. The following entries are taken from the 1973 volume:

	Abstract no.
Fibres	
production of, from films	1888
freezing of solvent solutions for	2848P
from thermoplastic resins,	
Forshaga process for	8746
spinning of	2648
Filaments	
production of, from films	1888
Films	
production of filaments and fibres from	1888
Resins	
thermoplastic, Forshaga process for	
production of fibres from	8746
Spinning	
of fibres	2648

The abstracts themselves are arranged under broad subject categories and are given a running number (e.g., 1888, 2648, 2848 and 8746 above—P refers to Patent). It will be seen that entries are made under most 'sought' headings, though the absence of entries under Forshaga process, Freezing, Solvents and Thermoplastics is perhaps unfortunate and something which one would not expect to happen using the *BTI* or PRECIS principles.

The Classified approach

There are, then, several different methods of compiling alphabetical subject indexes, but there is even more variety when it comes to systematic indexes because of the different classification schemes available for different disciplines. One of the original aims of the *Universal Decimal Classification* (UDC) was to provide a standard classification system which could be used for documents in all subject fields. This aim has not been achieved and in recent years a number of abstracting services which were originally arranged by UDC have changed their system of classification. Other services, which originally included UDC numbers with their abstracts, no longer do this. *World Fisheries Abstracts* is one service which does still include UDC numbers, as well as alphabetical subject headings and the United States Fish and Wildlife Classification System. These abstracts are arranged in random order, three entries to a page, and the entries can be cut to form five- by three- inch cards and arranged in one sequence according to one of these systems or indeed any other indexing system. Each issue of the abstracts also includes an alphabetical subject index.

A number of abstracting services are still arranged according to UDC or an amended version of UDC, including the Institution of Mining and Metallurgy's *IMM Abstracts* and *Technical Education Abstracts*, but the trend is towards specially developed classification systems.

One abstracting service of interest to the indexer is *Library and Information Science Abstracts* (*LISA*), which uses a special classification scheme for library and information science devised by the Classification Research Group as the basis of its arrangement with an alphabetical subject index compiled by the 'chain indexing' method to allow users to locate the class numbers.[10] The classification system has been criticised for its complexity and the class numbers can be somewhat frightening. For example, an article on MEDLARS (Medical Literature Analysis and Retrieval System) in Australia and New Zealand is given the class number RnOqM(61)D94+D931, where Rn means Information Services, Oq means Computers, M(61) means Medicine, D94 means Australia and D931 means New Zealand. The chain index allows users to locate this item reasonably quickly no matter what term they consult, even though the full context is not always given as would be the case with PRECIS entries:

```
Australia: MEDLARS        RnOqM(61)D94
New Zealand: MEDLARS      RnOqM(61)D94
MEDLARS                   RnOqM(61)
Medicine: Computerised information services
                          RnOqM(61)
Computerised information services RnOq
Information services      Rn
```

(For convenience and economy, an incorrect entry is given under New Zealand: the correct notation for an article on MEDLARS in New Zealand alone would be RnOqM(61)D931.)

The American counterpart of *LISA*, *Library Literature*, may be easier to use because of its alphabetical arrangement, but is less economical because it provides entries under three headings compared with *LISA's* one (though these entries are less full since *Library Literature* is an indexing service only and does not include abstracts). Entries are provided under

```
MEDLARS
INFORMATION SERVICES, Scientific and technical—
  Australia
INFORMATION SERVICES, Scientific and technical—
  New Zealand
```

with cross-references as follows:

```
COMPUTER-STORED INFORMATION see INFORM-
  ATION RETRIEVAL SYSTEMS
INFORMATION RETRIEVAL SYSTEMS—Medicine see
  also MEDLARS
AUSTRALIA see also INFORMATION SERVICES, Scientific
  and technical—Australia
NEW ZEALAND see also INFORMATION SERVICES,
  Scientific and technical—New Zealand
```

Once again the user is likely to locate the article eventually whatever term he consults, though (unlike the *LISA* classification, but like the other Wilson indexes) not one of the headings accurately specifies the subject of the article—MEDLARS in Australia and New Zealand. Also there is no cross-reference from MEDICINE in *Library Literature*, though it might be argued that this would file close enough to MEDLARS to make such a cross-reference unnecessary.

The classification system used for the five abstracting journals on management published by Anbar Publications Ltd.[11] is less complex than

the *LISA* system because no attempt is made to combine class numbers of multi-faceted topics. Instead each subject is entered separately in the alphabetical and classified indexes, the abstracts themselves being arranged in random order and given a running number. If, for example, the user is seeking information on information services in the petroleum industry from *Personnel + Training Abstracts* (1971), he first consults the alphabetical index, where he finds:

```
Information services        1.91
Petroleum                   1.50
```

He then consults the classified index, where he finds:

```
1.50 Oil, Petroleum, allied products
  Shell Research, information-using habits CH14
1.91 Libraries, etc., Translation Services
  Gate-opener as opposed to gatekeeper CH14, DA58
```

Abstract no. CH14 is an article on an investigation by Shell Research Ltd. of the information-using habits of their scientific staff aimed at identifying those individuals who are potentially 'technological gatekeepers'.

It is interesting to note that the ANBAR classification system, although designed specifically for a published abstracting service, is used in at least one library (that of the Institute of Practitioners in Work Study, Organisation and Methods) with few problems apart from occasional lack of specificity.

However unfamiliar the classification scheme, it should not be too difficult for a user to trace items on a specific subject in either *LISA* or the Anbar abstracting journals. Such, I fear, is not the case with *Sociology of Education Abstracts*, which are arranged alphabetically by author or title and supported by a classified index. The purpose of this index is not clear; certainly it would not help this particular layman in a retrospective search, especially as it lacks an alphabetical key.

The index has the following main sections:

```
ADMINISTRATION AND ORGANISATION (0)
CURRICULUM (1)
EDUCATIONAL RESEARCH AS AN ACTIVITY (2)
GOALS AND FUNCTIONS OF EDUCATION (3)
GUIDANCE AND COUNSELLING/SCHOOL PSYCH-
                                   OLOGY (4)
HISTORICAL DEVELOPMENT OF EDUCATION (5)
PERSONNEL (6)
THE TEACHING-LEARNING PROCESS (7)
TESTING AND MEASUREMENT (8)
I    SOCIOLOGICAL ANALYSIS
II   PRIMARY UNITS OF SOCIAL LIFE
III  BASIC SOCIAL INSTITUTIONS
```

It will be seen that the first nine of these broad subject headings are arranged alphabetically while the final three headings, presumably placed at the end because they deal with sociological aspects, seem to be arranged in an arbitrary order. As stated, there is no general alphabetical index, but each of the first nine headings, apart from HISTORICAL DEVELOPMENT OF EDUCATION, is subdivided into a number of alphabetically arranged subheadings, each of which is given a three-figure notation beginning with the figure which I have placed in parentheses after the main heading. Thus under ADMINISTRATION AND ORGANISATION we find:

001 Accreditations
002 Admissions
003 Administrative goals
004 Integration
005 Inter-agency relationships
006 Leadership development
007 Materials and supplies
008 Organisational patterns of educational institutions
009 Personnel employment practices
011 School finance
012 School plant
013 School-community relationships
014 Staff relations
015 Student services—health, financial aid, etc.
016 Transport
017 Other administration and organisation areas

The number of abstract numbers under some headings is staggering—for example, in the 1974 volume we find:

008 Organisational patterns of educational institutions:
11 14 15 16 26 33 39 40 48 54 61 71 72 91 92 95
98 108 110 111 118 127 131 135 145 146 159 174
185 186 198 210 236 239 244 245 251 257 273 275
277 278 279 295 302 306 315 329 331 335 336 341
352 353 355 359 361 373 390 409 424 425 430 451
462 471 478 479 481 484 486 510 512 530 531 543
548 550 551 567 572 574 580 592 594 600 615 620
628 629 637 640 641 658 659 665 666 710 711 726
737 749 754 755 756 771 783 792 801

This is a far cry from the five or six page references which we book indexers generally regard as the maximum without subdivision! The articles covered by these 109 abstracts cover a variety of topics including Florida's black school principals, experimental schools, racism and school staffing, resources of university departments, teacher training, school democracy, selection of pupils for secondary schools, the school and the community, children's behaviour problems, comprehensive schools and university reform. Let us look at one, number 710, in greater detail.

This article, from *Comparative Education Review*, vol. 18, 1974, deals with the attitudes of students and teachers to the establishment of school councils in secondary schools in Finland.

We find at the end of the abstract that it is also indexed at 310 (Education and social change), 523 (Political and legal) (under III Basic social institutions), 534 (Socialisation and indoctrination) (also under Basic social institutions) and 539 (Social change) (again under Basic social institutions). The listing of classification numbers at the end of each abstract suggests that the purpose of these numbers may be to indicate the subject of the article rather than to aid in retrospective searching, but surely the abstract itself should (and in this case certainly does) give a clear enough indication of the subject.

Lest it be thought that I have deliberately sought a poor example, I would mention that as many, or almost as many, abstract numbers are listed under the following headings:

301 Social distribution of education
310 Education and social change
750 Social factors
S13 Groups (including ethnic and class)
S30 Differentiation and stratification
S34 Socialism and indoctrination

and there are many more headings with thirty or more abstract numbers.

It may be that an educational sociologist would have no difficulty in finding his way around this index but I know that I, as a librarian, would not find it easy. What surprises me is that the editors of *Sociology of Education Abstracts* apparently rejected the PRECIS indexing system as being unsuitable, yet surely the following PRECIS style headings would enable abstract no. 710 to be located much more easily than does the present rather cumbersome system:

FINLAND
    Secondary schools. School councils. Attitudes of
    students and teachers
SECONDARY SCHOOLS. Finland
    School councils. Attitudes of students and teachers
SCHOOL COUNCILS. Secondary schools. Finland
    Attitudes of students and teachers
STUDENTS. Attitude to school councils. Secondary schools.
    Finland
TEACHERS. Attitude to school councils. Secondary schools.
    Finland

Conclusion

I have, as indicated at the beginning of the article, been very selective but the examples I have chosen clearly indicate the wide diversity of methods used for arranging indexes and abstracting services. Writing about documentation services in the field of business studies in 1969, Dews and Ford commented that 'diversified methods of arrangement' created difficulties when searching,[12] and this applied to one subject area only. How much more complicated is the situation facing the librarian or indexer having to use a large number of abstracting and indexing services in different subject areas.

Is there a solution and should there be a standardised system? The Universal Decimal Classification has been tried and apparently failed. The BTI system works very well in the field of technology; could it be equally successful in other areas? The PRECIS system certainly has possibilities and has been used for our national bibliography, covering all subjects, since 1971, but would it be reasonable to expect the many classification systems (those used for LISA and the Anbar journals as well as the many other systems used for services not mentioned in this article) to yield to it? I think not but, sticking my neck out, I would suggest (1) that a systematic method, be it the BTI approach, PRECIS or a classification scheme, generally makes life easier for the searcher than does a system of broad subject headings, and (2) that if classification is used, it is essential that there be a workable alphabetical index. This is the case with LISA and the Anbar journals but not with Sociology of Education Abstracts. In the case of the latter journal a considerable amount of the searcher's time must be wasted trying to find under which broad subject heading a specific subject is subsumed.

References.

1.   Coates, E. J. Aims and methods of the British technology index. The Indexer, 3 (4). Autumn 1963. pp. 146-52.

2.   Coates, E. J. Scientific and technical indexing. The Indexer, 5 (1). Spring 1966. pp.. 27-34.

3.   Coates, E. J. Computerised data processing for British technology index. The Indexer, 6 (3). Spring 1969. pp. 97-101.

4.   Singleton, A. Technical indexing at BTI (with a comment by E. J. Coates). The Indexer, 9 (2). Oct. 1974. pp. 37-52.

5.   Bakewell, K. G. B. The PRECIS indexing system. The Indexer, 9 (4). Oct. 1975. pp. 160-6.

6.   Austin, D. The development of PRECIS: a theoretical and technical history. Journal of Documentation, 30 (1). Mar. 1974. pp. 47-102.

7.   Personal communication from Christine Shaw.

8.   Lynch M. F. Computer-organised display of subject information. The Indexer, 7 (3). Spring 1971. pp. 94-100.

9.   Lynch, M. F. and Petrie, J. H. A program suite for the production of articulated subject indexes. The Computer Journal, 16 (1). Feb. 1973. pp. 46-51.

10.   Edwards, T. Indexing LISA: chains, KISS and the bold approach. The Indexer, 9 (4). Oct. 1975. pp. 133-46.

11.   Accounting + Data Processing Abstracts, Marketing + Distribution Abstracts, Personnel + Training Abstracts, Top Management Abstracts, Work Study + O and M Abstracts.

12.   Dews, J. D. and Ford, M. M. An investigation into existing documentation services in business studies. Manchester Business School. 1969. p.38.

Some Ideas on Indexing

J. Edwin Holmstrom

These are rather haphazard ideas, each described at the point to which reflection and a moderate amount of practical experience has carried it up to now but without trying to build them into a complete philosophy of the subject.

Indexing, in the wider sense of the word, includes any device for discovering or rediscovering in a book, or in a collection of papers or notes, such items of information or passages of text as may have a wanted relevance. This device is intended to perform the same sort of function as a person's memory. By comparison with natural memory it has the disadvantage that the wanted items do not spring spontaneously and instantly into focus but have to be searched for, with the liability of wasting time by searching in the wrong places. Furthermore the brain, it has been said[1]

> has one remarkable property which does not appear to be found in any mechanical system: namely, that the mesh of neurones can be polarised by the presentation of a new subject on which further information is required. A fresh focus is then created [upon which] the relevant data . . . may be said to converge automatically . . . The brain, therefore, possesses what may be termed an automatic adjustment of its cross-references.

On the other hand an artificial memory in the shape of an index offers several immense advantages over a natural one: its contents are accessible not only to the individual who apprehended them in the first place but also to other people who may not even have known that the data in question existed; it does not die when its possessor dies; its accuracy is potentially perfect and its capacity potentially limitless. These advantages are such as to make indexing of one kind or other an indispensable tool for any sort of research—and here we must include in "research" even such trivial operations as looking up a telephone number or consulting a guide book.

Indexing is effected by means of words or other graphical symbols which represent to the mind the topics under reference. Either these symbols may occur in random order so coded as to make it possible for those of them which relate to a given topic to be singled out from the rest by mechanical or electronic means, or they may be arranged in a classified sequence enabling them to be found by visual inspection. The first mentioned of these alternatives is very new. The second is very old, especially in the form of alphabetical classification, which no doubt is the form which the average reader of this journal understands by indexing.

It is important to appreciate the distinction between alphabetical and logical classification. The keywords, or index entries, used in the former are symbols not directly for the concepts under reference but for the sounds which people utter (each in his own language) when they talk about those concepts, or imagine when

Reprinted from *The Indexer* 1, no. 4 (Autumn 1959): 96–103.

they think about them, arranged in an arbitrary but conventional order known as the alphabet. Thus the hymn beginning " Lead, kindly light " may be indexed immediately before " lead pipes " whilst clay, copper, iron, etc., pipes may be scattered all over the index, according to the accident of the initial letters of these words, where the searcher whose life's passion is pipe-lore in all its rich variety may never notice them. Likewise, in an unsubdivided alphabetical index, the components of a motor car such as accumulator, brake, carburettor, dynamo, gear-box, steering, tyres and so on would appear in that order interspersed with the names of other things having no connection with motor cars ; whereas in a logical classification each of these would be given its proper place in some systematic scheme exhibiting either their functional or their constructional relationships and those of the assemblies to which they belong.

It was through the devising and progressive extension of systematic classifica-tions, whereof these are crude and incomplete examples, that the philosophic urge to arrange natural forms and phenomena in patterns gave rise to what we now call science and technology.

The examples, such as they are, may serve to bring out several important practical questions in alphabetical indexing. First, in such an index whose scope is not limited to motor cars, should those entries which do relate to that subject be grouped together ? If so, we avoid the dispersal of logically contiguous items but we lose that advantage of a single straight-through alphabetical sequence which consists in the certainty that the searcher will find what he is looking for (if it is there at all), provided only that he calls it by the same name as the indexer. Further we shall have to decide whether the sub-headings listed under the main heading of the group as a whole are to be arranged in alphabetical order among themselves or, alternatively, may be ramified systematically into sub-sub-headings, sub-sub-sub-headings and so forth—which seems logical, but which brings with it the disadvantages attaching to what the late Dr. S. C. Bradford, who was the protagonist in Britain of the Universal Decimal Classification, used to call " concealed " systematic classifications. These questions, important as they may become in indexing a technical treatise, textbook or periodical, need not how-ever arise in indexing a narrative work. For that purpose the plan which is easiest of all for the indexer to follow—namely that of simply referencing the various topics in the order they happen to be first mentioned in the text—will as a rule correspond roughly with the time sequence of the happenings related and, there-fore, be the most helpful to the reader also. The following entry in the index to Churchill's *The Second World War* may serve as an example :

> War Cabinet—Sir Archibald Sinclair and, 11 ; size of, 12 ; composition of, 13 ; meetings of, 15, 18 ; Secretariat of, 17-19 ; on need to retain air defences, 40 ; prepares for evacuation of Army, 52-3 ; determined to fight on, 80-157; and Italian appeasement, 190-191; in consultation on fall of France, 175-6, 180-1 ; . . . [etc.]

The bane of alphabetical indexing is the fact that terminology, except in a few specialised technical fields, is neither standardised nor defined. Generally, the words which have to be adopted as index heads are no more tools of precision than those used in textual composition. They have no clear limits of meaning but only a more or less generally agreed concentration of meaning tailing off into a penumbra of vagueness all round. The penumbras of words which suggest nearly but not quite the same things overlap one another, encouraging a currency of near-synonyms (like accumulator/battery and dynamo/generator in the above example) which are even more of a nuisance in indexing than real synonyms (like motor car/automobile). Where index headings, sub-headings and sub-sub-headings have synonyms or quasi-synonyms, should the indexer go on making multiple entries under each of these, or should he decide once and for all which of the synonyms he prefers, and enter everything under that alone, after making a single " see — " reference to it from the others ? If he adopts the first of these courses he may find he has let himself in for a lot of repetition (and checking !) which he might have avoided ; if he adopts the latter, some users of the index may be inconvenienced and annoyed. One way to prevent the indexer burying a reference under one heading and the searcher vainly looking for it under another is to provide both of them with a prefabricated list of headings which are the only ones allowed to be used, the terms in these lists being carefully chosen to ensure that their meanings are clearly delimited even in the minds of people having little knowledge of the subject field and, above all, so as to be mutually exclusive. All that the indexer has to do is to pick the term that most nearly fits the case arising ; or if, exceptionally, he is unable to find one which does fit he must apply to someone having the requisite knowledge and authority to add a new term to the list, chosen with the same care as the others. Examples of this practice exist particularly in the United States for cataloguing the titles and subjects of books in both general and special libraries, which is not quite the same thing as indexing the contents of any one book in detail but may nevertheless be useful in that connection also. (References to four such lists of subject headings may be found in the bibliography appended to one of my own books[2]).

Another of the moot points that arise in alphabetical indexing, particularly where corporate and geographical names and titles are concerned, is which of the following two sequences to adopt:

" Letter by letter "	" Word by word "
Oldbury	Old Cairo
Old Cairo	Old Catholics
Oldcastle, Sir John	" Old Charges " (Masonic)
Old Catholics	Old Cold Harbor
" Old Charges " (Masonic)	*Old Curiosity Shop, The*
Old Cold Harbor	Old Deerfield
Old Curiosity Shop, The	Oldbury
Old Deerfield	Oldcastle, Sir John
Oldenbarneveldt	Olden Times Inn
Oldenberg	Oldenbarneveldt
Oldenburg	Oldenberg
Olden Times Inn	Oldenburg

"Letter by letter" is used in such important works as the index to the *Encyclopaedia Britannica* and is in my view preferable because "word by word" may leave the searcher in doubt where to look for compound expressions which are sometimes printed as one word and sometimes split, like—

timekeeping	*as against*	time-lag
time-lag		time series
time series		timekeeping

The "word by word" (or "nothing before something") principle is tending, however, to be preferred, especially for names in directories, and since 1951 it has been embodied in the relevant British Standard[3] which determines also various other questions. On the outstanding questions, it may not very much matter what particular rules are adopted, but rules there must be, for the sake of consistency. Hence the fact that the Society of Indexers is engaged in drawing up a code is to be welcomed. Meanwhile, as being of possible interest although having no official sanction from any quarter, I reproduce below the rules I have suggested in another of my books[4] and which I myself at present follow:

(For "page numbers" read "paragraph numbers" if that system is adopted)

1. Begin every word, including the first, with a small letter unless it is a proper name or is part of the name of an organisation. Underline (for printing in italics) the titles of publications and also any words like *see, see also* or *and* not forming part of the material indexed but inserted as a direction to the reader.

2. Punctuate as in the examples below, using a comma before a page number, a semi-colon before a sub-heading, a semi-colon before *see also* if this follows a page number ; a colon before *see* if this directly follows a word and not a number ; no full stops anywhere.

3. If a main heading has one or more synonyms under which a user of the index might reasonably look instead of looking under the word preferred, repeat the index entries under the synonyms, provided that not more than four page numbers have to be repeated. If, however, more than four page numbers are affected, do not repeat them but give instead a *see* . . . reference from the non-preferred to the preferred synonym. If additional relevant material is indexed under another main heading which is not a synonym, give a *see also* . . . reference to this.

Exs.: assurance, 19, 32
       consumption, 84
       homotopic abstracts: *see* synopses
       insurance, 19, 32
       pthisis, 84
       preprints, 88, 93 ; *see also* separates
       shipping, 73, 89, 136 ; *see also* ports
       synopses, 26, 90, 92, 109, 112, 127, 153
       tuberculosis, 84
       zoology, 47, 83 ; *see also* biology

4. If the references to a subject named in the index extend over several continuous pages of the text, indicate the range of each continuity (repeating only the

minimum number of digits necessary).

Ex.: brickwork, 30-3, 148, 199-203

fenestration, 16, 48-50, 169-71

5. Index people by their surnames followed only by initials, unless they have honorific or territorial titles, in which case follow the rules of the Anglo-American Cataloguing Code. (Omit Prof., Dr., Mr., Mrs., Miss.) In the case of hyphenated names and in that of unhyphenated double names liable to doubt, give a cross-reference from the last part.

Ex.: Besançon, L. Justin-: *see* Justin-Besançon, L.

Bodet, J. Torres: *see* Torres Bodet, J.

6. Rearrange the names of societies and corporations and the titles of publications so as to begin with the first word in the name or title that indicates or qualifies the subject matter handled by the body or publication in question.

Ex.: Chemical Industry, Society of

Documentation, Journal of

Electroencephalography and Clinical Neurophysiology, International Federation of

Mental Health, World Federation for

Scientific and Industrial Research, (Australian) Council of

7. If such organisations are commonly known by abbreviations or initials, put these in brackets after the full names, without full stops between the capital letters.

Exs.: Economic and Social Council (ECOSOC)

Food and Agriculture Organisation (FAO)

Scientific and Industrial Research, Department of, (DSIR)

(Note, however, that certain organisations, such as Aslib since 1946, are officially registered under their abbreviated names and should be so indexed. In cases like Unesco where the user of the index may be in doubt, insert also a " *see* . . . " reference from the alternative to the preferred form.)

8. If several references are entered after one concept used as an index heading, some requiring it to be understood in the singular and some in the plural or with some other grammatical change, add the various alternative endings to the word in brackets.

Exs.: abstract(s)(ing)

Europe(an)

terminolog(y)(ies)

9. So as not to irritate the user of the index and waste his time by confronting him with a long string of page numbers without showing which are the ones he wants, subdivide main headings wherever possible by following them by sufficient sub-headings to entail not more than three page numbers after each sub-heading.

Ex.: India, 146 ; microfilm(s)(ing) in, 89, 91-2 ; statistics of periodicals, 146 ; time-lag in abstracting, 85 ; *see also* Pakistan

10. If, in carrying out Rule 9, the main heading reoccurs as part of a title used as a sub-heading, it may be replaced by . . . The sequence of the sub-headings may be either alphabetical as in the above example or numerical as in the following.

Ex.: Bank(s), 226, 304 ; statistics, 6 ; Midland, 22 ; of England, 226, 22 ;
    International . . . for Reconstruction and Development, 271

11. For the same reason as Rule 9, whenever several page numbers follow one heading or sub-heading, put the most important page reference first and follow this by the others in numerical order.

Ex.: industries, 86, 34, 53, 139 ; cocoa, 47, 19 ; primary, 87, 19 ; secondary, 87 ;
    secondary . . . as affecting balance of trade, 93, 34, 53, 143

(This rule is a departure from usual practice. It imposes additional responsibility and trouble on the indexer, but these should be accepted in order to maximise speed and convenience for the user.)

12. If the same concept occurs both as a main heading and as a sub-division of another main heading, repeat it or connect the two in accordance with Rule 3.

Exs.: alternators, 96

armoured fighting vehicles: cars, 16 ; tanks, 89-91

boiler(s), 36, 48-9 ; inspection of, 50 ; water-tube, 63, 87 ; descaling
    of water-tubes, 93

generators: alternating current, 96 ; direct current, 98

tanks, 89-91

water-tube boilers: *see* boilers

13. Explain what the user needs to know of these rules by the following note at the beginning of the index:

The most important reference to each subject is mentioned first and is followed by any others in the order of their occurrence in the text. A society, corporation or publication is indexed under the first word in its title which specifies the subject matter which it handles.

In technical fields there are many information bureaux or documentation centres which arrange their card files, and there are some periodicals which arrange their published indexes, not alphabetically but in accordance with what I called earlier in this article a " logical " or " systematic " scheme of classification. This enables a user to find his way about a field of knowledge and improve his familiarity with it just as he might find his way about country guided by a map, by identifying this or that feature in the landscape and proceeding from that to others. If the area covered is a large one he needs an alphabetical key—a gazetteer, so to speak, appended to the atlas of maps—indicating by symbols where to look for some starting point which he already knows of by name. The alphabetical key only has to be published once and for all ; and since it can list multiple names for the same thing—Automobile as well as Motor car, comparably to listing Copenhagen as well as København—the classification itself need take no account of these.

One great advantage of thus classifying index entries under symbols which indicate their places in a logical scheme is that it helps the searcher to orient himself and perceive cross-country journeys that might be worth making. Supposing, for instance, he looks to see if there is any reference to using Aluminium for a certain purpose but finds nothing under that head it may be helpful for him to be led from it to the higher collective " Light metals " and notice that there is another way down from that, labelled " Magnesium ", which might lead to something analogous although not identical with what he originally set out to find. In research and planning, such journeys as this may often be very suggestive. They approximate more closely to the spontaneous working of that incomparable instrument, the human brain, than does the act of consulting an alphabetical index.

For this purpose the Universal Decimal Classification, which Bradford made the basis of the various important services that are performed centrally in the Science Museum Library, offers advantages[5] in that it is internationally standard-ised, it is continually being extended and improved and its schedules giving the same class numbers for the same concepts are published in many languages (those in English by the British Standards Institution, 2 Park Street, London, W.1). Its principle of denoting subjects by decimal numbers which can be extended indefinitely, each decimal place corresponding to a further particularisation of what is denoted by the one on its immediate left, has been taken over from the Dewey classification which is used in many libraries for grouping books on the shelves according to subject. As far as the third or fourth decimal place the class numbers, too, are identical with Dewey, but those of the UDC can be extended much further into detail if that is required for the purpose of analytical indexing. Supporters of the system hope a time may come when every publication will be pre-indexed at its source by having the appropriate UDC numbers printed on it.

These numbers have also another possible function : several of them can be strung together with various marks of punctuation between them to indicate that in the document under reference the subjects they denote are treated conjointly. Thus 532.13:541.182.6:667.622 stands for something about " internal friction or viscosity " in relation to " suspensoid systems of a solid and a liquid " and to " pigments or lakes ". (The colon, as here, is the sign most frequently used, but others are available for indicating different kinds of interrelationship). Such an index entry made up of three UDC numbers being inserted at all three places in the numerical sequence, the reference to this very specific conjunction of ideas will be found with equal certainty from whichever aspect it is approached.

The UDC, however, also has many critics on various grounds and not all subject specialists find it the most suitable classification for their particular pur-poses. Moreover the device of " coloning " is in the nature of an afterthought to the system ; it was not originally designed for that and the strings of numbers may become inconveniently long as well as sometimes ambiguous. The Indian librarian S. R. Ranganathan has avoided these defects, secured other advantages and carried the principle of what he calls " facet analysis " very much further in his Colon Classification with its " chain procedure " for indexing, described by Foskett[6] and by Wells[7] but which there is not space to go into here.

Vickery, in his useful critical survey[8] of all these alternatives, considers it " clear that a large part in indexing in science and technology—perhaps by far the larger part—will continue to be alphabetical " ; and indeed the indexing of the American *Chemical abstracts*, probably the most extensive undertaking of its kind in the world, shows how well that system can be made to work if due attention is given to countering the liability of a searcher to look for terms which do not correctly describe the subjects he wants, or which differ from those which the indexer has used to describe those subjects. He also considers, however, that for some purposes systematic classifications are essential, and that the way to improve the efficiency of either kind is to make them multi-faceted. Mechanical or electronic selection is not, he points out, a new principle but a new tool for using either alphabetic or systematic classifications. " All that the machine does is to match a given code combination with the combinations in the index entries " just as a human searcher does in a visual index ; the question of their comparative economics in relation to speed and efficiency is one to be settled by cost analysis. But where punched card machines and electronic computers used as selectors are likely to show to greatest advantage is, in fact, for selecting those references that are of interest from multiple facets conjoined with one another.

Finally be it mentioned that under what is known as the Aslib-Cranfield Research Project 18,000 aeronautical documents are now in process of being indexed by four different systems simultaneously—UDC, alphabetical subject catalogue, faceted classification and the Uniterm system invented by M. Taube (see[2])—in order to compare their efficiencies under controlled conditions[9].

REFERENCES

[1] POTTS, H. E. Patents and special libraries. *Report of the Second Conference*, Aslib, 1926, pp. 161-6.

[2] HOLMSTROM, J. E. *Records and research in engineering and industrial science.* 3rd ed. London : Chapman & Hall. 1956.

[3] *Alphabetical arrangement.* BS 1749. London : British Standards Institution. 1951.

[4] HOLMSTROM, J. E. *Facts, files and action in business and public affairs. Part 2 : Filing, indexing and circulation.* London : Chapman & Hall. 1953.

[5] BRADFORD, S. C. *Documentation.* London : Crosby Lockwood. 1948.

[6] FOSKETT, D. J. The Colon classification. *Library Association Record*, 50, December, 1950, pp. 450-5.

[7] WELLS, A. J. The Colon classification. *Aslib Proceedings*, February, 1959, pp. 14-22.

[8] VICKERY, B. C. *Classification and indexing of science.* London : Butterworths Scientific Publications. 1958.

[9] Descriptive leaflet, inviting collaboration, obtainable from C. W. Cleverdon, Director, Aslib Cranfield Research Project, College of Aeronautics, Cranfield, Bletchley, Bucks.

Some Procedures in Indexing

J. Edwin Holmstrom

Whereas "Some ideas on indexing" in the Autumn, 1959, number of *The Indexer* dealt with principles, the present article, which is a sequel to that, will deal with some of the less usual of the practical methods that can be adopted for making alphabetical indexes to the contents of books and periodicals.

The possibility that makes the greatest demand on special equipment, which may or may not be economic as compared with using none at all, is that of using punched card or other machinery. The machines, usually rented from and serviced by their manufacturers, are very expensive and normally their use for indexing will not even be worth considering unless it can be fitted into otherwise wasted time between other jobs, such as accounting or statistical processing, which in any case are being performed in the same establishment. Even so, experience has shown that the cost of preparing and printing an author and title catalogue of books, which although not the same thing as preparing and printing an index to the contents of a single book is a comparable job, is likely to be greater by machine than by hand methods. What may render mechanisation economical is the case where it is desired to keep such a catalogue or index continuously up to date by intercalating new entries into the original alphabetical sequence with a view to revised editions or "cumulative indexes" to the contents of a periodical every few months or years. (A cumulative index is one which necessitates only a single search to discover everything that has been published by a given author or on a given topic from the first to the latest volume of a periodical. It is a very valuable tool of research, especially as it can be combined with the principle of a union catalogue so as to make any number of different journals or books searchable at once. The potential importance of this is clear from the consideration that in science and technology alone there are over 50,000 periodicals in existence, and that even if each of them issues its own index at the end of each annual volume nobody can search 50,000 n separate indexes, where n is the number of years back he wants to cover.)

An extract from a sample of what can be done by using punched cards is reproduced in Fig. 1 from a union catalogue under authors' names to the publications in a certain subject field available in certain American libraries, published by the New York State Library at Albany, N.Y., in 1956, under the title *Checklist of books and pamphlets in the Social Sciences*. The format is about 15½ x 10½ inches (like that of the small *Oxford Atlas*) and each of the 142 pages is divided into two columns, each column containing 156 lines, equivalent on the average to slightly less than that number of entries as some of them extend to two lines (requiring two cards), so the total number of entries in the book is well over 40,000. The names, titles, dates and class numbers were typewritten on punched cards which were sorted into alphabetical order roughly by machine and finally by hand so as to allow the necessary editing at the

Reprinted from *The Indexer* 2, no. 1 (Spring 1960): 20–30.

```
DEWHURST HENRY S    RAILROAD POLICE                          1955  S385.1     D519
DEXTER EMILY S      INTROD. TO FIELDS OF PSYCH.              1938  150.       D526
DEYOUNG JOHN E      VILLAGE LIFE IN MODERN THAILAND          1955  323.33     D529
DHUMY FERNAND E     WOMEN WHO INFLUENCED THE WORLD           1955  396.09     AD5
DIALECTICS 1V.                                               1939  335.05     D536
DIAMOND SIGMUND     REPUTATION OF AM. BUSINESSMAN            1955  330.92     AD
DICE LEE R    MAN'S NATURE AND NATURE'S MAN                  1955  301.       D546
DICKERSON REED      LEGISLATIVE DRAFTING                     1954  328.373    D549
DICKSON SARAH A     PANACEA OR PRECIOUS BANE                 1954  178.7      D554
DIEMAND JOHN A      INSURANCE COMPANY OF NORTH AMERICA       1953  368.065    159D
DIGEST OF PUBLIC RECORD OF COMMUNISM IN U.S.                 1955  351.75     QD572
DILLINGHAM WILLIAM P    FEDERAL AID TO VETERANS              1952  351.5      D578
DINERSTEIN HERBERT S    COMMUNISM AND RUSSIAN PEASANT        1955  323.33     D583
DISTRICT OF COLUMBIA BUDGET OFF. OF    REP. ON REORGAN. AND
    MGMT. IMPROVEMENT                                        1951  S353.9753D61
DITTMER HOWARD J    DEVELOPMENTAL ANATOMY                    1947  570.6      N55P
DITTMER HOWARD J    FERNS AND FERN ALLIES OF NEW MEXICO      1954  570.6      N55P
DITTMER HOWARD J    LAWN PROBLEMS OF SOUTHWEST               1950  570.6      N55P
DOBB MAURICE H    ON ECON. THEORY AND SOCIALISM              1955  330.4      D63ES
DOBZHANSKY THEODOSIUS G    EVOLUTION GENETICS AND MAN        1955  575.       D63E
DODD BELLA V    SCHOOL OF DARKNESS                           1954  335.4      D639
DODD STUART    SYSTEMATIC SOC. SC.                           1947  301.       D639S
DODDY HURLEY H    INFORMAL GROUPS AND THE COMMUNITY          1952  301.15     D642
DODMAN FRANK E    SHIPS OF THE CUNARD LINE                   1955  387.5065C792D
DODSON DAN W    BETWEEN HELL'S KITCHEN AND SAN JUAN HILL     1952  309.1747D647
DOLGE ALFRED AND SON    PRAC. APP. OF ECON. THEORIES IN
    FACTORIES                                                1896  N330.8     D664
DONAHUE WILMA T    EARNING OPPORTUNITIES FOR OLDER WORKERS   1955  331.113    D674
```

FIGURE 1.

same time; they were then reproduced by photo-offset in this reduced size. With equipment now available it is possible, however, to code-punch the cards directly from a typewriter-like keyboard and to depend on the machine to print out the entries in list form automatically after they have been sorted into the right order. The result, of course, is utilitarian rather than aesthetic, but although only capital letters can be so printed the appearance is less displeasing than it might have been, as blank spaces have judiciously been inserted instead of stops. Mr. C. F. Gosnell, who directed this project, states in his letter kindly giving permission for the sample to be reproduced here that if he were beginning over again he would consider using a machine which prepares the master copy for offset printing by photographing one-line or two-line entries typewritten along the tops of the cards. Without taking up any more space, this would allow both upper and lower case letters to be used and give much greater flexibility.

The total cost of editing and producing 1500 copies of the *Checklist* he gives as $14,032, whereof $6,568 was for editing and producing the 43,785 cards by the use of machines available in the State Education Department when not required for other purposes and the balance was spent on general editorial work, paper and printing, binding, etc. The $6,568 is more than it would have cost to prepare the copy for such a list by hand methods if there were to be only one edition; but supposing that new cards continue to be interfiled in the existing collection and it is re-used ten times for successive editions, each more comprehensive than the last, the cost of the original cards falls to only $657 for each edition. In point of fact this has not yet been done, but two supplements have been issued, the first reproducing the contents of new cards collected between April 1955 and December 1956, the second superseding the first supplement by incorporating in one alphabetical sequence all those from April 1955 to December 1958.

Punched card techniques, including those which can be adapted for accumulating references or index entries in carded form and converting them later into printed lists, are fully discussed in a book by a German limnologist, Dr. Martin Scheele, which the present writer has translated into English under the title *Punch-card methods in research and documentation, with special reference to biology* for publication this year by Interscience Publishers Inc., New York. Such techniques are not limited to those requiring elaborate machinery as described above, but there are several methods, two of which will now be briefly mentioned, which need only simple hand tools and are inexpensive enough to be usable by private workers.

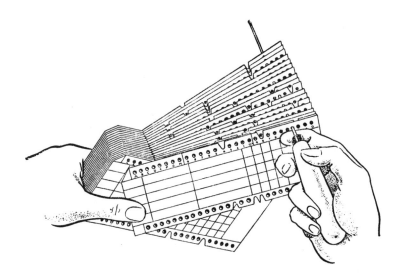

FIGURE 2.   (*By kind permission of The Copeland-Chatterson Co. Ltd.*)

The first is commonly known in Britain as Cope-Chat and in America as Keysort, a non-proprietory and more generic name being " edge-notched cards ". (Incidentally, the terminology of this subject stands badly in need of standardization and some proposals for that are put forward in Scheele's book.) They have rows of holes pre-punched close to the edge along all four sides of each card—not only along the top edge as shown in Fig. 2—and the holes are lettered or numbered to correspond with the indications it is desired to be able to spell out or otherwise record. These indications, typed or hand-written on the cards, are coded by converting the appropriate holes to slots open at the edge. (If so desired, it is possible to increase the coding capacity of the cards by providing two or even three rows of holes inside each edge so that combinations of "shallow", "medium" and "deep" slots can be cut, each with a different code meaning as printed below it.) The cards can then be stored in random order—which saves a great deal of time as compared with having to file them alphabetically or systematically—and those which have been coded in any particular way can be singled out from the rest, whenever required, by passing a wire needle through the appropriate holes in turn and lifting a pack several inches thick in one motion, whereupon those cards which have had the hole converted to a slot drop off but the others remain hanging on the needle.

The other hand-operated system is less well known but many consider it to have greater potentialities, especially from the standpoint of making it possible to pinpoint and retrieve any given reference according to a large number of different "features" ("facets" of interest; multiple "dimensions") at the same time. For this reason the cards used are best known as "feature cards"

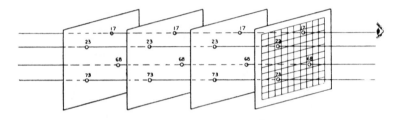

FIGURE 3.   From J. E. Holmstrom's *Facts, files and action*, part 2.
(*By kind permission of Chapman & Hall, Ltd.*)

(though here again the terminology is confused; in America they are called by the silly name "Peek-a-boo" but in Germany by the much better one *Sicht-lochkarten,* which expresses the fact that they are punched cards operated by visual inspection—not by machine). The principle as well as the advantages and the limitations are exactly opposite to those of machine-sorted and edge-notched cards: instead of, as in those systems, a separate card being provided for each reference or item of information so that the number of items is unlimited but the number of codable features restricted by the size of the cards, there is here a separate card for every feature that might occur (these being unlimited in number and the cards being kept filed in alphabetical order of features or in any other convenient way) and every one of the cards carries the same grid of punchable positions marked to correspond with the serial numbers of *all* the references that can ever be collected whatever their features of interest (the range of these numbers being limited by the size of the cards).

To give an illustratively simple example of how the system works, the documentary or indexing analogue of which the reader will easily perceive for himself, let us imagine that we have details of up to one hundred cases of apples classified in ten colour groups, eight varieties, twenty weight groups and ten suppliers, and we want to be able to select them according to combinations of these features. For this purpose we provide a feature card for each one of the $10+8+20+10=48$ different features and, supposing that the case of apples denoted by serial No. 23 belongs to colour No. 6, variety No. 5, weight No. 17 and supplier No. 9, we punch a hole at position No. 23 in the grid on the four cards that correspond to those particular features, as shown in Fig. 3. We proceed correspondingly for other cases and other features, but all the remaining positions in the grid are left unpunched.

If, now, the four cards shown in the illustration are picked out from the file, placed flat on one another and held up to the light, the searcher will be able to see through the positions which correspond to serial Nos. 17, 23, 68 and 73 because the holes in these positions on all four cards are in alignment. These, then, are indicated as being the numbers of the cases that share the desired four features. (There may happen to be other positions holed in one, two or three of the cards, but if so they do not satisfy the condition sought for, that all four features should be combined).

In practice, such cards can, of course, be made to contain many more than 100 punchable positions without becoming inconveniently large and liable to damage in handling. There is, for instance, a well-designed British make of 12 in. x 10 in. format printed with a grid which provides 2500 numbered positions in which holes can be punched, and another of the same size providing 10,000 positions for holes of $\frac{1}{16}$ in. diameter. There are several German makes approximately similar to the first mentioned and there is a French one in which the grid is like graph paper (that is, without individual position numbering) and the punching is reduced to mere pinholes, but accurately positioned by an ingenious device and perfectly visible with a light behind, accommodating no less than 12,500 positions within a format of 21 cm. x 15 cm. (roughly 8 in. x 6 in.). Once the total number of references collected exceeds the number or punchable positions it becomes necessary, of course, to start a complete new set of feature cards which must be searched independently of the foregoing. It may happen that the capacity of the cards corresponds with the maximum number of references likely to be collected in a year or other regular period plus a small margin, in which case it may be convenient to start a new set at the beginning of every such period and file it separately. Alternatively one may have successive cards of different colours for every feature, filing them in batches but being careful when searching always to lay red on red, blue on blue and so on.

J. L. Jolley has been studying refinements of "feature card" techniques, including one—as yet unpublished, but mentioned here with his permission—which is of interest in the present context as it can be used as a step in the compilation of ordinary page-printed indexes for books and periodicals and in appropriate cases may offer advantages for that. Each feature card is divided into two fields: firstly, a main field which is employed in the normal way for punching the numbers of whatever references are characterised by the feature to which the card relates, secondly an " extension field " in which numbers can be punched to identify other features possessed by some of the references whose serial numbers have been punched in the main field.

It would take too long to describe in detail here how this is done in such a way as to make it apparent at a glance which of the references combine which of the subsidiary features all punched in the same card, and how easy this makes it to build up classified alphabetical indexes containing sub-headings and sub-sub-headings. It must suffice to say that, although the punching operation takes longer than on feature cards used in the ordinary way, much time is saved through the indexer not having to do any writing at all until he is ready to begin typing out the copy he will send to the printer.

With the last mentioned system, what the user obtains from the punched cards is merely the serial numbers of the references (or of the documents them-selves) which he then has to turn up in a separate numerically-arranged file. With the other systems described his search leads him directly to cards which each contain one reference, as is the case with ordinary cards or slips such as (judging by several articles published in *The Indexer*) most indexers use for collecting and arranging index entries before these are converted into page form. Provided that the references which are to be used as index entries have been neatly typewritten immediately below the top edges of the cards or slips (so as not to waste space between them) it is possible to make this conversion by shingl-ing them over one another in some simple device which aligns and holds them accurately in place whilst photographing a pageful at a time, for reproduction by offset printing. The difficulty that cards may be too springy to type upon immediately below the edge without smudging can be overcome by obtaining special cards having a line of perforations half an inch below the top and by typing just below this line, afterwards tearing off the top before shingling the cards. The advantage of reproducing an index in page form directly from the separate cards by photography is not only that it saves the labour of typesetting or recopying on the typewriter but, above all, that it saves the need for further proof-reading and the time this takes if perfect accuracy is to be ensured, which in an urgent job may be an important consideration.

Turning now to unmechanised methods of indexing, the objection to writing the entries on separate cards or slips at the drafting stage is the amount of time wasted when filing these in alphabetical order through having to finger those already filed unless there are a great many " guide cards " with projecting tabs to show approximately where, for instance, the initial syllable " con " occurs amid the cards already put in after C, " inf " among those put in after I, and so on. It is possible to buy sets of guide cards with the first three letters of

English surnames printed on the tabs in the right average distribution so that the thickness of the cards or slips accumulating between successive guide cards tends to become equal. It is possible also to manufacture guides for oneself which will correspond to an average distribution of corporate mixed with personal surnames, by tearing out the pages of an old telephone directory and folding or cutting them so that the names printed in block capitals on the shoulders of the successive pages (or on every second, fifth, tenth, etc., page according to how many one wants) appear just over the tops of the cards or slips one is filing.

Even so, one still has to fumble among the cards or slips between the guides; moreover, for most books, the alphabetical average distribution of subject index entries will not be the same as for names. For these and other reasons it may be preferred to supplement the use of one, two or three-letter guide cards (according to the intended size of the index) with the following device for making the positions of the next two letters immediately apparent by a glance at tops of the cards themselves. Cards not smaller than the standard library cataloguing size (3 in. x 5 in.) must be used. Prepare a scale of divisions marked with the letters of the alphabet as shown at the top of Fig. 4 here (in which the 26 divisions are each 4 mm. wide) leaving about half an inch clear at each end. Assuming, for example, you are using two-letter guides and are about to insert after FR a card which is headed with the word " friction ", first put the top edge of this card against your scale, make a pencil mark on it opposite the letters I and C and, using a punch such as can be bought for the " edge-notched " system described earlier, notch these two letters. And, to indicate the fact that " i " comes before " c " in the word you are now indexing, notch the right-hand end of the card—had it been a word in which the third and fourth letters were in the order " ci " you would notch the left-hand end.

The notching takes very little time once the habit is acquired. Its effect, looking down on the thickness of cards between successive guides, is visible as continuous grooves on the left through the first part and on the right through the second part of the thickness, and between them an irregular sloping line made up partly of notches in single cards, partly of short grooves where the notches are continuous through several cards having the same initial groups of letters.

I have found a variant of this system valuable in a card index to names of correspondents, used for marking on the cards the file numbers and dates of letters exchanged with them. That, however, is another story and personally I do not use cards or slips for preparing book indexes. I prefer to do this in the form shown in Fig. 5 which, apart from the fact that it makes locating the entries almost instantaneous, offers the advantage of being easily portable so that one can do this kind of work at odd moments when travelling. The sheets, which should preferably be lined or squared, are wire-stapled into batches of ten

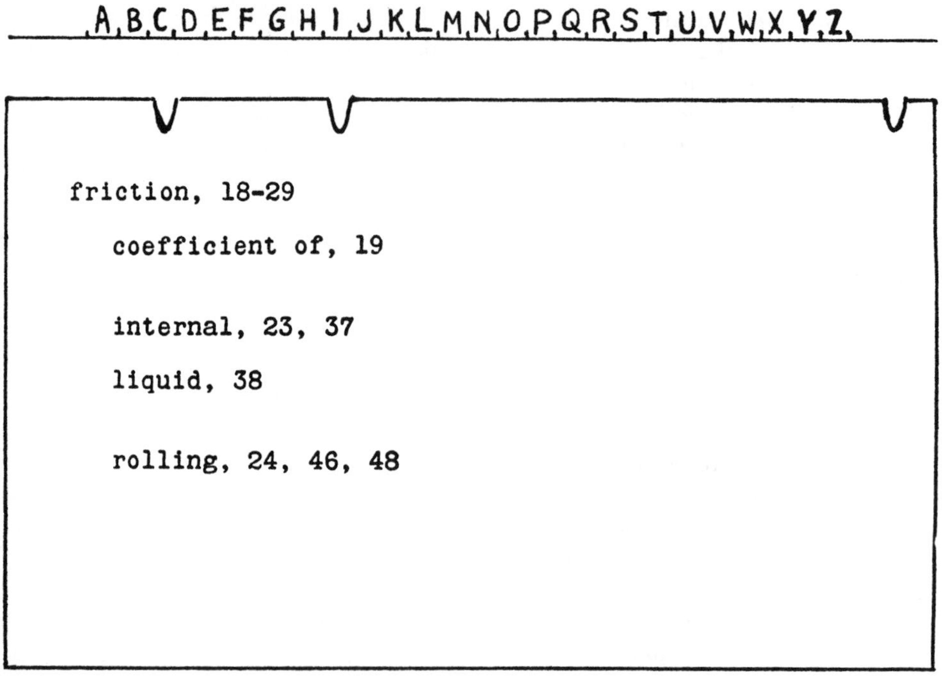

A, B, C, D, E, F, G, H, I, J, K, L, M, N, O, P, Q, R, S, T, U, V, W, X, Y, Z,

friction, 18-29

   coefficient of, 19

   internal, 23, 37

   liquid, 38

   rolling, 24, 46, 48

FIGURE 4.

with their bottom edges shingled over one another about a quarter of an inch. In the bottom right corner of each sheet are written the initial group of letters of whatever is to be the last word that may be indexed on that sheet. These markings, which serve the same purpose as those printed on the tabs of guide cards, are distributed in the right proportion of alphabetical range with the aim of ensuring that every sheet shall become about equally full. This is done by the simple device of copying them from the successive pages (or from every nth page, n being suitably chosen) in some existing index or dictionary relating to the same sort of subject matter.

Experience shows that it is always better to waste some paper than to run any risk of overcrowding the index entries. Further, since however much fore-sight is used in spreading the entries within each sheet there will sooner or later come a time when respect for the alphabet requires that a new one be interpolated between two already written on successive lines, it is best to crease the sheets down the middle and write only in the right-hand half until this occurs, leaving the left-hand half free for the interpolations.

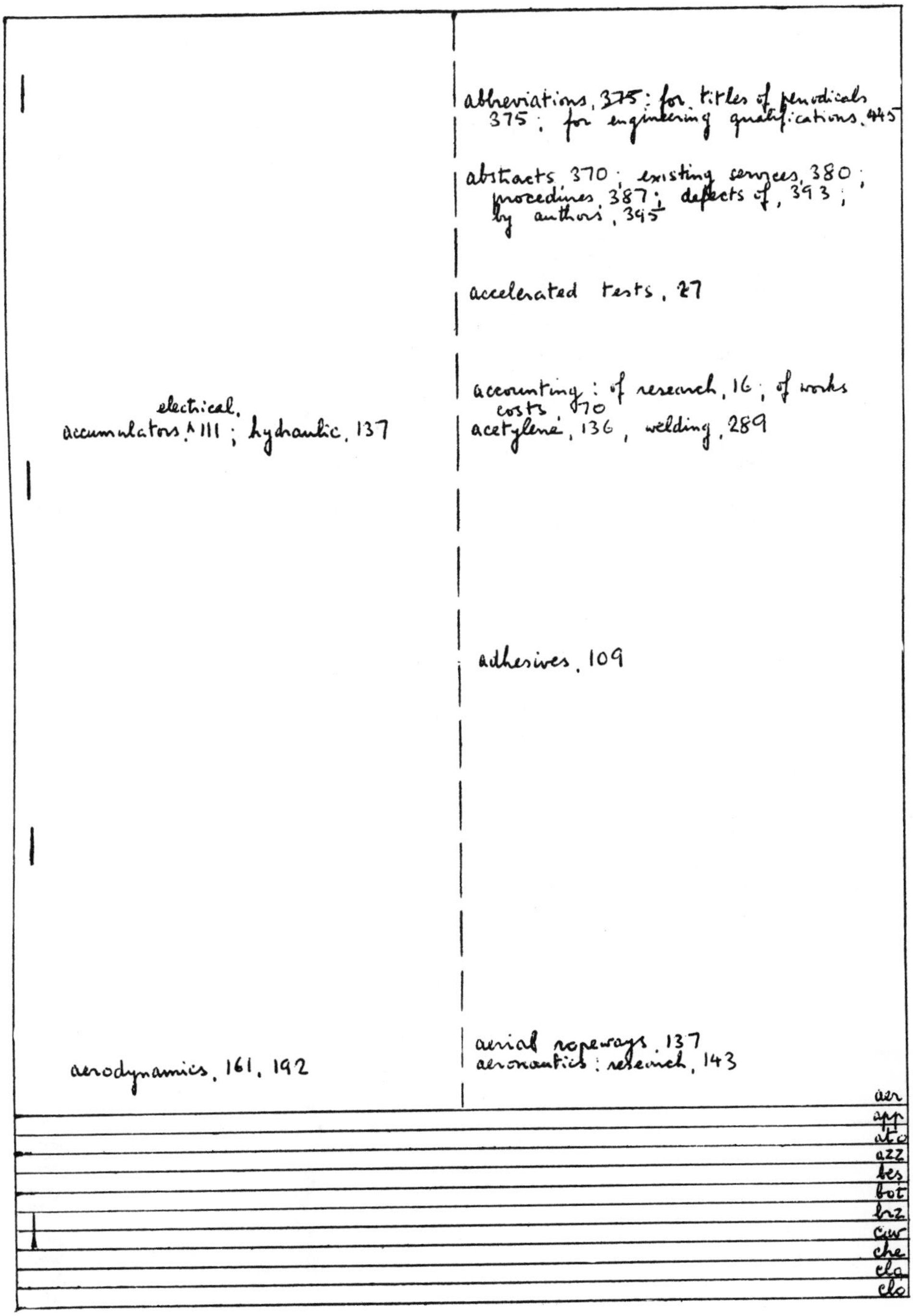

abbreviations, 375; for titles of periodicals 375; for engineering qualifications, 445

abstracts 370; existing services, 380; procedures 387; defects of, 393; by authors, 395

accelerated tests, 27

accounting: of research, 16; of works costs 170

acetylene, 136, welding, 289

electrical.
accumulators, 111; hydraulic, 137

adhesives, 109

aerodynamics, 161, 192

aerial ropeways, 137
aeronautics: research, 143

aer
app
ato
azz
bes
bot
brz
cur
che
cla
clo

FIGURE 5.

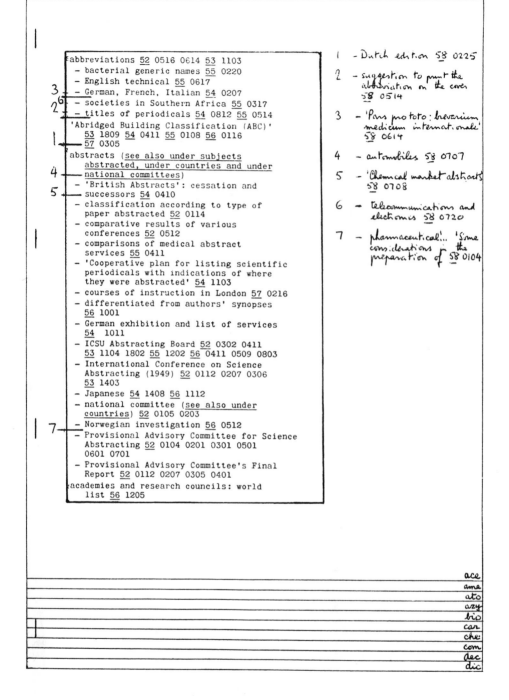

```
  │    abbreviations 52 0516 0614 53 1103          1  - Dutch edition 58 0225
       - bacterial generic names 55 0220
       - English technical 55 0617                 2  - suggestion to print the
 3  ┬  - German, French, Italian 54 0207              abbreviation on the cover
 2  ┤6 - societies in Southern Africa 55 0317          58 0514
    ┴  - titles of periodicals 54 0812 55 0514
       'Abridged Building Classification (ABC)'    3  - 'Pars proto toto : breverium
 1  ┬     53 1809 54 0411 55 0108 56 0116             medicum internationale'
    ┴     57 0305                                      58 0614
       abstracts (see also under subjects
          abstracted, under countries and under  4  - automobiles 58 0707
 4  ─     national committees)
       - 'British Abstracts': cessation and      5  - 'Chemical market abstracts'
 5  ┬     successors 54 0410                          58 0708
       - classification according to type of
          paper abstracted 52 0114               6  - telecommunications and
       - comparative results of various             electronics 58 0720
          conferences 52 0512
       - comparisons of medical abstract        7  - pharmaceutical... 'Some
          services 55 0411                          considerations in the
       - 'Cooperative plan for listing scientific    preparation of 58 0104
          periodicals with indications of where
          they were abstracted' 54 1103
       - courses of instruction in London 57 0216
       - differentiated from authors' synopses
          56 1001
       - German exhibition and list of services
          54  1011
       - ICSU Abstracting Board 52 0302 0411
          53 1104 1802 55 1202 56 0411 0509 0803
       - International Conference on Science
          Abstracting (1949) 52 0112 0207 0306
          53 1403
       - Japanese 54 1408 56 1112
       - national committee (see also under
          countries) 52 0105 0203
       - Norwegian investigation 56 0512
 7  ─  - Provisional Advisory Committee for Science
          Abstracting 52 0104 0201 0301 0501
          0601 0701
       - Provisional Advisory Committee's Final
          Report 52 0112 0207 0305 0401
       academies and research councils: world
          list 56 1205
```

ace
ama
ato
azy
bio
car
che
com
dec
dic

FIGURE 6.

Before actually starting to index a book it must be scanned right through and its list of contents be studied in order to appreciate its general plan ; then each chapter must be read attentively and judgment exercised in deciding, whilst the argument as a whole is fresh in one's mind, which are the words—neither too many nor too few—most serviceable to adopt as index headings. Skill in these preliminary stages of the work necessitates the indexer being generally familiar with the background to the subject of the book but, at the same time, circumspect enough to remember that the reader of the book and user of the index may be less familiar with the subject than he is himself. Such circumspection may be more difficult for the author of the book than for an independent indexer.

Finally Fig. 6 shows an adaptation of this system for the purpose of keeping a cumulative index to a periodical posted up to date immediately after each issue has appeared, so that no time need be lost in bringing out a new index covering the new and the preceding volumes as soon as each volume (or other run of the journal) is complete. The example reproduced here is part of the cumulative index to the mimeographed *Monthly Bulletin on Scientific Documentation and Terminology* which was started in 1952 and may at present be had free of charge by those constructively interested in its contents, from the Department of Natural Sciences in Unesco, 2 Place de Fontenoy, Paris 7E (but not through sales agents). A reference such as 54 0608 means item No. 8 in the issue of the 6th month of 1954. The index being mimeographed in two columns, the sheet here illustrated was made by cutting up that of the previous year into separate columns and pasting each column in the left-hand part of a sheet, hand-written current entries being thereafter interpolated month by month and the whole recopied on to new stencils at the end of the year. The sheets are shingled over one another in the same way as already described, but here the markings in the bottom right corner are simply copied from the entries at the foot of each column in last year's index.

A Curriculum in Indexing and Abstracting*

Richard A. Davis

How much I could assume about the background and knowledge of library schools in your diverse group was a problem, so I decided to begin at the beginning and risk that it will sound familiar to some of you. I am going to talk particularly about Rosary College's Graduate School of Library Science and more particularly about my indexing and abstracting course. Basically, this is my approach.

First, we must think about what the student is going to do with this training. Students come into the library school to prepare for various professional activities. Most of the indexing and abstracting group are probably going to a special library or a research library and will abstract and index for (1) internal publications and (2) the card catalogue or computer or other retrieval system. Bibliographic preparation and indexes for retrospective searching are also common. Let me emphasize that most of the output is used internally, not outside the organization. Consequently, it does not have to be as beautiful or as nicely prepared as something published for external consumption.

Many organizations over the years have accumulated in-depth indexes for their particular interest areas. A library in the petroleum field might cover petroleum chemistry, petroleum geology, the economics of petroleum, and so on. I recently visited the library at Standard Oil where a card catalogue index in great depth has been building up for a long time. Another common problem is proprietary materials, e.g. research reports prepared internally, laboratory notebooks, all of which must be indexed and the materials retained within the organization.

Our preparation is geared to this end product. There are a number of basic courses which people take prior to indexing and abstracting. The series of reference courses includes reference and bibliography, literature of the humanities, litera-

ture of the social sciences, and literature of the sciences. In all of these, students get involved with indexing and abstracting services, tools used in the literature and in reference. They are taught how to use them, how they are organized, how to evaluate them. When they come to my class, they are familiar with indexes from the wide range of *Reader's Guide* to *Science Citation Index* or *Chemical Abstracts*.

Most students, by the time they get to indexing and abstracting, have had at least one class in cataloguing and classification. This is basically the traditional Dewey and Library of Congress, but also introduced are how knowledge is organized, something of the history of classification systems, and subject headings which are a form of pre-coordinate indexing. Last of all, the student will probably take computer applications in libraries before he takes indexing and abstracting. This covers how a computer works and its satellite equipment, its capabilities and how to use them for library housekeeping chores and for organization of knowledge. While it does not go into the actual indexing and abstracting aspects of a computer, it does give students a familiarity with the concept.

At this point they come into my class, and I will tell you my policies on training for abstracting and indexing. First, in order to read the literature intelligently, people must understand the past, to see the growth and development of the field of organization of information for retrieval. Second, they must have practical, hands-on experience. You learn to write abstracts by writing abstracts, lots and lots of them; you learn to index by actually doing it. Within organizations where many of you work, I am sure this is the routine: abstracts are written, edited, and sent back, and the writers learn from this criticism; indexing is done, discussed, edited, and returned, and the indexers learn by doing. This is essentially what I am trying to do. We concentrate on the indexing of articles and research reports because this is the type of material which most of our students will handle in real-life situations. The subject of book indexing is touched on lightly.

*A paper read at the meeting of the American Society of Indexers held in Chicago on 6th May 1976.

Reprinted from *The Indexer* 10, no. 2 (October 1976): 75–77.

I start with background theory; what does this include? The history of how knowledge is organised could go back to the Babylonians; we do not go that far, but we consider some of the basic classification schemes, their construction and their faults. One of the original systems is the classified catalogue, still found in many libraries in Europe. Chicago has one of the few examples in the United States, the classified catalogue at John Crerar Library. New York has one at the Engineering Societies library, and a third is at Boston University.

Your typical subject-heading list is a pre-coordinate index. This course is concerned with post-coordinate indexing in the sense that we take terms and put them together for retrieval, not set them up ahead of time, because in most cases our people will be going into organizations which use post-coordinate indexes. We look at the history and development of co-ordinate indexing, its concepts, the construction of a thesaurus, and the construction and use of an index. My text is a book by A. C. Foskett called *The subject approach to information*, published by Linnet and in England by Bingley. After three or four years I still have not found anything I like better; it explains the organisation of knowledge and various schemes and it is fairly readable.

The elements included in the course itself are hard to describe in sequence because they do not happen in simple sequence; they mesh together and overlap. With this in mind I shall try to give you some idea of each.

First, we tackle the concept of abstracting. What is an abstract? How do you construct an abstract? How do you write an abstract? The text is a succinct paperback called *Abstracts and abstracting services* by Robert Collison, published by ABC-CLIO. It contains the gist of it all in about eighty pages. The students read articles on how to abstract, and then abstract the articles, several per week. These are edited extensively and returned. In just a few weeks the improvement is pleasing. The person who overflowed two pages with literary style tightens his sentences, simplifies his construction, gets it down to a paragraph and still covers the facts.

The next step is processing natural language. Each student indexes a set of abstracts using the natural language terms found in the abstracts and in the titles. Each person puts his index terms into a computer program which then combines all the entries and prints them out in alphabetical order. The result includes sequences like: information banks, information centre, information retrieval, information science, information scientists, information systems, information tech-

nology. Everyone expects this to be easy, but then the problems show up, synonyms, root words with different endings, overlap, inconsistency. They learn first hand the confusion from using natural language in the context of an uncontrolled vocabulary. Each gets a copy of the computer printout and the assignment to edit it.

KWIC (keyword in context) is a form of natural language index. They should know how it works and how to put one together, because in most special libraries it is a practical tool for producing a fast and cheap index to the titles of articles. The titles can be selected, enriched, manipulated to provide a frequent current awareness listing sent to everybody in the organization. The students feed their titles into the computer, then evaluate their printouts to see that the same natural language problems occur in KWIC indexes.

The use of a thesaurus for indexing is covered. Claire Schultz's *Thesaurus of information science terminology*, published by CSC/Pacific, is built for handling material on abstracting and indexing and is easy to use as the control vocabulary. They now start indexing the articles that they have been abstracting. In the cycle of learning they read material which tells them how to do what they are doing to the material they are reading. It works out pretty well.

As the class goes along through this whole procedure I have been outlining, I introduce the basic hand systems because many organizations do not have the facilities or funds for computer terminals. One is uniterm, basically a card which has ten columns. A subject heading is entered at the top of each card and the number of any document indexed with that subject is recorded in the columns. You retrieve by pulling out the pertinent subject cards and finding which documents appear on every one of the cards you pulled. Uniterm is a cheap and easy way to organize information. I generally tie this in with a natural language lesson so they see the problems of natural language and of uniterm simultaneously.

Optical coincidence systems also have one card per subject heading. I discuss the principles behind peek-a-boo and use demonstration materials, but do not assign a problem.

For extensive class work I use edge-notched cards. Each card is a unit record with all the elements present: the citation and abstract typed on the front, index terms listed on the back with their coding, and the coding punched around the edges. The whole thing is right there, and it makes a good teaching tool. Using a hand deck like this, they get an idea of how retrieval works. They needle their own decks and say, 'Why did

I get this false drop? Why didn't things co-ordinate properly?' The students themselves can analyse the process, which is hard to do when the information is in the computer.

Early in the course abstracts are typed on edge-notched cards which are turned in, edited, and returned. Index terms are added on the back and edited. Codings are punched around the edges. The students use the cards over and over through-out the course, slowly building a deck of about twenty-five. That is as many articles as they can comfortably handle in a semester's time. I find this a practical unit to demonstrate exactly how information gets from hand to machine to computer.

Last, we go into computer systems. They have had the course on automation in libraries, they have put a natural language index and a KWIC index in the computer. What I try to bring home to them now is that the computer systems merely speed up the hand techniques. You feed the information on the edge-notched cards into the computer. Instead of needling the deck to get information you query the computer and get back a printout.

I have developed a couple of data bases for the students to use; in addition we have access to Medline, Systems Development Corporation, and Lockheed. I hope students can have even more hands-on experience with these data bases because it expands their universe to see how the indexes work.

The course is not static, but is adjusted and altered each time I offer it to meet the challenge of changing aspects and improving techniques in the profession of indexing and abstracting.

VII. The Application of Modern Technology to Indexing

Computers and Indexes

Helen M. Townley

1. The nature of indexing and the nature of computing.

Essentially the preparation of an index falls into two sections—the intellectual work of deciding what a document is about, and the non-intellectual work of collating several references to the same thing.

Essentially a computer can perform two functions—analysis of information, normally by the use of some form of statistics, and manipulation of information.

The costs of human intellectual resources are rising; the costs of computing are falling. It was inevitable therefore that sooner or later someone would try to mechanise the indexing process; the odd thing (in retrospect) is that instead of separating out the two parts of indexing, the earlier efforts tried to treat simultaneously both the intellectual and the 'chore' parts of the job. But before we consider the actual processes involved we must take a look at the background against which this work was carried out.

2. Indexing and Information Retrieval.

An index is an information retrieval tool—one of the earliest and still one of the most important information retrieval tools. What is an information retrieval system but a means of locating information by using a special sub-set of language to identify the concepts and a series of unique references to identify the place in which these concepts are set out or discussed? For the lifetime of, I guess, every reader, it has been taken for granted that this special sub-set of the language can be used in indexing in two ways: either by the use of a subject heading list of some kind, or by the use of a classification code which is often (though it need not be) numerically expressed. What has, I think, been much less generally appreciated is the essential difference between the two.

It is a characteristic of a classification scheme that any one code number represents the co-ordination of a number of concepts; it is a characteristic of a subject heading list that the concepts are clearly distinguished one from another. So while we can write '372.215.6 = use of action songs as a teaching method in primary schools', we have to use 'action songs', 'teaching methods' and 'primary schools' simultaneously to identify the same concept from a subject heading list.

So our information retrieval tool can use either 372.215.6 or the combination of three phrases to define the concept, and by adding a reference to either can identify the location of the required information. If the retrieval tool is a pack of 5-in. x 3-in. cards, or a printed list, we need only the number to cover all three aspects of the concept; if subject headings are being used, provision has to be made for the possibility that a searcher might use as his own point of entry the term 'action songs' or the term 'teaching methods' or the term 'primary schools' and there must be three entry terms in the system to cater for him.

So a classification scheme pre-co-ordinates the elements of the indexed concept, whilst a subject heading list requires the user to exercise some form of co-ordination after the indexing has been done.

Now, pre-co-ordination imposes a point of view: the main field is subdivided into mutually exclusive fields, which are subdivided

Reprinted from *The Indexer* 6, no. 3 (Spring 1969): 102–107.

again and again and the sequencing of the subdivisions is important. Because teaching methods are subordinate to type of school, if we want action songs as a teaching method in secondary schools we must use a different class number, and if we just want ' action songs ' we must look in two different places. In fact, what matters is the *context* in which we are thinking about action songs, and in mechanised information retrieval systems (even down to the simplest of edge-notched card systems) it was early recognised that what was needed was a system which said : find me the references which are indexed by ' action songs ' *and* ' teaching methods ' *and* ' primary schools ' *or* ' kindergartens ' (i.e. but not ' secondary schools ').

Now, manually prepared indexes have always recognised this fact throughout their history : an entry under ' action songs ' will distinguish by means of sub-headings, between ' in primary schools ' and ' in kindergartens ', and have a further sub-heading ' as teaching methods '. If the index is required in great detail, ' teaching methods ' may appear as a further sub-heading both of ' in primary schools ' and of ' in kindergartens '. In any event, there will almost certainly be a corresponding entry ' Primary Schools, Action songs in '.

3. *Computer-prepared Indexes.*

It was this recognition that an entry term, generally speaking, ought not to stand alone but be given in its context that led to the earliest form of computer-prepared index, the KWIC (=Key Word in Context). This was an attempt to simplify the production of printed indexes to massive collections—primarily periodicals and in-house technical reports—by treating each of the significant words of the title (as opposed to the insignificant words such as ' the ', ' of ', etc.) as indexing terms. The computer's facility of manipulation was brought into play to bring each significant word in turn into the centre of the page, with the rest of the title spread around it (Fig. 1). No intellectual effort was involved except the preparation of the list of non-significant words, and large indexes could be prepared in a very short space of time. Of course, the success of the system depended on two unproved assumptions—that the words in the title fully represented the concepts in the document and that there would be few synonyms, so that a single word could serve efficiently as an entry point. In the event, neither of these has proved to be the case. There is the famous example of the paper on binary arithmetic entitled ' Fingers and Thumbs ' which, though properly (according to KWIC logic) indexed under both Fingers and under Thumbs, never served to lead the user to the concept of binary arithmetic; and KWICs have never been as useful as they might because of the lack of any form of vocabulary control, so that the user had to try to think of all the words for his sought concept which an author *might* have used in his title. However, KWICs have had quite an influence on the accuracy of titling of papers, and to solve the other points, programs have been written which perform the KWIC-type rotation (of the sentence round the indexing term) not on the title but on a descriptive phrase written by the indexer. Devotees of the original KWICs object that this defeats the main object of a KWIC, which is to produce an index with the minimum of human intervention, and KWICs still flourish; in highly specialised subjects, in which the terminology is controlled by the finiteness of the field, their speed of production and ease of use outweigh the disadvantages of an uncontrolled vocabulary and the rather ugly appearance on the printed page. KWOC (= Key Word Out of Context)—also illustrated in Fig. 1—does something to improve on the latter.

4. *Permuted Indexes.*

Programs for preparing indexes by computer went hand in hand with programs for information retrieval and by the early 1960s it was becoming widely recognised in the latter that IR systems had two functions to fulfil which were to some extent mutually exclusive—relevance and recall. In high relevance systems, the retrieved references were all required to be highly relevant to the

KWIC (KeyWord In Context) INDEXING

The five titles here to be KWICed are:-

Can Management Information be Automated
Source Data Collection in Automated Business Systems
Automatic Control — an Evaluation
Control through Information
Computer Management Control Systems.

Permuting the titles to bring to the middle each significant word results in :-

CAN MANAGEMENT INFORMATION BE AUTOMATED	1
SOURCE DATA COLLECTION IN AUTOMATED BUSINESS SYSTEMS	2
AUTOMATIC CONTROL — AN EVALUATION	3
E DATA COLLECTION IN AUTOMATED BUSINESS SYSTEMS SOURC	2
S SOURCE DATA COLLECTION IN AUTOMATED BUSINESS SYSTEM	2
COMPUTER MANAGEMENT CONTROL SYSTEMS	5
CONTROL THROUGH INFORMATION	4
AUTOMATIC CONTROL — AN EVALUATION	3
COMPUTER MANAGEMENT CONTROL SYSTEMS	5
YSTEMS SOURCE DATA COLLECTION IN AUTOMATED BUSINESS S	2
AUTOMATIC CONTROL — AN EVALUATION	3
CONTROL THROUGH INFORMATION	4
CAN MANAGEMENT INFORMATION BE AUTOMATED	1
COMPUTER MANAGEMENT CONTROL SYSTEMS	5
CAN MANAGEMENT INFORMATION BE AUTOMATED	1
INESS SYSTEMS SOURCE DATA COLLECTION IN AUTOMATED BUS	2
LLECTION IN AUTOMATED BUSINESS SYSTEMS SOURCE DATA CO	2
COMPUTER MANAGEMENT CONTROL SYSTEMS	5

The reference number at the end of each line leads the user to the correct document in the list, which gives full details of author, title and source.

There can also be provided an author index, giving merely author's name and the relevant document numbers.

KWOC INDEXES   Follow the same principle, but do not permute the title — they extract the keyword and put it at the beginning of the line, followed by the full title :-

INFORMATION	CONTROL THROUGH INFORMATION	4
	CAN MANAGEMENT INFORMATION BE AUTOMATED	1
MANAGEMENT	COMPUTER MANAGEMENT CONTROL SYSTEMS	5
	CAN MANAGEMENT INFORMATION BE AUTOMATED	1

FIGURE 1.

enquiry; in high recall systems the enquirer wanted an assurance that all the relevant material had been retrieved. At first it was thought that different retrieval languages (i.e. different sub-sets of the language, as in para. 1 of this paper) were needed for this, but experimental work began to show that it was not the languages, but how they were used in retrieval, that was critical, and this had its effect on the form of printed index programs. SLIC (= Selective Listing in Combination) made its appearance (Fig. 2), and though it has never had the popularity of KWIC it has had a considerable influence on index preparation programs. In the first place, it required the use of a controlled vocabulary with terms precisely defined; in the second, it was recognised that display—a good, readable, well laid-out page—was important. CELT (Classified Entries in Lateral Transposition) used faceted classification schemes, rotating the classification codes as did KWIC but (since the codes take up little space) printing the title alongside each rotation of the codes. 'Permuterm' took each pair of keywords from the string of keywords describing the document, and then sorted them, printing the reference numbers of documents to which each pair applied. Another form of permuted index printed across the top of the page a series of broad subject classes, and down the side of the keywords actually used, and then tabulated under each class/keyword combination the reference numbers of the documents to which it applied. Many other systems have been developed—too many to specify here; but the critical thing about all of them is the increasing recognition of the importance of the human intellectual effort in indexing.

But though the intellectual effort, excluded by KWIC, came back into prominence, there did not return the one thing KWIC did give—an indication of the relationships of the terms to one another; and it is these relationships that bring with them greater meaning and therefore higher relevance, in the retrieval process. This problem has been overcome only within the last two years.

SLIC INDEXES work on keywords chosen by the indexer, not on words from the title. The words are put into alphabetical order and permuted. Any permutation which repeats the first part of a previous permutation is omitted—thus, since we would find A B C under A B C D, there is no need to enter A B C separately. A SLIC on keywords A B C D E would be:—

A	B	C	D	E
A	B	D	E	
A	B	E		
A	C	D	E	
A	C	E		
A	D	E		
A	E			
B	C	D	E	
B	C	E		
B	D	E		
B	E			
C	D	E		
C	E			
D	E			
E				

FIGURE 2.

5. *Articulated Indexes.*

Analysis of a typical index entry shows that it is composed of a series of noun phrases articulated by prepositions:—

Indexes
    preparation of, by computer.

This can be 'normalised' into a sentence-like structure 'Preparation of indexes by computer'. The first programs for articulated indexes used the prepositions as 'articulation points' and the words between them as entry terms, so that the sentence above could be converted into

Computer
    preparation of indexes by
Indexes
    by computer, preparation of
Preparation
    of indexes by computer

Improvements came thick and fast. An early one was the recognition of the importance of 'of' in an index, so that the program was arranged to put terms preceded or followed by 'of' at the front of the entry. By this means, the second of the above examples became much clearer.

Indexes
    preparation of, by computer.

Then came the facility to split a long noun-phrase into two or more entry points. In the original version, for instance, 'preparation of pressed steel plates' could not be indexed under 'steel' or 'plates', but the current version allows the indexer to choose any or all or none of the components of a noun-phrase for use as entry terms. Another refinement was the ability to distinguish between two kinds of 'and'—that which is a true conjunction, linking noun-phrases wanted in every entry, and that which links noun-phrases to which the other indexing terms apply independently. Thus 'Relations between King and Parliament' needs both 'King' and 'Parliament' in every entry:—

King
    and Parliament, relations between
Parliament
    and King, relations between

On the other hand 'Preparation of Subject indexes and Author indexes' is satisfied with

    Subject Indexes
        Preparation of
and
    Author Indexes
        Preparation of

```
                    N.D.T. - INDEX LISTING              DATE  20/12/68      PAGE   13

   SUBJECT HEADING                                    INDEX ENTRY + CLASS/SERIAL NUMBER

RESONANCE FREQUENCY
              IDENTIFICATION OF BOND DEFECTS BY,  0003/0112
RESONATOR
              QUARTZ -, MEASUREMENT OF FILM THICKNESS BY,  0003/0095
RIVERS
              MEASUREMENT OF DEPTH OF, BY ULTRASONIC SCOUR METER,0003/0100
RODS
              STEEL - USING STRAIN GAUGES, THERMOTENSIMETRY FOR TESTING OF STRESS IN, 0002/0093
ROTATING PRODUCTS
              ULTRASONIC EXAMINATION OF, 0003/0105
ROTOR BLADES
              INFRARED, ULTRAVIOLET, ULTRASONIC + X-RAY TESTS OF,0001/0033
S
              PRESSURE LTRANSDUCE - WITH PIEZOELECTRIC RESPONSE TO FLUID FLOW,  0001/0060
SCATTERING
              MULTIPLE - OF LONGITUDINAL EFFECTIVE WAVE BY MICROHETEROGENEOUS MEDIA,  0003/0087
              PULSE-ECHO - EQUIPMENT, 0003/0109
SCINTISCANNING
              COMPARISON OF TECHNIQUES FOR, 0005/0058
SCOUR
              ULTRASONIC - METER, MEASUREMENT OF DEPTH OF RIVERS BY,0003/0100
                         METER, MANUAL FOR,0003/0101
SCREEN SENSORS
              USE OF, FOR EDDY-CURRENT MONITORING OF SHEET,0006/0027
SCREEN-FILM CONTACT
              INCREASE OF, WITH VACUUM PACK,0005/0050
SEALING
              OF TUBES FOR PRESSURE TESTING,0001/0082
SENSITIVITY
              DUAL - INSPECTION PENETRANTS, 0002/0094
SHADOW
              DEFECTOSCOPE, ACOUSTIC SECTION OF, WITH IMMERSION TESTING,  0003/0088
SHAPE
              MEASUREMENTOF, BY FLUID FLOW, 0001/0059
*SHARPE, *R,
              ON *N*D*T,  0001/0053
SHEAR
              TRANSDUCER FOR,0003/0091
SHEAR WAVES
              MICROWAVE - IN SOLIDS,  0001/0057
SHEET
              AUTOMATIC - GAUGES,  0003/0127
              EDDY-CURRENT MONITORING OF, USE OF SCREEN SENSORS FOR,0006/0027
              BY NORMAL WAVES, DETERMINATION OF COORDINATES + DEFECTS IN, 0003/0118
SIGNAL INTERPRETATION
              IMPROVEMENT OF,0006/0029
SILICA REFRACTORIES
              SONIC TESTING OF, IN QUALITY CONTROL,  0003/0096
SILICON
              X-RAY STRESS TOPOGRAPHY OF THIN FILMS ON, 0001/0085
SILVER
              MEASUREMENT OF MASS PER UNIT AREAOF, ON FILM BY X-RAY FLUORESCENCE,  0001/0063
SODIUM
```

FIGURE 3.

Finally, it is worth noting that articulated indexes are as suitable for book as for periodical literature indexing—provided, of course, that the book requires the detail of such an index. The preparation of indexing sentences for articulated indexing by computer requires no skills not at present possessed by the competent indexer. But if I may be flippant for a moment, I must emphasise one important characteristic—he must not make spelling mistakes! In the index of which Fig. 3 is a sample, the author succeeded in spelling 'emmission' in three of its four possible permutations. Fortunately the program prints out a proof-sheet (in fact, Fig. 3 is a copy of the proof, not of the final output), so the computer's inability to recognise that, for this indexer

emission = emmission = emision

was overcome in the final output.

(This particular program has the added advantage that the output may, if required, be a magnetic tape which can be fed to a photo-typesetting machine, thus eliminating all human activities (except proof-reading) between the writing of the individual indexing sentences and the production of the typeset page.)

6. *Auto-indexing.*

In my first sentence I distinguished between the human intellectual activity of recognising what a document is about and the non-intellectual work of generating, sorting and collating the several required entries. The intellectual part requires the expression of the meaning in a specialised sub-set of the total language.

I cannot close this article without making at least a passing reference to the experimental work now being done on auto-indexing. This is the use of the computer to identify this special sub-set and depends on statistical analysis of the frequency of the use of any given word. It can be assumed that if a word appears more frequently in a document than it does in its total usage in all communication, then it is significant to this document and is at least a candidate word for the special sub-set of indexing words.

At present, this work is wholly experimental and is designed to find words which can be used in computer information retrieval systems rather than in the less detailed printed indexing systems, but though results to date are not wholly satisfactory, it is beginning to appear that before long the selection of candidate words can be left to the computer. Other work on semantic analysis and further work on the way in which words are used together to form complex expressions is pointing the way to thesaurus generation and dictionary compilation and look-up programs which may eliminate much of the human part of the indexing process. But for myself, though my work lies wholly in the field of computerised documentation and though I have every confidence in its future, I do not see this ever taking the place of the human indexer of books.

I have little doubt that the time is approaching when technical papers now appearing in the periodical literature will be wholly computer-held, -indexed and -searched. A book, however, is something more than a report on a single piece of work, or even a state-of-the-art review: it is a synthesis by one man or a small group of men of the work of many men; one to which he has added something himself and his philosophy as well as his knowledge. As such, it is a thing one wishes to keep and to read again and again. And as such, it must have a printed index whose content must ultimately (whatever the computer processes which have subsequently manipulated it) be the work of a human.

I have not given a bibliography: this article covers a period of over ten years, and a multitude of techniques have been developed during this time on which I have no room to comment. If any reader would like to take the matter further, however, I shall be happy to suggest some further reading—though I should warn that little of it will be found in text-books and recourse will have to be had to the original papers.

A Computer-Generated Index Technique*

Brenda Hall

Indexing is not a new science. The preparation of indexes had reached a high peak of skill in the English world of letters by the mid-eighteenth century. In those more leisurely days an indexer had time to bring to his work much art as well as the necessary craft. Confronted with today's overwhelming volume of print in all fields of knowledge, however, indexers would be in danger of failing their public if forced to depend solely on conventional manual methods. The alternative—a marriage of convenience with the computer—seems to some indexers to be a treasonable alliance. But there are those who have been taking their first timorous steps in the direction of computer-generation of indexes.

It may help to understand progress in computer-generated indexing techniques if the usual process in making an index by the manual method is broken down into its components.

A Text to be indexed

B Trained indexer

C Material from A abstracted by B on to cards, making as many separate entries under different headings as are necessary to cover each concept

D Product of C arranged alphabetically by B

E Product of D edited by B‡

F Product of E typed into copy for printer

‡ The indexer may work on C, D and E more or less simultaneously; it is broken down into separate processes for the convenience of readers who may not know how an index is prepared.

The above processes are gone through in small or greater degree whether the desired end-project is a simple index of names or a highly organized index to a detailed work of scholarship. The latter type of index is sometimes called an articulated subject index.

The main advantage of an articulated subject index is that it provides a well-organized display of indexing phrases which it is easy to scan visually, because the technique of multiple indentation helps the reader to find what he is looking for quickly. Articulated subject indexes are used successfully with both large and small indexes.

* This paper is compiled from material originally published as two separate articles in the *Cartographic Journal* (Vol. 7 (2), page 70, and Vol. 9 (1), page 8). The material is here reproduced by permission of the Editor of the *Cartographic Journal*.

Reprinted from *The Indexer* 8, no. 3 (April 1973): 130–138.

The selection of the headings and modifying phrases, the manipulation of language, and word order to give the smoothest reading and the correct emphases, and the arrangement of common material in a logical system of heading, subheading, and sub-subheading, all in alphabetical order (i.e. the processes of A-F above), all these have been undertaken intuitively by the experienced indexer, taking into account the nature of the material and the needs of the reader who will consult the index. It is only recently that it has been discovered that indexes of this kind have a logical basis which can be expressed in mathematical terms and so be simulated by computer program. This logical basis is the point of common ground from which a happy marriage of art and science may spring.

Studies carried out in the Post-Graduate School of Librarianship in the University of Sheffield, under the direction of Dr. Michael Lynch, and with the assistance of grants from the Office for Scientific and Technical Information (Department of Education and Science) have led to the devising of a novel computer technique for the production of articulated subject indexes, the feasibility of which has been demonstrated in a number of trials. Some of the trials were based on samples submitted by the author of this paper, who acts as indexer of the *Cartographic Journal*, with the encouragement and support of the British Cartographic Society.

The first program used for these trials was written by Janet Armitage in Sheffield whose work formed the essential basis of subsequent studies. A later and more sophisticated version of Miss Armitage's program was developed by J. Howard Petrie, also in Sheffield. This is not the place to discuss (nor is the author of this paper competent to describe) the technical details of the program from the point of view of the computer scientist. Readers of this publication may however find the following account of the processes involved from the indexer's point of view both interesting and, it is hoped, reassuring.

The process may be summarised as follows:

Indexing phrases are derived by the indexer from the text to be indexed (compare stages A-C above). As many phrases are constructed as are necessary to extract all the material for the index . (In what follows, these phrases are referred to as the ' input '.) The input phrases, prepared on this basis, are then punched on to cards or tape ready for computer processing. The computer, having been instructed by the program then selects each heading in turn, produces an entry for each, and arranges them in appropriate alphabetical order. (Compare stages C-E above). The computer is linked to a line printer and the ' output ' may then be compared to stage F above, providing the basis of the printer's ' copy '.

The indexer first then, brings his expertise to bear on the abstraction of relevant material from the text in order to derive the indexing phrases which are to be punched on to cards. For example, it may be that the material to be indexed starts as the multiple concept

problems and techniques in land use mapping in Malawi, page 123

The indexer wishes to have entries under Land use, Mapping, land use, and Malawi. By the manual method he would write something like the following three cards:

Land use mapping
    problems and techniques in, in Malawi, 123
Mapping, land use
    problems and techniques in, in Malawi, 123
Malawi
    problems and techniques in land use mapping in, 123

To achieve a comparable result in the computer-generated index *one* ' input ' phrase is written and subsequently punched in exactly the following format

PROBLEMS AND TECHNIQUES IN <LAND USE <MAPPING>> in <MALAWI>, 123

The computer selects and alphabetizes the headings to give the following three entries

LAND USE MAPPING
   PROBLEMS AND TECHNIQUES IN – , IN MALAWI, 123
MAPPING, LAND USE
   PROBLEMS AND TECHNIQUES IN – , IN MALAWI, 123
MALAWI
   PROBLEMS AND TECHNIQUES IN LAND USE MAPPING IN, 123

The first obvious advantage is that for the effort of writing one phrase three entries are derived and arranged in alphabetical order. The second is that the 'nesting' of the parentheses (which it will have been noted are the symbols which indicate to the computer what words are to be selected for headings) is most helpful in subject matter where composite terminology is a characteristic (e.g. air photography, hydrographic charts, topographic mapping).

A further and sophisticated feature of the program is its capacity to select material common to several entries to produce alphabetically arranged and indented sub-headings. For example, in the following input phrases

USE OF <BENCHMARKS> IN <DATING> OF OLD MAPS
SIGNIFICANCE OF <WATERMARKS> IN <DATING> OF <ORDNANCE SURVEY MAPS>

<DATING> is common to both. The program generates the following entries:

BENCHMARKS
   DATING OF OLD MAPS, USE OF – IN
      OF ORDNANCE SURVEY MAPS, USE OF – IN

It will be seen that the common material has been selected by the computer to give a sub-heading, i.e. dating. A similar selection of common material will be brought forward to appear as a sub-heading under WATERMARKS and ORDNANCE SURVEY MAPS.

It may be desired to include the following material in the index:

representation of <rivers>, <roads>, <railways>, <urban areas> and <rural areas> in road maps.

The needs of the user of the index dictate that entries should be found under each of the bracketed terms, but not that all the material will be found repeated in each case. The typical entry should read

Rivers
   representation of, in road maps

not

Rivers
   representation of roads, railways, urban areas, rural areas and, in road maps

The earlier program required the indexer to write separate input phrases for each heading, five in all. By constructing the input phrase in the following way the five desired output phrases are generated from one input phrase:

representation of ! <rivers>, <roads>, <railways>, <urban areas> and <rural areas> ! in road maps

It is not, however, possible to use this technique for punctuated phrases or names or for phrases incorporating 'nested parentheses'. Separate input phrases have to be written, for example, if it is desired to generate headings from the following:

<Smith, D. G.>, <Jones, E. F.> and <Wilson, R. A.> paper on automated cartography
production of <hydrographic charts>>, <aeronautical charts>> and <bathymetric charts>>

Even with these limitations, however, this is a useful addition to the program.

Successful use of the program depends on (a) the prolific use of noun phrases separated by connective words like 'of', 'for', 'in', 'by', 'to' (referred to hereafter as function words), and (b) expertise born of study and practice in manipulating the word and phrase order in the input phrases. This is because the program operates on the basis of six hierarchical rules; if the first rule operates, rules two to six do not come into force, if the first rule does not apply, but the second one does, then rules three to six do not come into force, and so on. These rules are:

1 If the subject heading is first in the input phrase the modification appears in the natural order;

2 if the subject heading is part of a complex noun phrase the remainder of the noun phrase must occur first;

3 if the subject heading is followed by 'of' the preceding component comes first;

4 if the subject heading is preceded by 'of' the preceding component comes first;

5 if none of these apply, the most common component occurring in all phrases with this subject heading is selected to come first (to constitute a common subheading);

6 if the first component cannot be determined by rule 5 then the original order is preserved.

The *Cartographic Journal* which was the subject of some of the trials of this program is a learned periodical appearing twice yearly in issues of between 60 and 80 pages each, numbered consecutively (so that issue 2 of each volume starts with the page following the last page number of issue 1). The contents include learned articles, reviews, Cartographic Society proceedings and news, and miscellaneous items of interest to cartographers. The scope of the index is thus very diverse.

The earlier program was used to prepare an index to Volume 5 of the *Journal*. The later program was first used to prepare an index to Volume 6. Work of this comparatively limited scale and undertaken in a short span of time did not produce any very intractable problems for the indexer, other than those which are dealt with below. The program was then used to produce a cumulative index for Volumes 1-8. Problems arising at the input stage and the output stage will be discussed separately, but first it may be convenient to add a word about the actual mechanics of punching cards.

In the trials on the *Cartographic Journal* index the input phrases were prepared and punched by the indexer herself, who was fortunate enough to be given access to punching equipment at the Cripps Computing Laboratory at the University of Nottingham. The principal point to be made is that it is essential that the exact format has to be observed down to the last comma and space, and in particular, placing of $<$ $>$ symbols. Mistakes cannot be rectified except by punching a new card. This takes time and very accurate checking through, because a mis-type can cause a faulty entry and the computer cannot be programmed to correct a mistake; the most it can do is include in the output 'FAULTY ENTRY' and go on to the next card. Thereafter the only way to get the output correct is to replace the faulty cards with correct ones, and process the whole batch again. This is expensive and for practical purposes really rather impossible; the process can be stopped however, at the end of the feed-in of input, and faulty cards be detected from the print-out of the input material, provided facilities exist for this. What this amounts to is that an exceptionally high standard of accuracy is needed in preparation of the punched cards, which naturally takes quite a lot of time. The keyboards of the punching machines used are designed to provide upper case characters only, and so expert typists sometimes find it happens that mistakes arise out of old habits rather than lack of basic typing expertise. Bureaux specializing in punch card operating do provide this kind of service, but, of course at a cost.

Problems arising at the input and output stages may now be discussed.

A. *Input stage*.

The production of a cumulative index presents problems different from those which arise in handling a limited project such as a single volume. In this case the problems were aggravated because:—

1 Data were derived of necessity from five separate sources:

(a) the existing index to Volumes 1-4

(b) the computer output of the index to Volume 5 prepared in 1970 using the early program

(c) the computer output of the index to Volume 6 prepared early in 1971 using the later program

(d) the index to Volumes 7 and 8(1) existing as input phrases awaiting punching, prepared in June 1971

(e) the index to Volume 8(2) existing as input phrases awaiting punching, prepared in November 1971.

2 A great deal of work was involved in editing and streamlining the input material for the following reasons:

(a) the literary forms of the components listed in 1 (a)-(e) above were all different because of the different conditions in force at the times the work was originally done;

(b) it was necessary to establish consistency of form both in content and in punctuation of all words and phrases to be used as headings;

(c) recurrent material had to be traced through all issues and comprehensive entries compiled.

The need for consistency in form and punctuation may be illustrated. A journal compiled as a symposium of the work of different authors and editors may present particular difficulties. For example:

Smith, D. G.; Smith, David G.; Smith, David; Smith, D.; Smith, Dr. David; Smith, Dr. David G.; Smith, Dr.

If these variants were all to occur, the indexer operating manually might have cards written for all seven forms, particularly if they arose at widely spaced intervals of time. But they would be all filed together alphabetically, and in editing before printing, the queries as to identity would arise, investigation would take place, and the final entry would be determined according to an adopted principle, for instance, 'all known initials are given but no titles', so all entries would appear under Smith, D. G.

But in preparation of the computer index theoretically no alphabetical filing is necessary since the program does this part of the work. However, if the material is prepared over a long time, one of two situations may arise. Either the indexer will write eight separate input phrases giving rise to eight headings in the output, possibly some separated by intervening 'Smiths' with other alphabetical demands, or, the indexer, growing suspicious as yet another Smith is encountered, has to trace the earlier entries in order to collate them. Ideally the preparation of the input should not involve this type of search and no alphabetical filing should be necessary. But in practice, handling material of the scale of a cumulative index for the eight volumes of the *Journal* revealed the need for frequent searching of already-prepared input phrases. Therefore some alphabetical filing of input phrases had to be adopted, albeit reluctantly.

Need for consistency of punctuation may also be briefly illustrated. One paper may write of 'place names' and another of 'place-names'. Input phrases may be derived on widely separated occasions. In a manually prepared index two cards might be written but would be filed together, for example:

Place names, standardisation of Scottish
Place-names, transliteration of Arabic

In the production of the edited typescript only one heading will appear, with both phrases listed below it. Given two input phrases prepared one with hyphen and one without, the computer reproduces them separately, treating them as separate concepts. Unless they are filed together during the preparation of the input the discrepancy may not be revealed until it is too late. A modification to the program could be made to remove this type of difficulty, which exists at present.

In the matter of preparation of recurrent material the input phrases may take longer than the preparation of similar data by the manual method. For example, in approximately every second issue of the *Journal* there are references to the Cartographic Society Annual Report for the year. A manual index would contain one card:

British Cartographic Society
  Annual Reports
    1965/6 ......
    1966/7 ......
    1967/8 ......

To yield the same information underneath a single heading the program requires separate punched cards for each entry:

<British Cartographic Society> Annual Reports
  1965/6
<British Cartographic Society> Annual Reports
  1966/7
<British Cartographic Society> Annual Reports
  1967/8

Preparation of a cumulative index raises considerable problems of terminology for the indexer. The sort of problem encountered is illustrated by material arising from papers on automation in cartography. Scarcely touched on in Volume 1, it is getting under way in Volumes 2 and 3, and is in full flood by Volume 4. It starts to splinter into separate concepts. Automation applied to cartography becomes automated cartography, computer mapping, automated plotting, automated draughting, automated contouring, and so forth. Even the most intuitive indexer cannot always foresee how subjects will develop. Solutions to this problem are at the root and heart of successful cumulative indexing.

The problem was more acute when working with the computer program in preparation of the input phrases, because again it became necessary to search through previously prepared phrases for trends in terminology, and to edit to bring cognate material together. In practice in preparation of the cumulative index for Volumes 1-8 of the *Journal* it became necessary to devise a system to make easier the search. Two methods were tried.

1 input phrases were numbered in sequence and each phrase occurring as a heading was listed alphabetically with the number shown against it. This meant that a heading occurring frequently might occur in eight or ten phrases scattered through the input, each of which had to be consulted when adding additional material.

2 a system of modified alphabetical filing of the input phrases was adopted. It must be remembered that many phrases contained more than one concept to be used as a heading in the index, for example:

(a) <accuracy> of <sampling methods> in <population mapping>

(b) experimental <sampling methods> in <population mapping>

The practice followed was to file the input phrase under the alphabetically earliest heading it contained, whether or not it was the first in the phrase: (a) would therefore have been filed under Accuracy and (b) under Population mapping. But a further control had to be established because of the composite nature of the phrases. A search for population mapping would not automatically lead the indexer to look under Accuracy. Therefore a strictly alphabetical list was compiled of subject headings as they emerged, together with each other heading found in association with them:

A	B
Accuracy	Sampling methods
	Data banks
	Automated plotting
	Population mapping

Each item in list B had its own place in this alphabetical list in column A, with its particular associates under B:

A	B
Population mapping	Accuracy
	Sampling methods
	Data banks

Both these methods described in (1) and (2) had their advantages. The first was tried out successfully in preparation of the index for Volume 6. The second was preferred for the cumulative index because other reasons (see above) already pointed to the need for alphabetical filing of input phrases.

No doubt other controls could have been devised. Experience suggested that if an index generated this way was to be truly integrated and systematic, control of terminology and retrieval of input phrases during preparation of the input was most necessary. This added much to the indexing time and work involved, and was by way of making necessary a data retrieval system for a data retrieval system. This cancelled out the saving of indexing time which the program otherwise allows.

In fairness to the program, however, it must be stated that if the technique were used for a cumulative index right from the beginning, it would be possible to edit the input phrases for each volume as they were prepared, using either the previous volume index or a print-out of the volume file which is in effect a keyword out of context index. (Edit programs are available for deleting entries, but these would not be suitable for use on files of such a large scale as are needed for the cumulative index). The expansion of vocabulary could also be accommodated, using this technique, by deleting entries and inserting new input phrases using revised terminology. A modification to the program to bring about both these improvements could be introduced, and would provide a machine-stored authority file. But in either case a great deal of work is involved.

Before consideration of the computer output, it is relevant to refer briefly to problems arising from unstandardised terminology. This is closely linked to the problems of vocabulary control discussed above, and is a matter of such general concern that it is perhaps an impertinence for an indexer to animadvert at all on such a topic. However, the indexer of a periodical like the *Cartographic Journal* has the task of bringing to an integrated whole a précis of the thoughts and concepts of many different scholars who write using terms acceptable to themselves but not necessarily identical with those used by others to describe identical or very cognate matters. A very few examples from the

recent work will illustrate the difficulty:

Air photography	Aerial photography
Cartographic bibliography	Cartobibliography
Geologic maps	Geological maps
Line features	Lineal features
Topographic maps	Topographical maps

The list can be extended almost indefinitely. The position for the manual indexer is complex, but using the computer program the difficulties are highlighted by the problems of tracing input material and establishing control of vocabulary and punctuation.

B. *Output.*

It is a generally accepted principle in orthodox indexing, endorsed by the British Standards Institution pamphlet on preparation of indexes[1], that alphabetisation should be either letter-by-letter or word-by-word, e.g.:

Letter-by-letter	*Word-by-Word*
Newcastle	New Orleans
New Orleans	New York
New York	Newcastle

Which is adopted depends on the character of the material and the type of index desired. On the whole, word-by-word is suited to the material derived from the *Journal*. But in the computer-generated index there are complications arising from the hierarchical nature of the six selection rules which are intrinsic to the program, and the additional fact that in the operation of these selection rules the function word ('of', 'in', 'for', etc.) is subordinated to the first component of the modifying phrase which follows that function word. The application of these rules affects the output in three ways:

1 given the following input phrases:

use of <marginalia> in <dating> <ordnance survey maps>

use of <representation> of <railways> in <dating> <ordnance survey maps>

use of <price> in <dating> <ordnance survey maps>

use of <watermarks> in <dating> <ordnance survey maps>

the desired output under 'dating' is:

Dating
1 ordnance survey maps, use of marginalia in
2 use of price in
3 use of representation of railways in
4 use of watermarks in

In fact, however, the order which appears in the output is 4, 3, 1, 2. This is because at present the modification sort key covers only the first two subject word groups (and related function words). However, a modification could be introduced to make the alphabetisation word-by-word, and to extend it over all the word groups in each input phrase.

2 given the following input phrases:

<representation> of <footpaths>
<representation> of <ice features>
<representation> of <nomadic peoples>
<representation> of <railways>
<generalisation> and <representation> in <automated cartography>
methods of <representation> in <travel speed maps>
problems of <representation> in <aeronautical charts>

the desired output under 'representation' is:

Representation
1 generalisation and, in automated cartography
2 methods of, in travel speed maps
3 of footpaths
4 of ice features
5 of nomadic peoples
6 of railways
7 problems of, in aeronautical charts

In fact, however, the order which appears in the output is 3, 1, 4, 2, 5, 7, 6. This is because at present the function word is subordinated to the first component of the modifying phrase. This rule could be altered by introducing a further modification to the program.

3 A more complex problem arises on the selection of material which is common to several entries when the program can and should ideally bring it forward automatically as a sub-heading, and in

many situations this is carried out successfully. But given the following input phrases:

advantages, disadvantages of <mapping> by <computer>
principles of <mapping> by <computer>
<calcomp plotter> for <mapping> by <computer>
<census data> in <mapping> by <computer>

the sub-headings appear as desired under 'computer':

Computer
    mapping by, advantages, disadvantages of
        calcomp plotter for
        census data in
        choice of scale in
        principles of

But under 'mapping', where 'by computer' is common to all five phrases the output is:

Mapping
    advantages, disadvantages of, . . . by computer
    by computer
        calcomp plotter for
        census data in
    principles of, . . . by computer

The reason for this is that the rule requiring the program to select common material is the fifth of the six rules. If any of the rules 1-4 have come into operation the remainder are not checked. This gives inconsistent and unsatisfactory results. With further work, however, the sophistication of the algorithm which is basic to the program could be increased to ensure that words such as 'advantages', 'principles' did not become the first elements of a modifying phrase, and so would be disregarded in the selection of common material.

It may be asked why the input cannot be prepared using multi-case fonts instead of the upper case only which was used in Nottingham and Sheffield. In fact the machinery available for these trials did not make this possible; it would in theory have been possible to punch the input on tape which would have provided an output with built-in symbols indicating to the printer when to use capitals and when to use lower case. But punching equipment of this kind was not available. Even if it had been, a higher level of interpretation would have been required than most printers are able to give at commercially reasonable rates.

Summary

To sum up, the work at Sheffield, and the trials of the program on the index for the *Journal* must be regarded as academic research of which the index is in a sense a by-product, though it is hoped a very useful one. In preparing indexes for small and homogeneous batches of material which can be produced over a short time only it is simple to use and yields a reasonably satisfactory output. For large-scale indexes, particularly those dealing with very diverse material, derived over a long period of time, experience with the material from the *Journal* has shown that at present it needs a cumbersome system of controls, and at the preparation of the input stage it certainly did not save any indexing time; rather the reverse, because in practice the time spent on setting up controls, editing, searching, and checking for inconsistencies in content and punctuation was at least as great as that needed to write, file, and edit a manually prepared index. Even the punching of cards took longer than the preparation of a typescript because mistakes took longer to rectify.

Just as a manually produced articulated subject index, using multiple indentation and sub-headings is a much more complex structure, requiring a great deal more indexing expertise, than is an alphabetical list of paper titles, so the program is a very sophisticated concept of how to use automated techniques for data retrieval in depth. Its development is a considerable *tour de force*, and with the various modifications which the experience with the large samples from the *Journal, inter alia,* has revealed to be desirable, and some which as indicated could be introduced, most of the remaining problems could be removed. Indexing time would then be much reduced, and vocabulary control would be much simplified. Successful operation will continue to depend on the exercise of indexing expertise to bring the end product closer to the standard set by the linguistically polished and conceptually accurate excellence of the best manually produced indexes. The skills of the indexer should be willingly given in support of further research.

ACKNOWLEDGEMENTS

As before I am indebted to the Council of the Cartographic Society for its encouragement and support for this experimental work. Dr. Michael Lynch, Janet Armitage, J. Howard Petrie and Michael Snell of the Post-Graduate School of Librarianship at Sheffield have co-operated and encouraged with unfailing courtesy, though they would wish their thanks to the Council to be recorded as well, for allowing the program to be tried on the production of a cumulative index for the *Cartographic Journal.* It should be recorded here that the grant which supported their programme of research was made by the Office for Scientific and Technical Information. The thanks of the Society are also due to Dr. Eric Foxley of the Cripps Computing Laboratory at Nottingham University for giving access to the punching machinery which was used throughout.

REFERENCE

1 B.S.I. publication Nos. 1749, *Alphabetical Arrangement,* and 3700 *Preparation of Indexes.*

Computer-Aided Production of Book Indexes

Theodore C. Hines and Jessica L. Harris

Introduction

The Columbia University School of Library Service offers a course in indexing which is general in scope but includes book indexing both as an important area in its own right and as a type of indexing which is familiar to students and can be used to illustrate indexing principles.

The School also offers courses in information systems, with significant emphasis on computer applications.

For some years now, the authors of this paper have been using the computer as a tool for exploring information handling. This research and development work has been aimed at distinguishing unit operations in information handling, somewhat analogous to the unit operations of chemistry.

We have an advantage in that all of our programming is done by the authors of this paper; that is, the design and execution is done by experienced indexers and bibliographers rather than by systems analysts and programmers. Our theoretical approach cannot be considered adequately tested without production of actual, usable information tools of various kinds: journal indexes; thesauri; concordances; KWIC, KWOC, and other title-derivative indexes; and book indexes.

The research and development programme has now reached the point at which we can make computer programmes for the production of all of these types of tools available for use by students who have no knowledge of computers and computing, and who use the programmes as tools in learning about indexing and information systems. At present, this is done on an individual basis for those students with a special interest in these applications. We are in the process, however, of making use of the programmes a required part of course work.

Goals of Book Index Programme

In the case of the system for computer-assisted production of book indexes, we had two major goals in mind. In the first place we believed that, if we could define and codify a significant proportion of the work involved in producing book indexes so clearly and unambiguously that we could programme it for the computer without loss of index quality, this definition and codification would be an aid to further research into the indexing process. In the second place, we also believed that we could develop a system which would be immediately economic for production of indexes which are designed to be cumulated (such as the subject index to *Chemical abstracts*) or which are continuously revised for new editions or printings (such as those of many encyclopaedias).

Originally, we did not expect to develop, as we believe we have ended by developing, a system which would be economic and feasible for the production of book indexes generally, even when revision or cumulation is not expected. Of course, the terms economic and feasible must be taken with a grain of salt. The system will not compete with those free-lance indexers who, all too often, are forced to accept less than the going hourly rate for clerical workers for their time. Nor, for that matter, do most free-lance indexers as yet have access to keypunches or terminals, or to computer time on a rental basis when and as needed.

But, in saying that the system is economic, we are doing so against a background of studies in the clerical and professional labour costs of book indexing. We are also taking

362

Reprinted from *The Indexer* 7, no. 2 (Autumn 1970): 49–54.

into account the costs of the keypunch or terminal time used and the going rates for rental of computer time on a commercial basis in New York City.

Equipment Requirements

The assumptions that would underlie a decision to adopt this system for book index production are only that input equipment and computer time be available at the normal rates for such equipment today. While free-lance indexers would not be in this position unless they maintained a group of indexers working in-house, most publishers, at least in the U.S., and to a large extent in Britain, should currently be able to meet these requirements.

This estimate does not take into account possible savings to be derived from using the system's computer output to drive graphic arts composing equipment for the production of the final index. We are assuming only the production of a manuscript index for the printer, and our costs are compared with those of producing an index on cards, properly subordinated and consolidated, but not styled for the printer. We know that the output of our programmes could be used for graphic arts output devices, but have not used them thus and have no computer programme for this purpose. We have every reason to believe that this would be economic, too, but have no hard data on this phase of the operation.

Indexing Costs

It should also be noted that we have not included in our costs capital investment in programming. This investment is considerable, but we have done the work bit-by-bit over a long period of time, our programming is modular so that much of the cost would have to be allocated over other programmes for information handling, and we did not keep track of costs for programming.

Detailed costs are not of particular importance here, but benchmark figures are. The actual out-of-pocket cost, not counting overheads, for indexing the McGraw-Hill *Modern men of science*, Vol. I, in 1967, were very nearly $.25 per entry, with an entry

defined as a page reference or an inclusive page reference (e.g. 63-92). Most of the cost was in labour, and we allocated the very modest rates of $2.00 per hour for clerical time and $3.50 per hour for professional time. These rates would of course have changed by now. The labour involved was about 50 per cent clerical and 50 per cent professional and supervisory. While the procedures followed were not the most economic, the book was somewhat over-indexed, which should produce a lower cost per entry, and index design costs were not counted. This study of manual procedures was carried out by Alan Greengrass on an index designed by us. If the figure of $.25 per entry sounds high, we suggest costing actual index production on your own before communicating with us on it. We are willing to admit that more careful management might have lowered the costs by as much as 25 per cent, but not that most free-lancers are much more careful managers. Personnel costs in the U.K. might be somewhat lower. The computer-assisted indexing system discussed below is somewhat cheaper, and results in a manuscript index rather than the card index for which the cost figures were kept.

The Computer-Based Index System

How does the computer-based system work? Basically, the indexer marks or underlines the text and writes in the margins to indicate the entries he wishes made. There are no limits on the length of entries, or on their nature, but the styling of the entries must be precise so that they will file correctly by our computer filing procedures. Non-alphabetical classed groupings of entries are possible, but would require either hand filing of entries at extra cost or development of a numbering system for the classed groups so that filing could be on the basis of the numbers. We have recently found the latter method to work quite satisfactorily in a thesaurus for which we wanted classified sub-arrangement under several of the alphabetically-arranged main terms. The computer filing problem, some published opinion to the contrary notwithstanding, is a complex one, as any professional indexer who consults the sub-arrangement of entries in the *Index medicus* may see for himself. We have discussed computer filing at length elsewhere,[1] and shall not recapitulate that discussion here.

Keying of Entries

The keyboard operator keys the entries from the marked manuscript just as the typist would type cards. The programmes do not set any limitation on the kind of input equipment used. We have available to us 2260 consoles, a 2741 typewriter-terminal and 029 keypunches. We also had, for about a year, a Dura Mach 10 paper-tape typewriter. Aside from the latter, all our input equipment has been IBM-manufactured. We use, by preference, the 029 keypunch for input for indexes, since this gives us our entries on convenient, eye-readable cards.

We also prefer to key our input in all capitals. There is no programme limitation on using upper and lower case input, but we believe that we save considerable time and effort by using an automatic capitalization programme segment which gives us upper and lower case output by rule. The rule in this case is that all words not on a stop-list (such words as a, an, the, of, etc.) are always capitalized unless a special symbol is punched before them, and *vice versa*, with the additional exception that words on the stoplist are capitalized in any case if they are the first word of a subject, though not if they are the first word of a modifier or subdivision. A symbol may be similarly keyed before all acronyms which should appear in all-capitals, such as NASA, or a go list can be used for indexes intended to cumulate. We are in the process of developing a routine which will be the reverse of the above: that is, all initial letters not the first word of a subject, and not preceded by a special symbol, will be lower-cased.[2]

We have an alternative means of dealing with such capitalization exceptions as acronyms, which often seems preferable. This is simply to treat them as if they were keying errors and to punch a correction for them

after proof-reading so that they are handled with all other corrections and in the same manner. This is likely to be preferable because there are so few instances of this kind, and all of the occurrences of a single entry word (NATO, for instance) can be corrected by punching a single correction card.

The input configuration is quite flexible. Any convenient convention can be used to separate subjects from modifiers or subheads. For an index limited to a single modifier for each entry (e.g., *Chemical abstracts*) or to one level of subordination, subjects may be separated from the modifier by a colon and two spaces, e.g., TUNGSTEN: MEASUREMENT OF DUCTILITY.

The programme permits (and we may use) up to three levels of subject subdivision, and there would be no particular problem in providing for still more levels. Where more than one level of subdivision is required, we generally use the space, slash (solidus), space as a delimiter between subject and modifier, and between modifiers. Any symbol or sequence of symbols not occurring in the entries themselves could be used. This one was adopted because it is easy, logical, and unambiguous, and does not offend the eye in proof-reading input or checking cards.

It is also necessary to distinguish references (page numbers, for example), cross-references, and scope or other notes. Again, any convenient, non-ambiguous characters or sequences of characters can be used. We have used three spaces before references, e.g.,

TUNGSTEN   27

and four spaces before cross-references, scope notes, definitions, or other matter inserted in the index, e.g.,

WOLFRAM   SEE TUNGSTEN
WOLFRAMITE   SEE ALSO
        TUNGSTEN

Entries are keyed in the order of the text references; that is, the order in which they are made by the indexer. This has certain advantages, since (except in the case of inclusive page references such as 27-32) the page reference may be keyed only once for each page, and computer-posted to each entry for that page. A programme segment would then check the continuity of page numbers to be sure that the keyboard operator has not forgotten to change the page reference. We have not followed this procedure in doing indexes, since we have no regular keyboard operator but depend upon students without keyboarding experience to punch their own data. We have used it, however, in providing both line numbers and speaker designations in a concordance to Goethe's *Faust*.

We do find that the system allows us to do preliminary indexing of manuscript or galleys, providing page references at a later point. This does not save money and effort, but does permit considerable improvement of quality and saving of time over indexing after page proofs are in and publisher pressure is to have the index out yesterday.

The indexer must style his entries carefully so that they will file correctly, and keying must be accurate and careful.

After keying, entries are filed by the special sort routine, and the filed entries run through a final programme segment. This programme consolidates page references, e.g.,

TUNGSTEN 27-32
TUNGSTEN 44

become

TUNGSTEN 27-32, 44

It also subordinates modifiers under the appropriate subjects:

TUNGSTEN 27-32
TUNGSTEN 44
TUNGSTEN/MINING   211
TUNGSTEN/REFINING 38

become

Tungsten   27-32, 44
  mining   211
  refining   38

Page references may be right-justified, with or without leading dots, or be left ragged right. The indexer may specify whether he would like modifiers or subheadings for subjects with no page reference consolidated with the subject or not: that is, he may indicate whether he would like

ORES/MINING 311
ORES/REFINEMENT 17, 291, 312-3

to appear as

Ores, mining   311
  refinement   17, 291, 312-3

or as

Ores
  mining   311
  refinement   17, 291, 312-3

The indexer has a wide range of similar options, including numbering (and heading) as pages or leaves, and capitalization or non-capitalization of articles, conjunctions, and prepositions at the beginning of modifiers.

He may specify the number of columns to the page, page and column width, margins, indents, and so on by changing simple English-language definitions at the beginning of the programme.

Corrections are made either by removing offending cards in input and substituting correct cards or by keying enough of the error to identify it uniquely between corrections, followed by whatever is to replace it, e.g., a mispunching of 'Amurican Society of Indexers' could be corrected by

' Amurican '=' American '

A similar technique can add or delete entries.

Since the programme will accept upper and lower case, special symbols, and so on in input without affecting filing or organization of the material, any indications of italics or accents may be recorded. Unless requested, they do not appear in the manuscript index, but would be available for graphic arts output. Provision exists in the programme for inserting fount indications (boldface for subjects and italics for references, for example) by rule, so that much styling normally done by the indexer or editor could be done in this fashion.

Even for upper-and-lower case computer output, overprinting can be used for some accents, for boldface, and for underlining, so that the computer printout is equal in quality to good typing.

There are no limits on the length of any elements, no ' fixed fields ' in input, and no labelling of input (except that implicit in the styling conventions given).

Subject index entries may be added to abstracts when keyed. In this case, the abstract number is posted to the main entry and entries for the subjects created for input to the index system, along with author and title entries.

While other book indexing programmes have been written, those we know of are special purpose programmes which cannot handle complex entries, varying subordinations, and different output formats. An example is given in Reference [3].

Several indexes have been handled in this way, including the index to our own book on computer filing. Others are underway, as indicated by the sample (Figure 1) of Gail Persky's index to the American Library Association's Preconference on Subject Analysis, where the example is unedited and the references are to the manuscript papers. The sort routines have been tested on very large bodies of data, including a number of book catalogues and bibliographies. We have plans and preliminary runs at present, for use of the procedures on a consolidated index to the Library of Congress Classification, an index of more than 150,000 entries, and are confident of carrying it through if funding for input, editing, and production becomes available.

Figure 1. Sample page of index to Preconference Proceedings.

The programmes use procedures, or building blocks, Meccano-like sections, which are used very widely in all our other programming—the unit operations discussed earlier.

Of course, they deal only with the mechanical and clerical operations of book indexing. The identification and expression of indexable matter remain the province of the human indexer. But much of the handling of the entries, of repetitive typing, and of the styling of entries often done by the indexer or editor has been shifted to the broader back and faster fingers of the computer. At 1,000 entries per minute filing time and at about 20 pages per minute formatting time, a computer can give you quite a lot, including trial runs, before you go broke, even at $5.00 per minute, which is an outside upper limit. All of the figures in this report are loaded, if at all, *against* computer use.

We are happy with our production system. More important, however, is our feeling that pushing as much as we can regularize on to the computer leaves us freer to investigate what the indexing process itself actually is, and to work on our continuing series of studies in automatic indexing of various kinds. Working with the computer, with its requirement for rigour of definition, has taught us much indeed about filing and about entry form. Some of this we knew intuitively well enough to produce what we still think are good indexes—but intuitive knowledge only gets research started, and exact knowledge is required to advance it.

We do not think any system we or anyone else may devise can replace any professional indexers. We are convinced, however, that such work as we are doing may help indexers to become more professional, better indexers, and may free them from drudgery. Or at least, as a friend of ours has remarked in another context, while computers may not free us from drudgery, we will at least get more drudging done per drudge.

REFERENCES

[1] Hines, Theodore C., and Harris, Jessica L. *Computer filing of index, bibliographic and catalog entries.* Newark, New Jersey, USA: Bro-Dart Foundation, 1966.

[2] Since this article was submitted for publication, this routine has been written and is used in the index to a forthcoming book by one of the authors (Harris).

[3] Jordain, Philip B., and Breslaw, Michael, eds. *Condensed computer encyclopedia.* New York: McGraw-Hill, 1969. pp. 581-589.

The Moving Finger,

or: The Future of Indexing*

R. D. Gee

The theme of the Rubaiyat is the mystery of existence, doubt of the future, and belief in the present. I do not accept this philosophy. We cannot alter the past, but we can record it; and within reason we can use these records to anticipate and direct the future. We are irresponsible if we refuse to move from the interim present. Besides using the Rubaiyat to introduce comment on futurology, I will paraphrase it to provide a pertinence to indexing:—

'The moving finger hunts; and having hit,
Flips back: nor all thy piety and wit
Shall lure it back to check but half a line,
If what was indexed proves a proper fit.'

In marshalling my thoughts for this paper I met certain fundamental problems. In analysing them I found that I had created the very framework of the presentation. For instance, was I to state a future for indexers as I know you today—or for the applications of the craft of indexing, whoever is responsible for them? The overriding enigma is not conviction that indexes will exist, but the physical format of the material requiring indexing. This leads to questioning the aptitude of present methods for media yet to be developed.

I mention this because in the past five years I have worked with both a computer company and with a publishing group. My present work is related to research on printing and communications technology of future potential for publishing, and I am no longer prepared to accept paper as an *a priori* commodity for information transmission. Once one doubts the importance of crushed trees as the raw fuel, one begins to realise that all prognostication relies on the same confidence as that which guides an arm down a rabbit hole—to be bitten by an owl, which has no logical right to be there.

The future will be full of things that have no logical right to be where they appear—by today's concepts, that is. After all, we now accept that Stonehenge was built as an astronomical index, interwoven into a totally different culture to ours. To the builders of Stonehenge, Salisbury Cathedral has no right to exist.

A conference has just finished in New York, devoted to computers in printing, called COMPRINT 90. One paper was entitled 'The future isn't what it used to be' from a science fiction short story by Arthur C. Clarke[1]. The author, Arthur Gardner, introduced his paper with one of Clarke's predictions:

'Within ten years many households will be equipped with communications consoles. The con-

---

* A paper read at a meeting of the Society held on 3rd December, 1970.

Reprinted from *The Indexer* 7, no. 3 (Spring 1971): 101–113.

sole will consist of a television camera, a t.v. screen, a computer terminal, microfilm facilities, and a newspaper facsimile receiver—all linked to computers which, in turn, will be linked to communications satellites . . . Any newspaper in the world, from the *Wall Street Journal* to *Pravda,* would be available to any user of the console, no matter where he lives. And, thanks to microfilm storage and retrieval, any newspaper ever printed (back to the 18th century) would also be available, as well as any book, magazine or pamphlet worth saving. Such material would be called up from a global electronic library—a central data bank linked to the total electronic nervous system of the world.'

According to Arthur Gardner, Clarke's vision is as ridiculous as sending a man to the moon. The printing world has a future— but that future isn't what it used to be.

Certain technologies have remained stable because their physical presences have dominated an environment that in turn has conditioned them. Printing, as the oldest technology, has not changed much since the first steam presses of *The Times*—installed between the Retreat from Moscow and the Battle of Waterloo. This may have been because of the dominance of mechanical enginering, with electrical engineering as a support technology. The last decade, under the Svengali of space travel, has dictated that physical energy be transmitted with as few moving parts as possible. We are now at the beginning of not just an electronic age—but an opto-electronic age.

Don't accept my views as a prelude to a Wellsian technological Utopia. Our descendants will expend colossal effort and resources in converting the planet Venus into a human ecology, but our own deserts will still be deserts; our seas will still be inviolate beneath the surface; and the need to find a fresh planet will be stimulated by the polluted ruin that will be Earth.

In the meantime our future will be governed, not by the mere transmission of power, but of energetic senses. Sound has been conquered; vision has some problems left; and the future will tackle touch, smell, and intelligence. When we have identified the elusive sixth sense, that will be transmitted—

probably into the fourth dimension; and with suitable trumpeting from the fourth estate. All these labels refer to channels of information. The progress of man is measurable by his ability to transmit information, to record the process, and to recall it at will. Therefore, before I settle down to more mundane matters, I feel it necessary to break your conditioned responses to the printed word as it represents a concept. In fact, I read recently that the retreat from the word, or Gutenberg rut[2], is gaining momentum. Just consider that if a smell can be transmitted, stored, and retrieved—what logical processes can be used to index it? Somehow the brain manages it, and one day the method will be known and applied.

Since I am expected to foresee the passage of the moving finger, I intend to preface with some opinion on the subject known as 'technological forecasting'. This can be facetiously described as using statistical methods and computers to analyse chicken bones. One well-publicised system, developed by the Rand Corporation, is the Delphi technique—defined in one of its reports as 'a methodology used for the elicitation of opinions of experts'[3]. Isolated specialists forecast dates by which stated achievements will have been made. The correlated results are graphically presented as tabular catacombs of sarcophagi, the peak of each coffin representing the consensus of expert opinion. I choose this metaphor to remind me not to be misled by the cult of the expert—who too often listens to his own kind in order to cast more bones. I try to spot the living flesh. Future, like truth, is not shaped to fit into the hand of any person—or even into the cupped hands of a collective esotery. The problem is not new, and I remind you of a Shakespearean couplet:

'The mortal moon hath her eclipse endur'd
And the sad augurs mock their own presage.'

The Archivist of the United States recently prescribed the possible future of hard copy[4] I define this as 'information presented through conventional symbols on a paperlike base'. I use his comments here because of their relevance to any discussion of the future.

In 1950 (when people spoke in awe of electronic brains) 95 per cent of our records were on some form of paper. By the year 2000 this ratio will not be more than 50 per cent. Apart from the already known photographic film, we will have film bases which are diazo, vescicular, photochromic, ultra-high resolution, dry silver, or photopolymer. Paper will have been replaced or supplemented by thermoplastics or other plastics, either metallic- or magnetic-oxide based— which may have been imaged by video, hologram, or by magnetic-optical techniques.

To this, not only must be added materials and techniques yet undiscovered—but storage media intended purely for machine processing, such as tapes, discs and cassettes— and a yet undefined range of information to which I can only allude as 'soft-copy' (that is, disposable and short-lived) or 'palimpsest' (instantaneous display without copy).

It should be apparent that indexing, whether computer-assisted or not, has yet to face its greatest problems; and perhaps its greatest exponents are at present sucking tiny index fingers. Before you contemplate these problems, however, consider the following statements from experts:

'Space travel is utter bilge.'—
    Dr. Wooley, Astronomer Royal, 1956.
'As far as sinking a ship with a bomb is concerned, you just can't do it.'—
    U.S. Rear Admiral Woodward, 1939.
'Talking on the screen destroys the illusion. Devices for projecting the film actor's speech can be perfected, but the idea is not practical.'—
    Thomas Edison, 1926.

In every case, each expert was proved dramatically wrong within two years, although curiously these very events had already been rehearsed in some practical form. Edison himself had demonstrated the first public sound and motion experiment with his 'Kinetoscope' in 1894; while in the very year of this quotation the John Barry-

more film 'Don Juan' was released with an introductory speech from the screen and a synchronised musical accompaniment throughout.

And a word for the others. In 1877 the Tay Bridge was opened, designed badly, incorporating false data submitted to Sir Thomas Bouche by, among others, the Astonomer Royal of the day. (There must be something about Astronomers Royal.) As self-qualified eulogist and Dundee bard, William McGonagall burst forth:

'Beautiful Railway Bridge of the Silvery Tay !
I hope that God will protect all passengers
By night and by day,
And that no accident will befall them while crossing
The Bridge of the Silvery Tay,
For that would be most awful to be seen
Near by Dundee and the Magdalen Green.'

Two years later it fell down in a storm, together with a train and passengers, and was witnessed by many from 'nearby Dundee and the Magdalen Green'. Was McGonagall, as a complete non-expert, trying to say something that was common knowledge to all but experts? It is rather unusual to honour the opening of what was thought of as the finest engineering achievement in the world with even the slightest mention of accident.

Still, back to indexing.

The immediate, but improvable, present can be represented by those periodical indexes for which I have no responsibility whatever, because I am no part of the operational side of publishing. I am more concerned with the product as a consumer. With weeklies like New Scientist, European Chemical News, Computer Weekly, Electronics Weekly, or even Practical Gardener, Woman's Own, or Motor Cycle I feel that the Lynch programme could have some contribution to make. Despite the joint attitudes of editors and circulation managers I believe that an index can benefit circulation, and ultimately the advertising income. If regular readers were provided with an index, they may view their weekly expenditure as a contribution to a usable reference set—which, of course, must have no issues missing.

Unfortunately, editors see no value in yesterday's material, since easy retrieval may prevent a repetition in the future of a fresh feature. In the consumer magazine field, too much is made of the value of point-of-sale display, and not enough of the dynamic encouragement of regular subscription. The overlying economic principle for this attitude is historically justifiable, for as the domestic purse strings are tightened, the newsagents' orders are curtailed. It is up to publishers to ensure that the first cuts will be made elsewhere, because every system, however ideal, always faces fluctuations of economic stress. If I had the opportunity and energy to argue for an indexing policy within my company, I would pin my argument along those lines—not on utilitarian ideals. When the publisher of a serial refuses to recognise the value of an index, he has publicly admitted that his product has no value. Therefore his public cannot be blamed for purchasing from week to week, and breaking the habit on the shortcomings of one issue.

Certain weeklies could benefit by quarterly, bi-ennial, annual, and possibly further cumulated indexes, since services like British Technology Index and British Humanities Index cannot cope. In many cases the quantity of text in news items is too small for high-level indexing, although the information quotient is high enough for original editorial selection. Publishers see themselves as harvesters of ripe corn, rather than as purveyors of information. They should repeal their Corn Laws.

With monthlies I have less belief in the need for indexes, although I would like to use more five-year cumulations. Monthlies are well covered by commercial and institutional abstracts and indexes, by services which are professionally constructed, which are subject to less delay, and which cover other relevant publications. Where indexes to monthlies exist as separates, they are not amenable to sophisticated techniques. For

example, when twelve issues produce a total of eighty or so articles, an annual index has value only for library binding or to support microfilm files. If journals are kept boxed, which I prefer, a separate index is useful as a guide to missing copies, although even then an annual contents list is better. In other words, periodicals require individual indexes when the annual quantity of information is high, and such indexing is now possible by the use of data processing. The use of computers does not presuppose the by-passing of intellectual labour. The Lynch programme, for instance, demands a high level of analysis and heavy use of keypunching equipment.

The fault of individual journal indexes, for a librarian, is that one supposes the enquirer to have identified a source for his problem first. This is all well and good if you expect to find it there, because the journal is so specialist, or because it was remembered from an earlier reading. This sort of information work is too hit-and-miss, and publishers do not help by automatically providing indexes as a natural part of the subscription—even when they do exist.

You may reasonably wonder why I stand here and criticise my own industry, stating what is needed, but not converting from within. And since you are reasonable people, you will require a sort of reason. Publishing is a curious activity. Although tied to the first form of mass production, it stands on a cottage industry concept. Authors are often not employees, and are responsible for equipping themselves with the information they need—which probably accounts for their pressures for a Public Lending Right. Editors, illustrators, and indexers are hired in short doses like consultants or building labourers. A publisher does not maintain a reference library for staff, and the closest sort of information file is an inbred and empirically handled accumulation of cuttings previously generated by that publisher. Outside of that, 'stringers' are used—or the burden thrown at public libraries. And this accounts for some librarians' reaction to a

Public Lending Right. In general, all information is bought, begged, or scrounged from outside, and once used, is forgotten—so that the process can be repeated in the future. Although the situation is improving, you can appreciate the difficulty of spreading the gospel in such an environment. Arts-graduate-bound book publishers, failed-graduate-riddled magazine-houses, and anti-graduate newspapers all share one thing in common. They all survive by selling information, but they have little comprehension of it as a commodity, and none at all of it as an asset. The only consolation that I can masochistically offer, is that if the lesson is not learned within a decade they will not survive, and the commodity will be more efficiently handled by a new generation of alert enterprises—and electronics has nothing to do with it.

As a user of indexes, I have mixed feelings on the universal compendia like *British Technology Index* or *Engineering Index*. Headings become so complex that they face changes from year to year. Thus time-expansive searches become maddening. Better terms are discovered as one progresses, so constant re-searching becomes necessary. In highly specialist fields they become cumbersome, despite excellent design philosophy. Consider a typical pattern: assuming a search for a specific application of a programming language, FORTRAN IV, the searcher comes to grips with DIGITAL COMPUTERS: PROGRAMMING: LANGUAGES: FORTRAN: IV. This becomes more complicated if he seeks a sub-set when the original indexer is unaware of the hierarchical structure of some languages. For example, if COMPTRAN is an application sub-set of FORTRAN, is COMPTRAN IV a sub-set of FORTRAN IV, or a development of COMPTRAN I to III? This is where the subject abstracts win the day. It also indicates the need for the indexer to have a good grasp of the text.

It is regrettable that those publishers providing annual indexes to particular periodical titles have not appreciated the value of cumulation, nor the need to concentrate on the easier compilations for companies, products and trademarks from those infuriating pages at the back of commercial technical journals. The only real cumulation I know appearing regularly is that to the Economist Intelligence Unit's *Retail Business*. Each annual index covers back to issue 1, with 1-148 having just been published. Unfortunately the construction is crude, being title-based rather than subject; it is without cross-references, and it includes reports that have been superseded—without so indicating.

Certain periodicals have produced bumper bundles, such as *Scientific American* and *Engineering,* but these are rare and not part of a regular policy. *Computing Reviews* produces fairly regular cumulations for two or three year clumps—but true to the new traditions, they are in KWIC format, which does not endear me to them.

I also have to live with abstracts in printing, like that of PIRA whose latest annual index covers 1967—while they use their computer to produce an indifferent monthly printout of articles relevant to newspaper production. Since technology does not progress in annual cycles, I see no reason why subject indexes to abstracts should not cumulate in at least three-year compilations. On the other hand, an American equivalent of PIRA, the Graphic Arts Technical Foundation, does not index its monthly abstracts at all—and consequently wastes a great deal of work, because no one in their right mind would conduct a retrospective search through their chunky product.

Since I take over fifty subject indexes and abstracts in all fields of our research, I attach little value to the individual journal index, beyond that of a useful ' fill-in ' to literature searches. But consider the value of a ten-year cumulative index to the *Library Association Record* or *The Indexer*.

The reason for all these shortcomings is predominantly a shortage of full-time professional indexers.

The near future

I have mentioned some simple realisable improvements to today's efforts, which may need data processing assistance to handle the volume in sufficient time to make the progress worth-while.

There are now several comprehensive indexing services for news material that did not exist five years ago because no commercial need was recognised. Within five years these may be computer-driven. *Research Index*, with its crude production, disorganised subject headings, and lack of cumulative indexing, would be an incredible tool with computer support. It should compare itself with its American counterpart of Funk & Scott.

If any news index deserves more sophisticated techniques to match its impressive appearance, it is the *Official Index to the Times*—although it has improved enormously in the past decade. Its most unforgiveable fault is its tardiness. Too much editorial effort is thrown away by a production insistence on quality printing and prestige binding, thus destroying the prime motive of a news index—namely topicality. There is no reason why a paper-covered edition could not be produced, and cut out the eight-month delay which customers at present tolerate for relevant indexes. At the moment I receive my microfilm *Times* six months before they are indexed; this seriously affects the value of microfilm storage. I would suggest that the *Times* takes a close look at the H. W. Wilson publishing policy, and they may find their microfilm sales improving.

I will return later to what may be called 'case-hardened' book-publishing stupidity, but to introduce some coverage of computers I move on to a quotation from *Computing Reviews*, vol. 2, No. 9, September, 1970:

'In striving for a speedy method of organizing an index, the question arises as to which of various possible schemes is adaptable to fully automatic processing. Clearly, some means of ordering is required that is based on criteria extracted from the text itself rather than assigned in accordance with human judgment. The simplest format of a quickly assembled index might be an alphabetic listing of keywords, very much as in the index of a book. In dealing with a variety of subjects, the significance of such single keywords could, in most instances, be determined only by referring to the statement from which the keyword has been chosen. This somewhat tedious procedure may be alleviated to a significant degree by listing selected keywords together with surrounding words that act as modifiers pointing out the more specific sense in which a keyword has been applied. The added degree of information conveyed by such keyword-in-context indexes, or 'KWIC Indexes' for short, can readily be provided by automatic processing. Keyword-in-context indexing may be carried out on various levels, depending on the purpose an index is to serve. The process may be applied to the title of an article, its abstract or its entire text.'
    H. P. LUHN.
Keyword-in-Context Index for Technical Literature, 1959.

Before I move into the environment in which the computer may become a natural part of indexing, I will mention some services, which should be familiar, and which are using computer typesetting to get the information before the customer as quickly as possible. One is the Library Association's *British Technology Index*, another is the combined INSPEC service of the Institution of Electrical Engineers, and another is *Chemical Abstracts*. These three represent a whole range of similar systems.

An interesting pilot was the House of Commons index of last year, which I saw as the most significant contribution towards informing elected representatives of why they are there that the country has ever had. If penny-pinching prevents further examination of this service, then the British concept of democracy will have throttled itself in accepting the restriction of public spending as a worthwhile pursuit. It is essential that those who plan our future can quickly discover the knowledge that as voters we collectively have. Simply gaining more votes than an opponent does not transform a parliamentary candidate into an informed oracle. Democracy relies not only on the existence of information, but on the objective transmission of it. It has to be known to be instrumental.

If during the remainder of this paper I make statements about indexing that some of you may find quarrelsome, I hope you consider the particular contribution that indexing can make to an informed democracy—whether the process has been a human or a machine task. Countries that produce indexing are more democratic than those which do not. Even a Central Capability Unit needs organised guidelines to data before it divulges the benefits of its capability. It is equally important that *we* can assess the information that produces the judgments.

I see your members either as professional librarians whose daily function involves indexing a collection of some sort; or as freelancers compiling book indexes for authors or publishers. The librarian should have come to terms with the computer by now, and I hope he is well aware of the work that he needs to do in order to use the computer to ease his work. Strange, but true.

The other animal need fear nothing, because no one in their right minds will use a computer to index books, even where the book is computer typeset. All that would be produced would be a slab of 'over-indexing' of limited use, and taking up valuable collation. Extra book pages imply production difficulties with consequent increased cost. Such indexes would need meticulous editing and so the computer's contribution, although valuable, would be limited to providing an unpublished concordance—which the indexer could use as his starting point. It will be cheaper to have a human being read and compile from the start.

All this may seem an irrelevant and idealistic aside, but it introduces a thought which

I will expand later—the relative unimportance of books, compared with the volume of fresh knowledge transmitted through journals and reports. Modern society is more threatened by technological change than by the mystiques of economics, or by the applications of various shades of political dogma, although I appreciate that there may be a connection. If the layman is to argue convincingly for rational change, he must be able to comprehend what is happening, and all the possibilities and alternatives.

When governments and corporations blind him with science, he must not stick his head in the sand, or wear dark glasses. He must be able to give as good as he gets. To do this he should not have to rely on esoteric data banks, to which only a meritocracy will have access. He should be provided with public guidance through available scientific and technical abstracting services. No power of authority should exist from a consensus of ignorance, particularly when power comes from the counting of hands. It is therefore imperative that the walls of this establishment transmit the message to all public librarians who pass between them. Unless public authorities realise the necessary curiosity of the common man, they are failing in the responsibility that has been given them. Lip service is paid to the position of fount of all knowledge conferred on libraries, but as far as science and technology is concerned, there is a terribly conspiracy bordering on censorship by default.

It is extraordinary that most public authorities allow complete freedom for the professional librarians to select book stocks, but periodicals are subjected to tight scrutiny by gathered bands of shopkeepers. If you do not believe me, investigate any large reading-room where you will quickly see that to library committees, the definition of a technical journal is one that I would call ' trade '.

Since the higher level technical journals are not normally read as newspapers, but are produced to record ideas and endeavours, it follows that they must be supported by abstracts and indexes. It also follows that as disciplines cross-fertilize and as the flood grows, these tools must be as comprehensive and topical as possible. To me it is no *non sequitur* that such a target is impossible without computer-assistance at some stage, and fears of technical innovation allayed by the use of technology.

Since the computer is an indexing machine presenting the user with required information it has first to find it within itself. The processes of information retrieval that enable this to be done need to be specifically recognised and intellectually designed by a human brain. It is thus no accident that many terms of specific meaning within the computer world have been taken from the world of paper-based record. Any computer journal will be full of words like:

INDEXING LOOK-UP CROSS-REFERENCES
LIBRARY ROUTINES DIGIT PAGING
CUMULATIVE CONCORDANCE FILE
THESAURUS COMPILER TRANSLATOR

Even if they appear far removed from the meanings we first learnt. Before you wince pedantically, consider the origins of the words BOOK, PAPER, PARCHMENT, and PALIMPSEST, which I used before.

In a computer-bound world, the indexer may have something to offer of value. For instance, before programs become systems, much documentation is required, and the techniques used to analyse such procedures are akin to indexing. Without going into detail, it should be easy to visualise the type of intellectual effort needed to ensure that the output provides the required information in the right place at the right time.

Long before the computer has handled it, a human mind has defined sources from which the program will compute, or retrieve, or take as direct data input. Meticulously designed routines apply to all forms of data processing, from invoicing to automatic translation; from payroll to process control. Without this work the computer is as empty as a ream of paper before it becomes a book, and in most cases the programmer cannot start work until these paths have been mapped for him.

Too many computer installations are ineffective because the systems designers were ignorant of indexing principles. I think the historical basis for this is that the accountant mentality dominated for too long, and that left- and right-hand pages of ledgers became translated into input and output. In a simplified payroll system, a worker has a number which is matched with a name held in store for printout; and with a department; and with a known basic wage. Hours of work can be keyed in, or optically read from special forms; and from this a program will compute gross pay, take all deductions, and present net pay. All this information has come from different sources—from direct input, from files, and from computation. In what I call a 'ledger-minded' system the data punched-in will include name, number, department, grade, basic pay, &c., &c. The result of this is high volume of data preparation and costs to match; vast error rate or complex verification processes; much time consumption. And all to save costs on good programs and time on the central processor. If it is essential to save in this area, one might ask why it is felt worth using a computer at all.

To return to indexing: in order to use a computer for this purpose, input preparation requires an extravagance of labour. Therefore the prime reason for compute application must be to handle vast quantities of data with a flexibility previously impossible, and the need for this must be dominated by a sound economic or strategic reason. Otherwise it is just not worth it—as the editors of *European Chemical News* have decided with the Lynch program. It didn't increase the circulation, nor bring any new advertising, and it increased the administrative overheads. To meet these problems would have meant increasing the cover price, or selling the index independently at the full economic rate, or sharing costs by involving other journals.

The organisation of information will be an imperfect process long after computers have evolved into something else. But as we progress towards devices operating more like human brains, the whole philosophy of indexing will evolve, since I cannot believe that my own brain stores and retrieves information by crude word processing.

As far as current work is concerned, the computer is applied to five main areas in documentation, some of which are more developed than others. These areas are compiling, editing, producing, transmitting, and interrogating. As human indexers, you only really cover the first of these, and the most developed computer work is probably in the last three areas, with editing a fairly recent application. The computer cannot compile anything until a human interface has presented it in a machine-recognisable form—which also implies *selection*. In other words, the computer is an invaluable ally in handling vast amounts of data to pre-selected routines, but it has not, at present, much contribution to make to selecting the data it is to handle. Any future efforts to question the social impertinence of the computer will emphasise this problem, but I don't foresee a potential tyranny, because even selection routines will need human anticipation and control.

I have indicated that some data processing installations have not been as efficient as justifiably expected, through failure to organise detail in a systematic way, so that all contingencies were foreseen after close investigation and adequate record. Thus one future of indexing lies here, both within the field of systems design, and, in future, in the application areas of on-line time-sharing systems. If the jargon worries you, the concept is readily grasped.

An on-line system operates in the same way as a telephone network (in fact, in many examples the Post Office telephone complex is used), except that at the other end are computer services. The user's terminal will assess any service for which the subscriber has paid—and these may be offered by many different tele-processing agencies. Each customer may think that he is the sole recipient of the service at any specific moment, but the system is capable of serving all customers at once, apparently instantaneously. This is what is meant by time-sharing.

One number may be dialled for mathematical computation, another for stock market information, or another for accounting or stock control routines. The future will see thousands of various services accessed as readily as today's plumber through the Yellow Pages, offering from transport timetables to guides to restaurants; from entertainment information to remote library references—and all from one's home, or from public kiosks.

It should not need imagination to see the indexer contributing both to the design and to the use of such systems—as well as using them himself to compile, store and edit his products, which are then input into a processing network.

There is no difference between this electronic image and the process of using books and indexes to produce more books and indexes—some of which are classified directories. You are probably aware that the telephone directories now use computers to set them in type, operating on output produced by computers which have processed entries into classes and alphabetical subsorts. To make it sound less sinister, it is probably all done by the same installation through different peripherals. Even so, we all keep our own little lists of telephone numbers—and probably always will.

I would like to finish with the computer by quoting from a paper[5] presented at a Printing Industries of America conference in May, 1970; by an employee of *Time* magazine:—

' There was Mark I and ENIAC, UNIVAC and KWIC,
   UNITERM and PEEKABOO, POLYTERM and KIB,

KAD, KOV, KWOC and KWAC,
CRAM, CHRIS and COMAC,
WALNUT, CYPRESS, SAGE, FLIP,
Magnavue and Microchip,
Filesearch, Filmsort, Filmorex,
TWX, PERT, Computer decks,
Multics, JOSS, ARPA, DARE,
BMEWS, PILOT, ATLAS, SHARE,
MEDIBANK and Solomon, WHIRL-
    WIND and SPAAC (sounds like
    " smack "),
An ERA, SNOBOL, WATS, even
EDUAC.

The problem is that we are trying to use
these new engines and their programs for
very complex purposes—many of which we
barely understand. Man is trying to embed
machines into systems that are part-manual,
part-automatic, part-electronic. There is no
question that many investigations into new
business and editorial opportunities have
their roots in technology. Certainly the *New
York Times* Information Bank would never
be built without computerized microfilm and
computer-aided indexing. Publishers would
not enjoy subscribers in the millions without the electronic production of subscription
fulfilment. Time Inc. got two new businesses
that total over 100 million dollars as a by-
product of its first subscription service system
installed ten years ago, namely direct mail
sale of books and sale of complex regional
advertising.'

I have twice hinted at certain book concepts which must be challengeable. During
earlier discussion with the editor of your
journal on a possible approach to this paper,
it was suggested that I might comment on
the quality of certain book indexes, with
examples. However, I feel that some books
should not have indexes, and state this
heresy very firmly. I submit that a book can
be structured so that it works without an
index, and there are too many books that
are badly structured; thus needing an index
to sort out the mess. An example of a well-
planned reference work succeeding without
an index is the *Oxford companion to music,*
although all the Oxford Companions rely on

the cross-referring dictionary principle.
Another is Brewer's *Dictionary of phrase and
fable,* but again all dictionaries fit this. I
believe the Roget's *Thesaurus,* although indexed, can be used without one. Any trade
and commercial directory worthy of the
name is self-indexing, the secret of retrieval
lying in the user understanding the book.
One librarian I worked with always used
Whitaker's *Almanack* without needing the
index; and it was drummed into all librarians *never, never, never* to use the index to
the Dewey Decimal Classification in order
to classify. And, in truth, a good classifier
never needed it and a good librarian works
from his shelves, his catalogue, or his experience.

It might worry you to know that the first
man to compile an index, or concordance, to
the Bible was burnt at the stake—because by
doing so he had challenged the need for
ecclesiastical guidance. A restrictive practice
had been dented. I cannot help feeling that
the church's anger had some justification.
If you think about it, an index implies that
the book can be thrust together in any
order—scarcely an implication that should
be made of a holy book in darker times. It
is this implication that disturbs me. Just as
some books could be designed to be more
self-informative, there are others which
though needing an index, become over-indexed.

It is sad that a very fine Victorian practice
has been supplanted by the modern cruder
index. I refer to the full contents pages
carrying chapter synopses, which led to page
references carrying marginal guides alongside the pertinent passages.

I remember a *Times* crossword clue that
was an incomplete quotation from Byron's
Don Juan, and the compiler had ensured
that his ' light ' remained hidden within the
bushel of the *Oxford dictionary of quotations.*
I was forced to read the poem in some depth.
Of course, I could have waited for the solution the following day; but should I complain
of the lack of indexing that allowed this
experience? Are there not some books that

should be read, just as there are others that are to be used when needed?

I have an enjoyable social essay on railways by a respected author in which he pays tribute to his wife's index. It is a prime example of 'cottage industry' indexing. To the text covering 150 Penguin pages is appended fifteen pages of bad indexing. The book is predominantly British railway history, yet the index devotes one and a half of these fifteen pages to a subject heading RAILWAYS IN BRITAIN! To seek references to King's Cross, you have to be astute enough to refer to LONDON STATIONS. Since the author does not refer to Broad St., Liverpool St., Fenchurch St., Charing Cross, Victoria, Waterloo, Cannon St., or Blackfriars, I think the indexer is being too presumptuous in choosing a generic heading when a specific one is adequate. Faults are very easy to spot, but what is sad is that the single contents page is adequate enough to retrieve anything within 150 pages—particularly if one has already read the book. To add to a well-shaped effort a ten per cent index capacity seems to me a sacrilegious waste of time.

Meanwhile, John Prebble's absorbing account of the Tay Bridge disaster, *The high girders,* is not indexed—a state of affairs that aggravated me when seeking a point particular to this very paper. These comments lead me into the question which is not asked in polite society. Just why are books indexed? What policies exist within publishing houses to decree that some titles are treated and others not? Why do publishers spend much effort in producing house standardised packages from cover to cover—except that all their indexes are thrown together without any principle whatever?

I believe that every book should be closely analysed to decide whether an index is desired, or whether the author could structure his presentation more efficiently. If an index is necessary, then the type and level should be decided, and its production should be to house-specifications, at the very least. In other words, if the index is not presented as

an extension of the author's work *by the author,* then it should be an integral part of the book production process. I realise that I am sticking my neck out, but I am not convinced that the tradition of farming indexing out on a smallholding basis has given indexing the consideration it deserves.

You, as indexers, may worry about the machine. As a librarian, whose living comes from utilising published information, I ask that if your level of indexing is capable of economic replacement by machine, then it ought to be so replaced. As librarians, we never work for ourselves, since we are always servants to some style of organisation.

Too much book-indexing is soulless. Many indexers do not appear to have *read* the book in their charge, and merely match words with page numbers. This is *not* indexing. It does not aid the reader, and it confuses the searcher. In some cases it might even destroy the author's concept. Although I believe that indexing should be based on identifiable standards, I include within this philosophy the requirement that the index of a book should be part of the complete texture. If you study the *Oxford dictionary of quotations,* the index shows itself as the product of overall editorship—not as the work of isolated cottage labour.

Before a final comment on the rôle of the book in our future society, I would like to throw in an aside on indexing as a necessary craft—and one justifiable reason for indexes for the sake of indexing. In organising our own thoughts, studies, curiosity, or collections—to index is to learn. I think that if I were to index my own collection of science fiction short stories, I should not publish it. It is the duty of others with similar passions to undergo the same experience for themselves.

I will close the paper with my contribution to the fashionable debate on the future of the book. Everything I have read by experts I find wide of the mark that I gauge. One side forecasts books to be replaced by electronic or optical media; while the other side can see nothing other than the book as the only convenient form of communication, most suited to the time and privacy of the individual. Two technologies are trading blows.[2] [6] [7] The question should be, what type of presentation is suitable for book format? If fiction is a decayed fashion, how soon will it be replaced by a new imaginative art form based on, say, video cassettes? If directories are costly to compile, tortuous to typeset, expensive to distribute, expansive to shelve, diabolical to use, and difficult to rely on—at what stage will micro or digital formats service a happier market? Is poetry better borne by oral tradition than by the artificial formalities of the printed page? Will telephone directories be part of the hardware, rather than ergonomically bad, closely printed, floppy pages thrust periodically in bumper bundles through each door? Should not translating or grammatical dictionaries be provided through interactive on-line services, since it is constantly argued that language is a living organism changing daily? Printed dictionaries freeze a language, while today's electric global village needs greater flexibility in communication. If we are to class both novels and telephone directories as 'books' we are using a technical tradition to simplify a complex landscape.

Words are barriers where they prevent the transfer of a concept. Otherwise painting, sculpture, photography, and music would never have needed to exist. There will be a 'Newspeak', not as Orwell envisaged it, but so that communication can be more symbolic, more graphic, more cyphered, more conceptual. At the moment we are lacking the language, and a latter-day Chaucer will emerge—and he might even be a disciple of Marshall McLuhan.

Chaucer was a contemporary of Gutenberg—and McLuhan is ours as we move towards this perplexing future of the moving finger. I will close with my favourite quotation on futurology and the recalcitrance of man, aptly closing the chapter called 'Theories', in *Crotchet Castle*:

'The schemes for the world's regeneration evaporated in a tumult of voices.'

References

[1] GARDNER, A. E. The future isn't what it used to be. *Comprint 90.* October 1970. Offprint. Technical Information Inc. (Los Angeles).

[2] JOSEPH, E. C. A look at the future of computerized information technology. *IEEE Trans. Engg. Writing a Speech.* EWS-13, No. 2, September 1970. pp. 37-40. WISEMAN, T. Retreat from the word. *Guardian.* 13th October, 1970. p. 8.

[3] GORDON, T. J., *and* O. HELMER. Report on a long-range forecasting study. Rand Corp. P-2982. September 1964. DALKEY, N. C. Delphi. Rand Corp. P-3704. October 1967. (Also reprinted as AD 660 554.) BROWN, B. B. Delphi process: a methodology used for the elicitation of opinions of experts. Rand Corp. P-3925. September 1968. (Also reprinted as AD 675 981.)

[4] RHOADS, J. B. The future of hard copy. *Records Management Jnl.* 8. 1 Spring 1970. pp. 2-10.

[5] FISCHER, M. T. The production and composition of indexes. St. Paul, Minn. *PIA Computer Assn. Conference,* May 1970.

[6] BERNSTEIN, R. L. A publisher looks at publishing. *RCA Electronic Age.* Spring 1970. pp. 3-9.

[7] FRIEDLANDER, G. Automation comes to the printing and publishing industry. Newspaper manufacture and distribution, communications. *IEEE Spectrum.* April 1968. pp. 48-62. FRIEDLANDER, G. Automation comes to the printing and publishing industry. Production and distribution of magazines, periodicals, books. *IEEE Spectrum.* May 1968. pp. 53-62.

SUMMARY OF THE DISCUSSION ON MR. GEE'S PAPER

In the discussion which followed, the audience appeared reluctant to take up the big issues which the speaker had raised, nor did they attempt to rival him in prophecy about future developments.

The discussion opened with Mr. Neil Fisk objecting to Mr. Gee's criticisms to the index of Roget's *Thesaurus*. Mr. Fisk thought the index admirable and explained that he often used it more effectively by looking up two words approximating to the one he was trying to find an alternative for, and when he saw the same number under both, this generally referred him to the word he wanted. The speaker explained that he was a great browser in books and he found it difficult to consult Roget's great work at speed, but he always wanted to stay longer, so he found the index a great time consumer. Also when he first used Roget, he only possessed volume one of the Everyman edition and the index was in volume two; so he learnt how to find his way around without using the index. But he considered it such a well-structured book because every entry referred you to some other entry.

Mr. Molesworth Roberts asked Mr. Gee if he considered that many page entries under one heading indicated bad indexing. Mr. Gee said that many books could be much better structured than they were, thus less reliance could then be placed on the index to draw subjects together. Both questioner and speaker agreed that biographies demanded close indexing and Mr. Gee again regretted the passing of the Victorian habit of extended chapter headings and margin entries, which he thought a great help to the reader.

Mr. Raper pointed out that the area of subject matter in a technical index was voluminous, and instant rapid retrieval was better than browsing. Mr. Gee felt that personal browsing to find information for oneself was a different matter to finding facts for others and reiterated his feeling that too many books have indexes they don't need and many others which need them don't have them.

Mr. Gee also expressed concern at the pitifully small collection of journals on science and technology held by most public libraries, and thought they should spend more on these subjects. He also was very well aware of the mainly inadequate indexes (if any at all) produced for these journals, their usefulness being thereby greatly lessened.

Mr. Raper suggested that as knowledge was doubling every eight to ten years it was essential that libraries subscribed to more abstracting services. A response from the audience complained of the high cost of such services, exemplified by *Chemical Abstracts* at £400 per year. Mr. Gee felt that such expenses were essential to an efficient information service, but agreed that he could not justify *CA* although he spent £1,000 per annum on other abstracting services.

To the criticism from the audience that such scientific and technical journals would not be used sufficiently in public libraries to justify their cost, Mr. Gee pointed out that the same arguments were levelled against the provision of books when public libraries first came into being. He felt it was the fundamental task of libraries to educate and inform. This was particularly important at the present time as there was such a widespread ignorance of science and technology which was not improved, he felt, by the almost complete absence of information on these subjects in the national newspapers, the *Financial Times* excluded.

To a question put by Mr. Norman Knight on the necessity for the *I.E.E. Electronics Abstracts* to have a multiplicity of separate indexes, Mr. Gee pointed out the need to avoid confusion in a single-sequence dictionary index when covering 12 monthly collections of highly specific subjects; authors; institutions; companies; trade marks; and patents—particularly when each separate index was compiled by separate indexers. This problem implied computer assistance. Many visually attractive indexes were now being produced by computers with the use of both upper and lower case letters (previously held to be impossible) and also computer typesetting.

Mr. Gee ended by complaining that he thought that, for the most part, the state of British abstracting was abysmal, though there were one or two bright patches, especially the abstracting services of the Institute of Physics. It was also pointed out that the American Chemical Society had signed an agreement with the German and British chemical societies to provide information.

Nevertheless, Mr. Gee concluded that publishing in Britain is not an information-conscious industry; it is a selling industry, and the source of his salary.

The Role of Thesauri in Mechanized Systems*

Alan Gilchrist

There is a long history of research and development of thesaurus-type tools for various purposes including information retrieval, but vastly more money has been spent far more recently on mechanized information retrieval. This paper lightly reviews thesauri and mechanized systems and concludes with some observations about this apparent imbalance and the need for deeper thinking about concept formation and relationships, and more imaginative use of computers.

Introduction

As often happens, there was a long gap between the choice and announcement of the title of this talk and its writing. Consequently, I should start by indicating what it is I shall really be talking about, and try to convince you that I shall not be found guilty of transgressing the Trade Descriptions Act. As a consultant concerned with organizational problems, I have a strong interest in systems science and systems engineering. Consequently, my talk will be somewhat wider and more abstract than the title might suggest. I want to talk briefly about thesauri, briefly about mechanized information retrieval, even more briefly about mechanization in general and conclude with some observations about "A role for a thesaural concept in what would be bound to be a computer based system".

Thesauri

To those who profess to know little about librarianship or information science, the word thesaurus is probably exclusively linked with the name Roget. On the other hand, those who profess knowledge of information retrieval techniques are prone to argue about the exact nature of the beast and what elements must be present before it may be called a thesaurus and not something else. By the end of this talk I hope

I will have been able to convey an idea of what I mean by a thesuarus, but first I would like to take a brief look at the recent history of the thesaurus within information retrieval circles.

The word thesaurus comes from the Greek "thesauros", meaning a storehouse or treasury, and the Shorter Oxford English Dictionary records 1736 as the earliest known date when it was used, to mean "a treasury or storehouse of knowledge, as a dictionary, encyclopaedia or the like". But Karen Sparck-Jones[1] in an entertaining article has shown that the thesaurus is rooted in earlier ideas proposed by such philosophers as Sir Thomas Urquhart and Descartes. The former created a Universal Character (lost at the Battle of Worcester) of which he claimed that "for the affirmation, negation and infinitation of propositions, my language hath properties unknown to any other language" and that "in matters of Enthymems, Syllogisms, and all manner of illative ratiocination, it is the most compendious in the world". Sparck-Jones says that "The Universal Character would thus be distinguished by unambiguous, transparent and hence effective, signs". This in turn leads to the idea of a set of basic conceptual or semantic primitives, which can be used in combination for more complex concepts.

Ward, writing in 1654, and following ideas put forward by Descartes 25 years previously, said:

"My first proposal was to find whether other things might not as well be designed by Symbols (as in Mathematics), and herein I was presently resolved that Symbols might be found for every thing and notion . . . So that an Universal Character might easily be made wherein all Nations might communicate together, just as they do in numbers and in species . . . And the thing proposed is feasible, but the number of several Characters will be almost infinite . . . and the learning of them either impossible or very difficult . . . But it did

*A paper read at a meeting of the Society, 17th April 1975.

Reprinted from *The Indexer* 9, no. 4 (October 1975): 146–154.

presently occur to me, that by the help of Logic and Mathematics this might soon receive a mighty advantage, for all Discourses being resolved into sentences, those into words, words signifying either simple notions or being resolvable into simple notions, it is manifest, that if all the sorts of simple notions be found out, and have Symbols assigned to them, those will be extremely few in respect of the other . . . the reason of their composition easily known, and the most compounded ones at once will be comprehended, and yet will represent to the very eye all the elements of their composition, and so deliver the natures of things".

There is a somewhat salutary feeling of *déja vu* in these words, echoed again in the work of Ogden and Richards on Basic English in the earlier part of this century, and in more recent arguments put forward by experts in information retrieval. Well, these were early ideas, but the word thesaurus was brought into sudden prominence in information retrieval from late 1957 and the early 1960s. Helen Brownson[2] is credited with being the first person to use the word in print in its new application when she said, "The problem of [information retrieval], as some investigators see it at least, is to transform concepts and their relationships as expressed in the language of documents, into a somewhat more regularized language, with synonyms controlled and syntactic structures simplified . . . Now it is reasonable to think that the further we can go in routinizing and mechanizing the techniques of translating ordinary language into a regularized one and of coding for machine manipulation, the more will we be likely to achieve economically feasible machine searching on a large scale . . . Some investigators have come up with the thought that the best answer . . . may be the application of a mechanized thesaurus based on networks of related meanings". As with Urquhart, we have the idea of "regularizing language". And at about the same time Luhn of IBM was talking about "families of notions" and "dictionaries of notional families", expressions very reminiscent of Roget.

It is perhaps not surprising that these thesaural ideas were generated in the USA, a country which was both rich and clever enough to develop the computer; and a country which in its libraries had neglected classification in favour of the alphabetical subject heading approach. But, initially at least, the idea was simplistically applied. It was thought feasible by some that clerks could keypunch the words from titles, and perhaps abstracts, direct into the computer (thus dispensing with expensive indexers) and that the computer would then be powerful enough to digest and order these words for retrieval purposes—as in some vast, rapidly searchable alphabetical subject headings file. This optimism was soon dispelled, but I believe that the basic assumptions have persisted for many years. For example, the early days of MEDLARS were bedevilled by the attempt to combine computerized production of *Index Medicus*, using the Medical Subject Heading authority list, and to conduct post co-ordinate searches of the document file with the same subject headings list. Furthermore, the thought that classification was an unnecessary embellishment alongside the omnipotence of the computer gave rise to such poor pieces of work as the EJC thesaurus for science and technology and the ERIC thesaurus for education. If you think this judgement is harsh, consider the various auxiliary devices (categories, hierarchical listing and permuted compound terms) brought into the second edition of the EJC thesaurus (known as TEST), and for ERIC, take the several editions of this thesaurus and trace for yourselves the inconsistencies through those versions.

In my opinion, the best thesauri have been produced in this country, and now increasingly in Europe, because of our greater concern for classification. The work of Ranganathan, which the Classification Research Group did so much to foster in the West, made its greatest impact on thesaurus compilation methods with the production of the Thesaurofacet by Jean Aitchison. This is a thesaurus and faceted classification combined, linked by a notation and showing the principal hierarchies in the thesaurus section. The Thesaurofacet is a model which has been emulated in the Construction Industry Thesaurus and the recently completed Thesaurus/Classification for Planning.

But now that the thesaurus can be regarded as the alphabetical entry to a classification, in which either part may be used for information retrieval, we may perhaps wonder what a thesaurus really is. The ISO Standard on thesaurus compilation (which started life as the UNESCO Guidelines) defines a thesaurus in two ways:

"In terms of function, a thesaurus is a terminological control device used in translating from the natural language of documents, indexers, or users into a more constrained 'system language'.

"In terms of structure, a thesaurus is a controlled and dynamic vocabulary of semantically and generically related terms which covers a specific domain of knowledge".

I suspect Vickery[3] laid the foundations for these definitions in his review of the functions and structures of retrieval languages. He listed eight functions, the last being "to give aid to the searcher in his choice of search terms"—this being the function of thesauri. The point of his article was to stress that it was as futile to think that any one indexing language could satisfy all functions as to think that any one tool could satisfy all the needs of a carpenter. But these views of the thesaurus seem to me to be quite wide enough to make the thesaurus a powerful intellectual device—an arrangement of words showing relationships between concepts for the purposes of the system in which it is used—and in stressing the point about the purposes of the system I must add that purposes are likely to change and the indexing languages must evolve as well. In the article by Sparck-Jones to which I have already referred, she concludes by observing that her survey shows what a variety of approaches to conceptual vocabulary organization there are. Her final words are "We should not try to catch words and pin them down in neat little conceptual pigeonholes: such index terms will then be no more use for fertilizing library users' thoughts than dead butterflies are for fertilizing flowers".

Mechanized Information Retrieval

I am not going to attempt to give you a potted, evaluative, history of the use of computers for information retrieval. I just want to say a few things about the way in which computers are used, the ways in which thesauri and classifications feature in mechanized systems and to make some comments about them.

Broadly speaking, the computer is used for sorting and printing, so that mechanized systems are either engaged in the production of printed indexes or in performing very fast and complex searches of data files. The basic concepts of the printed index and the multi-entry catalogue are largely unchanged and the computer problems are mainly concerned with technology and economics.

Stevens[4] has classified automatic (or mechanized) indexing into three categories: automatic derived indexing, automatic assigned indexing, and automatic classification. The first of these is the approach in which the computer uses words in titles, abstracts or citations and sorts them into some predesigned format. Typical outputs of this exercise are the KWIC index and the *Science Citation Index*. No intelligence is involved in the operation and clerks can be used to input the material. The inadequacies of KWIC indexes have been widely documented, e.g.

erotic tendencies of Trappist monks. Atheroscl

and just as widely defended in economic terms. It therefore seems to me to be a contradiction to suppose that KWIC indexes can be improved by "enriching" titles, or by inducing authors or inputters to amend entries by reference to a thesaurus of preferred terms.

Most outputs of derived indexing are printed indexes, but of course it is possible to use the computer to manipulate automatically derived terms for search purposes. This is the principle of the free text input, in which the computer accepts everything but a short and simple list of terms on a "stop list". (Even here, one is in some trouble because the computer has to be told how to distinguish between "A" the preposition and the A which is a vitamin). If this procedure is used one needs a search thesaurus (as with UKCIS) and I shall return to this in a moment. If, on the other hand, it is preferred to impose concept control at the input stage (and some form of control is necessary at some stage of the process), then there are two possibilities. First of all, the subject analyst indexes documents in the conventional way, using a thesaurus (or a notated classification in a few systems), and the computer stores these against the bibliographic details. This method is used by INSPEC and by a growing number of international organizations like ILO (International Labour Office) who use a sophisticated computer system in conjunction with the OECD Macrothesaurus. Incidentally, this system has a number of features which illustrates the complexity of choice in computer systems. For each document, a subject analyst prepares a telegraphic abstract using preferred terms from the Macrothesaurus. For retrieval the computer can search through a file of these terms, or through any fields containing bibliographic details (author, organization, language, etc.), or it can perform a subject search through the whole file for uncontrolled terms appearing in titles or abstracts.

The second method in which thesaural control can be imposed is aided by the computer. Using this technique the computer scans all the terms input in a free or automatically-derived mode and prints out an alphabetical list of any terms it has not previously encountered. This list is then examined by subject specialists and again the decision can be made as to whether to impose control at the input or the output stage. In other words, either the computer can be instructed to treat synonyms or quasi-synonyms as equivalent, or such instructions can be recorded in a search thesaurus. This principle is employed in the ASSASSIN package developed by ICI. The arguments between the input control school and the output control school are still unresolved and probably cannot be generalized. I suspect the solution is again economic, resting on the assumption that as it is improbable that 100% of any library will be used it is not sensible to pay equal and detailed attention to the analysis of each item. It therefore appears to make better sense to accept whatever raw material is available and to use human intelligence to devise search strategies and to screen the output to discard false drops.

Most mechanized systems use Boolean logic in searching—that is to say, search teams are connected by the conditions AND OR and NOT, and very complex search statements can be built up. For example the expression

$$((((A+B) \mid (C \mid D \mid E \mid F))+\neg G) (H \times I)+\neg J)$$

would be legitimate where $+ =$ AND,
$$\mid = \text{OR},$$
$$\neg = \text{NOT}.$$

If there is no control language at the input stage, these expressions are likely to become complex as it may become necessary to include a string of OR connections to cover the various synonyms. A further problem arises because meanings are not always commensurate with words and the computer can only search for sets of letters in particular combinations. So it becomes possible to search for parts of words—where the part may have semantic value. This is known as truncation, and can be performed at the left, the right, or both at once. For example, the computer could be instructed to search for the occurrence of the letters *TIN*, where the asterisks indicate truncation. This search might retrieve the compounds tetraphenyltin, triethyltin

and bistributyltinoxide. It might also retrieve platinum and silver plating, because, as I said, those consecutive letters TIN do not always indicate that metal. Consequently a search thesaurus can be augmented by guides showing the occurrence of letter combinations to be found in the file, so that such confusion may be avoided. Williams[5] has described a number of such guides developed at the Illinois Institute of Technology Research Institute for use in searching a variety of data bases. One of these (Fig. 1) is composed of truncation guide entries for various terms: the one for analysis, for example, lists the 27 words in the file which start with Ana-, Anal-, Analy-, Analys-, Analysis, Analyt- and Analyz-. From this table it can be seen that terms 11 to 26 are the relevant ones—those starting with Analy-. Another device is known as the KLIC index (and this was invented at the University of Nottingham). As you might guess, this is a Key Letter in Context Index (Fig. 2) which enables one to look up any letter combinations to be found in descriptors held on the file. For example, the combination ALT is to be found in Salt, Cobalt, Walter, Alternating and Salts. By themselves these examples may seem fairly ridiculous, but in combination they provide quite powerful aids to retrieval. But it is important to recognize that they are aids which have been created to counter the innate idiocy of the computer, and furthermore are based on the assumption that this is the cheapest way we know of searching files. Imagine for a moment searching the alphetical subject index of a conventional catalogue for all entries containing the consecutive letters TIN!

If you can cast your mind back to my mention of the categories of automatic indexing enunciated by Stevens, you will remember that the third was automatic classification. I am not going to discuss this approach at length, because there are very few operational applications—so far as I know, none in this country. This approach uses the ability of the computer to form patterns of terms from the analysis of text, for example, by examining the statistical co-occurrence of terms or by syntactic analysis.

Before leaving the topic of mechanized information retrieval, I should like to say a word or two about costs and performance. I should like to, but unfortunately this is an almost impossible task to undertake with any confidence of objectivity. Looking at the largest data bases such as UKCIS, INSPEC, MEDLARS (UK), and BNB/MARC, it is certainly apparent that they have soaked up large sums of public money paid through OSTI, now known as the British Library Research and Development Department. In the five-year period 1966-1970, INSPEC took over £¼m, UKCIS a further £170,000 and BNB/MARC another £134,130. These three huge data bases accounted for something like a fifth of the total research funds available. In the period since 1970, it has been the intention to make INSPEC and UKCIS self-supporting, but even so they have had further grants of £¼m between them.

Mechanized systems are expensive, but what about their performance? Again, there are very few facts available, and what exists is difficult to get into perspective. For example, an evaluation of MEDLARS in the UK at the end of the 1960s showing overall average recall and precision ratios for 299 searches of 57.7% and 50.4% respectively.[6] Consequently, current awareness services have been preferred and a lot of work has gone into the compilation of search profiles. Even here, there have been complaints about the poor performance of these large systems. Now, I am quite aware that I may have unfairly overstated a case against mechanized information retrieval, but I wonder whether we are putting too much trust in computers, and whether we are spending enough research money on fundamental questions rather than on technology.

Mechanization in general

This thought is reinforced when one considers the history of mechanization in general. I am not referring to all the computer jokes, many of them apocryphal and many of them in fact trivial, such as the computer-produced bill for £0.0p which was followed up by summons for non-payment. But there have been enough failures of computer systems for there to be a discernible atmosphere of disenchantment in many places, for example from managers who are no longer given information by their subordinates, but have to contend instead with yards of computer print out. A short book by Brian Rothery[7] makes interesting reading. Rothery examines how computers come to be installed by companies in the first place, and makes the pertinent comment ". . . some of the finest and most intelligent minds I know work with computers. These people, however, do not buy computers for industry; they are hired to instal and supervise the computers bought by others". Then he goes on to

discuss the dreadful escalation in which management is trapped into spending more and more on peripherals and programming—and one begins to wonder whether the computer is serving the organization or *vice versa*. Among many problems he mentions I will mention just two: the concentration on computer problems to the exclusion of broader system considerations; and the inability to forecast the range of demand so that expensive one-off jobs have to be undertaken or manual methods adopted. Reverting to the library world, I can quote two examples of these problems. The first involves a mechanized system using a thesaurus for controlled input of indexing decisions, installed at great cost—and in danger of breaking down because nobody has thought to train the subject analysts who are independently making up their own keywords when dissatisfied with the choice offered by the thesaurus. The second problem is possibly exemplified by a study of manual versus mechanized searching.[8] The conclusions of this study in its own very specific situation were:

1. It was found to be in the region of 10 times cheaper to search manually than by the mechanized system, though in one case it was nearly 20 times cheaper.
2. Generally there was very little difference in the time taken by either method to locate and list relevant references.
3. The manual search produced a more comprehensive answer for the enquirer.

Now Rothery is talking about Management Information Systems, which have been concerned mainly with the handling of data—but he has this to say: "What is missing? Everything that matters. Most programmers, analysts and systems managers are only computer implementers. Left out are the systems analysts who understand the meaning of information systems . . . who know that only some of management's information is quantitative, the rest being qualitative and not easily expressed in data terms, who know that enterprises are steered as much with 'once-off' adaptive type information as they are with the recurring data-processing control type". And this statement must be even more true of the areas in which we work.

Information for what?

I've seen it said somewhere that information is collected for three purposes, (a) Leisure, (b)

Education, and (c) Decision-making. I don't discount the value of leisure, but if it can be regarded as personal, and as using browsing or serendipity, I shan't discuss it further. In education, I include the current-awareness function which is the updating of previous education. I am not going to embark on a lengthy discourse under the title "Whither education", but I would just make the comment that from an information point of view we are in some trouble. Boulding, the American economist and co-father of General Systems Theory, has succinctly described this problem in an article with the title "The diminishing returns of science".[9] The abstract states, "Within 100 years, the stock of human knowledge may be so large that the whole effort of the knowledge industry will have to be devoted to transmitting it from one generation to the next". Now, if Boulding is correct, and the basis of his argument is that no process of exponential growth goes on for very long, then it seems plausible that we should pay more attention to the exploitation of present knowledge in order to render decision-making more effective. And there are certain trends that support this contention. The switching of money from research to development; the growing interest in, and support for, the social sciences, after the long ride enjoyed by the earth and life sciences; the need for multidisciplinary teams to solve increasingly complex and widely-viewed problems; and the following more specific illustration which highlights a human problem. There is a growing interest in the establishment of world-wide information networks. After the large discipline-based services like CA, INSPEC, MEDLARS, came the discipline-based INIS, with decentralized input and centralized processing. This provided a model for AGRIS, which was described as being mission-oriented. Recently work has started on DEVSIS, which, covering the whole area of social and economic development in developing countries, can only be regarded as being problem-oriented. But problems give rise to missions which use disciplines for their solution, and the problem will be to design and relate information systems that cater for these needs. Unfortunately, and inevitably, we have created the systems in the wrong order and now have to deal with the inertia of large, established and often inflexible systems.

Conclusions

I spoke about thesauri, and tried to convey the impression that a vast amount of thought has been given to the relationships between concepts and words and to the organization of vocabularies. I think it is possible that, in the area of librarianship and information retrieval, we have assimilated a great deal of previous thought and have added some advances ourselves. At the same time, I believe we have far more to offer.

I then played the easy game of "knocking the computer", but must make my position clear. I am critical of the use of the computer and not of the computer itself. It's almost as though research grants were given to the computer rather than to the researchers. The computer systems and networks get larger, more expensive and faster— and yet we know little more about user *needs* as distinct from user *demands*.

I quoted Sparck-Jones on the variety of ways in which vocabularies can be organized, and Vickery on the variety of structures and functions of indexing languages. It is also apparent that indexing languages may often have to satisfy local and specific requirements. I don't believe in the Universal Indexing Language any more than I believe in Esperanto. I believe we have to accept the need for variety and to build our systems accordingly. (In parenthesis, let me say I do accept the sense of Dewey for public libraries, Dewey and LC for MARC records, and the possibility of a UDC-based roof-language being investigated by UNESCO.) But we need some compatibility, some ability to switch or translate between languages. And to do this I believe we have to understand three elements of the system.

(a) The documents containing information—the traditional province of our professions.
(b) The people requiring the information—and I believe we have made advances here in such things as user/librarian interaction, user studies and profile construction.
(c) The organization containing those people— and here I believe we need to do a lot more. And when I say "we" I mean our profession and the managers of the organizations who employ our services.

I don't think I am misusing the term "indexing" when I say that it is an act of describing our environment in systematic language. I believe that we can help the information process if we become involved in the task of "indexing" these elements. Some work is being done on personnel systems and expertise indexes, so that people may be described in terms of their experience, knowledge and information needs and habits.

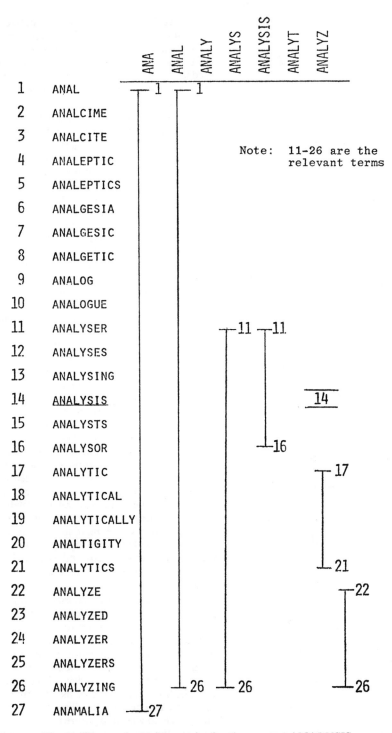

Fig. 1.—Truncation guide entries for the concept **ANALYSIS**

```
                DIH╫ ALIDES//

                     ALIGNED//

         PHTH    ALIMIDES//

       QUINOX    ALINE//

                     ALIPH//

                     ALIPHATIC//

          LOC    ALIZED//

                     ALKALI//

        MITRO    ALKANES//

        CYCLO    ALKENES//

                     ALKYL//

           DI    ALKYL//

  -CARBOXYI      ALKYL,//N

  UM//   TRI     ALKYLALUMIN

  UMS//           ALKYLALUMIN

                     ALKYLENE//

         POLY    ALKYLENE//

           SM    ALL-ANGLE//

                     ALLENE//

    /    CRYST   ALLINITIES/

         CRYST   ALLINITY//

    /    CRYST   ALLIZATION/

         CRYST   ALLIZED//

           NET   ALLORG//

    /      NET   ALLORGANIC/
```

Fig. 2.—Excerpt from CA Condensates
KLIC index.

McDonough,[10] some years ago, developed an alphanumerical code for the description of the mechanistic aspects of business—but at a recent Aslib Symposium, a psychologist argued that we needed to develop a language for the introspective description of organizations. This may well be an interdisciplinary problem.

Finally, I would like to describe very briefly some ideas generated in what was known as the "Data Coordination Project", sponsored by DoE, and in which Aslib was involved. The aim of the project was to improve the flow of information from designers to contractors by rationalizing the various information systems used by clients, architects, engineers, quantity surveyors, contractors and librarians. Three broad categories of information and their accompanying systems were included: General Information, available to everybody; Project Information, available to the project team, consisting mainly of drawings, specifications, bills of quantity; and Management Information, available to the specific organization. These three information systems were related to the various stages of the construction process in an ambitious diagram. We also examined the various conventions which are used in the construction industry to regulate the production, presentation, and handling of all forms of document in order to study what terms and classifications were being used. The conclusion was that there was a need for many classifications and for the flexible use of terms, but that fundamental guidelines could be devised so that the various conventions could be induced to evolve in similar ways. A further idea was that all these conventions could be gathered together and that all the terms and all the relationships between concepts could be analyzed and the significant terms and relationships stored on a computer together with their provenance. This was called a metasystem and was envisaged as the base for all the descriptor languages of the industry.

The metasystem is of course a form of thesaurus of a size requiring computer handling. As a start, the 14,000 terms of the Construction Industry Thesaurus are held on a computer and it is hoped that further work will investigate the relationships between the metasystem approach and the present knowledge of computer file organization. The power of the computer is such that we can envisage handling such a complex lattice. We now need to ensure that we are feeding sense to the computer, for if we do not we will be wasting precious resources.

References.

1. Sparck-Jones, K. "Some thesauric history", *Aslib Proceedings* **24** (7) July 1972, pp.400-411.
2. Brownson, Helen. "Current United States research on topics related to the Conference." In: *International study conference on classification for information retrieval. Proceedings.* Dorking, England, May 13-17, 1957. Aslib, and New York: Pergamon, 1957.
3. Vickery, B. C. "Structure and function in retrieval languages." *Journal of Documentation* **27** (2) June 1971, pp.69-82.
4. Stevens, M. E. *Automatic indexing: a state of the art report.* Washington, National Bureau of Standards. 1970.
5. Williams, M. E. "Experiences of IIT Research Institute in operating a computerized retrieval system for searching a variety of data bases." *Information Storage & Retrieval* **8** 1972, pp.57-78.
6. Lancaster, F. W. "MEDLARS: Report on the evaluation of its operating efficiency." *American Documentation* **20** (2) April 1969, pp.119-142.
7. Rothery, Brian. *The myth of the computer.* London, Business Books, 1971.
8. Goodliffe, E. C., and Hayler, S. J. "On-line information retrieval: Some comments on the use of Retrospec I in an industrial library." *Aslib Proceedings* **26** (5) May 1974, pp.177-188.
9. Boulding, K. "The diminishing returns of science." *New Scientist* 25/3/71, pp.682-4.
10. McDonough, A. *Information economics and management systems.* New York, McGraw Hill, 1963.

Computer-Organised Display of Subject Information*

Michael F. Lynch

Work has been in progress at the School in Sheffield for some years past on a topic which has come to be known as the articulated subject index. The present immediate objective of this work is readily defined; it is the design and implementation of a computer technique which can assist the indexer in the preparation of this particular type of subject index. The study, however, has a much wider scope as well, in that it is concerned with gaining insight into the processes of indexing and index use which may be of general value. The first part of this paper will be a factual account of progress towards the immediate objective; the second part will involve some speculation and perhaps provide something of a theoretical background to the work, based on certain of our findings.

The work began in 1965 with an examination of the Subject Indexes to *Chemical Abstracts*, in particular with a view to determining their potential for use in computer searches. Since magnetic tapes of these indexes are available this year for the first time, that was perhaps premature, but as it happened, a more immediate prospect became apparent, and this has largely occupied our time since then.

It seemed to us, five years ago, that the subject descriptions contained in the entries in CA indexes had many virtues for computer search, in particular a vocabulary which in part was closely controlled, and yet was hospitable to such ideas as had to be included for ample specification of the subject. Again, the representation took the form of natural language English phrases—somewhat rearranged, it is true, but none the less intuitively understandable. It seemed possible, at that time, that automatic syntactic analysis could be employed to help discern the relationships among the complex topics described there. As many of you know, syntactic analysis has not yet proved its worth in computer retrieval techniques. However, the need to straighten out the phrases, which appear in the index in a form which is often far from the natural order, led to the discovery of a simple rule, with the help of which the majority of entries in the indexes could be converted into the natural English phrase. The following example illustrates this point.

Calcium
> metabolism of, by bones, after administration of cortisone and its analogs, durabolin protection against, in bone disorders, *60*: 16173b

This entry, as printed in the index, consists of a number of parts: firstly the entry

* Paper read at a meeting of the Society held on 8th October, 1970.

Reprinted from *The Indexer* 7, no. 3 (Spring 1971): 94–100.

point, or subject heading, 'Calcium', and secondly the so-called modifying phrase, which together describe a far from simple topic. This particular phrase, which is of more than average complexity, contains no less than nine substantive words. The modifying phrase itself is divided into a number of components, separated from one another by commas. The regularity that was discovered was based, quite simply, on the fact that each of the components in this phrase either begins or ends with a common function word, usually a preposition, although connectives such as 'and' can also appear. The rule followed directly from this. It was that in building up the natural language phrase, the subject heading was taken first; each component of the modifying phrase was taken in turn, and placed before the heading if the function word came at the end of the component, or after it, if at the beginning. Thus, taking the first component, in which the preposition falls at the end, the first step led to:

'metabolism of calcium'

The second step led to:

'metabolism of calcium by bones',

and so on, until the whole phrase was reconstituted as:

'Durabolin protection against metabolism of calcium by bones after administration of cortisone and its analogs in bone disorders.'

This rule was merely a rationalisation of an intuitive and readily learned procedure performed by users of this type of index for many years. Indeed, Crestadoro may well be credited with the introduction of this form of indexing, with his work *The art of making catalogues of libraries*[1], which appeared as long ago as 1856.

This rule is applicable uniformly, and without exception, to all entries in the *CA* index, as well as many others of this type, provided that all components in the modifying phrase either begin or end with a function word. In certain circumstances, components may have two terminal func-

tional words, or none, and these cannot be dealt with by the simple rule. In the *CA* indexes, these account for 40 per cent of the entries. In other indexes, it can vary between 10 per cent and 90 per cent. However, since our work took a rather different direction, this is immaterial to the main purpose.

Thus far, we have considered an index entry, i.e., a subject heading and its modifying phrase, in isolation. Next we look at it in the context of the display in an index, when the purpose of the process of articulation becomes more clear. The following is a typical extract from the index.

Cesium. *(Other entries relating to cesium and its compounds can be found under the heading* Alkali metals *and under such headings as* Alkali metal chlorides.*)*
absorption by plants, fertilizer effect on, **60:** 13833f
  by plants, soil colloids and, **60:**11321h
  by roots, Ca and, **60:**12620b
adenosine triphosphatase response to, **60:** 4400b
adsorbed on Pt electrodes, hydroquinone-quinone system in relation to, **60:**3733g
adsorption of, by Hg electrodes, in presence of methylformamide, **60:**8668c
  from radioactive waste water by clay, **60:** 3865e
  from Na soln. by clinoptiolite, heat-treatment effect on, **60:**15482h
  from waste water by brown coal, clay and clinoptilolite, **60:**13009c
agaroid gel properties in presence of, **60:** 6246e

Here several characteristics are evident, in particular, a series of levels of indentations which guide the eye in scanning the display. The modifying phrases are indented, under the heading, continuing lines being set in deeply, with alphabetic arrangement according to the first significant word of each entry. When, as is frequently the case, an initial component is common to a series of phrases, it is not repeated, but the remainder of the succeeding phrases are again indented, and alphabetised again by the first non-function word. This technique further facilitates scanning. More recently, CAS, in an endeavour to break up highly populated headings, have introduced a further level, that of the subheading, which indicates the general area of interest, e.g., analytical, biochemical, etc.

It was clear, once we had identified the rule that enabled us to transform index phrases into the normal order—a process that was programmed for the computer at an early stage by Janet Ash—that a similar procedure was applied, but in reverse, by the indexer recording the entries. Since this held the prospect that we might be able to produce indexes of this type by a computer-aided procedure, we turned to this aspect. During examination of the display, the user enters the index at the heading, and adds successive components of the entry at either end to build up the complete phrase. Therefore, the indexer, having constructed an expression which describes the topic being indexed, must begin with the subject heading, and form the entry by splitting out successive components to form the modifying phrase. If the subject heading comes first, then there is no alternative but the natural order. Thus, starting with a phrase such as

'rain on plains in Spain'

when 'Rain' is taken as the heading, the entry must read

Rain
    on plains in Spain,

Taking 'Plains' as the heading, however, we have alternative possibilities:

Plains
    rain on, in Spain

and

Plains
    in Spain, rain on,

while with 'Spain' as the heading, we have again two possibilities, viz.

Spain
    plains in, rain on,

and

Spain
    rain on plains in.

All of these are equally intelligible. A choice between the alternatives must be made, since space dictates economy in the number of entries. It is quite clear that a human indexer, faced with the choice, may well make a decision based on his knowledge of the subject area, or context. Thus, if the index has climatological connotations, the entry:

Spain
    rain on plains in,

may well be preferable, while if it is topographical, that beginning with 'plains' may be better.

However, at this stage of the art, it is difficult, to say the least, to instruct the machine in such choices, and we must depend on a lesser, but computable rule, and one that is certainly of value in producing a well-organised display. Here we turned for guidance to the multiple levels of indentation characteristic of this type of index. As we have seen, the manipulation of the phrases to bring common components to the fore is carried out by human indexers. This is a manipulation which can also be carried out by computer, within the framework of the rules mentioned already.

Thus, if another indexing phrase to be dealt with reads as follows:

'rain on mountains in Spain'

then, at the heading 'Spain', we also have two possible modifying phrases:

Spain
    rain on mountains, in,

or

Spain
    mountains in, rain on,

It is possible to program a computer so that it makes a comparison of all possible first components for entries under the same heading, and gives precedence to those which have the same common components. Thus in the case in point, the result is as follows:

Spain
    rain on mountains in,
        on plains in,

each entry being followed by an appropriate document reference.

This is an oversimplified account of the algorism which we have developed, but this form of manipulation forms the nucleus of the technique. A complicating factor is the fact that not all function words are alike in allowing a full choice. Thus the preposition 'of', as we noted in the study of CA indexes, and subsequently in early stages of program development, insists on special treatment. Thus, if we have a heading with

' of ' on one side and another preposition on the other, the component linked to the heading by ' of ' must be given precedence, as in the following:

'errors in measurement of rainfall'

Here, when ' measurement' is chosen as the heading, no choice of component is possible; the entry must take the form:

Measurement
        of rainfall, errors in

Admitting the alternative form could result in ill-formed entries.

Again, the phrases instanced here consist of single nouns, concatenated by preposi-

tions. This is obviously an oversimplification, since title-like descriptive phrases take much more complex forms than this. To deal with these situations we have developed a means of editing input phrases which will be illustrated later.

Our initial programming effort, undertaken by Janet Ash, was concerned with the simple model, where it was assumed that the descriptive phrases consisted of noun phrases suitable for selection as subject headings and separated from one another by function words[2]. An example from this stage is given:

```
BIOLOGY
    CONFERENCE ON COMMUNICATION IN, AT INSTITUTE OF
        BIOLOGY AND ASLIB BIOLOGICAL GROUP, 67/
        1/6

BRITISH ASSOCIATION
    MEETING OF, DISCUSSION OF SCIENTIFIC AND TECHNI
        CAL INFORMATION AT, 66/2/2
    DISCUSSION OF SCIENTIFIC AND TECHNICAL INFORM
        ATION AT, 66/1/7

BRITISH STANDARDS INSTITUTION
    WORK ON DOCUMENTATION STANDARDS AT, 66/2/11

BRITISH TECHNOLOGY INDEX
    PRODUCTION OF, AT LIBRARY ASSOCIATION, STUDY OF
        COMPUTER TECHNIQUES FOR, 66/2/11

CAMBRIDGE UNIVERSITY
    DEVELOPMENT OF COMPUTER TECHNIQUES FOR INFORMAT
        ION RETRIEVAL IN GEOLOGY AT, 66/2/7, 67/
        4/2
    INFORMATION CENTRE FOR X-RAY CRYSTALLOGRAPHY DA
        TA AT, 66/1/2
```

The results were encouraging, and pointed out a number of possible improvements. For one thing, the assumption that each noun or compound was a candidate heading resulted in bodies of entries at headings such as 'Effect', 'Use', etc., and showed that either a stop-word list, as in the KWIC approach, or a means of differentiating words required as headings from others, was required. While we experimented briefly with the stop-word list, it became clear that the latter method offered much more potential. This became all the clearer as a result of co-operation with a number of individuals and organizations interested in matching the technique to their own requirements. With-

out the many helpful comments and suggestions from these collaborators, our progress would have been much slower.

One example of this was the work with Mr. M. Belton of the Safety in Mines Research Establishment, with a view to producing an index to the 3rd edition of their bibliography of publications[3]. Straining a program intended only for experimental use to its limits, a number of modifications were introduced which allowed the indexer to exercise a much finer degree of control over the form in which headings and services appeared. In particular, greater control over noun compounds was made possible by using editorial marks, sensed by the computer, and removed before printing. Thus, the use of parentheses in the following phrase:

explosions of carbonaceous (dust)

resulted in the entry shown below:

Dust

carbonaceous, explosions of,

The work of producing the index to this bibliography, and continued testing with other groups (Miss Townley read a paper on one such development to the Society last year)[4] helped define the requirements for a production program package, which Howard Petrie has now completed. This includes much more comprehensive editorial facilities during the preparation of the input, as well as error-correction and editing routines, which will not be detailed here. Computer typesetting routines will soon be added. This package is currently under trial with a number of organizations, including the Shirley Institute at Manchester, for use in the preparation of an index to *World Textile Abstracts*. We shall shortly be undertaking comparative trials of this technique with that currently used for *Food Science and Technology Abstracts,* which produces a KWAC index, and the tests will involve user studies with indexes in each format. Thus we hope soon to begin to investigate user reactions to varied formats in organised displays of information. In this respect, we feel that the ASI display technique must rank high.

The advantages of this technique for production of articulated subject indexes must be assessed from two points of view, that of the operator of the information service producing the index, and that of the user. In the first respect, we must first examine the circumstances in which ASIs, in general, are used. A useful four-way categorization of printed alphabetic subject indexes is on two bases.

	Derivative:	Assignment:
One stage:	KWOC, some KWIC	IM, BTI, PANDEX
Two stage:	KWIC, Permuterm	CA. Anal.Abs., NSA, etc.

The first categorization is self-evident; in assignment indexes, a human indexer assigns the descriptions within the context of the indexing language, while derivative indexes employ existing text, for instance, titles of documents.

The second categorization depends on whether the index itself contains a full or partially abbreviated bibliographic citation, so that consultation of the index can lead directly to a document, or whether, as in the two-stage index, reference is made to an intermediate stage such as an abstracts journal or bibliography. The ASI falls within this category, so that its use is indicated when some compilation other than the source documents is available.

The conventional manual or semi-automatic index production technique requires that the indexer produces each entry as it is to be printed in the display, although in many cases the content and terminology are identical. For the example cited earlier, this would entail creating the following three records:

Rain

on plains in Spain

Plains

rain on, in Spain

Spain

rain on plains in,

In our technique, however, the indexer need record only a single notation of content, for instance, as it would appear in current input:

<rain> on <plains> in <Spain>,

and the machine creates all three from this single record. As you will appreciate, much current effort in the rationalization of publishing techniques is being devoted to creating as many outputs as possible from a single input record, so this is certainly in accord with present trends in information handling. Again, the use of the single input record can be carried further, as in the production of issue, volume and cumulated indexes with little further intellectual effort. The practical implications of this are increased indexer efficiency, since the clerical aspects of his task are carried out automatically. It is perhaps worth mentioning in passing that, just as the indexer determines the content of the indexing expressions, generally with the help of an authority list or thesaurus, he also determines, in the light of experience, the cross-reference structure necessary for a particular application, and these cross-references can be automatically inserted in the final output.

From the users' viewpoint, the advantages are two-fold. On the one hand there are the factors of greater currency of indexes, and greater likelihood of having, for example, issue, volume and cumulative indexes, since these can be produced with little additional effort. The main advantages, however, are those of the articulated index itself, which can be seen as a widely accepted and adaptable form of display. It has a number of highly distinctive characteristics, which are present in greater or lesser measure in a number of existing, conventionally produced indexes. Foremost is the fact that the entries consist of natural language phrases, which permit the description of often highly complex topics with considerable precision, as evidenced by the calcium example above. While the entry vocabulary, i.e., the list of subject headings, is closely controlled, the technique is very hospitable in that the variety of construction and vocabulary available for description is virtually unlimited. The framework thus imposes no artificial constraints on the representation.

The second most distinctive feature is the articulation process itself. Here one can only speculate, for as yet we have no experimental work to help us in this. It appears that the function of this process is to provide the user with an easy means of entry to the descriptive phrases arranged under the subject heading, while the prepositions and connectives allow the interrelations of the terms to be built up logically. Thus the user inspecting the display enters first with the subject heading, then scans the initial component of

the entries arrayed under it. If his interest is triggered by it, he can scan further to the right, adding further components in turn to build up the full description. He need penetrate it only as far as necessary to determine irrelevancy, and can then resume his scanning of the next entry. He thus depends on his latent interest being triggered by the description. The function of the multiple levels of indentation is clear. It is to draw attention to a group of entries which, if the first component promises interest, must all be scanned at the second level, or, alternatively, if no interest attaches to it, this group can be skipped entirely.

It is surprising that so little attention has been paid thus far to methods of index use, and it seems highly probable that the display itself is as critical a factor as others, such as the choice of terminology. Indeed, it was with this thought in mind that the title of this paper was chosen to include the term ' display '. The terms index and indexing themselves imply the intermeshing of a number of factors, among which are the vocabulary and its interrelations, the structure of the descriptive notation in which the terms are embedded for display, and the form of organization of the display. Clearly, the computer-aided ASI technique relates primarily to the last of these, given a natural language, phrase-like notation.

We are limited to this, given our present understanding of instructing the computer in language and concept manipulation. We can differentiate clearly between our ability to perform operations on form and operations on content. By the former we mean symbol-manipulative operations, such as are used in publishing techniques; we understand these well, and they are providing substantial economic benefits. For example, by linking typographic style with the functions of different data elements in a record, we can produce economies by keyboarding information at a single level of detail, and enhance this automatically during a computer-driven typesetting operation.

Operations on content, however, are much less well understood. We cannot yet produce adequate abstracts, for example, by computer, nor can we analyze subject matter so as to assign subject headings at an acceptable level of performance. In this automatic ASI production technique, however, we are using operations on form which are in fact content-directed. It seems indeed that we must continue to seek and improve on techniques of this type so that with still limited understanding of language we can utilize the computer to its utmost in organising and displaying information for most effective use.

Acknowledgments

The work described here was supported by two grants from the Office for Scientific and Technical Information, London. Much of the work was ably carried out by Janet Ash (née Armitage) and J. Howard Petrie.

References

(1) Crestadoro, A., *The art of making catalogues of libraries*. London, The Literary, Scientific and Artistic Reference Office. 1856.

(2) Armitage, J. E., *and* M. F. Lynch, *J. Chem. Docum.*, 7, 170-8 (1967).

(3) SMRE Bibliography. 3rd edition, compiled by M. Betton. Sheffield, Safety in Mines Research Establishment. 1969.

(4) Townley, H. M., *The Indexer*, 6, 102-7 (1969).

Discussion

In the course of the discussion, Dr. Lynch indicated that he believed the rôle of the computer in the short term in information handling was to rationalise publication processes; there seemed little immediate prospect that computers could be used in producing abstracts or index entries for human perusal. Thus there would remain a continuing need for the indexer's skills well into the future.

Computer-Aided Production of the Subject Index to the *SMRE Bibliography**

M. Belton

At your Autumn meeting last year, Dr. Lynch spoke to you about the computer-organized display of subject information[1] and referred to a collaborative project between the Postgraduate School of Librarianship and Information Science at the University of Sheffield and the Safety in Mines Research Establishment (SMRE), also in Sheffield. This paper sets out to describe that part of the work which was undertaken at SMRE in the compilation of a subject index to the third edition of the *SMRE Bibliography*[2]. I will begin by giving some background information to SMRE and the *SMRE Bibliography*, followed by a description of the circumstances leading to our choice of this type of indexing, our experience in compiling and using the index, the subsequent modifications made and finally a brief indication of possible applications of this method of indexing.

Organized research into safety in mines in the United Kingdom dates from 1908 and a record of the published work (referred to as ' papers ') of the staff and of other workers associated with the Safety in Mines Research Establishment since this time is maintained in the SMRE Library. In 1953 this record

was published as the *SMRE Bibliography*[3] and a second revised edition appeared in 1960[4]. The third, and most recent edition was brought out in 1969[2]. Between successive editions of the *Bibliography*, a note of new publications is carried in SMRE's Annual Reports[5].

The first two editions of the *Bibliography* contained a main section in which the papers were listed, with full bibliographical references, alphabetically by author under broad subject headings, roughly corresponding to the appropriate schedules of the *Universal Decimal Classification* (UDC). This main section was supplemented by author and subject indexes and series lists. Each paper in the main section was numbered consecutively and references in the indexes and series lists were to these numbers.

By the time that we were ready to compile a third edition of the *Bibliography*, the number of publications to be indexed had increased to almost 1,700 and we had also gained a certain amount of experience in the use of the two previous editions. An analysis was made of the enquiries received which were best answered from the *Bibliography*, and it was decided, on the basis of the results, to investigate the various possibilities available to us with regard to the format, arrangement and indexing of the new edition.

---

* A paper read at a meeting of the Society on 19th October, 1971.

Reprinted from *The Indexer* 8, no. 1 (April 1972): 44–49.

At the same time we recognized that the compilation work had to be undertaken within the programme of normal library activities and therefore we would have to avail ourselves of existing methods. It would not have been practicable to look for a 'custom-built' bibliography.

It was also apparent that the major task in the compilation would be the indexing; material that could not be retrieved readily would be lost and this would defeat the whole object of the exercise, i.e. to bring together, in an accessible form, the published research work of the Establishment.

It was decided to arrange the main entries, which include full bibliographical details, in a single author sequence, thus obviating the need for an author index. At the same time, a means of referring from a proposed subject index to the main section was found, using the first-named author coupled with a number indicating the chronological order of publication of each paper. New material could thus be added without upsetting the reference system and as a useful by-product, we could produce, at a moment's notice, a full list of a particular author's works, which in our earlier investigation had been found to be a regular type of enquiry. Series lists presented no particular problem and the system of series numbers adopted in the first two editions was continued.

When we were gathering together the material for the *Bibliography,* much of which came from the earlier editions, with some from our Annual Reports and a little from hitherto overlooked sources, we were struck by the fact that in almost all cases the titles of the papers appeared to reflect accurately the content of the papers. It was this discovery that first led us to consider ways of using the titles as the basis for whatever form of subject-indexing we decided to have. The situation arises from the fact that since 1953, SMRE has had a professional editorial section whose attentions extend to the proposed titles of the papers they deal with.

Even before 1953, senior staff of the Establishment had considered the publication of

results to be sufficiently important to merit their attention to the editing and production of well-written papers. Such was the consistency which had been applied to the preparation of titles at the time papers were written that the exceptions were easily picked out; it was not quite so easy to put them right!

However, given a majority of full, explanatory titles, our initial task was to find the simplest (and cheapest) method of using them as a basis for a subject index. Several well-tried mechanized methods came to mind, KWIC, KWOC and KWAC being familiar and well-used examples, but two things happened at that time to divert us to the method finally chosen. In the first place we obtained access to a new tape-typewriter installed at SMRE. Knowing what these machines could do, we were ready to take full advantage of this facility. The second and more crucial factor was a discussion between Dr. Lynch and myself which showed that Dr. Lynch's team had reached the stage where a full-scale exercise was desirable to test the computer program which they had developed; on SMRE's part we had assembled a substantial amount of material which needed indexing. Discussions continued and a period of fruitful co-operation began.

Our first trial was with a group of fifty SMRE Research Report titles referring to our work in the fields of explosions and fires. We hoped that treatment of this sample would indicate some of the problems of computer-aided indexing and also, that the restricted subject-fields would show the effectiveness of the computer program when dealing with a comparatively high posting rate of entries to our selected entry words.

We experimented briefly with a 'stop-list' method, by which the computer chose all words and phrases between articulating points (mainly prepositions, conjunctions and certain punctuation marks) as index entry words but excluded from the print-out those words listed on a 'stop-list'. This was a satisfactory method for dealing with simple titles of the type 'Ignition of methane by friction ', but entailed very careful editing in titles only a little more complex. Our print-out using this method on our sample fifty titles produced some extraordinary looking entries and it was decided that the work on the ' go ' technique developed by Dr. Lynch and his team was much more likely to produce satisfactory results.

Dr. Lynch has already explained to you the principles on which his work is based and there is no need for me to repeat them here. Suffice it to say that in the ' go ' technique, emphasis is placed on the indexer making a positive identification of the index entry words to be used, leaving the computer to arrange the subsequent display and alphabetization of all the entries chosen.

The practical steps involved in using this technique, from the point of view of the indexer, can perhaps best be described by taking particular titles and showing how they are treated. For example, a very simple form is:

Asquith, S., Broomhead, G. and Burdekin, J. T.

Dust suppression by dust traps during drilling

SMRE Research Report no. 111 1955

The series entry (SMRE Research Report series) is dealt with by the simple listing of all reports in numerical order. For the authors, the main entry in the *Bibliography* is under Asquith. This happens to be the third paper written by this particular author and the author entry heading will be shown as:

Asquith, S. R. (3), Broomhead, G. and Burdekin, J. T.

followed by the title and full bibliographical details. At the end of the listings of papers by Broomhead and those by Burdekin appear lists of references amongst which will be one in each case ' *see also* Asquith S. R. (3) '.

For the subject index, it is sufficient to mark those words in the title which the indexer wishes to show as entry words. In this example, he may choose ' dust ' or ' dust

suppression ', ' dust traps ' or ' traps ', and ' drilling '. The main emphasis here lies in the fact that the human factor chooses the words to be used as index entries. At SMRE we found it convenient to compile a list of words chosen as index entries as we went along; we were able to modify this list in the light of experience and, since all the input data subsequently appear on punched paper tape it is a relatively easy matter to go back and change some of our initial decisions.

Having decided upon the choice of entry words, the next step was to mark the title clearly so as to show our library typist how the input data should be punched on the tape, e.g.:

<Dust> suppression by <dust traps> during <drilling>♯ Asquith S.R.(3)♯♯ shows how our first example appears ready for tape preparation. ' By ' and ' during ' are the articulating points and as a result we would expect to see index entries as follows:

Drilling
　　Dust suppression by dust traps during, Asquith S. R. (3)

Dust
　　Suppression by dust traps during drilling, Asquith S. R. (3)

Dust traps
　　Dust suppression by, during drilling, Asquith S. R. (3)

The signs < >, ♯ and ♯♯ are signals to the computer indicating the key-words chosen, title completion and entry completion respectively.

After the input data have been prepared on paper tape, the computer prepares an alphabetical list of entry words and lists the title for which each entry word has been chosen. This intermediate listing has been found to have several uses.

(a) It gives an overall picture of the extent of the index, showing, for example, superfluous entry words, that is, entry words with too many titles against them. (' Mining ' and ' safety ' are obvious examples in SMRE's field.) A separate print-out which the computer produced at this stage shows the number of titles containing each selected entry word (the posting rate).

(b) Errors in spelling are instantly revealed since the computer is meticulous in arranging words and phrases in alphabetical order.

(c) Additional 'see also' references may be introduced at this stage.

(d) Errors arising from inconsistencies are more readily corrected at this stage, e.g. a singular form of heading may have been chosen instead of the plural.

The following examples illustrate some of the problems that arise in compiling a computer-organized index, and the solutions devised.

(a) *Titles with sub-titles.* These may be dealt with, either

(i) by re-writing the two titles to form a new one, e.g. 'Research for safety: the metallurgist and the engineer' may be rewritten as:

The metallurgist and engineer in research for safety

or

(ii) by making two separate titles,

e.g. 'Mine rescue apparatus: the SMRB gas mask' is best split into its component parts:

Mine rescue apparatus,

and

SMRB gas mask

each referring to the same author.

(b) *Titles containing co-ordinate subjects.* The title, e.g.

'Effect of felspar, slate and quartz on the lungs of rats' is best treated by having index entries under each of the materials felspar, slate and quartz without showing all three in each entry:

> Felspar
> > Effect of, on lungs of rats
> Quartz
> > Effect of, on lungs of rats
> Slate
> > Effect of, on lungs of rats

In the published form of the *Bibliography*, it was not found possible to separate co-ordinate subjects such as these and rather cumbersome entries resulted:

> Felspar
> > Effect of, and slate and quartz, on lungs of rats

with similar entries at slate and quartz.

Happily, the shortened version is now part of the new program package, the title being marked:

> Effect of ! <felspar>, <slate> & <quartz>! on lungs of rats where ! . . . ! are symbols indicating that co-ordinate subjects are being processed.

(c) *Incomplete or misleading titles.* For reasons stated above, most of the titles to be included in the *Bibliography* represented accurately the content of the paper, but for a few exceptions it was found necessary either to rewrite the title completely or sometimes to add a descriptive word or phrase. An example here was the title 'Mechanical scanning of a circular field'. The addition of the words 'for photography' was enough to remove ambiguity. On the other hand, it is not difficult to recall titles in the general literature that would defy even the human indexer. In an American journal, I recall the short title 'Gas-eating bug' which dealt with Russian studies in the use of bacteria to absorb methane underground.

(d) *Changing terminology.* The period covered by our Bibliography is 60 years and obviously during this time terminology has changed. In addition variations in the terminology applied to equipment or materials may occur in different parts of the country. The two ways of dealing with this problem are, either to adopt one form consistently and refer from the ones not used, or to use the variations as they arise, and use 'see also' references to link them. This is a problem met in any type of indexing, and we found the first alternative to be better on the basis that with this method all related material together, rather than being in two places is linked with a 'see also' reference. A paper

'Laboratory tests on cogs' was changed at the input stage to 'Laboratory tests on chocks' and a 'see' reference 'cogs, *see* chocks' was made.

The production of references by the computer in the correct places in the subject-index presents no difficulty. They are prepared using the same format as for the papers, but using the second half of the reference as a simulated author.

Using the example above, the reference would be written

    <cogs>♯ see chocks ♯♯

and this would subsequently appear in the index as

    cogs
      see chocks

in its correct order in the alphabetical sequence.

Since the publication of the index in 1969, we have had a chance to assess its effectiveness as a working document. It has some shortcomings, but generally speaking it meets the majority of the demands made upon it.

Some of the apparent disadvantages arise directly from the method chosen to reproduce the index as part of the *Bibliography*. Our print order was not large enough to merit typesetting (neither computer-typesetting nor manual typesetting from computer print-out) but it was too large to justify either multiple runs through the computer or simple photocopying. Finally, the computer output was taken from a microfilm and hard-copy recorder, giving output in a form which when enlarged conveniently filled an A4 page. Copies were then produced photographically from master plates. Unfortunately the microfilm and hard-copy recorder divided up the output arbitrarily every 63 lines without taking into account whether or not an index entry was complete. This resulted in some entries being split between successive pages. Moreover no indication could be given of the fact that entries on a second or subsequent page were a continuation from a previous page. The pro-

gram has now been modified in such a way that these faults have been eradicated completely.

Other shortcomings can usually be met by changes in the wording of titles. We have found, not surprisingly, that long titles give rise to cumbersome index entries and already in a revised but unpublished subject-index we have been able to make substantial improvements with the minimum of indexing effort.

It is in this respect, i.e. a capacity for updating or revising an index, that I believe this particular computer-aided method shows its principal advantage. To extend our index to accommodate papers published since the publication of the *Bibliography* was a very simple procedure (from the indexer's point of view). A list of the new titles was prepared in the same way as the titles of the original 1,700 papers, any references needed were added and any errors that had come to our notice were corrected. The new tape was then merged with the old tapes and the revised subject-index was produced. With this facility we hope that we shall be able to maintain a reasonably up-to-date index as a working document; publication of such an index as part of a revised *Bibliography* would take place at less frequent intervals. This was our first experience with computer-aided indexing and during the early stages we maintained records showing the time and effort spent on compiling the index to the published *Bibliography*. We also carried out a simple comparison test to see how preparation of material for computer processing compared with the more traditional type of index preparation. Using a batch of titles chosen at random, it was found that the time taken to record index headings manually was twice that taken to edit and mark the same batch of titles in the way described above.

There is an obvious saving of clerical effort, and errors arising from misfiling are avoided. Since alphabetization is automatic, the time-consuming checking of the final order of an index is also dispensed with.

For the statistically minded, the revised subject-index contains 4,282 index entries (including 63 references) divided betwen 800 different index headings. These entries relate to 1,782 papers and an analysis of the index headings shows that 350 contain one entry only, 142 contain two entries and 75 three entries. At the other extreme, five subject headings contain over 100 entries. In the latter case, of course, the display of qualifying phrases as generated by the computer goes most of the way to meeting criticism that the headings chosen may be too wide in scope to be of value to the index user.

The wider application of this indexing method is currently under investigation, and indexes of the type described here are obvious candidates for consideration. Files of internal reports, registry files and collections of papers in restricted subject fields would also lend themselves to this technique. One of SMRE Library's publications is *Safety in Mines Abstracts* which contains information or papers dealing with aspects of the safety and health of miners, abstracted from periodical literature. At present this is indexed annually by a manual system but we hope to be able to see how far computer-aided indexing would be of help. Our first look at the prob-lem suggests that there is some way to go before we can index these abstracts using a computer owing to the ' uncontrolled ' language used in the titles of papers. One possible way of meeting this would be to re-write the title in a computer-acceptable form but at the present time we have not made any detailed investigation. There is little doubt in my mind, however, that the research into computer-aided indexing where the computer takes over the mechanical and repetitive tasks of indexing, leaving the human indexer to deal with the intellectual problems involved, has been amply justified by the benefits it has produced.

© Crown Copyright 1971

References

[1] Lynch, M. F. *The Indexer* 7, Spring, 1971, 94-100.

[2] *SMRE Bibliography.* 3rd ed. comp. by M. Belton. Sheffield, Safety in Mines Research Establishment. 1969.

[3] *SMRE Bibliography, 1921-1952.* Comp. by R. A. Dale. Sheffield, Safety in Mines Research Establishment. 1953.

[4] *SMRE Bibliography.* 2nd ed. comp. by E. B. Smith. Sheffield, Safety in Mines Research Establishment. 1960.

[5] *Safety in Mines Research :* Annual Report of the Safety in Mines Research Establishment. London, HMSO.

FLOW OF MATTER FROM SOURCES MOVING AT FLOW VELOCITIES, FLETCHER B.(2)
STEADY STATE -- IN TURBULENT FLOW IN PIPES, EXPERIMENTS ON, LEACH S.J.(11)
DIMETHYL ETHER
  N- BUTYL ACETATE + N- DIBUTYL ETHER +, WITH AIR, RELATION OF IGNITION CURRENT TO INDUCTANCE OF ELECTRICAL CIRCUITS FOR MIXTURES OF, JONES D.M.(11)
DIODES
  USE OF, AS SAFETY DEVICES FOR INTRINSIC SAFETY OF ELECTRICAL CIRCUITS, TOLSON P.
DIPHOSPHOPYRIDINE NUCLEOTIDE
  REDUCED FORMS OF, CONTROLLED POTENTIAL ELECTROLYTIC REDUCTION + POLAROGRAPHY OF OXIDIZED AND, BERGMAN I.(16)
DISPERSION
  CALCULATION OF, IN RECTANGULAR + TRIANGULAR DUCTS, USE OF MULTIPLE-IMAGE METHODS FOR, SEAGER J.S.(16)
  INTO TURBULENT FLOW IN PIPES, THEORETICAL TREATMENT OF, SEAGER J.S.(5)
  LONGITUDINAL -- OF AIRBORNE DUST CLOUDS IN TUNNELS, MEASUREMENT OF, LEACH S.J.(3)
  OF METHANE LAYERS, BAFFLES FOR, LEACH S.J.(10)
DISTILLATION
  DESTRUCTIVE --, WHEELER R.V.(50)
DIVIDERS
  FOR ANALOGUE COMPUTERS ON PRINCIPLE OF MILLER INTEGRATORS, GORDON R.L.(6)
  DECADE POTENTIAL --, WASS C.A.A.(4)
DOPPLERITE, TIDESWELL F.V.(3)
  OCCURRENCE OF, IN PEAT, FRANCIS W.(8)
DRIFT MINES
  OF BRITISH ISLES, INFESTATIONS OF BROWN RATS IN, TWIGG G.I.(1)
  POPULATION OF, STUDY OF RATS, TWIGG G.I.(2)
  SOUTH YORKSHIRE --, DISTRIBUTION OF UNDERGROUND POPULATION OF RATS IN, TWIGG G.I.(3)
DRIFTS
  STEEP --, MAN RIDING HAULAGE IN, TAIGEL P.G.(5)
DRILLING
  DURING --, DUST SUPPRESSION BY DUST TRAPS, ASQUITH S.R.(3)
  OPERATIONS IN MINES, STUDIES OF AIRBORNE DUST PRODUCED DURING, BURDEKIN J.T.(5)
  OF ROCK, RATE OF PRODUCTION AND FREE SILICA CONTENT OF FINE DUST FROM, SHAW A.(2)
DRILLING MACHINES, SEE ALSO ROCK DRILLS
  PNEUMATIC PERCUSSIVE -- FOR PRODUCTION OF DUST, TESTS OF, BURDEKIN J.T.(3)
  ROTARY --, DUST PRODUCED BY, ASQUITH S.R.(2)
  DUST FROM, ASQUITH S.R.(1)
DRILLS
  ELECTRIC ROTARY --, DUST PRODUCED BY, WATSON I.J.
DROPLETS
  LIQUID -- FROM ATOMIZERS BY PHOTOGRAPHY, OBSERVATION OF APPROXIMATE SIZE OF, BENTLEY R.A.
DUCTS
  MODELS OF, FOR RESEARCH IN MINE FIRES, ROBERTS A.F.(8)
  TRIANGULAR --, USE OF MULTIPLE-IMAGE METHODS FOR CALCULATION OF DISPERSION IN RECTANGULAR +, SEAGER J.S.(16)
  VENTILATED --, DEPOSITION OF AIRBORNE DUST IN, CRITCHLOW A.(1)

231

Ashley, T., Dixon, S.M. and Hogan, M.A.
Steel pit props
SMRB Paper no.58 1930

Ashmore, J.E. (1) and Wheeler, R.V.   The action of solvents
Studies in the composition of coal.
Jnl. Chem. Soc. 1933 1405

Ashmore, J.E. (2) and Wheeler, R.V.   The thermal decomposition of lignites
Studies in the composition of coal.
Jnl. Chem. Soc. 1934 474

Asquith, S.R. (1), Broomhead, G. and Burdekin, J.T.
Dust produced by rotary drilling machines
SMRE Res. Rep. no.55 1952

Asquith, S.R. (2), Broomhead, G. and Burdekin, J.T.   Part 2
The dust produced by rotary drilling machines:
power consumption in relation to dust production
SMRE Res. Rep. no.109 1955

Asquith, S.R. (3), Broomhead, G. and Burdekin, J.T.
Dust suppression by dust traps during drilling
SMRE Res. Rep. no.111 1955

Atherton, E.
See Guénault, E.M. (4)(5)(6)(8)(10)

Atkinson, F.S.
See Stafford, H. (4)

Atkinson, H.T. and Allsop, G.
An experiment in coal face lighting
Trans. Instn. Min. Engrs., Lond. 1935-36 90 270

Attygalle, D., King, E.J., Harrison, C.V. and Nagelschmidt, G.
The action of variable amounts of tridymite, and of tridymite combined with coal, on the lungs of rats
Br. Jnl. Ind. Med. Jan. 1956 13 41-50

Attygalle, D.
See also Nagelschmidt, G. (12)

TWO PAGES FROM THE *SMRE Bibliography*

Computerised Data Processing for *British Technology Index*

E. J. Coates

Indexing of all kinds inevitably calls for a certain amount of clerical work and, in the case of a periodically published index working to a dateline, careful apportionment of time between the indexing process proper and the necessary clerical tasks is a necessity. *British Technology Index* adopted computer assistance in the performance of clerical work in April 1968, after a research programme which dates back to 1964.* The motive for adopting computer assistance in this case was the need to maintain and if possible improve the currency of the index, which attempts to record articles from British technical journals within seven weeks of their original publication. Under the former manual regime indexing had to slow down at a point about two-thirds of the way through each month in order that the related clerical work could be accomplished in time. So much in the final publication depended upon the accurate carrying out of this work that it could not be allocated to clerks. It was in fact part of the indexers' work load.

Each month's issue of the *British Technology Index* comprises 2,000 to 2,500 en-

tries, plus 5,000 to 6,000 cross-references. The cross-references are generated or initiated by the subject index headings which are attached to entries. That is to say, if a particular subject heading is used in a given issue of the *Index* it calls up a particular set of cross-references which it will be necessary to include in the issue. Some of the cross-reference copy is used repeatedly and is kept in store until required; previously unused headings demand the production of fresh copy for the corresponding cross-references, and this was done concurrently with indexing. At the point mentioned above two-thirds of the way through the month, the file of entries and headings needed to be checked against the store of cross-references, and the necessary cross-reference copy withdrawn from store for the printer. This task of extracting 5,000 to 6,000 cross-references, including that of extracting cross-references to cross-references, took up many man-hours, and in minor emergencies such as staff sickness could bring the indexing process to a halt altogether.

It is this task of producing cross-reference copy from a given set of subject headings which has now been assigned to the computer. The complete process takes a little over an hour each month, and there is, in consequence of this saving, an increase of available time for indexing. A by-product of the main process is a monthly updated authority file of indexing decisions produced

* A feasibility study was undertaken by the University of Newcastle-upon-Tyne Computing Laboratory in 1966-67, with the support of the Office for Scientific and Technical Information. The University of Newcastle-upon-Tyne Computing Laboratory also undertake for BTI the production data processing described in this article.

Reprinted from *The Indexer* 6, no. 3 (Spring 1969): 97–101.

```
AUTHORITY FILE     PAGE  10

446    CASTINGS;STEEL-CHROMIUM;BLADES;TURBINES;WATER.     SEE WATER ****
447   *CATALYSTS,POROUS;CHEMICAL REATIONS,NON-ISOTHERMAL
448    CATALYSTS (( UNIT PROCESSES
449    CATALYSTS;REFORMING;HYDROCARBONS;TOWN GAS PRODUCTION.     SEE GAS ****
450    CATALYSTS;TRANSITION METALS;HYDROGENATION;HYDROCARBONS.     SEE HYDROCARBONS ****
451    CATHODE RAY TUBES;DIGITAL READ OUT DISPLAYS;OUTPUT UNITS;COMPUTERS.     SEE COMPUTERS ****
452    CATHODES (( ELECTRODES
453    CATHODES;MERCURY;SULPHATE SOLUTIONS (( ELECTROLYSIS
454   *CATHODES;MERCURY;SULPHATE SOLUTIONS;COUMARIN ADSORPTION
455    CATHODES;METALS;CAUSTIC SODA SOLUTIONS (( ELECTROLYSIS
456   *CATHODES;METALS;CAUSTIC SODA SOLUTIONS;HYDROGEN;ATOMIC;EVOLUTION
457    CATHODES;PLATINUM-RHODIUM;ACID SOLUTIONS (( ELECTROLYSIS
458   *CATHODES;PLATINUM-RHODIUM;ACID SOLUTIONS;OXYGEN;REDUCTION
459    CATHODES;PLATINUM-RUTHENIUM;ACID SOLUTIONS (( ELECTROLYSIS
460   *CATHODES;PLATINUM-RUTHENIUM;ACID SOLUTIONS;OXYGEN REDUCTION
461   -CATHODES;TEMPERATURE;EFFECT ON CURRENT;ANODES;PLANAR DIODES.     SEE DIODES ****
462    CATHODIC PROTECTION (( CORROSION
463    CATHODIC PROTECTION;CORROSION;WATER;SEA.     SEE SEA ****
464    CAUSTIC SODA (( ALKALIS
465    CAUSTIC SODA = SODIUM HYDROXIDE
466    CAUSTIC SODA;DECOMPOSITION;PHOSPHYLATED 2-PYRIDINE OXIMES.     SEE 2-PYRIDINE OXIMES ****
467    CAUSTIC SODA;SOLUTIONS;METALS;CATHODES.     SEE CATHODES ****
468   *CELLS,VOLTAIC (( ELECTROCHEMISTRY
469   *CELLS,VOLTAIC;ELECTRODES,POTASSIUM BISULPHATE,MOLTEN;POTENTIAL
470   *CELLS,VOLTAIC;ELECTRODES;ZINC AMALGAM;ZINC SALT SOLUTIONS
471    CELLULOSE (( POLYSACCHARIDES
472    CELLULOSE;ION EXCHANGE;SEPARATION;BIOLOGICAL MATERIALS.     SEE BIOLOGICAL MATERIALS ****
473    CELLULOSE ACETATE (( PLASTICS
474    CELLULOSE ACETATE (( THERMOPLASTICS
475    CELLULOSE ACETATE;FIBRES;YARNS;KNITTING.     SEE KNITTING ****
476    CELLULOSE ACETATE;MEMBRANES;REVERSE OSMOSIS;CONVERSION;WATER;SEA.     SEE SEA ****
477    CELLULOSE ACETATE,FABRICS.     SEE FABRICS ****
478    CEMENT BOUND BASE ;MOTORWAYS.     SEE MOTORWAYS. ****
479    CEMENTITE-AUSTENITE TRANSITION;STEEL.     SEE STEEL ****
480    CERAMICS (( CHEMICAL TECHNOLOGY
481    CERAMICS = CLAY PRODUCTS
482   *CERAMICS;MACHINING;DIAMOND
483    CERAMICS;NUCLEAR REACTORS COMPONENTS.     SEE NUCLEAR REACTORS ****
484    CERAMICS,STRUCTURAL     RH  BRICKS
485    CERAMICS,STRUCTURAL = CLAY,HEAVY;INDUSTRIES
486    CHARCOAL (( CARBON
487    CHARCOAL,(( WOOD;DISTILLATION
488    CHARCOAL;CHROMATOGRAPHY;BASIC AMINO ACIDS DETERMINATION;HYDROLYSATES;PROTEIN.     SEE PROTEIN ****
489    CHARGE STORAGE;PARAMETRIC DIODES;MULTIPLIERS;FREQUENCY.     SEE FREQUENCY ****
490    CHEMICAL ENGINEERING     RH  UNIT OPERATIONS
491    CHEMICAL ENGINEERING     RH  UNIT PROCESSES
492    CHEMICAL ENGINEERING = ENGINEERING,CHEMICAL
493    CHEMICAL ENGINEERING;PLANT   RH  BUBBLE BEDS
494    CHEMICAL ENGINEERING;PLANT   RH  BUBBLE CAP COLUMNS
```

1st indentation : Subject headings

2nd indentation: Cross references

3rd Indentation: Reversed synonym and 'related heading' cross references by the computer in print-out form. An authority file is of course needed continuously by indexers to check tentative headings and so ensure consistency. The manual authority file which the computer print-out forms will eventually supersede is in index-card form and up to April 1968 had accumulated nearly 250,000 records. Its maintenance was an increasingly heavy burden upon indexers' time, and it was becoming steadily more difficult to consult. Also there could be only one copy of it, whereas if it is found desirable each indexer can have his own copy of the print-out authority file. In the specimen reproduced the asterisked items are headings; lines which start at the second indentation from the left are cross-references, and those at the third indentation are reversed cross-references for synonyms and related terms. The latter do not appear in the final product.

To leave the by-product and return to a consideration of the main product, namely cross-reference copy, the general principle is that the editorial office punches coded subject headings to paper tape by means of a tape-output typewriter. On receiving these, the computer produces the appropriate cross-reference copy corresponding to the subject headings. The computer achieves this partly by extracting cross-references from a magnetic-tape store, which is closely analogous to the former manual store and partly by manipulating the component words in a subject heading according to prescriptions in the programme. The first process of extracting from magnetic-tape store, is easy to understand. The computer transfers the subject heading data to magnetic tape from the paper tape supplied and proceeds to sort it. It then compares this sorted file with another sorted file of coupled terms constituting the store of 'related heading' and synonym cross-references. When it discovers a term match between input subject heading and store terms, it copies the store terms concerned on to another magnetic tape and at the same time expands the information copied to the form required at the final output. An example will make this clear.

Let us suppose that part of the related heading and synonym store contains the following coupled terms

AIR COMPRESSORS/COMPRESSORS
AIR CONDITIONING/BUILDING
AIR CURTAINS/INSULATION, THERMAL
AIR GAPS/INSULATION, ELECTRICAL
AIR HEATING/HEATING
AIR MOTORS/PNEUMATIC MACHINERY
AIR POLLUTION/SANITARY ENGINEERING
AIR SPEED INDICATORS/AIRCRAFT,
   INSTRUMENTS

and let us suppose that part of the sorted file of the month's input subject headings reads as follows:

AGGREGATES
AGRICULTURAL MACHINERY
AIR HEATING
AIR TRANSPORT
AIR TURBINES

The computer systematically compares the two sets of terms until it discovers that there is an identity match at AIR HEATING. It then transfers AIR HEATING/HEATING to another tape, and performs a combined expansion and transposition operation on the terms to give the final output

HEATING   related headings
    AIR HEATING

It will be seen that under this system, *BTI* has to inform the store—by means of punched paper tape—when a subject heading is used for the first time and what the 'related heading' and synonym term is. Once the information is put into store it remains available for further use without any action by *BTI* beyond inputting the subject heading.

The second process—that of generating inversion 'See' cross-references, by computer manipulation of the component terms of the subject heading is much more complex and is probably an original concept in computer-assisted production of indexes. These manipulations were quite closely subject to rule under the manual system. It was necessary to refine and close any loopholes in the rules for the purpose of making a computer programme.

The simplest possible pattern of manipulation is illustrated by the following example:

For input subject heading
WATER   Flow   Pipes
Output cross-references
PIPES   Flow   Water
                    See   WATER   Flow   Pipes
FLOW   WATER   See   WATER   Flow

Computer package programmes which will perform a manipulation of this kind have been in existence for some time, and if this manipulation alone were all that is required, there would have been no problems. However, *British Technology Index* is designed primarily for the user whose interest is in highly specific subjects, and one corollary of this is that our cross-reference manipulation system must never result in loss of specificity in relation to a particular kind of thing or action. If we slightly change our example and employ the simple symmetrical pattern given above we have the following:

Input subject heading
WATER   Flow   Turbulent   Pipes
Output cross-references
PIPES   Turbulent   Flow   Water
        See   WATER   Flow   Turbulent   Pipes
TURBULENT   Flow   Water
                    See   WATER   Flow   Turbulent
FLOW   Water   See   WATER   Flow

The shortcoming in this result, from the point of view of a specific subject oriented index, is that at FLOW we have lost the idea of turbulent flow. It is quite true that the item is about Flow of water but the reference fails to say that it is about turbulent flow. In this case therefore where two consecutive terms in the subject heading string represent a Thing or Action (an Action in this case) followed by a term designating a Kind, then these are treated as inseparable and resort is made to permutation. Thus, the last cross-reference in the example above would read

FLOW   Turbulent   Water
                    See   WATER   Flow   Turbulent

The computer can perform this variant manipulation if we can find some way of informing it that Flow Turbulent in the subject heading string is a special situation requiring this variant manipulation, unlike Water Flow or Flow Pipes or Turbulent Pipes. The special signal required is in fact put in

by the indexer whenever he finds two consecutive terms in his subject heading exemplifying a Thing (or Action) plus Kind situation. The signal takes the form of differentiated punctuation in the input subject heading. Thus to produce the simple symmetrical pattern of cross-references given in the first example the input is punctuated with colons

WATER   : Flow, Turbulent   : Pipes

To produce the superimposed permutation required whenever a term specifies a Kind of the concept represented by the preceding term in the subject heading, the punctuation in front of the 'Kind' term is changed to a comma, giving

WATER   : Flow, Turbulent   : Pipes

The visual effect of this method of punctuation is to suggest that Flow and Turbulent are more tightly bound together than Water and Flow or Turbulent and Pipes, and indeed it is this relative inseparability which is reflected in the changed pattern of inversion references produced. One other thing has to be remembered by the computer by means of a special instruction in its programme. It reproduces the colons on the left hand side of the cross-references but not the comma, giving

PIPES   : Turbulent flow   : Water   See
TURBULENT FLOW   : Water   See

but yet again where the order of the permuted terms is the same as that in the subject heading, the comma is retained

FLOW, Turbulent   : Water   See

Frequently a type specifying term is not an adjective but the name of a material. In this case also the superimposed permutation pattern is used, but the signal is a semicolon, which is repeated in the output cross-references. For example, the flow of water in concrete pipes would be given as

WATER   : Flow   : Pipes ; Concrete

The computer programme can also cope with the fact that on occasion two or more kind-specifying terms may appear consecutively in a subject heading string. The second kind-specifying term may relate to the first kind-specifying term or to the entity being specified. Two contrasting subject heading inputs which show this effect are the following:

    PIPES ; Steel, Stainless
    PIPES ; Steel Ribbed

Stainless refers to steel, but ribbed refers to pipe.

In the examples given so far every term in the subject heading string initiates a cross-reference, but this is not always the case. In the example

    WATER : Flow : Measurement : Weirs
    WATER, Saline : Conversion : Ion exchange
    WATER : Extraction : Rivers

we make no cross-references beginning respectively with Measurement, Conversion, or Extraction, because we do not think that any user will need to look up everything on such pervasive concepts. We therefore need to signal to the computer whether or not each term in a subject heading string initiates a cross-reference. This is done by means of a second punctuation character (or 'second operator') between words, which having served its purpose is deleted on final output. The second operator is inserted in the following manner:

    WATER :.Flow :.Pipes

The full stop before Flow and Pipes instructs the computer that each of these words initiates a cross-reference.

In the example

    WATER : [Extraction :. Rivers

The bracket before extraction instructs the computer to make no cross-reference commencing with that term.

We have a list of about 40 terms which are so diffuse in their application that it is normally desirable that they should not appear either in the leading or second position in a cross-reference. These have a special code signal which conveys to the computer both an instruction that they do not initiate a cross-reference and a direction which 'relegates' them one place to the right in the inverted cross-reference string. This is illustrated by

    WATER :. Flow : Measurement :. Weirs

which gives on output cross-references beginning

    WEIRS : Flow measurement : Water. See
      WATER : Flow : measurement : weirs
    FLOW : Water. See WATER : Flow

Another second operator provides the facility for treating any two subject heading elements as one for manipulation purposes, wherever this may be necessary. The converse, the splitting up of a phrase forming part of a subject heading is also provided for in the programme. In all, the inversion reference programme comprises 28 separate instructions, and in practice these appear to cover about 98 per cent of requirements. The residual cases are fortunately easy to spot by the indexer at the pre-computer stage, and if missed they do not disrupt the other data-processing operations. They could probably be programmed but only at the cost of a considerable increase in the complexity of the present programme.

The adoption of the computer assistance in April led to a considerable rise in the productivity of the indexing staff. Some preliminary practice runs in using the special coding needed for the inversion references had been undertaken in 1967, and there were virtually no staff difficulties in coping with the change. After four months computer-assisted operation, the former backlog of work had been eliminated.

At the moment, for temporary technical reasons the extension of computer assistance to cover computer typesetting is in abeyance, but detailed plans for this further development are well advanced.

Appendix
Wheatley Medal Winners

The Library Association Wheatley Medal is awarded annually for an outstanding index published in the United Kingdom during the preceding three years. The award is made by a committee made up of representatives from both the Library Association and the Society of Indexers. Recommendations are invited from members of the Library Association, the Society of Indexers, publishers, and other individuals.

1962   Michael Maclagan, Index to *Clemency Canning* (Macmillan)

1963   J. M. Dickie, Index to *How to Catch Trout*, 3rd ed. (Chambers)

1964   Guy Parsloe, Index to *The Wardens' Accounts of the Worshipful Company of Founders of the City of London, 1497–1681* (Althone Press)

1965   Alison Quinn, "Modern Index" to *The Principall Navigations, Voiages and Discoveries of the English Nation* (Cambridge Univ. Press for the Hakluyt Society and the Peabody Museum of Salem)

1966   No Award

1967   G. Norman Knight, Index to *Winston S. Churchill, Vol. 2* (Heinemann)

1968   Doreen Blake and Ruth E. M. Bowden, Index to *The Journal of Anatomy: The First 100 Years, 1866–1966* (Cambridge Univ. Press)

1969   James C. Thornton, Index to *The Letters of Charles Dickens, Vol. 2: 1840–1841* (Clarendon Press, Oxford)

1970   E. L. C. Mullins, Index to *A Guide to the Historical and Archaeological Publications of Societies in England and Wales, 1901–1933* (Athlone Press)

1971–1972   No Awards

1973   K. Boodson, Index to *Non-ferrous Metals* (Macdonald Technical and Scientific)
       L. M. Harrod, Index to *The History of the King's Works, Vol. 6: 1782–1851* (Her Majesty's Stationery Office)

1974   C. C. Banwell, Index to *Encyclopedia of Forms and Precedents*, 4th ed. (Butterworths)

1975   Margaret D. Anderson, Index to *Copy-Editing: The Cambridge Handbook* (Cambridge Univ. Press)

1976   John A. Vickers, Index to Volume 11 of *The Works of John Wesley: The Appeals to Men of Reason and Religion and Certain Related Open Letters* (Clarendon Press)

1977   T. Rowland Powel, Index to *Archaeologia Cambrensis, 1901–1960* (Cambrian Archaeological Assn., Cardiff)

Index

NOTE: The treatment of titles in this index follows the practice of *The Indexer*. Titles of books and periodicals are set in italics; titles of articles are set in roman. Only the first word and proper names are capitalized in book and article titles; in periodical titles all main words are capitalized.